i

IF FOUND, please notify and arrange return to owner. This text is an important study guide for the owner's career and/or exam preparation.

Name: _____

Address: _____

City, State, ZIP: _____

Telephone: (_____) _____ Email: _____

GLEIM Exam Questions and Explanations Series

| Auditing & Systems EQE with Test Prep | Business Law/Legal Studies EQE with Test Prep | Federal Tax EQE with Test Prep | Financial Accounting EQE with Test Prep | Cost/Managerial Accounting EQE with Test Prep |

GLEIM Review Systems

GLEIM CPA Review System

GLEIM CIA Review System Updated for the New 3-Part Exam

GLEIM CMA Review System

GLEIM EA Review System

Use the order form provided at the back of this book, or contact us at www.gleim.com or (800) 874-5346.

REVIEWERS AND CONTRIBUTORS

Garrett W. Gleim, B.S., CPA (not in public practice), received a Bachelor of Science degree from The Wharton School at the University of Pennsylvania. Mr. Gleim coordinated the production staff, reviewed the manuscript, and provided production assistance throughout the project.

D. Scott Lawton, B.S., is a graduate of Brigham Young University–Idaho and Utah Valley University, and he has passed the EA exam. Mr. Lawton participated in the technical editing of the manuscript.

Kristina M. Rivet, CPA, CIA, graduated *cum laude* from Florida International University. She has extensive public accounting experience in the areas of financial accounting, tax, and consulting. Ms. Rivet provided substantial editorial assistance throughout the project.

A PERSONAL THANKS

This manual would not have been possible without the extraordinary effort and dedication of Jacob Brunny, Julie Cutlip, Eileen Nickl, Teresa Soard, Justin Stephenson, Joanne Strong, Elmer Tucker, and Candace Van Doren, who typed the entire manuscript and all revisions, and drafted and laid out the diagrams and illustrations in this book.

The authors also appreciate the production and editorial assistance of Jessica Felkins, Chris Hawley, Jeanette Kerstein, Katie Larson, Diana Leon, Cary Marcous, Shane Rapp, Drew Sheppard, and Martha Willis.

The authors also appreciate the critical reading assistance of Jared Armenti, Jeffrey Bennett, Ellen Buhl, Ray Busler, Ronny Chong, Stephanie Garrison, Bethany Harris, Eric Malinasky, Jerry Mathis, Dustin Wallace, Diana Weng, Kenneth Wilbur, and Hailun Zhu.

Finally, we appreciate the encouragement, support, and tolerance of our families throughout this project.

2014 EDITION

PART 2

BUSINESSES

by

Irvin N. Gleim, Ph.D., CPA, CIA, CMA, CFM, RTRP

and

James R. Hasselback, Ph.D.

ABOUT THE AUTHORS

Irvin N. Gleim is Professor Emeritus in the Fisher School of Accounting at the University of Florida and is a member of the American Accounting Association, Academy of Legal Studies in Business, American Institute of Certified Public Accountants, Association of Government Accountants, Florida Institute of Certified Public Accountants, The Institute of Internal Auditors, and the Institute of Management Accountants. He has had articles published in the *Journal of Accountancy*, *The Accounting Review*, and *The American Business Law Journal* and is author/coauthor of numerous accounting and aviation books and CPE courses.

James R. Hasselback is the Mary Ball Washington Eminent Scholar at the University of West Florida. A member of the American Accounting Association and the American Taxation Association, he has published over 160 papers in professional and academic journals, including *The Accounting Review*, *The Tax Adviser*, *Financial Management*, *Journal of Real Estate Taxation*, and the *American Business Law Journal*. Dr. Hasselback has presented papers at many national and regional professional meetings and has served as chairman at tax sessions of professional conferences. He regularly presents continuing education seminars for certified public accountants. In addition, he has been coauthor and technical editor of a two-volume introductory taxation series published by CCH, Inc., for the past 30 years and has served as technical editor of several publications by CCH and Harper-Collins. Dr. Hasselback has compiled 35 editions of the *Accounting Faculty Directory*.

Gleim Publications, Inc.
P.O. Box 12848
University Station
Gainesville, Florida 32604
(800) 87-GLEIM or (800) 874-5346
(352) 375-0772
Fax: (352) 375-6940
Internet: www.gleim.com
Email: admin@gleim.com

For updates to this 2014 edition of *EA Review: Part 2, Businesses*

Go To: www.gleim.com/EAupdate

Or: Email update@gleim.com with **EA 2 2014-1** in the subject line. You will receive our current update as a reply.

Updates are available until the next edition is published.

ISSN: 2168-3867

ISBN: 978-1-58194-344-3 *EA 1: Individuals*
ISBN: 978-1-58194-345-0 *EA 2: Businesses*
ISBN: 978-1-58194-346-7 *EA 3: Representation, Practices, and Procedures*
ISBN: 978-1-58194-349-8 *How to Pass the EA Exam: A System for Success*

ACKNOWLEDGMENTS

The authors appreciate and thank the Internal Revenue Service and Prometric for their cooperation. Questions have been used from the 1978-2005 Special Enrollment Examinations.

v

TABLE OF CONTENTS

DETAILED TABLE OF CONTENTS

PREFACE

The purpose of this book is to help **you** prepare to pass Part 2, Businesses, of the IRS Special Enrollment Exam, which we refer to as the EA (enrolled agent) exam. Our overriding consideration is to provide an inexpensive, effective, and easy-to-use study program. This book

1. Explains how to optimize your grade by focusing on Part 2 of the EA exam.

2. Defines the subject matter tested on Part 2 of the EA exam.

3. Outlines all of the subject matter tested on Part 2 in 20 easy-to-use-and-complete study units, reflecting 2013 tax law (which is what will be tested on the 2014 EA exam).

4. Presents multiple-choice questions from past EA examinations to prepare you for questions in future EA exams. Our answer explanations are presented to the immediate right of each question for your convenience. Use a piece of paper to cover our answer explanations as you study the questions.

5. Suggests exam-taking and question-answering techniques to help you maximize your exam score.

The outline format, the spacing, and the question-and-answer formats in this book are designed to facilitate readability, learning, understanding, and success on the EA exam. Our most successful candidates use the Gleim EA Review System*, which includes books, EA Test Prep, Audio Review, Gleim Online, Exam Rehearsals, and access to a Personal Counselor. Students who prefer to study in a group setting may attend Gleim Professor-Led Reviews, which combine the Gleim Review System with the coordination and feedback of a professor. (Check our website for live courses we recommend.) This review book and all Gleim EA Review materials are compatible with other EA review materials and courses that are based on Prometric's Exam Content Outlines.

To maximize the efficiency and effectiveness of your EA review program, augment your studying with *How to Pass the EA Exam: A System for Success.* This booklet has been carefully written and organized to provide important information to assist you in passing the EA examination.

Thank you for your interest in our materials. We deeply appreciate the thousands of letters and suggestions we have received from CIA, CMA, CPA, RTRP, and EA candidates and accounting students and faculty during the past 5 decades.

If you use the Gleim materials, we want YOUR feedback immediately after the exam and as soon as you have received your grades. The EA exam is NONDISCLOSED, and you must maintain the confidentiality and agree not to divulge the nature or content of any EA question or answer under any circumstances. We ask only for information about our materials, i.e., the topics that need to be added, expanded, etc.

Please go to www.gleim.com/feedbackEA2 to share your suggestions on how we can improve this edition.

Good Luck on the Exam,

Irvin N. Gleim
James R. Hasselback

February 2014

*Visit www.gleim.com or call (800) 874-5346 to order.

PREPARING FOR AND TAKING THE IRS ENROLLED AGENT EXAMINATION

FOLLOW THESE STEPS TO PASS THE EXAM

1. Read this **Introduction** to familiarize yourself with the content and structure of Part 2 of the EA exam. In the following pages, you will find

   a. An **overview of Part 2** and what it generally tests, including

      1) Prometric's exam content breakdown by section for Part 2, cross-referenced with the Gleim study units and subunits that contain each topic

   b. A detailed plan with **steps to obtain your EA certification**, including

      1) The order in which you should apply, register, schedule your exam, and buy your study materials

      2) How to organize your study schedule to make the most out of each resource in the Gleim EA Review System (i.e., books, EA Test Prep, Audio Review, Gleim Online, Exam Rehearsals, etc.)

   c. Tactics for your **actual test day**, including

      1) Time budgeting, so you complete all questions with time to review
      2) Question-answering techniques to obtain every point you can
      3) An explanation of how to be in control of your EA exam

2. Scan the Gleim *How to Pass the EA Exam: A System for Success* booklet and note where to revisit later in your studying process to obtain a deeper understanding of the EA exam.

   a. *How to Pass the EA Exam: A System for Success* has six study units:

      Study Unit 1: The EA Examination: An Overview and Preparation Introduction
      Study Unit 2: EA Exam Content Outlines
      Study Unit 3: Content Preparation, Test Administration, and Performance Grading
      Study Unit 4: Multiple-Choice Questions
      Study Unit 5: Preparing to Pass the EA Exam
      Study Unit 6: How to Take the EA Exam

    b.   If you feel that you need even more details on the test-taking experience, access Prometric's **Free Tutorial/Sample Test** at www.prometric.com/demos/irs/index.htm.

        1)   This tutorial is most useful to candidates who have little or no experience with computerized exams and have anxiety about performing well in unfamiliar circumstances.

3.   Follow the steps outlined on page 8, "How to Study a Study Unit Using the Gleim EA Review System." This is the **study plan** that our most successful candidates adhere to. Study until you have reached your **desired proficiency level** (e.g., 75%) for each study unit.

    a.   As you proceed, be sure to check any **Updates** that may have been released.

        1)   Gleim Online and EA Test Prep are updated automatically.

        2)   Book updates can be viewed at www.gleim.com/EAupdate, or you can have them emailed to you. See the information box on page iv for details.

    b.   **Review the *How to Pass the EA Exam: A System for Success* booklet** and become completely comfortable with what will be expected from you on test day.

4.   Shortly before your test date, take an **Exam Rehearsal** (complimentary with the EA Review System!) at www.gleim.com/RehearseEA.

    a.   This timed and scored exam emulates the actual EA exam and tests you not only on the content you have studied, but also on the question-answering and time-management techniques you have learned throughout the Gleim study process.

    b.   When you have completed the exam, study your results to discover where you should **focus your review during the final days before your exam**.

5.   **Take and PASS** Part 2 of the EA exam!

    a.   When you have completed the exam, please go to www.gleim.com/feedbackEA2 to give us your **suggestions, comments, and corrections**. We want to know how well we prepared you for your testing experience.

OVERVIEW OF EA EXAMINATION

The total exam is 10.5 hours of testing (12 hours total seat time to include tutorials and surveys). It covers **federal taxation; tax accounting; and the use of tax return forms for individuals, partnerships, corporations, trusts, estates, and gifts**. It also covers **ethical considerations and procedural requirements**.

The **exam consists of three parts, with 3.5 hours for each part** (4 hours total seat time to include tutorial and survey). The questions on the examination are directed toward the tasks that enrolled agents must perform to complete and file forms and tax returns and to represent taxpayers before the Internal Revenue Service. Each part of the examination consists of **100 multiple-choice questions** and covers the following tax topics:

Part 1 - Individuals
Part 2 - Businesses
Part 3 - Representation, Practices, and Procedures

Based on the experience of our customers who have taken all three parts of the exam, Gleim recommends that candidates sit for Parts 1 and 2 before taking Part 3. Feedback indicates that Part 3 candidates may be given questions related to topics covered in Parts 1 and 2.

EXAM CONTENT OUTLINES WITH GLEIM CROSS-REFERENCES

This section contains the Part 2 Exam Content Outlines.* The outlines are subdivided into sections, and each section has one or more topics, which are further divided into specific items. According to the IRS's *Candidate Information Bulletin* (available at www.prometric.com/irs), not every topic in the outlines will appear on the exam, and the list of topics may not be all-inclusive. However, the outlines are meant to reflect the knowledge needed for tasks performed by EAs.

Next to each topic, we have provided a cross-reference to the most relevant Gleim study unit(s)/subunit(s).

Section 1: Businesses (45 items)

a. **Business Entities**

1) Types of business entities and their filing requirements:

    a) Sole proprietorships – 1.1
    b) Partnerships – 1.1, 8.1, 8.2, 9.1
    c) Corporations – 1.1, 11.1, 11.2, 11.5
    d) S corporations – 1.1, 17.1
    e) Farmers – 1.2, 2.3
    f) LLCs – 1.1, 11.1
    g) Tax-exempt entities and associations – 20

2) Elections for type of entity – 17.1
3) Employer identification number – 1.1
4) Accounting periods (tax year) – 1.3
5) Accounting methods – 1.2

b. **Partnerships**

1) Partnership income, expenses, distributions, and flow-through (e.g., self employment income) – 2.2, 9
2) Family partnerships – 8.1
3) Partner's dealings with partnership (e.g., exchange of property, guaranteed payments, contribution of property to partnership) – 8.3, 9.3
4) Basis of partner's interest – 9.1
5) Disposition of partner's interest – 10.1
6) Partnership formation (e.g., partnership agreement, general vs. limited partners, capital contributions) – 1.1, 8.1, 8.3
7) Dissolution of partnership (e.g., sale, death of partner) – 9.1, 10.1
8) Filing requirements and due dates – 8.2
9) Services rendered in return for partnership interest – 8.3
10) Debt discharge – 8.3

c. **Corporations in General**

1) Filing requirements and due dates – 11.5
2) Earnings and profits – 15.1
3) Shareholder dividends, distributions, and recognition requirements – 15.2
4) Special deductions and credits (e.g., dividends received deductions, charitable deduction) – 14.1-14.3
5) Liquidations and stock redemptions – 16
6) Accumulated earnings – 11.7
7) Estimated tax payments – 11.8

d. **Forming a Corporation**

1) Services rendered to a corporation in return for stock – 12.2
2) IRC Section 351 exchange – 12.1
3) Transfer and/or receipt of money or property in addition to corporate stock – 12.1
4) Mortgaged property transferred – 12.1
5) Controlled groups – 11.2, 12.1
6) Closely held corporations – 1.1
7) Personal service corporations (e.g., 35% rate) – 11.3

*Note that, at time of print, Prometric has not released any changes to the Exam Content Outlines for the 2014-15 exam. If changes are made, Gleim will release updates to this cross-reference and anything else affected (i.e., outlines or questions) at www.gleim.com/EAupdate.

e.   **S Corporations**

   1)   Requirements to qualify – 17.1
   2)   S corp income, expenses and separately stated items – 17.2
   3)   Treatment of distributions (e.g., reasonable compensation) – 17.3
   4)   Shareholder's basis (e.g., loan basis, distributions and losses in excess of basis) – 17.2
   5)   Revocation, termination and reinstatement – 17.1
   6)   Debt discharge – 17.2
   7)   Non-cash distributions – 17.3
   8)   Election procedure – 17.1

Section 2: Business Financial Information (40 items)

a.   **Business Income**

   1)   Gross business income – 2.1
   2)   Cost of goods sold (e.g., inventory practices, expenditures included, uniform capitalization rules) – 3.2, 5.3, 5.4
   3)   Net income, net operating losses, and loss limitations including passive activity and at risk limitations – 7.3, 7.4, 9.1, 13.3, 17.2
   4)   Gain or loss on disposition of depreciable property – 2.1, 2.5, 2.6, 5.1, 5.2, 6, 13.4
   5)   Cancellation of business debt – 4.4

b.   **Business Expenses, Deductions and Credits**

   1)   Employees' pay (e.g., deductibility of compensation, fringe benefits, rules of family employment, statutory employee, necessary and reasonable) – 3.1, 4.7
   2)   Reporting requirements for contractors and employees (e.g., W-2, W-4, Form 1099) – 3.1
   3)   Business rental deduction – 3.4
   4)   Depreciation, amortization, IRC section 179, and depletion – 4.6, 6.1-6.4
   5)   Business bad debts – 4.4
   6)   Business travel, entertainment, and gift expenses – 4.1, 4.2, 4.5, 14.3
   7)   Interest expense – 3.3
   8)   Insurance expense – 4.3
   9)   Taxes (e.g., deductibility of taxes, assessments, and penalties; proper treatment of sales taxes paid) – 2.4, 3.5, 7.5, 11.6-11.8, 13.1, 15.4, 17.4
   10) Employment taxes – 3.5
   11) Federal excise tax – 3.5
   12) Casualties, thefts, and condemnations – 7.3, 14.3
   13) IRC section 199 deduction (domestic production activities) – 3.6
   14) Eligibility and deductibility of general business credits (e.g., disabled access credit, investment credit) – 7.1, 17.4
   15) Alternative minimum tax net operating loss deduction – 11.6
   16) Home office – 4.7

c.   **Business Assets**

   1)   Basis of assets – 5.1, 5.2
   2)   Disposition of depreciable property – 2.5, 2.6
   3)   Like kind exchange – 2.5

d.   **Analysis of Financial Records**

   1)   What type of business (e.g., service, retail, manufacturer, farm) – 1.1
   2)   Income statement – 8.2, 11.5
   3)   Balance sheet (e.g., proofing beginning and ending balances) – 8.2, 11.5
   4)   Method of accounting (e.g., accrual, cash, hybrid) – 1.2
   5)   Depreciation and amortization – 6
   6)   Depreciation recovery (e.g., recapture, Sec. 280F) – 6.5
   7)   Pass-through activity (e.g., K-1, separately stated items, non-deductible expenses) – 9.1, 17.2
   8)   Reconciliation of tax versus books (e.g., M-1, M-2, M-3) – 11.5, 14.4
   9)   Related party activity – 9.3, 13.5
   10) Loans to and from owners – 9.3

e.   **Advising the Business Taxpayer**

1)   Filing obligations (e.g., extended returns) – 8.2, 9.1, 11.5, 17.1, 17.2
2)   Deposit obligations (e.g., employment tax, excise tax) – 3.1
3)   Reporting obligations for businesses (e.g., 1099 series, 1031 exchanges, Form 8300) – 2.5, 3.1, 16.2
4)   Record-keeping requirements (e.g., mileage log, accountable plans) – 4.2
5)   Related party transactions – 9.3, 13.5
6)   Selection of business entity (e.g., benefits and detriments) – 1.1
7)   Comingling (e.g., personal usage of business accounts, separation of business and personal accounts) – 4.2
8)   Advice on accounting methods and procedures (e.g., explanation of requirements) – 1.2
9)   Transfer elections in or out of the business (e.g., contributed property, distributions) – 8.3, 9.2, 10, 12, 15.2, 16
10) Life cycle of the business (e.g., formation, dissolution) – 8.2, 10, 12, 16
11) Type of industry (e.g., personal service corporation) – 11.3
12) Worker classification – 3.1

Section 3: Specialized Returns and Taxpayers (15 items)

a.   **Trust and Estate Income Tax**

1)   Trust types (e.g., grantor, irrevocable, tax shelters) – 18.3
2)   Distributable net income and accounting income – 18.3
3)   Exclusions and deductions – 18.1
4)   Fraudulent trusts – 18.4
5)   Income in respect of a decedent – 18.2
6)   Income (e.g., allocations) – 18.1
7)   Separately stated items – 18.3
8)   Filing requirements – 18.2, 18.3

b.   **Exempt Organizations**

1)   Qualifying for and maintaining tax-exempt status (e.g., 501(c)) – 20.1
2)   Filing requirements (e.g., 1023, 1024, 990 series) – 20.1
3)   Unrelated business taxable income (UBTI) – 20.1

c.   **Retirement Plans**

1)   Employer and employee contributions – 19.1-19.3
2)   Reporting requirements – 19.1-19.3
3)   Plans for self-employed persons (e.g., SEP and SIMPLE) – 19.3
4)   Prohibited transactions – 19.3
5)   Qualified and non-qualified plans – 19
6)   Non-discrimination rules – 19.1

d.   **Farmers**

1)   Farm inventory – 2.3
2)   Depreciation for farmers – 2.3, 6
3)   Various disaster-area provisions – 2.3, 7.3
4)   Disposition of farm assets – 2.3
5)   Farm income (e.g., self-raised livestock, crop insurance proceeds) – 2.3
6)   Farm tax computation (e.g., Schedule J, Schedule SE, estimated tax) – 2.3

EA's NONDISCLOSURE AGREEMENT

The EA exam is nondisclosed. The following is taken verbatim from the IRS's *Candidate Information Bulletin* dated December 2013. It is reproduced here to remind all EA candidates about the IRS's strict policy of nondisclosure, which Gleim consistently supports and upholds.

This exam is confidential and proprietary. It is made available to you, the examinee, solely for the purpose of assessing your proficiency level in the skill area referenced in the title of this exam. You are expressly prohibited from disclosing, publishing, reproducing, or transmitting this exam, in whole or in part, in any form or by any means, verbal or written, electronic or mechanical, for any purpose, without the prior express written permission of the IRS.

You can use the past releases of EA questions (all of which are included in the Gleim EA test bank) as good indicators of what may be on your exam. The IRS released numerous nearly identical questions on certain topics. You should pay close attention to these questions and expect to see similar ones on your exam. The Gleim EA materials emphasize knowing exactly what will be expected of you during the EA exam and preparing you for what is required. To maintain our competitive edge, we ask you and other EAs and EA candidates for feedback and suggestions on how to improve our materials, with emphasis on topics to be strengthened and/or added. Please go to www.gleim.com/feedbackEA2 to provide us with your comments and suggestions.

DATES OF THE EXAMINATION/TAX LAW COVERED

The 2014 examination test window will begin May 1, 2014, and examinations will be offered continuously through February 28, 2015.

Each testing year's EA exam (up through February of the following year) covers the tax law in effect the previous December 31. For example, the May 1, 2014–February 28, 2015, testing window will test tax law in effect December 31, 2013.

EXAM COSTS

There are three fees you must pay to take the EA exam.

1. PTIN Application Fee - $64.25 (or PTIN Renewal Fee - $63.00)
2. Exam Scheduling Fee - $109.00 per part
3. Enrollment to Practice before the IRS Application Fee - $30.00

IRS STUDY MATERIAL

In studying for the examination, candidates may wish to refer to the Internal Revenue Code, Circular 230 (reproduced in Appendix A of *EA Review: Part 3*), IRS publications, and IRS tax forms and accompanying instructions, which can be found at www.irs.gov/Forms-&-Pubs or ordered from the IRS as a DVD for $30. You may order the IRS Tax Products DVD (Publication 1796) by calling 877-233-6767. There is an additional $6 handling fee if ordered by phone, fax, or mail. To avoid the handling fee, order online at www.ntis.gov/products/irsdvd.aspx. Use these IRS publications as references with the Gleim EA Review System.

STEPS TO BECOME AN EA

1. Become knowledgeable about the exam, and decide which part you will take first.

2. Purchase the **Gleim EA Review System** to thoroughly prepare for the EA exam. Commit to our systematic preparation for the exam as described in our review materials, including *How to Pass the EA Exam: A System for Success.*

3. Communicate with your Personal Counselor to design a study plan that meets your needs. Call (800) 874-5346 or email EA@gleim.com.

4. Apply and register to take the exam as far in advance as possible. To simplify this process, use www.irs.gov/ptin and www.prometric.com/irs. See www.gleim.com/EAsteps for detailed instructions.

5. Schedule your test with Prometric (online, or by calling the national 800 number or your local Prometric testing site). You have a window of 2 years from registration to schedule, but Gleim recommends you schedule immediately.

6. Work systematically through each study unit in the Gleim EA Review System.

7. Create an unlimited number of Practice Exams in Gleim EA Test Prep, which contains thousands of questions, all updated to the appropriate tax law. Listen to EA Audio Review as a supplement.

8. Sit for and PASS the EA exam while you are in control. Gleim Guarantees Success!

9. Enjoy your career and pursue multiple certifications (CIA, CMA, CPA, etc.), recommend Gleim to others who are also taking these exams, and stay up-to-date on your Continuing Education requirements with Gleim CE.

More specifically, you should focus on the following **system for success** on the EA exam:

1. **Understand the exam, including its purpose, coverage, preparation, format, administration, grading, and pass rates.**

   a. The better you understand the examination process from beginning to end, the better you will perform.

   b. Study the Gleim *How to Pass the EA Exam: A System for Success*. Be sure you have a copy of this useful booklet (also available at www.gleim.com/sfs).

2. **Learn and understand the subject matter tested.** The IRS's Exam Content Outlines for Part 2 are the basis for the study outlines that are presented in each of the 20 study units that make up this book.* You will also learn and understand the material tested on the EA exam by answering numerous multiple-choice questions from past EA exams. Multiple-choice questions with the answer explanations to the immediate right of each question are a major component of each study unit.

3. **Practice answering past exam questions to perfect your question-answering techniques.** Answering past exam questions helps you understand the standards to which you will be held. This motivates you to learn and understand while studying (rather than reading) the outlines in each of the 20 study units.

   a. Question-answering techniques are suggested for multiple-choice questions in Study Unit 4 of *How to Pass the EA Exam: A System for Success*.

   b. Our **EA Test Prep** contains thousands of additional multiple-choice questions that are not offered in our books. Additionally, EA Test Prep has many useful features, including documentation of your performance and the ability to simulate the exam environment and create as many Practice Exams as you want.

   c. Our **EA Gleim Online** is a powerful Internet-based program that allows EA candidates to learn in an interactive environment and provides feedback to candidates to encourage learning. It includes multiple-choice questions in Prometric's format. Each EA Gleim Online candidate has access to a Personal Counselor, who helps organize study plans that work with busy schedules.

   d. Additionally, candidates can access Prometric's free tutorial/sample test at www.prometric.com/demos/irs/index.htm.

4. **Plan and practice exam execution.** Anticipate the exam environment and prepare yourself with a plan: When to arrive? How to dress? What exam supplies to bring? How many questions and what format? Order of answering questions? How much time to spend on each question? Study Unit 6, Subunit 10, in *How to Pass the EA Exam: A System for Success* has detailed instructions on using the Gleim Time Management System.

   a. Expect the unexpected and adjust! Remember, your sole objective when taking an examination is to maximize your score. You must outperform your peers, and being as comfortable and relaxed as possible gives you an advantage!

5. **Be in control.** Develop confidence and ensure success with a controlled preparation program followed by confident execution during the examination.

---

*Please fill out our online feedback form (www.gleim.com/feedbackEA2) IMMEDIATELY after you take the EA exam so we can adapt to changes in the exam. Our approach has been approved by the IRS.

PRELIMINARY TESTING: GLEIM EA DIAGNOSTIC QUIZ

The Gleim EA Diagnostic Quiz provides a representative sample of 40 multiple-choice questions for Part 2. You should use this tool to determine how much time you need to devote to studying particular topic areas (i.e., what your strengths and weaknesses are).

When you have completed the quiz, you will be able to access a Review Session, where you can study answer explanations for the correct and incorrect answer choices of the questions you answered incorrectly. You will also have the option to consult with a Personal Counselor in order to better focus your review on any areas in which you have less confidence.

For smartphone users, there is also a Gleim Diagnostic Quiz App for iPhone, iPod Touch, and Android. More information can be found at www.gleim.com/QuizEA.

Candidates who have already purchased the Gleim EA Review System should skip the Diagnostic Quiz and immediately begin the steps provided below. These steps incorporate study-unit-specific diagnostic testing.

HOW TO STUDY A STUDY UNIT USING THE GLEIM EA REVIEW SYSTEM

To ensure that you are using your time effectively, we recommend that you follow the steps listed below when using all of the EA Review System materials together (books, EA Test Prep, Audio Review, and Gleim Online):

1. (30 minutes, plus 10 minutes for review) In the EA Gleim Online course, complete Multiple-Choice Quiz #1 in 30 minutes. It is expected that your scores will be lower on the first quiz than on subsequent quizzes.

    a. Immediately following the quiz, you will be prompted to review the questions you marked and/or answered incorrectly. For each question, analyze and understand why you were unsure or answered it incorrectly. This step is an essential learning activity to avoid repeating these or similar mistakes in the future.

2. (30 minutes) Use the online audiovisual presentation for an overview of the study unit. EA Audio Review can be substituted for audiovisual presentations and can be used while driving to work, exercising, etc.

3. (45 minutes) Complete the 30-question True/False quiz. It is interactive and most effective if used prior to studying the Knowledge Transfer Outline.

4. (60-80 minutes) Study the Knowledge Transfer Outline, particularly the troublesome areas identified from the multiple-choice questions in the Gleim Online course. The Knowledge Transfer Outlines can be studied either online or from the books.

5. (30 minutes, plus 10 minutes for review) Complete Multiple-Choice Quiz #2 in the Gleim Online course.

    a. Immediately following the quiz, you will be prompted to review the questions you marked and/or answered incorrectly. For each question, analyze and understand why you were unsure or answered it incorrectly. This step is essential to prepare for exam success.

6. (60 minutes) Complete two 20-question Practice Exams in EA Test Prep. Review as needed.

7. Continue taking customized Practice Exams in EA Test Prep until you approach your desired proficiency level, e.g., 75%+. Use Study Sessions as needed to get immediate feedback on questions in your problem areas.

The times mentioned above are recommendations based on prior candidate feedback and how long you will have to answer questions on the actual exam. Each candidate's time spent in any area will vary depending on proficiency and familiarity with the subject matter.

EA FINAL REVIEW

Final review is the culmination of all your studies and topics and should occur one week prior to when you sit for your exam. All study units in Gleim Online should be completed by this time.

Step 1: Take the EA Exam Rehearsal at the beginning of your final review stage. The Exam Rehearsal is 3.5 hours (210 minutes) long and contains 100 multiple-choice questions, just like the EA exam. This will help you identify any weak areas for more practice. Discuss your results with your Personal Counselor for additional guidance.

Step 2: Create Practice Exams in Gleim EA Test Prep, focusing on your weak areas identified from your Exam Rehearsal. Also, be sure to focus on all the material as a whole to refresh yourself with topics you learned at the beginning of your studies. View your performance chart to make sure you are scoring 75% or higher.

> **The following is a detailed description of how Gleim products will prepare you to pass the EA exam according to the steps given on the previous page and above (including the Final Review).**

EA GLEIM ONLINE

EA Gleim Online is a multi-platform, self-study review program delivered via the Internet. It is divided into three courses (one for each part of the EA exam) and contains IRS-released multiple-choice questions in an interface designed to emulate the EA exam.

EA Gleim Online contains

- Audiovisual presentations
- Comprehensive review book outlines
- Thousands of multiple-choice and true/false questions

EA Gleim Online provides you with access to a Personal Counselor, a real person who will provide support to ensure your competitive edge. EA Gleim Online is a great way to get confidence as you prepare with Gleim. This confidence will continue during and after the exam.

STUDYING WITH GLEIM BOOKS AND EA TEST PREP

EA Test Prep is an online question bank that offers unlimited Practice Exams to give you unprecedented studying potential. Twenty-question Practice Exams in EA Test Prep will help you focus on your weaker areas. Make it a game: How much can you improve?

Our EA Test Prep Practice Exams force you to commit to your answer choice before looking at answer explanations; thus, you are preparing under true exam conditions. They also keep track of your time and performance history for each study unit, which is available in either a table or graphical format. Using Cloud technology, your performance data can be synced to any computer or mobile device so you can study anywhere.

If you are using only the book and EA Test Prep to prepare, follow our suggested steps listed on the next page. DO NOT omit the step in which you diagnose the reasons for answering questions incorrectly; i.e., learn from your mistakes while studying so you avoid making similar mistakes on the EA exam.

1. Create and complete a 20-question diagnostic Practice Exam before studying any other information.

2. Study the Knowledge Transfer Outline for the corresponding study unit in your Gleim book.

    a. Place special emphasis on the weaker areas that you identified with the initial diagnostic Practice Exam in Step 1.

3. Take two or three 20-question Practice Exams after you have studied the Knowledge Transfer Outline.

4. Immediately following each Exam, you will be prompted to review the questions you marked and/or answered incorrectly. For each question, analyze and understand why you were unsure or answered it incorrectly. This step is an essential learning activity.

5. Continue this process until you approach a predetermined proficiency level, e.g., 75%+. Use Study Sessions as needed to get immediate feedback on questions in your problem areas.

6. Modify this process to suit your individual learning process.

    a. Learning from questions you answer incorrectly is very important. Each question you answer incorrectly is an **opportunity** to avoid missing actual test questions on your EA exam. Thus, you should carefully study the answer explanations provided so you understand why you chose the incorrect answer. This study technique is clearly the difference between passing and failing for most EA candidates.

    b. Reasons for missing questions include

        1) Misreading the requirement (stem)
        2) Not understanding what is required
        3) Making a math error
        4) Applying the wrong rule or concept
        5) Being distracted by one or more of the answers
        6) Incorrectly eliminating answers from consideration
        7) Not having any knowledge of the topic tested
        8) Employing bad intuition when guessing

    c. It is also important to verify that you answered correctly for the right reasons. Otherwise, if the material is tested on the EA exam in a different manner, you may not answer it correctly.

    d. It is imperative that you complete your predetermined number of study units per week (Study Unit 5, Subunit 4, in *How to Pass the EA Exam: A System for Success* has more information on study schedules) so you can review your progress and realize how attainable a comprehensive EA review program is when using the Gleim EA Review System. Remember to meet or beat your schedule to give yourself confidence.

GLEIM AUDIO REVIEWS

Gleim **EA Audio Reviews** provide an average of 30 minutes of quality review for each study unit. Each review provides an overview of the Knowledge Transfer Outline for each study unit in the *EA Review* book. The purpose is to get candidates started so they can relate to the questions they will answer before reading the study outlines in each study unit. The reviews are available via download from our website.

The audios get to the point, as does the entire **Gleim System for Success**. We are working to get you through the EA exam with minimum time, cost, and frustration. You can listen to sample audio reviews on our website at www.gleim.com/accounting/demos.

TIME-BUDGETING AND QUESTION-ANSWERING TECHNIQUES FOR THE EXAM

The following suggestions are to assist you in maximizing your score on multiple-choice questions. Remember, knowing how to take the exam and how to answer individual questions is as important as studying/reviewing the subject matter tested on the exam.

1. **Budget your time.** We make this point with emphasis. Just as you would fill up your gas tank prior to reaching empty, so too should you finish your exam before time expires.

   a. You will have 3 hours and 30 minutes (210 minutes) to answer 100 multiple-choice questions.

   b. As you work through the individual multiple-choice items, monitor your time. Your goal is to answer all of the items and achieve the maximum score possible.

   c. If you allocate 1.5 - 2 minutes per question, you will require 150 - 200 minutes to finish all questions, leaving 10 - 60 minutes to review your answers and "marked" questions (see item 2.b. below). Spending 2 minutes should be reserved for only the most difficult questions. You should complete 10 questions every 15 - 20 minutes. If you pace yourself during the exam, you will have adequate time.

   d. On your Prometric computer screen, the time remaining (starting with 03:30:00) appears in the top right corner of the screen.

   e. Gleim recommendation: Feedback from individuals who have taken Part 2 and at least one other part shows Part 2 to be more time-consuming. Plan accordingly.

2. **Answer the items in consecutive order.**

   a. Do **not** agonize over any one item. Stay within your time budget.

   b. Note any items you are unsure of by clicking the "mark" button and return to them later if time allows. Plan on going back to all marked questions.

   c. Never leave a question unanswered. Make your best guess in the time allowed. Your score is based on the number of correct responses. You will not be penalized for guessing incorrectly.

3. **For each multiple-choice question,**

   a. **Try to ignore the answer choices at first.** Do not allow the answer choices to affect your reading of the question.

      1) If four answer choices are presented, three of them are incorrect. These incorrect answers are called **distractors** for good reason. Often, distractors are written to appear correct at first glance until further analysis.

      2) In computational items, distractors are carefully calculated such that they are the result of making common mistakes. Be careful, and double-check your computations if time permits.

   b. **Read the question** carefully to determine the precise requirement.

      1) Focusing on what is required enables you to ignore extraneous information, focus on the relevant facts, and proceed directly to determining the correct answer.

         a) Be especially careful to note when the requirement is an **exception**; e.g., "Which of the following is **not** includible in gross income?"

   c. **Determine the correct answer** before looking at the answer choices.

      1) However, some multiple-choice items are structured so that the answer cannot be determined from the stem alone. See the stem in b.1)a) above.

   d. **Read the answer choices carefully.**

      1) Even if the first answer appears to be the correct choice, do not skip the remaining answer choices. Questions often ask for the "best" of the choices provided. Thus, each choice requires your consideration.

      2) Treat each answer choice as a true/false question as you analyze it.

  e. **Click on the best answer.**

    1) You have a 25% chance of answering the question correctly by guessing blindly; improve your odds with educated guessing.

    2) For many of the multiple-choice questions, two answer choices can be eliminated with minimal effort, thereby increasing your educated guess to a 50/50 proposition.

 4. After you have answered all 100 questions, return to the questions that you marked. Then, verify that all questions have been answered.

 5. **If you don't know the answer,**

  a. Make an educated guess, which means selecting the best possible answer. First, rule out answers that you think are incorrect. Second, speculate on what the IRS is looking for and/or the rationale behind the question. Third, select the best answer or guess between equally appealing answers. Your first guess is usually the most intuitive. If you cannot make an educated guess, read the stem and each answer, and pick the most intuitive answer. It's just a guess!

  b. Make sure you accomplish this step within your predetermined time budget.

IF YOU HAVE QUESTIONS

Content-specific questions about our materials will be answered most rapidly if they are sent to us via the easily accessible feedback forms within the online study components. For inquiries regarding your Review book or Test Prep Software Download, please visit www.gleim.com/questions and complete the on-screen form. Our team of accounting experts will give your correspondence thorough consideration and a prompt response.

Questions regarding the information in this Introduction (study suggestions, studying plans, exam specifics) should be emailed to personalcounselor@gleim.com.

Questions concerning orders, prices, shipments, or payments should be sent via email to customerservice@gleim.com and will be promptly handled by our competent and courteous customer service staff.

For technical support, you may use our automated technical support service at www.gleim.com/support, email us at support@gleim.com, or call us at (800) 874-5346.

HOW TO BE IN CONTROL

Remember, you must be in control to be successful during exam preparation and execution. Perhaps more importantly, control can also contribute greatly to your personal and other professional goals. Control is a process whereby you

 1. Develop expectations, standards, budgets, and plans.
 2. Undertake activity, production, study, and learning.
 3. Measure the activity, production, output, and knowledge.
 4. Compare actual activity with expected and budgeted activity.
 5. Modify the activity to better achieve the desired outcome.
 6. Revise expectations and standards in light of actual experience.
 7. Continue the process.

Exercising control will ultimately develop the confidence you need to outperform most other EA candidates and PASS the EA exam! Obtain our *How to Pass the EA Exam: A System for Success* booklet for a more detailed discussion of control and other exam tactics.

STUDY UNIT ONE
ENTITY TYPES, METHODS, AND PERIODS

(11 pages of outline)

One of the most important decisions a business can make is its choice of entity type. Each type of business form has advantages and disadvantages from both tax and liability perspectives. Each taxpayer must figure taxable income on an annual accounting period called a tax year. The calendar year is the most common tax year. Each taxpayer must also use a consistent accounting method, which is a set of rules for determining how and when to report income and expenses. The most commonly used accounting methods are the cash method and the accrual method.

1.1 BUSINESS ENTITIES

Several different forms of businesses have been made available to taxpayers over the years. Each of these business forms has characteristics that are favorable or unfavorable to the taxpayer.

Sole Proprietorship

1. The sole proprietorship is the most common form of business entity.

   a. A sole proprietorship is not a legal entity separate and apart from its owner.
   b. The income or loss is reported by the taxpayer on Schedule C of the owner's Form 1040.
   c. The owner has unlimited liability with regard to the sole proprietorship.
      1) The owner's personal assets are exposed without limitation to any and all liabilities related to the business.
   d. Sole proprietorships are easy to establish and require no special forms.
   e. The business cannot be transferred.
      1) If the business is sold, the owner reports the sale as if each asset were sold.
   f. Spouses filing a joint return may elect out of partnership treatment by choosing to be a **qualified joint venture**. Each spouse is treated as a sole proprietor, allowing both to receive Social Security benefits.

Corporations

2. Corporations were created to allow for the limited liability of the owners. The owners' personal assets are protected from creditors. Creditors can only look to the assets of the corporation for settlement of the debts.

   a. Regular corporations are referred to as C corporations.
      1) C corporations have double taxation.
         a) First, the income is taxed to the corporation as it is earned.
         b) Second, the income is taxed when the corporation distributes the income in the form of dividends.
   b. The corporation files a return separate from its owners. The tax return is due the 15th day of the 3rd month following the end of its tax year.

    c.   Closely held corporations are subject to the at-risk rules. A corporation is closely held if both of the following apply:

        1)   It is not a personal service corporation.

        2)   At any time during the last half of the tax year, more than 50% of the value of its outstanding stock is directly or indirectly owned by or for five or fewer individuals. "Individuals" includes certain trusts and private foundations.

S Corporations

3.   The S corporation is a special type of corporation that first became available as a business form in 1958.

    a.   The S corporation is not taxed, and the income is taxed to the shareholders when earned by the S corporation.

    b.   The S corporation has the limited liability feature of the C corporation. However, there are several ownership restrictions placed on the S corporation.

    c.   S corporations comprise over one-half of all corporations.

        1)   S corporations tend to be small in size and number of owners.

        2)   Over half of all S corporations have only one owner.

        3)   For the most part, S corporations are required to be on a calendar tax year.

Partnerships

4.   There are several forms of partnerships available for taxpayers.

    a.   Partnerships have the advantage that income is taxed only once.

        1)   The partnership does not pay tax; the income flows through and is taxed on each owner's personal tax return.

        2)   The main disadvantage of the partnership form of organization is that the owners can be held liable for the partnership's debts if there are not enough assets to cover the partnership liabilities. This form of partnership is referred to as a **general partnership**.

        3)   Partnership tax returns are due by the 15th day of the 4th month following the close of the partnership tax year.

    b.   **Limited partnerships** were created in the 1970s to allow for the limited liability feature of the corporation while at the same time retaining the single form of taxation.

        1)   The owners were divided into general partners and limited partners. Only the limited partners had the limited liability feature.

            a)   However, the limited partner was not allowed to participate in the operations of the business.

    c.   The **limited liability partnership** quickly followed the limited liability company in adoption by all states and is very similar to the limited liability company.

        1)   The limited liability partnership is primarily used by personal service taxpayers.

        2)   Several states require that the owners remain personally liable for the contracted debts of the entity.

Limited Liability Companies (LLCs)

5.   An LLC is a noncorporate hybrid business structure that combines the limited liability of a corporation with the tax advantages of a general partnership.

6.   An LLC is a domestic entity that is not specifically classified as a corporation is classified as a partnership (if it has two or more members), or is disregarded as an entity separate from its owner (if it has only one owner) [Reg. 301.7701-3(b)(1)]. Thus, for federal tax purposes, the default classification for a domestic LLC with at least two members is to be treated as a partnership. However, the check-the-box regulations discussed below allow an LLC to elect to be treated as a corporation.

   a.   LLCs are the only business entities that allow

      1)   Complete pass-through tax advantages and the operational flexibility of a partnership,
      2)   Corporation-style limited liability under state law,
      3)   No restrictions on the number or types of members, and
      4)   Management participation by all members. Members are the owners or shareholders of the LLC.

   b.   Most states follow Federal taxation of LLCs. Texas and Tennessee tax LLCs as corporations. Michigan has a unified business tax on all forms of business.

   c.   There is no uniform LLC agreement among states; an LLC doing business out of state may have to live with unacceptable uncertainty as to its legal status. Every state and the District of Columbia permit a single-member LLC.

Single-Member Limited Liability Companies

7.   Single-member LLCs are generally treated as disregarded entities unless they elect otherwise.

8.   For individuals, the profit or loss from a disregarded entity is simply reported on Schedule C of the member's Form 1040 along with Schedule SE. Rental real estate operation reports its income or loss on Schedule E.

   a.   For businesses, the profit or loss from a disregarded entity is reported on the member's return as an unincorporated branch or division of the member.

Entity Classification Election -- Check-the-box Regulations

9.   An eligible entity can use Form 8832 to elect how it will be classified for federal tax purposes: as a corporation, a partnership, or an entity disregarded as separate from its owner.

   a.   An eligible entity is classified for federal tax purposes under the default rules unless it filed Form 8832 or Form 2553 to elect a classification or change its current classification.

   b.   Unless an election is made on Form 8832, a domestic eligible entity is

      1)   A partnership if it has two or more members
      2)   Disregarded as an entity separate from its owners if it has a single owner

   c.   Unless an election is made on Form 8832, a foreign eligible entity is

      1)   A partnership if it has two or more members and at least one member does not have limited liability
      2)   An association taxable as a corporation if all members have limited liability
      3)   Disregarded as an entity separate from its owner if it has a single owner that does not have limited liability

   d.   A corporation organized under a state law can only be taxed as a corporation. However, the entity may be eligible to be classified as an S corporation.

Summary of Business Entities

Business Entity	Owner's Liability	Taxation
Sole Proprietorship	Unlimited	Flow through to individual.
Corporations	Limited	At corporate level.
S Corporations	Limited	Flow through taxation on a per-day and per-share basis.
Partnership	General partners – Unlimited Limited partners – Limited	Flow through to partner.
Limited Liability Company (LLC)	Limited	Default is flow through to member. However, may elect to be treated as a different type of entity.
Single-Member LLC (disregarded entity)	Limited	Default is flow through to member. However, may elect to be treated as a different type of entity.

Trusts and Estates

10. Trusts and estates are separate entities from their owners.

    a. Trusts may be created to hold assets for the beneficiaries.

    b. The trust income is usually distributed to the beneficiaries.

    c. The beneficiary pays an income tax on the income of the trust that is required to be distributed.

    d. The trust only pays tax on income that is not required to be distributed. Thus, the income of a trust is taxed only once.

11. An estate comes into place after the taxpayer dies.

    a. The estate is required to pay tax on income that is earned on the assets of the decedent before the assets are distributed to the beneficiaries.

    b. Similar to the trust, the beneficiaries pay the tax on any income that is distributed and the estate pays tax on the remaining income.

Employer Identification Number

12. An employer identification number (EIN) is the business/entity equivalent of a taxpayer identification number (TIN).

    a. Use Form SS-4 to apply for an EIN. An EIN is a nine-digit number assigned to sole proprietors, corporations, partnerships, estates, trusts, and other entities for tax filing and reporting purposes.

    b. A sole proprietorship or self-employed farmer who establishes a qualified retirement plan or is required to file excise, employment, alcohol, tobacco, or firearms returns must have an EIN.

    c. A partnership, corporation, REMIC, nonprofit organization, or farmers' cooperative must use an EIN for any tax-related purposes even if the entity does not have employees.

    d. Generally, a sole proprietor should file only one Form SS-4 and needs only one EIN, regardless of the number of businesses operated as a sole proprietorship or trade names under which a business operates.

        1) If the proprietorship incorporates or enters into a partnership, a new EIN is required.

        2) Each corporation in an affiliated group must have its own EIN.

e. Generally, a single-member domestic LLC should use the name and EIN of its owner for all federal tax purposes.

1) The reporting and payment of employment taxes for employees of the LLC may be made using the name and EIN of the LLC.

f. Do not apply for a new EIN if the existing entity only

1) Changed its business name,

2) Elected on Form 8832 to change the way it is taxed (or is covered by the default rules), or

3) Terminated its partnership status because at least 50% of the total interests in partnership capital and profits were sold or exchanged within a 12-month period. The EIN of the terminated partnership should continue to be used.

g. Do not use the EIN of the prior business unless a taxpayer became the owner of a corporation by acquiring its stock.

1) An existing corporation that is electing or revoking S corporation status should use its previously assigned EIN.

Stop and review! You have completed the outline for this subunit. Study questions 1 and 2 on page 23.

1.2 ACCOUNTING METHODS

An accounting method is a set of rules used to determine the tax year in which an item is includible or deductible in computing taxable income. The method must clearly reflect income and remain the same from year to year. The cash method and the accrual method are the most common. However, other methods are allowed. Specific provisions of the Internal Revenue Code (IRC) may override and require specific treatment of certain items.

Change in Methods

1. Change in accounting methods generally requires consent of the IRS, including change in either the overall system of accounting for gross income or deductions or treatment of any material item used in the system.

a. The taxpayer should file Form 3115 to request consent for such changes.

2. IRS consent is not required for the following changes:

a. Adopting LIFO inventory valuation

1) Switching/changing to LIFO inventory requires IRS consent.

b. Switching from declining-balance depreciation to straight-line

c. Making an adjustment in useful life of certain assets

d. Correcting an error in computing tax, e.g., omission

3. Rev. Proc. 2002-9 provides the procedures by which taxpayers may obtain automatic consent to change certain methods of accounting without having to pay a user fee, e.g., changing depreciation methods.

4. **Cash Method**

a. A cash-method taxpayer accounts for income when one of the following occurs:

1) Cash is actually received

2) A cash equivalent is actually received

3) Cash or its equivalent is constructively received

b. **Cash equivalent.** At the time a person receives noncash forms of income, such as property or services, the fair market value is included in gross income. This applies even if the property or service can be currently converted into cash at an amount lower than face value.

    1) A cash equivalent is property that is readily convertible into cash and typically has a maturity of 3 months or less. Cash equivalents are so near to maturity that the risk of loss due to a change in value is immaterial. The following are considered cash equivalents:

        a) Checks, valued at face
        b) Property, e.g., land, transferable at current FMV
        c) Promissory notes, valued at FMV

    2) If the value of property received cannot be determined, the value of what was given in exchange for it is treated as the amount of income received.

EXAMPLE

An accountant performs various services for a start-up company in exchange for stock options. If the value of the stock options cannot be determined, the value of the services performed is included in income.

---

    3) If both the property received and the property given are impossible to value, e.g., an unsecured promise to pay from a person with unknown creditworthiness, the transaction is treated as open, and the consideration is not viewed as income until its value can be ascertained.

c. **Constructive receipt.** Under the doctrine of constructive receipt, an item is included in gross income when a person has an unqualified right to immediate possession.

    1) A person constructively receives income in the tax year during which it is credited to his or her account, set apart for him or her, or otherwise made available so that (s)he may draw upon it at any time.

        a) It is more than a billing or an offer, or mere promise, to pay.
        b) It includes ability to use on demand, as with escrowed funds subject to a person's order.
        c) Deferring deposit of a check does not defer income. However, dishonor retroactively negates the income.

    2) Income is not constructively received if the taxpayer's control of its receipt is subject to substantial restrictions or limitations, e.g., a valid deferred compensation agreement.

EXAMPLE

John is awarded a $10,000 bonus in 2013. If only half of the bonus is payable in 2013 with the other half paid at the end of 2014, contingent upon John completing another year of service for his employer, only $5,000 is taxable in 2013.

---

d. Receipt or constructive **receipt by an agent** is imputed to the principal.

e. **Economic benefit.** The courts have interpreted the definition of gross income to include any economic or financial benefit conferred on an employee as compensation. This economic benefit theory is applied by the IRS in situations in which an employee or independent contractor receives a transfer of property that confers an economic benefit that is equivalent to cash.

EXAMPLE

The fair rental value of a car that a dealership provides for the personal use of its president is gross income.

---

    1) The economic benefit theory applies even when the taxpayer cannot choose to take the equivalent value of the income in cash.

f. Dividends are constructively received when made subject to the unqualified demand of a shareholder.

 1) If a corporation declares a dividend in December and pays such that the shareholders receive it in January, the dividend is not treated as received in December.

g. **Bonds.** When a bond is sold between interest payment dates, the interest accrued up to the sale date is added to the selling price of the bond. The seller includes the accrued interest in gross income.

h. **Prepaid rent** is gross income when received.

 1) Security deposits are not considered income.
 2) Tenant improvements, in lieu of rent, are included.
 3) Lease cancelations are included.
 4) Advance rental payments must be deducted by the payee during the tax periods to which the payments apply.

i. **Tips.** An employee who receives $20 or more in tips a month working for any employer must report the tips to the employer by the 10th day of the following month. The tips are gross income when reported.

j. **Deductions.** A cash-method taxpayer deducts expenditures when actually paid, except for prepaid rent.

 1) A promise to pay, without more, is not payment.
 2) A check represents payment when delivered or sent.
 3) A third-party (e.g., bank) credit card charge transaction represents current payment with loan proceeds. A second-party (e.g., store) credit card charge transaction is not paid until the charge is paid off.
 4) Bad debt. Adjusted basis in accounts receivable is deductible when the debt becomes worthless. Since a cash-method taxpayer usually has no basis in accounts receivable, (s)he may not deduct bad debts.
 5) **Interest on a loan** issued at discount, or unstated (imputed) interest, is deductible pro rata over the life of the loan.
 6) A person who uses the cash method to report gross income must use the cash method to report expenses.

Advance Payment of Expenses

k. In general, expenses that you pay in advance can be deducted only in the year to which they apply, even under the cash method of accounting.

 1) However, an exception exists for farmers (but not farming syndicates). They may deduct prepaid feed when the expenditure is incurred even if it is to be consumed by the livestock in a subsequent year. Sec. 464(f) limits the deduction to 50% of other farm expenses.

l. The cash method cannot be used by corporations (other than S corporations), partnerships having a corporation (other than an S corporation) as a partner, or tax shelters.

 1) However, an exception allows the following entities to use the cash method:

 a) A family farm corporation with gross receipts of $25 million or less
 b) Other farming corporations whose gross receipts for each tax year beginning after 1975 are $1 million or less
 c) Corporations whose business is operating nurseries or sod farms (other than fruit and nut trees)
 d) Qualified personal service corporations
 e) A corporation or partnership with a corporate partner, other than a tax shelter, with average annual gross receipts of $5 million or less.

5. **Accrual Method**

    a. An accrual-method taxpayer accounts for income in the period it is actually earned.

    b. The accrual method is required of certain persons and for certain transactions.

        1) If the accrual method is used to report expenses, it must be used to report income items.

        2) A taxpayer that maintains inventory must use the accrual method with regard to purchases and sales.

            a) Exceptions to this inventory rule include

                i) **Qualifying taxpayers** who satisfy the gross receipts test for each test year.

                    ● The average annual gross receipts (consisting of the test year and the preceding 2 years) for each test year must be $1 million or less.

                ii) **Qualifying small business taxpayers** who satisfy the gross receipts test for each test year (i.e., tax year ending on or after December 31, 2000).

                    ● The average annual gross receipts must be $10 million or less.
                    ● The taxpayer must not be a corporation (other than an S corp) or a partnership with a corporate partner.
                    ● The principal business activity cannot be mining, manufacturing, wholesale trade, retail trade, or information industries.

        3) Generally, C corporations, partnerships with a C corporation as a partner, and tax shelters must use the accrual method.

            a) Tax shelters include any arrangement for which the principal purpose is avoidance of tax, any syndicates, and any enterprise in which the interests must be registered as a security.

            b) Exceptions to the general rule allow the following taxpayers to use the cash method if the entity is not a tax shelter:

                i) Qualified personal service corporations
                ii) Entities that meet the gross receipts test by having $5 million or less average gross receipts in the 3 preceding years
                iii) Farming or tree-raising businesses

    c. Income is included when all the events have occurred that fix the right to receive it and the amount can be determined with reasonable accuracy.

        1) A right is not fixed if it is contingent on a future event.

        2) The all-events test is satisfied when goods shipped on consignment are sold.

        3) Only in rare and unusual circumstances, in which neither the FMV received nor the FMV given can be ascertained, will the IRS respect holding a transaction open once the right to receive income is fixed. In those circumstances, income is accrued upon receipt.

            a) Proceeds from settlement of a lawsuit are determinable in amount with reasonable accuracy when received.

    d. Prepaid income must generally be included in income when received.

        1) Prepaid rent is includible in gross income in the year received. This rule applies to both cash-method and accrual-method taxpayers.

        2) Prepaid income for services may be accrued over the period for which the services are to be performed, but only if it does not extend beyond the end of the next tax year.

           a) If the taxpayer does not complete the performance within that period, the prepaid income is included in the year following receipt.

        3) Merchandise sales. The right to income is fixed when it is earned, e.g., when goods are shipped.

           a) Prepayments for goods must be included when reported for accounting purposes if reported earlier than when earned.

        4) Taxpayers who use an accrual method of accounting, derive all their income from services, and do not charge interest or penalties for late payments may use the nonaccrual-experience method to report bad debts.

           a) For example, a corporation may accrue 2% of gross sales as bad debt expense when, over the last 8 years, roughly 2% of gross sales have been uncollectible.

    e. Deductions. Expenses are generally deductible in the period in which they accrue.

        1) The accrual-method taxpayer may claim an allowable deduction when both of the following requirements are met:

           a) All events have occurred that establish the fact of the liability, including that economic performance has occurred.

           b) The amount can be determined with reasonable accuracy.

        2) To the extent the amount of a liability is disputed, the test is not met. But any portion of a (still) contested amount that is paid is deductible.

        3) Economic performance occurs as services are performed or as property is provided or used.

        4) Under current case law, reserves for contingent liabilities (such as product warranties) are not determinable in amount with reasonable accuracy.

        5) Accrued vacation pay is generally deductible when paid.

        6) Deduction of an amount payable to a related party is allowed only when includible in gross income of the related party.

Hybrid Methods

6. Any combination of permissible accounting methods may be permitted if the combination clearly reflects income and is consistently used.

    a. If inventory is used, the accrual method must be used for purchases and sales. The cash method may be used for other receipts and expenses if income is clearly reflected.

    b. A person may use different methods for separate businesses as long as the method used for each business clearly reflects the income of that particular enterprise.

    c. Any hybrid method for reporting expenses that includes the cash method is treated as the cash method and is subject to the limitations that apply to the cash method.

Related Parties

7. The Code requires matching of a deduction claimed by a payor and income reported by a payee in related-party cases of expense or interest transactions.

    a. Typically, if the payee is a cash-basis taxpayer, (s)he will include the payment in income in the taxable year received, and the payor will then deduct the payment in the same year.

    b. Related parties include your spouse, child, grandchild, parent, brother/sister (half or whole), or a related corporation, S corporation, partnership, estate, or trust.

Stop and review! You have completed the outline for this subunit. Study questions 3 through 24 beginning on page 24.

1.3 ACCOUNTING PERIODS

The taxpayer adopts a tax year when the first income tax return is filed.

Tax Year

1. The term "tax year" is defined as follows:

    a. The annual accounting period regularly used by a taxpayer for keeping records of income, whether it be a calendar year or a fiscal year;

    b. The calendar year, if the taxpayer keeps no books, has no annual accounting period, or has an annual accounting period other than a calendar year that does not qualify as fiscal year; or

    c. The period for which the return is made, if for a period of less than 12 months.

Available Tax Years

2. The tax year may be either a calendar or fiscal year or the period for which a return is made, if the return is made for a period of less than 12 months (a short-period tax year).

    a. A calendar year is a period of 12 months ending on December 31.

    b. A fiscal year is a period of 12 months ending on the last day of any month other than December, or a 52- or 53-week tax year.

        1) A fiscal year will be recognized only if it is established as the taxpayer's annual accounting period and only if the books are kept in accord with it.

        2) A 52- or 53-week tax year. The taxpayer may elect to use a fiscal tax year that varies from 52 to 53 weeks if such period always ends on the same day of the week, either

            a) The last such day in a calendar month (e.g., January 31) or

            b) The closest such day to the last day of a calendar month (e.g., the last Friday in January).

Short Tax Year

    c. A return for a period of less than 12 months may be filed by a taxpayer that

        1) Existed during only part of what would otherwise be the taxable year or

        2) Changed the annual accounting period, e.g., from fiscal to calendar year.

            a) In calculating the tax for a short tax year, the income must first be annualized. Then the tax on the annualized income is calculated, and the final step is to determine the short tax year portion of tax.

$$\text{Annualized income} = \text{Short tax year income} \times \frac{12 \text{ months}}{\text{Short tax year months}}$$

Calculate tax:

$$\text{Short tax year tax} = \text{Annualized income tax} \times \frac{\text{Short tax year months}}{12 \text{ months}}$$

    d. Form 1128 is generally filed with the IRS to request the change in tax years.

        1) The form must be filed by the due date (not including extensions) of the federal income tax return for the first effective year.

        2) Permission to change tax years is normally granted when a substantial business purpose exists.

        3) When the sole purpose of the change is to obtain a favorable tax status, the substantial business purpose test is not met.

e. Form 8716 is filed with the IRS by partnerships, S corporations, and PSCs to request a change in tax years other than a required tax year.

1) This is called a Sec. 444 election.

2) A Sec. 444 election may be made without first requesting permission to use the tax year and being denied permission.

EXAMPLE

A partnership has a calendar year. Corporation X acquires over 50% ownership in the partnership. Corporation X has a June 30 tax year. Form 1128 is filed to change the partnership to a June 30 year end. June 30 is a required year end of the partnership. Form 8716 is filed instead of Form 1128 if the change is to a year end other than a required one.

Stop and review! You have completed the outline for this subunit. Study questions 25 through 27 beginning on page 30.

QUESTIONS

1.1 Business Entities

1. A domestic limited liability company with at least two members that does not file Form 8832, *Entity Classification Election*, is classified as

A. An entity disregarded as an entity separate from its owners by applying the rules in regulations section 301.7701-3.

B. A partnership.

C. A corporation.

D. A non-entity that requires members to report the income and related expenses on Form 1040.

Answer (B) is correct.

REQUIRED: The default entity classification of a domestic limited liability company with at least two members.

DISCUSSION: An eligible entity is classified for federal tax purposes under the default rules unless it filed Form 8832 or Form 2553 to elect a classification or change its current classification:

1. A partnership if it has two or more members

2. Disregarded as an entity separate from its owners if it has a single owner

3. Unless an election is made on Form 8832, a foreign eligible entity is

   a. A partnership if it has two or more members and at least one member does not have limited liability

   b. An association taxable as a corporation if all members have limited liability

   c. Disregarded as an entity separate from its owner if it has a single owner that does not have limited liability

Answer (A) is incorrect. An entity disregarded as an entity separate from its owner applies to an entity with a single owner. Answer (C) is incorrect. An association taxable as a corporation applies to foreign (not domestic) eligible entities. Answer (D) is incorrect. A domestic limited liability company with at least two members is classified as a partnership.

2. LLCs may be an attractive small business alternative as opposed to an S corporation because LLCs offer the following advantage(s) not available in S corporations:

A. Inclusion of entity-level liabilities in tax basis.

B. Pass-through taxation.

C. Flexibility in types of owners and ownership interests.

D. Both inclusion of entity-level liabilities in tax basis and flexibility in types of owners and ownership interests.

Answer (D) is correct.

REQUIRED: The advantages available to LLCs but not S corporations.

DISCUSSION: The basis of each member in an LLC, like a partnership, is increased or decreased by the allocable share of the LLC's liabilities (IRC Sec. 752). This allows for tax loss claims in excess of capital investment and greater tax-free distributions of money and property to members. A corporation's debt may not be used by an S corporation shareholder to increase their basis, regardless of guaranteeing the debt. LLCs have no limitations on the number of owners allowed. S corporations are limited to 100 shareholders. LLCs also do not have any restrictions as to the type of owners. S corporations are restricted to estates, certain tax-exempt organizations, certain trusts, and to individuals.

Answer (A) is incorrect. Flexibility in types of owners and ownership interests are also advantages of an LLC not available to S corporations. Answer (B) is incorrect. Both LLCs and S corporations have the advantage of pass-through taxation. Answer (C) is incorrect. Inclusion of entity-level liabilities in tax basis is also an advantage of an LLC not available to S corporations.

1.2 Accounting Methods

3. Which of the following accounting changes do not require the filing of Form 3115 to request a change in accounting method?

A. Correction of a math error.

B. Change from accrual method to cash method.

C. Change in the method inventory is valued.

D. Change from cash method to accrual method.

Answer (A) is correct.

REQUIRED: The accounting change that does not require the filing of Form 3115.

DISCUSSION: Sec. 446(e) requires the taxpayer to obtain permission from the IRS to change a method of accounting. A change from the accrual method to the cash method of accounting, or vice-versa, and the change in the method of inventory valuation are changes in the method of accounting that would require the filing of Form 3115. However, a correction of an error in calculating tax is not a change in accounting method [Reg. 1.446-1(e)(2)(ii)(b)].

Answer (B) is incorrect. A change from the accrual method to the cash method would require the filing of Form 3115. Answer (C) is incorrect. In general, a change in the method of inventory valuation would require the filing of Form 3115. A change to LIFO, however, does not require consent from the IRS (this is a special exception and not applicable to this general question). Answer (D) is incorrect. A change from the cash method to the accrual method would require the filing of Form 3115.

4. Which of the following accounting methods is not an acceptable method of reporting income and expenses?

A. If an inventory is necessary to account for your income, you must use an accrual method for purchases and sales. You can use the cash method for all other items of income and expenses.

B. If you use the cash method for figuring your income, you can use the accrual method for figuring your expenses.

C. Any combination that includes the cash method is treated as the cash method.

D. You can use different accounting methods for reporting business and personal items.

Answer (B) is correct.

REQUIRED: The unacceptable method of reporting income and expenses.

DISCUSSION: If the accrual method is used to report expenses, it must be used to report income items. (See Publication 538.)

Answer (A) is incorrect. If inventory is used, the accrual method must be used for purchases and sales. The cash method may be used for other receipts and expenses if income is clearly reflected. Answer (C) is incorrect. Any hybrid method for reporting expenses that includes the cash method is treated as the cash method and is subject to the limitations that apply to the cash method. Answer (D) is incorrect. A taxpayer may use different methods for separate businesses as long as the method used for each business clearly reflects the income of that particular enterprise.

5. Which of the following statements regarding accounting methods is false?

A. If inventories are necessary, the accrual method is used for sales and purchases.

B. A combination (hybrid) method is not an acceptable method of accounting.

C. A change from the accrual to the cash method of accounting requires consent from the IRS.

D. Under the cash method of accounting, gross income includes all items of income actually or constructively received during the year.

Answer (B) is correct.

REQUIRED: The false statement regarding accounting methods.

DISCUSSION: Under Sec. 446, one or more hybrid methods of accounting may be authorized by regulation. The regulations permit the use of a combination of methods if the combination clearly reflects income and is consistently used.

Answer (A) is incorrect. If inventory is used, the accrual method must be used for purchases and sales. The cash method may be used for other receipts and expenses if income is clearly stated. Answer (C) is incorrect. A change in accounting methods generally requires consent of the IRS, including change in the overall system of accounting. Answer (D) is incorrect. Under the cash method, all cash and constructive cash is considered income.

6. You can compute your taxable income under which of the following accounting methods?

A. Hybrid method.

B. Accrual method.

C. Special method for certain items.

D. All of the answers are correct.

Answer (D) is correct.

REQUIRED: The permissible accounting method(s) used to compute taxable income.

DISCUSSION: A taxpayer is permitted to use the hybrid method, accrual method, and other special methods for certain items when computing taxable income subject to specific rules. (See Publication 538.)

7. The following methods of accounting for inventory are considered acceptable except

   A. Cost.

   B. First-in, first-out.

   C. Last-in, first-out.

   D. Trade discount method.

Answer (D) is correct.

   REQUIRED: The unacceptable method to account for inventory.

   DISCUSSION: The cost method is used when the actual cost can be identified and matched to the items in inventory. The first-in, first-out and last-in, first-out methods are used when items cannot be specifically identified with their costs. A trade discount is not a method of accounting for inventory but rather an adjustment made to the cost method.

   Answer (A) is incorrect. Cost is an acceptable method used to account for inventory. Answer (B) is incorrect. First-in, first-out is an acceptable method used to account for inventory. Answer (C) is incorrect. Last-in, first-out is an acceptable method used to account for inventory.

8. Generally, all of the following entities may use the cash method of accounting except

   A. A family farming corporation with gross receipts of $25 million or less.

   B. An entity with no inventories and average annual gross receipts of $5 million or less.

   C. A qualified personal service corporation.

   D. A corporation that has long-term contracts.

Answer (D) is correct.

   REQUIRED: The entity prohibited from using the cash method of accounting.

   DISCUSSION: Corporations that have long-term contracts must use a special method of accounting (which is neither a pure cash nor accrual method). The following entities, however, may use the cash method of accounting: a family corporation with gross receipts of $25 million or less for each prior tax year beginning after 1985, any corporation or partnership (other than a tax shelter) that meets the gross receipts test for all tax years after 1985, and a qualified personal service corporation (Publication 538, page 9).

   Answer (A) is incorrect. A family farming corporation with gross receipts of $25 million or less may use the cash method of accounting. Answer (B) is incorrect. An entity with no inventories and average annual gross receipts less than $5 million may use the cash method of accounting. Answer (C) is incorrect. Qualified service corporations may use the cash method of accounting.

9. A cash-basis taxpayer should report gross income

   A. Only for the year in which income is actually received in cash.

   B. For the year in which income is either actually or constructively received in cash only.

   C. Only for the year in which income is actually received whether in cash or in property.

   D. For the year in which income is either actually or constructively received, whether in cash or in property.

Answer (D) is correct.

   REQUIRED: The timing of income of a cash-method taxpayer.

   DISCUSSION: A cash-method taxpayer accounts for an item of income when the first of the following occurs: (1) Cash is actually received, (2) an equivalent of cash is actually received, or (3) constructive receipt of cash or its equivalent occurs.

10. Erin earned $1,000 in interest in 2011. Erin withdrew $700 in 2012 and $300 in 2013. How much of the original $1,000 should Erin report as interest earned in 2013?

   A. $0

   B. $300

   C. $700

   D. $1,000

Answer (A) is correct.

   REQUIRED: The amount of interest Erin should report in gross income.

   DISCUSSION: Sec. 61(a) states that interest is considered income and is included on the taxpayer's tax return the year it is earned. The interest income of $1,000 earned in 2011 will have been included in Erin's 2011 tax return without regard to when the interest was withdrawn.

   Answer (B) is incorrect. The full $1,000 of interest earned in 2011 was taxed, and the $300 will not be taxed again in 2013. Answer (C) is incorrect. The full $1,000 of interest earned in 2011 was taxed, and the $700 will not be taxed again in 2013. Answer (D) is incorrect. The $1,000 was taxed in 2011 when it was earned; it will not be taxed again in 2013.

11. Which of the following statements is not correct?

A. Under an accrual method of accounting, you generally report income in the year earned and deduct or capitalize expenses in the year incurred.

B. Under an accrual method of accounting, you generally report receipt of an advance payment for services to be performed over 3 or more years as income in the year you receive the payment.

C. Under an accrual method of accounting, business expenses and interest owed to a related person who uses the cash method of accounting are deductible when the all-events test has been met.

D. Under an accrual method of accounting, you can take a current deduction for taxes when economic performance occurs.

Answer (C) is correct.

REQUIRED: The false statement about the accrual method of accounting.

DISCUSSION: Sec. 267 requires the matching of the deduction claimed by a payor and the income reported by a payee in the case of expense or interest transactions with related parties. This rule prevents an accrual method taxpayer taking a deduction in the year the expense accrued and the cash method taxpayer recognizing income from this in a latter year.

Answer (A) is incorrect. Under an accrual method of accounting, you generally report income in the year earned and deduct or capitalize expenses in the year incurred. Answer (B) is incorrect. Under an accrual method of accounting, you generally report receipt of an advance payment for services to be performed in a later tax year as income in the year you receive the payment if the service extends beyond the end of the next tax year. Answer (D) is incorrect. Under an accrual method of accounting, you can take a current deduction for taxes when economic performance occurs.

12. Generally, a substantial business inventory requires use of which method of accounting?

A. Cash.

B. Hybrid.

C. Accrual.

D. None of the answers are correct.

Answer (C) is correct.

REQUIRED: The required method of accounting when a substantial business inventory is present.

DISCUSSION: Reg. 1.446-1(c)(2) states that, when inventory is used, the accrual method of accounting must be used for purchases and sales.

Answer (A) is incorrect. Generally, the accrual, not the cash, method is required. Answer (B) is incorrect. Generally, the accrual, not the hybrid, method is required. Answer (D) is incorrect. The accrual method of accounting must be used.

13. John is a cash-basis taxpayer. He received the following items of income in December 2013:

1. The loan on his truck was forgiven because he performed accounting work for the dealer. He owed $2,000 at the time.

2. A retainer of $500 from a new client to guarantee that his services would be available in February when the client would need help preparing financial statements.

3. The $800 for work he completed in November of 2012.

How much of this income must John include on his 2013 tax return?

A. $500

B. $1,300

C. $2,500

D. $3,300

Answer (D) is correct.

REQUIRED: The amount of income a taxpayer must include on his or her tax return.

DISCUSSION: Gross income means all income from whatever source derived unless specifically excluded (Sec. 61). A taxpayer who is solvent generally realizes income to the extent that debts are forgiven (Sec. 108). Cash-basis taxpayers must report prepaid income when received.

Answer (A) is incorrect. The forgiven debt and the retainer are both included as gross income. Answer (B) is incorrect. The forgiven debt is included in gross income. Answer (C) is incorrect. The $800 received is included in 2013 because it is actually received in 2013.

14. Mark is an accrual-method taxpayer. He shipped $500 worth of merchandise to Ralph on December 30, 2013. Mark sent Ralph an invoice January 2, 2014, that was payable in 30 days. Ralph mailed his check to Mark on February 2, 2014. Mark deposited the check on February 6, 2014. Mark received and reconciled his bank statement March 3, 2014. When does Mark record the $500 in income?

A. January 2, 2014, because that is when he invoiced Ralph.

B. March 3, 2014, because that is when Mark verified that the $500 check had been accepted as a deposit.

C. December 30, 2013, the date when he shipped the merchandise to Ralph.

D. February 6, 2014, because that is when Mark deposited the check from Ralph.

Answer (C) is correct.

REQUIRED: The date that Mark should record income when using the accrual method.

DISCUSSION: An accrual-method taxpayer accounts for income in the period it is actually earned. Income is included when all the events have occurred that fix the right to receive it and the amount can be determined with reasonable accuracy. Because Mark has performed all activities necessary for the income to be earned, he must include the $500 as of December 30.

Answer (A) is incorrect. The date the invoice is sent out is irrelevant. Answer (B) is incorrect. The date Mark reconciles his bank statement is irrelevant. Answer (D) is incorrect. The date the merchandise is shipped, not the date Ralph deposited the check, is used in determining when to include the amount in gross income.

15. Linda is not deemed to have constructively received income in 2013 in which of the following situations?

A. Linda receives a check for her services on December 20, 2013, but waits until January 5, 2014, to cash the check.

B. In 2013, a third party promises to pay all of her debts to Linda in the near future. On January 2, 2014, Linda receives all of the payments due.

C. Linda's compensation payment is automatically deposited into her checking account on December 28, 2013. However, Linda does not draw any of the funds from her account until February 3, 2014.

D. In 2013, Linda receives payments subject to substantial restrictions. On December 27, 2013, the restrictions lapsed, and on January 18, 2014, Linda withdrew the funds.

Answer (B) is correct.

REQUIRED: The situation that is not constructive receipt.

DISCUSSION: Under the doctrine of constructive receipt, an item is included in gross income when a person has an unqualified right to immediate possession. However, constructive receipt involves more than a billing, an offer, or a mere promise to pay. Therefore, amounts promised to be paid do not need to be included in income until actually received.

Answer (A) is incorrect. Deferring deposit of a check does not defer income. Answer (C) is incorrect. Linda has the ability to use the funds in 2013. When she actually uses the funds is irrelevant. Answer (D) is incorrect. Constructive receipt occurs when substantial restrictions lapse.

16. Given the fact patterns below, which of the following entities may not use the cash method of accounting?

A. The Acme Partnership had gross receipts of $3,500,000 in 2013. Its gross receipts for 2012 were $8,000,000, and its gross receipts for 2011 were $3,000,000.

B. John Jones manufactures and sells fans. His average annual gross receipts since 2013 are $975,000.

C. Dallas Partnership has two partners in 2013 -- Joe Dallas, an individual, and Deer, Inc., a corporation. Dallas Partnership averaged annual gross receipts of $6,500,000.

D. John Gibb files his 2013 Form 1040 with an attached Schedule C reflecting $11,000,000 in gross receipts from selling real estate.

Answer (C) is correct.

REQUIRED: The entity that may not use the cash method of accounting.

DISCUSSION: A cash-method taxpayer accounts for an income item when the first of the following occurs: Cash is actually received; an equivalent of cash is actually received; and cash or its equivalent is constructively received. The cash method cannot be used by corporations (other than S corporations), partnerships having a corporation (other than an S corporation) as a partner, and tax shelters.

Answer (A) is incorrect. The partnership may use the cash method of accounting. Answer (B) is incorrect. A sole proprietor may use the cash method of accounting. Answer (D) is incorrect. A sole proprietor selling real estate may use the cash method of accounting.

17. Peter is an auto mechanic. On November 25, 2013, he made some major auto repairs on Harry's Mercedes. Harry is an attorney. In exchange for the service, Harry is going to draft Peter's will and represent him when he settles on his new house. Harry will perform all of these services in 2014. The repair bill for the Mercedes came to $1,200. Both Peter and Harry are cash-basis taxpayers. How do they report this income?

A. Both report $1,200 income in 2013.

B. Both report $1,200 income in 2014.

C. Harry reports $1,200 in 2013 and Peter reports $1,200 in 2014.

D. Peter reports $1,200 in 2013 and Harry reports $1,200 in 2014.

Answer (C) is correct.
REQUIRED: The amount of income reported for parties exchanging services.
DISCUSSION: Under Sec. 451(a) and Reg. 1.451-1(a), a cash-basis taxpayer generally includes an item in income when it is actually or constructively received. Under Sec. 461(a) and Reg. 1.461-1, a cash-basis taxpayer generally reports income only in the year of actual receipt. Constructive receipt is equivalent to actual receipt. The services performed for Harry were completed in 2013, and therefore he reports $1,200 of income in 2013. The services performed for Peter were completed in 2014, and therefore he reports $1,200 of income in 2014.
Answer (A) is incorrect. Peter receives services in 2014. Answer (B) is incorrect. Harry receives services in 2013. Answer (D) is incorrect. Harry receives services in 2013, and Peter receives services in 2014.

18. In September 2013, Charlie, a self-employed lawyer, performed legal services for a client that has a men's clothing store. In payment for his services, Charlie received store credit of $3,500 in 2013. Charlie uses $1,500 of his store credit in 2013 and the balance in 2014. How should Charlie include the income?

	2013	2014
A.	$3,500	$0
B.	$1,500	$2,000
C.	$0	$3,500

D. None of the answers are correct.

Answer (A) is correct.
REQUIRED: The amount includible in gross income in the respective year.
DISCUSSION: The taxpayer is to include in gross income amounts received as salary or wages. If a taxpayer is an accrual method payor, items are included when the amounts receivable are reasonably estimable and all necessary events have occurred to ensure the taxpayer's right to receive income. On the other hand, a cash-method taxpayer includes items in gross income when actually or constructively received. Specifically, constructive receipt occurs when payment is made available to the taxpayer without restriction; actual possession is not necessary. Therefore, regardless of Charlie's method of accounting, all $3,500 would be included in 2013. (See Publication 334.)
Answer (B) is incorrect. All $3,500, not just $1,500, is included in 2013. Answer (C) is incorrect. All is included in 2013, not 2014. Answer (D) is incorrect. One of the answers is correct.

19. Ms. Dee owns and operates a dance studio. On December 1, 2012, she received an advance payment of $2,400 from Angie to give her 12 dance lessons. The agreement stated that one lesson would be given in 2012 and 11 lessons in 2013. However, due to Angie's health, one lesson scheduled for June 2013 was postponed until January 2014. Ms. Dee uses the calendar year and the accrual method of accounting. Assuming Dee elects to defer the advance payments, when must she include the payment received from Angie in income?

A. $2,400 in 2013.

B. $200 in 2012 and $2,200 in 2013.

C. $200 in 2012, $2,000 in 2013, and $200 in 2014.

D. $2,400 in 2012.

Answer (B) is correct.
REQUIRED: The amount and timing of the recognition of prepaid income.
DISCUSSION: Generally, amounts that are paid for future services are required to be included in the year of receipt. However, accrual-basis taxpayers may elect to defer recognition until the time of performance. The amount of the deferral is proportionate to the portion of services remaining unperformed at the end of the tax year of receipt. The amount deferred must be included in income in the tax year following the tax year of receipt regardless of whether the remaining services are all performed in that tax year. Ms. Dee must recognize $200 in 2012 ($2,400 × 1/12) and the remainder, $2,200, in 2013.
Answer (A) is incorrect. The portion of the contract performed in 2012 must be recognized in that year. Answer (C) is incorrect. The full amount of the payment must be recognized by the end of the year following the year of receipt. Answer (D) is incorrect. The prepayment for future services may be deferred until the time of performance.

20. Candice operates a business giving art lessons at her studio. On October 3, 2012, she collected $800 from Robbie under a 1-year contract. The contract provided for 40 1-hour weekly lessons beginning that day. During 2012, Candice gave Robbie 10 lessons. In 2013, Robbie received 28 lessons, and in 2014, he received the remaining two. Candice uses a calendar tax year and the accrual method of accounting. She elects to defer the advance payments. When should she report the income from these lessons?

	2012	2013	2014
A.	$0	$800	$0
B.	$200	$600	$0
C.	$200	$560	$40
D.	$800	$0	$0

Answer (B) is correct.
REQUIRED: The amount an accrual-basis taxpayer includes in income from prepaid services.
DISCUSSION: Generally, an accrual-basis taxpayer must recognize prepaid income when received. However, prepaid income for services may be accrued over the period for which the services are to be performed provided that the period does not extend past the end of the next tax year (Rev. Proc. 71-21).
Here, the services are to be performed during a 1-year period under the contract. Therefore, the income is recognized in that 1-year period. The first 10 lessons are given in 2012, so $200 [(10 lessons ÷ 40 lessons) × $800] is includible in 2012. The remaining income of $600 must be reported by December of 2013, even though two lessons are given in 2014.
Answer (A) is incorrect. The portion of the contract performed in 2012 must be recognized in that year. Answer (C) is incorrect. The remaining income must be recognized by the end of the 2013 tax year. Answer (D) is incorrect. The taxpayer elects to defer the advance payments.

21. Alayna is a voice and singing coach. She is a calendar-year taxpayer using the accrual method of accounting. On November 2, 2012, she received $3,200 for a 2-year contract for 64 1-hour voice and singing lessons beginning on that date. The contract provided that Alayna give eight lessons in 2012 and 48 lessons in 2013, with the remaining lessons to be given in 2014. What is the amount that Alayna should report on her 2013 return?

A. $0

B. $2,800

C. $3,200

D. $2,400

Answer (B) is correct.
REQUIRED: The amount and timing of the recognition of prepaid income.
DISCUSSION: Amounts that are paid for future services are required to be included in the year of receipt. This rule applies whether the taxpayer is on the cash or accrual method of accounting. There is an exception that allows an accrual method taxpayer to defer recognition of advance payments up to 1 year. Alayna must recognize $400 in 2012 for the eight lessons given. She must recognize the balance of $2,800 in 2013 because the income cannot be deferred more than 1 year (Rev. Proc. 2004-34).
Answer (A) is incorrect. Recognition of the prepayment for future services may be deferred up to 1 year for accrual method taxpayers. Answer (C) is incorrect. The income for services rendered in 2014 may not be deferred beyond 2013. Answer (D) is incorrect. The prepaid amounts for 2013 and 2014 may be deferred to 2013.

22. The Kilometer Partnership sells computers and maintains its accounting system on the accrual basis. Kilometer sold and delivered a computer on December 29, 2012, and billed the customer $3,250 on January 7, 2013. Kilometer received the $3,250 payment on February 15, 2013. The check cleared on February 22, 2013. On which date will Kilometer recognize this income?

A. January 7, 2013.

B. February 15, 2013.

C. December 29, 2012.

D. February 22, 2013.

Answer (C) is correct.
REQUIRED: The date an accrual-basis taxpayer recognizes income.
DISCUSSION: A sale is included in gross income on the date in which all the events that fix the taxpayer's right to receive income have occurred and an amount can be determined with reasonable accuracy. Kilometer Partnership recognizes the sale of the computer on December 29, 2012. This is the date of the sale and delivery of the product. Both the right to receive income and a reasonably accurate estimate of the amount to be received arise on this date (Publication 538, page 10).
Answer (A) is incorrect. The date on which a bill is sent to the customer is generally not the earliest date that a taxpayer can include a sale in gross income. Answer (B) is incorrect. Kilometer would recognize the sale on February 15, 2013, if it were a cash-basis taxpayer. Answer (D) is incorrect. The date on which a customer's check clears does not represent the time when all the events to secure the taxpayer's right to receive income occurs.

23. Eric, a cash-basis taxpayer, owned 25% of Watson, Inc., stock. Watson files a calendar-year *U.S. Corporation Income Tax Return*, Form 1120, employing the accrual method of accounting. Eric loaned Watson $100,000 at the beginning of 2012. The accrued interest on this loan was $5,000 as of December 31, 2012. Watson paid Eric the $5,000 in January of 2013. How should Eric report the interest income and Watson, Inc., report the interest expense from this transaction?

A. Watson reports the expense in 2012, and Eric reports the income in 2012

B. Watson reports the expense in 2012, and Eric reports the income in 2013.

C. Watson reports the expense in 2013, and Eric reports the income in 2013.

D. None of the answers are correct.

Answer (B) is correct.
    REQUIRED: The recognition of interest income and expense when using the cash and accrual methods.
    DISCUSSION: A cash-basis taxpayer accounts for an income item when the first of the following occurs: Cash is actually received; an equivalent of cash is actually received; and cash or its equivalent is constructively received. An accrual-method taxpayer generally would account for an expense in the period when the expense was incurred. Because Eric does not own a controlling stake in the corporation he made the loan to, these rules apply. Thus, Watson would report the expense in the period incurred, 2012, and Eric would report the income in the period received, 2013.
    Answer (A) is incorrect. Eric is cash-basis taxpayer and would report the income in the period received. Answer (C) is incorrect. Watson can report the expense when incurred, in 2012. Because Eric does not own a controlling stake in Watson, these rules apply. Answer (D) is incorrect. Watson reports the expense in 2012, and Eric reports the income in 2013.

24. Farmer John, a cash-basis taxpayer, bought $3,000 of cattle feed in Year 1 for use in Year 2. John's other farming expenses for Year 1 amounted to $2,000. In prior years, he also had prepaid expenses in excess of nonprepaid expenses. How much and when is the cattle feed deductible?

	Year 1	Year 2
A.	$0	$1,000
B.	$0	$3,000
C.	$1,000	$2,000
D.	$3,000	$0

Answer (C) is correct.
    REQUIRED: The amount of prepaid feed a farmer may deduct.
    DISCUSSION: Reg. 1.162-12 provides that farmers (but not farming syndicates) may deduct prepaid feed when the expenditure is incurred even if it is to be consumed by the livestock in a subsequent year. After 1986, even an individual farmer's deduction of prepaid farm supplies is limited by Sec. 464(f) to 50% of other farming expenses incurred during the taxable year. Farmer John's deduction of prepaid cattle feed for Year 1 is thus limited to $1,000 ($2,000 other expenses × 50%).
    If the farmer has a principal residence on a farm or his or her principal occupation is farming, and if the aggregate of prepaid farm supplies for the prior 3 taxable years is less than 50% of the aggregate of other deductible farming expenses, the 50% limitation does not apply for the current year.
    Answer (A) is incorrect. The farmer is permitted to deduct a portion of the expenses in Year 1. Answer (B) is incorrect. The farmer is permitted to deduct a portion of the expenses in Year 1. Answer (D) is incorrect. The farmer's deduction in Year 1 is limited to 50% of other farming expenses incurred during the taxable year.

1.3 Accounting Periods

25. In order to adopt a fiscal tax year on its first federal income tax return, the taxpayer must

A. Maintain books and records and report income and expenses using that tax year.

B. Attach a completed Form 1128 to his or her fiscal-year-basis income tax return.

C. File a short-period return.

D. Get IRS approval.

Answer (A) is correct.
    REQUIRED: The procedure that a taxpayer must follow to adopt a fiscal tax year on its first tax return.
    DISCUSSION: Permission from the IRS is generally not needed to place a taxpayer's first tax year on either a calendar- or a fiscal-year basis. A taxpayer's first tax year is selected on the initial return. However, in order to adopt a fiscal year, the new taxpayer must adopt that year on the books and records before the due date for filing the return for that year (not including extensions).
    Answer (B) is incorrect. A completed Form 1128 is not required to adopt a fiscal tax year on a taxpayer's first federal income tax return. Answer (C) is incorrect. A short-period tax year return is for a period of less than 12 months for taxpayers with special circumstances. Answer (D) is incorrect. IRS approval is not necessary on the initial return.

26. Which of the following dates would not be considered the end of a tax year?

A. The last Friday in June.

B. September 30, 2013.

C. April 15, 2013.

D. December 31, 2013.

Answer (C) is correct.
　　REQUIRED: The date not considered the end of a tax year.
　　DISCUSSION: A calendar year is a period of 12 months ending on December 31. A fiscal year is a period of 12 months ending on the last day of any month other than December, or a 52- or 53-week tax year. A fiscal year will be recognized only if it is established as the taxpayer's annual accounting period and only if the books are kept in accord with it. The taxpayer may elect to use a fiscal tax year that varies from 52 to 53 weeks if such period always ends on the same day of the week, either the last such day in a calendar month or the closest such day to the last day of a calendar month. (See Publication 538.)
　　Answer (A) is incorrect. It could be an end of tax year date under a 52- or 53-week tax year. Answer (B) is incorrect. It could be an end of tax year date under a fiscal year or 52- or 53-week tax year. Answer (D) is incorrect. It is the end of a calendar-year tax year.

27. Mr. Jones has an adjusted gross income of $40,000 and itemized deductions of $16,000 for the 6-month period from January 1 through June 30, 2013. He is allowed to claim exemptions of $15,600 (four people). Mr. Jones received an approved change to his tax year, and he must file a short tax year return. What is the taxable income amount that Mr. Jones must use to compute his short year return?

A. $8,400

B. $16,200

C. $32,400

D. $24,000

Answer (C) is correct.
　　REQUIRED: The amount of taxable income for a short tax year.
　　DISCUSSION: Publication 538 states, "Income tax for a short tax year must be annualized. . . . An individual must figure income tax for the short tax year as follows.

1.　Determine your adjusted gross income for the short tax year and then subtract your actual itemized deductions for the short tax year. (You must itemize deductions when you file a short-period tax return.)

2.　Multiply the dollar amount of your exemptions by the number of months in the short tax year and divide the result by 12.

3.　Subtract the amount in (2) from the amount in (1). This is your modified taxable income.

4.　Multiply the modified taxable income in (3) by 12, then divide the result by the number of months in the short tax year. This is your annualized income."

Therefore, the taxable amount of income he must report on his short year tax return is $32,800.

1.	$40,000 − $16,000	=	$24,000
2.	$15,600 × 6 ÷ 12	=	7,800
3.	$24,000 − $7,800	=	$16,200
4.	$16,200 × 12 ÷ 6	=	$32,400

　　Answer (A) is incorrect. This amount subtracts the full personal exemptions, does not annualize AGI, and does not follow steps 2-4. Answer (B) is incorrect. This amount does not annualize income by following step 4. Answer (D) is incorrect. This amount does not annualize the personal exemptions.

Use the additional questions in Gleim **EA Test Prep** to create Practice Exams that emulate Prometric!

STUDY UNIT TWO
INCOME, FARMS, AND PROPERTY TRANSACTIONS

(12 pages of outline)

Businesses define gross income the same as individuals. Also like individuals, some business transactions do not currently recognize or indefinitely exclude recognition of income, but instead defer recognition until a later period. This study unit also covers unique aspects of self-employment income, farm income, small business stock, like-kind exchanges, and involuntary conversions.

2.1 GROSS INCOME

The IRC (Internal Revenue Code) defines gross income as all income from whatever source derived except as otherwise provided.

1. Sec. 61(a) enumerates types of income that constitute gross income. The list is not exhaustive.

   a. Compensation for services, including fees, commissions, and fringe benefits
   b. Gross income derived from business
   c. Gains derived from dealings in property
   d. Interest
   e. Rents
   f. Royalties
   g. Dividends
   h. Alimony and separate maintenance payments
   i. Annuities
   j. Income from life insurance and endowment contracts
   k. Pensions
   l. Income from discharge of indebtedness
   m. Distributive share of partnership gross income
   n. Income in respect of a decedent (income earned but not received before death)
   o. Income from an interest in an estate or trust

2. Other types of income also constitute gross income unless a statute specifically provides for their exclusion.

Business Income

3. Gross income includes all income from a trade or business.

   a. Gross income from a business that sells products or commodities is

   ```
     Gross sales (receipts)
   − Cost of goods sold
   + Other gross income (e.g., rentals)
   = Gross income from the business
   ```

    b.   Cost of goods sold is essentially treated as a return of capital. A return of capital is not income for tax purposes. Typically, cost of goods sold for a tax year is

              Beginning inventory
        + Inventory purchased during year
        − Year-end inventory
        = Cost of goods sold

    c.   Cost of goods sold should be determined in accordance with the method of accounting consistently used by the business.

Bad Debt Recovery

4.   The recovery of an amount previously deducted as a bad debt is included in gross income to the extent that the prior deduction reduced taxes.

Prepaid Income

5.   Generally, amounts that are received in advance for future services are required to be included in the year of receipt. However, accrual-basis taxpayers can elect to defer recognition until the time of performance, up to the year after the payment date.

Discharge of Debt

6.   Income is not recognized from a canceled debt to the extent the payment would have been a deduction when paid.

    a.   An unpaid business debt of a cash-basis taxpayer is not income when canceled.

    b.   The canceled debt of an accrual-basis taxpayer would be income because the deduction has already been taken.

7.   **Examples of Other Taxable Income**

    a.   Prizes and awards

    b.   Gambling winnings (e.g., lottery and raffle winnings)

    c.   Jury duty fees

    d.   Income from the rental of personal property if the taxpayer engages in the activity for profit but is not in the business of renting property

    e.   Income from an activity not engaged in for profit (e.g., hobby income)

        1)   Hobby-related expenses are deductible (to the extent of hobby income) as itemized deductions.

    f.   Reimbursements for items deducted in an earlier tax return (e.g., state income taxes, bad debts, and medical expenses)

    g.   Supplemental wages, which are compensation paid in addition to an employee's regular wages

        1)   They do not include payments for travel reimbursements paid at the federal government per diem rate.

Assignment of Income

8.   Gross income includes income attributable to a person even though the income is received by other persons. This doctrine imposes the tax on income on those who earn it, produce the right to receive it or enjoy the benefit of it when paid, or control property that is its source.

EXAMPLE

Swift, a life insurance salesperson, directs his employer to pay his commissions to his daughter. The commissions paid to Swift's daughter are gross income to Swift.

---

    a.   The doctrine applies to income earned by personal services or derived from property.

EXAMPLE

Taxpayer makes a gift of interest earned on securities to her 20-year-old daughter who attends college. The interest is gross income to Taxpayer.

---

    b.   Assignment of an income-producing asset is effective to shift the gross income to the assignee.

EXAMPLE

Taxpayer gives the underlying securities to her 20-year-old daughter. Interest earned after the transfer is gross income to the daughter.

---

    c.   Effective assignment requires that

        1)   The transfer of property be complete and bona fide,
        2)   No control retained over either the property or the income it produces, and
        3)   The transfer take place before the income is actually earned.

Stop and review! You have completed the outline for this subunit. Study questions 1 through 5 beginning on page 44.

2.2 SELF-EMPLOYMENT INCOME

A FICA tax liability is imposed on net earnings from self-employment (SE).

Included

    1.   Net earnings from self-employment include

        a.   Net income from a trade or business,
        b.   General distributive share of the ordinary income or loss of a partnership (whether active or not),
        c.   Guaranteed payments for services from a partnership,
        d.   Corporate director's fees, and
        e.   Payments for lost earnings.

Excluded

    2.   Net earnings from self-employment do not include

        a.   Salaries, fees, etc., subject to Social Security or Medicare tax that a taxpayer received for performing services as an employee
        b.   Rent from real estate and personal property leased with real estate unless services are provided to tenants

            1)   Services generally are provided for the occupants if they are primarily for their convenience and not services normally provided with the rental of rooms for occupancy only. (See Publication 334.)

        c.   Dividends and interest from any bond, debenture, note, certificate, or other indebtedness issued with interest coupons or in registered form by a corporation unless they are received by a dealer in stocks or securities in the ordinary course of his or her business
        d.   An S corporation shareholder's distributive share of income or loss
        e.   The sale, exchange, involuntary conversion (gains resulting from casualty or theft losses), or other disposition of property unless the property is stock in the business or property that is considered inventory primarily held for sale to customers in the ordinary course of business
        f.   Fees received for services performed as a notary public

Self-Employment Tax

3.   The FICA tax liability is imposed on net earnings from self-employment is twice the rate that applies to an employer, that is, 15.3% [2 × (6.20% Social Security tax + 1.45% Medicare tax)].

   a.   Net earnings from self-employment are tentative net earnings from self-employment, minus .0765 times tentative net earnings from self-employment.

   b.   Self-employed individuals can deduct 50% of FICA taxes paid to arrive at AGI.

   c.   The self-employment tax is computed using the total earnings from self-employment; therefore, no change in computation is necessary if the self-employed person has more than one trade or business.

   d.   For 2013, the maximum amount of wages subject to Social Security tax is $113,700. However, the Medicare component does not have a cap amount.

   e.   In 2013, self-employed persons may deduct 100% of amounts paid for health insurance from gross income (AGI). The insurance can be for themselves, their spouses, or their dependents.

   f.   Contributions to a qualified retirement plan for a self-employed individual do not constitute a business expense. Therefore, they are not deductible when computing self-employment tax.

Religious Exemptions

4.   A religious exemption for self-employment tax is available for a duly ordained, commissioned, or licensed minister of a church; a member of a religious order; or a Christian Science practitioner if (s)he files an exemption certificate (Form 4361).

Stop and review! You have completed the outline for this subunit. Study questions 6 through 8 on page 46.

2.3 FARMING INCOME AND EXPENSE

   Gross income from farming includes gross farm income, gross farm rental income, and gains from the sale of livestock that were raised on the farm or purchased for resale.

Gross Income from Farming

1.   Gross farm income includes

   a.   Income from farming -- amounts received from cultivating the soil or raising or harvesting agricultural commodities.

   b.   Gains from the sale of livestock -- amounts received for livestock raised on the farm or purchased for resale. The basis of livestock is generally the cost of the animals.

   c.   Income reported on Schedule F.

Gross Farm Rental Income

2.   Rent received from the use of farmland is generally rental income unless it is rent received from crop shares or unless the taxpayer materially participates in the lessee's operations.

Gains from the Sale of Livestock

3.   Gains from the sale of livestock used for draft (hauling), dairy, breeding, or sporting purposes generally result in capital gains and are not reported on Schedule F.

   a.   Gains on the sale of these types of livestock are reported on Form 4797, Part I.

Where to Report Sales of Farm Products

Items Sold	Schedule F	Form 4797
Farm products raised for sale	X	
Farm products bought for resale	X	
Farm assets not held primarily for sale, such as livestock held for draft, breeding, sport, or dairy purposes (bought or raised)		X

4. Agriculture program payments are reported on Form 1040, Part I, Schedule F and are subject to self-employment taxes.

Capitalization and Depreciation

5. If the taxpayer produced real or tangible personal property or acquired property for resale, certain expenses must be included in inventory costs or capitalized. These expenses include the direct costs of the property and the share of any indirect costs allocable to that property.

   a. However, these rules generally do not apply to expenses of

      1) Producing any plant that has a preproductive period of 2 years or less;
      2) Raising animals; or
      3) Replanting certain crops if they were lost or damaged by reason of freezing temperatures, disease, drought, pests, or casualty.

   b. A farmer can deduct depreciation of buildings, improvements, cars and trucks, machinery, and other farm equipment of a permanent nature. Do not deduct depreciation on a home, furniture or other personal items, land, livestock bought or raised for resale, or other property in inventory. A farmer can also elect under Section 179 to expense a portion of the cost of certain property bought during the year for use in a farming business.

Section 1231 Gains

6. Schedule F does not include gains and losses from sales or other dispositions of farm land (Section 1231 property), depreciable farm equipment (Section 1245 property), and buildings and structures (Section 1250 property).

Farm Income Averaging

7. If a taxpayer is engaged in a farming or fishing business, (s)he may be able to average all or some of his or her current year's farm income by shifting it to the 3 prior years (base years).

   a. An individual, a partner in a partnership, or a shareholder in an S corporation may elect farm income averaging on a timely filed return (including extensions) or later if the IRS approves.

      1) The taxpayer need not have engaged in a farming business in any base year.

   b. Corporations, partnerships, S corporations, estates, and trusts cannot use farm income averaging.

   c. To elect farm income averaging as a tax computation method, you must file a Schedule J with your income tax return for the election year.

      1) This includes late or amended returns if the period of limitations on filing a claim for credit or refund has not expired.

8.   **Special Circumstances**

Weather-Related Gains

a.   The gain from sales caused by drought, flood, or other weather-related conditions (causing the affected area to be eligible for assistance by the federal government) can be postponed for 4 years. If, because of the weather-related conditions, a farmer who uses the cash method of accounting sells more livestock (including poultry) than (s)he would have sold under normal business conditions, the farmer may choose to include the gain from the sale of the additional livestock in income next year instead of the current year.

1)   The election applies to all livestock, whether held for resale or other purposes. It applies even if the livestock was actually exchanged or sold before an area is designated as eligible for federal assistance, as long as the weather-related condition caused the exchange or sale.

Crop Insurance and Disaster Payments

b.   Crop insurance and disaster payments are generally included in income in the year they are received.

1)   An election is available to include the proceeds in income for the tax year following the tax year in which the crops were damaged.

a)   The taxpayer must prove that the income from such crops would have been reported in the following taxable year.

b)   The taxpayer must attach a statement to the return to verify this requirement has been met.

Estimated Taxes

9.   If a taxpayer qualifies as a farmer by receiving at least two-thirds of the total gross income from farming in the current year or the preceding tax year, the following special rules apply:

a.   The taxpayer shall pay all estimated taxes by January 15 and then file the 1040 return and pay any additional taxes by April 15. The required annual payment is the smaller of two-thirds of the current year's tax or 100% of the previous year's tax.

b.   In lieu of estimated payments described in 9.a., the taxpayer may file the 1040 return and pay all taxes due by March 1.

c.   The taxpayer should be sure to include any alternative minimum tax that (s)he expects to owe in the calculation for estimated tax.

Stop and review! You have completed the outline for this subunit. Study questions 9 through 16 beginning on page 47.

2.4   SMALL BUSINESS STOCK

Section 1202 and Section 1244 stock provisions are both designed to encourage investment in small business corporations. However, there are major differences between the two. Under Section 1202, a taxpayer may be allowed to exclude from taxable income all or a portion of the capital gain realized on the sale of qualified small business stock. Under Section 1244, owners of a qualified small business corporation are able to deduct as ordinary losses any losses sustained when they dispose of their small business stock up to an annual limit.

1.   Sec. 1244 stock is stock (common or preferred, voting or nonvoting) of a small business corporation held since its issuance (e.g., not acquired by gift or subsequent purchases) and issued for money or other property (not stock or securities).

a. Up to $50,000 ($100,000 if joint return) of loss realized on disposition or worthlessness of Sec. 1244 stock is treated as an ordinary loss.

   1) The limit applies to Sec. 1244 stock held in all corporations.
   2) The limit is applied at a partner level, if applicable.
   3) The loss is considered to be from a trade or business for NOL purposes.

b. To be classified as a small business corporation, the aggregate amount of money and other property received by the corporation for stock, as a contribution to capital and as paid-in surplus, cannot exceed $1 million.

   1) However, even if the paid-in capital exceeds $1 million, part of the stock (up to $1 million) may be designated by the corporation as qualifying for Sec. 1244 ordinary loss treatment.

c. Any excess of basis over FMV of depreciated property at the time of its contribution in exchange for Sec. 1244 stock is treated as capital loss (to the extent thereof) before any other realized loss may be treated as ordinary.

   1) Basis in the stock is equal to the property's basis in the hands of the transferor when contributed.
   2) When an owner of Sec. 1244 stock makes an additional capital contribution but does not receive any additional shares of stock, the additional investment cost is added to the basis of the previously held stock.

      a) The additional basis does not qualify for the Sec. 1244 ordinary loss treatment.
      b) Any future loss must be apportioned between the qualifying Sec. 1244 stock and the additional capital interest.

Sec. 1202 Stock Qualified Small Business Stock

2. When a taxpayer sells or exchanges Sec. 1202 small business stock that the taxpayer has held for more than 5 years, 50% of the gain may be excluded from the taxpayer's gross income.

   a. If the small business stock qualifies for this 50% exclusion, any recognized gain from the sale or exchange of the stock is subject to a maximum capital gains rate of 28%.

3. The general requirements for stock to be treated as Sec. 1202 qualified small business stock are as follows:

   a. The stock is received after August 10, 1993.
   b. The issuing corporation is a domestic C corporation.
   c. The seller is the original owner of the stock.
   d. The corporation's gross assets do not exceed $50 million at the time the stock was issued.

4. If the stock is acquired after February 17, 2009, and before September 28, 2010, 75% of the gain may be excluded. The exclusion increases to 100% for stock acquired after September 27, 2010, and before January 1, 2014.

Stop and review! You have completed the outline for this subunit. Study questions 17 through 19 beginning on page 49.

2.5 LIKE-KIND EXCHANGES

Sec. 1031 defers recognizing gain or loss to the extent that property productively used in a trade or business or held for the production of income (investment) is exchanged for property of like-kind. Realized gain (loss) is the gain (loss) from the sale or exchange. Recognized gain (loss) is the amount reported on the tax return.

Like-Kind Property

1. Like-kind property is alike in nature or character but not necessarily in grade or quality.

    a. Properties are of like kind if each is within a class of like nature or character, without regard to differences in use (e.g., business or investment), improvements (e.g., bare land or house), location (e.g., city or rural), or proximity.

General Asset Classes	
Office furniture, fixtures, and equipment (asset class 00.11)	Light general-purpose trucks (asset class 00.241)
Information systems (computers and peripheral equipment) (asset class 00.12)	Heavy general-purpose trucks (asset class 00.242)
Data handling equipment, except computers (asset class 00.13)	Railroad cars and locomotives, except those owned by railroad transportation companies (asset class 00.25)
Airplanes (airframes and engines), except those used in commercial or contract carrying of passengers or freight, and all helicopters (airframes and engines) (asset class 00.21)	Tractor units for use over-the-road (asset class 00.26)
Automobiles, taxis (asset class 00.22)	Trailers and trailer-mounted containers (asset class 00.27)
Buses (asset class 00.23)	Vessels, barges, tugs, and similar water transportation equipment, except those used in marine construction (asset class 00.28)
Industrial steam and electric generation and/or distribution systems (asset class 00.4)	

EXAMPLE

Taxpayer C transfers a railroad car (asset class 00.25) to D in exchange for a tractor-trailer container (asset class 00.27). The properties exchanged are not of a like class because they are within different General Asset Classes. Therefore, the exchange does not qualify for nonrecognition of gain or loss under section 1031.

Examples of like-kind exchanges are car for truck, unimproved farm property for office building, store building for parking lot, investment for business real property.

    b. Real property is of like kind to other real property, except foreign property.
    c. Personal property and real property are not of like kind.
    d. A lease of real property for 30 or more years is treated as real property.

Liabilities

2. Liabilities are not qualified property, whether incurred or relieved of.

    a. They are treated as money paid or received.
    b. If each party assumes a liability of the other, only the net liability given or received is treated as boot.

Unqualified Property

3. The following property types do not qualify for Sec. 1031 nonrecognition:

   a. Money
   b. Liabilities
   c. Inventory
   d. Partnership interest in different partnerships, e.g., general for general
   e. Securities and debt instruments, e.g., stocks, bonds
   f. Livestock (if different sexes)

Boot

4. Boot is all nonqualified property transferred in an exchange transaction.

   a. Gain is recognized equal to the lesser of gain realized or boot received.
   b. Boot received includes cash, net liability relief, and other nonqualified property (its FMV).

5. If some qualified property is exchanged, loss realized with respect to qualified or other property is not recognized.

Basis

6. Qualified property received in a like-kind exchange has an exchanged basis adjusted for boot and gain recognized.

   AB of property given
   + Gain recognized
   + Boot given (cash, liability, incurred, other property)
   − Boot received (cash, liability relief, other property) + legal fees incurred
   = Basis in acquired property

Realized Gain

7. Under Sec. 1031, realized gain is usually recognized only to the extent of boot (cash + FMV of other property + net liability relief) received.

8. The realized gain when not like-kind property is received is calculated as follows (see Form 8824 Part III):

   FMV of like-kind property received
   + Cash received
   + FMV of other property received (not like-kind)
   + Liability relief
   − Expenses incurred (e.g., closing cost)
   − AB of like-kind property given
   − Net amounts paid
   = Realized gain

   a. **Sec. 1245** ordinary income is limited to the sum of the following:

      1) Gain recognized and
      2) FMV of property acquired that is not Sec. 1245 property and is not included in computing the recognized gain.

   b. **Sec. 1250** ordinary income is limited to the greater of the following:

      1) Recognized gain or
      2) Excess of the potential Sec. 1250 ordinary income over the FMV of Sec. 1250 property received.

   c. Basis in property acquired is increased for gain recognized.

Deferred Like-Kind Exchanges

9.   If a taxpayer sells property and buys similar property in two mutually dependent transactions, the taxpayer may have to treat the sale and purchase as a single nontaxable exchange.

Qualified Exchange Accommodation Agreement

10. With a qualified exchange accommodation agreement, the property given up or the replacement property is transferred to an exchange accommodation titleholder. The exchange accommodation titleholder is considered the beneficial owner of the property.

   a.   This arrangement allows a transfer in which a taxpayer acquires replacement property before transferring relinquished property to qualify as a tax-free exchange.

   b.   The following requirements must be met:

      1)   Time limits for identifying and transferring the property are satisfied.
      2)   A written agreement exists.
      3)   The exchange accommodation titleholder has the qualified indications of ownership of the property.

Related Parties

11. Like-kind exchanges between related parties are subject to special restrictions.

   a.   Related parties include members of a family, a grantor of a trust, a corporation in which the taxpayer has more than 50% ownership, or a partnership in which the taxpayer directly or indirectly owns more than 50% interest in the capital or profits.

Reporting

12. A taxpayer must substantiate the existence of a like-kind exchange.

13. Sec. 1031 like-kind exchanges are reported annually on Form 8824 and include the following:

   a.   Description of property exchanged
   b.   Dates of acquisition, transfer, property identification, and actual receipt
   c.   Related party exchange information
   d.   Realized gain (loss) and basis in property received

Depreciation

14. Generally, a taxpayer must depreciate MACRS (Modified Accelerated Cost Recovery System) property that was acquired in a like-kind exchange of other MACRS property over the remaining period of the exchanged property and continue to use the same depreciation method.

Stop and review! You have completed the outline for this subunit. Study questions 20 through 27 beginning on page 50.

2.6 INVOLUNTARY CONVERSIONS

A taxpayer may elect to defer recognition of gain if property is involuntarily converted into money or property that is not similar or related in use under Sec. 1033. Nonrecognition of gain is contingent on the involuntarily converted property being reinvested in qualified replacement property. Losses on involuntary conversions are not deferred.

1.   An involuntary conversion of property results from destruction, theft, seizure, requisition, condemnation, or the threat of imminent requisition or condemnation.

2.   When property is converted involuntarily into nonqualified proceeds and qualified property is purchased within the replacement period, an election may be made to defer realized gain.

   a.   The deferral is limited to the extent that the amount realized is invested in qualified replacement property.

   b.   Basis in the qualified replacement property is decreased by the amount of any unrecognized gain.

3.   Taxpayers may meet the replacement of property test by acquiring a controlling interest in a corporation that owns replacement property. Taxpayers who must reduce the basis in the corporation's stock as a result of applying the involuntary conversion rules must also reduce the basis of the corporation's assets (but not below the basis in the stock after it has already been adjusted).

   a.   Recognized gain is limited to any excess of any amount realized over any cost of qualified property.

   b.   Sec. 1245 or Sec. 1250 may require recognition of ordinary income.

4.   Sec. 1033 does not apply to any realized losses.

   a.   Loss from condemnation or requisition of a personal-use asset is not deductible. But certain casualty losses are deductible.

   b.   When loss is realized, basis is determined independently of Sec. 1033.

Direct Conversion

5.   Proceeds of an involuntary conversion are qualified property.

   a.   Nonrecognition is mandatory, not elective, on direct conversion to the extent of any amount realized in the form of qualified replacement property.

   b.   Basis in the proceeds (property) is exchanged, i.e., equal to the basis in the converted property.

6.   The replacement period begins on the earlier of the date of disposition or the threat of condemnation and ends 2 years after the close of the first tax year in which any part of the gain is realized.

   a.   Regarding real property used in business or held for investment (not inventory, dealer property, or personal-use property), if conversion is by condemnation or requisition, or threat thereof, 3 years is allowed.

   b.   Construction of qualified property must be complete before the end of the replacement period for its cost to be included.

7.   "Similar or related in service or use" means the following:

Owner-User

a.   For an owner-user, that the property has functional similarity, i.e., meets a functional use test that requires the property to

   1)   Have similar physical characteristics
   2)   Be used for the same purpose

      a)   For example, for an owner-user, a warehouse used to store parts for a bicycle manufacturer is not similar or related in service to a warehouse rented out for storage of household goods.

Owner-Investor

b.   For an owner-investor, that the service or use of the property has a close relationship to the service or use the previous property had to the investor, such that the owner-investor's

   1)   Risks, management activities, services performed, etc., continue without substantial change.

      a)   For example, for an owner-investor, the following types of investment are not similar or related in service or use: passive leasing investment; investment in actively managed rental apartments; speculative investment in a silver mine.

c.   For **owners (in general)** that, if property held for investment or for productive use in a trade or business is involuntarily converted due to a Presidentially declared disaster, any tangible replacement property will be deemed similar or related in service or use.

8.   For real property used in business or held for investment (not inventory, dealer property, personal-use property, etc.), if conversion is by condemnation or threat thereof, like-kind property qualifies as replacement. This standard is less stringent.

a.   Conversion must be direct. There is no indirect ownership allowance (i.e., stock).

9.   To recap, on a Sec. 1033 involuntary conversion, realized gain is generally recognized only to the extent that any amount realized exceeds the cost of the similar or related-in-service property. Gain recognized is subject to classification as ordinary income under Sec. 1245 or Sec. 1250.

Stop and review! You have completed the outline for this subunit. Study questions 28 and 29 on page 53.

QUESTIONS

2.1 Gross Income

1. Mr. Zum owns an apartment house for which he provides no services to his tenants. On December 1, 2013, he received a $2,400 payment for the first 6 months' rent in 2014. He also received a security deposit of $400. What is the amount of gross rental income Mr. Zum should include on his 2013 income tax return?

A. $400

B. $800

C. $2,400

D. $2,800

Answer (C) is correct.

   REQUIRED: The landlord's rental income.
   DISCUSSION: Both cash- and accrual-basis taxpayers must include amounts in gross income upon actual or constructive receipt if the taxpayer has an unrestricted claim to such amounts under Reg. 1.61-8(b). Since Mr. Zurn has an unrestricted claim to the $2,400 of rent paid in advance, it would be included in his rental income. The security deposit of $400 would not be included in rental income since it was not intended as an advance rental payment. (Mr. Zurn does not have an unrestricted claim since it must be returned unless there are damages or rent is not paid.) Therefore, Mr. Zurn's gross rental income is $2,400.
   Answer (A) is incorrect. The full amount of prepaid rent is included in current-year income. Answer (B) is incorrect. The full amount of prepaid rent is included in current-year income. Answer (D) is incorrect. Mr. Zurn does not have an unrestricted claim to the security deposit, so it is not included in income.

2. Gross income from a hobby activity of an individual is

A. Not reported if less than $400.

B. Reported as other income on line 21, Form 1040.

C. Reported as gross income on line 1, Schedule C (Form 1040).

D. Netted against related expenses, and the excess, if any, is reported as other income on line 21, Form 1040.

Answer (B) is correct.
REQUIRED: The reporting of hobby income on Form 1040.
DISCUSSION: Income from activities from which a profit is not expected must be included on the tax return. Such activities include hobbies and farm activities operated for recreation and pleasure. Related expenses are deductible to the extent that they do not exceed the reported income. The income is reported on line 21 of Form 1040, and the related expenses are reported as itemized deductions on Schedule A.
Answer (A) is incorrect. There is no minimum amount that does not need to be reported. Answer (C) is incorrect. Income from a hobby activity is classified as other income. Answer (D) is incorrect. The related expenses are deducted separately on Schedule A as an itemized deduction.

3. In 2012, the Birch Company had gross income of $163,000, a bad debt deduction of $5,000, and other allowable deductions of $58,500. Birch uses the accrual method of accounting and the specific charge-off method for bad debts. In 2013, Birch recovered $1,600 of the bad debt that had been deducted in 2012. What portion of the bad debt recovery should be included in Birch's income for 2013?

A. $0

B. $1,600

C. $3,400

D. $5,000

Answer (B) is correct.
REQUIRED: The amount of bad debt recovery that must be included in gross income.
DISCUSSION: The recovery of an amount previously deducted as a bad debt is included in gross income to the extent that the prior deduction reduced taxes (Sec. 111). Since the prior deduction reduced taxable income by $5,000, the full amount of the $1,600 recovery is included in gross income.
Answer (A) is incorrect. The full amount of the recovery must be included in gross income because bad debt was taken as a business deduction. Answer (C) is incorrect. Only the amount that is recovered should be included in income. Answer (D) is incorrect. Only the amount that is recovered should be included in income.

4. In 2012, the Hydrangea Company (a sole proprietorship) had gross income of $158,000, a bad debt deduction of $3,500, and other allowable deductions of $49,437. The business reported on the accrual method of accounting and used the specific charge-off method for bad debts. The entire bad debt deduction reduced the taxable income on the 2012 return. In 2013, the business recovered $2,000 of the $3,500 deducted in 2012. How should the recovery be treated?

A. Include $2,000 in income on the 2013 return.

B. Include $3,500 in income on the 2013 return.

C. Amend the 2012 return to add the $2,000.

D. None of the answers are correct.

Answer (A) is correct.
REQUIRED: The proper treatment of the recovery of an amount previously deducted as a bad debt.
DISCUSSION: The recovery of an amount previously deducted as a bad debt is included in gross income to the extent that the prior deduction reduced taxes (Sec. 111). Since the prior deduction reduced taxable income by $3,500, the full amount of the $2,000 recovery is included in gross income.
Answer (B) is incorrect. Only the amount of the bad debt expense recovered should be included in income in 2013. Answer (C) is incorrect. The amount of the recovery should be included in the return for 2013. Answer (D) is incorrect. A correct answer is given.

5. Shawn Smith, sole proprietor, had the following transactions during 2013:

Received rental income	$ 7,500
Performed legal services for ATI Corporation in return for 10 shares of stock	24,000
Recovered accounts receivable that had been written off and deducted in 2011 (did not reduce tax)	20,000

What amount must Mr. Smith include in gross income for 2013?

A. $44,000

B. $27,500

C. $31,500

D. $51,500

Answer (C) is correct.
REQUIRED: The amount includible in gross income.
DISCUSSION: Income is included in the taxable year in which all the events have occurred that fix the right to receive such income and in which the amount can be determined with reasonable accuracy. The rental income is included in gross income. The payment for legal services performed is also included in gross income. The fair market value of the stock is the amount included [Sec. 83(a)]. Under Sec. 111, the recovery of a bad debt is excluded from income if the previous deduction did not reduce taxes. Therefore, $31,500 ($7,500 + $24,000) is included in gross income.
Answer (A) is incorrect. The recovered accounts receivable is not included and the rental income is included. Answer (B) is incorrect. The recovered accounts receivable is not included and the stock for services rendered is. Answer (D) is incorrect. The accounts receivable recovered is not included.

2.2 Self-Employment Income

6. Which type of income is not subject to self-employment tax?

A. Wages, salaries, and tips received as an employee.

B. Non-employee compensation.

C. Net profits from sole proprietorship.

D. Distributive share of partnership income.

Answer (A) is correct.

REQUIRED: The type of income not subject to self-employment tax.

DISCUSSION: In some instances, a self-employed individual may also earn wages while working as a full- or part-time employee. In such a case, the income is not subject to self-employment tax but is subject to withholding.

Answer (B) is incorrect. It is a type of income subject to self-employment tax. Non-employee compensation is a source of income that must be reported by the taxpayer at its full amount; in other words, no taxes have been withheld on this source of income. Answer (C) is incorrect. It is a type of income subject to self-employment tax. Net profits from a sole proprietorship is a source of income that must be reported by the taxpayer at their full amounts; in other words, no taxes have been withheld on this source of income. Answer (D) is incorrect. It is a type of income subject to self-employment tax. A partner's distributive share of partnership income is a source of income that must be reported by the taxpayer at its full amount; in other words, no taxes have been withheld on this source of income.

7. Mike owns a four-family apartment building and actively participates in the rental activity. Mike advertised, rented the apartments to the tenants, collected rents, and made repairs. His brother, Bryan, also owns an apartment building. Bryan spends more than half his time developing, constructing, renting, managing, and operating his apartment building as well as providing regular cleaning, linen service, and maid service for the convenience of the tenants. Which brother has self-employment income from his apartment building?

A. Mike.

B. Bryan.

C. Both brothers.

D. Neither.

Answer (B) is correct.

REQUIRED: The self-employment income obtained from the rental of an apartment building.

DISCUSSION: Rent from real estate and personal property leased with real estate is not self-employment income unless services are provided to tenants. Services generally are provided for the occupants if they are primarily for their convenience and not services normally provided with the rental of rooms for occupancy only. (See Publication 334.) Since Bryan, but not Mike, provides these services, he is the only brother that has self-employment income from his apartment building.

Answer (A) is incorrect. Tentative net earnings from self-employment do not include rents from real estate or from personal property leased with the real estate, gain (or loss) from disposition of business property, capital gain (or loss), nonbusiness interest, or dividends. Answer (C) is incorrect. Mike does not have self-employment income. Answer (D) is incorrect. One brother does have self-employment income.

8. Based on the following information, what is the amount of Beth's self-employment income?

Salary from her S corporation	$15,000
Partnership income (inactive general partner)	8,000
Corporate director's fees	1,500
Payment from insurance company for lost income	10,000

A. $1,500

B. $9,500

C. $19,500

D. $24,500

Answer (C) is correct.

REQUIRED: The amount of self-employment income.

DISCUSSION: Under Sec. 1402(a) and Reg. 1.1402(a)-1, net earnings from self-employment include the net income from a trade or business, guaranteed payments for services from a partnership, and a partner's distributive share of income from a partnership (whether the partner is active or not). Director's fees are self-employment income. Rev. Rul. 91-19 held that payments received for lost earnings were included in net earnings from self-employment. A bona fide salary is income from employment, not self-employment.

Beth's self-employment income is computed as follows:

Corporate director's fees	$ 1,500
Distributive share of partnership income	8,000
Payment for lost earnings	10,000
Self-employment income	$19,500

Answer (A) is incorrect. Partnership income and insurance payments for lost income are self-employment income. Answer (B) is incorrect. Insurance payments for lost income are included as self-employment income. Answer (D) is incorrect. Salaries are not included in self-employment income, but insurance payments for lost income are included as self-employment income.

2.3 Farming Income and Expense

9. Dan, a calendar-year taxpayer, has the following amounts of gross income for 2013:

Wages -- $10,000
Interest -- $2,000
Farm income -- $200,000

Dan has tax, including self-employment tax, of $20,000, and withholding of $1,000. To avoid any filing or estimated tax penalties, Dan must

    A. File an estimated tax payment by January 15, 2014, and pay 60% of the tax due.

    B. File his tax return and pay all tax due by March 1, 2014.

    C. File an estimated tax payment by March 1, 2014, and pay 66 2/3% of the tax due.

    D. File his tax return and pay all tax due by April 15, 2014.

Answer (B) is correct.
    REQUIRED: The required filings and payments by a farmer to avoid penalties.
    DISCUSSION: Dan is a qualified farmer since at least two-thirds of his gross income for 2013 was from farming (Publication 225). A qualified farmer has two filing options. The first option is to make a required payment by January 15 and file Form 1040 by April 15. The second option is to file Form 1040 and pay all tax due by March 1.

10. Farmer John, a cash-basis farmer, operates a cow-calf breeding operation. The breeder cows are not primarily held for sale. In addition to the calves raised on his farm, John also purchases calves for resale. During 2013, John had the following acquisitions and dispositions of cattle:

Purchase of 30 calves for resale	$ 3,420
Sale of 30 calves purchased for resale	6,100
Sale of 45 calves raised by John	10,400
Sale of 10 breeder cows	6,750
Original cost of breeder cows	5,500
Accumulated depreciation on breeder cows	2,860

What amount should John include in gross income on his Schedule F for 2013?

    A. $13,080

    B. $14,510

    C. $16,500

    D. $18,580

Answer (A) is correct.
    REQUIRED: The total amount of income reported on Schedule F.
    DISCUSSION: Income from farming reported on Schedule F includes amounts that the farmer receives from cultivating the soil or raising or harvesting any agricultural commodities, including income from the sale of livestock. Sale of livestock held for draft, breeding, or sporting purposes generally results in capital gains. John should include $13,080 [$10,400 + ($6,100 – $3,420)] in gross income on his Schedule F.
    Answer (B) is incorrect. The sale of the breeder cows produces capital gains, not ordinary income. Answer (C) is incorrect. The original purchase price of the calves bought for resale is deducted from gross income. Answer (D) is incorrect. The gross income does not include the original cost of the breeder cows.

11. The receipt of agricultural program payments by a farmer for refraining from growing crops should be reported as

    A. Miscellaneous income on Form 1040.

    B. Farm income, not subject to self-employment tax.

    C. Rental income, not subject to self-employment tax.

    D. Farm income, subject to self-employment tax.

Answer (D) is correct.
    REQUIRED: The proper place to report agricultural program payments.
    DISCUSSION: An agricultural program payment should be reported on the appropriate line of Part I of Schedule F (farm income) (Publication 225). The full amount of the payment should be reported even if it is returned to the government for cancelation. A self-employed individual usually has to pay self-employment tax (Publication 225). Farmers are considered to be self-employed if they operate their own farm on land they own or rent.

12. Bobby Rice is an unincorporated grain farmer in Louisiana with a calendar year end. Bobby does not live or farm in a disaster area. Bobby computed an estimated tax liability of $25,000 for 2013. To avoid the failure to pay estimated tax penalty, Bobby should

    A. Make his first 2013 estimated tax payment by March 1, 2014.

    B. Pay all his 2013 estimated taxes by February 15, 2014, and file his tax return by April 15, 2014.

    C. Include any alternative minimum tax he expects to owe in his calculation of 2013 estimated taxes.

    D. Pay all of his 2013 estimated taxes by the due date of his return.

Answer (C) is correct.

    REQUIRED: The proper way for a farmer to avoid paying a penalty when (s)he owes an estimated tax.

    DISCUSSION: If a taxpayer qualifies as a farmer by receiving at least two-thirds of the total gross income from farming in the current year or the preceding tax year, the taxpayer shall pay all estimated taxes by January 15 and then file the 1040 return and pay any additional taxes by April 15, or the required annual payment is two-thirds of the current year's tax or 100% of the previous year's tax. The taxpayer shall file the 1040 return and pay all taxes due by March 1. In addition, the alternative minimum tax that the taxpayer expects to owe should be included in the calculation of the estimated tax owed.

13. If you sell more livestock than you normally would in a year because of a drought, flood, or other weather-related condition, you may be able to postpone reporting the gain from selling the additional animals until the next year. You must meet all of the following conditions to make the election except

    A. You can show that, under your usual business practices, you would not have sold the animals this year except for the weather-related conditions.

    B. The weather-related conditions caused an area to be designated as eligible for assistance by the federal government.

    C. You use the accrual method of accounting.

    D. Your principal trade or business is farming.

Answer (C) is correct.

    REQUIRED: The condition not required for the election related to the postponement of the gain from a sale due to a drought, flood, or other weather-related condition.

    DISCUSSION: Publication 225 states, "If you sell more livestock, including poultry, than you normally would in a year because of a drought, flood, or other weather-related condition, you may be able to postpone reporting the gain from selling the additional animals until the next year. You must meet all the following conditions to qualify.

- Your principal trade or business is farming.
- You use the cash method of accounting.
- You can show that, under your usual business practices, you would not have sold the animals this year except for the weather-related condition.
- The weather-related condition caused an area to be designated as eligible for assistance by the federal government."

14. If at least two-thirds of your gross income for 2012 or 2013 was from farming, only one estimated tax payment is due. The required annual payment is the

    A. Larger of two-thirds of your total tax for 2013 or 100% of the total tax shown on your full-year 2012 return.

    B. Smaller of two-thirds of your total tax for 2012 or 100% of the total tax shown on your full-year 2013 return.

    C. Larger of two-thirds of your total tax for 2012 or 100% of the total tax shown on your full-year 2013 return.

    D. Smaller of two-thirds of your total tax for 2013 or 100% of the total tax shown on your full-year 2012 return.

Answer (D) is correct.

    REQUIRED: The estimated tax payments required by farmers.

    DISCUSSION: If a taxpayer qualifies as a farmer by receiving at least two-thirds of the total gross income from farming in the current year or the preceding tax year, the taxpayer shall pay all estimated taxes by January 15 and then file the 1040 return and pay any additional taxes by April 15. The required annual payment is the smaller of two-thirds of the current year's tax or 100% of the previous year's tax.

15. Who of the following may use farm income averaging, assuming farm income rules are met?

A. A natural person filing a Form 1040, a partner in a partnership, and a shareholder in an S corporation.

B. A natural person filing a Form 1040, a partnership, an S corporation, and a C corporation.

C. A natural person filing a Form 1040, a partner in a partnership, and a shareholder in a C corporation.

D. A natural person filing a Form 1040, a partner in a partnership, an estate, and a trust.

Answer (A) is correct.
    REQUIRED: The taxpayer eligible to use farm income averaging.
    DISCUSSION: Under Sec. 1301, a taxpayer engaged in a farming business in the year of election as an individual, a partner in a partnership, or a shareholder in an S corporation can elect to use farm income averaging. Corporations, partnerships, S corporations, estates, and trusts cannot use farm income averaging.
    Answer (B) is incorrect. Partnerships, S corporations, and C corporations cannot elect farm income averaging. Answer (C) is incorrect. A shareholder in a C corporation cannot elect farm income averaging. Answer (D) is incorrect. Estates and trusts cannot elect farm income averaging.

16. Farm income averaging is computed on Schedule J, which may be filed

A. For the current year when a taxpayer files Schedule F showing a farm loss.

B. For the current year that includes Schedule F showing net income from farming.

C. Only by IRS after the taxpayer's return is completed and reviewed.

D. On a family farming corporation with less than $25 million in gross receipts.

Answer (B) is correct.
    REQUIRED: The appropriate time to file Schedule J.
    DISCUSSION: If a taxpayer is engaged in a farming business, (s)he may be able to average all or some of his or her farm income by allocating it to the 3 prior years (base years). Farm income averaging can be used to figure the tax for any year in which the taxpayer was engaged in a farming business as an individual, a partner in a partnership, or a shareholder in an S corporation (Publication 225).

2.4 Small Business Stock

17. Frank files a joint return with his wife, Rose. Frank incurred a loss of $125,000 on the sale of his qualifying small business stock (Sec. 1244) in 2013. How much of this loss is deductible on their joint return as an ordinary loss?

A. $125,000

B. $3,000

C. $100,000

D. $50,000

Answer (C) is correct.
    REQUIRED: The ordinary loss on the sale of qualifying small business stock that is deductible.
    DISCUSSION: Up to $50,000 ($100,000 if joint return) of loss realized on disposition or worthlessness of Sec. 1244 stock is treated as an ordinary loss. The limit applies to Sec. 1244 stock held in all corporations. The limit is applied at a partner level, if applicable. The loss is considered to be from a trade or business for NOL purposes.
    Answer (A) is incorrect. The loss is limited to $100,000 for a joint return. Answer (B) is incorrect. A loss of Sec. 1244 stock is not limited to the $3,000 capital loss deduction. Answer (D) is incorrect. The limit for a loss on Sec. 1244 stock is $100,000 for a joint return.

18. Ms. Witherby purchased 100 shares of qualifying small business (Sec. 1244) stock for $10,000 on January 2, 2013. On July 1, 2013, Ms. Witherby had to make an additional $2,000 contribution to capital, which increased her total basis in the 100 shares to $12,000. On November 9, 2013, Ms. Witherby sold the 100 shares for $9,000 to an unrelated party. What are the amount and the character of the gain or loss Ms. Witherby may claim on her 2013 income tax return?

	Ordinary Loss	Capital Gain or Loss
A.	$(12,000)	$9,000
B.	$(3,000)	$0
C.	$(2,500)	$(500)
D.	$0	$(3,000)

Answer (C) is correct.
    REQUIRED: The amount and the character of the gain or loss on the sale of Sec. 1244 stock.
    DISCUSSION: If an owner of Sec. 1244 stock invests additional capital but is not issued additional shares of stock, the amount of the additional investment is added to the basis of the originally issued stock, but this subsequent increase to the basis of the originally issued stock does not qualify for ordinary loss treatment. Any resulting loss must then be apportioned between the qualifying Sec. 1244 stock and the nonqualifying additional capital interest (Code Sec. 1244). Since the additional capital interest of $2,000 is one-sixth of the total basis of $12,000, the $3,000 loss is apportioned as follows: $500 of capital loss (one-sixth of $3,000) and $2,500 of qualifying ordinary loss.
    Answer (A) is incorrect. She has a total loss on the sale of $3,000. Answer (B) is incorrect. An increase in basis of the originally issued stock does not qualify for ordinary loss treatment. Answer (D) is incorrect. A proportionate share of original basis qualifies for ordinary loss treatment.

19. During 2013, Gabrielle, whose filing status is single, sold all of her Sec. 1244 stock in two small business companies. None of the stock qualifies for 1202 treatment. Her records reflect the following:

1,000 shares Nebulus Corp. purchased June 2, 2008	$20,000
1,000 shares Schyst, Inc., purchased March 6, 2011	60,000
1,000 shares Nebulus Corp. sold July 16, 2013	80,000
1,000 shares Schyst, Inc., sold August 4, 2013	5,000

What is the amount of Gabrielle's recognized gain or loss for 2013?

A. $55,000 capital gain.

B. $(50,000) ordinary loss; $55,000 capital gain.

C. $(50,000) ordinary loss; $60,000 capital gain.

D. $(55,000) ordinary loss; $60,000 capital gain.

Answer (B) is correct.
REQUIRED: The amount and the character of loss to be reported from Sec. 1244 stock.
DISCUSSION: An individual taxpayer is entitled to recognize the loss on Sec. 1244 stock as an ordinary loss, subject to a maximum amount of $50,000 per year ($100,000 per year for a husband and wife filing a joint return). Gabrielle realizes a $60,000 gain on the sale of Nebulus stock and a $55,000 loss on the sale of Schyst stock. Of the loss, $50,000 can qualify for ordinary loss treatment, while the remaining $5,000 loss is a capital loss. The capital loss is netted with the $60,000 capital gain for a total capital gain of $55,000.
Answer (A) is incorrect. An ordinary loss may be recognized up to a $50,000 limit. Answer (C) is incorrect. The remaining $5,000 of loss is a capital loss and is netted against capital gains. Answer (D) is incorrect. Only $50,000 of loss may be recognized as ordinary.

2.5 Like-Kind Exchanges

20. Which of the following transactions qualifies as a like-kind exchange?

A. The exchange of a copyright on a novel for a copyright on a song.

B. An exchange of the "goodwill or going concern value" of a business for the "goodwill or going concern value" of another business.

C. An exchange of land improved with an apartment house for land improved with a store building.

D. An exchange of personal property used predominantly in the United States for personal property used predominantly outside the United States.

Answer (C) is correct.
REQUIRED: The transaction that qualifies as a like-kind exchange.
DISCUSSION: Sec. 1031 defers recognizing gain or loss to the extent that property productively used in a trade or business or held for the production of income (investment) is exchanged for property of like-kind. Like-kind property is alike in nature or character but not necessarily in grade or quality. Properties are like-kind if each is within a class of like nature or character, without regard to differences in use, improvements, location, or proximity. Thus, an exchange of land improved with an apartment house for land improved with a store building qualifies as a Sec. 1031 exchange.
Answer (A) is incorrect. The underlying assets, the novel and the song, are not like-kind. Answer (B) is incorrect. The going concern value of one entity is never like-kind as the going concern value of another entity. Answer (D) is incorrect. Sec. 1031 does not apply to foreign personal or foreign real property.

21. Nelson, Inc., owned a manufacturing building with a fair market value of $95,000 and an adjusted basis of $75,000. Nelson, Inc., entered into an agreement to exchange the manufacturing building for a warehouse with an adjusted basis of $80,000 and a fair market value of $90,000 with Roberts Corporation. In addition, Nelson, Inc., would pay Roberts Corporation $5,000 in cash. Nelson, Inc., also incurred and paid attorney and deed preparation fees of $5,000 on this exchange. What is Nelson's basis in the warehouse it received in this like-kind exchange?

A. $85,000

B. $90,000

C. $95,000

D. $100,000

Answer (A) is correct.
REQUIRED: The basis of property acquired in a like-kind exchange.
DISCUSSION: Sec. 1031 defers recognizing gain or loss to the extent that property productively used in a trade or business or held for the production of income (investment) is exchanged for property of like-kind. The basis in the property equals the adjusted basis of the property given plus any gain recognized, boot given, and legal fees incurred, and less any boot received. Thus, the basis in the new property equals $85,000 ($75,000 adjusted basis of property given + $5,000 boot given + $5,000 legal fees incurred).
Answer (B) is incorrect. The basis in the new property does not equal the FMV of that property. Answer (C) is incorrect. The basis in the new property does not equal the FMV of the transferred property. Answer (D) is incorrect. The basis of the new property does not equal that property's FMV plus boot given and legal fees incurred.

22. Rebecca exchanges real estate held for investment with an adjusted basis of $400,000 and a mortgage of $100,000 for other real estate to be held for investment. The other party agrees to assume the mortgage. The fair market value of the real estate Rebecca receives is $500,000. She pays exchange expenses of $10,000. What amount of gain does Rebecca realize?

A. $100,000

B. $190,000

C. $90,000

D. $200,000

Answer (B) is correct.
REQUIRED: The realized gain on the sale of property.
DISCUSSION: This transaction is a like-kind exchange. The real estate had an adjusted basis of $400,000 and was exchanged for property that has a FMV of $500,000. She was also relieved of a $100,000 mortgage, which is the same as receiving cash, and the $10,000 in expenses reduces the realized gain. So the realized, not recognized, gain is the $100,000 in the exchange of properties plus the $100,000 in mortgage relief minus the $10,000 in expenses to give a total gain of $190,000.
Answer (A) is incorrect. The realized amount that is received is $590,000. The $100,000 mortgage that is taken over is equivalent to receiving cash. This $100,000 is added to the $500,000 FMV and then is reduced by the $10,000 exchange expense to get a total of $590,000. Subtract $400,000 from the $590,000 and you get the $190,000 realized gain. Answer (C) is incorrect. It does not take into account the $100,000 mortgage that is assumed. When someone takes over your debt, it is the same as receiving cash. This $100,000 is added to the gain realized. Answer (D) is incorrect. The amount of $200,000 fails to take into account the $10,000 exchange expense. Expenses incurred in acquiring property are added to the basis of the property, thus reducing the amount of gain realized.

23. Sylvester owns farm machinery that has a fair market value of $157,000 and an adjusted basis of $90,000. The farm machinery is subject to a liability of $47,000. Dorene would like to purchase Sylvester's farm machinery and makes the following offer:

- Cash -- $15,000
- Assumption of Sylvester's liability
- Farmland owned by Dorene having a fair market value of $95,000; the land is not encumbered by any liabilities

What is the amount of Sylvester's recognized gain if he accepts Dorene's offer?

A. $15,000

B. $20,000

C. $62,000

D. $67,000

Answer (D) is correct.
REQUIRED: The gain recognized in an exchange when properties that are not of a like-kind are exchanged.
DISCUSSION: Sec. 1031(b) provides that, if boot is received in addition to like-kind property, the amount of recognized gain is the lesser of the amount of boot received or the amount of gain realized. However, an exchange of farming real property (land) for farming machinery does not qualify as a like-kind exchange. Therefore, the entire realized gain of $67,000 ($157,000 FMV of property received – $90,000 basis) must be recognized.

24. Kayla exchanged her unimproved land with an adjusted basis of $80,000 and a fair market value of $130,000 for unimproved land with a fair market value of $100,000 and $10,000 in cash. Kayla also paid $5,000 in closing costs. The unimproved land that Kayla gave up was subject to a $30,000 mortgage for which she was liable. The other party assumed this mortgage. What is Kayla's realized gain on this exchange?

A. $40,000

B. $55,000

C. $35,000

D. $25,000

Answer (B) is correct.
REQUIRED: The gain realized in a Sec. 1031 transaction.
DISCUSSION: Unfair trade -- exchanging $130,000 – $30,000 for $100,000 + $10,000. The IRS exam does this all the time. The best way to work the problem is to ignore the FMV of the asset given up. The realized gain is $55,000 ($100,000 + $10,000 + $30,000 – $80,000 basis – $5,000 closing costs).

25. Joe traded a truck with an adjusted basis of $10,000 and received a new truck with a fair market value of $9,000 and $1,500 cash. What is the basis of Joe's new truck?

A. $8,500

B. $10,500

C. $10,000

D. $9,000

Answer (D) is correct.

REQUIRED: The correct basis of a property in a like-kind exchange.

DISCUSSION: Qualified property received in a like-kind exchange has an exchanged basis adjusted for boot and gain recognized. The adjusted basis of the property given is increased by the gain recognized and the boot given, and then it is decreased by the boot received. A gain in a like-kind exchange is recognized equal to the lesser of gain realized or boot received. The truck has a basis of $10,000 and is exchanged for a truck with a FMV of $9,000 and $1,500 in cash; thus, there is a gain of $500. This gets added to the adjusted basis of the truck given up and the $1,500 in boot is subtracted to get $9,000.

Answer (A) is incorrect. The $8,500 does not account for the $500 recognized gain. This must be added to the adjusted basis of the property. Answer (B) is incorrect. This number does not subtract the $1,500 boot that was received. Answer (C) is incorrect. The adjusted basis of the property given up in a like-kind exchange must be adjusted by increasing it by the gain recognized, then by decreasing it for the boot that is received.

26. The Andee Partnership traded its panel truck with an adjusted basis of $10,000 for a pickup truck with a fair market value of $15,000. Andee also received $3,500 cash on the trade. What is the gain, if any, on this trade?

A. $0

B. $3,500

C. $8,500

D. $1,500

Answer (B) is correct.

REQUIRED: The realized gain on the exchange of trucks.

DISCUSSION: A partially nontaxable exchange occurs when cash or unlike property are received in addition to like-kind property. If boot (cash or nonqualified property) is received in addition to like-kind property, the amount of recognized gain is the lesser of the amount of boot received or the amount of gain realized. In this case, Andee Partnership received boot of $3,500 cash in addition to the like-kind truck received. The realized gain of $8,500 ($15,000 fair market value of the pickup truck + $3,500 cash received – $10,000 adjusted basis of the panel truck) is taxed only to the extent of the cash received, or $3,500. Thus, the gain on the trade is $3,500 (Publication 544, page 13).

Answer (A) is incorrect. Andee Partnership received boot in addition to the like-kind property in the exchange. Answer (C) is incorrect. Realized gain is taxed only to the extent of the boot received ($3,500). Answer (D) is incorrect. The gain is equal to the amount of boot received, but not exceeding realized gain.

27. The Post and Rail Partnership traded a piece of farm land with an adjusted basis of $4,000 for a farm tractor that has a fair market value of $9,000 and an adjusted basis of $8,000. What is the recognized gain or loss?

A. $5,000

B. $4,000

C. $1,000

D. None; it is a like-kind exchange.

Answer (A) is correct.

REQUIRED: The recognized gain or loss on the exchange.

DISCUSSION: The definition of fair market value (FMV) is the price at which property would change hands between a buyer and a seller, neither having to buy or sell, and both having reasonable knowledge of all necessary facts (Publication 551). Since the transaction does not qualify for a like-kind exchange, the gain should be determined by subtracting the adjusted basis of the amount given up ($4,000) from the FMV of the amount received ($9,000).

2.6 Involuntary Conversions

28. A tornado destroyed Ian's forklift in 2013. Ian had purchased the forklift for $8,000 and had correctly deducted $6,000 of depreciation. Ian's adjusted basis in the forklift was $2,000. Ian's insurance company reimbursed him $9,000, and he spent $7,500 for a new forklift. How much ordinary income should Ian report on his 2013 income tax return?

    A. $0

    B. $1,500

    C. $6,000

    D. $7,000

Answer (B) is correct.

REQUIRED: The gross income resulting from the involuntary conversion of insured property.

DISCUSSION: Ian received insurance proceeds of $9,000 on destroyed property with an adjusted basis of $2,000 and thereby realized a gain of $7,000. Since the replacement property was similar, under Sec. 1033(a)(2), Ian may elect to recognize the gain only to the extent that the amount realized ($9,000) exceeds the cost of the replacement property ($7,500), or $1,500.

Answer (A) is incorrect. A gain must be recognized to the extent that the amount realized exceeds the cost of the replacement property. Answer (C) is incorrect. The gain that is recognized is limited to the amount that the amount realized exceeds the cost of the replacement property. Answer (D) is incorrect. The gain that is recognized is limited to the amount that the amount realized exceeds the cost of the replacement property.

29. Sally's business office was condemned to make way for an expanded highway on May 1, 2013. Sally's adjusted basis in her building was $20,000 ($80,000 original cost less $60,000 in depreciation). Her proceeds from condemnation were $220,000. Sally replaced her office on November 10, 2013, at a cost of $185,000. Sally must recognize a gain of

    A. $200,000

    B. $0

    C. $35,000

    D. $60,000

Answer (C) is correct.

REQUIRED: The gain recognized on an involuntary conversion.

DISCUSSION: When property is converted involuntarily into nonqualified proceeds and qualified property is purchased within the replacement period, an election may be made to defer realized gain to the extent that the amount realized on the conversion is reinvested in qualified replacement property. The basis in qualified replacement property is decreased by any unrecognized gain. Sally's gain on the involuntary conversion is the $220,000 proceeds received less the cost of the replacement property of $185,000 for a gain of $35,000. The $35,000 of gain recognition will most likely be classified as recapture gain.

Answer (A) is incorrect. The gain is based upon the proceeds received and the replacement property purchased, not the basis of the old property. Answer (B) is incorrect. Sally must recognize a gain if the replacement property does not cost as much as the proceeds received from the involuntary conversion. Answer (D) is incorrect. The entire $60,000 of depreciation will not be recaptured.

Use the additional questions in Gleim **EA Test Prep** to create Practice Exams that emulate Prometric!

STUDY UNIT THREE
BUSINESS EXPENSES

(12 pages of outline)

A deduction from gross income is allowed for all ordinary and necessary expenses paid or incurred during a tax year in carrying on a trade or business. The deduction is allowed to a sole proprietor, a partnership, or a corporation. A sole proprietor claims these deductions on Schedule C.

A trade or business is a regular and continuous activity that is entered into with the expectation of making a profit. "Regular" means the taxpayer devotes a substantial amount of business time to the activity. An activity that is not engaged in for a profit is a hobby (personal). An activity that results in a profit in any 3 of 5 consecutive tax years (2 out of 7 for the breeding and racing of horses) is presumed not to be a hobby.

An expense must be **both** ordinary and necessary to be deductible. An expense is ordinary if it normally occurs or is likely to occur in connection with businesses similar to the one operated by the person claiming the deduction. The expenditures need not occur frequently. "Necessary" implies that an expenditure must be appropriate and helpful in developing or maintaining the trade or business. Implicit in the "ordinary and necessary" requirement is a requirement that the expenditures be reasonable. For example, if the compensation paid a shareholder exceeds that ordinarily paid for similar services (reasonable compensation), the excessive payment may constitute a nondeductible dividend.

3.1 COMPENSATION

A deduction is generally allowed for salaries, wages, and other forms of payment made to employees.

1. Compensation must meet all of the following tests to be deductible:

Ordinary and Necessary

    a. Payments must be ordinary and necessary expenses directly related to the trade or business.

        1) Certain wages or salaries paid by a company may be considered direct or indirect costs of producing property.

            a) If the property is inventory, the wages are added to inventory.
            b) The costs are capitalized and depreciated for any other property.

Reasonable

    b. Reasonable pay is the amount that would ordinarily be paid for the services by a like enterprise under similar circumstances at the time the services are contracted.

For Services Performed

    c. There must be proof that services were actually performed.

Paid or Incurred

    d. The expenses must have been paid or incurred during the tax year.

Paid to Employees

    e.   Employees are generally individuals who perform services for a company, and the company controls when and how the work is performed.

        1)   Individuals in business for themselves are generally not considered employees (Publication 15).

        2)   Direct sellers and qualified real estate agents are considered nonemployees.

2. **Cash Payments**

    a.   Bonuses paid to an employee for services actually performed may be deductible if they are reasonable for the type of services performed.

    b.   Loans or advances made to employees may be deducted if it is doubtful that the employee will repay the loan.

    c.   Vacation pay is income to the employee whether or not the employee chooses to go on vacation.

        1)   Cash- and accrual-basis taxpayers deduct vacation pay when it is paid.

        2)   The deduction for accrual-basis taxpayers of amounts vested and paid within 2 1/2 months after the close of the tax year is no longer allowed (Publication 535).

    d.   Unpaid salaries may be deducted by accrual-basis taxpayers if

        1)   Economic performance has occurred in the tax year,
        2)   There is an unconditional agreement to pay an employee, and
        3)   The payments are made within 2 1/2 months after the close of the tax year.

            a)   Payments made to cash-basis related taxpayers (i.e., brothers, sisters, spouses, and lineal descendants) as wages are not deductible until the tax year in which the payment is made.

    e.   Sick pay is deductible but limited to amounts not compensated by insurance or other means.

3. **Noncash Payments**

    a.   Gifts of nominal value are deductible as nonwage business expenses.

    b.   Transfers of property to an employee can also be considered compensation, and the fair market value of such property on the date of transfer is deductible.

        1)   A gain or loss is recognized on the transfer of the difference between fair market value and the adjusted basis.

4. **Employee Benefit Programs**

    a.   Cafeteria plans allow employees to choose among two or more benefits consisting of cash and qualified benefits.

        1)   The participant does not include any benefit amounts in gross income unless the cash is chosen.

        2)   If a cafeteria plan discriminates in favor of certain employees as to eligibility to participate in the plan, the employees are taxed on the taxable benefits they could have received under the plan.

    b.   When an employer makes payments or reimbursements for an employee's qualified educational expenses, the employer generally is allowed to deduct the expenses.

        1)   Under an employer's educational assistance program, the employee may exclude up to $5,250 from his or her gross income.

        2)   The courses do not have to be job-related.

        3)   Graduate and undergraduate coursework qualify for the deduction.

   c.   Dependent care assistance can be deducted when

      1)   The employer provides a dependent care facility for employees,

      2)   The employer contracts for services with a third-party dependent care provider, or

      3)   Employees are reimbursed for dependent care services. The maximum amount excludable from an employee's gross income cannot exceed $5,000 per year.

   d.   Group-term life insurance does not have to be included in an employee's income if the employer does not provide more than $50,000 of coverage.

   e.   An employer may deduct contributions paid or accrued to a welfare benefit fund, as long as the contributions for the year do not exceed benefits actually paid out during the year.

5. **Fringe Benefits**

   a.   An employer can exclude from the employee's income certain qualified fringe benefits provided by the employer. Examples include

      1)   No-additional-cost services, e.g., standby flights to flight attendants

      2)   Qualified employee discounts

      3)   De minimis fringe benefits

      4)   Qualified transportation fringes -- $245 per month for commuter or transit passes and $245 per month for parking

      5)   On-premises athletic facilities

      6)   Qualifying adoption expenses of $12,970

      7)   Occasional tickets to sporting events

   b.   Employer car for personal use is included in wages

      1)   For automobiles first made available in 2013, the maximum fair market automobile value for using the cents-per-mile valuation rule is $16,000 (Notice 2013-27).

6. **Rules of Family Employment**

Child Employed by Parents

   a.   Payments for the services of a child under age 18 who works for his or her parents in a trade or business are not subject to Social Security and Medicare taxes if the trade or business is a sole proprietorship or a partnership in which each partner is a parent of the child.

      1)   If these services are for work other than in a trade or business, such as domestic work in the parent's private home, they are not subject to Social Security and Medicare taxes until the child reaches age 21.

          a)   However, see "Covered Services of a Child or Spouse" on the next page.

      2)   Payments for the services of a child under age 21 who works for his or her parent are not subject to federal unemployment (FUTA) tax.

          a)   Although not subject to FUTA tax, the wages of a child may be subject to income tax withholding.

One Spouse Employed by Another

   b.   The wages for the services of an individual who works for his or her spouse in a trade or business are subject to income tax withholding and Social Security and Medicare taxes, but not to FUTA tax.

      1)   The services of one spouse employed by another in other than a trade or business, such as domestic service in a private home, are not subject to Social Security, Medicare, and FUTA taxes.

Covered Services of a Child or Spouse

    c.   The wages for the services of a child or spouse are subject to income tax withholding as well as to Social Security, Medicare, and FUTA taxes if (s)he works for

        1)   A corporation, even if it is controlled by the child's parent or the individual's spouse;

        2)   A partnership, even if the child's parent is a partner, unless each partner is a parent of the child;

        3)   A partnership, even if the individual's spouse is a partner; or

        4)   An estate, even if it is the estate of a deceased parent.

Parent Employed by Child

    d.   The wages for the services of a parent employed by his or her child in a trade or business are subject to income tax withholding and Social Security and Medicare taxes. Social Security and Medicare taxes do not apply to wages paid to a parent for services not in a trade or business, but they do apply to domestic services if

        1)   The parent cares for a child who lives with a son or daughter and who is under age 18 or requires adult supervision for at least 4 continuous weeks in a calendar quarter due to a mental or physical condition and

        2)   The son or daughter is a widow or widower, divorced, or married to a person who, because of a physical or mental condition, cannot care for the child during such period.

    Wages paid to a parent employed by his or her child are not subject to FUTA tax, regardless of the type of services provided.

Statutory Employees

    7.   An employer should indicate on the worker's Form W-2 whether the worker is classified as a statutory employee.

        a.   Statutory employees report their wages, income, and allowable expenses on Schedule C (or Schedule C-EZ), Form 1040.

        b.   Statutory employees are not liable for self-employment tax because their employers must treat them as employees for Social Security tax purposes.

    8.   **Documentation of Compensation Deductions**

W-2 & W-3

        a.   Employers must file Form W-2 for wages paid to each employee from whom income, Social Security, or Medicare tax was withheld or income tax would have been withheld if the employee had claimed no more than one withholding allowance or had not claimed exemption from withholding on Form W-4, *Employee's Withholding Allowance Certificate*.

        1)   Every employer engaged in a trade or business who pays remuneration for services performed by an employee, including noncash payments, must furnish a Form W-2 to each employee even if the employee is related to the employer.

        2)   Anyone required to file Form W-2 must file Form W-3 to transmit Copy A of W-2 forms.

           a)   Make a copy of Form W-3.

           b)   Keep it and Copy D (For Employer) of Form W-2 with your records for 4 years.

           c)   Be sure to use Form W-3 for the correct year.

        3)   File Copy A of Form W-2 with the entire page of Form W-3 by February 28, 2014.

           a)   If you file electronically, the due date is April 2, 2014.

           b)   You may owe a penalty for each Form W-2 that you file late.

4) Furnish Copies B, C, and 2 of Form W-2 to your employees generally by January 31, 2014.

a) You will meet the "furnish" requirement if the form is properly addressed and mailed on or before the due date.

b) If employment ends before December 31, 2013, you may furnish copies to the employee at any time after employment ends, but no later than January 31, 2014.

c) If an employee asks for Form W-2, give him or her the completed copies within 30 days of the request or within 30 days of the final wage payment, whichever is later.

Form W-4

b. Before an employee is entitled to any withholding allowances, (s)he must file a withholding allowance certificate, **Form W-4**, with his or her employer. If an employee fails to furnish such a certificate, (s)he is considered as claiming "0" exemptions.

1) Marital status has a bearing on the withholding rate.

a) Tax is withheld at different rates for single and married persons.

b) Newly married persons are required to file a new W-4 form showing their changed marital status if they desire the lower withholding rate applied to married taxpayers.

2) In the case of new employment, a new certificate should be furnished to the employer by the employee on or before the date such employment begins.

3) Near the end of each year, every employer should request employees to file new W-4 forms for the coming year if their allowance status has changed since the filing of their latest certificates.

4) Form W-4 provides for employees to claim withholding allowances on account of estimated deductions, losses or credits.

5) An employee who incurred no income tax liability for his or her preceding tax year and anticipates no such liability for his or her current tax year may include statements to this effect on Form W-4. In such case, the employer may not withhold income tax from the employee's wages.

Form 1099

c. In general, by January 31 of the current year, employers/payers must provide employees/recipients with the following forms, either paper or electronic:

1) W-2, *Wage and Tax Statement*

2) 1099-R, *Distributions From Pensions, Annuities, Retirement or Profit-Sharing Plans, IRAs, Insurance Contracts, etc.*

3) 1099-INT, *Interest Income*

4) 1099-MISC, *Miscellaneous Income*

Form 8300 – $10,000

9. Each person engaged in a trade or business who, in the course of that trade or business, receives more than $10,000 in cash in one transaction or in two or more related transactions, must file Form 8300. Any transactions conducted between a payer (or its agent) and the recipient in a 24-hour period are related transactions. Transactions are considered related even if they occur over a period of more than 24 hours if the recipient knows, or has reason to know, that each transaction is one of a series of connected transactions.

10. Depositing Obligations (e.g., employment tax)

Employment Tax Deposits

a.   Employment taxes are withheld income tax, FICA contributions, and backup withholding on reportable payments.

   1)   Generally, an employer must make either **monthly or semi-weekly** deposits during a calendar year based upon the aggregate amount of employment taxes paid during the "lookback" period.

   a)   The lookback period for each calendar year is the 12-month period that ended the preceding June 30.

   b)   An employer's obligation to make deposits in 2013 will be based upon the aggregate employment taxes paid during the period July 1, 2011, through June 30, 2012.

   c)   New employers are considered to have an aggregate tax liability of zero for any calendar quarter in which the employer did not exist.

Nonemployee Exemption

   2)   An employer does not withhold federal income tax for workers who are not common-law employees.

Monthly Deposits

b.   Monthly deposits are required if the aggregate amount of employment taxes reported by the employer for the lookback period is $50,000 or less. Monthly deposits are due on the 15th day of the following month in which the payments were made.

Semi-Weekly Deposits

c.   An employer is a semi-weekly depositor for the entire calendar year if the aggregate amount of employment taxes during the lookback period exceeds $50,000.

   1)   A monthly depositor will become a semi-weekly depositor on the first day after the employer becomes subject to the one-day rule, discussed below.

   2)   Semi-weekly deposits are generally due on either Wednesday or Friday, depending upon the timing of the employer's payperiod.

   3)   Employers with payment dates (paydays) that fall on Wednesday, Thursday, or Friday must deposit the employment taxes on or before the following Wednesday.

   4)   Employers with payment dates that fall on Saturday, Sunday, Monday, or Tuesday must make their deposit on or before the following Friday.

   5)   An employer will always have 3 banking days in which to make the deposit.

   a)   Thus, if any of the 3 weekdays following the close of a semi-weekly period is a holiday, then the employer will have an additional banking day in which to make the deposit.

One-Day Rule

d.   If an employer has accumulated $100,000 or more of undeposited employment taxes, then the taxes must be deposited by the close of the next banking day.

Federal Unemployment Taxes

e.   The calendar year is divided into four quarters for purposes of determining when deposits of federal unemployment tax are necessary.

   1)   The periods end on March 31, June 30, September 30, and December 31.

   2)   If the employer owes more than $500 in undeposited federal unemployment tax at the end of a quarter, then the tax owed must be deposited by the end of the next month.

f. **Additional Employment Tax Deposit Information**

1) The two methods of depositing employment taxes are by Electronic Federal Payment System (EFTPS) and by using Federal Tax Deposit (FTD) coupons, Form 8109.

Employers are required to make electronic deposits using EFTPS for all tax liabilities in 2013 if total deposits of all federal depository taxes were more than $200,000 in 2011 or the employer was required to use EFTPS in 2012.

2) If the employer is not required to use EFTPS, the employer can use FTD coupons to make required deposits at a financial institution or Federal Reserve Bank (FRB) that is an authorized depository.

a) An authorized depository is a financial institution (e.g., a commercial bank) that is authorized to accept federal tax deposits.

3) Timeliness of deposits. A tax deposit received by an authorized depository (no longer including Federal Reserve Banks) after the due date for the deposit is timely if it has been properly mailed at least 2 days before the prescribed due date.

a) If any person is required to deposit tax more than once a month and the deposit amounts to $20,000 or more, the deposit must be received on or before the prescribed due date in order to be timely.

Stop and review! You have completed the outline for this subunit. Study questions 1 through 11 beginning on page 66.

3.2 COST OF GOODS SOLD (COGS)

Cost of goods sold is the value of inventory sold during the course of the tax year. Cost of goods sold is not a "business deduction," but it does reduce gross revenues.

1. Cost of goods sold is calculated using the following formula:

Beginning inventory		$ XXX
Plus:		
Raw materials	$XXX	
Labor	XXX	
Materials and supplies	XXX	
Overhead	XXX	
Cost of goods in inventory		XXX
Less:		
Ending inventory		(XXX)
COGS		$ XXX

a. Beginning inventory is the ending inventory from the previous year.

b. Raw materials include the cost of all materials or parts purchased for manufacture into a finished product. Raw materials also include the cost of freight-in.

c. Labor includes all direct and indirect labor costs that are attributable to the manufacturing of a product and are included in COGS.

1) Any labor costs not properly attributable to COGS may be deducted as selling or administrative expenses.

d. Materials and supplies used in manufacturing goods, such as hardware or chemicals, are charged to COGS.

e. Overhead expenses that are necessary for the manufacturing of a finished product are charged to COGS.

f. The cost of inventory must be reduced by any trade discounts received.

2.   Manufacturers are required to use the full absorption method of costing. Therefore, both direct and indirect production costs must be included in cost of goods sold (Sec. 263A).

Stop and review! You have completed the outline for this subunit. Study questions 12 through 14 beginning on page 69.

3.3 INTEREST EXPENSE

Generally, the amount of interest agreed upon by the lender and the borrower can be deducted when paid or accrued.

1.   **Current Deductible Interest**

   a.   Interest on debt whose proceeds were used to purchase or finance a business-related property

   b.   A prepayment penalty on a loan

   c.   Unstated interest to the extent that the difference between interest under the contract at the applicable federal rate and the contract interest reduces the basis of the purchased property

   d.   Investment interest to the extent of investment income

2.   **Noncurrent Deductible Interest**

   a.   Points or loan origination fees

   b.   Capitalized interest

      1)   When real property is produced for use in trade or business or for sale to customers, the uniform capitalization rules require some interest expense to be capitalized.

         a)   The amount of interest that is generally capitalized is an amount equal to expenditures made to produce the property.

         b)   The production period must either exceed 2 years or exceed 1 year and have a cost exceeding $1 million.

   c.   Interest on income tax owed

Refinancing

3.   When a debt is refinanced, the deductibility of the interest is determined by how the new loan proceeds are used.

   a.   If the refinanced loan proceeds are used for personal reasons (e.g., to buy a sports boat for recreational purposes), the related interest is not deductible.

   b.   If the loan proceeds are used for business purposes, the corresponding interest will be deductible as business interest expense.

4.   Interest on borrowed funds used to purchase an interest in assets used in a trade or business may be deductible.

   a.   The interest deduction allowed on the borrowed funds attributed to an active trade or business is limited to the proportion of the assets devoted to an active trade or business.

5.   If a taxpayer borrows money from a third party to pay off a loan already outstanding and the interest is otherwise deductible, the individual may deduct the interest portion of the payment.

   a.   If a cash-basis individual borrows money from the same person to whom the already outstanding loan is owed so that (s)he could pay off that first loan, then the borrower cannot deduct the interest.

Stop and review! You have completed the outline for this subunit. Study questions 15 through 17 on page 71.

3.4 RENT EXPENSE

Rent is any amount paid for property that is not owned. Rent that is not unreasonable is deductible.

1. Prepaid rent and lease payments are deductible only for amounts that apply to the use of rented property during the tax year. The balance can be deducted only over the period to which it applies.

2. The costs of acquiring a lease (i.e., commissions, bonuses, and fees) are capitalized and amortized over the life of the lease. If less than 75% of the cost of acquisition is attributable to the basic term of the lease, the term of the lease includes all renewal options.

3. Rent for construction equipment used to build a new building is capitalized as part of the building.

Stop and review! You have completed the outline for this subunit. Study questions 18 through 25 beginning on page 72.

3.5 TAXES

Taxes paid or accrued in a trade or business are deductible. Taxes paid to purchase property are treated as part of the cost of the property.

Sales Tax

1. Sales tax is treated as part of the property's cost.

   a. If capitalized, the sales tax may be recoverable as depreciation.
   b. If the cost of the property is currently expensed and deductible, so is the tax.

Occupational License

2. Occupational license taxes are deductible. The Occupational License Tax and Wagering Tax are both imposed on wagering activities.

Property Tax

3. State or local personal property taxes are an itemized deduction for individuals. Tax on business property is a business expense.

   a. Local improvements. Taxes assessed for local benefit that tend to increase the value of real property are added to the property's adjusted basis and are not currently deductible as tax expense.

      1) Examples are taxes assessed for streets, sidewalks, sewer lines, public parking facilities, etc.

Income Taxes

4. State and local taxes imposed on net income of an individual are deductible.

   a. They are not a business expense of a sole proprietorship.

      1) They are a personal, itemized deduction not subject to the 2% exclusion.

   b. Federal income taxes generally are not deductible.
   c. Individual taxpayers may claim an itemized deduction for either general state and local sales taxes or state income taxes, but not both.

      1) Taxpayers can deduct either their actual sales tax amounts or a predetermined amount from an IRS table.

Employment Taxes

5. An employer may deduct the employer portion of FICA taxes. An employee may not deduct FICA taxes.

    a. Self-employed persons deduct the employer portion of FICA (self-employment) taxes to arrive at AGI based on net earnings.

Federal Excise Tax

6. Excise taxes are levied on transactions, not on income or wealth.

    a. Federal gasoline and excise taxes and import duties are not deductible as taxes.

        1) If they are paid or incurred in connection with a trade or business or with income-producing property, they may be deducted as an expense.

    b. When manufacturers' or retailers' excise taxes are reflected in the price of an article that is purchased for business or income-producing purposes, the entire price paid for such article is deductible.

        1) This applies even if the excise tax is separately stated.
        2) If the purchase price is deductible currently, the tax included in the purchase price is also deductible.
        3) If the purchase price is capitalized and amortized/depreciated, the tax included in the purchase price is also amortized/depreciated.

    c. The federal tax on automobiles may not be deducted by the ultimate purchaser.

    d. See Publication 510 for additional information.

    e. Common Excise Taxes

        1) Environmental taxes on the sale or use of ozone-depleting chemicals and imported products containing or manufactured with these chemicals
        2) Communications and air transportation taxes
        3) Fuel taxes
        4) Tax on the first retail sale of heavy trucks, trailers, and tractors
        5) Manufacturers' taxes on the sale or use of a variety of different articles

    f. The manufacturer of an item may be eligible for a credit or refund of the manufacturer's tax for certain uses, sales, exports, and price readjustments. The claim must set forth in detail the facts upon which it is based.

    g. A credit or refund (without interest) of the taxes on heavy trucks and trailers, gas guzzler vehicles, tires, gasoline, diesel fuel, kerosene, coal, vaccines, and sporting goods may be allowable if a tax-paid article is, by any person,

        1) Exported,
        2) Used or sold for use as supplies for vessels (except for coal and vaccines),
        3) Sold to a state or local government for its exclusive use (except for coal, gas guzzlers, and vaccines),
        4) Sold to a not-for-profit educational organization for its exclusive use (except for coal, gas guzzlers, and vaccines), or
        5) Used for further manufacture of another article subject to the manufacturer's taxes (except for coal).

    h. Excise taxes are added to the basis of the asset purchased and are deductible either through depreciation or when the asset is sold.

Real Estate Taxes

7.   Any state, local, or foreign taxes on real property are deductible when paid.

   a.   If real estate is sold, the deduction for real estate taxes must be divided between the buyer and the seller according to the number of days in the real property year.

   b.   Real estate taxes paid into an escrow account are deductible when the funds are withdrawn and paid to the taxing authority.

Penalties

8.   Penalty taxes are generally not deductible.

Stop and review! You have completed the outline for this subunit. Study questions 26 through 28 beginning on page 74.

3.6 MANUFACTURING DEDUCTION

Gross Receipts

1.   Domestic production gross receipts (DPGR) are defined by Section 199 as gross receipts that are derived from

   a.   The sale, exchange, or other disposition or any rental, lease, or licensing of

   1)   Qualified production property that is manufactured, produced, grown, or extracted in the United States by the taxpayer in whole or in significant part.

   2)   Any qualified film produced by the taxpayer in the United States.

   3)   Electricity, natural gas, or potable water produced by the taxpayer in the United States.

   b.   Construction performed in the United States.

   c.   Engineering and architectural services performed in the United States for a construction project located in the United States.

   NOTE: Through 2013, the manufacturing deduction is extended to include Puerto Rico.

Production Property

2.   Qualified production property generally includes tangible personal property, computer software, and sound recordings.

Personal Property

3.   Gross receipts from the sale or lease of personal property that is manufactured in the United States are considered DPGR.

   a.   The gross receipts from the lease, rental, or license of property to a related party do not qualify as DPGR.

   1)   Employees are considered related parties to an employer.

   2)   All employees of a company and its subsidiaries are considered to be employed by a single employer.

Domestic Activity

4.   When determining the income attributable to domestic activities, a company does not include any gross receipts from nondomestic production in the calculation of DPGR.

   a.   If nondomestic production gross receipts are less than 5% of the total gross receipts for the company, the company may treat all gross receipts as though they are DPGR.

U.S. Production Deduction

5.   The U.S. Production Deduction applies to firms that perform manufacturing, production, or extraction activities in the United States.

a.   The deduction for income attributable to domestic gross income for 2013 is equal to 9% of the least of the following:

1)   The qualified production activities income (QPAI),

a)   QPAI is calculated by taking the DPGR and subtracting the sum of the following from it:

i)   The cost of goods sold attributable to DPGR;

ii)   Other deductions, expenses, or losses that are directly attributable to DPGR; and

iii)   A proper share of other deductions, expenses, or losses that are not directly allocatable to DPGR or another class of income.

2)   The taxable income of the taxpayer, or

3)   50% of the W-2 wages for the year allocable only to qualified production activities income instead of all wages.

Stop and review! You have completed the outline for this subunit. Study questions 29 and 30 on page 76.

QUESTIONS

3.1 Compensation

1. Which of the following tests is not used to determine whether an employee's pay is deductible as an expense?

A.   Payments for services an employee rendered are reasonable. This test is based on the circumstances at the time you contract for the services, not on those existing when the amount of pay is questioned.

B.   Payments for services an employee rendered are ordinary and necessary and are directly or indirectly connected with your trade or business.

C.   Payments are made for services actually performed.

D.   Depending upon the taxpayer's method of accounting, payments are made or expenses are incurred for services rendered during the year.

Answer (B) is correct.

REQUIRED: The test not used to determine whether an employee's pay is deductible.

DISCUSSION: Sec. 162(a)(1) allows a deduction for a reasonable allowance of salaries or other compensation for personal services actually rendered. The salary, wage, or other payment for services an employee renders must be an ordinary and necessary expense and directly connected with your trade or business.

Answer (A) is incorrect. Sec. 162(a)(1) specifically requires the amount to be reasonable and the services to be actually rendered in order to deduct compensation. Answer (C) is incorrect. Sec. 162(a)(1) specifically requires the amount to be reasonable and the services to be actually rendered in order to deduct compensation. Answer (D) is incorrect. Sec. 162 requires the expense to be paid or incurred during the year.

2. Mr. Aspen, a cash basis CPA, pays Gail Smith to work during tax season as a data entry clerk. Mr. Aspen pays Gail the following:

Hourly wages	$6,275
Bonuses	500
Loan	150

How much can Mr. Aspen deduct as compensation?

A. $6,275

B. $6,775

C. $6,925

D.   None of the answers are correct.

Answer (B) is correct.

REQUIRED: The amount deductible as compensation.

DISCUSSION: Sec. 162(a)(1) permits a deduction for a reasonable allowance for salaries or other personal services actually rendered, including bonuses. The loan is deductible only if it is doubtful the employee will repay. Otherwise, it is treated as a loan and cannot be deducted. Therefore, the wages and bonuses are deductible, but the loan is not.

Answer (A) is incorrect. The permitted deduction includes both the wages and bonuses, not just wages. Answer (C) is incorrect. The loan is not deductible because there is no indication for personal services actually performed. Answer (D) is incorrect. There is a correct answer given.

3. Michelle Nicole is the chief executive officer of It'll Rain Someday, Inc., a publicly held company that sells umbrellas and rainwear. During the year, Ms. Nicole was paid $1.5 million in compensation, which included a $600,000 excess golden parachute payment. What is the amount that It'll Rain Someday can deduct for Ms. Nicole's compensation?

A. $1,500,000

B. $900,000

C. $400,000

D. $1,000,000

Answer (B) is correct.
REQUIRED: The amount of compensation that can be deducted.
DISCUSSION: A corporation that enters into a contract whereby it agrees to pay an employee amounts in excess of the employee's usual compensation in the event that control or ownership of the corporation changes is barred from taking a deduction for an "excess parachute payment made to a disqualified individual." A disqualified individual is an employee who performs services for any corporation and is an officer, a shareholder, or other highly compensated individual. Therefore, the entire golden parachute payment is not deductible, and It'll Rain Someday, Inc., will deduct only $900,000.

4. Payments made to employees are normally currently deductible as business expenses except

A. Vacation pay paid to an employee even when the employee chooses not to take a vacation.

B. Wages paid to employees for constructing a new building to be used in the business.

C. Reasonable salaries paid to employee-shareholders for services rendered.

D. Payments made to the beneficiary of a deceased employee that are reasonable in relation to the employee's past services.

Answer (B) is correct.
REQUIRED: The payment to an employee not currently deductible.
DISCUSSION: Normally, Sec. 162(a)(1) allows a deduction for a reasonable allowance for salaries or other compensation for personal services actually rendered. However, Sec. 263A requires all direct costs and a proper share of indirect costs allocable to property produced by the taxpayer to be capitalized. Wages paid to employees for constructing a new building would be direct costs allocable to that building. Those costs are capitalized and depreciated as part of the cost of the building rather than currently deductible.

5. Mr. Holiday is a calendar-year, accrual-basis taxpayer. His records concerning vacation pay for his employees reflect the following:

- $20,000 paid January 30, 2013, for vacations earned in 2012. Nothing was vested by December 31, 2012.
- $100,000 vacation pay accrued and paid in 2013.
- $14,000 accrued in 2013 but vested by December 31, 2013; paid by February 28, 2014.
- $10,000 accrued but not vested by December 31, 2013.

What amount can Mr. Holiday deduct as a business expense for 2013?

A. $114,000

B. $124,000

C. $120,000

D. $154,000

Answer (C) is correct.
REQUIRED: The amount of vacation pay deductible in the current year.
DISCUSSION: Accrual-basis taxpayers deduct vacation pay when it is paid. Therefore, Mr. Holiday can deduct $120,000 in the current year.

6. Allyn transferred office equipment used in his business to Wilson, an employee, as payment for services. At the time of the transfer, the equipment had a fair market value of $4,000 and an adjusted basis to Allyn of $4,750. How should Allyn report this transfer on his income tax return?

A. Wage expense $4,750; loss on sale $0.

B. Wage expense $4,000; loss on sale $750.

C. Wage expense $4,000; loss on sale $0.

D. Wage expense $0; loss on sale $4,750.

Answer (B) is correct.
REQUIRED: The proper treatment of a transfer of property as payment for services.
DISCUSSION: When property is transferred to an employee as compensation, the employer is entitled to a deduction of its fair market value on the date of the transfer. A gain or loss is realized on the date of the transfer as the difference between the fair market value and adjusted basis. Allyn will deduct $4,000 as wages and recognize a $750 loss on the sale of the equipment ($4,000 – $4,750).
Answer (A) is incorrect. A loss on sale must be recognized separately, not as a component of wage expense. Answer (C) is incorrect. A loss on sale must be recognized. Answer (D) is incorrect. The fair market value of the equipment transferred may be deducted as wages.

7. Which of the following statements is true in respect to determining when fringe benefits are deductible?

A.   Education expenses paid for employees are deductible as fringe benefits whether or not job related.

B.   Cafeteria plans are written plans that allow employees to choose among two or more benefits consisting of cash and qualified benefits.

C.   Only those fringe benefits that are includible in an employee's wages are deductible.

D.   If an employer transfers a capital asset to an employee, no gain or loss is recognized by the employer or the employee.

Answer (B) is correct.

   REQUIRED: The true statement regarding fringe benefits.
   DISCUSSION: Cafeteria plans are employer-sponsored benefit packages that offer employees a choice between taking cash and receiving qualified benefits, such as accident and health coverage or group-term life insurance coverage. No amount is included in the gross income of the participant unless cash is chosen.
   Answer (A) is incorrect. Educational expenses in the amount of $5,250 are deductible as noncompensating expenses. Answer (C) is incorrect. Some fringe benefits, like de minimis fringes, are not included as income by the employee but are still deductible. Answer (D) is incorrect. A gain or loss must be recognized on the transfer of an asset as the difference between the fair market value and its adjusted basis.

8. Which of the following statements describes an incorrect treatment of employee benefit programs?

A.   A qualified benefit can be excluded from income because of specific provisions of law.

B.   An employer provides qualifying dependent care assistance to his or her employees. The employer can exclude from the employees' wages up to $5,000 in assistance for each employee.

C.   The cost of group term life insurance coverage, up to $50,000, is excluded from income.

D.   A cafeteria plan that discriminates in favor of certain employees as to eligibility to participate in the plan results in the employees being taxed on the sum of the value of all of the benefits offered by the plan.

Answer (D) is correct.

   REQUIRED: The false statement regarding the treatment of employee benefit programs.
   DISCUSSION: Sec. 125 defines a cafeteria plan as a written plan under which all participants are employees and the participants may choose among benefits consisting of cash and qualified benefits. If a cafeteria plan discriminates in favor of certain employees as to eligibility to participate in the plan, the employees are taxed on the taxable benefits they could have received under the plan.
   Answer (A) is incorrect. Due to provisions of law, a qualified benefit can be excluded. Answer (B) is incorrect. The maximum amount excludable from an employee's gross income cannot exceed $5,000 per year. Answer (C) is incorrect. Group-term life insurance does not have to be included in an employee's income if the employer does not provide more than $50,000 of coverage.

9. Which of the following fringe benefits cannot be excluded from an employee's income?

A.   Transportation up to $245 per month for combined commuter highway vehicle transportation and transit passes, and $245 per month for qualified parking.

B.   Holiday gifts, other than cash, with a low fair market value.

C.   Qualified employee discounts given employees on certain property and services offered to customers in the ordinary course of the line of business in which the employees perform services.

D.   Memberships in municipal athletic facilities for employees, their spouses, and their dependent children.

Answer (D) is correct.

   REQUIRED: The fringe benefit that cannot be excluded.
   DISCUSSION: Sec. 132 excludes certain qualified fringe benefits that are provided to an employee from the employee's income. Excludable fringe benefits include qualified employee discounts, de minimis fringes, and qualified transportation fringes. Membership in an athletic facility qualifies only if it is for an on-premises facility available to all employees. Memberships in municipal facilities cannot be excluded as wages.
   Answer (A) is incorrect. Qualified transportation fringe benefits include $245 per month for commuter or transit passes and $245 per month for parking. Answer (B) is incorrect. Holiday gifts with a low fair market value are de minimis fringe benefits. Answer (C) is incorrect. Qualified employee discounts are fringe benefits.

10. Karla operates a clothing store and paid $24,000 in wages to two employees ($12,000 each). She also provided for child care for their children valued at $3,600 for each employee. The employees also received clothing from the store, having a total value of $800, for working 5 extra days. How much is deductible by Karla?

A. $24,000

B. $24,800

C. $31,200

D. $32,000

Answer (D) is correct.
    REQUIRED: The amount deductible for wages, child care, and inventory received by employees.
    DISCUSSION: Sec. 162(a)(1) allows a deduction for reasonable compensation for personal services actually rendered. Sec. 83(a) allows the deduction to an employer equal to the fair market value of property given to the employee when the property is transferable or is not subject to a substantial risk of forfeiture. The value of the child care services provided by the employer also constitutes compensation for the employee's services and is deductible by the employer (up to $5,000 per employee).
    Answer (A) is incorrect. The child care and the clothes may also be deducted. Answer (B) is incorrect. The child care for the other employee may also be deducted. Answer (C) is incorrect. The clothes given may also be deducted.

11. Which of the following fringe benefits is not excludable from an employee's wages?

A. Qualifying adoption expenses of $12,970 provided through an adoption assistance program.

B. Educational assistance expenses of $5,250 provided through an educational assistance program.

C. $60,000 of group term life insurance covering the death of an employee.

D. Dependent care assistance of $5,000 provided through a dependent care assistance program.

Answer (C) is correct.
    REQUIRED: The fringe benefit not excludable from an employee's wages.
    DISCUSSION: Under Sec. 79, the cost of qualified group term life insurance paid by an employer is included in the employee's gross income to the extent that such cost exceeds the cost of $50,000 of such insurance. The includible cost is determined on the basis of uniform premiums prescribed by regulations, rather than actual cost.
    Answer (A) is incorrect. Qualifying adoption expenses of $12,970 are excludable. Answer (B) is incorrect. Under an employer's educational assistance program, the employee may exclude up to $5,250 from his or her gross income. Answer (D) is incorrect. Dependent care assistance of $5,000 is excludable.

3.2 Cost of Goods Sold (COGS)

12. The FX Partnership manufactures garden hoses for sale. In the month of January, its sales were $80,000. During that month, the partnership had:

Beginning inventory, January 1	$ 0
Raw materials purchased January 1	35,000
Raw materials shipping costs	1,585
Direct labor (production)	27,000
Factory overhead	6,000
Ending inventory, January 31	10,000

What is the cost of goods sold for the FX Partnership for the month of January?

A. $58,000

B. $59,585

C. $69,585

D. $53,585

Answer (B) is correct.
    REQUIRED: The amount reported as cost of goods sold.
    DISCUSSION: Cost of goods sold is computed by starting with the beginning inventory, adding the cost of materials purchased during the year and the cost of production, and subtracting the ending inventory. Under Sec. 263A, manufacturers are required to use the full absorption method of costing, which means that both direct and indirect production costs must be included. Freight charges are always added to the cost of the goods purchased.
    Costs to ship to the purchaser are selling expenses, not costs of inventory.

Beginning inventory		$ 0
Raw materials and labor:		
Direct labor	$27,000	
Raw materials	36,585	
Production overhead	6,000	69,585
Goods available for sale		$69,585
Less ending inventory		(10,000)
Cost of goods sold		$59,585

    Answer (A) is incorrect. Raw material shipping costs are added to the cost of the goods purchased. Answer (C) is incorrect. Ending inventory must be subtracted from the goods available for sale. Answer (D) is incorrect. Factory overhead is an indirect production cost that must be included.

13. Lisa Arsenault operates a small basket weaving business as a sole proprietor. She incurred the following expenses in 2013:

Beginning inventory raw material	$ 5,000
Beginning inventory finished goods	10,000
Ending inventory raw material	6,250
Ending inventory finished goods	4,700
Purchases	17,500
Fabric used in finished goods	2,350
Building rent	12,000
Freight in on fabric	300
Freight out on sale of finished goods	475

What was her cost of goods sold?

A. $24,375

B. $24,675

C. $21,850

D. $24,200

Answer (D) is correct.

REQUIRED: The cost of goods sold for a manufacturing company.

DISCUSSION: Cost of goods sold is computed by starting with the beginning inventory, adding the cost of materials purchased during the year and the cost of production, and subtracting the ending inventory. Under Sec. 263A, manufacturers are required to use the full absorption method of costing, which means that both direct and indirect production costs must be included. Freight charges are always added to the cost of the goods purchased. Freight out on sale of finished goods are selling expenses, not costs of inventory.

Beginning inventory (raw materials and finished goods)		$15,000
Materials and labor:		
Fabric used	$ 2,350	
Freight-in	300	
Purchases	17,500	
Goods available for sale		20,150
		$35,150
Less ending inventory (raw materials and finished goods)		(10,950)
Cost of goods sold		$24,200

Authors' note: This is a former EA exam question. The answer choices indicate that building rent is a Selling, General, and Administrative (SG&A) expense, i.e., not included in overhead and therefore not included in COGS.

Answer (A) is incorrect. Freight out are selling expenses, not cost of inventory. Answer (B) is incorrect. Freight out are selling expenses, not cost of inventory. Answer (C) is incorrect. The fabric used must be included in cost of goods.

14. XYZ Corporation, a clothing retailer, showed the following expenses in 2013:

Clothing purchased for resale	$72,000
Freight-in	3,550
Freight out to customers	1,750
Beginning inventory	55,650
Ending inventory	42,500

What is XYZ's cost of goods sold?

A. $88,700

B. $175,450

C. $90,450

D. $86,900

Answer (A) is correct.

REQUIRED: The calculated cost of goods sold.

DISCUSSION: Cost of goods sold is computed by starting with the beginning inventory, adding the cost of materials purchased during the year and the cost of production, and subtracting the ending inventory. Under Sec. 263A, manufacturers are required to use the full absorption method of costing, which means that both direct and indirect production costs must be included. Freight charges are always added to the cost of the goods purchased. Costs to ship to the purchaser are selling expenses, not costs of inventory. Therefore, the cost of goods sold is $88,700.

Beginning inventory	$ 55,650
Clothing purchased for resale	72,000
	$127,650
Less ending inventory	42,500
	$ 85,150
Freight-in	3,550
	$ 88,700

Answer (B) is incorrect. The ending inventory is subtracted, not added, and the freight out to customers is not included to arrive at cost of goods sold. Answer (C) is incorrect. Freight out to customers is a selling expense, not an item in cost of goods sold. Answer (D) is incorrect. Freight out to customers is a selling expense, not an item in cost of goods sold.

3.3 Interest Expense

15. On June 30, 2013, Sally, who uses the cash method of accounting, borrowed $25,000 from a bank for use in her business. Sally was to repay the loan in one payment with $2,000 interest on December 30, 2013. On December 30, 2013, she renewed that loan plus the interest due. The new loan was for $27,000. What is the amount of interest expense that Sally can deduct for 2013?

- A. $0
- B. $333
- C. $1,000
- D. $2,000

Answer (A) is correct.
REQUIRED: The amount of interest deduction permitted for a cash-method taxpayer.
DISCUSSION: If a taxpayer borrows money from a third party to pay off a loan already outstanding and the interest is otherwise deductible, the individual may deduct the interest portion of the payment. However, if a cash-basis individual borrows money from the same person to whom the already outstanding loan is owed so that (s)he could pay off that first loan, then the borrower cannot deduct the interest. Thus, Sally cannot deduct interest expense for 2013.

16. On June 30, 2013, Cindy, who uses the cash method of accounting, borrowed $30,000 from Bank 1 to use in her business. Cindy was to repay the loan in one payment with $2,000 interest due on December 30, 2013. She took out a new loan from Bank 1. The new loan was for $32,000 (the original unpaid loan and unpaid interest). How much can Cindy deduct as interest expense for 2013?

- A. $2,000
- B. $1,000
- C. $0
- D. $500

Answer (C) is correct.
REQUIRED: The deductibility of interest on a loan used to pay off another loan.
DISCUSSION: If a taxpayer borrows money from a third party to pay off a loan already outstanding and the interest is otherwise deductible, the individual may deduct the interest portion of the payment. However, if a cash-basis individual borrows money from the same person to whom the already outstanding loan is owed so that (s)he could pay off that first loan, then the borrower cannot deduct the interest. Thus, Cindy cannot deduct interest expense for 2013.

17. You buy an interest in a partnership for $20,000 using borrowed funds. The partnership's only assets include machinery used in the business valued at $60,000 and stocks valued at $15,000. In 2013, you paid $2,000 interest on the loan. How much interest is deductible as interest attributed to a trade or business?

- A. $0
- B. $400
- C. $1,600
- D. $2,000

Answer (C) is correct.
REQUIRED: The deduction for interest on borrowed funds.
DISCUSSION: The interest deduction allowed on the borrowed funds attributed to an active trade or business is limited to the proportion of the partnership assets devoted to an active trade or business. The machinery consists of 80% ($60,000 ÷ $75,000) of the business assets used in an active trade or business. The stocks are not considered part of an active trade or business. Therefore, 80% of the $2,000, or $1,600, is deductible as interest attributed to an active trade or business.
Answer (A) is incorrect. The portion of the interest expense attributed to assets used in an active trade or business in the partnership will be deductible. Answer (B) is incorrect. The 20% of the interest attributed to the stock ownership by the partnership will not be deductible as interest attributed to a trade or business. Answer (D) is incorrect. The entire $2,000 is not deductible. Only the portion of the interest expense attributed to assets used in an active trade or business in the partnership will be deductible.

3.4 Rent Expense

18. Wilma Smith leased a building for 4 years beginning in March of the current year for $1,500 per month. On March 1 of the current year, Mrs. Smith paid her landlord $33,000 in rent. How much can she deduct on her current-year tax return?

A. $33,000

B. $18,000

C. $0

D. $15,000

Answer (D) is correct.

REQUIRED: The allowable deduction for prepaid rent.

DISCUSSION: If rent is paid in advance, only the portion that applies to the current year may be deducted. The rest of the prepayment is deductible in the year in which the rent applies. Therefore, $15,000 is deductible in the current year ($1,500 × 10 months).

Answer (A) is incorrect. Only rent attributable to the current year may be deducted, not the entire amount. Answer (B) is incorrect. Only the rent for the remaining 10 months ($15,000) may be deducted, not an entire year's rent of $18,000 ($1,500 × 12 months). Answer (C) is incorrect. The amount of $15,000 is permitted as a deduction in the current year.

19. On March 1 of the current year, Sharon, a cash-basis sole proprietor, leased a dance studio from Shelby Room Rentors for 3 years at $1,200 per month. During the current year, Sharon paid $28,800 on the lease. What is the amount Sharon can deduct on her income tax return for the current year?

A. $26,400

B. $12,000

C. $14,400

D. $28,800

Answer (B) is correct.

REQUIRED: The amount of rent that can be deducted in the current year.

DISCUSSION: Rental expenses are generally deductible by a cash-basis taxpayer-lessee in the tax year in which they are paid. However, the general rule does not apply to advance rental payments. Advance rental payments made by a cash-basis taxpayer-lessee are generally not deductible in the tax year in which they are made but must be allocated over the period of time for which the premises may be used as a result of such payments. Sharon will deduct $12,000 of rent expense in the current year (10 months of current year rent × $1,200 rent per month).

20. Clyde operated a food distribution business. He leased a small warehouse in 2012 for $60,000 per year for a 3-year term. The lease was to start on July 1, 2012. Clyde paid the first year's rent in advance in May 2012. Clyde then began to make monthly payments of $5,000 starting on July 1, 2013, and continuing on the first of the month for the balance of 2013. What rent expense may Clyde claim in 2013?

A. $60,000

B. $50,000

C. $30,000

D. None of the answers are correct.

Answer (A) is correct.

REQUIRED: The amount of rent that can be deducted.

DISCUSSION: Assuming that Clyde is a cash-basis taxpayer, generally, rental expenses are deductible by a cash-basis taxpayer-lessee in the tax year in which they are paid. However, the general rule does not apply to advance rental payments. Advance rental payments made by a cash-basis taxpayer-lessee are generally not deductible in the tax year in which they are made but must be allocated over the period of time for which the premises may be used as a result of such payments. Clyde will be able to deduct $60,000 of rent because he can deduct the allocated portion of the $30,000 prepaid rent and the $30,000 of current rent expenses paid.

21. In 2013, Charlie purchased a lease on an office building for 4 years, beginning January 1. Charlie paid $27,000 in advance rent, of which $3,000 was for the purchase of the existing lease. The remaining was for monthly lease payments. How much can Charlie deduct for 2013?

A. $6,750

B. $0

C. $3,000

D. $9,000

Answer (A) is correct.

REQUIRED: The amount deductible as prepaid rent.

DISCUSSION: Rent paid in your trade or business is deductible in the year paid or accrued. If you pay rent in advance, you can deduct only the amount that applies to your use of the rented property during the tax year. You can deduct the rest of your payment only over the period to which it applies. If you get an existing lease on property or equipment for your business, you must amortize any amount you pay to get that lease over the remaining term of the lease. (See Publication 535.)

Answer (B) is incorrect. A deduction is allowed. Answer (C) is incorrect. The $3,000 lease is required to be allocated over the 4 years. Answer (D) is incorrect. The $3,000 lease must be allocated over the 4 years.

22. On July 1 of the current year, Mel leased property for 2 years for $700 a month. On September 30 of the current year, the owner of the property told him if he paid the total in advance for the remainder of the lease the rent would be reduced to $675 a month. Mel accepted his offer and on October 1 of the current year, he paid the owner $14,175. How much can Mel deduct as rental expense in the current year?

A. $2,025

B. $4,050

C. $4,125

D. $16,300

Answer (C) is correct.

REQUIRED: The deductible amount of rental expense.

DISCUSSION: Prepaid rent may not be deducted by either a cash-basis or an accrual-basis taxpayer. To do so would violate the requirement that the taxpayer's method of accounting must clearly reflect income [Sec. 446(b)]. Furthermore, an expenditure that creates an asset having a useful life extending substantially beyond the close of the taxable year is not deductible [Reg. 1.461-1(a)]. Only the $4,125 of rental expense allocable to the current year is deductible. The amount that Mel can deduct is calculated as follows:

July	$ 700
August	700
September	700
October	675
November	675
December	675
Total rental expense	$4,125

Answer (A) is incorrect. The amount of $2,025 does not account for the rent paid for July, August, and September. Answer (B) is incorrect. The reduced rent does not take effect until October. Answer (D) is incorrect. Prepaid rent is deductible to the current year on an allocable basis, not a cash or accrual basis.

23. On January 1, 2013, Carrie leased property for her business for 5 years for $6,200 per year. Carrie paid the full $31,000 during the first year of the lease. What is Carrie's rental deduction for the year 2013?

A. $31,000

B. $6,200

C. $15,500

D. $24,800

Answer (B) is correct.

REQUIRED: The deduction for prepaid lease payments.

DISCUSSION: Rent is any amount paid for property that is not owned. Rent that is not unreasonable is deductible. Prepaid rent and lease payments are deductible only for amounts that apply to the use of rented property during the tax year. The balance can be deducted only over the period to which it applies. Since Carrie's payment for the first year would be $6,200, that is all she is able to deduct for the current tax year. In the remaining 4 years of the lease, she will be able to deduct the remainder.

Answer (A) is incorrect. The full $31,000 paid is not deductible in the current year. Carrie must allocate the lease payments over the 5-year term of the lease. Answer (C) is incorrect. Half of the advance lease payment is not deductible in the current year. Carrie must allocate the lease payable over the 5-year term of the lease. Answer (D) is incorrect. Only 1 year's worth of lease payments will be currently deductible, not 4 years' worth of lease payments.

24. In 2012, Bob purchased a lease for an office for 4 years, beginning January 1, 2013, to use in his tax practice. Of the $21,600 he paid, $5,000 was for the purchase of the existing lease with 4 years remaining and no options to renew. The remaining amount was for monthly lease payments paid in advance. How much can Bob deduct for 2013?

A. $0

B. $1,500

C. $3,800

D. $5,400

Answer (D) is correct.

REQUIRED: The amount of rent that can be deducted.

DISCUSSION: Assuming that Bob is a cash-basis taxpayer, generally, rental expenses are deductible by a cash-basis taxpayer-lessee in the tax year in which they are paid. However, the general rule does not apply to advance rental payments. Advance rental payments made by a cash-basis taxpayer-lessee are generally not deductible in the tax year in which they are made but must be allocated over the period of time for which the premises may be used as a result of such payments. Bob can deduct $5,400 in 2013 ($21,600 prepaid rent ÷ 4 years).

Answer (A) is incorrect. Prepaid rent is allocated over the life of the lease. Answer (B) is incorrect. The current year's rent deduction is calculated by allocating the prepaid rent over the life of the lease. Answer (C) is incorrect. The current year's rent deduction is calculated by allocating the prepaid rent over the life of the lease.

25. On January 1, 2013, Adam, a cash-basis sole proprietor, acquired a lease on a machine for $55,000. In addition, Adam paid a $5,000 finder's fee to obtain the lease. There are 10 years remaining on the lease with no option to renew. What amount can Adam deduct for 2013?

A. $5,000

B. $5,500

C. $6,000

D. $10,500

Answer (C) is correct.

REQUIRED: The deductible amount of rent in the current year.

DISCUSSION: Generally, rental expenses are deductible by a cash-basis taxpayer-lessee in the tax year in which they are paid. However, the general rule does not apply to advance rental payments. Advance rental payments made by a cash-basis taxpayer-lessee are generally not deductible in the tax year in which they are made but must be allocated over the period of time for which the premises may be used as a result of such payments. Costs of acquiring a lease, such as commissions, bonuses, and fees, are capitalized and amortized over the life of the lease as a rent expense.

Answer (A) is incorrect. The finder's fee does not reduce the amount of prepaid rent. Answer (B) is incorrect. The finder's fee is added to the amount of prepaid rent in determining its allocation. Answer (D) is incorrect. The current-year rent deduction is calculated by allocating the prepaid rent over the life of the lease.

3.5 Taxes

26. During 2013, Ms. Smith had the following expenditures relating to commercial real estate she owns:

- County property tax, $1,975
- State property tax, $980
- Assessment for sewer construction, $1,500
- Charges for sewer and water service, $810

What is the amount Ms. Smith may deduct as real estate taxes on her commercial real estate for 2013?

A. $2,955

B. $4,455

C. $3,765

D. $5,265

Answer (A) is correct.

REQUIRED: The correct amount to be deducted as real estate taxes.

DISCUSSION: Sales and/or local property taxes are an itemized deduction for individuals and a business expense for businesses. Thus, the $1,975 and the $980 are deductions as real estate taxes. Assessments for sewer construction are local improvements. These are taxes for things not currently deductible as a tax expense that tend to increase the value of real property and are added to the property's adjusted basis. Charges for sewer and water service would not be deducted as real estate tax.

Answer (B) is incorrect. Assessments for sewer construction are local improvements. These are taxes for things that tend to increase the value of real property and are added to the property's adjusted basis. These are not currently deductible as tax expense. Answer (C) is incorrect. Charges for sewer are not deductible as real estate tax. These are taxes for things not currently deductible as a tax expense that tend to increase the value of real property and are added to the property's adjusted basis. Answer (D) is incorrect. Assessments for sewer construction are local improvements. These are taxes for things not currently deductible as a tax expense that tend to increase the value of real property and are added to the property's adjusted basis. Charges for sewer and water would not be deducted as real estate tax.

27. Which of the following statements regarding deductible taxes is correct?

1) Local benefit taxes for business assets are deductible only if they are for maintenance, repair, or interest charges related to those benefits.

2) Real estate taxes on business property included in monthly mortgage payments placed in escrow cannot be deducted unless the lender actually paid the taxing authority.

3) Taxes on gasoline, diesel fuel, and other motor fuels that you use in your business should be deducted as part of the cost of the fuel.

4) Any tax imposed by a state or local government on personal property used in your trade or business is deductible.

    A. 1, 2, and 4.

    B. 2 and 4.

    C. 1 and 3.

    D. 1, 2, 3, and 4.

28. Rudy, a plumber, paid the following taxes: $800 on the purchase of a new truck, $1,500 for the current year's property tax, $150 sales tax on miscellaneous office supplies, $600 sales tax on merchandise he purchased for resale. How much can he deduct as a current business expense for tax purposes?

    A. $150

    B. $1,650

    C. $2,250

    D. $3,050

Answer (D) is correct.

REQUIRED: The correct statement about deductible taxes.

DISCUSSION: Local benefit taxes for businesses are deductible if the local benefit does not increase the value of the property. When real estate taxes are paid into an escrow account with the monthly mortgage payment, the taxes cannot be deducted until the escrow funds are withdrawn and paid to the taxing authority. Taxes on gasoline, diesel fuel, and other motor fuels are expensed. The rule is if the cost of the property is currently expensed and deductible, so is the tax. Any tax by state or local government on personal property in a trade or business is deductible.

Answer (A) is incorrect. Taxes on gasoline, diesel fuel, and other motor fuels are expensed. The rule is, if the cost of the property is currently expensed and deductible, so is the tax. Answer (B) is incorrect. Local benefit taxes for businesses are deductible if the local benefit does not increase the value of the property and because taxes on gasoline, diesel fuel, and other motor fuels are expensed. The rule is, if the cost of the property is currently expensed and deductible, so is the tax. Answer (C) is incorrect.. When real estate taxes are paid into an escrow account with the monthly mortgage payment, the taxes cannot be deducted until the escrow funds are withdrawn and paid to the taxing authority. Also, any tax by state or local government on personal property in a trade or business is deductible.

Answer (B) is correct.

REQUIRED: The type of taxes deductible as a current business expense.

DISCUSSION: Sec. 1012 outlines general rules for certain types of commonly capitalized costs. The $800 paid in taxes on the purchase of a new truck is capitalized and added to the basis of the truck and depreciated. The $600 sales tax on merchandise purchased for resale is added to the cost basis of the merchandise and used to determine the cost of goods sold. The $1,500 for the current year's property tax (assuming the tax is related to the business) is deductible as a current business expense. The $150 in sales tax for the office supplies is deductible as a current business expense because the supplies are deemed to be consumed during the year. Therefore, the total amount Rudy may deduct during the current year as a current business expense is $1,650. However, due to the vagueness of the relationship of the property tax to the business, the IRS accepted both $150 and $1,650 as answers for this question.

Answer (A) is incorrect. The $1,500 of property tax may be deductible as a current business expense. Answer (C) is incorrect. The $600 of sales tax on the merchandise purchased for resale is capitalized as part of the cost of the merchandise. Answer (D) is incorrect. The $600 of sales tax on the merchandise purchased for resale is capitalized as part of the cost of the merchandise. Also, the $800 of tax on the purchase of the new truck is capitalized as part of the cost of the truck and will be depreciated.

3.6 Manufacturing Deduction

29. The gross receipts from which of the following activities would not qualify as domestic production gross receipts (DPGR)?

A. Sale of a qualified movie that was filmed by the taxpayer in Minnesota.

B. Sale of a house that was constructed in Miami, FL, by the taxpayer.

C. Receipts from an architectural consultation by the taxpayer in Austin, TX, about the construction of a building in Mexico.

D. Sale of corn grown in Durand, MI, when the taxpayer did not participate in 5% of the procedures required to grow the corn.

Answer (C) is correct.

REQUIRED: The gross receipts that would not qualify as domestic production gross receipts.

DISCUSSION: Sec. 199 defines DPGR as gross receipts that are derived from

1. The sale, exchange, or other disposition, or any rental, lease, or licensing of

    a. Qualified production property that is manufactured, produced, grown, or extracted in the United States by the taxpayer in whole or in significant part

    b. Any qualified film produced by the taxpayer in the United States

    c. Electricity, natural gas, or potable water produced by the taxpayer in the United States

2. Construction performed in the United States

3. Engineering and architectural services performed in the United States for a construction project located in the United States

Qualified production property generally includes tangible personal property, computer software, and sound recordings. Thus, the gross receipts from the architectural consultation in Austin, TX, about the construction of a building in Mexico do not qualify as DPGR because the construction of the building will not take place in the United States.

Answer (A) is incorrect. Gross receipts from a qualified movie that was filmed in the U.S. qualify as DPGR. Answer (B) is incorrect. Construction performed in the U.S. qualifies as DPGR. Answer (D) is incorrect. Gross receipts from qualified production property that is grown in whole or significant part by the taxpayer qualify as DPGR. Since the taxpayer participated in 95% of the growth of the corn, (s)he is considered to have significantly participated in growing the corn.

30. Woodburg, Inc., has domestic production gross receipts (DPGR) of $200,000. His total expenses include $100,000 of cost of goods sold and $40,000 of other expenses. The portion of cost of goods sold and other expenses that are allocable to domestic production is 60%. Woodburg's taxable income is $150,000 and the W-2 wages allocable only to qualified production activities income for 2013 are equal to $240,000. What is Woodburg's deduction for income attributable to domestic activities?

A. $10,440

B. $10,800

C. $13,500

D. $18,000

Answer (A) is correct.

REQUIRED: The deduction for income attributable to domestic activities.

DISCUSSION: The deduction for income attributable to domestic gross income for 2013 is equal to 9% of the least of the following:

1. The qualified production activities income (QPAI),
2. The taxable income of the taxpayer, or
3. 50% of the W-2 wages allocable only to qualified production activities income for the year.

QPAI is calculated by taking the DPGR and subtracting the sum of the following from it:

1. The cost of goods sold allocable to DPGR,

2. Other deductions, expenses, or losses that are directly allocable to DPGR, and

3. A proper share of other deductions, expenses, or losses that are not directly allocable to DPGR or another class of income.

Thus, Woodburg's QPAI is equal to $116,000 {$200,000 − [($100,000 × 60%) + ($40,000 × 60%)]}. Since this is less than the taxable income ($150,000) and 50% of the W-2 wages ($120,000), the deduction for income attributable to domestic gross income is 9% of the QPAI, or $10,440 ($116,000 × 9%).

Answer (B) is incorrect. The deduction is 9% of the lesser of QPAI, taxable income, or 50% of the W-2 wages. QPAI is less than 50% of the W-2 wages. Answer (C) is incorrect. The deduction is 9% of the lesser of QPAI, taxable income, or 50% of the W-2 wages. QPAI is less than the taxable income. Answer (D) is incorrect. The allocable portion of the cost of goods sold and the expenses should be deducted from DPGR before the 9% for the deduction is taken.

STUDY UNIT FOUR
OTHER DEDUCTIONS

(14 pages of outline)

This study unit continues the discussion of business expenses. A deduction from gross income is allowed for all ordinary and necessary expenses paid or incurred during a tax year in carrying on a trade or business. The deduction is allowed to a sole proprietor, a partnership, or a corporation. A sole proprietor claims these deductions on Schedule C.

4.1 ENTERTAINMENT EXPENSES

1. Entertainment includes recreation, e.g., entertaining guests at a nightclub, sporting event, or theater; supplying vacations, trips, etc.; and furnishing a hotel suite, automobile, food and beverages, or the like to a customer or a member of the customer's family.

   a. Club dues for social gatherings are not deductible. Dues paid to professional clubs (e.g., Kiwanis) are deductible if they are paid for business reasons and if the principal purpose of membership is professional and not for entertainment.

2. The expense must be either **directly related to** or **associated with** the active conduct of a trade or business. The predominant purpose must be the furthering of the trade or business of the taxpayer incurring the expense. A taxpayer is not required to verify that business income or some other business benefit resulted from each entertainment expense.

Directly Related

   a. **"Directly related"** means that business is actually conducted during the entertainment period.

   1) The taxpayer must have had more than a general expectation of deriving income, or some other specific business benefit, at some indefinite future time.

   2) The taxpayer must engage in the active conduct of business with the person being entertained.

   3) The active conduct of business must have been the principal aspect of the combined business and entertainment.

   a) A restaurant owner providing an occasional free meal to a loyal customer is considered a directly related expense (Pub. 463).

Associated with

   b. **"Associated with"** means that the entertainment must occur directly before or after a business discussion.

Deduction Limit

3. The amount deductible for meal and entertainment expense is 50% of the actual expense. The limit also applies to the taxpayer's own meals. Related expenses, such as taxes, tips, and parking fees, but not transportation to and from a business meal, are also subject to the 50% limit.

a.   The IRS has denied deductions for any meal or entertainment expense over $75 for which the claimant did not provide substantiating evidence, i.e., documented dates, amounts, location, purpose, and business relationship.

b.   An exclusion for employee meals furnished on the business premises of the employer applies if they are furnished to the employee for the convenience of the employer.

1)   The meals are deductible by the employer as an ordinary and necessary business expense.

EXAMPLE

ABC Accounting Firm requires its employees to work until 11 p.m. every evening the month prior to tax filing deadlines. ABC contracts a catering service to provide the employees with meals every evening on the company's premises. Such meals are for the convenience of the employer and are excluded from the employee's income. ABC would be allowed a deduction for the cost of the meals.

---

c.   The cost of a skybox that is leased for more than one event is disallowed to the extent that it exceeds the cost of nonluxury box seat tickets multiplied by the number of seats in the skybox.

4.   Meal expenses are not deductible if neither the taxpayer nor an employee of the taxpayer is present at the meal.

Entertainment Facility

5.   Generally, no deduction is allowed for any expenses for entertainment facilities, such as yachts, hunting lodges, swimming pools, tennis courts, or bowling alleys [Sec. 274(a)(1)(B)]. The membership or initiation fee is a capital expenditure that is not currently deductible, and any gain upon sale is a capital gain.

Stop and review! You have completed the outline for this subunit. Study questions 1 through 6 beginning on page 90.

4.2 TRAVEL EXPENSES

While away from home overnight on business, ordinary and necessary travel expenses, including meals and entertainment (subject to the 50% limit), are deductible.

1.   No deduction is allowed for the following:

a.   Travel that is primarily personal in nature (if more days are spent for personal purposes than for business purposes)

b.   The travel expenses of a taxpayer's spouse unless there is a bona fide business purpose for the spouse's presence, the spouse is an employee, and the expenses would be otherwise deductible

c.   Commuting between home and work

1)   A taxpayer's "home" is considered to be

a)   The taxpayer's regular or principal (if there is more than one regular) place of business, or

b)   If the taxpayer has no regular or principal place of business because of the nature of the work, the taxpayer's regular place of abode in a real and substantial sense.

2)   If the period of work in a new location is or becomes indefinite, travel expenses are not deductible because the individual is treated as though (s)he changed the location of his or her tax homes to his or her work location.

d.   Travel for attending investment meetings

e.   Travel as a form of education

2. For employees subject to Department of Transportation hours of service rules, the deductible meals percentage is 80%.

Automobile Expenses

3. Actual expenses for automobile use are deductible (e.g., services, repairs, gasoline, etc.). Alternatively, the taxpayer may deduct the standard mileage rate of $.565 per mile for 2013, plus expenses, such as parking fees and tolls, that are not actual automobile expenses.

Domestic Travel

4. For travel within the U.S., expenses other than transportation (e.g., airfare) are allocated based on personal or business purpose. Transportation expenses are

    a. 100% deductible if the primary purpose is business or

    b. 0% deductible if the primary purpose is personal (i.e., no proportional allocation for transportation costs when traveling within the U.S.).

Foreign Travel

5. Generally, traveling expenses (including meals and lodging) of a taxpayer who travels outside of the United States and away from home must be allocated between time spent on the trip for business and time spent for pleasure.

    a. A trip is considered entirely for business if the traveler did not have substantial control over arranging the trip.

    b. When the trip is for not more than 1 week and a personal vacation was not the major consideration, or when the time spent for personal reasons on the trip is less than 25% of the total time away from home, no allocation is required.

    c. When the foreign trip is longer than a week (7 consecutive days counting the day of return but not the day of departure) or 25% or more of the time away from home is spent for personal reasons, a deduction for travel expenses will be denied to the extent that they are not allocable to the taxpayer's business (or the taxpayer's management of income-producing property).

Convention Expenses

6. Deductible travel expenses include those incurred in attending a convention related to the taxpayer's business even though the taxpayer is an employee.

    a. The fact that an employee uses vacation or leave time or that attendance at the convention is voluntary will not necessarily negate the deduction.

    b. Expenses for a convention or meeting in connection with investments, financial planning, or other income-producing property are not deductible.

    c. A limited deduction is available for expenses incurred for conventions on U.S. cruise ships.

        1) This deduction (limited to $2,000 with respect to all cruises beginning in any calendar year) is only allowed if

            a) All ports of such cruise ships are located in the U.S. or in U.S. possessions,

            b) The taxpayer establishes that the convention is directly related to the active conduct of his or her trade or business, and

            c) The taxpayer includes certain specified information in the return on which the deduction is claimed.

        2) A taxpayer can show that his or her attendance at a convention benefits his or her trade or business by comparing the convention agenda with the official duties and responsibilities of his or her position. The fact that the convention agenda does deal with his or her specific duties lends support for the travel being ordinary and necessary in the conduct of a trade or business.

Reimbursed Employee Expenses

7. If reimbursements equal expenses and the employee makes an accounting of expenses to the employer, the reimbursements are excluded from the employee's gross income, and the employee may not deduct the expenses (accountable plan).

   a. This rule also applies if reimbursements exceeding expenses are returned to the employer and the employee substantiates the expenses.

   b. If excess reimbursements are not returned or if the employee does not substantiate them, the reimbursements are included in the employee's gross income, and all the expenses are deducted from AGI (below-the-line-deductions).

      1) These expenses are a miscellaneous itemized deduction subject to the 2% floor (nonaccountable plan).

Stop and review! You have completed the outline for this subunit. Study questions 7 through 10 beginning on page 92.

4.3 INSURANCE EXPENSES

1. Ordinary and necessary trade or business insurance expense paid or incurred during the tax year is deductible.

   a. A cash-method taxpayer may not deduct a premium before it is paid.

   b. Prepaid insurance of more than 1 year must be apportioned over the period of coverage.

Ordinary & Necessary Trade/Business Insurance Expenses		
Casualty insurance: -Fire -Accident -Storm -Theft -Other	Credit insurance: -Losses from unpaid debts	Group hospitalization & medical insurance costs paid for employees
Accident & health insurance premiums paid for partners as guaranteed payments made to the partners in a partnership or the shareholders in an S corporation	Workers' Compensation Premiums for: Deduct as: Employees Business insurance Partners Guaranteed payment S corp shareholders Wages	Overhead insurance -Long periods of disability from taxpayer's injury/illness (i.e., owner, not employee)
Malpractice and nonperformance insurance	Liability insurance -Covers injury to employee/client	Life insurance -Covers officers & employees -Taxpayer is not the beneficiary
Self-employed (SE) health insurance (post-2002) -100% of costs -Covers SE/spouse/dependents -Deduction limit = Earnings from related business	Compensation for employees injured at work	
SUTA fund contributions -If state considers as tax	Business auto insurance -No deduction if mileage rate for car expenses is used	Business interruption insurance -Profit loss due to shutdown

2. A taxpayer may not deduct the following:

   a. Loss of earnings except for certain overhead insurance expenses
   b. Self-insurance reserve funds
   c. Premiums on a life insurance policy covering the taxpayer, an employee, or any person with a financial interest in the taxpayer's business if the taxpayer is directly or indirectly a beneficiary

3. Self-employed health insurance is not deductible on Schedule C. It would be deducted on Form 1040, line 29.

Stop and review! You have completed the outline for this subunit. Study questions 11 through 14 beginning on page 94.

4.4 BAD DEBTS

Bad Debt Deduction

1. A bad debt deduction is allowed only for a bona fide debt arising from a debtor-creditor relationship based upon a valid and enforceable obligation to pay a fixed or determinable sum of money.

   a. Worthless debt is deductible only to the extent of adjusted basis in the debt.
   b. A cash-basis taxpayer has no basis in accounts receivable and generally has no deduction for bad debts.

Business Bad Debt

2. A business bad debt is one incurred or acquired in connection with or closely related to the taxpayer's trade or business.

   a. A debt is closely related if the primary motive for incurring the debt is business related.
   b. The bad debts of corporations are always business bad debts.
   c. Partially worthless business debts may be deducted to the extent they are worthless and specifically written off.
   d. A business bad debt is treated as an ordinary loss.
   e. A bad debt written off in a previous tax year but recovered in the current tax year should be reported as other income on Schedule C.
   f. If a taxpayer sells a business but keeps its receivables, these debts are business debts since they arose out of a trade or business.
   g. If a taxpayer makes a loan to a client, supplier, or distributor for a business reason and it becomes worthless, (s)he has a business bad debt.
   h. Any guarantee made by an employee to protect or improve his or her job is closely related to his or her trade or business and is deductible to the extent it is written off.

Nonbusiness Bad Debt

3. A nonbusiness bad debt is a debt other than one incurred or acquired in connection with the taxpayer's trade or business.

   a. Investments are not treated as a trade or business.
   b. A shareholder loan to protect his or her investment in the corporation is not treated as a business loan.
   c. A partially worthless nonbusiness bad debt is not deductible.
   d. A wholly worthless nonbusiness debt is deducted in the year it becomes worthless, and it is then treated as a short-term capital loss.

    e.   A debt becomes worthless when there is no longer any chance the amount owed will be paid.

        1)   It is not necessary to go to court if a taxpayer can show that a judgment from court would be uncollectible.

        2)   Taxpayers must only show that reasonable steps to collect the debt have been taken.

        3)   Bankruptcy of the debtor is generally good evidence of the worthlessness of at least part of an unsecured and unpreferred debt.

4.   Taxpayers cannot take a bad debt deduction for a loan made to a corporation if, based on the facts and circumstances, the loan is actually a contribution to capital.

    a.   Worthless corporate securities are not considered bad debts. They are generally treated as a capital loss.

5.   Taxpayers can take a bad debt deduction only if the amount owed was previously included in gross income. This applies to amounts owed from all sources of taxable income, including sales, services, rents, and interest.

    a.   If a taxpayer uses the cash method of accounting, (s)he generally reports income when payment is received. A taxpayer cannot take a bad debt deduction for amounts owed because those amounts were never included in income.

Specific Write-off Method

6.   The specific write-off method must be used for tax purposes. The reserve method is used only for financial accounting purposes.

    a.   If the specific write-off method is used, taxpayer can deduct specific bad debts that become either partly or totally worthless during the tax year.

    b.   Taxpayers can deduct specific bad debts that become partly uncollectible.

    c.   The tax deduction is limited to the amount charged off on the books during the year.

Nonaccrual-Experience Method

7.   The nonaccrual-experience method of accounting allows a taxpayer to exclude income that is not expected to be collected.

    a.   This method applies only to accounts receivable for services the taxpayer performs (e.g., accounting, actuarial science, consulting, engineering, health, law, or performing arts) or if the taxpayer meets the $5 million annual gross receipts test for all prior years.

    b.   This method cannot be used for amounts earned by selling goods or for amounts owed for which the taxpayer charges interest or late penalties.

    c.   The nonaccrual-experience method does not apply to cash-method taxpayers.

Stop and review! You have completed the outline for this subunit. Study questions 15 through 21 beginning on page 95.

4.5 BUSINESS GIFTS

Expenditures for business gifts are deductible. They must be ordinary and necessary.

1.   Deduction for business gift expenditure is disallowed unless the taxpayer substantiates, by adequate records, the following:

    a.   Amount (cost) of the gift
    b.   Date of the gift
    c.   Description of the gift
    d.   Business purpose for the gift
    e.   Business relation of the recipient to the taxpayer

2.   Deduction is limited to $25 per recipient per year for items excludable from income.

    a.   A husband and wife are treated as one taxpayer, even if they file separate returns and have independent business relationships with the recipient.

    b.   The $25 limit does not apply to incidental items costing (the giver) not more than $4 each.

Employee Achievement Awards

3.   Up to $400 of the cost to the employer (not FMV) of employee achievement awards is deductible by an employer for all nonqualified plan awards. (Deduction of qualified plan awards is limited to $1,600 per year.)

    a.   An employee achievement award is tangible personal property awarded to an employee as part of a meaningful presentation for safety achievement or length of service.

    b.   A qualified plan award is an employee achievement award provided under an established written program that does not discriminate in favor of highly compensated employees.

        1)   If the average cost of all employee achievement awards is greater than $400, it is not a qualified plan award.

Stop and review! You have completed the outline for this subunit. Study questions 22 through 24 beginning on page 97.

4.6 OTHER BUSINESS EXPENSES

Some other items of business-related expense follow:

Depreciation

1.   Deduction for obsolescence or wear and tear of property used in a trade or business has generally been tested in the context of corporations. However, depreciation can be a deductible expense of any business.

Start-Up/Organization Costs

2.   Start-up/organization costs in general are capitalized and amortized proportionally over the 180-month (15-year) period beginning with the month in which the active trade or business begins. Examples of start-up costs are costs of investigating the creation or acquisition of a trade or business and costs to prepare to enter into the trade or business, to secure suppliers and customers, and to obtain certain supplies and equipment (noncapital). Examples of organization costs are accounting and legal fees to prepare and file a partnership agreement and to incorporate a business.

    a.   Taxpayers can deduct up to $5,000 of start-up and $5,000 of organizational expenditures in the taxable year in which the business begins.

        1)   The $5,000 is reduced, but not below zero, by the cumulative cost of the start-up expenditures that exceed $50,000.

        2)   A taxpayer is deemed to have made the election; therefore, a taxpayer is not required to attach a separate statement to the return.

Vacant Land

3.   Interest and taxes on vacant land are deductible.

Demolition

4.   If a structure is demolished, demolition costs, undepreciated (remaining) basis, and any losses sustained are not deductible. They are allocated to the land.

Abandoned Assets

5.   A loss is deductible in the year the assets are actually abandoned with no claim for reimbursement. The amount of the loss is the adjusted basis for determining a loss on the sale or other disposition of the property.

COGS

6.   Cost of goods sold is not deductible. It reduces gross income.

Medical Reimbursement Plans

7.   The cost of such a plan for employees is deductible by the employer.

Political Contributions

8.   Contributions to a political party or candidate are not deductible.

EXAMPLE

Craft Store pays for advertising in the program for a political party's convention. Proceeds are used for the party's activities. The expense is a political contribution, which is not deductible.

---

   a.   However, expense in connection with appearances before and communications with any **local** council or similar governing body with respect to legislation of direct interest to the taxpayer is deductible.

   1)   Up to $2,000 of direct cost of such activity at the state or federal level is deductible.

   a)   This does not include payments to professional lobbyists.

   b)   If total direct costs exceed $2,000, this de minimis exception is entirely unavailable.

Debt of Another

9.   Payment of a debt of another party is generally not ordinary for a trade or business and thus is not deductible.

   a.   A legal obligation or definite business requirement, e.g., if required by suppliers to stay in business, renders the payment deductible.

Intangibles

10.   The cost of intangibles must generally be capitalized.

   a.   Amortization is allowed if the intangible has a determinable useful life, e.g., a covenant not to compete or if a code section specifically so provides.

   b.   Generally, Sec. 197 intangibles have a 15-year life.

Tax-Exempt Income

11.   An expenditure related to producing tax-exempt income, e.g., interest on a loan used to purchase tax-exempt bonds, is not deductible.

Public Policy

12.   Certain trade or business expenditures that are ordinary, necessary, and reasonable may be nondeductible if allowing the deduction would frustrate public policy. The following are examples of expenditures disallowed as deductions:

   a.   Fines and penalties paid to the government for violation of the law
   b.   Bribes and kickbacks (including Medicaid and Medicare referrals)
   c.   Two-thirds of damages for violation of federal antitrust law
   d.   Expenses of dealers in illegal drugs

Environmental Clean-Up Costs

13. Environmental clean-up costs paid or incurred before January 1, 2012, are generally deductible as a business expense.

    a. Those costs incurred after January 1, 2012, generally must be treated as capital expenditures.

Moving Expenses

14. An employee or self-employed individual may deduct moving expenses as an adjustment from gross income.

    a. Generally, the expenses must be related to starting work in a new location, and the expenses must be reasonable.

    b. When an employer reimburses an employee, gross income does not include qualified moving expense reimbursements.

        1) For the exclusion of the reimbursements to apply, the employee may not deduct the moving expenses from gross income.

Research Expenses

15. A taxpayer may deduct all research and experimental costs connected with a trade or business.

    a. The expenses must be incurred to fund qualified research and must not be incurred for a tax-avoidance purpose.

Miscellaneous Business Expenses

16. Miscellaneous ordinary and necessary business expenses are deductible. Examples include costs of office supplies, advertising, professional fees, and bank fees.

Fines for Nonperformance of a Contract

17. Although fines and penalties paid to a government are generally not deductible, the payment of a penalty for nonperformance of a contract is generally deductible.

    a. This penalty usually represents damages that one contracting party was willing to incur in order to avoid performing under the contract.

    b. Payment of the penalty is a business decision, and the damages are deductible.

Costs of Removing Barriers to the Disabled and the Elderly

18. The costs of making a facility or public transportation vehicle more accessible to those who are disabled or elderly can be deducted.

    a. The facility or vehicle must be owned or leased by the taxpayer and used in his or her trade or business.

    b. The most that can be deducted for any year is $15,000.

    c. The costs incurred above the limit can be added to the basis of the property and depreciated.

Charitable Contributions

19. Sole proprietorships, shareholders in S corporations, and partners in partnerships may be able to deduct charitable contributions made by their business entities.

    a. The deduction is taken on Schedule A of Form 1040 (see Publication 526).

Government-Granted License

20. Taxpayer must amortize the capitalized costs of acquiring, issuing, or renewing a license granted by a governmental unit or agency.

Education Expenses

21. Education expenses (e.g., correspondence courses, travel, supplies, books, and tuition) may be deductible only if incurred to maintain or improve skills that are required in the taxpayer's current employment context or if incurred to meet legal requirements or employer requirements.

    a. In contrast, the expense of education to enter a trade, business, or profession or to meet the minimum education requirements is not deductible, even if state law requires the education.

    b. Travel as a form of education is not deductible (i.e., the travel itself is the educational purpose).

    c. Educational expenses that are personal or constitute an inseparable aggregate of personal and capital expenditures are not deductible.

    d. Veterans and other students may not deduct education expenses to the extent the amounts expended are allocable to the tax-exempt income.

Deductions on Schedule C

22. A statutory employee's business expenses are deductible on Schedule C or Schedule C-EZ (Form 1040) and are not subject to the reduction of 2% of adjusted gross income (AGI).

Reforestation Cost

23. Up to $10,000 may be expensed in the current year. Any remaining balance is amortized over 7 years.

Stop and review! You have completed the outline for this subunit. Study questions 25 through 28 beginning on page 98.

4.7 BUSINESS USE OF HOME

1. Expenses incurred for the use of a person's home for business purposes are deductible only if strict requirements are met.

    a. The portion of the home must be used exclusively and regularly as

        1) The principal place of business for any trade or business of the taxpayer;

        2) A place of business that is used by patients, clients, or customers in the normal course of the taxpayer's trade or business; or

        3) A separate structure that is not attached to the dwelling unit that is used in the taxpayer's trade or business.

    b. If the taxpayer is an employee, the business use of the home must also be for the convenience of the employer.

Exclusive-Use Test

2. Any personal use of the business portion of the home by anyone results in complete disallowance of the deductions. There are two exceptions to the exclusive-use test:

    a. Retail/wholesale. A retailer or wholesaler whose **sole** location of his or her business is his or her home need not meet the exclusive-use test.

        1) The ordinary and necessary business expenses allocable to an identifiable space used regularly for inventory or product sample storage by a taxpayer in the active pursuit of his or her trade or business are deductible.

    b. Day care. If the business portion of a home is used to offer qualifying day care, the exclusive-use test need not be met.

Multiple Locations

3. If the taxpayer has more than one business location, the primary factor in determining whether a home office is a taxpayer's principal place of business is the relative importance of the activities performed at each business location.

    a. If the primary location cannot be determined by the relative importance test, then the amount of time spent at each location will be used.

Principal Place of Business

4. A home office qualifies as a "principal place of business" if used by the taxpayer to conduct administrative or management activities of the taxpayer's trade or business and there is no other fixed location where the taxpayer conducts such activities.

Limitation

5. A taxpayer's deduction of otherwise nondeductible expenses, e.g., insurance, utilities, and depreciation (with depreciation taken last), is limited to

    a. Gross income derived from the use; minus

    b. Deductions related to the home, allowed regardless of business or personal use, e.g., interest or taxes; and

    c. Deductions allocable to the trade or business for which the home office is used that are not home office expenses, e.g., employee compensation.

Carryover

6. Any currently disallowed amount is deductible in succeeding years, subject to the same limitations.

Simplified Option

7. A new simplified option allows taxpayers to claim $5 per square foot of home office space, up to 300 feet^2, for a maximum deduction of $1,500.

Stop and review! You have completed the outline for this subunit. Study question 29 on page 99.

4.8 STATUTORY EMPLOYEES/NONEMPLOYEES

Worker Classification

1. It is critical that business owners correctly determine whether the individuals providing services are employees or independent contractors. Generally, employers must withhold income taxes, withhold and pay Social Security and Medicare taxes, and pay unemployment tax on wages paid to an employee. Employers do not generally have to withhold or pay any taxes on payments to independent contractors. Before an employer can determine how to treat payments made for services, the employer must first know the business relationship that exists between the employer and the person performing the services. In determining whether the person providing service is an employee or an independent contractor, all information that provides evidence of the degree of control and independence must be considered.

Common Law Rules

2. Facts that provide evidence of the degree of control and independence fall into three categories:

    a. Behavioral: Does the company control or have the right to control what the worker does and how the worker does the job?

b.   Financial: Are the business aspects of the worker's job controlled by the employer (e.g., how the worker is paid, whether expenses are reimbursed, who provides tools/supplies)?

c.   Type of Relationship: Are there written contracts or employee-type benefits (e.g., pension plan, insurance, vacation pay)? Will the relationship continue, and is the work performed a key aspect of the business?

3.   Employers must weigh all these factors when determining whether a worker is an employee or independent contractor. Some factors may indicate that the worker is an employee, while other factors indicate that the worker is an independent contractor. There is no "magic" or set number of factors that "makes" the worker an employee or an independent contractor, and no one factor stands alone in making this determination. Also, factors that are relevant in one situation may not be relevant in another.

a.   The keys are to look at the entire relationship, consider the degree or extent of the right to direct and control, and, finally, to document each of the factors used in coming up with the determination.

b.   If, after reviewing the three categories of evidence, it is still unclear whether a worker is an employee or an independent contractor, Form SS-8, *Determination of Worker Status for Purposes of Federal Employment Taxes and Income Tax Withholding*, can be filed with the IRS. The form may be filed by either the employer or the worker. The IRS will review the facts and circumstances and officially determine the worker's status. It can take at least 6 months to get a determination, but an employer who continually hires the same types of workers to perform particular services may want to consider filing the Form SS-8.

Employment Tax Obligations

4.   Once a determination is made (whether by the employer or by the IRS), the next step is filing the appropriate forms and paying the associated taxes.

Misclassification of Employees/Consequences of Treating an Employee as an Independent Contractor

5.   If an employer classifies an employee as an independent contractor and there is no reasonable basis for doing so, the employer may be held liable for employment taxes for that worker.

Relief Provisions

6.   If an employer has a reasonable basis for not treating a worker as an employee, the employer may be relieved from having to pay employment taxes for that worker. To get this relief, the employer must file all required federal information returns on a basis consistent with the employer's treatment of the worker. The employer must not have treated any worker holding a substantially similar position as an employee for any period beginning after 1977.

Misclassified Workers Can File Social Security Tax Form

7.   Workers who believe they have been improperly classified as independent contractors by an employer can use Form 8919, *Uncollected Social Security and Medicare Tax on Wages*, to figure and report the employee's share of uncollected Social Security and Medicare taxes due on their compensation.

Voluntary Classification Settlement Program

8.   The Voluntary Classification Settlement Program (VCSP) is a new optional program that provides taxpayers with an opportunity to reclassify their workers as employees for future tax periods for employment tax purposes with partial relief from federal employment taxes for eligible taxpayers that agree to prospectively treat their workers (or a class or group of workers) as employees. To participate in this new voluntary program, the taxpayer must meet certain eligibility requirements, apply to participate in the VSCP by filing Form 8952, *Application for Voluntary Classification Settlement Program*, and enter into a closing agreement with the IRS.

Statutory Employees

9.   If workers are independent contractors under the common law rules, such workers may still be treated as employees by statute (statutory employees) for certain employment tax purposes if they fall within any one of the following four categories and meet the three conditions described under "Social Security and Medicare Taxes" below.

   a.   A driver who distributes beverages (other than milk) or meat, vegetable, fruit, or bakery products; or who picks up and delivers laundry or dry cleaning, if the driver is the payer's agent or is paid on commission.

   b.   A full-time life insurance sales agent whose principal business activity is selling life insurance, annuity contracts, or both, primarily for one life insurance company.

   c.   An individual who works at home on materials or goods that the payer supplies and that must be returned to the payer or to a person the payer names if the payer also furnishes specifications for the work to be done.

   d.   A full-time traveling or city salesperson who works on the payer's behalf and turns in orders to the payer from wholesalers, retailers, contractors, or operators of hotels, restaurants, or other similar establishments. The goods sold must be merchandise for resale or supplies for use in the buyer's business operation. The work performed for the payer must be the salesperson's principal business activity.

Social Security and Medicare Taxes

10.   Payers withhold Social Security and Medicare taxes from the wages of statutory employees if all three of the following conditions apply:

   a.   The service contract states or implies that substantially all the services are to be performed personally by the statutory employees.

   b.   The statutory employees do not have a substantial investment in the equipment and property used to perform the services (other than an investment in transportation facilities).

   c.   The services are performed on a continuing basis for the same payer.

Statutory Nonemployees

11.   There are three categories of statutory nonemployees: direct sellers, licensed real estate agents, and certain companion sitters. Direct sellers and licensed real estate agents are treated as self-employed for all federal tax purposes, including income and employment taxes, if

   a.   Substantially all payments for their services as direct sellers or real estate agents are directly related to sales or other output rather than to the number of hours worked and

   b.   Services are performed under a written contract providing that they will not be treated as employees for federal tax purposes.

Direct Sellers

12. Direct selling includes activities of individuals who attempt to increase direct sales activities of their direct sellers and who earn income based on the productivity of their direct sellers. Such activities include providing motivation and encouragement; imparting skills, knowledge, or experience; and recruiting. Direct sellers include persons falling within any of the following three groups:

    a. Persons engaged in selling (or soliciting the sale of) consumer products in the home or place of business other than in a permanent retail establishment

    b. Persons engaged in selling (or soliciting the sale of) consumer products to any buyer on a buy-sell basis, a deposit-commission basis, or any similar basis prescribed by regulations, for resale in the home or at a place of business other than in a permanent retail establishment

    c. Persons engaged in the trade or business of delivering or distributing newspapers or shopping news (including any services directly related to such delivery or distribution)

Licensed Real Estate Agents

13. Licensed real estate agents include individuals engaged in appraisal activities for real estate sales if they earn income based on sales or other output.

Companion Sitters

14. Companion sitters are individuals who furnish personal attendance, companionship, or household care services to children or to individuals who are elderly or disabled. A person engaged in the trade or business of putting the sitters in touch with individuals who wish to employ them (i.e., a companion sitting placement service) will not be treated as the employer of the sitters if that person does not receive or pay the salary or wages of the sitters and is compensated by the sitters or the persons who employ them on a fee basis. Companion sitters who are not employees of a companion sitting placement service are generally treated as self-employed for all federal tax purposes.

Stop and review! You have completed the outline for this subunit. Study question 30 on page 100.

QUESTIONS

4.1 Entertainment Expenses

1. With regard to the directly related test for entertainment, which of the following statements is false?

   A. If the entertainment takes place in a clear business setting and is for the taxpayer's business, the expenses are considered directly related.

   B. It is not necessary to devote more time to business than to entertainment during the entertainment period.

   C. The taxpayer is required to show that business income or some other business benefit resulted from each entertainment expense.

   D. If business and entertainment are combined on a hunting or fishing trip, business is not considered to be the main purpose unless the taxpayer can show otherwise.

Answer (C) is correct.
   REQUIRED: The false statement regarding the directly related test for entertainment expenses.
   DISCUSSION: A taxpayer is not required to verify that business income or some other business benefit resulted from each entertainment expense. However, the taxpayer must have had more than a general expectation of deriving income or some other specific business benefit at some indefinite future time. The taxpayer must engage in the active conduct of business with the person being entertained. Also, the active conduct of business must be the principal aspect of the combined business and entertainment.
   Answer (A) is incorrect. The phrase "directly related" means that business is actually conducted during the entertainment period. Answer (B) is incorrect. The taxpayer need not devote more time to business while entertaining. Answer (D) is incorrect. The predominant purpose must be the furthering of the trade or business of the taxpayer incurring the expense.

2. When an employer reimburses an employee for meals under an accountable plan while the employee is away from home, the employer must

   A. Include 50% of the cost of meals as income to the employee.

   B. Do nothing.

   C. Deduct only 50% of the reimbursement on his or her tax return.

   D. Add 100% of the meals as income to the employee.

Answer (C) is correct.
   REQUIRED: The true statement regarding meal reimbursements.
   DISCUSSION: Publication 334 states, "You can take a deduction for travel, meals, and entertainment expenses if you reimburse your employees for these expenses under an accountable plan. The amount you deduct for meals and entertainment, however, may be subject to a 50% limit." Meals purchased while away from home that are reimbursed by an employer are not gross income to the employee.
   Answer (A) is incorrect. Meals purchased while away from home that are reimbursed by an employer are not gross income to the employee. Answer (B) is incorrect. The employer may deduct only 50% of the reimbursement on his or her tax return, not 100%. Answer (D) is incorrect. Meals purchased while away from home that are reimbursed by an employer are not gross income to the employee.

3. Which of the following fringe benefits for meals is subject to the 50% deduction limit?

   A. Meals furnished to your employees at the work site when you operate a restaurant.

   B. Meals furnished to your employees as part of the expense of a company picnic.

   C. Meals furnished to your employees at your place of business when more than half of these employees are provided the meals for your convenience.

   D. Meals furnished to a customer during a business discussion.

Answer (D) is correct.
   REQUIRED: The fringe benefits for meals subject to the 50% deduction limit.
   DISCUSSION: The amount deductible for meal and entertainment expenses is 50% of the actual expense. The limit also applies to the taxpayer's own meals. Thus, meals furnished to a customer during a business discussion qualify.
   Answer (A) is incorrect. Sec. 119 provides an exclusion for meals furnished on the business premises of the employer if they are furnished to the employee for the convenience of the employer. Answer (B) is incorrect. These amounts would not be deductible. They are not directly related or associated with the active conduct of a trade or business. Answer (C) is incorrect. Sec. 119 provides an exclusion for meals furnished on the business premises of the employer if they are furnished to the employee for the convenience of the employer.

4. You are a self-employed caterer. To encourage the continuation of an existing business relationship, you took one of your clients to a Broadway show. The visit to the show occurred directly after a substantial business discussion with that client. You paid a ticket broker $300 for two tickets to that show. The face value of each ticket was $100 ($200 total). What is your total deductible expense for both tickets?

   A. $100

   B. $150

   C. $200

   D. $300

Answer (A) is correct.
   REQUIRED: The total deduction for entertainment expenses.
   DISCUSSION: Entertainment expenses are deductible but are subject to a 50% limit of the face value of an entertainment ticket. The expense must be either directly related or associated with the active conduct of a trade or business. The predominant purpose must be the furthering of the trade or business of the taxpayer incurring the expense. Because the event occurred after a substantial business discussion, 50% of the expense is deductible. Thus, you may deduct $100 ($200 × 50%). You cannot deduct service fees paid to ticket brokers (Pub. 463).
   Answer (B) is incorrect. There is no option to deduct 50% for one ticket and 100% for the other. Answer (C) is incorrect. The expenses are subject to the 50% limitation. Answer (D) is incorrect. The fair market value is irrelevant. The amount deductible is 50% of the face value.

5. During the current year, Mr. Tripper paid $10,000 in membership dues to a local country club. His records reflected that he used the club as follows:

Personal use	25%
"Directly related" entertainment	40%
"Associated with" entertainment	35%

His records also show that he paid $3,000 for meals and entertainment that were either directly related to or associated with his trade or business. How much of the dues, meals, and entertainment can Mr. Tripper deduct in the current year?

- A. $1,500
- B. $3,000
- C. $5,250
- D. $6,500

Answer (A) is correct.
    REQUIRED: The taxpayer's allowable deduction for country club dues and entertainment.
    DISCUSSION: Sec. 274 disallows a deduction for expenditures made with respect to a facility used in connection with entertainment or recreation (e.g., a country club). The only deduction available to Mr. Tripper is for the business entertainment expenses of $3,000. The deduction is limited to 50%, or $1,500.
    Answer (B) is incorrect. The deduction must be limited to 50% of the entertainment expenses. Answer (C) is incorrect. Country club dues are no longer deductible under Sec. 274. Answer (D) is incorrect. Country club dues are no longer deductible.

6. All of the following statements about the 50% limit on business-related meal and entertainment expenses are true except

- A. Employees are not subject to the 50% limit if the employer reimburses the employees under an accountable plan and does not treat the reimbursement as wages.
- B. A self-employed accountant is not subject to the 50% limit if (s)he was reimbursed and provided the payer with adequate records of the expenses.
- C. The cost of a package deal that includes a ticket to a regular season professional baseball game is not subject to the 50% limit.
- D. A pizza parlor's cost in providing free slices of pizza to the public, as a form of advertisement, is not subject to the 50% limit.

Answer (C) is correct.
    REQUIRED: The false statement regarding the 50% limitation on business-related meal and entertainment expenses.
    DISCUSSION: Entertainment includes recreation, e.g., entertaining guests at a nightclub, sporting event, or theater; supplying vacations, trips, etc.; and furnishing a hotel suite, an automobile, food and beverages, or the like to a customer or a member of his or her family. The amount deductible for meal and entertainment expense is 50% of the actual expense. The limit also applies to the taxpayer's own meals. Related expenses, such as taxes, tips, and parking fees, but not transportation to and from a business meal, are also subject to the 50% limit.
    Answer (A) is incorrect. When a taxpayer is reimbursed for the meal or entertainment, the limitation is imposed on the party making reimbursement, not the taxpayer. Answer (B) is incorrect. When a taxpayer is reimbursed for the meal or entertainment, the limitation is imposed on the party making reimbursement, not the taxpayer. Answer (D) is incorrect. The cost of advertisement, even though considered food, is not subject to the 50% limit.

4.2 Travel Expenses

7. With regard to deductible travel expenses when attending a convention, all of the following statements are correct except:

- A. If you can show that your attendance benefits your trade or business, you can deduct your travel expenses if the expenses are reasonable.
- B. You cannot deduct expenses for attending a convention, seminar, or similar meeting held outside of the U.S. area unless the meeting is related to your trade or business.
- C. If you establish that a meeting held on a cruise ship is directly related to your trade or business, you may be able to deduct expenses of up to $2,000 per trip.
- D. You must reduce otherwise deductible travel expenses that you pay by the reimbursements not reported on your Form W-2 that you receive from others for these expenses.

Answer (C) is correct.
    REQUIRED: The incorrect statement about deductible travel expenses when attending a convention.
    DISCUSSION: A limited deduction is available for expenses incurred for conventions on U.S. cruise ships. This deduction is limited to $2,000 with respect to all cruises beginning in any calendar year. Thus, you are not able to deduct expenses of $2,000 per trip, but $2,000 total can be deducted for cruise conventions.
    Answer (A) is incorrect. Deductible travel expenses include those incurred in attending a convention related to the taxpayer's business. Answer (B) is incorrect. Deductible travel expenses include those incurred in attending a convention related to the taxpayer's business. If a person is attending a convention that is not related to his or her business, then they are not deductible. Answer (D) is incorrect. Travel expenses must be reduced by the reimbursements that are received for these expenses.

8. Bart, a partner in the B & A Partnership, attended the Comdex Computer Convention in Las Vegas. The partnership repairs and upgrades commercial computers for business use. At the convention, a new advanced computer hard drive was introduced that would make current machines run faster and more efficiently. Bart is responsible for purchasing hard drives for the computers used in the partnership. Bart's travel expenses, excluding meals, were $950. Part of that amount includes a rental car of $100 incurred to visit his mother and $50 for flowers and candy he bought for her. How much is deductible as a business expense?

A. $950

B. $900

C. $800

D. $850

Answer (C) is correct.
REQUIRED: The amount of travel expenses deductible as business expenses.
DISCUSSION: A taxpayer may deduct ordinary and necessary expenses incurred when traveling away from home on business. A business deduction is not allowed for personal expenses. Bart must divide the total travel expenses between the business related expenses and personal expenses. He may only deduct as a business expense the business related travel expenses. Therefore, Bart may deduct $800 ($950 − $100 − $50) of the travel expenses excluding meals as a business expense.
Answer (A) is incorrect. The $150 of personal expenses incurred during travel are not deductible as business expenses. Answer (B) is incorrect. The $100 Bart incurred to visit his mother is a personal travel expense and is not deductible. Answer (D) is incorrect. The $50 Bart spent on flowers and candy for his mother is a personal expense and is not deductible.

9. With regard to deductible travel expenses when attending a convention, which of the following statements is true?

A. If the taxpayer attends conventions, seminars, or similar meetings held on cruise ships, (s)he may be able to deduct up to $3,000 per year of the expenses if (s)he establishes that the meeting is directly related to his or her trade or business.

B. If the taxpayer can show that his or her attendance benefits his or her trade or business, (s)he can deduct his or her and his or her family's travel expenses providing the expenses are reasonable.

C. The agenda of the convention has to deal specifically with his or her official duties or responsibilities of his or her position or business.

D. The fact that the taxpayer has been appointed or elected as a delegate to a convention does not, in itself, entitle him or her to a deduction.

Answer (D) is correct.
REQUIRED: The true statement regarding deductible travel expenses.
DISCUSSION: A taxpayer's appointment as a delegate to a convention does not, in itself, entitle the taxpayer to a deduction. A deduction is allowed for ordinary and necessary traveling expenses incurred by a taxpayer while away from home in the conduct of a trade or business.
Answer (A) is incorrect. The deduction for conventions on U.S. cruise ships is limited to $2,000 for the calendar year. Answer (B) is incorrect. It is an incorrect statement regarding deductible travel expenses. Answer (C) is incorrect. It is an incorrect statement regarding deductible travel expenses.

10. During the current year, Mark attended a seminar that was held on a U.S.-registered cruise ship on the Mississippi River. The seminar was directly related to his trade or business, i.e., the construction of docks and wharves on rivers such as the Mississippi. Mark incurred the following expenses while on the cruise ship:

Lodging	$2,000
Meals	1,200

How much of the expenses incurred can Mark deduct in the current year, provided he attaches the proper statements to the current year's tax return?

A. $0

B. $2,000

C. $2,600

D. $3,200

Answer (B) is correct.
REQUIRED: The amount of deductible travel expenses incurred when attending a convention on a U.S. cruise ship.
DISCUSSION: A limited deduction is available for expenses incurred for conventions on U.S. cruise ships. This deduction is limited to $2,000 with respect to all cruises beginning in any calendar year. The deduction applies only if all ports of such cruise ships are located in the U.S. or in U.S. possession. Also, the taxpayer must establish that the convention is directly related to the active conduct of his or her trade or business, and the taxpayer includes certain specified information on the return.
Answer (A) is incorrect. A portion of the travel expenses are deductible. Answer (C) is incorrect. The travel expenses incurred on a U.S. cruise ship are subject to a specialized limitation. Answer (D) is incorrect. The travel expenses incurred on a U.S. cruise ship are subject to a specialized limitation.

4.3 Insurance Expenses

11. You operate a business and file your tax return on a calendar-year basis. You bought a fire insurance policy on your building effective November 1, Year 1, and paid a premium of $1,200 for 2 years of coverage. How much can you deduct on your Year 1 return?

A. $1,200

B. $600

C. $100

D. $50

Answer (C) is correct.

REQUIRED: The amount of insurance policy premium deductible in the current year.

DISCUSSION: A premium paid for insurance against losses from fire, accident, storm, theft, or other casualty is deductible if it is an ordinary and necessary expense of a business. When an insurance premium is paid in advance for more than 1 year, only a pro rata portion of the premium is deductible for each year, regardless of the taxpayer's method of accounting. A portion of the premium paid in Year 1 is deductible in Year 2. On the Year 1 return, only the part of the total premium that applies to the 2 months of coverage in Year 1 is deductible. Therefore, the permitted deduction is $100 [($1,200 ÷ 24 months) = $50 × 2 months].

Answer (A) is incorrect. The policy was purchased for a 2-year period. Thus, only the portion of the prepaid premium attributable to Year 1 is deductible, not the entire policy. Answer (B) is incorrect. The attributable portion of the policy to the year is 2 months ($100) worth of the policy, not 1 year. Answer (D) is incorrect. The attributable portion is 2 months, not 1 month.

12. All of the following insurance premiums are ordinarily deductible as an insurance expense except

A. Workers' compensation on behalf of partners in a business partnership.

B. Life insurance on the life of an employee with the employee's wife as the beneficiary.

C. Group health insurance that does not contain continuation coverage to employees.

D. Malpractice insurance covering a professional's personal liability for negligence resulting in injury to business clients.

Answer (A) is correct.

REQUIRED: The insurance premium not ordinarily deductible as a business expense.

DISCUSSION: Workers' compensation insurance premiums paid on behalf of employees are deductible as a business expense. However, for this purpose, partners are not considered employees of the partnership (they are considered self-employed owners), and the insurance premiums on their behalf are deductible as guaranteed payments, not as an insurance expense.

Answer (B) is incorrect. Life insurance premiums paid on the life of an employee are deductible as long as the employer is not the beneficiary. These life insurance premiums are effectively compensation to the employee unless excluded as part of a group term life insurance plan. Answer (C) is incorrect. The premiums are deductible by the employer. However, an excise tax is imposed under Sec. 4980B if an employer has group health insurance not containing continuation coverage for employees. Answer (D) is incorrect. Malpractice insurance is deductible as an ordinary business expense.

13. During the current year, WHOOS Partnership paid insurance premiums for the following coverage:

Use and occupancy and business interruption insurance	$2,000
Overhead insurance	1,000
Accident and health insurance paid for its partners as guaranteed payments made to the partners	800
Group term life insurance on the lives of all the partners with the partnership as beneficiary	500
Life insurance on the lives of all the partners in order to get or protect a loan	700

What is the amount of WHOOS's deductible expense for the current year?

A. $5,000

B. $3,800

C. $3,700

D. $3,000

Answer (B) is correct.

REQUIRED: The amount of the partnership's deductible insurance expense.

DISCUSSION: Sec. 162(a) allows a deduction for all ordinary and necessary expenses paid or incurred during the taxable year in carrying on any trade or business. Insurance premiums paid for carrying on a trade or business are deductible. Under the terms of a use and occupancy insurance contract, a taxpayer may be insured for the loss of the use and occupancy of property damaged by fire. This expense is deductible. Premiums paid for overhead insurance are also deductible. Guaranteed payments are recorded as income by the partners and are deductible by the partnership. The deduction for the group term life insurance is not available because the partnership is the beneficiary. Finally, insurance premiums paid on a taxpayer's own life are personal expenses and are not deductible.

Answer (A) is incorrect. All of the expenses are not deductible. Answer (C) is incorrect. The life insurance is not deductible. Answer (D) is incorrect. The accident and health insurance is deductible.

14. John owned a small advertising company, the operations of which he included on Schedule C of his current-year individual income tax return. What type of insurance may John not deduct on his current-year return?

A. Fire, theft, and flood insurance.

B. Employer's liability insurance.

C. Loss of earnings due to sickness or disability.

D. Overhead insurance, which pays John's overhead expenses in the event of his long period of disability caused by his sickness or injury.

Answer (C) is correct.

REQUIRED: The insurance that may not be deducted on the taxpayer's return.

DISCUSSION: A premium on a personal disability insurance policy is not deductible when it applies to insurance for the self-employed owner.

Answer (A) is incorrect. Fire, theft, and flood insurance is an ordinary and necessary trade or business insurance expense. Answer (B) is incorrect. Employer's liability insurance is an ordinary and necessary trade or business insurance expense. Answer (D) is incorrect. Overhead insurance is an ordinary and necessary trade or business insurance expense.

4.4 Bad Debts

15. Which is a false statement regarding business bad debts?

A. The debt does not have to be due to be worthless.

B. A bad debt can result from a loan to a supplier.

C. Cash-basis taxpayers can take a deduction for amounts never received or collected.

D. A debt can arise from the guarantee of a debt that becomes worthless.

Answer (C) is correct.

REQUIRED: The false statement regarding business bad debts.

DISCUSSION: A taxpayer may deduct a loss from a bad debt only if (s)he has a basis in the debt. For this reason, cash basis taxpayers who normally do not report income until it is required are not entitled to deductions for payments they cannot collect. Their loss is represented by the unrecovered expenses incurred in providing the goods or services.

Answer (A) is incorrect. The debt is worthless when it is determined the borrower cannot pay the debt. Answer (B) is incorrect. Sec. 166 includes debts that arise from the sale of goods or services. Answer (D) is incorrect. The guarantee of a debt that becomes worthless is legally enforceable as a debt.

16. Jennifer Jones, an attorney, made loans of $5,000 and $2,000 to two of her clients in order to keep their business. She also made a loan of $1,000 to her cousin John to whom she had provided free legal advice regarding the start of his own business. If all three loans become uncollectible, what amount may Jennifer deduct as a business bad debt?

A. $8,000

B. $1,000

C. $7,000

D. $2,000

Answer (C) is correct.

REQUIRED: The correct amount deductible as business bad debt.

DISCUSSION: A business bad debt is one incurred or acquired in connection with the taxpayer's trade or business. The two loans to her clients are treated as business bad debt because these loans are associated with her business. Since Jennifer provided free legal advice to her cousin, this loan is a nonbusiness bad debt because there is no connection to her business. Thus, $7,000 is the business bad debt.

Answer (A) is incorrect. The $1,000 loan to Jennifer's cousin is a nonbusiness bad debt. This debt was not acquired in connection with the trade or business of Jennifer. She was not compensated for her advice to her cousin. Answer (B) is incorrect. The $5,000 and $2,000 loans are business loans because they were made in connection with Jennifer's business. Answer (D) is incorrect. The $5,000 loan is also a business bad debt.

17. With regard to the correct treatment of business bad debts, which of the following statements is false?

    A. Tom deducted a bad debt in a prior tax year and later recovered part of it. He may have to include the amount recovered in gross income for the year of recovery.

    B. Bill can deduct his business bad debt as a short-term capital loss.

    C. Sally received property in a partial settlement of a debt. She should reduce the debt by the fair market value of the property received. She can deduct the remaining amount as a bad debt in the year she determines it to be worthless and charges it off.

    D. Jane may deduct only the difference between the amount owed to her by a bankrupt entity and the amount received from the distribution of its assets as a bad debt.

Answer (B) is correct.

    REQUIRED: The false statement concerning the treatment of business bad debts.

    DISCUSSION: A loss from a business debt is an ordinary loss, while a loss from a nonbusiness debt is treated as a short-term capital loss.

    Answer (A) is incorrect. Recovery of a bad debt is generally included in the current year's income. Answer (C) is incorrect. Partially worthless business debt may be deducted to the extent they are worthless and specifically written off. Answer (D) is incorrect. Partially worthless business debt may be deducted to the extent they are worthless and specifically written off.

18. Mary, a seamstress, made loans of $5,000 and $1,000 to Buttons & Bows and Thread Bare, respectively. Both of these establishments are partnerships. Mary also made a loan of $2,000 to her cousin Sarah, who was starting her own business as a proprietorship. The loans to both partnerships improved Mary's business, which was the reason Mary made the loans. If all three loans become uncollectible, what amount may Mary deduct as a business bad debt?

    A. $5,000

    B. $6,000

    C. $1,000

    D. $2,000

Answer (B) is correct.

    REQUIRED: The amount that can be deducted as a business bad debt.

    DISCUSSION: Publication 535 states, "A business bad debt is a loss from the worthlessness of a debt that was either

- Created or acquired in your trade or business, or
- Closely related to your trade or business when it became partly or totally worthless.

A debt is closely related to your trade or business if your primary motive for incurring the debt is business related. . . . If you make a loan to a client, supplier, employee, or distributor for a business reason and it becomes worthless, you have a business bad debt." The loans to both partnerships improved Mary's business, so they are deductible. However, Mary's loan to Sarah is not deductible because it was made for personal reasons instead of business reasons.

    Answer (A) is incorrect. Mary's loan to Thread Bare is deductible since it was made to improve her business. Answer (C) is incorrect. Mary's loan to Buttons & Bows is deductible since it was made to improve her business. Answer (D) is incorrect. Mary's loan to Sarah was not for business reasons, so it is not deductible.

19. Dr. K, a dentist and calendar-year taxpayer, has consistently reported income and expenses from his business on the cash basis. All cash and checks he receives are deposited and included in income. K's records for the current year reflect the following information:

Uncollectible receivables	$2,000
Patients' uncollectible returned checks	500
Recovery of an uncollectible receivable from 3 years ago	1,000
Business-related loan to a supplier that became totally worthless	3,000

What is the amount of K's bad debt expense for the current year?

    A. $2,500

    B. $3,500

    C. $4,500

    D. $5,500

Answer (B) is correct.

    REQUIRED: The amount of bad debt expense.

    DISCUSSION: Dr. K has consistently reported income and expenses on the cash basis, and cash and checks received are deposited and included in income. Therefore, the $2,000 in accounts receivable has not been included in income, and accordingly, no deduction will arise from uncollectible receivables. The recovery of an uncollectible receivable from 3 years ago of $1,000 will be included in income and will not be netted against bad debt expense. Bad debt expense for the current year will be $3,500; the $500 in returned checks has been included in income, so a bad debt deduction is proper, and the $3,000 business bad debt is also deductible.

    Answer (A) is incorrect. The receivables have not been included in income, and a deduction cannot be claimed yet for the uncollectible receivables. However, the totally worthless business bad debt (loan to the supplier) may be deducted. Answer (C) is incorrect. The recovery of a bad debt does not increase bad debt expense. Instead, it is added to gross income. Answer (D) is incorrect. Uncollectible receivables should not be included in bad debt expense unless they were realized as income.

20. Mr. Benson, who operates a small tools supply company, guaranteed payment of a $10,000 note for Black Hardware store, one of Mr. Benson's largest clients. Black Hardware later filed for bankruptcy and defaulted on the loan. Mr. Benson made full payment to satisfy the note. Mr. Benson's payment should be considered a(n)

A. Business bad debt.

B. Nonbusiness bad debt.

C. Gift.

D. Investment.

Answer (A) is correct.
REQUIRED: The characterization of a loss on a guarantee of a customer's debt.
DISCUSSION: A business bad debt is deductible in full as an ordinary loss under Sec. 166. A loss on a guarantee of a debt is treated the same as a primary debt in determining whether it is business or nonbusiness. To be a business bad debt, it must be closely related to one's trade or business. However, guaranteeing the debt of a primary customer does not necessarily make it a business debt. If making the guarantee was required to retain the customer, the payment on the guarantee would be a business bad debt.
Authors' Note: This question does not specify that the guarantee was required to retain the customer. But the Special Enrollment Exam seems to assume that guaranteeing the debt of a primary customer is closely related to one's trade or business. On that basis, it would be a business bad debt.

21. Ms. R lent her sister money to buy a new personal-use automobile. The understanding was that the loan was to be repaid. The debt was subsequently forgiven since Ms. R's sister could not repay the debt. This is an example of

A. A business bad debt.

B. A nonbusiness bad debt.

C. A gift.

D. A specific charge-off.

Answer (C) is correct.
REQUIRED: The character of a forgiven debt owed by a related party.
DISCUSSION: A bad debt deduction may be taken only for a bona fide debt arising from a valid debtor-creditor relationship based upon a valid and enforceable obligation to pay a fixed or determinable sum of money [Reg. 1.166-1(c)]. Ms. R made a gift to her sister of the balance of the debt owed. Therefore, no bad debt exists, and no deduction is available.

4.5 Business Gifts

22. William Roberts sells products to unrelated XYZ Corporation. He gave XYZ five cheese packages to thank them for their business. Mr. Roberts paid $100 for each package for a total of $500. Five of the XYZ Corporation executives took the packages home. How much can William deduct for the gifts?

A. $125

B. $500

C. $0

D. $250

Answer (A) is correct.
REQUIRED: The amount of deductible business gifts.
DISCUSSION: Deductions for business gifts, whether made directly or indirectly, are limited to $25 per recipient per year. Since William gave five gifts to five executives, he is allowed to deduct $25 per recipient, or $125.
Answer (B) is incorrect. He is not allowed to deduct the entire cost of the gifts. Answer (C) is incorrect. He is allowed a deduction for the gifts. Answer (D) is incorrect. He is limited to $25 per recipient.

23. Derek Dunn received three employee achievement awards during the year: a nonqualified plan award of a watch that cost $250, two qualified plan awards of a computer that cost $1,500, and a radio that cost $400. The requirements for qualified plan awards are satisfied. What amount, if any, must Derek include in income?

A. $0

B. $1,150

C. $550

D. $1,500

Answer (C) is correct.
REQUIRED: The amount of business gifts included in gross income.
DISCUSSION: Employees must include in gross income the amount of nonqualified plan awards and qualified plan awards exceeding $1,600 for a tax year. Derek Dunn's $250 watch from the nonqualified plan would be fully deductible (under $400) if the other two gifts had not been given. However, because the other two were given, the watch is added to the total amount of gifts for the year. Therefore, the total included in his gross income is $550 [($250 + $1,500 + $400) − $1,600 deduction].
Answer (A) is incorrect. The total amount of gifts ($2,150) in excess of $1,600 deduction is included in income. Answer (B) is incorrect. The limit on qualified awards is $1,600 a year, not $1,150. Answer (D) is incorrect. The total amount of gifts ($2,150) in excess of $1,600 deduction is included in income, not just the cost of the computer.

24. During the current year, Frank gave the following gifts to business clients. (Note: None of the employees of the receiving companies were to receive more than one gift.)

100 pens with Frank's company name imprinted on them, valued at $4 each, to Corporation X	$400
25 bottles of wine valued at $30 each to Corporation Y	750
Wrapping for the 25 bottles of wine	50
15 floral arrangements valued at $25 each to Z Company	375

The amount that Frank can deduct for business gifts for the current year is

A. $1,575

B. $1,450

C. $1,400

D. $1,250

Answer (B) is correct.

REQUIRED: The amount of deductible business gifts.

DISCUSSION: Deductions for business gifts, whether made directly or indirectly, are limited to $25 per recipient per year. However, items clearly of an advertising nature, such as pens embossed with the company name, that cost $4 or less do not figure in the $25 limitation. Since none of the employees of the receiving companies were to receive more than one gift, each gift given to each company employee is deductible up to $25. The pens costing $4 each are completely deductible. The 25 bottles of wine are deductible up to $25 each, or an amount of $625 (25 bottles at $25 each). The wrapping is completely deductible because incidental costs such as gift wrapping, mailing, and delivery of gifts and certain imprinted gift items costing $4 or less are excluded. The floral arrangements are also fully deductible. The total amount of deductible business gifts is $1,450 [$400 + $625 (25 bottles at $25 each) + $50 + $375].

Answer (A) is incorrect. The bottles of wine are only deductible up to $25 each, not $30. Answer (C) is incorrect. The wrapping for the bottles is deductible as an incidental cost. Answer (D) is incorrect. The business gift limitation limits the wine deduction to $625, not $425.

4.6 Other Business Expenses

25. All of the following "Sec. 197 intangibles" acquired after August 10, 1993, must be amortized over 15 years except a

A. Covenant not to compete entered in connection with the acquisition of an interest in a trade or business.

B. Patent that you created, but not in connection with the acquisition of assets constituting a trade or business or a substantial part of a trade or business.

C. Fast food franchise.

D. Governmental license including renewals.

Answer (B) is correct.

REQUIRED: The Sec. 197 intangible that is not required to be amortized over 15 years.

DISCUSSION: Under Sec. 197, the cost of acquiring any intangible assets, including non-compete covenants, is amortizable over a 15-year period, beginning in the month of acquisition. The actual useful life of the covenant is ignored. Sec. 197(c)(2) states that, generally, a Sec. 197 intangible created by the taxpayer is not amortizable unless it is created in connection with a transaction or series of related transactions that involves the acquisition of assets constituting a trade or business or a substantial part of a trade or business.

26. Tina owns a car dealership. Her books and records reflect the following items for the current year:

Reserve for anticipated expenses associated with service contracts sold in the current year	$10,000
Expenses paid in an attempt to influence legislation of the local city council	1,000
Expenses paid for admission to an inaugural ball for a candidate for mayor	500
Cost to demolish a building used in her business	3,000
Undepreciated basis of demolished building	5,000

What is the amount Tina can deduct on her income tax return for the current year?

A. $1,000

B. $9,500

C. $18,000

D. $20,500

Answer (A) is correct.

REQUIRED: The amount of deductible expenses.

DISCUSSION: The reserve for anticipated expenses is not deductible in the current year. The taxpayer also may not deduct the expenses paid for admission to the inaugural ball. Political contributions, even indirect contributions such as attending a fund-raiser, are generally not deductible. In addition, the taxpayer may not deduct either the demolition expenses or the undepreciated basis of the demolished building. However, these expenses may be added to the basis of the land. Although there is generally a denial of deduction for lobbying expenses, there is an exception for lobbying expenses that pertain to local legislation. The taxpayer may deduct the $1,000 expense paid to influence the legislation of the local city council.

Answer (B) is incorrect. The admission to the ball and the demolition expenses are not deductible. Answer (C) is incorrect. The reserve and the demolition expenses are not deductible. Answer (D) is incorrect. Only the local lobbying is deductible.

27. Mr. R is a self-employed over-the-road trucker who uses the cash method of accounting. Which one of the following expenses paid during the current year would be deductible on Mr. R's Schedule C?

    A. Penalty for late delivery of cargo paid to Corporation V.

    B. Fine for speeding in business truck paid to City A.

    C. Overweight fine paid to State B.

    D. Contribution to Bull Moose political party in an attempt to receive a trucking contract.

Answer (A) is correct.
    REQUIRED: The deductible business expense.
    DISCUSSION: Although fines and penalties paid to a government are generally not deductible, the payment of a penalty for nonperformance of a contract is generally deductible. This penalty usually represents damages that one contracting party was willing to incur in order to avoid performing under the contract. This is a business decision, and the damages are deductible under Sec. 162(a).
    Answer (B) is incorrect. It is a fine or penalty paid to a government or governmental agency and is specifically not deductible under Sec. 162(f). Answer (C) is incorrect. It is a fine or penalty paid to a government or governmental agency and is specifically not deductible under Sec. 162(f). Answer (D) is incorrect. Political contributions are not deductible as business expenses.

28. With regard to "other" business expenses for the tax year 2013, all of the following statements are true except

    A. Reimbursements you make to job candidates for transportation or other expenses related to interviews for possible employment are deductible business expenses.

    B. Legal fees paid to acquire a new office building are ordinary and necessary expenses directly related to operating your business and are deductible as business expenses.

    C. You may deduct your own education expenses, including certain related travel that is related to your trade or business.

    D. None of the answers are correct.

Answer (B) is correct.
    REQUIRED: The false statement regarding "other" business expenses for the tax year.
    DISCUSSION: In order for the expenses to be deductible, they must be ordinary, necessary, and directly related to the operations of the business. The legal fees to acquire a new office building do not meet this requirement because the acquisition is not deemed to be an "ordinary" expense in the operations of the company. The legal fees would be capitalized as part of the basis of the building and depreciated over 39 years.

4.7 Business Use of Home

29. Which of the following is a true statement about the exclusive-use test for business use of a home?

    A. Generally, any personal use of the business portion of the home by anyone results in complete disallowance of the deductions.

    B. A retailer whose sole location of the business is the retailer's home must meet the exclusive-use test.

    C. If the business portion of a home is used to offer qualifying day care, the exclusive-use test must be met.

    D. A wholesaler whose sole location of the business is the wholesaler's home must meet the exclusive-use test.

Answer (A) is correct.
    REQUIRED: The true statement about the exclusive-use test.
    DISCUSSION: Any personal use of the business portion of the home by anyone results in complete disallowance of the deductions. There are two exceptions to the exclusive-use test:

1. A retailer or wholesaler whose sole location of the business is the retailer's/wholesaler's home need not meet the exclusive-use test.

2. If the business portion of a home is used to offer qualifying day care, the exclusive-use test need not be met.

    Answer (B) is incorrect. Retailers with no other location are exempt from the test. Answer (C) is incorrect. Use by a qualifying day care is exempt from the test. Answer (D) is incorrect. Wholesalers with no other location are exempt from the test.

4.8 Statutory Employees/Nonemployees

30. Which of the following is a statutory employee?

A. A person engaged in selling consumer products in homes, and all service payments are for sales, not hours worked.

B. A companion sitter who pays the placement service out of the payments from the sitter's client.

C. A soda beverage distribution driver who performs all the services on a continuing basis for the same payer, and does not own any of the equipment.

D. A real estate appraiser with earnings based on sales who is contracted as not being an employee.

Answer (C) is correct.

REQUIRED: The statutory employee.

DISCUSSION: If workers are independent contractors under the common-law rules, such workers may still be treated as employees by statute for certain employment tax purposes. An example of a statutory employee is a driver who distributes beverages (other than milk) if the driver is the payer's agent or is paid on commission. Other requirements include substantial performance of all services, no substantial investment in the equipment, and the continual performance of the services.

Answer (A) is incorrect. Direct sellers are statutory nonemployees. Answer (B) is incorrect. The placement service will not be treated as the employer of the sitter if the service does not receive or pay the salary or wages of the sitter and is compensated by the sitter. Answer (D) is incorrect. Nonemployee licensed real estate agents include those engaged in appraisal activities for real estate sales if earnings are based on sales or other output.

Use the additional questions in Gleim **EA Test Prep** to create Practice Exams that emulate Prometric!

STUDY UNIT FIVE
BASIS

(7 pages of outline)

The concept of basis is important in federal income taxation. The assigned value of property at any particular time is the property's **basis**. Multiple factors may require a taxpayer to adjust the basis of his or her property during the time (s)he owns it. Uniform capitalization rules determine if a cost is allocated to the basis of the property or expensed in the current year. Inventory has unique rules for identification and valuation.

5.1 BASIS

When a taxpayer acquires property, his or her basis in the property is initially cost, substituted, transferred, exchanged, or converted basis.

1. **Cost basis** is the sum of capitalized acquisition costs.

   a. Cost basis includes the FMV of property given up. If it is not determinable with reasonable certainty, use FMV of property received.

   b. A rebate to the purchaser is treated as a reduction of the purchase price. It is not included in basis or in gross income.

2. **Substituted basis** is computed by reference to basis in other property.

3. **Transferred basis** is computed by reference to basis in the same property in the hands of another.

4. **Exchanged basis** is computed by reference to basis in other property previously held by the person.

5. **Converted basis** is when personal-use property is converted to business use; the basis of the property is the lower of its basis or the FMV on the date of conversion.

Capitalized Acquisition Costs

6. Initial basis in purchased property is the cost of acquiring it. Only capital costs are included, i.e., those for acquisition, title acquisition, and major improvements.

   a. Capital acquisition expenditures may be made by cash, by cash equivalent, in property, with liability, or by services.

Common Capitalized Costs (for Sec. 1012)

Purchase Price (Stated)

NOTE: Not unstated interest
Liability to which property is subject

Closing Costs

Brokerage commissions
Pre-purchase taxes
Sales tax on purchase
Title transfer taxes
Title insurance
Recording fees
Attorney fees
Document review, prep.

Miscellaneous Costs

Appraisal fees
Freight
Installation
Testing

Major Improvements

New roof
New gutters
Extending water line to property
Demolition costs and losses
New electrical wiring

---

b.   Expenses not properly chargeable to a capital account. Costs of maintaining and operating property are not added to basis, e.g., interest on credit related to the property, insurance (e.g., casualty), ordinary maintenance or repairs (e.g., painting).

Liabilities

7.   Acquisition basis is

   a.   Increased for notes to the seller (minus unstated interest)
   b.   Increased for liabilities to which the acquired property is subject

Property for Services

8.   The FMV of property received in exchange for services is income (compensation) to the provider when it is not subject to a substantial risk of forfeiture and not restricted as to transfer. The property acquired has a tax cost basis equal to the FMV of the property.

   a.   Sale of restricted stock to an employee is treated as gross income (bonus compensation) to the extent that any price paid is less than the stock's FMV.

      1)   While restricted, the basis is any price paid other than by services.
      2)   Upon lapse of the restriction, the recipient has ordinary gross income of the spread between FMV on that date and any amounts otherwise paid.

         a)   Basis is increased by that same amount.
         b)   The transferee may elect to include the FMV minus the cost spread in gross income when the stock is purchased.

            i)   Basis includes tax cost, but no subsequent deduction (recovery of tax cost) is allowed if the stock is forfeited by operation of the restriction.

Lump Sum

9.   When more than one asset is purchased for a lump sum, the basis of each is computed by apportioning the total cost based on the relative FMV of each asset.

$$Allocable\ cost\ (basis) = \frac{FMV\ of\ asset}{FMV\ of\ all\ assets\ purchased} \times Lump\ sum\ purchase\ price$$

   a.   Under Code Sec. 1060, the purchase price of assets that constitute a trade or business must be allocated for tax purposes using the residual method to determine the amount allocable to each of the assets.

   b.   The residual method, particularly relevant to goodwill and going concern value, allocates purchase price for both transferor and transferee to asset categories up to FMV in the following order:

      1)   Cash and cash equivalents
      2)   Near-cash items, such as CDs, U.S. government securities, foreign currency, and other marketable securities
      3)   Accounts receivable, mortgages, and credit card receivables acquired in the ordinary course of business
      4)   Property held primarily for sale to customers in the ordinary course of a trade or business or stocks included in dealer inventory
      5)   Assets not listed in 1) through 4) above
      6)   Sec. 197 intangibles, such as patents and covenants not to compete except goodwill and going-concern value
      7)   Goodwill and going-concern value

   NOTE: When the purchase price is lower than the aggregate FMV of the assets other than goodwill and going-concern value, the price is allocated first to the face amount of cash and then to assets 2) through 6) above, according to relative FMVs.

   c.   The purchaser and seller of a group of assets subject to Code Sec. 1060 must file asset acquisition statements on Form 8594 with their income tax returns for the taxable year that includes the purchase date. The agreement is binding on the parties unless the IRS deems it improper.

Gifts

10. The donee's basis in property acquired by gift is the donor's basis, increased for any gift tax paid attributable to appreciation. The donor's basis is increased by

$$\text{Gift tax paid} \times \left[\frac{\text{FMV (at time of gift)} - \text{Donor's basis}}{\text{FMV (at time of gift)} - \text{Annual exclusion}} \right]$$

   a.   If the FMV on the date of the gift is less than the donor's basis, the donee has a dual basis for the property.

      1) Loss basis. The FMV at the date of the gift is used if the property is later transferred at a loss.

      2) Gain basis. The donor's basis is used if the property is later transferred at a gain.

      3) If the property is later transferred for more than FMV at the date of the gift but for less than the donor's basis at the date of the gift, no gain (loss) is recognized.

   b.   Depreciable basis is transferred basis adjusted for gift taxes paid. If converted from personal to business use, it is FMV on the date of conversion if less than adjusted basis.

Inherited Property

11. Basis is the FMV on the date of death or 6 months thereafter if the executor elects the alternate valuation date for the estate tax return. The FMV basis rule also applies to the following property:

   a.   Property received prior to death without full and adequate consideration (if a life estate was retained in it) or subject to a right of revocation. Reduce basis by depreciation deductions allowed the donee.

   b.   One-half of community property interests.

   c.   Property acquired by form of ownership, e.g., by right of survivorship, except if consideration was paid to acquire the property from a nonspouse.

   d.   The FMV rule does not apply to

      1) Income in respect of a decedent or

      2) Appreciated property given to the decedent within 1 year of death (use AB in the property immediately prior to death).

   e.   A shareholder must report his or her ratable share of any corporate income that is income in respect to a decedent as if (s)he had received it directly from the decedent.

      1) For example, the shareholder's basis in the inherited S corporation stock is its FMV on the date of death reduced by his or her ratable share of any income in respect to a decedent attributable to such stock.

Property Converted into Business Use

12. Basis for depreciation is the lesser of the FMV of the property at the conversion date or the adjusted basis at conversion.

Leasehold Improvements

13. Lessors may use the adjusted basis of a leasehold improvement made by the lessor to calculate their gain or loss upon termination of the lease.

    a. Lessors may then report that gain or loss even though the property underlying the lease on which the leasehold improvements are situated is not sold or otherwise exchanged.

    b. Lessees may also do this upon termination of the lease if they created and abandoned a leasehold improvement.

Stop and review! You have completed the outline for this subunit. Study questions 1 through 11 beginning on page 107.

5.2 ADJUSTMENTS TO BASIS

Initial basis is adjusted consistent with tax-relevant events. Adjustments include the following:

1. Certain expenditures subsequent to acquisition are property costs, and they increase basis, e.g., legal fees to defend title or title insurance premiums.

2. Basis must be increased for expenditures that prolong the life of the property by at least 1 year or materially increase its value.

    a. Assessments that increase the value of property should be capitalized.
    b. If the assessments do not add value to the property, they are deductible.

        1) Examples include major improvements (e.g., new roof, addition to building) and zoning changes.
        2) Maintenance, repair, and operating costs are not capitalized.

3. Increase to basis may result from liability to the extent it is secured by real property and applied to extend its life.

4. Basis must be reduced by the larger of the amount of depreciation allowed or allowable (even if not claimed). Unimproved land is not depreciated.

    a. Sec. 179 expense is treated as a depreciation deduction.

        1) The Sec. 179 amount is $500,000 for 2013.

5. A shareholder does not recognize gain on the voluntary contribution of capital to a corporation.

    a. The shareholder's stock basis is increased by the basis in the contributed property.
    b. The corporation has a transferred basis in the property.

6. The basis of stock acquired in a nontaxable distribution (e.g., stock rights) is allocated a portion of the basis of the stock upon which the distribution was made.

    a. If the new and old shares are not identical, basis is allocated in proportion to the FMV of the original stock and the distribution as of the date of distribution.

    b. If the new and old shares are identical (e.g., stock splits), the old basis is simply divided among the new total of shares.

    c. If the FMV of the stock rights is less than 15% of the FMV of the stock upon which it was issued, the rights have a zero basis (unless an election is made to allocate basis).

EXAMPLE

A taxpayer exercises (sells) rights to purchase stock at $50 per share when the rights are worth $6 per share. Since the rights are worth less than 15% of the FMV of the stock, the taxpayer is not required to allocate a portion of old basis of the stock to the stock rights.

Tax Benefit Adjustments

7. Basis adjustment is required for certain specific items that represent a tax benefit. Four examples follow:

Casualty Losses

a. Basis is reduced by the amount of the loss, minus any amounts for which no tax benefit was received, e.g., $100 floor for individuals.

Debt Discharge

b. Specific exclusion from gross income is allowed to certain insolvent persons for debt discharged. Reduction in basis is required for certain amounts excluded.

Credits for Building Rehabilitation

c. Sometimes, the full amount of the credit must be deducted from the basis; other times, only one-half of credit must be deducted. In the case of low-income housing, no reduction is required.

d. Exclusions from income for energy conservation. Exclusions from income of subsidies for energy conservation measures decrease the basis of property.

Partial Disposition of Property

8. The basis of the whole property must be equitably apportioned among the parts; relative FMV is generally used.

Stop and review! You have completed the outline for this subunit. Study questions 12 through 17 beginning on page 110.

5.3 UNIFORM CAPITALIZATION RULES

Costs of constructing real or tangible personal property to be used in trade or business and costs of producing or acquiring property for sale to customers are capitalized.

1. Costs (both direct and most allocable indirect costs) necessary to prepare the property for its intended use must be capitalized, e.g., for permits, materials, equipment rental, compensation for services (minus any work opportunity credit), and architect fees.

a. Costs and losses associated with demolishing a structure are allocated to the land. The costs include the original cost (not FMV) of the structure and demolition costs.

2. Construction period interest and taxes must be capitalized as part of building cost.

3. Uniform capitalization rules do not apply if property is acquired for resale and the company's annual gross receipts (for the past 3 years) do not exceed $10 million.

4. Uniform capitalization rules do not apply to the following:

a. Property produced for personal purposes

b. Qualified creative expenses incurred by an individual as a freelance writer, photographer, or artist

c. Property produced under a long-term contract

d. Research and development expenses

e. Intangible drilling and development costs

f. Trees

1) Specifically, timber and certain (more than 6 years old) ornamental trees raised, harvested, or grown, and the underlying land.

g. Any animal

1) The uniform capitalization rules do apply to animals if the taxpayer is a corporation, partnership, or tax shelter that is required to use an accrued method of accounting.

Stop and review! You have completed the outline for this subunit. Study questions 18 through 24 beginning on page 112.

5.4 INVENTORY VALUATION

Identification Methods

1. There are three methods of identifying items in inventory:

Specific

    a. The specific-identification method is used to identify the cost of each item of inventory by matching it with its cost of acquisition.

FIFO

    b. The FIFO method assumes that the items first acquired are the first sold. Thus, the items remaining in inventory are the last items acquired.

LIFO

    c. The LIFO method assumes that the latest goods to be acquired are the first to be sold. Thus, the oldest goods are considered to remain in inventory, and the cost of the oldest goods is used for valuing inventory.

Valuation Methods

2. The fundamental requirements for inventory valuation are that it conforms as nearly as possible to the best accounting practice in the trade or business and that it clearly reflects income. There are three approved methods:

Cost Method

    a. The cost method includes all direct and indirect costs associated with the inventory.

        1) For beginning inventory, cost means the value of goods held at the end of the prior year.

        2) For inventory purchased, cost means the price, minus discounts, plus freight-in and other costs of acquisition.

            a) If the merchant purchased inventory items and withdrew some of these items for personal use, the merchant must reduce the cost of purchases by the cost of the personal-use items.

        3) For inventory produced, cost means all direct and indirect costs that are required to be capitalized under the uniform capitalization rules.

Lower-of-Cost-or-Market

    b. The lower-of-cost-or-market method values inventory at the lesser of the market value of the inventory or its cost at year end.

        1) Each item in the inventory must be valued separately.
        2) The lower-of-cost-or-market method cannot be used in conjunction with LIFO.

Rolling Average

    c. As of 2008, taxpayers using rolling-average inventory valuation for financial accounting purposes may use the same valuation method for federal income tax purposes. Use of this method is only allowed if

        1) The taxpayer recomputes the rolling average cost of an inventory item on one of the following bases:

            a) Each time the taxpayer purchases or produces an additional unit or units of that item or

            b) On a regular basis but no less frequently than once per month, and

2) The taxpayer satisfies one of the following conditions:

a) The variance percentage does not exceed 1% [(rolling average cost – actual cost) ÷ rolling average cost] or

b) The entire inventory of a taxpayer's trade or business turns at least four times per year (COGS ÷ average inventory).

NOTE: Once a valuation method is chosen, it cannot be changed without consent from the IRS.

FOB Shipping or Destination

3. FOB shipping point indicates that the buyer is responsible for the goods as soon as the goods are shipped.

4. FOB destination implies that the seller is responsible for the goods, and a sale is not recognized until the goods have reached the designated destination.

Consignment

5. Inventory out on consignment is included in ending inventory. The sale of consignment inventory is contingent on a future event (the person holding the inventory selling it).

Stop and review! You have completed the outline for this subunit. Study questions 25 through 30 beginning on page 114.

QUESTIONS
5.1 Basis

1. Several years ago, you paid $150,000 to build your home on a lot that cost you $50,000. Before converting the property to rental use last year, you paid $30,000 for permanent improvements to the house. You received a $5,000 easement payment from the State of California for use of the land for a power line. The county indicates the FMV of the house is $250,000 and the land is $100,000. What is your basis for depreciation?

A. $150,000

B. $175,000

C. $180,000

D. $250,000

Answer (C) is correct.

REQUIRED: The basis of converted property.

DISCUSSION: For property converted into business use, the basis for depreciation is the lesser of the FMV of the property at the conversion date or the adjusted basis at conversion. The adjusted basis in the house on the date of conversion is $180,000 ($150,000 + $30,000). The FMV of the house on the date of conversion is $250,000. Accordingly, the depreciable basis for the house is $180,000. The $5,000 easement is related to the land, which is not depreciated (Publication 551).

Answer (A) is incorrect. The original basis of the house is $150,000. Answer (B) is incorrect. The $5,000 easement is related to the land, which is not depreciated. Answer (D) is incorrect. The FMV of the house at the date of conversion is $250,000.

2. Arthur is a proprietor of Arthur's Pizza Emporium. He bought a commercial building several years ago. He made a down payment of $20,000 in cash and assumed a mortgage for $100,000. After he paid off the mortgage, Arthur later sold the building for $180,000. Straight-line depreciation taken up to the date of sale was $18,000. What is the total gain on the sale?

A. $78,000

B. $80,000

C. $60,000

D. $160,000

Answer (A) is correct.

REQUIRED: The gain on the sale of property.

DISCUSSION: The adjusted basis of property is typically the cost basis increased by certain items, such as boot given. The cost basis for the commercial building is the $20,000 down payment of cash by Arthur, increased by the assumption of the $100,000 mortgage. Therefore, Arthur's basis in the commercial building is $120,000. However, this basis is reduced by the $18,000 of depreciation taken. When Arthur sells the commercial building for $180,000, he must recognize a gain on the difference between the amount realized of $180,000 and his adjusted basis of $102,000 for a total of $78,000.

Answer (B) is incorrect. The down payment of $20,000 increased Arthur's basis in the commercial building, and the $18,000 of depreciation taken reduced Arthur's basis in the commercial building. Answer (C) is incorrect. The $18,000 of depreciation taken reduces Arthur's adjusted basis from $120,000 to $102,000. Answer (D) is incorrect. The assumption of the $100,000 mortgage increases Arthur's adjusted basis in the commercial building.

3. Larry purchased an office building and land on February 1 of the current year for $1,000,000. No liabilities were assumed. The assessed value of the assets for real estate purposes at the time of the purchase were as follows:

	Assessed Value
Land	$300,000
Building	500,000

What is the basis of the building?

A. $500,000

B. $600,000

C. $625,000

D. $700,000

Answer (C) is correct.
    REQUIRED: The building's basis in a lump sum purchase.
    DISCUSSION: When more than one asset is purchased for a lump sum, the basis of each is computed by apportioning the total cost based on the relative FMV of each asset. The allocable cost (basis) for each asset is calculated as follows:

$$\frac{FMV\ of\ asset}{FMV\ of\ all\ assets\ purchased} \times Lump\ sum\ purchase\ price$$

Assuming the assessed value of the assets for real estate purposes reflects the FMV of the assets, the basis of the building is $625,000 [$1,000,000 × ($500,000 ÷ $800,000)] (Publication 551).
    Answer (A) is incorrect. The basis is the proportion of total purchase price based on the relative FMV of each asset. It is not the FMV of the building. Answer (B) is incorrect. The basis is the proportion of the total purchase price based on the relative FMV of each asset purchased. Answer (D) is incorrect. The basis is the proportion of the total purchase price based on the relative FMV of each asset purchased.

4. George purchased a business on May 31 of the current year for a lump sum price of $1,400,000. The values of the assets on the seller's books were as follows:

	Book Value	Fair Market Value
Cash	$200,000	$200,000
Land	150,000	150,000
Building	300,000	450,000
Equipment	250,000	300,000
Covenant not to compete	0	100,000

George did not assume any loans. What is his basis for goodwill and the equipment?

	Goodwill	Equipment
A.	$0	$300,000
B.	$200,000	$300,000
C.	$200,000	$350,000
D.	$0	$350,000

Answer (B) is correct.
    REQUIRED: The basis of goodwill and equipment acquired in a lump sum purchase.
    DISCUSSION: Under Sec. 1060, both the buyer and the seller involved in a transfer of assets that amount to a trade or business must allocate the purchase price among the assets using the residual method. The residual method requires the purchase price to be allocated first to cash; then to near-cash items, such as CDs, government securities, and other marketable securities; and then to other tangible and intangible assets, such as equipment, buildings, land, accounts receivable, and covenants not to compete. The allocation of the purchase price may not exceed the FMV for each of these categories. Finally, any residual purchase price is allocated to intangible assets, such as goodwill and going-concern value. In this case, goodwill is equal to $200,000 ($1,400,000 – $1,200,000). The purchase price is allocated to each asset listed based on its FMV.
    Answer (A) is incorrect. Goodwill is equal to the excess of the purchase price over the sum of the assets' FMVs, or $200,000 ($1,400,000 – $1,200,000). Answer (C) is incorrect. The equipment cannot be valued above its FMV. Answer (D) is incorrect. Goodwill is equal to the excess of the purchase price over the sum of the assets' FMVs, or $200,000 ($1,400,000 – $1,200,000), and the equipment cannot be valued above its FMV.

5. John purchased a new gasoline-electric hybrid automobile on July 2, 2005, for $18,000. He also claimed a $2,000 clean-fuel vehicle deduction on his 2005 tax return for that vehicle. From 2005 through 2012, John used this automobile only for personal purposes. On January 1, 2013, he began using the hybrid automobile exclusively for business purposes. The fair market value of the automobile on that day was $17,000. What is the automobile's depreciable basis as of January 1, 2013?

A. $15,000

B. $16,000

C. $17,000

D. $18,000

Answer (B) is correct.
    REQUIRED: The automobile's depreciable basis upon conversion of property from personal use to business use.
    DISCUSSION: Basis for depreciation is the lesser of the FMV of the property at the conversion date or the adjusted basis at conversion. The FMV on the date of conversion was $17,000. The basis was $16,000 ($18,000 purchase price – $2,000 deduction). Thus, the basis equals $16,000.
    Answer (A) is incorrect. The FMV at the date of conversion is not reduced by the amount of the deduction. Answer (C) is incorrect. The basis used is the lesser of the adjusted basis and the FMV on the date of conversion. Answer (D) is incorrect. The purchase price is irrelevant in this problem. The adjusted basis and FMV on the date of conversion are all that matter.

6. Mike purchased a building lot in Year 1 for $25,000 and constructed his primary residence there for an additional $175,000. In Year 4, Mike moved to a different city but kept the house he constructed in Year 1 and converted it to a rental property. On the date Mike made this change, the fair market value of the converted property was $225,000. For depreciation purposes, what is Mike's basis in this rental property?

A. $150,000

B. $175,000

C. $200,000

D. $225,000

Answer (B) is correct.

REQUIRED: The basis of property converted into business use.

DISCUSSION: Property converted into business use uses a basis of depreciation of the lesser of the FMV of the property at the conversion date or the adjusted basis at conversion. Because Mike's adjusted basis is less than the FMV at the date of conversion, the adjusted basis is used.

Answer (A) is incorrect. The basis of the rental property is not reduced by the basis of the land. Answer (C) is incorrect. The basis in rental property does not include the basis in the land. Answer (D) is incorrect. The basis used is the lower of FMV or adjusted basis on the date of conversion.

7. Bob purchased a building and land to use in his business for a price of $1,000,000. The land was valued at $300,000 (included in the price). He then incurred $90,000 to replace the roof of the building. The city replaced the sewage lines to his business and assessed Bob $20,000. Bob had been slow in getting insurance coverage on the real property and incurred a small fire loss of $10,000, which he plans to deduct on his business tax return. What is Bob's basis for depreciation after deducting the loss?

A. $1,100,000

B. $810,000

C. $800,000

D. $720,000

Answer (C) is correct.

REQUIRED: The depreciation basis in a purchase of a business.

DISCUSSION: To determine the basis of the building for depreciation, the land ($300,000) must be subtracted from the $1,000,000 to get $700,000. The $90,000 spent to replace the roof and the $20,000 spent to replace the sewage lines must be capitalized because they are capital expenditures, and they increase the value of the property. The $10,000 fire loss should reduce the basis because casualty losses reduce the basis by the amount of the loss. This gives $700,000, plus $90,000, plus $20,000, minus $10,000 to equal $800,000.

Answer (A) is incorrect. The amount of $1,100,000 includes the value of the land. Land is not depreciated. Answer (B) is incorrect. This number does not include the $10,000 loss due to the fire. Answer (D) is incorrect. It does not capitalize the $90,000 to replace the roof, and it does not deduct the $10,000 loss due to the fire.

8. Gwen owned a duplex and lived in one half. The other half was rental property. The cost of the property was $80,000, of which $70,000 was allocated to the building and $10,000 to the land. In the current year, the property was condemned by the city. Up to that time, she had allowed (allowable) depreciation of $23,000. The city paid Gwen $70,000. She bought another duplex for $85,000. Gwen lived in one half, and the other half is a rental. What is the basis of the replacement property?

A. $62,000

B. $67,000

C. $72,000

D. $85,000

Answer (B) is correct.

REQUIRED: The basis of the replacement property.

DISCUSSION: Gwen has two assets: one for rental and one for personal use. Each asset must be computed separately. The basis of the rental building before the sale was $17,000 ($40,000 purchase price – $23,000 depreciation taken). That portion of the building was sold for $35,000, leaving a gain of $18,000. The gain is deferred, leaving a basis of $24,500 ($42,500 – $18,000). The personal-use building has a $5,000 loss ($35,000 selling price – $40,000 basis). That loss is a nondeductible personal loss. The replacement portion has a basis of $42,500, the purchase price. The total basis is $67,000 ($24,500 rental portion + $42,500 personal-use portion).

Answer (A) is incorrect. The loss does not reduce the basis. Answer (C) is incorrect. The loss is not deferred. Answer (D) is incorrect. The deferred gain reduces the basis of the new asset.

9. P&L Partnership purchased a building for commercial purposes on July 1 for $200,000. Carpeting was installed at a cost of $8,000 on August 30. Furniture was purchased at a cost of $10,000 on September 1. Legal fees of $700 and recording fees of $100 were incurred at the time the building was purchased. What is the cost basis of the building?

A. $218,800

B. $200,000

C. $200,800

D. $218,000

Answer (C) is correct.
REQUIRED: The cost basis of the building.
DISCUSSION: Cost basis is the sum of capitalized acquisition costs. Capitalized acquisition costs include purchase price, closing costs, major improvements, and miscellaneous costs, e.g., freight. Examples of closing costs are legal fees and recording fees. Since the carpeting was newly installed and it did not replace old carpeting, it cannot be considered a major improvement. The carpet and the furniture are newly acquired assets and must be capitalized separate from the building.
Answer (A) is incorrect. The carpeting and furniture are newly acquired assets and must have separate accounts created for them. Answer (B) is incorrect. The legal fees and recording fees are closing costs and must be capitalized as part of the initial basis of the building. Answer (D) is incorrect. The carpeting and furniture cannot be capitalized as part of the building. The legal and recording fees must be capitalized with the purchase price of the building to determine the building's initial basis.

10. Dianne's Desserts, a sole proprietorship, bought a building for $350,000 cash in January. Settlement costs were $12,500. The business placed $15,000 in escrow for future payment on taxes and insurance and assumed an existing mortgage of $20,000 on the property. Legal fees of $7,500 were incurred for defending and perfecting title in a lawsuit that occurred during the same year. What is the adjusted basis of the building on December 31?

A. $390,000

B. $405,000

C. $385,000

D. $377,500

Answer (A) is correct.
REQUIRED: The circumstances in which certain fees and other expenses become part of the cost basis in property.
DISCUSSION: The basis of the property purchased can include settlement fees and closing costs for purchasing the property. Some settlement fees and closing costs that are specifically included are abstract fees, legal fees, transfer taxes, and any amounts that the seller owes that you agree to pay. Settlement costs do not include amounts placed in escrow for the future payment of items, such as taxes and insurance (Publication 551, page 2).

11. A used car lot owner sold an adjacent lot on June 9, Year 4, for $125,000. He purchased this lot on August 6, Year 1, for $65,000. He did not pave this lot or make any improvements to it. He paid $4,600 in closing costs at the sale. How much gain does he have, and what type of gain is it?

A. $55,400, Section 1250 gain.

B. $55,400, Section 1231 gain.

C. $4,600, Section 1245 gain; $50,800, Section 1231 gain.

D. $55,400, Schedule D gain.

Answer (B) is correct.
REQUIRED: The amount and character of the gain.
DISCUSSION: Publication 544 states, "When you dispose of business property, your taxable gain or loss is usually a Section 1231 gain or loss." Additionally, Publication 544 states that if closing costs are incurred, the taxpayer should "subtract these expenses from the consideration received to figure the amount realized on the exchange."
Authors' Note: It is assumed that the used car lot owner held the asset for use in his business. If the asset were held as a capital asset, there would be a $55,400 Schedule D gain.
Answer (A) is incorrect. The lot cannot be Section 1250 property. Section 1250 property is all depreciable real property that is not Section 1245 property. Answer (C) is incorrect. The lot cannot be Section 1245 property. Section 1245 property generally is depreciable personal property. Land is not depreciable. Answer (D) is incorrect. The lot could only have a Schedule D gain if it were being held as a capital asset.

5.2 Adjustments to Basis

12. Which of the following items does not decrease the basis of property?

A. Capitalized value of a redeemable ground rent.

B. Sec. 179 deduction.

C. Rebate from manufacturer or seller.

D. Amount of insurance received due to a casualty and any deductible loss not covered by insurance.

Answer (A) is correct.
REQUIRED: The item that does not decrease basis.
DISCUSSION: The basis of property must be increased by the amount of any expenditure or other item properly chargeable to a capital account. The capitalized value of redeemable ground rent is an addition to basis.
Answer (B) is incorrect. A Sec. 179 deduction in 2013 reduces basis by a maximum of $500,000. Answer (C) is incorrect. A rebate from a manufacturer or seller reduces basis. Answer (D) is incorrect. The amount of insurance received due to a casualty and any deductible loss not covered by insurance decreases basis.

13. All of the following items decrease the basis of property except

A. Casualty or theft loss deductions and insurance reimbursements.

B. The cost of defending and perfecting a title.

C. Section 179 deduction.

D. The exclusion from income of subsidies for energy conservation measures.

Answer (B) is correct.
REQUIRED: The item that does not decrease the basis of property.
DISCUSSION: According to Reg. 1.212-1(k), the expenses paid or incurred in defending or perfecting title of property constitute a part of the cost of property. The expenses are not deductible, and the cost is added to the basis of the property.
Answer (A) is incorrect. Casualty or theft loss deductions decrease the basis of property. Answer (C) is incorrect. Sec. 179 deductions decrease the basis of property. Answer (D) is incorrect. Exclusions from income of subsidies for energy conservation measures decrease the basis of property.

14. Rich, Inc., a calendar-year taxpayer employing the accrual method of accounting, acquired a business warehouse building in Year 1 for $100,000. Rich deducted $3,000 in warehouse asset depreciation expense on December 31, Year 1. In January of Year 2, Rich incurred a $2,000 legal bill, successfully defending its title to the building. Later in the year, a second-floor office was added to the warehouse at a cost of $10,000. Rich deducted $5,000 in warehouse asset depreciation expense on December 31, Year 2. What is Rich, Inc.'s adjusted basis in the warehouse asset on January 1, Year 3?

A. $100,000

B. $104,000

C. $110,000

D. $112,000

Answer (B) is correct.
REQUIRED: The adjusted basis in the warehouse asset.
DISCUSSION: Initial basis is adjusted consistent with tax-relevant events. Adjustments made for certain expenditures subsequent to acquisition are property costs, such as legal fees to defend title. Basis must be increased for expenditures that prolong the life of the property by at least 1 year or materially increase its value. Basis must be reduced by the larger of the amount of depreciation allowed or allowable. Thus, Rich, Inc.'s basis in the warehouse equals $104,000 ($100,000 purchase price – $3,000 depreciation in Year 1 + $2,000 legal fees + $10,000 expansion – $5,000 depreciation in Year 2).
Answer (A) is incorrect. The adjusted basis and original basis may not necessarily be equal. In this instance, they are not. Answer (C) is incorrect. The only adjustment made to the original basis is the expansion. Basis must also be reduced for the legal fees incurred and depreciation. Answer (D) is incorrect. The adjusted basis has not been reduced for depreciation.

15. Which of the following items does not increase the basis of property?

A. Freight and installation costs.

B. Legal fees to perfect the title.

C. Zoning costs.

D. Missed depreciation deductions in tax years barred by the statute of limitations.

Answer (D) is correct.
REQUIRED: The item that does not increase basis.
DISCUSSION: The basis of property must be decreased by any item that represents a return of capital for the period during which the property has been held. The basis is adjusted for depreciation in the amount that was claimed or could have been claimed on the owner's return. This reduction of basis must be taken, whether or not the taxpayer actually claimed it and even if the statute of limitations for claiming the deduction has expired.

16. Michael wants to convert his personal residence to a rental property. He paid $300,000 for the property, and the allocation of value for tax assessment has always been 2/3 building and 1/3 land. Over the years, he incurred $50,000 in permanent improvements to the house. He claimed a casualty loss deduction of $5,000 in 1 year. On the date of conversion, the fair market value of the property was $600,000. What is the basis for depreciation of this rental?

A. $600,000

B. $345,000

C. $245,000

D. $400,000

Answer (C) is correct.
REQUIRED: The adjusted basis in property converted from personal use to business use.
DISCUSSION: Property converted into business use has a basis for depreciation of the lesser between the FMV of the property at the conversion date and the adjusted basis. Two-thirds of the $300,000 is allocated to the building. The $50,000 in permanent improvements is capitalized, and the $5,000 claimed as a casualty loss is subtracted.
Answer (A) is incorrect. Property converted into business use has a basis for depreciation of the lesser between the FMV ($600,000) of the property at the conversion date and the adjusted basis ($245,000). Answer (B) is incorrect. The $345,000 does not subtract out the value of the land. The land is 1/3 of the $300,000, and it is subtracted because land is not depreciated. Answer (D) is incorrect. The personal residence's basis for depreciation is valued at 2/3 of the cost, not the FMV.

17. Which of the following does not reduce the basis of property?

    A. Credit for qualified electric vehicles.

    B. Depreciation.

    C. Zoning costs.

    D. Section 179 deductions.

Answer (C) is correct.
    REQUIRED: The item that does not reduce the basis of property.
    DISCUSSION: Publication 551 provides examples of items that increase and decrease a taxpayer's basis in property. Zoning costs do not decrease, but rather increase, the basis. Conversely, a credit for qualified electric vehicles, depreciation, and Sec. 179 deductions do decrease basis.

5.3 Uniform Capitalization Rules

18. The uniform capitalization rules will apply in all of the following situations except

    A. Produce real or tangible personal property for sale to customers.

    B. Acquire property for resale, and average annual gross receipts exceed $10,000,000.

    C. Produce real or tangible personal property for use in a business or activity carried on for profit.

    D. Produce property under a long-term contract other than a home construction.

Answer (D) is correct.
    REQUIRED: The situation where uniform capitalization rules do not apply.
    DISCUSSION: Uniform capitalization rules determine the costs and expenditures, including interest, that must be capitalized by a taxpayer. These uniform capitalization rules apply to all real and tangible personal property that is produced by a taxpayer and to all real or personal property that is acquired by a taxpayer for resale. However, these rules apply only to property used in a taxpayer's trade or business or in an activity engaged in for profit. They do not apply to property that is used for personal purposes, to timber, or to any property that is being produced under a long-term contract.

19. Which of the following is not subject to the uniform capitalization rules?

    A. Real property or tangible personal property that an individual produces for sale to customers.

    B. Real property or tangible personal property that an individual produces for use in a trade or business.

    C. Personal property acquired for resale if an individual has average annual gross receipts of more than $10 million.

    D. Property produced under a long-term contract.

Answer (D) is correct.
    REQUIRED: The type of property not subject to the uniform capitalization rules.
    DISCUSSION: Uniform capitalization rules determine the costs and expenditures, including interest, that must be capitalized by a taxpayer. These uniform capitalization rules apply to all real and tangible personal property that is produced by a taxpayer and to all real or personal property that is acquired by a taxpayer for resale. However, these rules apply only to property used in a taxpayer's trade or business or in an activity engaged in for profit. They do not apply to property that is used for personal purposes, to timber, or to any property that is being produced under a long-term contract.

20. Which of the following classes of property is (are) excepted from the uniform capitalization rules?

    A. Timber and certain ornamental trees raised, harvested, or grown, and the underlying land.

    B. Intangible drilling and development costs of oil and gas or geothermal wells.

    C. Qualified creative expenses incurred as a self-employed writer, photographer, or artist that are otherwise deductible.

    D. All of the answers are correct.

Answer (D) is correct.
    REQUIRED: The class(es) of property excepted from the uniform capitalization rules.
    DISCUSSION: Uniform capitalization rules determine the costs and expenditures, including interest, that must be capitalized by a taxpayer. These uniform capitalization rules apply to all real and tangible personal property that is produced by a taxpayer and to all real or personal property that is acquired by a taxpayer for resale. The uniform capitalization rules do not apply to timber, to research and experimental costs, to intangible drilling costs, to mining exploration and development costs, to costs (other than circulation expenditures) subject to a 10-year amortization election made to minimize alternative minimum tax liability, or to the "qualified creative costs" of freelance artists, authors, and photographers.

21. Farmer Bob sold a breeding cow on March 8 for $2,500. Expenses related to the sale were $250. Farmer Bob deducted $1,000 in costs of raising the cow during the years the cow was raised. What is Farmer Bob's gain (loss) on the sale of the breeding cow, without regard to the Uniform Capitalization Rules?

A. $(350)

B. $1,150

C. $2,250

D. None of the answers are correct.

Answer (C) is correct.
REQUIRED: The gain (loss) reported without regard to the uniform capitalization rules.
DISCUSSION: Farmer Bob sold a breeding cow for $2,500. Because Farmer Bob had already received a tax benefit from the costs of raising the cow, he cannot offset those costs against the proceeds received from selling the cow. The only expenses he can deduct against the proceeds are the selling expenses. Thus, Farmer Bob's gain is $2,250 ($2,500 – $250).
Answer (A) is incorrect. The gain is calculated based on the selling price minus the selling expenses incurred. Answer (B) is incorrect. The gain is calculated based on the selling price minus the selling expenses incurred. Answer (D) is incorrect. The gain reported is $2,250.

22. The uniform capitalization rules apply to all of the following business-related costs except

A. Direct materials.

B. Indirect materials.

C. Direct labor.

D. Research.

Answer (D) is correct.
REQUIRED: The cost not subject to the uniform capitalization rules.
DISCUSSION: Uniform capitalization rules determine the costs and expenditures, including interest, that must be capitalized by a taxpayer. These uniform capitalization rules apply to all real and tangible personal property that is produced by a taxpayer and to all real or personal property that is acquired by a taxpayer for resale. However, these rules apply only to property used in a taxpayer's trade or business or in an activity engaged in for profit. They do not apply to property that is used for personal purposes, to timber, or to any property that is being produced under a long-term contract. The uniform capitalization rules also do not apply to research and experimental costs.

23. Which of the following activities would subject a taxpayer to the uniform capitalization rules?

A. Taxpayer produces real or tangible property for non-business use.

B. Taxpayer acquires property not for resale.

C. Taxpayer produces real or tangible personal property for sale to customers.

D. None of the answers are correct.

Answer (C) is correct.
REQUIRED: The activity that would subject a taxpayer to the uniform capitalization rules.
DISCUSSION: Under Sec. 263A(b)(1), the uniform capitalization rules apply to real or tangible personal property produced by the taxpayer. Property produced for the taxpayer's own use is excepted, unless the use is in a trade or business or an activity conducted for profit [Sec. 263A(c)(1)]. In addition, the taxpayer is subject to the rules if property is acquired for resale (unless the property is personal property and average annual gross receipts are $10 million or less) (Publication 538).
Answer (A) is incorrect. The property produced for non-business uses is an exception. Answer (B) is incorrect. The rules only apply if it is acquired for resale (unless the gross receipts test is passed). Answer (D) is incorrect. The uniform capitalization rules apply to real or tangible personal property produced by the taxpayer.

24. Amounts paid or incurred to demolish a structure are

A. Deductible as a casualty loss.

B. Capitalized and amortized over a 180-month period.

C. Treated as a reduction of the basis of the structure.

D. Capitalized and added to the basis of the land where the demolished structure was located.

Answer (D) is correct.
REQUIRED: The tax treatment of demolition expenditures.
DISCUSSION: Initial basis is adjusted consistent with tax-relevant events. An adjustment is made for demolition of a structure. Costs and losses associated with demolishing a structure are allocated to the land. The costs include the original cost (not FMV) of the structure and demolition costs.
Answer (A) is incorrect. The costs are capitalized to the cost of the land. Answer (B) is incorrect. No amortization is allowed. The cost is recovered when the land is sold and any subsequent gain is reduced by the increased basis or any loss is increased by the increase basis. Answer (C) is incorrect. The costs and losses associated with the demolition are added to the basis of the land.

5.4 Inventory Valuation

25. Which of the following statements with respect to methods of valuing or identifying items in inventory is false?

A. Under the lower-of-cost-or-market method, a business compares the market value of each individual item on hand at the inventory date with its cost and uses the lower value as its inventory value.

B. If a taxpayer uses the specific-identification (cost) method or the lower-of-cost-or-market method to value inventory, (s)he may switch between the cost and the lower-of-cost-or-market methods anytime (s)he wishes, as long as the method (s)he chooses is used for a complete tax year.

C. You may adopt the LIFO method by filing either Form 970, *Application to Use LIFO Inventory Method*, or a statement that has all the information required in Form 970.

D. Deducting a reserve for price changes or an estimated amount for depreciation in the value of your inventory is not a recognized inventory practice for tax purposes.

Answer (B) is correct.
 REQUIRED: The false statement regarding inventory valuation methods.
 DISCUSSION: The two most common methods to value inventory are the cost method and the lower-of-cost-or-market method. Once a method is chosen, it may not be changed to another method without consent from the IRS.
 Answer (A) is incorrect. Under the lower-of-cost-or-market method, a business compares the market value of each individual item on hand at the inventory date with its cost and uses the lower value as its inventory value is a correct statement. Answer (C) is incorrect. You may adopt the LIFO method by filing either Form 970, *Application to Use LIFO Inventory Method*, or a statement that has all the information required in Form 970 is a correct statement. Answer (D) is incorrect. Deducting a reserve for price changes or an estimated amount for depreciation in the value of your inventory is not a recognized inventory practice for tax purposes is a correct statement.

26. Williams Manufacturing has the following account information at year end. Compute ending inventory using the following information:

Physical inventory at 12/31 at cost	$300,000
Reserve for estimated depreciation of inventory	15,000
Stock shipped FOB destination 12/30	5,000
Raw materials ordered 12/20, invoiced and payable (not yet received)	10,000

A. $300,000

B. $305,000

C. $310,000

D. $315,000

Answer (D) is correct.
 REQUIRED: The ending inventory for a manufacturing company.
 DISCUSSION: The stock shipped FOB destination has not arrived and should be included in inventory. Also, the raw materials ordered should be included in inventory since title has passed. The reserve is specifically prohibited from reducing inventory according to Reg. 1.471-2(c). Therefore, the total inventory is $315,000 ($300,000 beginning inventory + $5,000 stock + $10,000 raw materials).
 Answer (A) is incorrect. The stock shipped FOB destination has not arrived and should be included in inventory. The raw materials ordered should be included in inventory also. The reserve is specifically prohibited from reducing inventory according to Reg. 1.471-2(c). Answer (B) is incorrect. The raw materials that are not received should be included in ending inventory when they are invoiced and payable. Answer (C) is incorrect. Raw materials that are not received should be included in ending inventory when they are invoiced and payable. Also, the stock shipped FOB destination should be included in Williams Manufacturing's ending inventory.

27. Under the lower-of-cost-or-market method, what is the value of the following items that should be included in closing inventory?

Item	Cost	Market
X	$450	$700
Y	$250	$100
Z	$300	$250
Total	$1,000	$1,050

A. $800

B. $1,000

C. $1,050

D. $1,250

Answer (A) is correct.
 REQUIRED: The value of the closing inventory using the lower-of-cost-or-market method.
 DISCUSSION: The fundamental requirements for inventory valuation are that they conform as nearly as possible to the best accounting practice in the trade or business and that they clearly reflect income. There are two approved methods: the cost method and the lower-of-cost-or-market method. Using the lower-of-cost-or-market method, each item of inventory must be valued separately. Thus, the total value of inventory is $800 ($450 cost of item X + $100 market value of item Y + $250 market value of item Z).
 Answer (B) is incorrect. The aggregate cost of the items is $1,000. Answer (C) is incorrect. The aggregate market value of the items is $1,050. Answer (D) is incorrect. This $1,250 uses the greater of cost or market.

28. Mr. and Mrs. Hammer own a retail hardware store. Which of the following items should they include in their December 31 current year inventory?

A. Envelopes and stationery used in the office.

B. A lawnmower that was sold to, and paid for by, a customer and has not yet been picked up.

C. In-transit C.O.D. shipment of nails to a customer.

D. Goods consigned to Mr. and Mrs. Hammer.

Answer (C) is correct.
REQUIRED: The item that is included in inventory.
DISCUSSION: Reg. 1.471-1 provides that inventory should include all finished goods, work-in-process, and raw materials and supplies that will physically become a part of merchandise intended for sale. Merchandise should be included in inventory only if title thereto is vested in the taxpayer. The title to items shipped C.O.D. does not pass to the purchaser until the items are delivered. Therefore, the Hammers still have title to the inventory.
Answer (A) is incorrect. The envelopes and stationery were not acquired for sale. Answer (B) is incorrect. The title has been transferred to the purchaser. Answer (D) is incorrect. The title remains with the consignor.

29. A taxpayer is a merchant who has purchased inventory items. He withdrew some of these items for personal use. He must

A. Increase his sales by the cost of the items withdrawn.

B. Reduce the cost of purchases by the cost of the personal-use items.

C. Reduce the cost of purchases by the fair market value of the personal-use items.

D. Reduce beginning inventory by the cost of the personal-use items.

Answer (B) is correct.
REQUIRED: The cost of inventory items used for personal use.
DISCUSSION: Publication 334 states, "If you withdraw merchandise for your personal or family use, you must exclude this cost from the total amount of merchandise you bought for sale. Do this by crediting the purchases or sales account with the cost of merchandise you withdraw for personal use. You should charge the amount to your drawing account."

30. Which of the following items are generally included in inventory?

A. Goods for sale that someone else has consigned to you.

B. Equipment used in your business to manufacture goods.

C. Goods you have sent out on consignment for someone else to sell.

D. Goods in transit to you for which title has not yet passed to you.

Answer (C) is correct.
REQUIRED: The items included in inventory.
DISCUSSION: Ending inventory includes the cost of the raw materials, the direct and indirect labor costs that are attributable to the manufacturing of a product and are included in COGS, overhead costs, and materials and supplies used in manufacturing goods, such as hardware or chemicals. Inventory out on consignment is included in ending inventory. The sale of consignment inventory is contingent on a future event (the person holding the inventory selling it).
Answer (A) is incorrect. The inventory you hold on consignment for someone else is properly included in the other entity's inventory, not your own. Answer (B) is incorrect. This equipment is depreciable property and should not be included in inventory. The overhead associated with those machines should be charged to COGS and/or added to inventory. Answer (D) is incorrect. Those goods would properly be included in the shipping company's inventory, not your own.

Use the additional questions in Gleim **EA Test Prep** to create Practice Exams that emulate Prometric!

STUDY UNIT SIX
DEPRECIATION

(14 pages of outline)

Depreciation is a business deduction that allows a taxpayer to recover the cost or other basis of certain business-use property with a useful life in excess of 1 year. It is an annual allowance for the wear and tear, deterioration, or obsolescence of the property. Related cost recovery methods include amortization and depletion. Sec. 179 is a special election that allows for immediate, limited expensing of depreciable property.

6.1 DEPRECIATION METHODS

Tax accounting methods of depreciation that allow a deduction in excess of a current year's decline in economic value are accelerated cost recovery (ACR) methods.

1. Property subject to the allowance for depreciation is tangible property used in trade, in business, or for production of income and has a determinable, limited useful life.

   a. The amount of a current depreciation deduction is computed by applying a rate to depreciable basis.

      1) The rate is determined under a mandatory or elected depreciation method.
      2) The basis of property is decreased by the greater of the amount of depreciation allowed or allowable.

         a) Allowable depreciation is the amount that a taxpayer is entitled to deduct under any proper method.
         b) Allowed depreciation is the deduction claimed on the tax return.

2. Depreciation of property begins in the taxable year that it is placed in service. Property is considered placed in service when it is ready and available for a specific use. Even if the taxpayer does not begin using the property, it is in service when it is available and ready for its specific use.

Straight-Line Depreciation (S-L)

3. The annual amount allowable is the depreciable basis reduced for salvage value (SV) and divided by the useful life of the asset.

$$(Basis - SV) \div Useful\ life$$

150% Declining Balance

4. Basis (not reduced by SV) minus previously allowable deductions, which is adjusted basis (AB), is multiplied by 1 1/2 times the straight-line rate.

$$AB \times (150\% \div Useful\ life)$$

   a. The rate is constant. It is applied to declining basis.
   b. It is generally applicable to used property with a useful life of at least 3 years and used depreciable real property.

200% Declining Balance

5.   The constant rate is twice the straight-line rate.

$$AB \times (200\% \div Useful\ life)$$

    a.   It is generally allowable for property with a useful life of at least 3 years.

Sum-of-the-Years' Digits

6.   A changing rate is applied to a constant, the cost of the property (unadjusted basis) reduced by salvage value. The rate is the number of years of the useful life remaining divided by the sum of the numbers of the years of the estimated useful life, the latter being $n(n+1)/2$.

2nd of 5 years: Rate = $4 \div (1 + 2 + 3 + 4 + 5) = 4/15$

MACRS

7.   The modified accelerated cost recovery system (MACRS) applies to property placed in service in 1987 or later.

    a.   The 200%-declining-balance method is used for MACRS recovery periods of 3, 5, 7, and 10 years; 150% is used for 15 and 20 years.

        1)   A switch is made to a straight-line rate on adjusted (reduced for allowable depreciation) basis when it yields a higher amount.

        2)   Real property costs are recovered using a straight-line rate on unadjusted basis.

            a)   Salvage value is ignored.

    b.   Mid-year (personal property) and mid-month (real property) conventions apply.

        1)   A mid-quarter convention applies when asset acquisition is bunched at the end of the year.

            a)   Each asset is treated as placed in service at the midpoint of the quarter in which it actually was placed in service.

            b)   Apply the convention to all depreciable personal property acquired during the tax year when the sum of the bases of all depreciable personal property placed in service during the last quarter of the year exceeds 40% of those placed in service during the entire year.

        2)   The first year depreciation is calculated by multiplying the full-year amount by the following percentages based on the placed-in-service quarter:

            a)   87.5% for the first quarter
            b)   62.5% for the second quarter
            c)   37.5% for the third quarter
            d)   12.5% for the fourth quarter

EXAMPLE

The formula for 3-year property placed in service in the third quarter is AB × (200% ÷ Useful life) × 37.5%.

---

    c.   IRS tables provide rates to be applied to the unadjusted basis (except for Sec. 179 expense) for each year of service.

        1)   The rate incorporates applicable methods, applicable recovery periods, and conventions.

    d.   Depreciation is allowed during a disposition year.

    e.   Personal property is assigned a recovery period of either 3, 5, 7, 10, 15, or 20 years, according to the midpoint of the asset depreciation range (ADR) class life applicable to the type of property.

        1)   The half-year or mid-quarter convention is applied.

MACRS Recovery Period # of Years	Midpoint of ADR for Class # of Years	DB Rate Applicable Percent	Examples
		MACRS RECOVERY PERIODS (Personal Property)	
3	≤4	200	Special tools, e.g., for rubber manufacturing Most race horses
5	>4, <10	200	Computers, office machinery (e.g., copier) Cars, trucks Research and experimentation (R&E) equipment
7	≥10, <16	200	Most machinery Office furniture and equipment Agricultural structures (single-purpose) Property without ADR midpoint & not otherwise classified
10	≥16, <20	200	Water vessels, e.g., barge Petroleum processing equipment Food & tobacco manufacturing
15	≥20, <25	150	Data communication plants, e.g., for phone Sewage treatment plants Billboards, improvements to land
20	≥25	150	Utilities, e.g., municipal sewers (pre 6/13/1996) Not real property with ADR midpoint ≥ 27.5 years

Real Property

    f.   The straight-line method and the mid-month convention apply. The mid-quarter convention does not apply.

Residential Rental Property

    1)   The straight-line rate is based on a 27 1/2-year recovery period (Publication 527).

        a)   It is real property with at least 80% of gross rents coming from dwelling units. Partial use by the owner is included. Transient use of more than half the units excludes the property, e.g., a motel.

    2)   Nonresidential real estate is assigned a 39-year (31 1/2-year for property placed in service before May 13, 1993) recovery period.

        a)   It is real property that is not residential rental property.

        b)   It also includes real property with an ADR midpoint of less than 27 1/2 years.

15-Year Depreciation

3) The following three real properties qualify for 15-year-straight-line depreciation:

    a) Qualified Leasehold Improvement Property

        i) The improvement must be to the interior portion of a building.

        ii) The building must be nonresidential real property.

        iii) The improvement must be made pursuant to or under a lease by either the lessee (or sublessee) or the lessor to property that will be occupied exclusively by the lessee (or sublessee).

        iv) The improvement must be placed in service more than 3 years after the date the building was first placed in service.

        v) Leases between related taxpayers do not qualify.

    b) Qualified Restaurant Property

        i) Qualified restaurant property includes a new building as well as a used building placed in service after 2008 and before 2014.

        ii) The restaurant must use more than half of the building's square footage.

            • This applies to all improvements attached to the building.

    c) Qualified Retail Improvement Property

        i) The property must be an improvement to an interior portion of a building that is nonresidential real property.

        ii) The interior portion of the building must be open to the general public and used in the retail trade or business of selling tangible personal property to the general public.

        iii) The improvement must be placed in service more than 3 years after the building was first placed in service.

        iv) Businesses primarily engaged in providing services, such as professional services, health services, and entertainment services, will not qualify.

            • Examples of qualifying businesses are grocery, hardware, convenience, and clothing stores.

g. Most tangible depreciable property falls within the general rule of MACRS, also called the general depreciation system (GDS). The major differences between GDS and the alternative depreciation system are the recovery period and the depreciation method used to figure the deduction.

Alternative Depreciation System (ADS)

h. MACRS is mandatory unless ADS is required or elected. ADS uses a straight-line rate based on longer recovery periods. Examples of ADS recovery periods follow:

# Years	Items
5	Cars, light trucks, certain technological equipment
12	Personal property with no class life
15	Agricultural structures (single-purpose)
40	Residential rental and nonresidential real estate

1) ADS is required for each of the following:

    a) Listed property

    b) Property used, leased, or financed by tax-exempt organizations

    c) Tangible property used predominantly outside the U.S.

    d) Imported property from a country that engages in discriminatory trade practices

Elective Methods

    i. By election, one of the following two alternative methods may be used:

      1) Straight-line rates based on ADS recovery periods may be used for (tangible) personal property.

      2) The 150%-declining-balance method (or straight-line rate for real property) and recovery periods of GDS may be used.

    This election is irrevocable once made and is applied to all property in the MACRS class (recovery period) for which the election is made that is placed in service in the tax year of election.

    NOTE: Nonresidential real property and rental property elections are applied on a property-by-property basis.

Listed Property and Automobiles

8. Recapture income may result from modified use. Timing of capital recovery is even more specifically regulated in the case of luxury automobiles.

Passenger Automobiles

a. Rules with priority over those applicable to listed property, and to property generally, spread cost recovery for passenger automobiles that cost more than a base amount.

    1) Passenger automobiles are generally four-wheeled, made for use on public roads, below the weight threshold of 6,000 pounds, not used to transport for compensation, and not otherwise exempt.

      a) Passenger automobiles include trucks and vans with a gross vehicle weight of 6,000 pounds or less.

    2) Deduction, otherwise allowable, is limited to the business-use percentage of the dollar limitation amount applicable with reference to the year placed in service.

    3) The lease of a car for business use is deductible.

      a) Gross income includes certain amounts when a business lease exceeds 30 days.

      b) This balances the lease expenditure deduction with the limited depreciation deduction allowable to a purchaser.

b. Depreciation of listed property is limited by reference to qualified business use (QBU). Listed property includes the following:

    1) Passenger automobiles,

    2) Other transportation vehicles (e.g., truck under 6,000 pounds),

    3) Entertainment or recreational property (e.g., video camera), and

    4) Computers and peripherals not exclusively used at a regular place of business (e.g., home office).

c. Rules for QBU include the following:

    1) Use by an employee of his or her own property is QBU only if it is in the employer's trade or business, for the convenience of the employer, and required as a condition of employment (it enables proper performance of duties). Not included is use

      a) For investment purposes

      b) By a 5%-or-more owner as compensation or under a lease

      c) As other compensation, unless it is reported and tax is withheld

    2) If QBU exceeds 50% in the tax year in which listed property is placed in service, Sec. 179 current expensing and MACRS depreciation are allowable with respect to the QBU portion.

3)   If QBU is not more than 50% during the year in which listed property is placed in service,

    a)   Sec. 179 expense election is not allowable
    b)   ADS depreciation is used (S-L over the class-life)

NOTE: Specifically prescribed periods apply to certain property, e.g., 5 years for automobiles and computers.

4)   When QBU exceeds 50% in the first year but not in a subsequent year, the taxpayer must recapture as gross income

    a)   Any excess of depreciation allowed over
    b)   ADS depreciation for prior year(s).

NOTE: ADS depreciation is used for all years once QBU does not exceed 50% for any year.

c)   In addition to the business-use requirements, limits are placed on the maximum MACRS deduction allowable for most passenger automobiles. The depreciation limits depend upon the year the automobile was placed in service and on the recovery (depreciation) year.

Placed in Service	1st Recovery Year	2nd Recovery Year	3rd Recovery Year	4th & Succeeding Recovery Years
2013	$3,160*	$5,100	$3,050	$1,875
2012	3,160*	5,100	3,050	1,875
2011	3,060*	4,900	2,950	1,775
2010	3,060*	4,900	2,950	1,775
2009	2,960*	4,800	2,850	1,775
2008	2,960*	4,800	2,850	1,775
2007	3,060	4,900	2,850	1,775

*The first-year limit may be increased by a bonus depreciation of $8,000 for 2008 through 2014 (Sec. 168).

Incorrect Depreciation

9.   When a taxpayer deducts an incorrect amount of depreciation in any year, the taxpayer may be able to make a correction by filing an amended return for that year.

a.   An amended return can be filed to correct the amount of depreciation for any property in any of the following situations:

1)   There was an incorrect amount because of a mathematical error.
2)   There was an incorrect amount because of a posting error.
3)   The taxpayer has not adopted a method of accounting for the property.

b.   If the error is discovered after the statute of limitations has expired, the taxpayer may qualify to correct the error through a change of accounting method under Rev. Proc. 2011-14.

Stop and review! You have completed the outline for this subunit. Study questions 1 through 8 beginning on page 131.

6.2 SEC. 179 EXPENSE

A person may elect to deduct all or part of the cost of Sec. 179 property acquired during the year, up to a maximum of $500,000 in 2013.

1. Sec. 179 property is

    a. Tangible personal property that is

        1) Recovery property (depreciable) and
        2) Sec. 1245 property

    b. Acquired

        1) By purchase,
        2) From an unrelated party, and
        3) For use in the active conduct of a trade or business.

        NOTE: Specifically excluded from the Sec. 179 election are investment property, air-conditioning and heating units, property used for lodging, property used by tax-exempt organizations, land and land improvements, and property used outside the United States.

2. The recent expanded definition of qualified Sec. 179 property includes qualified real property, which is defined as qualified leasehold improvement property, qualified restaurant property, and qualified retail improvement property.

    a. Taxpayers are limited to expensing up to $250,000 of the total cost of these properties.
    b. Limitations apply to the carryover of qualified real property deductions.

3. Sec. 179 expense is treated as depreciation. It reduces basis in the property (but not below zero) prior to computation of any other depreciation deduction allowable for the first year, but only if and to the extent that Sec. 179 deduction is elected.

    a. It is subject to recapture under Sec. 1245 as depreciation.

4. Apply the following limits in the order presented:

    a. For pass-through entities, apply each limit on Sec. 179 expense first at the entity level and then at the partner/shareholder level.
    b. Trusts and estates may not claim a Sec. 179 deduction.
    c. Only the business-use portion of the cost of Sec. 179 property may be expensed.
    d. Cost of Sec. 179 property does not include the basis determined by reference to other property held by the taxpayer.
    e. No more than the statutory amount may be deducted as depreciation on cars and certain luxury items. Excess over the limit may not be expensed under Sec. 179.
    f. Taxpayers cannot claim a Sec. 179 expense over $25,000 for SUVs weighing 14,000 pounds or less. If a vehicle meets one of the three exceptions listed below and exceeds 6,000 pounds, it remains eligible for the full $500,000 Sec. 179 deduction.

        1) Any vehicle designed to have a seating capacity of more than nine persons, excluding the driver's seat
        2) Any vehicle equipped with a cargo area of at least 6 feet that is designed to be an open area and not readily accessible from the passenger department
        3) Any vehicle that has an integral enclosure, does not have seating rearward of the driver's seat, and does not have a body section that exceeds more than 30 inches from the windshield

      g.   For 2013, a deduction may be for no more than either

          1) $500,000 minus the excess of tangible personal property purchases for the year over $2,000,000 or

          2)   Taxable income (TI) from the active conduct of any trade or business during the tax year.

      h.   The date the Sec. 179 property is placed in service is irrelevant to the amount of the Sec. 179 expense deduction allowed. However, the number of days the Sec. 179 property is in service may be a factor when determining the eligibility of property.

   5.   Current-year excess over TI may be carried forward and treated as Sec. 179 cost in a subsequent year.

Bonus Depreciation

   6.   A first-year depreciation (also called bonus depreciation) of 50% of the adjusted basis is allowed for qualified property.

      a.   This is in addition to the Section 179 deduction.

      b.   The deduction is permitted for both regular and AMT purposes.

      c.   Qualifying property must be new, generally have a 20-year or less recovery period, and be placed into service after September 10, 2001, and before January 1, 2005, or after December 31, 2007, and before January 1, 2014 (ATR Act of 2012). Qualifying property includes leasehold improvements.

      d.   One hundred percent first year depreciation is allowed after September 8, 2010, and before January 2012.

Recapture

   7.   Sec. 179 property need not be used to elect the deduction. The amount of allowed Sec. 179 deduction may be allocated to Sec. 179 property as desired. But, if Sec. 179 property is disposed of prior to the end of the MACRS recovery period, gross income includes any

      a.   Excess of Sec. 179 deduction over
      b.   MACRS deductions allowable notwithstanding Sec. 179.

      NOTE: Recapture also applies when the business use of the Sec. 179 property changes to less than 50% of total use.

Stop and review! You have completed the outline for this subunit. Study questions 9 through 14 beginning on page 133.

6.3 AMORTIZATION

    Amortization accounts for recovery of capital ratably (in equal installments over the useful life of the property).

   1.   An amortizable asset, generally, is property that

      a.   Is intangible,
      b.   Is personal (as opposed to real),
      c.   Has a determinable useful life, and
      d.   Is used in a trade or business or for the production of income.

   2.   Examples of nonpersonal-use assets are patents, leases, covenants not to compete, customer lists, and mortgages.

   3.   A deduction is allowed for assets used in a trade or business or for the production of income. The deduction is ratable (straight-line) over the useful life of the asset, starting with the month the asset is acquired.

      a.   The useful life of a patent is the 20 years for which it is afforded legal protection.

      b.   Federal copyright protection extends from the time the work is fixed in a tangible medium of expression for the life of the author plus 70 years.

Indefinite Life

4. Capital costs attributable to intangible personal property with an indeterminable life are generally accounted for by a reduction in gain realized or an increase of loss incurred on disposition of the asset.

   a. Examples are unimproved land and rare collectibles.

   b. If a going concern is purchased in the absence of specific allocation to a covenant not to compete (determinable useful life), any excess of cost over the FMV of tangible assets may be determined allocable to goodwill.

Intangibles

5. The cost of certain intangibles acquired (not created) in connection with the conduct of a trade, business, or income-producing activity is amortized over a 15-year period, beginning with the month in which the intangible is acquired.

   a. Qualified intangibles do not include intangibles that result from the taxpayer's own efforts, unless they are in connection with the acquisition of a trade or business.

      1) The basis of an intangible is usually the cost to buy or create it.

         a) Cost includes all costs of acquisition and expenditures necessary to make the intangible asset ready for its intended use.

         b) The basis does not include unsubstantiated expenses for creative effort, only identifiable expenses.

   b. Qualified intangibles include the following:

      1) Acquired goodwill and going-concern value
      2) Intangible assets relating to the work force, information base, know-how, customers, suppliers, or similar items
      3) Licenses, permits, or other rights granted by governmental units
      4) Covenants not to compete
      5) Any franchise, trademark, or trade name

   c. Intangible amortization applies generally to property acquired after August 10, 1993.

      1) This new intangible amortization does not apply to amounts that are otherwise currently deductible under current law.

   d. Loss realized on disposition of a qualified intangible is disallowed if the taxpayer retains other qualified intangibles acquired in the same (set of) transaction(s).

      1) The amount disallowed is added to the basis of the intangibles retained.

   e. Certain intangibles are subject to amortization only if acquired in connection with acquisition of a trade or business. They include the following:

      1) Covenants not to compete
      2) Patents
      3) Copyrights
      4) Sound recordings
      5) Computer software

   f. Excluded from intangible amortization treatment are the following:

      1) Interests in corporations, partnerships, trusts, estates
      2) Interests in land
      3) Most financial instruments and contracts
      4) Leases of intangible personal property
      5) Professional sports franchises

Start-Up Costs

6. Start-up costs of business may be amortized over 180 months or more, starting with the month when business begins (eligible expensing is discussed in item 8. below).

    a. Start-up costs are both

        1) Paid or incurred in connection with starting or investigating the start or acquisition of an active trade or business and

        2) Allowed as a current deduction if for expansion of an existing business (i.e., not capital and fully deductible in current year).

    b. Examples are research of a product or market, books relevant to start-up, advertising for opening the business, setting up an accounting system, travel to secure distributors, and salaries and other expenses of training employees.

    c. Not included is the purchase price of property to be used in the trade or business, e.g., land, building, and equipment.

    d. If the business is not started or acquired, the costs are not deductible.

    e. If the person is already engaged in a similar line of business, the expenses are currently deductible without regard to eventual acquisition.

Organizational Expense

7. Organizational expense of a corporation or a partnership is generally capitalized. Amortization over at least 180 months may be elected. If not, it is recoverable only upon dissolution of the entity (eligible expensing is discussed in item 8. below).

8. Up to $5,000 of start-up expenses and organization costs may be deducted in the first year.

    a. If the costs exceed $50,000, the $5,000 is reduced dollar-for-dollar above $50,000.

    b. A taxpayer is deemed to have made the election and is not required to attach a separate statement to the return.

Construction Period Interest

9. Construction period interest must be capitalized and recovered under applicable depreciation rules. Amortization is not permitted.

Lease Costs

10. Costs of acquiring a lease are amortized over the lease term. Examples are the purchase price paid to the current holder, commissions, and finders' fees.

    a. Renewal options are included in the term if less than 75% of the cost is attributable to the period prior to renewal.

        1) Allocate the cost over the original and renewal term, i.e., cost ÷ n years, unless the contract (reasonably) specifies otherwise.

    b. Improvements by the lessee are deducted under the MACRS method (according to the type of improvement).

        1) For a lease entered into before September 26, 1985, the lessee could elect to recover the costs over the remaining lease term.

Leasehold Improvements

11. Leasehold improvements qualify for bonus depreciation for 2013, and the remaining basis is amortized over 15 years.

Stop and review! You have completed the outline for this subunit. Study questions 15 through 19 beginning on page 134.

6.4 DEPLETION

Depletion accounts for recovery of investment in natural resources property.

1. Only a person who has an economic interest in a (mineral) property is entitled to deductions for depletion.

    a. A person has an economic interest if (s)he

        1) Acquires by investment an interest in the mineral in place,
        2) Derives income from extraction of the mineral, and
        3) Looks to the extracted mineral for return of capital.

    b. Investment need not be in cash and could, for example, be in

        1) Land that ensures control over access to the mineral or
        2) Stationary equipment used to extract and produce the mineral.

Cost Depletion

2. Cost depletion is computed as follows:

[Adjusted basis in mineral property ÷ Estimated mineral units available at year's start] × Mineral units sold during year

NOTE: The total deductions are limited to unrecovered capital investment.

Percentage Depletion

3. Percentage depletion, which allows deduction in excess of capital investment, is the lower of

    a. 50% of the person's TI before depletion (100% for oil and gas) or

    b. A percentage (specified by statute) of gross income from the property less related rents or royalties paid or incurred.

4. For mineral property, the taxpayer generally must use the method that gives the largest deduction.

Stop and review! You have completed the outline for this subunit. Study questions 20 and 21 on page 136.

6.5 DEPRECIATION RECAPTURE

1. Secs. 1231, 1245, and 1250 recharacterize gain or loss. Sec. 1245 also accelerates recognition of certain installment gain that would otherwise be deferred.

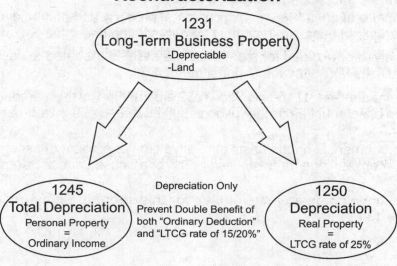

Figure 6-1

Sec. 1245 Ordinary Income

2. Gain on the disposition of Sec. 1245 property is ordinary income to the extent of the lesser of all depreciation taken or gain realized. The realized gain in excess of the depreciation taken may be treated as a gain from the sale or exchange of Sec. 1231 property.

    a. Sec. 1245 property generally is depreciable personal property.

        1) It is tangible or intangible depreciable personal property; recovery property, including specified real property; and tax benefit property.

    b. Other tangible property (excluding a building or its structural components) includes property used as an integral part of a trade or business, e.g., manufacturing or production equipment used in a trade or business.

    c. Intangible amortizable personal Sec. 1245 property examples include

        1) Leaseholds of Sec. 1245 property
        2) Professional athletic contracts, e.g., baseball
        3) Patents
        4) Goodwill acquired in connection with the acquisition of a trade or business
        5) Covenant not to compete

    d. Particular types of property are treated as Sec. 1245 property due to an attributable tax benefit. An example is amortized pollution control facilities.

Sec. 1250 Ordinary Income (OI)

3. Sec. 1250 property is all depreciable real property that is not Sec. 1245 property, such as a building or its structural components.

    a. Sec. 1250 property is subject to its own recapture rules. For the two items listed below, the aggregate gain realized on the sale or disposition of Sec. 1250 property is ordinary income.

        1) For corporations, the gain must be computed under both Sec. 1245 and Sec. 1250. If Sec. 1245 gain is larger than Sec. 1250 gain, 20% of the difference is characterized as ordinary income (see Section 291).
        2) For property held less than 1 year, all depreciation is recaptured.

    b. Land is not Sec. 1250 property, but leases of land are Sec. 1250 intangible properties. Certain improvements to land may be treated as land, e.g., dams and irrigation systems.

    c. Examples of Sec. 1250 property include shopping malls, an apartment or office building, low-income housing, rented portions of residences, and escalators or elevators (placed in service after 1986).

    d. Recapture of post-1986 residential rental property and nonresidential real property is not required because they must be depreciated under the S-L method.

4. Income received or accrued for more than one asset is allocated to each asset by agreement, by FMV, or by the residual method.

    a. To compute Sec. 1245 and Sec. 1250 ordinary income, an amount realized allocable to an asset must be further allocated to each use of a mixed-use asset for each tax year.

    b. Apportionment is on the basis of relative time or amount of asset usage, e.g., 5% of automobile usage for business or 50% of a house used as rental property.

Gift Property

5. Neither Sec. 1245 nor Sec. 1250 applies to a gift disposition.

   a. Any gain realized by the donee upon a subsequent taxable disposition is subject to Sec. 1245 and Sec. 1250 characterization up to the sum of (1) any potential Sec. 1245 and Sec. 1250 OI at the time of the gift and (2) any Sec. 1245 and Sec. 1250 OI potential arising between gift and subsequent disposition.

Inherited Property

6. Neither Sec. 1245 nor Sec. 1250 applies to a disposition by bequest, devise, or intestate succession.

   a. Exceptions. Sec. 1245 and Sec. 1250 OI are recognized for a transfer at death to the extent of any income in respect of a decedent (IRD).

      1) Sec. 1245 OI potential also results from depreciation allowed to a decedent because the depreciation does not carry over to the transferee.

Sec. 1231 Property

7. Unlike the recapture provisions in Secs. 1245 and 1250, Sec. 1231 is beneficial to the taxpayer. When Sec. 1231 property gains exceed losses (a net Sec. 1231 gain), each gain or loss is treated as being from the sale of a long-term capital asset. However, if Sec. 1231 property losses exceed gains (a net Sec. 1231 loss), each gain or loss is considered ordinary.

   a. Sec. 1231 property is property held for more than 1 year and includes

      1) All real or depreciable property used in a trade or business
      2) Involuntarily converted capital assets held in connection with a trade or business or in a transaction entered into for a profit

   b. Examples of Sec. 1231 property include apartment buildings, parking lots, manufacturing equipment, and involuntarily converted investment artwork.

   c. Examples of property that is not Sec. 1231 property include personal-use property and inventory.

   d. Sec. 1231 has a two-step test:

      1) Step 1 -- Determine net gain or loss from all casualties or thefts of Sec. 1231 property for the tax year. Gain or loss from involuntary conversions by other than casualty or theft is included in Step 2 but not Step 1.

         a) If the result is a net loss, each gain or loss is treated as ordinary income or loss.
         b) If the result is a net gain, each gain or loss is included in Step 2.

      2) Step 2 -- Determine net gain or loss from all dispositions of Sec. 1231 property for the year, including the property included in Step 1 only if Step 1 resulted in a net gain.

         a) If the result is a net loss, each gain or loss is treated as ordinary income or loss.
         b) If the result is a net gain, each gain or loss is treated as a long-term capital gain or loss.

Allocation

    e.   Allocation is required when Sec. 1245 or Sec. 1250 property is also Sec. 1231 property and only a portion of gain recognized is Sec. 1245 or Sec. 1250 OI.

EXAMPLE

The taxpayer sold a second residence for $800,000. The land had a cost of $100,000, and the house had a cost of $300,000. The selling price was allocated as follows: $200,000 to the land and $600,000 to the house. The taxpayer also sold a residential rental building and land for $1,200,000. The land had a basis of $200,000, and the building had a basis of $200,000. The building cost $400,000 and had been depreciated using accelerated depreciation under ACRS. The excess of accelerated depreciation over straight line was $50,000. The selling prices of the land and building were $400,000 and $800,000, respectively. In addition, the taxpayer had a $600,000 casualty loss on a business-use aircraft.

	Personal Use		Prod. of Income/Bus.		
	Land	Improvements	Land	Depreciable	Total
Cost	$100,000	$300,000	$200,000	$ 400,000	$1,000,000
Depreciation taken	0	0	0	(200,000)	
Amount realized	200,000	600,000	400,000	800,000	2,000,000
Gain realized	100,000	300,000	200,000	600,000	1,200,000
Sec. 1250 OI				$ 50,000	
Sec. 1231 gain				550,000	
Other Sec. 1231 loss (casualty 100% business-use aircraft)				$(600,000)	
Sec. 1231 ordinary loss				(50,000)	
LTCG	$100,000	$300,000	$200,000	$ 0	$ 600,000

- The taxpayer has a $100,000 gain ($200,000 – $100,000) on the sale of the personal land.
- There is a $300,000 gain ($600,000 – $300,000) on the sale of the second residence.
- The business land has a $200,000 gain ($400,000 – $200,000).
- The residential rental building has a $600,000 gain ($800,000 – $200,000).
  - The $50,000 accelerated depreciation over the straight-line depreciation is recaptured as ordinary income.
- The remaining $550,000 gain on the rental property is offset by the business casualty loss, creating an ordinary loss of $50,000 ($550,000 – $600,000).
  - The $50,000 ordinary income from the depreciation recapture is offset by the $50,000 Sec. 1231 ordinary loss.

---

    f.   The installment method can apply to Sec. 1231 property.

        1)   Sec. 1231 merely characterizes gain or loss.

        2)   Any Sec. 1231 gain that is recharacterized as capital gain will first consist of 28% gain, then 25% gain, and finally 15% gain.

Recapture

    g.   Net gain on Sec. 1231 property is treated as ordinary income to the extent of unrecaptured net Sec. 1231 losses from preceding tax years.

        1)   Unrecaptured net Sec. 1231 losses are the total of net Sec. 1231 losses for the last 5 tax years, reduced by net Sec. 1231 gains characterized as ordinary income under Sec. 1231(c).

        2)   Sec. 1245 and 1250 recapture is computed before Sec. 1231 recapture, but Sec. 1231 recapture is computed before Steps 1 and 2 on the previous page.

Stop and review! You have completed the outline for this subunit. Study questions 22 through 30 beginning on page 136.

QUESTIONS

6.1 Depreciation Methods

1. In 2011, Nancy leased a building for use in her business. She signed a 6-year lease with an option for an additional 3 years. In 2013, she made leasehold improvements to the building, costing a total of $8,200. Nancy must

    A. Amortize the improvements over the remaining term of the initial lease period.

    B. Amortize the improvements over the remaining term of the initial lease period, plus the option period.

    C. Depreciate the improvements using the modified cost recovery system (MACRS).

    D. Deduct the cost of the improvements as a current expense.

Answer (C) is correct.
    REQUIRED: The proper method of capital recovery for leasehold improvements.
    DISCUSSION: The cost of an addition or improvement made by the lessee to real property subject to MACRS is depreciated in the same manner as the property would be if the property had been placed in service at the same time as the addition or improvement without regard to the lease term.

2. In order to determine the MACRS deduction using the percentage tables, all of the following must be determined except

    A. The basis of the property.

    B. The recovery period.

    C. The declining balance rate.

    D. The placed-in-service date.

Answer (C) is correct.
    REQUIRED: The item not used in the MACRS percentage tables.
    DISCUSSION: The percentage tables are based on the depreciation method, recovery period, and convention. An applicable percentage is determined each year by matching the year of the recovery period with the placed-in-service date. The percentages in the tables are applied to the unadjusted basis of the property each year to determine the MACRS deduction. Any declining balance rate is built into the tables.

3. In 2011, Paige signed a 6-year lease for a building to use in her business. In 2013, she installed shelves and made other leasehold improvements to the building for a total of $3,200. She can

    A. Deduct $3,200 as a current expense.

    B. Depreciate the $3,200 using MACRS.

    C. Depreciate the $3,200 using the straight-line method.

    D. Amortize the $3,200 over the remaining term of the lease.

Answer (B) is correct.
    REQUIRED: The proper method of capital recovery for leasehold improvements.
    DISCUSSION: The cost of an addition or improvement made by the lessee to real property subject to MACRS is depreciated in the same manner as the property would be if the property had been placed in service at the same time as the addition or improvement without regard to the lease term.
    Answer (A) is incorrect. Paige cannot deduct the entire $3,200 in 2013 because the shelves are depreciable personal property. Answer (C) is incorrect. Straight-line depreciation is the basis reduced for salvage value divided by the useful life of the asset. This method is not allowed for leasehold improvements for tax purposes. This answer choice is not referring to MACRS straight-line, which uses a GDS/ADS recovery period and ignores salvage value. Answer (D) is incorrect. The shelves are depreciated using MACRS, not the term of the lease.

4. Burt bought a 2013 BMW 525i for $64,000 on March 2, 2013. He will use the automobile 100% of the time in his business. The recovery period for passenger autos is 5 years. Burt elected out of additional first-year depreciation. What is Burt's depreciation for the year 2013?

    A. $12,800

    B. $3,160

    C. $3,200

    D. $640

Answer (B) is correct.
    REQUIRED: The amount of depreciation allowed for an automobile used 100% in business.
    DISCUSSION: If qualified business use exceeds 50% in the tax year in which listed property is placed in service, Sec. 179 current expensing and MACRS depreciation are allowable with respect to the qualified business use. However, in addition to the business-use requirements, limits are placed on the maximum MACRS deduction allowable for most passenger automobiles. For a vehicle placed in service in 2013, the depreciation limit in its first recovery year is $3,160 when election out of additional bonus depreciation is taken.
    Answer (A) is incorrect. The amount of $12,800 is depreciation calculated under MACRS for the automobile without taking the limit of $3,160 into account. Answer (C) is incorrect. Burt may take depreciation of $3,160 since regular MACRS exceeds the limit. Answer (D) is incorrect. Burt may take depreciation of $3,160 since regular MACRS exceeds the limit.

5. During 2013, Nancy, a calendar-year taxpayer, acquired and placed in service the following business assets:

January:	Delivery trucks	$ 50,000
March:	Warehouse building	150,000
June:	Computer system	30,000
September:	Automobile	30,000
November:	Office equipment	90,000

Which convention(s) can Nancy use to figure depreciation for 2013?

A. Mid-quarter for all assets except the warehouse building, which uses mid-month.

B. Half-year for all of the assets.

C. Mid-quarter for all of the assets.

D. Half-year for all assets except the warehouse building, which uses mid-month.

6. The K&L Partnership owned the following tangible property. Which one is not considered listed property?

A. An automobile.

B. A video camera.

C. A computer used for personal use 40% of the time.

D. A truck weighing 17,000 pounds designed to carry cargo.

7. The D&L Partnership bought a truck for $28,000 and a trailer for $4,000 on January 10, 2011, to be used in the business. D&L uses the straight-line method and a 5-year life to recover its cost for tangible property. In 2011 and 2012, D&L took depreciation of $6,400 and $4,600, respectively. In January 2013, D&L discovered that it under-claimed depreciation of $1,800 on its tax return for 2012. What can D&L do to recover the $1,800?

A. Claim $8,200 depreciation in 2013.

B. Make a pro-rata adjustment to the basis of the equipment.

C. Amend the tax return for 2012.

D. It cannot be recovered.

8. Most tangible depreciable property falls within the general rule of MACRS. However, the law requires use of the ADS for certain property. ADS must be used for all of the following except

A. Tax-exempt use property.

B. Tax-exempt bond-financed property.

C. Tangible personal property.

D. Tangible property used predominantly outside the United States during the year.

Answer (A) is correct.

REQUIRED: The convention(s) to be used in calculating depreciation.

DISCUSSION: Under the MACRS rules, the mid-quarter convention must be used for all personal property placed in service during the year if substantial property was placed in service during the last 3 months of the year [Sec. 168(d)(3)]. Substantial property is defined as greater than 40% of the aggregate bases of property placed in service during the year. The $90,000 office equipment constitutes 45% ($90,000 ÷ $200,000) of all personal property placed in service, so the mid-quarter convention must be used. A mid-month convention is used in the year of acquisition for real property. Therefore, the mid-month convention is used for the warehouse building.

Answer (B) is incorrect. The mid-quarter convention must be used for the personal property, whereas the mid-month convention must be used for the warehouse. Answer (C) is incorrect. The mid-month convention must be used for the warehouse. Answer (D) is incorrect. The mid-quarter convention must be used for the personal property.

Answer (D) is correct.

REQUIRED: The item that is not considered listed property.

DISCUSSION: Depreciation of listed property is limited by reference to qualified business use. Listed property includes the following: passenger automobiles, other transportation vehicles (e.g., truck under 6,000 lbs.), entertainment or recreational property (e.g., video camera), and computers and peripherals not exclusively used at a regular place of business (e.g., home office).

Answer (C) is correct.

REQUIRED: The recovery of under-claimed depreciation.

DISCUSSION: Publication 946 states, "If you deducted an incorrect amount of depreciation in any year, you may be able to make a correction by filing an amended return for that year. . . . You can file an amended return to correct the amount of depreciation claimed for any property in any of the following situations.

- You claimed the incorrect amount because of a mathematical error made in any year.
- You claimed the incorrect amount because of a posting error made in any year.
- You have not adopted a method of accounting for property. . . ."

In addition, even if you do not claim depreciation you are entitled to deduct, "you must still reduce the basis of the property by the full amount of depreciation allowable."

Answer (A) is incorrect. The under-claimed depreciation may not be added to current-year depreciation. Answer (B) is incorrect. The basis of the property must be reduced by the full amount of the depreciation D&L was entitled to take. Answer (D) is incorrect. The under-claimed depreciation can be recovered by filing an amended return.

Answer (C) is correct.

REQUIRED: The property not required to use ADS.

DISCUSSION: MACRS provides two systems for depreciating property: the general depreciation system (GDS) and the alternative depreciation system (ADS). Although GDS is used for most property, ADS is required by law for any tangible property used predominantly outside the United States, any tax-exempt use property, and any tax-exempt bond-financed property. Use of ADS for tangible personal property is an election, not a requirement.

6.2 Sec. 179 Expense

9. The maximum Sec. 179 expense you can elect to deduct for property you placed in service in tax year 2013 is

A. $2,000,000

B. $250,000

C. $500,000

D. $25,000

Answer (C) is correct.
REQUIRED: The maximum Sec. 179 expense for 2013.
DISCUSSION: A person may elect to deduct all or part of the cost of Sec. 179 property. Sec. 179 expense is treated as depreciation and it reduces the basis in the property prior to any computation for depreciation for the year. The Sec. 179 expense for 2013 is $500,000.
Answer (A) is incorrect. The Sec. 179 expense for 2013 is $500,000. The maximum amount of investment allowed is $2,000,000. Answer (B) is incorrect. The maximum Sec. 179 expense in 2008 and 2009 was $250,000. Answer (D) is incorrect. The Sec. 179 expense for 2013 is $500,000.

10. In 2013, Mary Jane placed in service a machine that cost $2,320,000. If she placed no other Sec. 179 property in service during the year and forgoes additional first-year depreciation, how much is her Sec. 179 maximum dollar limit?

A. $250,000

B. $500,000

C. $0

D. $180,000

Answer (D) is correct.
REQUIRED: The allowable Sec. 179 expense deduction.
DISCUSSION: Sec. 179 allows a taxpayer to treat up to $500,000 of the cost of Sec. 179 property acquired in 2013 as an expense rather than as a capital expenditure. There are certain limitations that can reduce the allowable deduction. One limitation is that the amount deductible under Sec. 179 must be reduced by the amount by which the cost of Sec. 179 property placed in service during the year exceeds $2,000,000. Mary Jane's deduction is reduced from $500,000 to $180,000 [$500,000 – ($2,320,000 – $2,000,000)].
Answer (A) is incorrect. The amount of $250,000 is the 2009 limit before reduction for purchases exceeding $2,000,000. Answer (B) is incorrect. The entire $500,000 must be reduced by personal property placed in service exceeding $2,000,000 and limited to taxable income. Answer (C) is incorrect. A Sec. 179 deduction is available for 2013.

11. James bought and placed in service computer equipment in 2013. He paid $15,000 cash and received a $3,000 trade-in allowance for his old computer equipment. James had an adjusted basis of $4,000 in the old computer equipment. He used both the old and new computer equipment 90% for business and 10% for personal purposes. His allowable Sec. 179 expense deduction is

A. $16,200

B. $13,500

C. $17,100

D. $15,000

Answer (B) is correct.
REQUIRED: The allowable amount of Sec. 179 expense.
DISCUSSION: Only 90% of the boot given is eligible for the Sec. 179 deduction ($13,500 = $15,000 × 90%).
Answer (A) is incorrect. The amount of $16,200 is 90% of both boot given and the $3,000 trade-in allowance. Only the $15,000 cash (boot given) qualifies for Sec.179 expense deduction ($13,500 = $15,000 × 90%). Answer (C) is incorrect. The amount of $17,100 is 90% of $19,000, which is the sum of the boot given and the AB of the old computer. Only the $15,000 cash (boot given) qualifies for Sec.179 expense deduction ($13,500 = $15,000 × 90%). Answer (D) is incorrect. The amount of $15,000 is 100% of boot given; however, only 90% of boot given is eligible for Sec.179 deduction ($13,500 = $15,000 × 90%).

12. On January 15, 2013, Amber purchased a car for $20,000. She used the car 75% for business during 2013. What is the maximum Sec. 179 deduction and depreciation Amber may elect to claim on her income tax return for 2013, assuming she forgoes additional first-year depreciation?

A. $2,370

B. $3,160

C. $15,000

D. $20,000

Answer (A) is correct.
REQUIRED: The Sec. 179 expense deduction in 2013.
DISCUSSION: In 2013, Sec. 179 allows a taxpayer to treat up to $500,000 of the cost of Sec. 179 property acquired as an expense. Only the 75% portion of the automobile used for business will qualify, however. Therefore, the Sec. 179 expense would normally be $15,000 ($20,000 × 75%).
But Sec. 280F limits the first-year capital recovery deduction for automobiles to $3,160 for 2013 (Rev. Proc. 2013-21). The capital recovery deductions include the amount expensed under Sec. 179 and depreciation. This amount must be reduced by personal use for the automobile during the year. The redetermined amount is the limit times the percentage of business/investment use during the year ($2,370 = $3,160 × 75%).
Answer (B) is incorrect. The deduction is limited to the percentage used in business. Answer (C) is incorrect. The limit on first-year capital recovery deduction for automobiles is $3,160. Answer (D) is incorrect. The limit on first-year capital recovery deduction for automobiles is $3,160, and only the percentage used in business is allowed.

13. Which of the following is a true statement concerning depreciation of automobiles placed in service during 2013?

A. The amount of depreciation and Sec. 179 expense is limited to $11,160 in the first year.

B. The amount of depreciation is limited to $11,160 per year.

C. If the automobile is used 50% or less for business use, no depreciation is allowed.

D. If the use of an automobile for business decreases to 50% or less after the first year, only the current and subsequent years' depreciation will be affected.

Answer (A) is correct.
    REQUIRED: The true statement concerning depreciation of automobiles placed in service in 2013.
    DISCUSSION: Sec. 280F limits the depreciation on automobiles. The maximum amount of depreciation deductible in the first year for automobiles acquired in 2013 is $11,160 (Rev. Proc. 2013-21) if no election out of the bonus depreciation is made. This amount is reduced if business use is less than 100%.
    Answer (B) is incorrect. Depreciation after the first year is limited to $5,100 in the second year, $3,050 in the third year, and $1,875 per year thereafter. Answer (C) is incorrect. Depreciation for an automobile used 50% or less in business is computed by the alternative depreciation system. Answer (D) is incorrect. If an automobile's use decreases to 50% or less in subsequent years, any depreciation in prior years in excess of the alternative depreciation system is included in gross income for the years in which the business use decreased to 50% or less.

14. On January 1, 2013, Sally Jefferson purchased an auto for $18,000. Her business use was 60% during 2013. She is electing $1,000 Sec. 179 deduction on the auto, but is electing not to claim any bonus depreciation. What is her total deduction for calendar tax year 2013?

A. $18,000

B. $3,160

C. $10,800

D. $1,896

Answer (D) is correct.
    REQUIRED: The depreciation limit on automobiles placed in service during 2013.
    DISCUSSION: In 2013, Sec. 179 allows a taxpayer to treat up to $500,000 of the cost of Sec. 179 property acquired as an expense. Only the 60% portion of the automobile used for business will qualify, however. Therefore, the Sec. 179 expense would normally be $10,800 ($18,000 × 60%).
    But Sec. 280F limits the first-year capital recovery deduction for automobiles to $3,160 for 2013. The capital recovery deductions include the amount expensed under Sec. 179 and depreciation. This amount must be reduced by personal use for the automobile during the year. The redetermined amount is the limit times the percentage of business/investment use during the year ($1,896 = $3,160 × .60).
    Answer (A) is incorrect. The depreciation limit for 2013 must be reduced for business use only. Additionally, automobiles are limited to $3,160 of first-year recovery for 2013. Answer (B) is incorrect. The depreciation limit for 100% business-use cars in 2013 is $3,160. This amount must be reduced by personal use for the automobile. Answer (C) is incorrect. Automobiles are limited to $3,160 of first-year recovery for 2013.

6.3 Amortization

15. Jeanne incurred start-up costs for her new business, which opened October 1, 2013. The costs were for advertising of $1,000, a market analysis survey of $2,500, employee training costs of $6,000, and travel costs for securing prospective distributions of $2,500. What is the maximum amount of the amortizable costs that may be deducted in 2013?

A. $12,000

B. $5,000

C. $5,117

D. $800

Answer (C) is correct.
    REQUIRED: The deduction of amortizable start-up expenses.
    DISCUSSION: Taxpayers may elect to deduct start-up expenditures paid or accrued up to $5,000 in the tax year the trade or business begins. A taxpayer is deemed to have made the election. The $5,000 deduction amount is reduced dollar-for-dollar when start-up costs exceed $50,000. Taxpayers must amortize the remaining balance over 180 months.

Advertising	$ 1,000
Market analysis survey	2,500
Employee training costs	6,000
Travel costs	2,500
Total start-up expenditures	$12,000
Initial deduction	$ 5,000
Current-year amortization ($7,000 × 3/180 months)	$ 117
Total 2013 deduction	$ 5,117

    Answer (A) is incorrect. After the initial $5,000 deduction, the remaining cost must be amortized over 180 months. Answer (B) is incorrect. Jeanne is able to include the current year's amortization as well as the $5,000. Answer (D) is incorrect. The amount of $800 is 1 full year's amortization of the $12,000 and does not include the $5,000 initial deduction.

16. All of the following are considered Sec. 197 intangibles except

    A. Goodwill.

    B. An interest under an existing lease of tangible property.

    C. A trademark or trade name.

    D. Information bases, including lists or other information, regarding current or future customers.

Answer (B) is correct.
    REQUIRED: The item that is not a Sec. 197 intangible.
    DISCUSSION: The following intangibles are Sec. 197 intangibles: goodwill, going-concern value, and covenants not to compete entered into in connection with a trade or business acquisition; workforce in place; information base; know-how; any customer- or supplier-based intangible; any license, permit, or other right granted by a governmental unit or agency; and any franchise, trademark, or trade name.

17. Michael James purchased a travel agency on July 1, 2013, and immediately took over the business. The purchase contract included the following items as part of the purchase price:

- Goodwill valued at $60,000.
- Workforce in place valued at $30,000.
- Trademark valued at $60,000.
- Government permit valued at $30,000.

What is the proper amount of Michael's Internal Revenue Code Sec. 197 amortization expense for 2013, assuming Michael is a calendar-year taxpayer?

    A. $90,000

    B. $30,000

    C. $6,000

    D. $12,000

Answer (C) is correct.
    REQUIRED: The amount of amortization expense of intangibles for 2013.
    DISCUSSION: Sec. 197 states that the cost of certain intangibles acquired in connection with the conduct of a trade or business or income-producing activity is amortized over a 15-year period, beginning with the month in which the intangible is acquired. The total cost of the intangibles equals $180,000 ($60,000 goodwill + $30,000 workforce + $60,000 trademark + $30,000 government permit). This amount is amortized over 180 months. Michael James may only deduct $6,000 in 2013 [$180,000 (6 months ÷ 180 months)].
    Answer (A) is incorrect. Half of the total amount of intangibles capitalized is $90,000. These intangibles must be amortized over the 180-month period. Answer (B) is incorrect. The amortization period is not 6 years. Answer (D) is incorrect. The business was not acquired until July 1, 2013. Thus, only 6 months of amortization expense can be taken in 2013.

18. The Adams & Baker Partnership bought Nico's B&B restaurant, which was located in an exclusive section of town. The goodwill associated with the purchase of this business was valued at $60,000. Per Sec. 197, what is the number of years over which goodwill can be amortized?

    A. 5 years.

    B. 10 years.

    C. 15 years.

    D. 20 years.

Answer (C) is correct.
    REQUIRED: The number of years over which goodwill can be amortized.
    DISCUSSION: The cost of certain intangibles acquired in connection with the conduct of a trade or business or income-producing activity is amortized over a 15-year period, beginning with the month in which the intangible is acquired. Qualified intangibles include acquired goodwill and going-concern value.

19. On March 1, 2013, you purchased a business with the following asset values for $250,000:

Equipment	$175,000
Goodwill	60,000
Cash	15,000

What is the amortization deduction only for 2013?

    A. $333

    B. $0

    C. $28,320

    D. $3,330

Answer (D) is correct.
    REQUIRED: The amortization in the first year of business.
    DISCUSSION: The cost of certain intangibles acquired in connection with the conduct of a trade or business or income-producing activity is amortized over a 15-year period, beginning with the month in which the intangible is acquired. Qualified intangibles include acquired goodwill and going-concern value. The amortization deduction is determined as follows:

Goodwill	$60,000
Divided by years	÷ 15
Amortization deduction per year	$ 4,000
Multiplied by fraction of year	× 10/12
Amortization deduction	$ 3,330

    Answer (A) is incorrect. The deduction per month is $333. Answer (B) is incorrect. An amortization deduction is allowed for 2013. Answer (C) is incorrect. Only the goodwill is amortizable.

6.4 Depletion

20. Mark, a 50% partner in the X & Y Partnership, uses the percentage method to compute his depletion allowance for the gas and oil property owned by the partnership. His allocable share of the property is $100,000. The fair market value of the property also is $100,000. His taxable income for 2013 equals $65,000. The percentage depletion rate is 15% for natural gas and oil sold. X & Y is a small producer, and the average daily production does not exceed the depletable oil and gas quantity. Mark's share of the gross sale of oil and gas deposits was $30,000. What is Mark's depletion deduction for 2013?

A. $4,500

B. $9,750

C. $9,000

D. $5,250

Answer (A) is correct.

REQUIRED: The amount of depletion deduction for a partner using the percentage method.

DISCUSSION: Percentage depletion, which allows deduction in excess of capital investment, is the lower of 50% of the person's TI before depletion (100% in the case of oil and gas) or a percentage (specified by statute) of gross income from the property less related rents or royalties paid or incurred. Publication 535 states, "If you are an independent producer or royalty owner, you figure percentage depletion using a rate of 15% of the gross income from the property based on your average daily production of domestic crude oil or domestic natural gas up to your depletable oil or natural gas quantity." Accordingly, 15% of the gross profit is $4,500 ($30,000 × 15%). Since $4,500 is less than $65,000 (100% of taxable income limit), $4,500 is the amount of depletion Mark may take in 2013.

Answer (B) is incorrect. This amount is 15% of 65% of Mark's taxable income. Answer (C) is incorrect. This amount is 30% of the partnership's gross profit. Answer (D) is incorrect. This amount is 17.5% of the partnership's gross profit.

21. Which of the following would not qualify for a depletion deduction?

A. Gas well.

B. Timber lot.

C. Oil refinery.

D. Stone quarry.

Answer (C) is correct.

REQUIRED: The property not qualifying for a depletion deduction.

DISCUSSION: Depletion accounts for recovery of investment in natural resource property. A gas well, timber lot, and stone quarry are all natural resource properties and thereby qualify for the depletion deduction. The oil refinery, however, is a facility used to refine oil obtained from mineral property. It is depreciable property and does not qualify for the depletion deduction.

6.5 Depreciation Recapture

22. Maria owns a custom curtain/drapery business. She purchased three new sewing machines and, in a separate transaction, sold her three old machines for $6,000. She had bought the old machines for $5,000 and had properly claimed depreciation of $3,000. What is the amount and character of Maria's gain?

A. $0 ordinary gain and $4,000 Sec. 1231 gain.

B. $2,000 ordinary gain and $4,000 Sec. 1231 gain.

C. $3,000 ordinary gain and $1,000 Sec. 1231 gain.

D. $4,000 ordinary gain and $0 Sec. 1231 gain.

Answer (C) is correct.

REQUIRED: The amount and character of gain.

DISCUSSION: A gain on the sale or other disposition of Sec. 1245 property is taxed as ordinary income to the extent of all depreciation or amortization deductions previously claimed on the property. The amount treated as ordinary income is the lower of the excess of the amount realized or fair market value over the adjusted basis of the Sec. 1245 property or the previously allowed or allowable depreciation or amortization. Maria realizes a $4,000 gain on the sale and had previously allowable depreciation of $3,000. Therefore, Maria recognizes $3,000 of ordinary income and $1,000 of Sec. 1231 gain.

Answer (A) is incorrect. The sewing machines are subject to Sec. 1245 recapture. Answer (B) is incorrect. The realized gain is only $4,000. Answer (D) is incorrect. The previously allowable depreciation is less than the realized gain.

23. In 2010, Ben purchased a truck for $15,000. In 2010, he claimed a $3,000 Sec. 179 deduction and began depreciating the truck. He sold the truck in 2013 for $13,000. Prior to the sale, Ben claimed MACRS deductions of $8,000. Had Ben claimed straight-line depreciation, he would have claimed $6,000 prior to the sale. What amount of gain on the sale is treated as ordinary income in 2013?

A. $2,000

B. $8,000

C. $9,000

D. $11,000

Answer (C) is correct.

REQUIRED: The amount and character of the gain on the sale of the truck.

DISCUSSION: Since this property is depreciable business property that is personal in nature, under Sec. 1245, any realized gain must be recognized as ordinary income to the extent of any depreciation previously taken. Ben realizes a $9,000 gain [$13,000 amount realized – ($15,000 basis – $11,000 depreciation)]. He will recapture $9,000 of this gain as ordinary income because the realized gain is less than the previously allowable depreciation ($11,000).

Answer (A) is incorrect. A truck is not Sec. 1250 property. Answer (B) is incorrect. Sec. 179 deductions are treated as previously allowable depreciation. Answer (D) is incorrect. The realized gain is less than the previously allowable depreciation.

24. Sam files a calendar-year return. In February 2011, he purchased and placed in service for 100% use in his business a light-duty truck (5-year property) for a cost of $10,000. He used the half-year convention and figured his MACRS deductions for the truck were $2,000 in 2011 and $3,200 in 2012. He did not take the Sec. 179 deduction on it. He sold the truck in May 2013 for $7,000. The MACRS deduction in 2013, the year of sale, is $960 (1/2 of $1,920). How much of the gain will be treated as ordinary income in 2013?

A. $3,160

B. $2,200

C. $3,840

D. None of the answers are correct.

Answer (A) is correct.
REQUIRED: The amount of gain treated as ordinary income.
DISCUSSION: Sam purchased the truck for $10,000 and took $6,160 in depreciation, leaving a basis of $3,840. The gain on the sale is $3,160. Under Sec. 1245, if the gain is less than the depreciation taken, the entire gain is reported as ordinary income.
Answer (B) is incorrect. Sam is allowed to decrease his basis in the truck by the MACRS deduction he took in 2013 ($960). Answer (C) is incorrect. The amount of $3,840 represents the basis, not the amount treated as ordinary income. Answer (D) is incorrect. Sam purchased the truck for $10,000 and took $6,160 in depreciation, leaving a basis of $3,840. The gain on the sale is $3,160. Under Sec. 1245, if the gain is less than the depreciation taken, the entire gain is reported as ordinary income.

25. A taxpayer acquired a rental house several years ago for $190,000. The taxpayer sold his rental house for $190,000 in May 2013. Under an accelerated method, the taxpayer's depreciation is $67,840. Under the S-L method, the taxpayer's depreciation is $64,960. How much Sec. 1250 gain did this taxpayer have classified as ordinary income when the house was sold?

A. $0

B. $2,880

C. $64,960

D. $67,840

Answer (A) is correct.
REQUIRED: The amount of Sec. 1250 gain that is recaptured as ordinary income.
DISCUSSION: Recapture of residential rental property as ordinary income is not required because it must be depreciated under the S-L method.
Answer (B) is incorrect. Accelerated depreciation does not apply to residential rental property. Answer (C) is incorrect. S-L depreciation is not recaptured if the property is held for more than 1 year. Answer (D) is incorrect. Recapture of residential rental property as ordinary income is not required because it must be depreciated under the S-L method.

26. During 2013, Wendy sold low-income housing property for $320,000. Her original purchase price was $275,000, and she had properly deducted $148,500 of depreciation. What is the amount and character of Wendy's gain?

	Ordinary Income	Sec. 1231 Gain
A.	$148,500	$45,000
B.	$0	$126,500
C.	$45,000	$148,500
D.	$0	$193,500

Answer (D) is correct.
REQUIRED: The amount and character of gain to be recognized on the sale of low-income housing.
DISCUSSION: Low-income housing is Sec. 1250 property. Under Sec. 1250, realized gain must be recognized as ordinary income to the extent of any depreciation taken in excess of depreciation under the straight-line method. This excess is $0. The realized gain on the sale of the property was $193,500, so the lesser of these two amounts is recognized as ordinary income. The remainder ($193,500) is treated as Sec. 1231 gain.
Answer (A) is incorrect. Only excess depreciation is ordinary income. Real property is depreciated under the S-L method. Answer (B) is incorrect. Realized gain is sale price minus the excess of purchase price over depreciation taken. Answer (C) is incorrect. Low-income housing is Sec. 1250 property and depreciated under the S-L method.

27. ABC Corp., a corporation that is not an S corporation, acquired a residential rental building on June 1, 2012, for $500,000. It sold the building March 1, 2013, for $700,000. In 2012, $9,850 of depreciation was deducted using the S-L method. What portion of ABC's gain is treated as ordinary income?

A. $0

B. $4,545

C. $9,850

D. $200,000

Answer (C) is correct.
REQUIRED: The allowed depreciation deduction.
DISCUSSION: The sale of the office building resulted in a realized gain of $200,000. The building is Sec. 1250 residential real property since it is excluded from Sec. 1245 property by Sec. 1245(a)(3) as in effect prior to the 1986 Tax Act. The depreciation for residential rental property is calculated using the S-L method; however, if held less than 1 year, all depreciation is recaptured as ordinary income.
Answer (A) is incorrect. The sale of the building results in Sec. 1231 gain less any depreciation recapture. Answer (B) is incorrect. The $4,545 for the first 3 months of 2013 was never taken. Answer (D) is incorrect. The ordinary income is the depreciation previously taken, not the realized gain.

28. Which of the following statements is not true concerning residential rental property placed in service in 2013?

- A. For property held less than 1 year, all depreciation is recaptured.
- B. Depreciation is determined using the S-L method.
- C. Depreciation is determined using an accelerated method.
- D. Recovery period is 27 1/2 years.

Answer (C) is correct.

REQUIRED: The false statement concerning residential rental property.

DISCUSSION: Only residential rental property placed in service prior to 1987 used accelerated depreciation. For property placed in service after 1987, the S-L method applies.

Answer (A) is incorrect. Depreciation is recaptured when the property is held for less than a year. Answer (B) is incorrect. All post-1986 residential rental property uses the S-L method. Answer (D) is incorrect. The S-L recovery period for residential rental property is 27 1/2 years.

29. With regard to Sec. 1250 and Sec. 1245 property, which of the following statements is false?

- A. Property may start out as Sec. 1250 property and later be converted into Sec. 1245 property. Once this conversion takes place, the property can never be reconverted into Sec. 1250 property.
- B. Under Sec. 1245, there is depreciation recapture on disposition by death.
- C. Sec. 1250 excludes disposition by gift from causing recapture. However, the depreciation potential carries over to the donee.
- D. Neither Sec. 1245 nor Sec. 1250 applies to a gift disposition.

Answer (B) is correct.

REQUIRED: The false statement regarding Sec. 1250 and Sec. 1245 property.

DISCUSSION: Under Sec. 1245(b)(2), depreciation recapture is not recognized on disposition by death.

Answer (A) is incorrect. Sec. 1250 property may later be converted into Sec. 1245 property. Answer (C) is incorrect. Sec. 1250 excludes disposition by gift from causing recapture. However, the depreciation potential carries over to the donee. Answer (D) is incorrect. Neither Sec. 1245 nor Sec. 1250 applies to a gift disposition.

30. With regard to Sec. 1250 and Sec. 1245 property, which of the following statements is false?

- A. Property may start out as Sec. 1250 property and later be converted into Sec. 1245 property. Once this conversion takes place, the property can never be reconverted into Sec. 1250 property.
- B. When a taxpayer dies, ordinary income because of depreciation must be reported on property that is transferred to his or her estate or beneficiary.
- C. When making a gift of property, the donor does not have to report on the transaction. However, if the donee sells the property in a disposition that is subject to recapture, the donee must take into account the depreciation the donor deducted in figuring the gain to be reported as ordinary income.
- D. A like-kind exchange will not result in the reporting of ordinary income because of depreciation unless money or unlike property is also received in the transaction.

Answer (B) is correct.

REQUIRED: The false statement regarding Sec. 1245 and Sec. 1250 property.

DISCUSSION: The depreciation recapture rules do not apply in the case of disposition by gift or to transfers at death. The beneficiary will recognize the amount of ordinary income upon later sale.

Use the additional questions in Gleim **EA Test Prep** to create Practice Exams that emulate Prometric!

STUDY UNIT SEVEN
CREDITS, LOSSES, AND ADDITIONAL TAXES

(11 pages of outline)

This is the final study unit to discuss reductions in tax liability that apply to all business entities. Business-specific credits may reduce an entity's tax due amount, while losses may reduce an entity's taxable income. Losses come from operations, casualty, and theft. When the activity is not considered for profit, it is a hobby and is subject to specific limits.

This study unit concludes with a brief explanation of additional business-related taxes for heavy vehicle use, farmers, and tanning services.

7.1 GENERAL BUSINESS CREDIT

Tax credits are used to achieve policy objectives, such as encouraging energy conservation. A $1 credit reduces gross tax liability by $1.

1. Most credits are nonrefundable, meaning that once tax liability reaches zero, no more credits can be taken to produce refunds.

2. The General Business Credit (GBC) is a set of several credits commonly available to businesses (Form 3800).

   a. The GBC includes, among others, credits for investment, research, work opportunity, disabled access, alcohol fuels, pension plan start-up, childcare facilities, and alternative motor vehicles.

Overall Limit [Sec. 38(c)]

3. The GBC is limited to net income tax minus the greater of the tentative minimum tax or 25% of net regular tax over $25,000.

   a. On Form 1040, the regular tax (line 44) is the tax computed on taxable income.

   b. The income tax (line 46) is the regular tax (line 44) plus the AMT (line 45).

   c. The net income tax is the income tax (line 46) minus the nonrefundable credits other than the GBC.

   d. The GBC will not be available when the tentative minimum tax exceeds the regular tax.

EXAMPLE

A taxpayer has a regular tax of $60,000 and a tentative minimum tax of $57,000. The taxpayer also has $10,000 of potential general business credits. Since the regular tax exceeds the tentative minimum tax, there is no alternative minimum tax. The taxpayer is allowed a General Business Credit computed as follows:

$60,000	Regular tax
+ -0-	Alternative minimum tax
$60,000	Income tax
− -0-	Nonrefundable credits other than General Business Credit
$60,000	Net income tax
−57,000	Greater of tentative minimum tax or 25% of net regular tax over $25,000
$ 3,000	General Business Credit

---

e. Net income tax is the sum of regular income tax and minimum tax liability, reduced by nonrefundable credits other than those that comprise the General Business Credit.

f. Tentative minimum tax is an amount used in computing the alternative minimum tax.

g. Net regular tax is the taxpayer's regular income tax liability (i.e., without alternative minimum tax) reduced by nonrefundable credits.

h. Excess over the limit may be allowable as a current deduction to the extent it is attributable to the Work Opportunity Credit and the Alcohol Fuels Credit.

i. Any excess of the combined GBC over the limit (and not allowed as a current deduction) may be carried back 1 year and forward 20 as a credit. It is carried to the earliest year to which it could be used, then to the next, and so on.

Small Employer Insurance Credit

4. Effective for tax years beginning after December 31, 2009, and before 2014, the Small Employer Health Insurance Tax Credit provides a 35% credit for the cost of premiums paid toward health insurance coverage.

a. The small employer must contribute at least 50% of the premium cost.

1) Any premium paid under a salary reduction arrangement is not treated as paid by the employer for purposes of the credit.

b. The **full** credit is available to small employers with 10 or fewer employees and average annual wages of less than $25,000 (2013).

c. The credit is reduced by 6.667% for each full-time employee in excess of 10 and by 4% of each $1,000 that average annual compensation exceeds $25,000 (2013).

d. A sole proprietor, a partner, a shareholder owning more than 2% of an S corporation, and any owner of more than 5% of other businesses are not employees for purposes of the credit. Family members of any business are generally excluded. Seasonal employees who work for 120 days or fewer for the business in a year are excluded.

e. The number of full-time equivalent employees is basically the total number of hours worked by all employees, divided by 2,080. The result, if not a whole number, is then rounded to the next lowest whole number (IR-2010-48).

1) The total hours for any single employee will not exceed 2,080.

f. The maximum credit for a tax-exempt employer is 25% for tax years beginning in 2010 through 2013.

g. The credit reduces the deduction for health insurance premiums.

Disabled Access Credit (Sec. 44)

5. A credit for a portion of qualifying expenditures to provide access to disabled persons is available as a General Business Credit.

a. Eligible persons are small businesses, including partnerships and S corporations, that, during the preceding tax year, did not have either more than 30 full-time employees or more than $1 million in gross receipts.

b. Examples of qualifying access expenditures are payments to remove physical barriers, to modify equipment, and to install access ramps.

c. The credit is equal to 50% of qualifying expenditures that fall between a $250 threshold and a $10,250 cap.

d. The credit is limited to $5,000 [($10,250 – $250) × 50%] for the tax year.

e. The credit is not allowed for new buildings.

f. The credit is computed on Form 8826, *Disabled Access Credit*.

Work Opportunity Tax Credit (WOTC) (Sec. 51)

6. Employers may take a credit equal to 40% of the first $6,000 paid to each employee from certain targeted groups. The credit is taken on Form 5884.

    a. The employees must work at least 400 hours during the year.

        1) If an employee works more than 120 hours but less than 400, the credit is reduced to 25% of the first $6,000 paid to each employee.

        2) No credit is available for employees who work less than 120 hours.

    b. If the employee is a long-term (LT) family assistance recipient, the credit is equal to 40% of the first $10,000 in wages.

    c. If the employee is a qualified summer youth employee, the credit is equal to 40% of the first $3,000 paid.

        1) The wages must be paid during any 90-day period between May 1 and September 15.

    d. The maximum credit is

        1) $4,000 for LT family assistance recipients ($10,000 × 40%)
        2) $1,200 for qualified summer youth employees ($3,000 × 40%)
        3) $2,400 for all other targeted groups ($6,000 × 40%)

    e. Targeted groups include

        1) Qualified recipients of temporary assistance to needy families
        2) Qualified veterans
        3) Qualified ex-felons
        4) Designated community residents
        5) Vocational rehabilitation referrals
        6) SNAP recipients (food stamp recipients)
        7) SSI recipients
        8) LT family assistance recipients
        9) Qualified summer youth employees
        10) Unemployed veterans

    f. The second-year credit allowed only for LT family assistance recipients is 50% of the first $10,000. The maximum credit for both years is $9,000 ($4,000 + $5,000).

        1) Qualified wages include

            a) Remuneration for employment
            b) Amount received under accident and health plans
            c) Contributions by employers to accident and health plans
            d) Educational assistance
            e) Dependent care expenses

    g. Any business deduction for the wages must be reduced by the amount of the credit.

7. **Investment Tax Credit**

    a. The credit is claimed on Form 3468 and consists of the following five parts:

        1) (Business) Energy Credit
        2) Rehabilitation Credit
        3) Qualifying Advanced Coal Project Credit
        4) Qualifying Gasification Project Credit
        5) Qualifying Advanced Energy Project Credit

(Business) Energy

b.   The credit is available to businesses that invest in energy-conserving property.

   1)   The original use of the property must begin with the taxpayer.

   2)   Basis (of energy property placed in service during the year)

   $$\frac{\times \text{ Energy \%}}{\text{Energy Credit}}$$

   3)   Qualified property and their corresponding energy percentages are

   a)   Property using geothermal energy, 10%

   b)   Property using solar illumination/energy, 30%

   c)   Qualified fuel cell property, 30%

   i)   The credit is limited to $1,500 per .5 kilowatt capacity of the property.

   d)   Qualified microturbine property, 10%

   i)   The credit is limited to $200 per kilowatt capacity of the property.

   e)   Small wind energy property, 30%

   4)   The property's basis for depreciation is reduced by 50% of the credit taken.

Rehabilitation

c.   The credit is equal to 10% of rehabilitation expenditures for structures placed in service before 1936 and 20% for certified historic structures.

   1)   Construction costs are for rehabilitation if

   a)   At least 50% of the structure's existing external walls are retained as external walls,

   b)   At least 75% of the structure's existing external walls are retained as internal or external walls, and

   c)   At least 75% of the structure's existing internal framework remains in place.

   2)   The expenditures must exceed the larger of $5,000 or the structure's adjusted basis.

   3)   The structure's basis for depreciation is reduced by the amount of the credit taken.

Qualifying Advanced Coal Project

d.   The credit is available for investment in qualified property that is used in a qualified advanced coal project. The details of a qualified project are beyond the scope of the EA exam.

   1)   The original use of the property must begin with the taxpayer.

   2)   Basis (of property placed in service for an advanced coal project)

   $$\frac{\times \text{ Credit \%}}{\text{Advanced Coal Project Credit}}$$

   3)   Qualified property and their corresponding credit percentages are

   a)   Integrated gasification combined cycle, 20%
   b)   Other advanced coal-based projects, 15%
   c)   Advanced coal-based generation technologies, 30%

Qualifying Gasification Project

    e.   The credit is available for investments in qualified property used in a qualified gasification project. The credit is 20% of the basis, with an increase to 30% if 75% of carbon dioxide emissions are captured.

        1)   Credit is disallowed for property if an Advanced Coal Credit is allowed.

Qualifying Advanced Energy Project

    f.   The Qualified Advanced Energy Project Credit is available for investment in qualified property used in a qualifying advanced energy project.

        1)   The credit is 30% of the basis.

        2)   Credit is disallowed for property available for the Energy Credit, the Advanced Coal Project Credit, or the Gasification Project Credit.

Research Credit

    8.   A tax credit can be claimed for expenses relating to increasing research activities in a trade or business.

        a.   The following is a calculation of the credit for research:

$$\begin{array}{l} 20\% \times (\text{Qualified expenses for the year} - \text{Base period expenses}) \\ + \ 20\% \times (\text{Basic research payments}) \\ \hline \text{Research Credit claimed} \\ \hline\hline \end{array}$$

            1)   Qualified expenses represents all research expenses (not just in-house) for the taxpayer incurred while carrying on any trade or business.

                a)   Wages taken into account in determining the Work Opportunity Credit from qualified research expenses are excluded.

            2)   Basic research payments are calculated by multiplying the taxpayer's average gross receipts from the 4 preceding years by the taxpayer's fixed-base percentage.

                a)   The fixed-base percentage depends on whether the taxpayer is an existing company or a start-up company.

                b)   The maximum fixed-base percentage is 16%, and start-up companies must use a 3% fixed-base percentage.

        b.   Taxpayers may elect an alternative simplified credit equal to 14% of expenses in excess of 50% of the average expense for the preceding 3 years.

        c.   The credit is included as part of the General Business Credit described in Sec. 38 and may be subject to limitation and carryforward and carryback rules.

        d.   Unused Research Credit that remains at the end of the carryforward period is allowed to be deducted in the year subsequent to expiration, according to Sec. 196.

        e.   Seventy-five percent of amounts paid to a qualified research consortium (65% for unqualified consortiums and 100% for energy research consortiums) are treated as qualified research expenditures.

            1)   A qualified research consortium is a tax-exempt organization with a primary objective to conduct scientific research.

        f.   The cost of acquiring someone else's product or process does not qualify for the credit.

Alcohol Fuels Credit

9.   The Alcohol Fuels Credit was composed of the Alcohol Mixture Credit, the Alcohol Credit, the Small Ethanol Producer Credit, and the Second Generation Biofuel Producer Credit. It provided incentives to use alternative fuels. The Second Generation Biofuel Producer is the only portion of the credit that has continued past 2011.

Pension Plan Start-Up Costs

10. A Pension Plan Start-Up Costs Credit for small employers may be taken by the taxpayer.

   a.   The credit amount equals 50% of the start-up costs incurred to create or maintain a new employee retirement plan.

   b.   The credit limit is $500 in any tax year.

Employer-Provided Childcare Facilities Credit

11. The Employer-Provided Childcare Credit was designed to create an incentive for small and medium-sized businesses to provide childcare for their employees.

   a.   This credit applies to 25% of qualified expenses paid for employee childcare and 10% of qualified expenses paid for childcare resource and referral services.

   b.   This credit is limited to $150,000 each year, and it is filed on Form 8882.

Alternative Motor Vehicle Credit

12. A credit is allowed for qualifying vehicles. Credit for vehicles subject to depreciation is taken as a part of the General Business Credit. Form 8910, *Alternative Motor Vehicle Credit*, is used to compute the Alternative Motor Vehicle Credit.

   a.   Qualified fuel cell vehicles are the only remaining component of the Alternative Motor Vehicle Credit. Qualified fuel cell vehicles are vehicles powered by electricity converted from chemical energy by combining oxygen with hydrogen fuel.

   b.   The following are additional requirements:

      1)   Original use begins with the taxpayer
      2)   Purchased for use or lease but not for resale (except to exempt organizations)

         a)   Sellers claiming the credit for sales to an exempt organization must also claim the credit as part of the General Business Credit.

      3)   Primarily used in the U.S.
      4)   Placed in service after 2005

   c.   The IRS publishes a list of the qualifying vehicles.

      1)   In general, a taxpayer may rely on the manufacturer's certification that a specific make, model, and model year vehicle qualifies for the credit and on the manufacturer's certification of the maximum amount of the credit for which a vehicle qualifies.

FICA Tip Credit

13. A nonrefundable tax credit is allowed for an employer's portion of FICA taxes paid (incurred) on employee cash tips exceeding the tips satisfying minimum wage requirements.

Stop and review! You have completed the outline for this subunit. Study questions 1 through 10 beginning on page 150.

7.2 NET OPERATING LOSS (NOL)

A net operating loss occurs when business expenses exceed business income. The NOL is deductible when carried to a year in which there is taxable income. Generally, NOLs are first carried back for 2 years and then carried forward up to 20 years.

1. Remember that an NOL is limited to a loss from business operations. Although NOLs are typically business deductions, an individual may have an NOL.

    a. NOLs relating to casualty and theft losses for an individual may be carried back for 3 years.

    b. NOLs associated with federally declared disaster areas and incurred by a small business or a farmer may be carried back for 3 years.

    c. NOLs attributable to farming business may be carried back for 5 years.

2. Calculation. Start with taxable income (a negative amount) and make the following adjustments:

    a. NOLs either carried forward or backward into the current tax year are added back.

    b. Personal exemptions must be added back.

    c. Excess of nonbusiness deductions over nonbusiness income must be added back. For this purpose,

        1) Nonbusiness deductions are alimony, contributions to self-employed retirement plans, loss from the sale of investment property, and either the standard deduction or all itemized deductions.

        2) Business deductions include all (even personal) casualty losses as well as losses associated with rental property.

        3) Nonbusiness income includes interest, dividends, gain on the sale of investment property, and treasure trove. Rent and wages are business income.

    d. Capital losses. The amount of capital loss (CL) included in the NOL of a noncorporate taxpayer is limited. Before the limit is applied, the CL must be separated into business CL and nonbusiness CL. Capital losses are included in the NOL only as follows:

        1) Nonbusiness CL is deducted to the extent of nonbusiness capital gain (CG). Any excess nonbusiness CL is not deductible.

        2) If nonbusiness CG exceeds nonbusiness CL, such excess is applied against any excess of nonbusiness deductions over nonbusiness income.

        3) If nonbusiness CG exceeds excess nonbusiness deductions, the excess nonbusiness CG may offset business CL. Business CL may also be deducted to the extent of business CG.

EXAMPLE

For 2013, Sally, a filing single taxpayer, realized a $10,000 net loss (sales of $95,000 less expenses of $105,000) from operating a sole proprietorship without regard to dispositions of property other than inventory. Other than this, the income tax return showed gross income of $5,000 ($2,500 of wages, $500 interest on personal savings, and a $2,000 long-term capital gain on business property). The excess of deductions over income was $16,000 ($5,000 gross income – $10,000 loss from business operations – $1,000 nonbusiness short-term capital loss on the sale of stock – $6,100 standard deduction – $3,900 personal exemption).

To compute Sally's NOL, (1) the $3,900 personal exemption amount is added back, (2) the $5,600 excess of nonbusiness deductions over nonbusiness income ($6,100 standard deduction – $500 interest) is added, and (3) the $1,000 nonbusiness capital loss is added because there is no nonbusiness capital gain to offset it. Thus, Sally's NOL for the current tax year is $(5,500) [$(16,000) negative taxable income + $3,900 + $5,600 + $1,000]. Note that the capital gain on the business property is not offset by the nonbusiness capital loss or by nonbusiness deductions in computing the net operating loss.

3.   If the NOL is carried back, the taxpayer files for a tax refund. Carrying back the NOL may require a recomputation of taxable income.

   a.   A taxpayer may elect to forgo carrying back the NOL and may carry forward the total NOL amount.

4.   If the NOL is carried forward, it is a deduction to arrive at AGI.

Stop and review! You have completed the outline for this subunit. Study questions 11 through 16 beginning on page 152.

7.3 CASUALTY AND THEFT LOSSES

The IRC allows deductions for losses caused by theft or casualties, whether business or personal.

Casualty

1.   Casualty loss arises from a sudden, unexpected, or unusual event caused by an external force, such as fire, storm, shipwreck, earthquake, sonic boom, etc.

   a.   Not deductible are losses resulting from ordinary accidents, e.g., dropping a vase, or from progressive deterioration, e.g., rust, insect damage.

   b.   A casualty loss on inventory, including items held for sale to customers, can be claimed through the increase in cost of goods sold by properly reporting opening and closing inventories.

Theft

2.   Theft includes robbery, larceny, and the like. It also may include loss from extortion, blackmail, etc. Not generally included in the definition of theft is misplacing or losing items or having them confiscated by a foreign government.

Personal Casualty or Theft Losses

3.   Taxpayers who itemize may deduct a limited amount for casualty losses to nonbusiness property that arise from theft, fire, storm, shipwreck, or other casualty.

   a.   Limitation. Only the amount of each loss over $100 is deductible. Only the aggregate amount of all losses (over $100 each) in excess of 10% of AGI is deductible.

      1)   If the loss was covered by insurance, timely filing of an insurance claim is prerequisite to deduction.

   b.   If the net amount of all personal casualty gains and losses after applying the $100 limit (but before the 10% of AGI threshold) is positive, each gain or loss is treated as a capital gain or loss. If the net amount is negative, the excess over 10% of AGI is deductible as an itemized deduction.

   c.   Cost of appraising a casualty loss is treated as a cost to determine tax liability (a miscellaneous itemized deduction subject to the 2%-of-AGI exclusion).

   d.   The cost of insuring a personal asset is a nondeductible personal expense.

Business or Income-Producing Property

4.   If a taxpayer has business or income-producing property, such as rental property, and it is stolen or completely destroyed, the decrease in FMV is not considered. The loss is calculated as follows:

$$
\begin{aligned}
&\text{Adjusted Basis} \\
&-\text{ Salvage Value} \\
&\underline{-\text{ Insurance Reimbursement}} \\
&=\text{ Deductible Loss}
\end{aligned}
$$

   a.   When business property is partially destroyed, the deductible amount is the lesser of the decline in FMV or the property's adjusted basis (prior to the loss).

Federally Declared Disaster Election

5. A taxpayer is subject to a special rule if (s)he sustains a loss from a federally declared disaster. Disaster loss treatment is available when property is rendered unsafe due to the disaster in the area and is ordered to be relocated or demolished by the state or local government.

   a. The 10%-of-AGI limitation applicable to personal casualty loss deductions is waived for personal casualty losses that are "net disaster losses."

      1) Net disaster losses are the excess of federally declared disaster losses over personal casualty gains.

   b. The taxpayer has the option of deducting the loss on

      1) The return for the year in which the loss actually occurred or
      2) The preceding year's return (by filing an amended return).

         a) Revocation of the election may be made before expiration of time for filing the return for the year of loss.

         b) A disaster loss deduction is computed the same as a casualty loss.

   c. The IRS grants administrative relief to taxpayers who are affected by a federally declared disaster area by suspending examination and collection actions.

      1) Examination and collection actions that can be precluded or suspended include tax return audits, mailings of notices, and other actions involving the collection of overdue taxes.

      2) The IRS may abate the interest on the underpaid income tax for the length of any extension period granted for filing income tax returns. However, abatement of interest is not mandatory.

Stop and review! You have completed the outline for this subunit. Study questions 17 through 21 beginning on page 154.

7.4 HOBBY LOSSES

Losses incurred by individuals, S corporations, partnerships, and estates and trusts that are attributable to an activity not engaged in for profit are generally deductible only to the extent of income produced by the activity. A few factors used to determine whether an activity is carried on for profit are

1. The manner in which the taxpayer carries on the activity;
2. The expertise of the taxpayer or advisors;
3. The time and effort expended by the taxpayer in carrying on the activity;
4. The expectation that assets used in the activity may appreciate in value;
5. The success of the taxpayer in carrying on other similar or dissimilar activities;
6. The taxpayer's history of income or losses with respect to the activity;
7. The amount of occasional profits, if any, that are earned;
8. The financial status of the taxpayer; and
9. Elements of personal pleasure or recreation.

Hobby Activity

10. An activity is presumed to be a hobby if losses result in any 3 of 5 (2 of 7 for activities involving horses) consecutive tax years ending with the tax year in question.

Deductible Expenses

11. Hobby expenses must be deducted in the following order:

    a. Taxes, interest, and casualty losses are deductible even if they exceed hobby income.

        1) These expenses reduce the amount of hobby income against which other hobby expenses can be offset.

    b. Other expenses, such as insurance or maintenance, can then be used to reduce income.

    c. Any remaining hobby income can then be offset by depreciation and other basis adjustment items.

12. The itemized deduction for hobby expenses to the extent of income derived from the activity is subject to the 2% floor on miscellaneous deductions.

13. Gross income from a hobby is placed as other income on Form 1040.

Vacation Home

14. The deduction of expenses related to the rental of a vacation home is similar to hobbies.

    a. No deduction is allowed if the home is rented for less than 15 days. Any rental income received is excluded from gross income.

    b. The deductions are limited to gross rental income if the vacation home is rented for 15 or more days and is used for personal purposes for more than the greater of

        1) 14 days or
        2) 10% of the number of days the home is rented.

    c. The deductions must be taken in the same order as hobby deductions. However, the deductions are limited by the percentage of days rented over days used.

    d. Any interest and tax expenses that are not allowed as vacation rental expenses may still be deducted as an itemized deduction.

Stop and review! You have completed the outline for this subunit. Study questions 22 through 27 beginning on page 156.

7.5 ADDITIONAL TAXES

Heavy Vehicle Use Tax

1. Taxpayers operating qualified vehicles are subject to an excise tax for highway use based on weight.

    a. A person is subject to the highway use tax if his or her vehicle meets all of the following tests:

        1) It is a highway motor vehicle.
        2) It is registered for highway use.
        3) It is used on public highways.
        4) It has a taxable gross weight of at least 55,000 pounds.

    b. The taxable gross weight of a vehicle (other than a bus) is the total of

        1) The actual unloaded weight of the vehicle fully equipped for service,
        2) The actual unloaded weight of any trailers or semitrailers fully equipped for service customarily used in combination with the vehicle, and
        3) The weight of the maximum load customarily carried on the vehicle and on any trailers or semitrailers customarily used in combination with the vehicle.

    c.   Filing requirements. Every person with a highway motor vehicle registered in his or her name at the time of its first taxable use must file a Form 2290, *Heavy Highway Vehicle Use Tax Return*. The tax period runs from July 1 of the current year through June 30 of the next year.

    d.   If a vehicle is purchased from another registered vehicle owner who had used the vehicle during the tax period, the original owner owes the tax for the whole tax period.

        1)   If the tax is not paid and the new owner uses the vehicle, the new owner is liable for the tax.

    e.   If a vehicle is expected to be used on public highways for 5,000 miles or less (7,500 miles or less for agricultural vehicles) during a certain period, the liability for the heavy vehicle use tax can be suspended for that period.

Farmers' Other Taxes

2.   Farmers are subject to unique tax laws for fuel tax credits and employment taxes.

    a.   A farmer may claim a credit or refund of excise taxes included in the price of fuel used on a farm for farming purposes if (s)he is the owner, tenant, or operator of a farm.

        1)   The credit is available for excise taxes on gasoline, special motor fuel, compressed natural gas, and aviation fuel used on a farm for farming purposes.

        2)   A credit cannot be claimed for a tax on diesel fuel.

    b.   Employment taxes. Farmers who have employees may have to pay employer taxes, withhold employee Social Security and Medicare taxes, and withhold income tax.

        1)   A farmer-employer may have to pay Social Security and Medicare taxes if (s)he has one or more agricultural employees, including parents, children 18 years of age or older, or a spouse, and the farmer meets either of the following tests:

            a)   Paid the employee $150 or more in cash wages during the year
            b)   Paid wages of $2,500 or more during the year to all employees

Tanning Excise Tax

3.   A 10% excise tax applies to tanning services.

    a.   The excise tax is imposed on the total amount paid by an individual for indoor tanning service, including any amount paid by insurance (TD 9486).

    b.   Full payment is due at the time the provider timely files Form 720, *Quarterly Federal Excise Tax Return*.

    c.   The cost of other goods may be excluded from the excise tax if they are separable, do not exceed the fair market value of such other goods, and are shown in the exact amounts in the records pertaining to the indoor tanning service charge.

    d.   Certain medical procedures are exempt from the excise tax. These include phototherapy service for the treatment of dermatological conditions, sleep disorders, seasonal affective disorder, or other psychiatric disorders; neonatal jaundice; wound healing; and other qualified procedures if performed by a licensed medical professional on the medical professional's premises.

    e.   No portion of a membership fee is subject to the tax if the facility meets the definition of a qualified physical fitness facility (QPFF).

        1)   In this case, the indoor tanning service is treated as incident to the physical fitness facility's predominant business, and no liability for the excise tax attaches.

        2)   A tanning salon cannot qualify as a QPFF by allowing users access to exercise classes or equipment.

Stop and review! You have completed the outline for this subunit. Study questions 28 through 30 beginning on page 159.

QUESTIONS

7.1 General Business Credit

1. Your General Business Credit is limited to your net income tax minus

    A. Your alternative minimum tax.

    B. Your tentative minimum tax.

    C. Your net income tax.

    D. The greater of the tentative minimum tax or 25% of net regular tax liability above $25,000.

Answer (D) is correct.
    REQUIRED: The limit on the General Business Credit.
    DISCUSSION: The amount that may be claimed as the General Business Credit is limited based on tax liability. The General Business Credit may not exceed net income tax minus the greater of the tentative alternative minimum tax or 25% of net regular tax liability above $25,000.
    Answer (A) is incorrect. The limit is the tax liability minus 25% of tax liability larger than $25,000. Answer (B) is incorrect. The tentative minimum tax is only a component of the limit on General Business Credits. Answer (C) is incorrect. The limit is the tax liability minus 25% of tax liability larger than $25,000.

2. During 2013, Mark had a General Business Credit of $45,000. His net income tax is $65,000. His tentative minimum tax figured on Form 6251 was $30,000. What is the maximum amount of General Business Credit Mark can claim in 2013?

    A. $30,000

    B. $35,000

    C. $45,000

    D. $55,000

Answer (B) is correct.
    REQUIRED: The maximum General Business Credit that may be taken in the current year.
    DISCUSSION: Sec. 38(c) states that the General Business Credit is limited to the taxpayer's net income tax over the greater of the tentative minimum tax or 25% of the net regular tax liability exceeding $25,000. Applying this formula, Mark's General Business Credit is limited to $65,000 minus the greater of $30,000 or $10,000 [($65,000 – $25,000) × 25%]. Thus, the General Business Credit is limited to $35,000 ($65,000 – $30,000). Any General Business Credit greater than $35,000 would reduce the income tax below $30,000, which would then be brought back up to $35,000 by the AMT.
    Answer (A) is incorrect. The amount of $30,000 is the tentative minimum tax, which represents the maximum reduction in the income tax. Answer (C) is incorrect. The General Business Credit is limited to $35,000. Answer (D) is incorrect. The General Business Credit is limited to $35,000.

3. The General Business Credit consists of the following conditions except

    A. Investment Credit.

    B. Credit for alcohol used as fuel.

    C. Work Opportunity Credit.

    D. Qualified Electric Vehicle Credit.

Answer (D) is correct.
    REQUIRED: The credit that is not a component of the General Business Credit.
    DISCUSSION: The General Business Credit (GBC) is a set of several credits commonly available to businesses. The GBC includes credits for investment, research, work opportunity, and disabled access. It does not include a credit for qualified electric vehicles. In addition, the Qualified Electric Vehicle Credit expired after 2006 (Publication 334).

4. The General Business Credit cannot lower your tax below

    A. The poverty level for the year.

    B. The taxpayer's tax for the prior year.

    C. A number IRS announces each year.

    D. The taxpayer's alternative minimum tax for the tax year.

Answer (D) is correct.
    REQUIRED: The threshold amount for which the General Business Credit can no longer lower tax.
    DISCUSSION: The General Business Credit (GBC) is limited to net income tax minus the greater of the tentative minimum tax or 25% of net regular tax over $25,000. The amount that may be claimed as the GBC is limited based on tax liability. Hence, the GBC cannot lower a taxpayer's tax below his or her alternative minimum tax for the tax year. A credit cannot lower a taxpayer's liability below zero.
    Answer (A) is incorrect. The General Business Credit (GBC) is limited based on tax liability. It is not limited to the poverty level for the year. Answer (B) is incorrect. The GBC may not lower the taxpayer's liability below the alternative minimum tax for the tax year. The taxpayer's tax for the prior year is not used in determining the GBC limit for the current year. Answer (C) is incorrect. The IRS does not announce a number each year regarding the amount the General Business Credit cannot lower your tax below. The GBC may not exceed net income tax minus the greater of tentative alternative minimum tax or 25% of the net regular tax liability above $25,000.

5. An employee who qualifies for the Work Opportunity Credit must be a member of a targeted group. All of the following are considered targeted groups except

A. Qualified veterans.

B. Qualified relatives of the employer.

C. Qualified summer youth employees.

D. Qualified food stamp recipients.

Answer (B) is correct.
REQUIRED: The party that is not classified as a targeted group for purposes of the Work Opportunity Credit.
DISCUSSION: Publication 954 defines a member of a targeted group to be any employee who has been certified by your state employment security agency (SESA) as a

1) Qualified recipient of temporary assistance to needy families
2) Qualified veteran
3) Qualified ex-felon
4) Designated community resident
5) Vocational rehabilitation referral
6) SNAP recipient (food stamp recipient)
7) SSI recipient
8) LT family assistance recipient
9) Qualified summer youth employee
10) Unemployed veteran

6. The F&E Partnership spent $100,000 on eligible access expenditures that qualify for the Disabled Access Credit. The partnership had gross receipts of $1 million and 30 full-time employees during the preceding tax year. What is the amount of the Disabled Access Credit for the year 2013?

A. $5,000

B. $10,000

C. $250

D. $50,000

Answer (A) is correct.
REQUIRED: The amount of the Disabled Access Credit for the year 2013.
DISCUSSION: Publication 535 states, "The disabled access credit is a nonrefundable tax credit for an eligible small business that pays or incurs expenses to provide access to persons who have disabilities." Form 8826 defines, "For purposes of the credit, an eligible small business is any business or person that (a) had gross receipts for the preceding tax year that did not exceed $1 million or had no more than 30 full-time employees during the preceding tax year . . ." The credit equals 50% of eligible expenditures in excess of $250 and less than $10,250.
Answer (B) is incorrect. The credit equals 50% of eligible expenditures in excess of $250 and less than $10,250, or $5,000. Answer (C) is incorrect. The credit equals 50% of eligible expenditures in excess of $250 and less than $10,250, not limited to only $250. Answer (D) is incorrect. The credit equals 50% of eligible expenditures in excess of $250 and less than $10,250, or $5,000.

7. The Barrow and Jones partnership incurred qualified rehabilitation expenses of $50,000 on a certified historic structure. What is the Rehabilitation Investment Credit before tax limitations are applied?

A. $5,000

B. $10,000

C. $7,500

D. $6,000

Answer (B) is correct.
REQUIRED: The Rehabilitation Investment Credit before tax limitations are applied.
DISCUSSION: Instructions for Form 3468 state, "You are allowed a credit for qualified rehabilitation expenditures made for any qualified rehabilitated building. The credit is 10% of the expenditures for any qualified rehabilitated building other than a certified historic structure and 20% of the expenditures for a certified historic structure."

8. Ryan runs a manufacturing business employing several people with young children. These employees require daycare as both parents work. He decided that, in order to make it easier for his employees to come to work each day, he would allocate some of the unused space in his manufacturing facility to a childcare facility. In 2013, he incurred $20,000 in qualified childcare facility expenditures. He had no qualified childcare resource and referral expenditures and had no pass-through credits. What is Ryan's credit for 2013?

A. $20,000

B. $2,000

C. $10,000

D. $5,000

Answer (D) is correct.
REQUIRED: The amount of the Employer-Provided Childcare Facilities Credit.
DISCUSSION: The Employer-Provided Childcare Facilities Credit was established to create an incentive for small- and medium-sized businesses to provide childcare for their employees. This credit applies to 25% of qualified expenses paid for employee childcare. Thus, Ryan can use a credit of $5,000 ($20,000 × 25%).
Answer (A) is incorrect. The credit is limited to 25% of qualified expenses. Answer (B) is incorrect. The 10% rule applies to qualified expenses paid for employee childcare resource and referral services. Answer (C) is incorrect. The correct percentage is 25%, not 50%.

9. A company increased its research expenses by $3,600. What is the maximum credit it qualifies for on its tax return for tax year 2013?

A. $360

B. $900

C. $2,700

D. $720

Answer (D) is correct.

REQUIRED: The maximum Research Tax Credit.

DISCUSSION: Publication 334 states, "The research credit is designed to encourage businesses to increase the amounts they spend on research and experimental activities. The credit is generally 20% of the amount by which your research expenses for the year exceed your base amount."

10. In 2013, Santergraph, Inc., remodeled and converted a portion of its building into a licensed childcare facility open for the care of any of its employees' children. The cost of this remodeling qualifies for which of the following?

A. An asset to be depreciated over the remaining useful life of the building.

B. An adjustment to income of 75% of the costs, with the balance depreciable.

C. A tax credit of 25% of the qualified expenses, maximum credit of $150,000, with the balance depreciable.

D. Sec. 179 expensing election.

Answer (C) is correct.

REQUIRED: The correct amount of credit for employer-provided childcare.

DISCUSSION: Employers may receive a 25% credit for childcare expenses up to a maximum credit of $150,000. The costs of Santergraph, Inc., to remodel and convert a portion of its building into a licensed childcare facility for the care of any of its employees' children are qualified childcare expenses (Publication 553, page 13).

Answer (A) is incorrect. The cost of remodeling the building into a licensed childcare facility qualifies as a credit to the employer. The balance is depreciable as part of the capitalized cost of the building. Answer (B) is incorrect. The costs do not qualify as an adjustment to income of 75% of the costs. The Employer-Provided Childcare Credit is equal to 25% of the qualified expenses. Answer (D) is incorrect. Costs do not qualify for a Sec. 179 expensing election.

7.2 Net Operating Loss (NOL)

11. Jason sustained a net operating loss for the current year. If Jason does not elect to forgo the carryback period, to what years may he carry the NOL?

A. Back 3 years; forward 5 years.

B. Back 3 years; forward 15 years.

C. Back 2 years; forward 15 years.

D. Back 2 years; forward 20 years.

Answer (D) is correct.

REQUIRED: The years to which an NOL may be carried.

DISCUSSION: The Taxpayer Relief Act of 1997 changed the carryforward and carryback periods for NOLs. A net operating loss may now be carried back to each of the 2 taxable years preceding the taxable year of such loss (oldest first) and may be carried forward to each of the 20 taxable years following the taxable year of the loss [Sec. 172(b)(1)(A)]. Alternatively, the taxpayer may elect to forgo the carryback entirely and carry forward only the net operating loss [Sec. 172(b)(3)].

12. Which of the following statements about forgoing the net operating loss (NOL) carryback period is false?

A. The election should be made as a written statement attached to the tax return for the NOL year citing the appropriate Internal Revenue Code section.

B. Once the election is made, the taxpayer cannot later revoke it for that tax year.

C. A taxpayer may amend a prior year's return to include the election as long as the election is made before the expiration of the statute of limitations.

D. A taxpayer who wants to forgo the carryback period for more than one NOL must make a separate election for each NOL year.

Answer (C) is correct.

REQUIRED: The false statement about forgoing the NOL carryback period.

DISCUSSION: Under Sec. 172(b)(3), an NOL election may be made on an amended return if the return is filed on or before the due date for filing returns for the year the election is sought. An election, once made for any tax year, is irrevocable.

13. Sam had a net operating loss (NOL) in 2013. He did not elect to forgo the carryback. He can first carry the loss to which one of the following years?

A. 2007

B. 2009

C. 2010

D. 2011

Answer (D) is correct.

REQUIRED: The years to which a net operating loss may be carried.

DISCUSSION: The Taxpayer Relief Act of 1997 changed the carryforward and carryback periods for NOLs so that a net operating loss may be carried back to each of the 2 taxable years preceding the taxable year of such loss (oldest first) and may be carried forward to each of the 20 taxable years following the taxable year of the loss [Sec. 172(b)(1)(A)]. Alternatively, the taxpayer may elect to forgo the carryback entirely and carry forward only the net operating loss [Sec. 172(b)(3)].

14. Based on the following information, compute the 2013 net operating loss (NOL) that an individual can carry over to 2014 if the proper election to forgo the carryback is taken.

2012 NOL	$(15,000)
Wages	25,000
S corporation loss	(40,000)
Schedule C net profit	7,000
Interest income	500
Standard deduction	12,200
Personal exemptions	11,700

A. $7,500

B. $8,000

C. $19,700

D. $31,400

Answer (B) is correct.

REQUIRED: The taxpayer's 2013 NOL carryover.

DISCUSSION: A net operating loss is defined as the excess of allowable deductions (as modified) over gross income [Sec. 172(c)]. An NOL generally includes only items that represent business income or loss. Personal casualty losses and wage or salary income are included as business items. Nonbusiness deductions in excess of nonbusiness income must be excluded. Interest and dividends are not business income.

Wages	$25,000
Schedule C net profit	7,000
S corporation ordinary loss	(40,000)
Net operating loss	$ (8,000)

Nonbusiness deductions (the standard deduction) are not allowed because there is only $500 of nonbusiness income. No deduction for personal exemptions is allowed. The NOL carryover from 2012 is not allowed in arriving at the 2013 NOL. If the proper election to forgo the carryback is taken, the entire NOL can be carried over to 2014.

Answer (A) is incorrect. Nonbusiness income of $500 is not included. Answer (C) is incorrect. Interest income and the standard deduction are not included in the NOL calculation. Answer (D) is incorrect. Interest income, standard deduction, and personal exemptions are not included in the NOL calculation.

15. A net operating loss (NOL) may be carried forward if a proper election is made. Which of the following statements about the election is not correct?

A. Once the election is made, you can use the net operating loss only in the 20-year carryforward period.

B. To make the election, you attach a statement to your tax return filed by the due date (including extensions) for the net operating loss year.

C. Once the election is made to waive the carryback period for one net operating loss, it remains in effect for all subsequent net operating losses.

D. If you filed your return timely but did not attach the election statement, you have 6 months from the due date of your original return (excluding extensions) to file the statement with an amended return for the net operating loss year.

Answer (C) is correct.

REQUIRED: The incorrect statement about the NOL election.

DISCUSSION: NOLs are first carried back for 2 years and then carried forward up to 20 years. A taxpayer may elect not to carry back the NOL but to carry the loss forward. The election to waive the carryback period applies only to each individual NOL. Making this election for one NOL does not affect other NOLs.

Answer (A) is incorrect. Once the election is made not to carry back the NOL, you can only use the NOL in the 20-year carryforward period. Answer (B) is incorrect. In order to make this election to carry forward the NOL, you must attach a statement to your tax return filed by the due date for the net operating loss year. Answer (D) is incorrect. If you filed your return timely but did not attach the election statement, you have 6 months from the due date of the original return to file the statement with an amended return for the net operating loss year.

16. For 2013, Able Corporation had $700,000 of gross income from business operations and $750,000 of allowable business expenses. It also received $100,000 in dividends from a domestic corporation for which it can take an 80% deduction. Based on this information, compute Able's net operating loss for 2013.

- A. Able Corporation did not have an NOL for 2013.

- B. $(30,000)

- C. $(50,000)

- D. $(150,000)

Answer (B) is correct.
REQUIRED: The corporation's net operating loss when there is dividend income and an NOL carryover.
DISCUSSION: Sec. 172(c) defines a net operating loss as the excess of deductions over gross income, with certain modifications. One modification is that the dividends-received deduction is computed without regard to the Sec. 246(b) limitation of 80% of taxable income if taking the full 80% deduction creates or increases an NOL. Also, a deduction for a net operating loss carryover is not allowed in computing a current NOL. Consequently, Able Corporation's NOL is computed as follows:

Gross income from business operations	$700,000
Dividends received	100,000
Gross income	$800,000
Less: Business expenses	(750,000)
Dividends-received deduction ($100,000 × 80%)	(80,000)
Net operating loss	$ (30,000)

Answer (A) is incorrect. A $30,000 NOL exists at year end. Answer (C) is incorrect. The NOL is calculated as gross income less business expenses and the dividends-received deduction. Answer (D) is incorrect. The NOL is calculated as gross income less business expenses and the dividends-received deduction.

7.3 Casualty and Theft Losses

17. A taxpayer suffered an $11,000 loss of inventory when his cooler malfunctioned. He had no insurance for this type of loss. He shows this loss on his tax return by

- A. Taking a bad debt deduction of $22,000, the amount he would have sold the inventory for.

- B. Taking an ordinary loss on Form 4797 of $11,000.

- C. Taking a business loss on his Schedule C as reflected by an increase of $11,000 in cost of goods sold.

- D. Taking a loss of $11,000 as a bad debt on Schedule D.

Answer (C) is correct.
REQUIRED: The correct method of presenting an inventory loss on the tax return.
DISCUSSION: Publication 547 states, "There are two ways you can deduct a casualty or theft loss of inventory, including items you hold for sale to customers.
"One way is to deduct the loss through the increase in the cost of goods sold by properly reporting your opening and closing inventories. Do not claim this loss again as a casualty or theft loss. If you take the loss through the increase in the cost of goods sold, include any insurance or other reimbursement you receive for the loss in gross income.
"The other way is to deduct the loss separately. If you deduct it separately, eliminate the inventory items from cost of goods sold by making a downward adjustment to opening inventory or purchases. Reduce the loss by the reimbursement you received. Do not include the reimbursement in gross income. If you do not receive the reimbursement by the end of the year, you may not claim a loss to the extent you have a reasonable prospect of recovery."
Answer (A) is incorrect. The deduction cannot be greater than the cost basis of the property. Answer (B) is incorrect. Form 4797 is used for sales and exchanges of property used in a trade or business from other than casualty or theft. Answer (D) is incorrect. To take the loss on Schedule D, it must be a bad debt from sales or services. Losses on inventory do not fall under this category.

18. Fran's car, which she used 75% for business, was stolen in Year 3. It cost $30,000 in Year 1. She had properly claimed depreciation of $5,220. The insurance company reimbursed her $19,000, which was the fair market value at the time of the theft. What is the amount of the business portion of Fran's theft loss for Year 3?

A. $3,030

B. $4,030

C. $4,335

D. $5,780

Answer (A) is correct.

REQUIRED: The amount of business casualty loss in the current year.

DISCUSSION: When property is used partly for personal purposes and partly for business purposes, the casualty loss deduction must be figured separately for the personal-use portion and for the business portion because the losses attributed to these two uses are figured in two different ways. When figuring the business loss, allocate the adjusted basis, the salvage value after the casualty loss, and the insurance or other reimbursement based on the use of the property. Since the FMV after a theft is considered $0, there is no salvage value. The loss is figured using the adjusted basis. The casualty loss would be determined as follows:

Allocated cost to business portion ($30,000 × 75%)	$22,500
Less depreciation	5,220
Adjusted basis	$17,280
Loss (AB $17,280)	$17,280
Less salvage value	0
Less insurance reimbursement ($19,000 × 75%)	14,250
Deductible business casualty loss	$ 3,030

Answer (B) is incorrect. Only 75% of loss is deductible as a business casualty loss. Answer (C) is incorrect. One hundred percent of the properly claimed depreciation should be used to calculate the adjusted basis when determining the casualty loss. Answer (D) is incorrect. The cost and the insurance reimbursement must be allocated to the business portion.

19. In June of Year 1, you paid $82,600 for real property to be used as a manufacturing plant. You allocated the cost to land as $10,325 and to building as $72,275. From Year 1 to Year 4, you incurred the following expenses related to this property:

Building remodeling before placed in service	$20,000
Depreciation expense	14,526
Casualty loss not covered by insurance	5,000
Fire damage restoration	5,500

What is the adjusted basis of the building and land as of January 1, Year 5?

A. Building, $77,749; land, $10,825.

B. Building, $88,249; land, $10,825.

C. Building, $78,249; land, $10,325.

D. Building, $92,275; land, $20,825.

Answer (C) is correct.

REQUIRED: The amount of the adjusted basis of the building and land.

DISCUSSION: Basis is adjusted by capitalizable costs minus depreciation and deductions. The basis of the building is computed as follows:

Original cost of building		$72,275
Adjustments to basis		
Add:		
Improvements		20,000
Repair of fire damage		5,500
		$97,775
Subtract:		
Depreciation	$14,526	
Deducted casualty loss	5,000	19,526
Adjusted basis on January 1, Year 5		$78,249

The basis of the land, $10,325, remains unchanged. It is not affected by any of the above adjustments, which affect only the basis of the building.

Answer (A) is incorrect. The basis of the land remains unchanged. Answer (B) is incorrect. The casualty loss is deducted from the basis. Answer (D) is incorrect. Depreciation is deducted from the basis in the building.

20. A hurricane destroyed Frank's tractor in the current year. Frank had purchased the tractor for $8,000 and had correctly deducted $6,000 of depreciation. His adjusted basis in the tractor was $2,000. Frank's insurance company reimbursed him $9,000, and he spent $7,500 for a new tractor later in the year. How much ordinary income should Frank report on his current year income tax return?

A. $0

B. $1,500

C. $6,000

D. $7,000

Answer (B) is correct.

REQUIRED: The gross income resulting from the involuntary conversion of insured property.

DISCUSSION: Frank received insurance proceeds of $9,000 on destroyed property with an adjusted basis of $2,000 and thereby realized a gain of $7,000. Since the replacement property was similar, under Sec. 1033(a)(2), Frank may elect to recognize the gain only to the extent that the amount realized ($9,000) exceeds the cost of the replacement property ($7,500), or $1,500.

Answer (A) is incorrect. A gain must be recognized to the extent that the amount realized exceeds the cost of the replacement property. Answer (C) is incorrect. The gain that is recognized is limited to the amount that the amount realized exceeds the cost of the replacement property. Answer (D) is incorrect. The gain that is recognized is limited to the amount that the amount realized exceeds the cost of the replacement property.

21. In the current year, Ms. Brown's building was damaged by an earthquake. The building was on land Ms. Brown owned. She used 75% of the building for business purposes and lived in the other 25%. For the current year, her books and records reflect the following:

Cost of building	$400,000
Depreciation on building before earthquake	130,000
Fair market value before earthquake	800,000
Fair market value after earthquake	200,000
Insurance reimbursement	200,000

What is Ms. Brown's deductible business casualty loss for the current year?

A. $20,000

B. $40,900

C. $170,000

D. $250,000

Answer (A) is correct.

REQUIRED: The deductible business casualty loss.

DISCUSSION: When property is partially destroyed, the loss is the lesser of the adjusted basis less any reimbursement or the decrease in the FMV less any reimbursement. When the property is used only partially for business, the casualty loss is calculated separately for business and personal purposes.

	Business (75%)	Personal (25%)
Cost of building	$300,000	$100,000
Depreciation	130,000	
(1) Adjusted basis	$170,000	$100,000
(2) Decrease in FMV ($800,000 – $200,000)	$450,000	$150,000
Lesser of (1) or (2)	170,000	100,000
Less insurance	(150,000)	(50,000)
Loss	$ 20,000	$ 50,000

Therefore, Ms. Brown's business casualty loss is $20,000.

7.4 Hobby Losses

22. In determining whether an activity is engaged in for profit, the relevant facts and circumstances are taken into account. All of the following may indicate you are carrying on the activity for profit except

A. You carry on the activity in a businesslike manner.

B. You depend on income from the activity for your livelihood.

C. You can expect to make a future profit from the appreciation of assets used in the activity.

D. Despite your lack of profitability, you continue to use the same methods of operation to prove that you are serious and the activity is not just a hobby.

Answer (D) is correct.

REQUIRED: The incorrect statement about determining whether an activity is engaged in for profit.

DISCUSSION: In general, expenses incurred in a profit-motivated activity, such as a business or an investment, are deductible, whereas most expenses associated with personal activities, such as hobbies, are not. Reg. Sec. 1.183-2(b) lists the factors used to determine whether an activity is profit-motivated. These factors include the amount of occasional profits that are earned and the history of income or losses with respect to the activity. Having a lack of profitability and not trying to fix this is not an indication of carrying on the activity for profit. There has not been a history of profitability, and there has not been any change made to increase profitability.

Answer (A) is incorrect. Carrying on an activity in a businesslike manner is an indication you are carrying on the activity for profit. Answer (B) is incorrect. Dependence on income from the activity for your livelihood is an indication you are carrying on the activity for profit. Answer (C) is incorrect. Expectation of future profits from the appreciation of assets used in the activity is an indication you are carrying on the activity for profit.

23. During 2013, Flint rented out his vacation home for 90 days and used the home for personal purposes for 30 days. His income and expenses relating to the vacation home were as follows:

Rental income	$3,000
Mortgage interest	1,500
Real estate taxes	800
Maintenance and insurance	1,500
Depreciation	1,200

Without regard to the limitation on itemized deductions, what amount is deductible as a vacation home expense by Flint on his 2013 income tax return?

	Interest and Taxes	Maintenance and Insurance	Depreciation
A.	$1,500	$1,500	$1,200
B.	$1,725	$1,125	$900
C.	$2,300	$1,125	$150
D.	$2,300	$700	$0

Answer (C) is correct.

REQUIRED: The amount of deductions allowed for a not-for-profit activity.

DISCUSSION: Limitations apply to the allowable deductions that may be taken by a taxpayer who rents out a vacation home or other dwelling unit that (s)he uses as his or her residence during the tax year. The limitations apply if the vacation home is rented for 15 or more days during the tax year and is used by the taxpayer for personal purposes for the greater of 14 days or more than 10% of the number of days the home is rented. In such a case, the amount of the rental activity deductions is limited to gross income and must be taken in the following order: (1) taxes and interest allocable to rental use, (2) operating expenses, and (3) depreciation. The allocation of expenses is based on 75% (90 days rented ÷ 120 days used). Therefore, the allocation of expenses is calculated as follows:

Gross rental income	$ 3,000
Less: Interest and taxes (75% of $2,300)	(1,725)
Less: Maintenance and insurance (75% of $1,500)	(1,125)
Remaining income	$ 150
Less depreciation allowed	(150)
Remaining income	$ 0

The $575 of interest and taxes allocated to personal use can be deducted as itemized deductions for a total of $2,300.

Answer (A) is incorrect. Interest and tax expenses are deducted before maintenance, insurance, and depreciation deductions. Answer (B) is incorrect. The deductions are limited to rental income. Answer (D) is incorrect. A portion of the interest expense is allocated to personal use before limiting total vacation home expenses to $3,000.

24. Samboni, an individual, is engaged in a not-for-profit activity. The income and expenses of the activity are as follows:

Gross income		$ 4,500
Less expenses allocated to activity		
Real estate taxes	$1,800	
Home mortgage interest	1,200	
Utilities	300	
Maintenance	700	
Depreciation on an automobile	1,600	
Depreciation on equipment	1,400	
Total expenses		(7,000)
Loss		$(2,500)

Compute the amount of depreciation expense, if any, that Samboni can deduct for the year.

A. $0

B. $500 as a miscellaneous itemized deduction on Schedule A (Form 1040), subject to the 2%-of-adjusted-gross-income limit.

C. $500 as a Schedule C expense.

D. $848 as a miscellaneous itemized deduction on Schedule A (Form 1040), not subject to the 2%-of-adjusted-gross-income limit.

Answer (B) is correct.

REQUIRED: The amount of automobile depreciation expense that can be deducted for a not-for-profit activity.

DISCUSSION: If a business is carried on as a not-for-profit activity, there is a limit on the amount of deductions that are available. There are three categories of deductions, and the deductions must be taken in order.

Category 1: Deductions that are for personal as well as for business activities are allowed in full. These include mortgage interest, taxes, and casualty losses.

Category 2: Deductions that do not result in an adjustment to the basis of property are allowed next but only to the extent that the gross income from the activity exceeds the deduction taken under the first category. These include utilities, insurance, advertising, etc.

Category 3: Business deductions that decrease basis are allowed last but only to the extent the gross income exceeds the deductions taken from the first two categories. When more than one asset is involved, depreciation should be divided proportionately among those assets.

Therefore, Samboni's deduction for depreciation on the automobile is calculated as follows:

Limit on deduction	$ 4,500
Category 1, taxes and interest	(3,000)
Category 2, utilities and maintenance	(1,000)
Available for category 3	$ 500

Answer (A) is incorrect. Deductions are allowed to the extent of gross income from a not-for-profit activity. Answer (C) is incorrect. Not-for-profit activities are shown on Schedule A. Answer (D) is incorrect. Utilities and maintenance are allowed as deductions to the extent of gross income.

25. In determining whether you are carrying on an activity for profit, all the facts and circumstances are taken into account. All of the following are factors to consider except

A. You are carrying on two different business activities. When you combine the income and expenses together, you have a net profit.

B. Your losses are due to circumstances beyond your control.

C. You can expect to make a future profit from the appreciation of the assets used in the activity.

D. You were successful in making a profit in similar activities in the past.

Answer (A) is correct.

REQUIRED: The factor that does not determine whether you are carrying on an activity for profit.

DISCUSSION: Publication 535 states, "In determining whether you are carrying on an activity for profit, all the facts are taken into account. No one factor alone is decisive. Among the factors to consider are whether

1. You carry on the activity in a businesslike manner,
2. The time and effort you put into the activity indicate you intend to make it profitable,
3. You depend on income from the activity for your livelihood,
4. Your losses are due to circumstances beyond your control (or are normal in the start-up phase of your type of business),
5. You change your methods of operation in an attempt to improve profitability,
6. You, or your advisors, have the knowledge needed to carry on the activity as a successful business,
7. You were successful in making a profit in similar activities in the past,
8. The activity makes a profit in some years, and how much profit it makes, and
9. You can expect to make a future profit from the appreciation of the assets used in the activity."

Answer (B) is incorrect. Losses due to circumstances beyond your control are a factor to consider in determining whether you are carrying on an activity for profit. Answer (C) is incorrect. Expectations of a future profit from the appreciation of the assets used in the activity are a factor to consider in determining whether you are carrying on an activity for profit. Answer (D) is incorrect. Successfully making a profit in similar activities in the past is a factor to consider in determining whether you are carrying on an activity for profit.

26. Fred, an individual, is engaged in a not-for-profit activity. The income and expenses of the activity are as follows:

Gross income	$ 4,500
Less expenses allocated to activity	
Real estate taxes	1,800
Home mortgage interest	1,200
Utilities	300
Maintenance	700
Depreciation on automobile	1,600
Depreciation on equipment	1,400
Total expenses	$ 7,000
Loss	$(2,500)

Based on the information provided above, on what schedule, if any, can Fred deduct the real estate tax expense?

A. As an itemized tax expense on Schedule A (Form 1040).

B. As a miscellaneous itemized deduction on Schedule A (Form 1040), subject to the 2%-of-adjusted-gross-income limit.

C. As an expense for the business use of his home on Part II, Schedule C (Form 1040).

D. None of the answers are correct.

Answer (A) is correct.

REQUIRED: The schedule on which a taxpayer should deduct real estate taxes.

DISCUSSION: Sec. 164 allows a deduction for real estate taxes. Since this is not a deduction allowable in arriving at adjusted gross income as defined in Sec. 62, it is an itemized deduction as defined in Sec. 63(d). Itemized deductions are reported on Schedule A. These amounts include the personal and not-for-profit part of the real estate taxes. For-profit business taxes are deducted on Schedule C.

Answer (B) is incorrect. Real estate taxes for not-for-profit activity are an itemized tax deduction on Schedule A. Answer (C) is incorrect. According to IRS Publication 587, "Business Use of Your Home," the portion of real estate taxes that relate to the taxpayer's trade or business should be deducted on Schedule C (Form 1040). The remainder is deductible on Schedule A (Form 1040). Answer (D) is incorrect. Real estate taxes for not-for-profit activity are an itemized tax deduction on Schedule A.

27. Ida is engaged in a not-for-profit activity. The income and expenses of the activity are as follows:

Gross income		$3,200
Less expenses		
Real estate tax	$700	
Home mortgage interest	900	
Insurance	400	
Utilities	700	
Maintenance	200	
Depreciation on an automobile	600	
Depreciation on a machine	200	
Total expenses		(3,700)
Loss		$ (500)

The amount of allowable depreciation for the automobile is

A. $600

B. $300

C. $225

D. None of the answers are correct.

Answer (C) is correct.

REQUIRED: The amount of allowable depreciation a taxpayer may take for an automobile.

DISCUSSION: Allowable depreciation is the amount that a taxpayer is entitled to deduct under any proper method. The amount of allowable depreciation may not create or increase a net operating loss. Total expenses excluding depreciation are $2,900, so Ida's total allowable depreciation is $300 ($3,200 – $2,900). The $300 is allocated to the automobile and the machine. Therefore, the amount of allowable depreciation for the automobile is $225 [$300 × ($600 ÷ $800)].

Answer (A) is incorrect. The amount of allowable depreciation may not create or increase a net operating loss. Answer (B) is incorrect. The $300 is allocated to the automobile and the machine. Answer (D) is incorrect. One of the answers is correct.

7.5 Additional Taxes

28. Which of the following vehicles are eligible for suspension of the heavy highway motor vehicle use tax?

A. Heavy highway motor vehicles with a gross weight of 55,000 pounds or more.

B. Commercial buses.

C. Agriculture vehicles used 7,500 or fewer miles.

D. Trucks and tractors.

Answer (C) is correct.

REQUIRED: The vehicle eligible for suspension of the heavy highway motor vehicle use tax.

DISCUSSION: Highway motor vehicles that have a taxable gross weight of 55,000 pounds or more are taxable. A highway motor vehicle includes any self-propelled vehicle designed to carry a load over public highways, whether or not also designed to perform other functions. Examples of vehicles that are designed to carry a load over public highways include buses, trucks, and truck tractors. Generally, vans, pickup trucks, panel trucks, and similar trucks are not subject to this tax because they have a taxable gross weight less than 55,000 pounds. If a vehicle is expected to be used on public highways for 5,000 miles or less (7,500 miles or less for agricultural vehicles) during a certain period, the liabilities for the heavy vehicle use tax can be suspended for that period.

29. For a tax period beginning July 1, a truck with taxable gross weight of 60,000 lbs., registered to Mason Corp., was first used on a public highway on July 10. On December 10, the truck was sold to Mr. Diaz, who registered and used it in the tax period. The total federal highway use tax for the period was $232. Which of the following statements is false in respect to who is liable for the tax?

A. Mason Corp. is liable for the full tax of $232 since it first placed the truck in service.

B. Mr. Diaz is liable for the full tax of $232 to the extent Mason has not paid the tax.

C. Mr. Diaz is the only one of the two owners during the tax period with any liability for the tax due from December through June.

D. To the extent that either Mason or Mr. Diaz pays the $232, the other party is relieved, although the truck changed ownership.

Answer (C) is correct.

REQUIRED: The false statement regarding the liability for heavy vehicle use tax.

DISCUSSION: If a heavy vehicle is purchased from another registered owner, the first owner (Mason) owes the tax for the tax period the vehicle is used. However, if the first owner owed the tax but did not pay it, the second owner (Diaz) is liable for the tax if it is used during the period that unpaid tax is due.

Answer (A) is incorrect. The first owner owes the tax for the whole tax period the vehicle is used. Answer (B) is incorrect. Mr. Diaz is liable for the full tax of $232 to the extent Mason has not paid the tax. Answer (D) is incorrect. To the extent that either Mason or Mr. Diaz pays the $232, the other party is relieved, although the truck changed ownership.

30. With regard to excise taxes and their effect on farmers, which of the following statements is false?

A. A farmer can claim a credit for diesel fuel used on the highway in the transportation of livestock, feed, crops, or equipment.

B. Effective October 1, 1993, an excise tax was imposed on compressed natural gas. A credit can be claimed for this fuel if it is used on a farm for farming purposes.

C. If any other person performs services to cultivate the soil or harvest any agricultural commodity for a farmer, the farmer can claim the credit or refund for the fuel used in the performance of such services.

D. Since 1994, farmers have not been permitted to apply for credits or refunds of tax on diesel fuel sold for use on a farm for farming purposes.

Answer (A) is correct.
　REQUIRED: The false statement regarding excise taxes and their effect on farmers.
　DISCUSSION: A credit may be claimed only for the tax on gasoline, special motor fuel, and compressed natural gas used on a farm for farming purposes. A credit may not be claimed for the tax on diesel fuel or for any off-the-farm use, such as on the highway, even if the fuel is used in transporting livestock, feed, crops, or equipment.

Use the additional questions in Gleim **EA Test Prep** to create Practice Exams that emulate Prometric!

STUDY UNIT EIGHT
CONTRIBUTIONS TO A PARTNERSHIP

(7 pages of outline)

Partnerships are collaborative ventures governed by the partnership agreement. Ownership interest in a partnership is determined by contributions to the partnership and the operations of the partnership, including assumptions of liability. Despite the flow-through nature of partnerships, filing requirements do exist, with the required tax year determined by several guidelines.

8.1 PARTNERSHIP DEFINED

1. A partnership is the relationship between two or more entities who join together to carry on a trade or business. An entity, when used in this context, may refer to an individual, a corporation, a trust, an estate, or another partnership.

   a. For federal tax purposes, the term "partnership" includes a syndicate, group, pool, or joint venture that is carrying on a trade or business and is not classified as a trust, an estate, a qualified joint venture, or a corporation.

      1) Per-se corporations, such as insurance companies, cannot be classified as partnerships.
      2) Tax-exempt organizations cannot be classified as partnerships.
      3) A domestic LLC with at least two members that does not file Form 8832 is classified as a partnership for federal income tax purposes.

   b. An agreement to share expenses does not constitute a partnership.

   c. Co-ownership of rental property is not a partnership unless services are provided to the tenants.

   d. A partnership is allowed to be excluded from treatment as a partnership if it is not in the active conduct of a business, for example, a partnership of individuals who pool their money for investment purposes.

      1) All partners must elect for this treatment to apply.
      2) Each member must separately include his or her share of the income and deductions.

   e. A single-member domestic limited liability company (LLC) is treated as a disregarded entity but alternatively may elect treatment as a corporation for tax purposes.

Partnership Agreement

2. A partnership agreement includes the original agreement that determines the partner's share of income, gains, losses, deductions, and credits.

   a. The agreement must be agreed to by all partners.

   b. The agreement may be modified for a particular tax year after the close of that year but not later than the date for filing the partnership return for that year (excluding any extensions of time).

   c. The agreement must have substantial economic effect; otherwise, the allocation will be made based on the partner's interest in the partnership.

      1) There must be a reasonable possibility that the allocation will substantially affect the dollar amount of the partner's share of ownership.

    2)   The partner to whom an allocation is made actually receives the economic benefit or burden corresponding to that allocation.

Family Partnership

3.   A family partnership is one consisting of a taxpayer and his or her spouse, ancestors, lineal descendants, or trusts for the primary benefit of any of them. Siblings are not treated as members of the taxpayer's family for these purposes. Income or loss from a family partnership should be reported on Form 1065 rather than on Schedule C of Form 1040.

    a.   In Publication 541, under *Family Partnership*, family members will be recognized as partners only if one of the following requirements is met:

        1)   If capital is a material income-producing factor, they acquired their capital interest in a bona fide transaction (even if by gift or purchase from another family member), actually own the partnership interest, and actually control the interest.

        2)   If capital is not a material income-producing factor, they joined together in good faith to conduct a business. They agreed that contributions of each entitle them to a share in the profits, and some capital or service has been (or is) provided by each partner.

    b.   Services. A services partnership is one in which capital is not a material income-producing factor. In a family partnership, a family member is treated as a services partner only to the extent (s)he provides services that are substantial or vital to the partnership.

    c.   Capital. A family member is treated as a partner in a partnership in which capital is a material income-producing factor, whether the interest is acquired by gift or purchase.

        1)   However, the partnership agreement is disregarded to the extent a partner receives less than reasonable compensation for services.

EXAMPLE

R gives Son a gift of $250,000. Son contributes it in exchange for a 50% interest in a newly formed partnership with R. R&R Partnership continues what was R's sole proprietorship. The reasonable value of R's services the following tax year is $75,000. Of R&R's gross income of $125,000, $75,000 must be allocated to R for his services. Son's distributive share attributable to his capital interest is no more than $25,000.

---

        2)   The recipient of gifted interest may not receive income greater than the proportionate share of the donor.

        3)   This rule applies to all, not just some, family members.

    d.   Spouses filing a joint return may elect out of partnership treatment by choosing to be a qualified joint venture.

        1)   The only members of the joint venture must be the husband and wife, and both must materially participate and make the election.

        2)   Each spouse will be treated as a sole proprietor, allowing both to receive Social Security benefits.

Constructive Ownership

4.   An individual is treated as owning the interest owned by his or her spouse, brothers and sisters, children, grandchildren, and parents.

    a.   An interest directly or indirectly owned by or for a corporation, partnership, estate, or trust is considered to be owned proportionately by or for its shareholders, partners, or beneficiaries.

    b.   See Study Unit 13, Subunit 5, and item 13 in Study Unit 16, Subunit 1, for additional coverage of related party and constructive ownership.

Stop and review! You have completed the outline for this subunit. Study questions 1 through 8 beginning on page 168.

8.2 FILING REQUIREMENTS

Tax Year

1. A partner reports his or her distributive share of partnership items, including guaranteed payments, in that tax year of the partner within (or with) which the partnership's tax year ended.

    a. Unless an exception applies (see b. on the next page), the partnership must use a required tax year.

        1) The required tax year is the first of 3), 4), or 5) below that applies.
        2) The partners, not the partnership, are obligated to make any estimated tax payments.

Majority Interest

        3) Majority interest tax year is the tax year of partners owning more than 50% of partnership capital and profits if they have had the same tax year on the first day of the partnership tax year.

Principal Partner

        4) Principal partners' tax year is the same tax year of all principal partners, i.e., partners owning 5% or more in capital and profits.

Least Aggregate Deferral

        5) Least aggregate deferral tax year is determined by multiplying each partner's ownership percentage by the number of months of income deferral for each possible partnership tax year and then selecting the tax year that produces the smallest total tax deferral.

            a) The deferral period begins with the possible partnership tax year-end date and extends to the partner's tax year-end date.

EXAMPLE

A and B each have a 50% interest in a partnership that started business on July 1. A uses a calendar year, while B has a fiscal year ending September 30. Because ownership is split 50/50 and different year endings are used, the least aggregate deferral year must be used. The two calculations are as follows:

12/31 Year End	Year End	Interest in Partnership	Months of Deferral for 12/31 Year End	Interest × Deferral
A	12/31	.5	0	0
B	9/30	.5	9	4.5
			Total deferral	4.5

9/30 Year End	Year End	Interest in Partnership	Months of Deferral for 9/30 Year End	Interest × Deferral
A	12/31	.5	3	1.5
B	9/30	.5	0	0
			Total deferral	1.5

A September 30 year end is the least aggregate deferral year end for the partnership.

b.   A year other than one required may be adopted for a business purpose with IRS approval. Income deferral is not a business purpose.

Natural Business Year

1)   Accounting for a natural business year, e.g., in a seasonal line of business, can be an acceptable business purpose.

a)   It is any 12-month period for which at least 25% of annual gross receipts were received during the last 2 months of each of the preceding 3 years.

Fiscal Year

2)   Under Sec. 444, a partnership may elect a tax year that is neither the required year nor a natural business year. The year elected may result in no more than 3 months of deferral (between the beginning of a tax year elected and the required tax year).

a)   The partnership must also pay an amount approximating the amount of additional tax that would have resulted had the election not been made.

b)   Under Sec. 444, the partnership may make the election only if the partnership is not a member of a tiered structure and it did not previously make a Sec. 444 election other than to change to a shorter deferral period.

Return Due Date

2.   Generally, the return is due by the 15th day of the 4th month following the close of the tax year.

a.   An application for an extension of a partnership tax return is filed on Form 7004. The extension is for 5 months after the original due date of the return.

Domestic Partnership

3.   Every domestic partnership must file Form 1065, unless it neither receives income nor incurs any expenses treated as deductions or credits for federal income tax purposes.

4.   Partnerships having gross receipts under $250,000 and assets under $1,000,000 are not required to file a balance sheet per books (Form 1065, Schedule L), a reconciliation of book income with return income (Schedule M-1), or an analysis of partner's capital accounts (Schedule M-2).

Stop and review! You have completed the outline for this subunit. Study questions 9 through 16 beginning on page 170.

8.3 CONTRIBUTIONS TO A PARTNERSHIP

Contribution of Property

1.   Generally, no gain or loss is recognized on the contribution of property in exchange for a partnership interest. The contribution may occur at the formation of the partnership or after it has been in existence for some time.

a.   Gain or loss is recognized when the following situations occur:

1)   The partnership would be treated as an investment company if it were a corporation. Also, 80% or more of the partnership's assets are marketable securities, and the partner's interest in securities has diversified by the contribution [Code Sec. 721(b)].

2)   The contributed property is distributed to a different partner within 7 years of the contribution date. The contributing partner's recognized gain is the lesser of the precontribution gain or the gain that would result if the property were sold at FMV.

3) When a partner contributes property to a partnership and immediately receives a distribution, the transaction is essentially a sale. Gain realized is recognized to the extent the contributed property is deemed purchased by the other partners.

EXAMPLE

P and Q contributed land with FMVs of $250,000 and $500,000, respectively, each in exchange for a 50% interest in PQ Partnership. PQ mortgaged the land for $550,000 and distributed $250,000 of the proceeds to Q. Q recognizes any gain realized on 50% of the land she contributed. Fifty percent of the AB in the land is included in Q's basis in her partnership interest.

---

4) A partner who contributed property receives a distribution of a different property (other than money) within 7 years of his or her contribution. The contributing partner recognizes gain on the lesser of

    a) FMV of the distributed property over the partner's basis in his or her partnership interest or

    b) The difference between the FMV and the AB of the contributed property on the contribution date.

EXAMPLE

C is a partner in CD Partnership. CD Partnership holds three assets: property #1, property #2, and property #3. C contributed property #1, with an AB of $5,000 and a FMV of $10,000, to the partnership in the current year. The other two properties were acquired by the partnership. C's basis in his partnership interest is $2,000. In Year 5, C receives property #3 (FMV $8,000) in a distribution from the partnership. C's gain is the lesser of (1) $6,000 ($8,000 FMV property distributed – $2,000 AB in partnership interest) or (2) $5,000 ($10,000 FMV property #1 at contribution date – $5,000 AB property #1 at contribution date). C recognizes $5,000 of gain on the distribution.

---

5) A partner acts in an individual capacity in a transaction with the partnership.

  b. The basis of contributed property is the same in the hands of the partnership as it was in the hands of the partner. The holding period is carried over as well.

Contributions of Services

2. The value of a capital interest in a partnership that is transferred to a partner in exchange for services is taxable as ordinary income.

  a. The income recognized is added to the basis of the partnership interest.

  b. The receipt of a profits interest is generally not taxable as ordinary income (Rev. Proc. 93-27).

Liabilities

3. When a partner contributes property subject to a liability or the partnership assumes a liability of the contributing partner, the partner is treated as receiving a distribution of money from the partnership in the amount of the liability.

  a. A distribution reduces the partner's basis in the partnership interest.

EXAMPLE

John contributed an office building with an AB of $500,000 for a share in the partnership. The office building currently has a mortgage with a balance of $200,000. John's basis in the partnership is $300,000 ($500,000 AB – $200,000 mortgage).

Recognized Gain

  b. To the extent liabilities assumed by the partnership exceed the partner's aggregate AB in all property contributed, the partner recognizes gain (and basis in the partnership interest is zero).

    1) Note that a partner still bears responsibility for his or her share of the liabilities assumed by the partnership.

2) If the contributed property was Sec. 1245 or 1250 recapture property, the gain recognized will be characterized as ordinary income to the extent of the recapture gain. Ordinary income recapture potential in excess of the amount of gain recognized remains with the property in the hands of the partnership.

EXAMPLE

In 2013, Albert acquired a 20% interest in a partnership by contributing a parcel of land and $10,000 in cash. At the time of Albert's contribution, the land had a fair market value of $50,000, had an adjusted basis to Albert of $20,000, and was subject to a mortgage of $70,000. Albert's relinquished liability is a gain. When Albert became a 20% partner, he was relieved of 80% of the mortgage debt. Thus, 80% of his $70,000 mortgage, or $56,000, is a benefit to Albert because the other partners are assuming part of the mortgage obligation. Therefore, Albert has a recognized gain of $26,000 ($56,000 benefit – $10,000 cash – $20,000 AB of property).

Stop and review! You have completed the outline for this subunit. Study questions 17 through 23 beginning on page 173.

8.4 PARTNERSHIP INTEREST

1. The original basis of a partner's interest acquired in exchange for contributions of property is the sum of

    a. The money contributed,
    b. The adjusted basis of property contributed, and
    c. The amount of any recognized gain by the partner under Sec. 721(b) on the contribution.

2. The assumption of liabilities by the partner is treated as a contribution of money to the partnership and increases basis.

3. The amount of liabilities assumed by the partnership is treated as a distribution to the contributing partner and reduces basis.

4. A partner's basis in a cash-basis partnership includes liabilities only to the extent that the liability

    a. Creates or increases the partnership's basis in its assets
    b. Gives rise to a current deduction
    c. Gives rise to a nondeductible, noncapital expense of the partnership

5. Accrued but unpaid expenses and accounts payable are not included in the basis of a partner's interest in a cash-basis partnership.

6. A partner includes a liability only to the extent that the partner bears the economic risk of loss.

Partner's Basis

7. A partner's basis in contributed items is exchanged for basis in the partnership interest received, adjusted for gain recognized and liabilities. Using the previous example, the calculation follows:

FORMULA	EXAMPLE
Cash contributed	$10,000
+ AB of property contributed	20,000
+ Any gain recognized on contributed property or services	26,000
+ Share of partnership liabilities	14,000
– Partner's liability assumed by partnership	(70,000)
= **Basis in partnership interest**	$ 0

Partnership's Gain

8. The partnership realizes neither gain nor loss when it receives contributions of money or property in exchange for a partnership interest.

Partnership's Basis

9. The partnership's basis in contributed property is equal to the contributing partner's AB in the property immediately before contribution, increased by any gain recognized by the partner. It is not adjusted for liabilities.

   a. The rule is different if a person provides services to a sole proprietorship in exchange for the sole proprietor's promise that the service provider will become a partner in the business at some future date.

      1) When the partnership is formed, the service provider has gross income of his or her partnership interest percentage times the fair market value of each asset (net of liabilities) of the proprietorship.

      2) The partnership's basis in the assets then includes the amount of gross income recognized by the service provider.

Holding Periods

10. The holding period (HP) of the partner's interest includes the HP of contributed capital and Sec. 1231 assets. If the interest was received in exchange for ordinary income property or services, the HP starts the day following the exchange.

    a. The partnership's HP in contributed property includes the partner's HP, even if the partner recognized gain.

Partner Purchased Interest

11. The basis in a partnership interest purchased from a partner is its cost, which is the sum of the purchase price and the partner's share of partnership liabilities.

    a. The partnership may elect to adjust the basis in its assets by the difference between the transferee's basis in his or her partnership interest and his or her proportionate share of the partnership's adjusted basis (AB) in its assets. This is referred to as a Sec. 754 election.

       1) The difference is allocated first to Sec. 1231 property and capital assets and then to other partnership property (usually ordinary assets). Finally, allocation is made to assets within each of the two classes.

          a) For upward adjustment, allocation is on the basis of relative appreciation of classes and assets. No adjustment is made to a depreciated class or asset.

          b) For downward adjustment, allocation is on the basis of relative depreciation of classes and assets. No allocation is made to an appreciated class or asset.

       2) Sec. 743 provides that this adjustment to basis will apply only for the transferee partner.

Stop and review! You have completed the outline for this subunit. Study questions 24 through 30 beginning on page 175.

QUESTIONS

8.1 Partnership Defined

1. For federal tax purposes, the term "partnership" includes all of the following except a

- A. Syndicate.
- B. Pool.
- C. Joint venture.
- D. Trust.

Answer (D) is correct.
   REQUIRED: The item not included in the term "partnership."
   DISCUSSION: Subchapter K is the part of the Code containing most of the tax rules that apply to partnerships. A partnership is defined under Sec. 761(a) as including a syndicate, group, pool, joint venture, or other unincorporated organization that carries on a business and is not a corporation, a trust, or an estate.

2. Which of the following statements about partnership agreements is false?

- A. Modifications to the partnership agreement must be agreed to by all the partners or adopted in any other manner provided by the partnership agreement.
- B. The agreement or modifications can be oral or written.
- C. The partnership agreement can be modified for a particular tax year after the close of the year but not later than the date for filing the partnership return for that year, including extensions.
- D. A partner's share of income, gains, losses, deductions, or credits is usually determined by the partnership agreement.

Answer (C) is correct.
   REQUIRED: The false statement about partnership agreements.
   DISCUSSION: A partnership agreement may be modified with respect to a particular tax year after the close of the year but not later than the date for filing the partnership return for that year (excluding any extensions) [Reg. 1.761-1(c)].
   Answer (A) is incorrect. A partnership agreement includes the original agreement and any modifications agreed to by all the partners or adopted in any other manner provided by the partnership agreement. Answer (B) is incorrect. A partnership agreement and/or modifications to it can be oral or written. Answer (D) is incorrect. Allocations of partnership items of income, loss, etc., in the partnership agreement are generally respected for federal income tax purposes.

3. A domestic limited liability company with at least two members that does not file Form 8832, *Entity Classification Election*, is classified as

- A. An entity disregarded as an entity separate from its owner by applying the rules in Reg. 301.7701-3.
- B. A partnership.
- C. A corporation.
- D. A non-entity, which requires members to report the income and related expenses on Form 1040.

Answer (B) is correct.
   REQUIRED: The correct classification of an LLC that does not file Form 8832.
   DISCUSSION: An organization formed after 1996 is classified as a partnership for federal tax purposes if it has two or more members. However, certain entities with two or more members are not partnerships if they are classified as something else, such as any other organization that elects to be classified as a corporation by filing Form 8832. A domestic LLC with at least two members that does not file Form 8832 is classified as a partnership for federal income tax purposes.

4. Jane gave each of her two children, Jake and Jeff, a 30% interest in her clothing store. Capital is a material income-producing factor. Jeff is 21 and has worked in the store since he was 15, has developed significant sales skills, and helps his mom with the management duties. Jake is 25, is married, has a job in another state, and does not participate in any of the store's management decisions. Who is(are) recognized as a partner(s)?

- A. Jane.
- B. Jane and Jake.
- C. Jane, Jake, and Jeff.
- D. Jane and Jeff.

Answer (C) is correct.
   REQUIRED: The recognized partners in a family partnership.
   DISCUSSION: Sec. 704 defines a family partnership as one consisting of a taxpayer and his or her spouse, ancestors, lineal descendants, or trusts for the primary benefit of any of them. A family member is treated as a partner in a partnership in which capital is a material income-producing factor, whether the interest is acquired by gift or purchase. However, the partnership agreement is disregarded to the extent a partner receives less than reasonable compensation for services.
   Answer (A) is incorrect. Jeff and Jake are also considered partners because capital is a material income-producing factor and Jeff and Jake acquired their interest by gift. Answer (B) is incorrect. Jeff is a partner since he acquired his interest by gift. Answer (D) is incorrect. Jake is a partner since he acquired his interest by gift.

5. John sold his daughter 50% of his business partnership. The partnership had an $80,000 profit this year before deducting any compensation to the partner as a guaranteed payment. Capital is a material income-producing factor. John performed services worth $55,000, which is reasonable compensation. The daughter performed no services. How much income will John claim on his individual tax return?

A. $40,000

B. $55,000

C. $67,500

D. $80,000

Answer (C) is correct.

REQUIRED: The amount of income a partner who receives compensation will claim on the individual return.

DISCUSSION: In a partnership in which a partner performs services for compensation and capital is a material-producing factor, the compensation is first allocated from profits to the respective partner. Any remaining profits are then distributed to each partner in their respective share. Therefore, John must claim $67,500 ($55,000 + $12,500) on his return (Publication 541).

Answer (A) is incorrect. The compensation must first be deducted before profits are distributed. Answer (B) is incorrect. John's share of profits due to capital of 50%, or $12,500, must also be claimed. Answer (D) is incorrect. John's daughter must receive his portion of profits attributable to the capital, $12,500.

6. Andrew is a 40% partner in the ABC Partnership, in which capital is a material income-producing factor. He gives one-half of his interest to his brother, John. During the current year, Andrew performs services for the partnership for which reasonable compensation is $65,000 but for which he accepts no pay. Andrew and John are each credited with a $100,000 distributive share of the partnership's ordinary income. How much should Andrew report?

A. $132,500

B. $100,000

C. $67,500

D. $105,000

Answer (A) is correct.

REQUIRED: The maximum amount of profit a partner can report in the tax year in which he gave an interest to his brother.

DISCUSSION: The partnership agreement is disregarded to the extent a partner receives less than reasonable compensation for services. Of ABC's $200,000 gross income credited to Andrew and John, $65,000 must be allocated to Andrew for his services. The remaining $135,000 is split between the two. Thus, Andrew should report $132,500 [($65,000 + ($135,000 × 1/2)].

Answer (B) is incorrect. Of ABC's $200,000 gross income credited to Andrew and John, $65,000 must be allocated to Andrew for his services. The remaining $135,000 is split between the two. Answer (C) is incorrect. The amount of $65,000 for services must also be allocated to Andrew. Answer (D) is incorrect. The partnership agreement is disregarded to the extent a partner receives less than reasonable compensation for services. Of ABC's $200,000 gross income credited to Andrew and John, $65,000 must be allocated to Andrew for his services. The remaining $135,000 is split between the two.

7. In determining the ownership rules of partnerships, which one of the following combinations would total more than 50% ownership of The Peach Company for Jake?

A.	Jake	30%
	Jake's wife	10%
	Jake's aunt	60%
B.	Jake	45%
	His uncle's trust	55%
C.	Jake	10%
	Jake's wife's corporation	90%
D.	Jake	30%
	Jake's father	10%
	Jake's nephew	60%

Answer (C) is correct.

REQUIRED: The constructive ownership percentages of a partnership.

DISCUSSION: An individual is treated as owning the stock owned by his or her spouse, siblings, children, grandchildren, and parents. If 50% or more in value of the interest in a partnership is owned, directly or indirectly, by or for any person, that person is considered to own the interest, directly or indirectly, by or for his or her partnership in the proportion that the value of the stock (s)he owns bears to the value of all the stock in the partnership. Stock owned, directly or indirectly, by or for a trust is considered to be owned by its beneficiaries in proportion to their actuarial interest in the trust. Stock owned, directly or indirectly, by or for an estate is considered to be owned proportionately by the beneficiaries. Jake is considered to own more than 50% of the partnership only in the answer choice stating that Jake has 10% direct ownership plus 90% indirect ownership from his wife's corporation.

Answer (A) is incorrect. Jake's aunt's ownership is not constructively owned by Jake. Answer (B) is incorrect. Jake's uncle's trust is not constructively owned by Jake. Answer (D) is incorrect. Jake's nephew's ownership is not constructively owned by Jake.

8. Dianne owns 10% interest in DJJ Partnership and 20% of the outstanding stock of PAD Corporation. Her son, Nick, owns 60% of the outstanding shares of PAD Corporation. The PAD Corporation owns 50% interest in the DJJ Partnership. Dianne's sister, Dolores, owns 40% interest in the DJJ Partnership. Using the constructive ownership rules for partnerships, Dianne is considered to own how much of DJJ Partnership?

A. 80%

B. 50%

C. 90%

D. 20%

Answer (C) is correct.

REQUIRED: The total interest a partner owns under the constructive ownership rules.

DISCUSSION: An individual is treated as owning the stock owned by his or her spouse, brothers and sisters, children, grandchildren, and parents. If 50% or more in value of the stock in a corporation is owned, directly or indirectly, by or for any person, that person is considered to own the stock, directly or indirectly, by or for his or her corporation in the proportion that the value of the stock (s)he owns bears to the value of all the stock in the corporation. Dianne is considered to own 90% of the partnership: 10% direct ownership, plus 80% indirect ownership (made up of her 20% ownership of the corporation plus her son's 60% ownership of the corporation times the 50% corporate ownership of the partnership), plus her sister's 40% ownership.

Answer (A) is incorrect. Dianne's indirect ownership must be included (20% × 50%). Answer (B) is incorrect. The stock the sister owns must be included. Answer (D) is incorrect. Twenty percent is the percentage of stock that Dianne owns in PAD Corporation.

8.2 Filing Requirements

9. Bytes, Ltd. is a partnership formed by Warren Corporation, JCL Corporation, and Mike (an individual) to build and repair personal computers. The partners' profits interest in Bytes and their respective taxable years are stated below. Assuming there is no business purpose for any particular year and no Sec. 444 election has been made, determine the partnership's required taxable year.

Partner	Profits & Capital Interests	Taxable Year End
Warren Corporation	25%	May 31
JCL Corporation	40%	August 31
Mike	35%	Calendar

A. Since no business purpose to establish a particular year exists, the partnership must adopt the calendar taxable year.

B. The partnership may adopt a taxable year ending either May 31 or August 31.

C. Under the required tax year rules, the partnership must adopt a taxable year ending August 31.

D. Under the required tax year rules, the partnership must adopt a calendar year.

Answer (B) is correct.

REQUIRED: The correct taxable year of a partnership.

DISCUSSION: A partnership's required tax year is that of the partner(s) owning more than 50% of the partnership's capital and profits. If the majority partner(s) do(es) not have the same year, the tax year of all principal (5%) partners must be adopted. If all principal partners do not have the same taxable year, the partnership must adopt the tax year of the partner that results in the least aggregate deferral of income to the partners. Least aggregate deferral tax year is determined by multiplying each partner's ownership percentage by the number of months of income deferral for each possible partnership tax year and then selecting the tax year that produces the smallest total tax deferral. Using Warren's tax year would result in aggregate deferral of 3.65 [(3 × 40%) + (7 × 35%) + (0 × 25%)]. Using Warren's tax year of May 31, JCL would have a deferral of 3 months (June, July, and August). Mike would have a deferral of 7 months (June through December). Using JCL's tax year would result in aggregate deferral of 3.65 [(4 × 35%) + (9 × 25%) + (0 × 40%)]. Using Mike's tax year would result in aggregate deferral of 4.45 [(5 × 25%) + (8 × 40%) + (0 × 35%)]. Because Warren and JCL's tax years result in the least deferral of income, the partnership can choose either one.

Answer (A) is incorrect. Partnership's required tax year is first of the partner(s) owning more than 50%, then of all principal partners, and lastly of the partner that results in the least aggregate deferral. Answer (C) is incorrect. JCL and Warren's tax year result in the least aggregate deferral of income, so the partnership must choose one of these two and is not obligated to either one. Answer (D) is incorrect. Under the required tax year rules, the partnership must pick a tax year of first of the partner(s) owning more than 50%, then of all principal partners, and lastly of the partner that results in the least aggregate referral.

10. Alpha Partnership is on a fiscal year ending March 31. Partner Alf reports income on the fiscal year ending March 31, and Partner Omega reports income on the fiscal year ending September 30. Both partners have a 50% interest in partnership profits. Assuming the partnership does not make a Sec. 444 election and does not establish a business purpose for a different period, what tax year must the partnership use to file its tax return?

A. Any month end.

B. March 31.

C. September 30.

D. December 31.

Answer (B) is correct.

REQUIRED: The tax year the partnership must use to file its tax return.

DISCUSSION: A partnership's required tax year is that of the partner(s) owning more than 50% of partnership capital and profits. If the majority partner(s) do(es) not have the same year, the tax year of all principal (5%) partners must be adopted. If all principal partners do not have the same taxable year, under Temp. Reg. 1.706-1T(a)(1) and (2), the partnership must adopt the tax year of the partner that results in the least aggregate deferral of income to the partners. Aggregate deferral is the sum of the products of deferral for each partner and each partner's interest in partnership profits. Using Alf's tax year results in aggregate deferral of 3.0 [(0 × 50%) + (6 × 50%)]. Using Omega's tax year would result in aggregate deferral of 3.0 [(6 × 50%) + (0 × 50%)]. Temp. Reg. 1.706-1T(a)(2) further provides that, if one or more than one qualifying tax year is also the partnership's existing tax year, the partnership must maintain its existing tax year.

Answer (A) is incorrect. Temp. Reg. 1.706-1T(a) requires that the partnership adopt a tax year that results in the least aggregate deferral of income to the partners. Answer (C) is incorrect. If one or more than one qualifying tax years is also the partnership's existing tax year, the partnership must maintain its existing tax year. Answer (D) is incorrect. Temp. Reg. 1.706-1T(a) requires that the partnership adopt a tax year that results in the least aggregate deferral of income to the partners.

11. Abraham becomes an equal partner in the Kit, Kat, and Kidd Partnership in 2013. In 2012, he filed his personal tax return on the calendar tax year basis. The partnership reports income and expenses on the fiscal tax year basis. How should Abraham report partnership income or loss distributed to him?

A. Abraham may choose a fiscal year to report income and expenses.

B. Abraham must report income and expenses on the calendar year basis.

C. Abraham may choose either a calendar tax year or fiscal tax year to report income and expenses.

D. Abraham may choose a fiscal tax year and later obtain IRS approval if he wishes to change to a calendar tax year for reporting income and expenses.

Answer (B) is correct.

REQUIRED: The appropriate tax year for a new partner to report partnership income or loss.

DISCUSSION: A partner can only change his or her tax year with approval from the IRS. Although Abraham, a calendar-year taxpayer, joins as a partner into a fiscal-year partnership, he must continue to use the calendar year when filing his tax returns (Publication 541).

Answer (A) is incorrect. Abraham must continue to use the calendar year when filing his tax returns unless he receives IRS approval to change to a fiscal year. Answer (C) is incorrect. Abraham must continue to use the calendar year when filing his tax returns unless he receives IRS approval to change to a fiscal year. Answer (D) is incorrect. Abraham must report income and expenses on the calendar-year basis and then later obtain IRS approval if he wishes to switch to fiscal year.

12. Which of the following is one of the conditions a partnership must meet to be eligible to make a Sec. 444 election (election to use a tax year that is different from a required tax year)?

A. The partnership must not choose a tax year with a deferral period that is longer than 6 months or with the deferral period of the tax year being changed, if this period is shorter.

B. The partnership has not previously had a Sec. 444 election other than to change an election to a shorter deferral period.

C. The partnership establishes a business purpose for a different period.

D. The partnership is a member of a tiered structure.

Answer (B) is correct.

REQUIRED: The item that is a condition to make the Sec. 444 election.

DISCUSSION: A partnership may elect to use a tax year other than the tax year required. Under Sec. 444, the partnership may make the election only if the partnership is not a member of a tiered structure, it did not previously make a Sec. 444 election, and the deferral period is not longer than 3 months.

Answer (A) is incorrect. The deferral period must not be longer than 3 months. Answer (C) is incorrect. The partnership does not have to establish a business purpose to make a Sec. 444 election. Answer (D) is incorrect. The partnership must not be a member of a tiered structure.

13. A partnership, S corporation, or personal service corporation can elect to use a tax year other than its required tax year if it

    A. Elects a year that meets the deferral period requirement.

    B. Is not a member of a tiered structure as defined by the regulations.

    C. Has not previously had an election in effect to use a tax year other than its required tax year.

    D. All of the answers are correct.

Answer (D) is correct.
    REQUIRED: The tax year election.
    DISCUSSION: A partnership, S corporation, or personal service corporation can elect to use a tax year other than its required tax year if it elects a tax year that meets the deferral period requirement, is not a member of a tiered structure as defined by the regulations, and has not previously had an election in effect to use a tax year other than its required tax year.

14. Which of the following is a true statement with respect to a partnership electing under Sec. 444 a fiscal year that is not normally a required tax year and for which a business purpose does not exist?

    A. The election requires the partners to pay an additional tax on their income from the partnership.

    B. The election requires a payment to approximate the tax the partners would have paid if the partnership had switched to its required year.

    C. The election requires minimum distributions to be made to the partners.

    D. Any fiscal year may be selected if the required payment is made.

Answer (B) is correct.
    REQUIRED: The true statement concerning a partnership's election of a fiscal year under Sec. 444.
    DISCUSSION: A partnership may elect, under Sec. 444, a fiscal year that is not normally a required tax year and for which a business purpose does not exist. However, for the election to be effective, Sec. 7519 requires a payment intended to approximate the tax the partners would have paid if the entity had switched to its required year.
    Answer (A) is incorrect. The partnership makes the additional payment (similar to a deposit), not the partners. Answer (C) is incorrect. Minimum distributions are required of a personal service corporation to elect a fiscal year, not a partnership. Answer (D) is incorrect. The fiscal year may not result in more than a 3-month deferral unless the partnership existed in 1986 and is retaining the fiscal year it had at that time.

15. New ABC Partnership is organized in the current year with three general partners. The partners include a corporation with a tax year ending on March 31 and a 60% interest in partnership capital and profits, and two individuals, each having a calendar tax year and a 20% interest in partnership capital and profits. The partnership's required tax year ends on

    A. March 31.

    B. September 30.

    C. October 31.

    D. December 31.

Answer (A) is correct.
    REQUIRED: The tax year of a partnership.
    DISCUSSION: Unless an exception applies, the partnership must use a required tax year. The first required tax year stipulated by the IRC is the majority interest tax year. The majority interest tax year is the tax year of partners owning more than 50% of partnership capital and profits if they have had the same tax year on the first day of the partnership tax year. Since the corporate partner owns 60% of the interest in ABC Partnership, the partnership must use a tax year ending on March 31.

16. DCS Partnership, formed on July 8, Year 1, elected to use a fiscal year ending September 30. DCS is required to file its return by which of the following dates?

    A. December 15, Year 1.

    B. January 15, Year 2.

    C. February 15, Year 2.

    D. April 15, Year 2.

Answer (B) is correct.
    REQUIRED: The required due date for a partnership tax return.
    DISCUSSION: Generally, Form 1065 must be filed by the 15th day of the 4th month following the close of the partnership's tax year. For a tax year ending September 30, the return must be filed by January 15 of the following year. The dates may be adjusted for weekends and holidays.

8.3 Contributions to a Partnership

17. Generally, no gain or loss is recognized by the partnership or a partner when the partner contributes property to the partnership, unless

    A. The partnership is being formed.

    B. A gain is realized on the transfer of property to a partnership that would be treated as an investment company if the partnership were incorporated.

    C. The partnership is already operating.

    D. Unencumbered depreciable property is contributed.

Answer (B) is correct.
    REQUIRED: The correct time to record a gain or loss on contributed property to a partnership.
    DISCUSSION: Generally, no gain or loss is recognized on the contribution of property in exchange for a partnership interest. However, there are exceptions to this rule. One exception is if the partnership would be treated as an investment company if it were a corporation.
    Answer (A) is incorrect. No gain or loss is recognized when property is contributed during the partnership's formation. Answer (C) is incorrect. No gain or loss is recognized when the partnership is already running. Answer (D) is incorrect. It does not matter if the property is unencumbered depreciable property.

18. Scott contributed property having an adjusted basis to him of $10,000, to LMN Partnership for a 45% interest in the partnership. At the time of the contribution, the property had a fair market value of $20,000. What is the amount and character of Scott's gain on this transaction to be reported on his tax return?

    A. $0

    B. $4,500 long-term capital gain.

    C. $10,000 ordinary income.

    D. $10,000 long-term capital gain.

Answer (A) is correct.
    REQUIRED: The gain reported on a contribution of capital to a partnership.
    DISCUSSION: When property is contributed to a partnership in exchange for a partnership interest, the general rule is that no gain or loss is recognized by the partner or the partnership [Sec. 721(a)]. This rule applies even though the contributed property is appreciated and the partner receives a disproportionate interest in the partnership. For assets contributed after March 31, 1984, precontribution gain on the asset is allocated to the contributing partner when the partnership later sells the asset.

19. Patti and Kae formed a partnership in which they share income and loss equally. Kae contributes land on which there is a recourse mortgage of $18,000. The land has an adjusted basis to Kae of $15,000 and a fair market value of $20,000 at the time of the contribution. Patti contributes $2,000 to the partnership in cash. What amount of gain should Kae recognize as a result of the contribution of property?

    A. $0

    B. $9,000

    C. $5,000

    D. $2,000

Answer (A) is correct.
    REQUIRED: The amount of gain to be recognized on the contribution of property.
    DISCUSSION: Generally, no gain or loss is recognized on the contribution of property in exchange for a partnership interest; however, a gain or loss could be recognized to the extent liabilities assumed by the other partner exceed the partner's aggregate adjusted basis in all property contributed. The only other partner, Patti, assumed a liability of half the mortgage, or $9,000, and the aggregate adjusted basis is $15,000 from the land plus $2,000 from the cash contributed. The liability reduces Kae's adjusted basis, but there is no gain on this transaction because the liability assumed does not exceed Kae's adjusted basis.
    Answer (B) is incorrect. The liability that is assumed by the partnership is $9,000. Because Kae's AB is bigger than this amount, no gain is recognized. Answer (C) is incorrect. No gain is recognized on contributed property when the FMV exceeds the AB. This gain is deferred until the partnership sells the property. Answer (D) is incorrect. Kae's AB is larger than the amount of liability assumed; thus, there is no gain or loss recognized on this transaction.

20. Sharon provides services to a partnership during the year in exchange for a capital interest of 30% worth $25,000. Sharon's basis in the partnership is

A. Zero since she exchanged services for her interest.

B. $25,000, which must be reported by her as income in the year of receipt if the interest is vested.

C. The present value of $25,000, computed over the lesser of Sharon's remaining life or the average remaining life of the other partners.

D. Considered a profits interest and has a zero basis.

Answer (B) is correct.
   REQUIRED: The correct basis in a partnership when the interest is exchanged for services.
   DISCUSSION: The value of a capital interest in a partnership that is transferred to a partner in exchange for services is taxable as ordinary income. The income recognized is added to the basis of the partnership interest.
   Answer (A) is incorrect. Services can be exchanged for a capital interest in a partnership. Answer (C) is incorrect. A capital interest in a partnership that is transferred to a partner in exchange for services is valued at what they are worth today, and it is not discounted over any period of time. Answer (D) is incorrect. A profits interest is when the partner's only interest is in the future earnings of the partnership, with no interest in the current partnership assets.

21. On April 10, Year 1, Reuben contributed land in exchange for a 25% partnership interest in Larson Partners. The fair market value of the land at that time was $60,000, and Reuben's adjusted basis was $25,000. On November 1, Year 5, Larson distributed that land to another partner. The fair market value at that time was $65,000. What is the amount of Reuben's recognized gain from the transfer of the land by Larson to another partner?

A. $5,000

B. $25,000

C. $35,000

D. $40,000

Answer (C) is correct.
   REQUIRED: The amount of precontribution gain when a partnership distributes contributed property.
   DISCUSSION: For property contributed to a partnership after 10/3/89 that had a deferred precontribution gain or loss, the contributing partner must recognize the precontribution gain or loss when the property is distributed to any other partner within 7 years of its contribution [Sec. 704(c)(1)(B)]. The precontribution gain or loss that is recognized equals the remaining precontribution gain or loss which would have been allocated to the contributing partner if the property had instead been sold for its fair market value on the distribution date. Reuben recognizes a $35,000 gain ($60,000 FMV at contribution date − $25,000 adjusted basis).
   Answer (A) is incorrect. The gain is not calculated by subtracting the fair market value at distribution from the fair market value at the time of contribution. Answer (B) is incorrect. The $25,000 is the adjusted basis of the property when it is contributed. Answer (D) is incorrect. The difference between the fair market value of the property when distributed and the adjusted basis of the property at contribution is $40,000.

22. Taxpayer A contributed stock with a FMV of $10,000 and a basis of $5,000 to ABC Partnership (which would be treated as an investment company if it had been incorporated) for a 50% interest. What is the partnership's basis in the stock?

A. $0

B. $2,500

C. $5,000

D. $10,000

Answer (D) is correct.
   REQUIRED: The basis of property contributed to a partnership by a partner to the partnership.
   DISCUSSION: The partnership's basis of property contributed to a partnership by a partner is the adjusted basis of the property to the contributing partner at the time of the contribution. However, if the partnership is an investment company partnership, the partnership's basis for property contributed is increased by the amount of gain recognized by the contributing partner. Therefore, ABC's basis in the stock is $10,000 ($5,000 adjusted basis + $5,000 gain recognized by Taxpayer A).
   Answer (A) is incorrect. The partnership does have a basis in the stock. Answer (B) is incorrect. The basis is not limited to 50% of the partner's basis. Answer (C) is incorrect. The basis would carry over for a company that was not an investment company. However, since this partnership is, the gain recognized by the taxpayer must be added.

23. Audra acquired a 50% interest in a partnership by contributing property that had an adjusted basis of $20,000 and a fair market value of $50,000. The property was subject to a liability of $44,000, which the partnership assumed for legitimate business purposes. Which of the following statements is true?

A. Audra must include a gain from the sale or exchange of a capital asset on her individual return, and her basis in her partnership interest increases.

B. Audra must include a gain on her individual return, and her basis in her partnership interest is zero.

C. Audra is not required to include a gain on her individual return, and her basis in her partnership interest is zero.

D. Audra is not required to include a gain on her individual return, but the gain increases her basis in her partnership interest.

Answer (B) is correct.
  REQUIRED: The true statement regarding gain recognition on a contribution to a partnership.
  DISCUSSION: When encumbered property is contributed to a partnership, a partner recognizes gain to the extent the partner is deemed to be relieved of a portion of the debt. Audra has a $42,000 basis upon contribution ($20,000 property basis plus $22,000, which is half of the $44,000 debt). She is also deemed to receive a cash distribution of $44,000 (the amount of the debt), creating a gain of $2,000. The distribution also reduces the basis in her partnership interest to zero.
  Answer (A) is incorrect. The gain recognized does not affect the basis in the partnership interest. Answer (C) is incorrect. A gain is recognized when a distribution exceeds the partner's basis in the partnership interest. Answer (D) is incorrect. A gain is recognized when a distribution exceeds the partner's basis in the partnership interest.

8.4 Partnership Interest

24. If the partner's distributive share of a partnership item cannot be determined under the partnership agreement, it is determined by his or her interest in the partnership. The partnership interest is determined by taking into account all of the following items except the

A. Partner's relative contributions to the partnership.

B. Interests of all partners in economic profits and losses (if different from interests in taxable income or loss) and in cash flow and other nonliquidating distributions.

C. Amount of the partnership's nonrecourse liabilities.

D. Right of the partners to distributions of capital upon liquidation.

Answer (C) is correct.
  REQUIRED: The factor that does not determine a partnership interest.
  DISCUSSION: Publication 541 states, "If a partner's distributive share of a partnership item cannot be determined under the partnership agreement, it is determined by his or her interest in the partnership. The partner's interest is determined by taking into account all of the following items:

● The partners' relative contributions to the partnership.

● The interests of all partners in economic profits and losses (if different from interest in taxable income or loss) and in cash flow and other nonliquidating distributions.

● The rights of the partners to distributions of capital upon liquidation."

  Answer (A) is incorrect. The partner's relative contributions to the partnership are taken into account in determining a partnership interest. Answer (B) is incorrect. The interests of all partners in economic profits and losses (if different from interests in taxable income or loss) and in cash flow and other nonliquidating distributions are taken into account in determining a partnership interest. Answer (D) is incorrect. The right of the partners to distributions of capital upon liquidation is taken into account in determining a partnership interest.

25. Marlene acquired a 30% interest in a partnership by contributing property that had an adjusted basis to her of $25,000, a fair market value of $50,000, and a $40,000 mortgage. The partnership assumed the liability. What is Marlene's gain or loss on the contribution of her property to the partnership?

A. $0

B. $3,000 gain.

C. $12,000 gain.

D. $10,000 loss.

Answer (B) is correct.
  REQUIRED: The gain or loss recognized on the contribution of encumbered property to a partnership.
  DISCUSSION: To the extent liabilities assumed by the partnership exceed the partner's aggregate adjusted basis in all property contributed, the partner recognizes gain. Accordingly, Marlene recognizes a $3,000 gain [($40,000 × 70%) – $25,000]. Note that a partner still bears responsibility for his or her share of the liabilities assumed by the partnership.
  Answer (A) is incorrect. The partnership recognizes no gain or loss, but Marlene does because she received boot from the partnership's assumption of her mortgage. Answer (C) is incorrect. The gain is not calculated on the mortgage assumed. Answer (D) is incorrect. The fair market value of the property exceeds the mortgage.

26. A partner who acquired a part of his partnership in a sale may be able to choose a special basis adjustment for the property. Which of the following is true?

A. The distribution must be made within 1 year after the partner acquired the partnership interest.

B. The partner's basis for the property distributed is the same as it would have been if the partnership had chosen the optional adjustment to basis.

C. The partnership may also choose the optional adjustment to basis when the partner acquired the partnership interest.

D. All of the answers are correct.

Answer (B) is correct.
REQUIRED: The effect on property basis acquired in a sale to the partner.
DISCUSSION: The partnership may not choose the optional adjustment to basis.
Answer (A) is incorrect. The distribution must be made within 2 years, not 1 year. Answer (C) is incorrect. This question is asking the rules when a partner receiving a distribution from the partnership can qualify for a special basis adjustment. This question is applying the rules of Sec. 732, not Sec. 754. These rules are discussed in Publication 541. Answer (D) is incorrect. "The partner's basis for the property distributed is the same as it would have been if the partnership had chosen the optional adjustment to basis" is the only true statement taken directly from the publication.

27. Josephine acquired a 20% interest in a partnership by contributing property that had an adjusted basis to her of $8,000 and a $4,000 mortgage. The partnership assumed payment of the mortgage. What is the basis of Josephine's interest?

A. $1,600

B. $4,000

C. $4,800

D. $8,000

Answer (C) is correct.
REQUIRED: The taxpayer's basis in a partnership interest when mortgaged property is contributed.
DISCUSSION: Under Sec. 722, the basis of a partnership interest acquired by the contribution of property is the adjusted basis of the property to the contributing partner. Under Sec. 752(b), the assumption by a partnership of a partner's individual liabilities is treated as a distribution of money to the partner, which reduces the basis of the partner's interest (Sec. 733). Josephine's basis is the $8,000 adjusted basis of the equipment contributed less the relieved individual liability ($4,000 × 80% = $3,200). The basis is $4,800 ($8,000 – $3,200).
Answer (A) is incorrect. The basis is not calculated by multiplying the percent interest times the adjusted basis of the contributed property. Answer (B) is incorrect. The basis is the adjusted basis of the equipment less the percentage of the mortgage actually relieved. Answer (D) is incorrect. The basis is the basis of the equipment less any relieved individual liability.

28. Three individuals formed a partnership sharing in profits and losses equally. Mr. Aardvark contributed $10,000 cash. Mr. Baboon contributed $5,000 in cash and land worth $5,000 with an adjusted basis of $4,000. Mr. Camel contributed machinery with a fair market value of $16,000 subject to a mortgage of $6,000, which the partnership assumed, and with an adjusted basis of $16,000. The partnership has no other liabilities. The adjusted basis of Mr. Baboon's interest in the partnership is

A. $5,000

B. $9,000

C. $10,000

D. $11,000

Answer (D) is correct.
REQUIRED: The adjusted basis of a partner's interest received in exchange for cash and property.
DISCUSSION: The basis of a partnership interest acquired by a contribution of property and money is the adjusted basis of property contributed plus the amount of money contributed (Sec. 722). An increase in a partner's share of partnership liabilities is treated as an additional cash contribution [Sec. 752(a)], which increases the partner's basis. Mr. Baboon's adjusted basis is

Money contributed	$ 5,000
Adjusted basis of land contributed	4,000
Share of partnership's liabilities (1/3 of $6,000)	2,000
Baboon's adjusted basis	$11,000

Answer (A) is incorrect. The adjusted basis of the property and the partner's share of the partnership liabilities also increase basis. Answer (B) is incorrect. The partner's share of the partnership liabilities also increases basis. Answer (C) is incorrect. The basis does not equal the cash and the fair market value of the land.

29. Bob acquired a 50% interest in a partnership by contributing depreciable property that had an adjusted basis of $15,000 and a fair market value of $45,000. The property was subject to a liability of $32,000, which the partnership assumed for legitimate business purposes. What is the partnership's basis in the property for depreciation?

A. $0

B. $13,000

C. $15,000

D. $16,000

30. The holding period of property acquired by a partnership as a contribution to the contributing partner's capital account

A. Begins with the date of contribution to the partnership.

B. Includes the period during which the property was held by the contributing partner.

C. Is equal to the contributing partner's holding period prior to contribution to the partnership.

D. Depends on the character of the property transferred.

Answer (D) is correct.
 REQUIRED: The partnership's basis in contributed property.
 DISCUSSION: Under Sec. 723, the partnership's basis for contributed property is the adjusted basis of such property to the contributing partner at the time of contribution, provided it is not an investment partnership plus any gain recognized by the partner. Bob is required to recognize $1,000 upon contribution of the asset in order to bring his basis in the partnership up to zero. Upon contribution, Bob's basis in the partnership equals $1,000 [($15,000 – $32,000) + (50% × $32,000)]. This triggers the $1,000 gain.
 Answer (A) is incorrect. The partner's basis is $0, and the basis of the contributing partner carries over to the partnership. Answer (B) is incorrect. The FMV of the property less the assumed mortgage is not the basis of the property. Answer (C) is incorrect. The basis of the property must be increased by any gain recognized.

Answer (B) is correct.
 REQUIRED: The holding period of contributed property.
 DISCUSSION: The partnership's holding period for contributed property includes the period of time the property was held by the contributing partner [Sec. 1223(2)]. The holding period of the partner "tacks on" because the partnership receives a carryover basis in the contributed property. This is true even if the contributing partner recognizes a gain or loss.

Use the additional questions in Gleim **EA Test Prep** to create Practice Exams that emulate Prometric!

STUDY UNIT NINE
PARTNERSHIP OPERATIONS

(11 pages of outline)

A partnership is a business organization, other than a corporation, a trust, or an estate, co-owned by two or more persons and operated for a profit.

The partnership, as an untaxed, flow-through entity, reports taxable income or loss and separately stated items. When computing his or her personal income tax liability, an individual partner must consider his or her distributive share of the partnership's taxable income or loss and every other separately stated item for the partnership, regardless of whether any distributions were made from the partnership to the partner. The same applies in computing alternative minimum tax (AMT) liability.

Nonseparately and separately stated partnership items are currently taxed to the partners, but distributions are generally received tax-free. You should identify the different loss limitation rules. Partnership inventory and unrealized receivables are very important because they can trigger ordinary income to one partner when another partner receives a distribution (even of money). Similarly, precontribution gain must be identified as it can trigger and recharacterize otherwise unrecognized capital gain. Partnership liability fluctuations also have special significance because they vary the partners' bases in their partnership interests and affect treatment of distributions. Be prepared to identify a payment to a partner as a guaranteed payment, as a distributive share, or in a nonpartner capacity, and the effect of the classification, e.g., a deduction to the partnership passed through ratably to all partners.

9.1 PARTNERSHIP OPERATIONS AND PARTNER'S TAXABLE INCOME

Partnership-Incurred Liabilities

1. A partner's share of partnership liabilities affects the partner's basis in his or her partnership interest and can result in increased gain being recognized by the partner.

Recourse Liabilities

   a. A liability is a recourse liability if the creditor has a claim against the partnership or any partner for payment if the partnership defaults.

   1) Partners generally share recourse liabilities based on their ratio for sharing losses.

   a) However, regulations allocate a recourse liability to the partner(s) who would be liable for it if, at the time, all partnership debts were due, all partnership assets (including cash) had zero value, and hypothetical liquidation occurred.

   b) A partner who pays more than his or her proportionate share of a partnership debt that becomes uncollectible is permitted to take a bad debt deduction equal to the amount in excess of that partner's share of the debt.

   2) A limited partner cannot share in recourse debt in excess of any of his or her obligations to make additional contributions to the partnership and any additional amount(s) that (s)he would actually lose if the partnership could not pay its debt.

Nonrecourse Liabilities

b.   The creditor has no claim against the partnership or any partners. At most, the creditor has a claim against a particular secured item of partnership property.

1)   All partners share in nonrecourse liabilities based on their ratio for sharing profits.

2.   **Organization and Syndication Fees**

a.   Generally, organization costs are not deductible as a current expense but reduce gain on dissolution.

1)   However, up to $5,000 of organization costs may be currently deducted.

a)   This $5,000 is reduced by the amount that such expenditures exceed $50,000.

b)   The remainder of the organizational expenditures may be deducted over the 180-month period beginning when the organization begins business.

c)   Organizational expenses are costs incurred in forming the partnership.

d)   Examples are legal fees for drafting a partnership agreement, costs of state filings, and cost of required notice publications.

e)   A partnership on the cash basis of accounting is not allowed a deduction for organization expenses until the expenses are actually paid.

f)   A taxpayer is deemed to have made the election; therefore, a taxpayer is not required to attach a separate statement to the return.

b.   Syndication fees are not amortizable.

1)   They are costs of issuing and marketing partnership interests.

a)   Examples are prospectus preparation costs and commissions on sales of limited partnership interests.

2)   They might alter the amount of gain or loss when the partnership is terminated.

Partners' Capital Accounts

3.   A capital account is maintained for each partner at the partnership level.

a.   A partner's initial capital account balance is the adjusted basis of the assets (net of liabilities) (s)he contributed to the partnership.

b.   It is separate from the partner's AB in his or her partnership interest.

Partner's Taxable Income

4.   A partner's taxable income may be affected by his or her share of a partnership interest in several ways. Examples include

a.   His or her distributive share of partnership income and separately stated items
b.   Sale of his or her partnership interest
c.   Dealings with the partnership (e.g., guaranteed payments)

5.   A partner reports his or her distributive share of partnership items for the partnership's tax year that ends with or within the partner's tax year.

Partnership Taxable Income

6.   Partnership taxable income is determined in the same way as for individuals except that certain deductions are not allowed for a partnership, and other items are required to be separately stated.

Separately Stated Items

7. Each partnership item of income, gain, deduction, loss, or credit that may vary the tax liability of any partner (if reported separately on the partner's personal return) must be separately stated. Items that must be separately stated include the following:

    a. Sec. 1231 gains and losses
    b. Net STCG and net LTCG or loss from the sale or exchange of capital assets
    c. Dividends that are eligible for a corporate dividends-received deduction
    d. Tax-exempt income and related expenses
    e. Investment income and related expenses
    f. Rental activities, portfolio income, and related expenses
    g. Recovery items (e.g., prior taxes, bad debts)
    h. Charitable contributions
    i. Foreign income taxes paid or accrued
    j. Depletion on oil and gas wells
    k. Sec. 179 deductions

Ordinary Income

8. This is all taxable items of income, gain, loss, or deduction that are not separately stated.

    a. Ordinary income is different from taxable income, which is the sum of all taxable items, including the separately stated items and the partnership ordinary income or loss.

        1) Ordinary income includes such items as gross profit, administrative expenses, and employee salaries.

Deductions

9. Certain deductions, e.g., charitable contributions, are disallowed in computing partnership taxable income. These are items that must be separately stated by the partnership.

    a. Each partner may be entitled to a deduction for his or her distributive share of these items in computing his or her personal tax liability.

Contributions to Employee Retirement Accounts

10. Contributions made by a partnership for its employees under a qualified SEP, SIMPLE IRA, pension, profit sharing plan, annuity plan, or another deferred compensation plan may be deducted subject to limitations.

    a. Contributions to an employee's IRA are included in the employee's salaries and wages.

Partner's Distributive Share

11. Each partner is taxed on his or her share of partnership income whether or not it is distributed.

    a. A partner's distributive share of any partnership item is allocated by the partnership agreement as long as the allocation has substantial economic effect, which means the allocation is not for tax avoidance. The partnership agreement includes modifications up to the partnership return due date (without extensions).

        1) For example, allocation of tax-exempt income to one partner and taxable interest (equal in amount) to another partner in a lower tax bracket has no substantial economic effect; i.e., it is motivated by tax avoidance.

    b. If the partnership agreement does not allocate a partnership item or the agreement lacks substantial economic effect, the item must be allocated to partners according to their interests in the partnership.

    c. Substantial economic effect is present for any allocation that may substantially affect the amount of the partners' shares of total partnership income or loss independently of tax consequences of the allocation.

Precontribution Gain or Loss

    d.   To the extent of gain not recognized on contribution of property to the partnership, gain or loss subsequently recognized on the sale or exchange of an asset by the partnership must be allocated to the contributing partner.

        1)   Postcontribution gain or loss is allocated among partners as distributive shares, i.e., as any other gain or loss.

EXAMPLE

Tony and Mary form a partnership as equal partners. Tony contributes cash of $100,000, and Mary contributes an asset with a basis of $80,000 and a FMV of $100,000. Two years later, the partnership sells the asset for $110,000. The $30,000 gain ($110,000 selling price – $80,000 basis) is allocated, $25,000 to Mary [$20,000 precontribution gain + (50% partnership interest × $10,000 postcontribution gain)] and $5,000 to Tony (50% partnership interest × $10,000 postcontribution gain).

---

        2)   Accounting for variation between the property's FMV and AB immediately before contribution also applies to related deductions. For example, depreciation must be apportioned and allocated.

            a)   Depreciation deductions are allowed for a noncontributing partner.

            b)   The contributing partner, however, cannot take a depreciation deduction.

            c)   This method, the traditional method, tries to prevent the shifting of tax consequences with respect to appreciated property.

                i)   Disallowing the depreciation deduction essentially forces the contributing partner to recognize a portion of the built-in gain.

Character

    e.   The character of distributive shares of partnership items is generally determined at the partnership level.

        1)   Any capital loss (FMV < AB) inherent at contribution is capital loss to the extent of any loss realized when the partnership disposes of the property. This applies for 5 years after contribution.

        2)   To the extent of variations between FMV and AB on contribution, partnership gain or loss on inventory and unrealized receivables is ordinary income. This taint on the inventory (but not the receivables) disappears 5 years after contribution.

    f.   If the size of a partner's interest in the partnership varies (e.g., by sale, purchase, exchange, liquidation) during a partnership tax year, the distributive shares of partnership items must be apportioned on a daily basis.

        1)   The partnership may change profit and loss ratios up to the date of the return. However, certain items (such as cash-paid interest) must be allocated based on the number of days of ownership.

        2)   Furthermore, the following items of a cash-basis partnership must be accounted for on an accrual basis: payments for services or the use of property, interest, and taxes. Note that this is only for apportioning distributive shares.

Elections by Partnership or Partner

    12.   A few of the elections available to partnerships are made at the partnership level:

        a.   Partnerships make all elections available (except for those listed in b. on the next page), such as

            1)   Methods of accounting
            2)   Computing depreciation
            3)   Installment method election
            4)   Expensing intangible drilling and development costs

These elections apply equally amongst all partners; however, no election made by a partnership has any force or effect with respect to any partner's nonpartnership interests.

    b.   Partners make the following elections on the individual income tax return:

        1)   Deduction or credit of foreign income taxes paid

            a)   The amount is limited to the partner's distributive share from the partnership.

        2)   Treatment of mining and exploration expenditures

        3)   Basis reduction following discharge of indebtedness

Adjustments to Basis

13.   The basis of a partner's interest in a partnership is adjusted each year for subsequent contributions of capital, partnership taxable income (loss), separately stated items, variations in the partner's share of partnership liabilities, and distributions from the partnership to the partner.

```
      Initial basis
 +    Subsequent contributions of capital
+/–   Distributive share of partnership taxable income (loss)
 +    Separately stated taxable and nontaxable income
 –    Separately stated deductible and nondeductible expenditures
 +    Increase in allocable share of partnership liabilities
 –    Decrease in allocable share of partnership liabilities
 –    Distributions from partnership
 =    Adjusted basis in partnership interest
```

EXAMPLE

The taxpayer's ownership and basis in the partnership are 50% and $15,000, respectively, at the beginning of the year. The partnership has ordinary income of $8,000, made charitable contributions of $3,000, and made a $5,000 distribution to the taxpayer. The taxpayer's basis at the end of the year is $12,500 [$15,000 beginning basis + ($8,000 ordinary income × 50% ownership) – ($3,000 charitable contribution × 50% ownership) – $5,000 distribution].

---

    a.   Basis is adjusted for variations in a partner's allocable share of partnership liabilities during the year, e.g., by payments on principal.

        1)   Partner capital accounts are not adjusted for partnership liability variations.

    b.   Basis is not reduced below zero.

    c.   Basis is reduced without regard to losses suspended under passive activity loss rules and at-risk rules.

    d.   No adjustment to basis is made for guaranteed payments received.

Loss Limits

14.   A partnership ordinary loss is a negative balance of taxable income.

Basis Limit

    a.   A partner's distributive share of a partnership ordinary loss is allowable as a deduction to the partner only to the extent of the partner's AB in his or her interest in the partnership at the end of the year. Excess loss is deductible in a subsequent year in which AB is greater than zero.

        1)   To recognize a loss beyond the partner's AB in his or her interest in the partnership, the distribution must also

            a)   Liquidate the partner's entire interest in the partnership and

            b)   Be made in the form of money, unrealized receivables, or inventory items.

At-Risk Rules

    b.   Each partner may deduct only a partnership ordinary loss to the extent (s)he is at risk with respect to the partnership.

        1)   The amount of a partnership loss currently deductible (up to an amount for which the partnership bears economic risk of loss with respect to each partnership activity) is allocated to partners as a deductible distributive share.

            a)   Only partnership liabilities for which a partner is personally liable can be considered in a partner's at-risk limit.

        2)   A limited partner is at risk in the partnership to the extent of contributions and his or her share of qualified nonrecourse financing, that is, the amount the partner would lose if the partnership suddenly became worthless.

    c.   Passive activity losses are deductible in the current tax year only to the extent of gains from passive activities (in the aggregate).

        1)   Partnership ordinary loss is generally passive to a partner unless the partner materially participates in the partnership activity.

Gift of a Partnership Interest

15.   Generally, no gain is recognized upon the gift. However, if partnership liabilities allocable to the gifted interest exceed the AB of the partnership interest, the donor must recognize gain. No loss is recognized on the gift.

    a.   The donee's basis in the interest is the donor's basis after adjustment for the donor's distributive share of partnership items up to the date of the gift.

    b.   For purposes of computing a loss on a subsequent sale of the interest by the donee, the FMV of the interest immediately prior to the gift is used.

    c.   Generally, when there is a direct gift of a partnership interest to a related minor, it is presumed that the minor is controlled by others. Therefore, there are limits on the amount that can be allocated to a related minor as a distributive share of income from the partnership.

Inheritance

16.   The tax year of a partnership closes with respect to a partner whose entire interest in the partnership terminates, whether by death, liquidation, or otherwise.

    a.   The successor has a FMV basis in the interest.

    b.   The partnership tax year does not close with respect to the other partners.

Reporting Requirements

17.   A partnership, as a conduit, is not subject to federal income tax. But it must report information that includes partnership items of income, loss, deduction, and credit to the IRS.

    a.   A partnership is required to file an initial return for the first year in which it receives income or incurs expenditures treated as deductions for federal income tax purposes.

    b.   A partnership engaged in a trade or business or has gross income must file an information return on Form 1065. The return must be signed by a general partner.

        1)   A limited liability company that is treated as a partnership must file Form 1065, and one of its members must sign the return.

    c.   A partnership with more than 100 partners is required to file a partnership return on magnetic media.

    d.   Any partnership item that may vary tax liability of any partner is separately stated on Schedule K. For separately stated Sec. 1231 gains and losses, a copy of the partnership Form 4797, *Sales of Business Property*, should be attached to each partner's K-1.

    e.   A Schedule K-1 is prepared for each partner and contains the partner's distributive share of partnership income and separately stated items to be reported on the partner's tax return.

    f.   A partnership return is due (postmark date) on or before the 15th day of the 4th month following the close of the partnership's tax year.

    g.   Signature by any partner is evidence that the partner was authorized to sign the return.

    h.   Inadequate filing. Penalty is imposed in the amount of the number of persons who were partners at any time during the year, multiplied by \$195 for each of up to 12 months (including a portion of one) that the return was late or incomplete.

    i.   When a partnership is notified of an exchange of partnership interests involving unrealized receivables or inventory items, the partnership must file Form 8308, *Report of a Sale or Exchange of Certain Partnership Interests*.

        1)   Form 8308 is filed with Form 1065 for the tax year that includes the last day of the calendar year in which the exchange took place.

        2)   If notified of an exchange after filing Form 1065, the partnership must file Form 8308 separately, within 30 days of the notification.

18. Each partner must report his or her share of items consistently with their treatment on the partnership return, unless

    a.   The partner identifies inconsistency on a filed statement or

    b.   The partnership has no more than 10 partners and no estate or nonresident alien is a partner.

19. When a partner dies, his or her distributive share of the partnership income (or loss) is figured through the end of the month in which the death occurs.

    a.   This is true even though the decedent's estate or heirs may succeed to rights in the partnership.

    b.   The partnership income (or loss) for the year is treated as though it was earned in equal amounts each month.

Partnership Tax Administration

20. The IRC provides for designation of a tax matters partner (TMP), e.g., the general partner holding the largest partnership interest.

    a.   When the IRS enters into a settlement agreement with any partner, it must offer consistent settlement terms to any other partner who so requests.

    b.   Each partner is bound to a settlement agreement entered into between the IRS and the TMP, unless the partner files notice otherwise.

    c.   Small partnerships. Consistent and binding settlements do not apply to a small partnership, i.e., one that has no more than 10 partners, each being a natural person or an estate.

Stop and review! You have completed the outline for this subunit. Study questions 1 through 13 beginning on page 190.

9.2 DISTRIBUTION OF PARTNERSHIP ASSETS

A distribution is a transfer of value from the partnership to a partner in reference to his or her interest in the partnership. A distribution may be in the form of money, liability relief, or other property. A draw is a distribution.

Current Distributions

1. A current (or operating) distribution reduces the partner's basis in the partnership interest.

    a. A decrease in a partner's allocable share of partnership liabilities is treated as a distribution of money.

Money Distributions

    b. The partnership recognizes no gain on money distributions.

        1) A partner recognizes gain only to the extent the distribution (FMV) exceeds the AB in the partnership interest immediately before the distribution.

            a) Gain recognized is capital gain.
            b) Basis in the interest is decreased, but not below zero.
            c) Loss is not recognized.

    c. Property distributions.

        1) The partnership. Generally, no gain or loss is recognized by the partnership when it distributes property, including money. Sec. 1245 and Sec. 1250 do not trigger recognition on the distribution.

            a) Precontribution gain or loss. If property is distributed to a noncontributing partner within 7 years of contribution, the partnership recognizes gain or loss realized to the extent of any unrealized gain or loss, respectively, that existed at the contribution date.

                i) Allocate this recognized gain (loss) to the contributing partner.
                ii) The contributing partner's basis in his or her partnership interest is increased.
                iii) Basis in the property is also increased.
                iv) The distributee has a transferred basis.

            b) Disproportionate distributions of unrealized receivables or substantially appreciated inventory result in gain recognition.

        2) Partner. The distributee partner generally recognizes gain only to the extent that money (including liability relief) exceeds his or her AB in his or her partnership interest.

    d. The partner's basis in the distributed property is the partnership's AB in the property immediately before distribution, but it is limited to the distributee's AB in his or her partnership interest minus any money received in the distribution.

        1) When the above limit applies, allocate basis

            a) First to unrealized receivables and inventory, up to the partnership's AB in them, and
            b) Second to other (noncash) property.

        2) If the available basis is too small, the decrease (partnership basis in assets – basis in partnership interest) is allocated to the assets. The decrease is allocated by the following steps:

            a) Assign each asset its partnership basis.
            b) Calculate the decrease amount.
            c) Allocate the decrease first to any assets that have declined in value.
            d) Allocate any remaining decrease to the assets based on relative adjusted basis at this point in the calculation.

EXAMPLE

Karen has a $6,000 basis in the BK Partnership immediately before receiving a current distribution (there is no remaining precontribution gain). The distribution consists of $5,000 cash, a computer with an FMV of $1,500 and a $4,000 basis to the partnership, and a desk with an FMV of $500 and a $1,500 basis to the partnership. Karen's basis in the distributed property is determined as follows:

Beginning basis in partnership interest	$6,000
Less: Money received	(5,000)
Remaining basis to allocate	$1,000

		Computer	Desk
Step 1: Allocate partnership basis to each asset.	Partnership basis in assets	$ 4,000	$1,500
Step 2: Calculate decrease.			

Total partnership basis	$5,500	
Basis to allocate	(1,000)	
Decrease amount	$4,500	

		Computer	Desk
Step 3: Allocate decrease to assets with a decline in FMV.	Decline in FMV	(2,500)	(1,000)
	Relative adjusted basis	$ 1,500	$ 500
Step 4: Allocate remaining decrease of $1,000 ($4,500 – $2,500 – $1,000) based on relative adjusted basis.	Remaining decrease	(750)*	(250)*
	Karen's basis in distributed property	$ 750	$ 250

* $750 = (1,500 ÷ 2,000) × $1,000
$250 = (500 ÷ 2,000) × $1,000

---

    e.   The partner's holding period in the distributed property includes that of the partnership.

    f.   The partner's basis in his or her ownership interest in the partnership is reduced by the amount of money and the AB of property received in the distribution.

Disproportionate Distributions

2.   Gain is recognized on a distribution of property that is disproportionate with respect to unrealized receivables (URs) or substantially appreciated inventory (SAI).

    a.   The distribution will be recharacterized as if the URs or SAI were distributed.

Stop and review! You have completed the outline for this subunit. Study questions 14 through 17 beginning on page 194.

9.3 PARTNERS DEALING WITH THEIR OWN PARTNERSHIP

    The Code recognizes that a partner can engage in property, services, and loan transactions with the partnership in a capacity other than as a partner, i.e., as an independent, outside third party. The tax result, in general, is as if the transaction took place between two unrelated persons after arm's-length negotiations.

Customary Partner Services

1.   When a partner performs services for the partnership that are customarily performed by a partner, the partner's return is generally his or her share of profits of the partnership business.

    a.   A partner's allocable share of partnership items is the partner's "compensation" for acting to perform the normal functions of a partner, e.g., driving the truck and keeping books of an ice cream vending partnership.

        1)   It is gross income, not as compensation, but as a distributive share of partnership income.

        2)   The value of the services is not deductible by the partnership.

Guaranteed Payments

2. A guaranteed payment (GP) is a payment to a partner for services rendered or capital used that is determined without regard to the income of the partnership. It is used to distinguish payments that are a function of partnership income and payments connected with partners acting in a nonpartner capacity.

    a. Services. The services must be a customary function of a partner. They are normal activities of a partner in conducting partnership business.

    b. Use of capital. The payment may be stated to be interest on the partner's capital account or to be rent on contributed property.

        1) Interest on a bona fide loan is not a GP.

    c. Fixed amount stated. If the partnership agreement provides for a GP in a fixed amount, e.g., annual salary amount, the GP amount is the stated amount.

    d. Stated minimum amount. The partnership agreement may allocate a share of partnership income to the partner but guarantee payment of not less than a stated amount to the partner even if the allocable share is less.

        1) If so, the GP amount is any excess of the guaranteed minimum amount over the distributive share allocable to the partner.

    e. For purposes of determining the partner's gross income, the GP is treated as if made to a nonpartner.

        1) The partner separately states the GP from any distributive share.
        2) The payment is always ordinary income to the partner (compensation, interest, possibly rent).
        3) The GP is reported in the recipient partner's tax year that includes the end of the partnership tax year (in which the GP was made or deducted by the partnership).
        4) Receipt of the GP does not directly affect the partner's AB in his or her partnership interest.

    f. For purposes of determining deductibility by the partnership, a GP is treated as if made to a nonpartner.

        1) The payment is deductible if it would have been deductible if made to a nonpartner.
        2) Usually, deductible GPs are for a general business expenditure that need not be separately stated.

            a) Investment interest expense, however, should be separately stated even if it is a GP and even if it is deductible by a partner.

        NOTE: If the GP exceeds the partnership's ordinary income, the resulting ordinary loss is allocated among the partners (including the partner who receives the GP).

    g. For all other purposes, the GP is treated as if made to a partner in his or her capacity as a partner.

        1) A partner is not an employee of the partnership.
        2) Partnership contributions to a self-employment retirement plan are not deductible by the partnership.

Nonpartner Capacity

3. Payments to a partner without regard to income of the partnership for property or for services not customarily performed by a partner are generally treated as if the transaction took place between two unrelated persons after arm's-length negotiations.

   a. Loans. Interest paid to a partner on a (true) loan is all gross income to the partner and a deductible partnership item.

   b. Services. Payments to the partner for services rendered (of a nature not normally performed by a partner) to or for the partnership are gross income to the partner and generally an ordinary deductible expense of the partnership.

   c. Property. A partner acting as a nonpartner (independent third party, outsider) can sell (or exchange) property to (or with) the partnership and vice versa. Gain or loss on the transaction is recognized unless an exception applies.

EXAMPLE

Partnership sells land to Partner. Partnership recognizes loss unless the sale is to a related party. The loss is a partnership item allocable to partners as distributive shares. Partner takes a cost basis in the property.

---

   d. Character and loss limit rules.

      1) Applicability. These loss limits apply to any transaction between the partnership and either

         a) A partner who owns more than 50% of the partnership or

         b) Another partnership if more than 50% of the capital or profits interest of each is owned by the same persons.

      2) Character. Any gain recognized is OI if the property is held as other than a capital asset by the acquiring partner or partnership.

EXAMPLE

Dora has held a capital asset for several years. The asset has a basis of $16,000 and a FMV of $24,000. She sells the asset to a partnership in which she is more than a 50% owner. The partnership will hold the property as a depreciable asset. Her gain of $8,000 ($24,000 − $16,000) will be ordinary income since she sold a capital asset to a more-than-50%-owned partnership that is not a capital asset to the partnership. If the partnership were to hold the asset as a capital asset, her gain would be capital gain.

---

      3) Related party sales.

         a) The acquiring party has a cost basis, and a subsequent taxable disposition event results in no more gain recognition than any excess of realized gain over the loss previously disallowed.

         b) Expenditures are deductible when, and not before, the amount is includible in gross income by the payee, even if the payor is an accrual-method taxpayer.

Stop and review! You have completed the outline for this subunit. Study questions 18 through 30 beginning on page 195.

QUESTIONS

9.1 Partnership Operations and Partner's Taxable Income

1. Bridget and Brenda formed B & B Partnership in Year 1 as equal partners. They closed the business during Year 5 because it was not profitable. After the partnership closed, they had debts to pay. Because Bridget was insolvent, she paid only part of her share of the partnership's debts. Brenda was required to pay all of the remaining debts during Year 5. Which of the following statements reflects the correct treatment of the debts paid by Brenda on her tax return for Year 5?

A. She cannot deduct any of the debt she paid.

B. She can deduct only her payment of her share of the debt as a bad debt.

C. She can deduct all of the debt she paid as a bad debt.

D. She can deduct only her payment of Bridget's share of debt as a bad debt.

Answer (D) is correct.

REQUIRED: The correct treatment of debts paid by a partner due to an insolvent partnership.

DISCUSSION: A partner who pays more than his or her proportionate share of a partnership debt that becomes uncollectible is permitted to take a bad debt deduction equal to the amount in excess of that partner's share of the debt.

Answer (A) is incorrect. She can deduct part of her payment as a bad debt. Answer (B) is incorrect. She can only deduct her payment of Bridget's share of debt as a bad debt. Answer (C) is incorrect. She cannot deduct the entire payment as a bad debt.

2. John owns a residential contracting business. Capital is a material income-producing factor. John's services to the business for Year 1 were worth $30,000. John's son, Alex, is interested in eventually working in his father's business. On January 1, Year 1, Alex receives a gift of 20% of his father's interest in the business. Alex performed no services for the business in Year 1. If the resulting partnership had a profit of $100,000 for tax year Year 1, how much of the partnership profit should be allocated to Alex?

A. $20,000

B. $35,000

C. $50,000

D. $14,000

Answer (D) is correct.

REQUIRED: The partnership profit allocated to Alex.

DISCUSSION: In a gift of a partnership interest, the donee's distributive share must be determined after due allowance has been made for the services contributed by the donor. Thus, the 20% gift is taken from the $100,000 profit minus John's services of $30,000. The calculation is [($100,000 − $30,000) × .20].

3. All of the following items must be separately stated on the partnership's Schedule K (Form 1065) and included as separate items on the partner's return except

A. Ordinary gains and losses from Form 4797, Part II.

B. Gains and losses from sales or exchanges of capital assets.

C. Guaranteed payments to the partners.

D. Interest income.

Answer (A) is correct.

REQUIRED: The item not required to be separately stated.

DISCUSSION: Each partnership item of income, gain, deduction, loss, or credit that may vary the tax liability of any partner (if reported separately on the partner's personal return) must be separately stated. Items that must be separately stated include the following: (1) Sec. 1231 gains and losses; (2) net short- and net long-term capital gain or loss from the sale or exchange of capital assets; (3) dividends that are eligible for a corporate dividends-received deduction; (4) tax-exempt income and related expenses; (5) investment income and related expenses; (6) rental activities, portfolio income, and related expenses; (7) recovery items (e.g., prior taxes, bad debts); (8) charitable contributions; (9) foreign income taxes paid or accrued; (10) depletion on oil and gas wells; and (11) Sec. 179 deductions. (See Publication 541, Form 1065 Schedule K, and the instructions to Form 1065.)

4. Comfy Chairs Manufacturing, Ltd. operates as a partnership and files Form 1065. Comfy manufactures inflatable lounge chairs. During the current tax year ended December 31, Comfy generated income and expenses as stated below. What is the correct amount of ordinary income (loss) from trade or business activities Comfy should report on Schedule K for the current year?

Employee wages	$15,000
Income from rental real estate	20,000
Charitable contributions	500
Cost of goods sold	10,000
Income from chair sales	75,000

   A. $65,000

   B. $69,500

   C. $50,000

   D. $30,000

Answer (C) is correct.
REQUIRED: The correct amount of ordinary income to be reported on a Schedule K.
DISCUSSION: Included in the partnership's ordinary income are such items as gross profit on sales, administrative expenses, and employee expenses. Thus, income from chair sales, employee wages, and cost of goods sold are included in ordinary income to give $50,000 ($75,000 – $15,000 – $10,000). Charitable contributions and income from rental real estate have to be separately stated. Ordinary income is different from partnership taxable income in that partnership taxable income is the sum of all taxable income items, including separately stated items and ordinary income items.
Answer (A) is incorrect. Employee wages are deductible as ordinary income of a partnership. Answer (B) is incorrect. Income from rental real estate and charitable contributions are not included as ordinary income/expense of a partnership. Answer (D) is incorrect. Ordinary income includes gross profit on sales, administrative expenses, and employee expenses.

5. Juan and Adelfo are equal partners in a music store. In 2013, they bought an amplifier for use in the store to demonstrate certain instruments. The amplifier cost $30,000. The partnership's taxable income before the Sec. 179 deduction is $25,000. What amount of Sec. 179 expense can Juan and Adelfo each deduct if neither has any other Sec. 179 deductions?

   A. $0

   B. $12,500

   C. $500,000

   D. $25,000

Answer (B) is correct.
REQUIRED: The amount of Sec. 179 expense each partner can deduct if neither has any other Sec. 179 deductions.
DISCUSSION: Several types of deductions must be reported separately by the partners, and Sec. 179 deductions are one of these types of deductions. With regard to elections to expense Sec. 179 property, the dollar limitations apply both to the partnership and to each individual partner. The maximum Sec. 179 deduction is $500,000 for 2013. The deduction for the $30,000 cost of the amplifier is further limited to the partnership's taxable income of $25,000, which is then split between the two partners.
Answer (A) is incorrect. The partners are entitled to a limited Sec. 179 deduction. Answer (C) is incorrect. The maximum deduction for 2013 for the partnership is $500,000. Answer (D) is incorrect. The partners split the $25,000 deduction.

6. Which of the following statements about partnership agreements and a partner's distributive share of items is false?

   A. The partnership agreement generally determines a partner's distributive share of income, gain, loss, deductions, and credits.

   B. If the partnership agreement provides for a partner with a 50% capital interest to share in 60% of the profits and 90% of the losses, the agreement will be disregarded even though the allocation has substantial economic effect.

   C. A partner's distributive share is determined by his or her interest in the partnership if the partnership agreement does not provide for the allocation of income, gain, loss, deductions, or credits.

   D. If the partnership agreement or any modification is silent on any matter, the provisions of state law are treated as part of the agreement.

Answer (B) is correct.
REQUIRED: The false statement regarding partnership distributive share and the partnership agreement.
DISCUSSION: The partnership agreement usually sets out the partners' distributive shares of income, gains, losses, deductions, and credits. If the partnership agreement does not provide each partner's distributive share of such items, the partners' shares are determined according to each partner's interest in the partnership, taking all the pertinent facts and circumstances into account.
Although the partnership agreement normally controls the allocation of partnership income, gains, losses, deductions, and credits to the partners, the allocations provided in the agreement are disregarded if they lack "substantial economic effect." If the partnership agreement is silent on any matter, state law provisions are automatically treated as if they are part of the agreement.

7. On January 1, 2011, Thomas contributed real estate he held for investment to Fog Partnership, a dealer in real estate. The real estate had an adjusted basis to Thomas of $50,000 and a fair market value at the time of the transfer of $43,000. On June 1, 2013, Fog sold the real estate for $40,000. What are the amount and the character of the partnership's loss?

A. $3,000 capital loss; $7,000 ordinary loss.

B. $7,000 capital loss; $3,000 ordinary loss.

C. $10,000 ordinary loss; $0 capital loss.

D. $10,000 capital loss; $0 ordinary loss.

Answer (B) is correct.

REQUIRED: The amount and the character of the partnership's loss on the sale of contributed property.

DISCUSSION: The partnership's basis in the property was $50,000 under Sec. 723. The loss realized and recognized on its sale was $10,000 (Sec. 1001). If property is contributed that would have generated a capital loss if sold by the partner, a loss on the disposition of the property within 5 years of its contribution is a capital loss [Sec. 724(c)]. The amount of the loss characterized as capital is the amount of capital loss the contributing partner would have recognized if (s)he had sold the property on the contribution date ($50,000 – $43,000 = $7,000). The remaining loss has the character it would have to the partnership.

Answer (A) is incorrect. The amount of the loss characterized as capital is the amount of capital loss the contributing partner would have recognized if (s)he had sold the property on the contribution date. Answer (C) is incorrect. When property is contributed that would have generated a capital loss if sold by the partner, a loss on the disposition of the property within 7 years of its contribution is a capital loss. Answer (D) is incorrect. The amount of the loss characterized as capital is the amount of capital loss the contributing partner would have recognized if (s)he had sold the property on the contribution date.

8. The adjusted basis of Carol's partnership interest is $50,000. She receives a distribution of $10,000 cash, land that has an adjusted basis of $30,000, and a FMV of $50,000. What is Carol's adjusted basis in the land?

A. $20,000

B. $30,000

C. $40,000

D. $50,000

Answer (B) is correct.

REQUIRED: The partner's adjusted basis for distributed property.

DISCUSSION: Publication 541 states, "Unless there is a complete liquidation of a partner's interest, the basis of property (other than money) distributed to the partner by a partnership is its adjusted basis to the partnership immediately before the distribution. However, the basis of the property to the partner cannot be more than the adjusted basis of his or her interest in the partnership reduced by any money received in the same transaction." Therefore, Carol's adjusted basis in the land is $30,000, the adjusted basis to the partnership immediately before the distribution.

Answer (A) is incorrect. The amount of $20,000 is not the adjusted basis to the partnership immediately before the distribution. Answer (C) is incorrect. Carol's partnership interest less the cash distribution is $40,000. Answer (D) is incorrect. The FMV of the distributed property is $50,000.

9. The adjusted basis of Paul's partnership interest is $10,000. He receives a distribution of $4,000 cash and property that has an adjusted basis to the partnership of $8,000. (This was not a distribution in liquidation.) What is the basis of the distributed property in Paul's hands?

A. $8,000

B. $6,000

C. $14,000

D. $2,000

Answer (B) is correct.

REQUIRED: The basis of property distributed to a partner.

DISCUSSION: Sec. 732(a) provides that the basis of property distributed to a partner is the property's adjusted basis to the partnership immediately before such distribution. This basis, however, cannot exceed the adjusted basis of the partner's interest in the partnership minus any money received in the same distribution [Sec. 732(a)(2)]. Paul's basis in the property distributed is

Basis of partnership interest	$10,000
Less: Cash received	(4,000)
Basis in distributed property	$ 6,000

Answer (A) is incorrect. The basis of his partnership interest cannot be reduced below zero. Answer (C) is incorrect. The cash received reduces Paul's partnership; it does not increase his basis. Answer (D) is incorrect. The basis in the property is not equal to the difference between the basis in the partnership and the partnership's basis in the property.

10. Partnership LIFE's profits and losses are shared equally among the four partners. The adjusted basis of Partner E's interest in the partnership on December 31, Year 1, was $25,000. On January 2, Year 2, Partner E withdrew $10,000 cash. The partnership reported $200,000 as ordinary income on its Year 2 partnership return. In addition, $5,000 for qualified travel, meals, and entertainment was shown on a separate attachment to E's Schedule K-1 of Form 1065. Due to the limitation, $2,500 of the $5,000 is unallowable as a deduction. What is the amount of E's basis in the partnership on December 31, Year 2?

A. $60,000

B. $61,000

C. $65,000

D. $71,000

Answer (A) is correct.

REQUIRED: The adjusted basis of a partner's partnership interest.

DISCUSSION: The adjusted basis of a partner's interest is the original basis of such interest, increased by the partner's distributive share of the partnership's income and allocable portion of liabilities, and decreased by the partner's distributive share of partnership loss and distributions (Secs. 705, 733, and 752). Partnership basis is also reduced by both deductible and nondeductible expenses.

Beginning basis	$ 25,000
Ordinary income ($200,000 × 25%)	50,000
Cash distribution	(10,000)
Travel, meals, entertainment expense	(5,000)
Year-end basis	$ 60,000

11. At-risk rules apply to most trade or business activities, including activities conducted through a partnership. The at-risk rules limit a partner's deductible loss to the amounts for which that partner is considered at risk in the activity. Select the statement below that is false. A partner is considered at risk for

A. The money and adjusted basis of any property (s)he contributed to the activity.

B. The partner's share of net income retained by the partnership.

C. Certain amounts borrowed by the partnership for use in the activity if the partner is personally liable for repayment or the amounts borrowed are secured by the partner's property (other than property used in the activity).

D. 90% of the total expected tax for the current year.

Answer (D) is correct.

REQUIRED: The false statement concerning at-risk limitations on losses.

DISCUSSION: Sec. 465 generally limits losses from an activity for each year to the amount the taxpayer has at risk in the activity at year end. A taxpayer is generally considered at risk for money and the adjusted basis of property contributed to the activity and amounts borrowed for use in the activity. However, amounts borrowed for use in the activity are not at risk if the lender has no recourse against the borrower personally, except for certain qualified financing with respect to real property. Also, the partner's share of net income not distributed is considered in whether or not a taxpayer is at risk. However, estimated tax payments are not considered for at-risk purposes.

12. A partner is considered not at risk for which of the following amounts?

A. The money and adjusted basis of any property the partner contributed to the activity.

B. The partner's share of net income retained by the partnership.

C. An allocation of a loss, deduction, or expense attributable to a partnership nonrecourse liability.

D. Certain amounts borrowed by the partnership for use in the activity if the partner is personally liable for repayment.

Answer (C) is correct.

REQUIRED: The amount for which a partner is considered not at risk.

DISCUSSION: Sec. 465 states that each partner may deduct only a partnership ordinary loss to the extent (s)he is at risk with respect to the partnership. The at-risk limits also apply at the partnership level with respect to each partnership activity. The amount of a partnership loss currently deductible (up to an amount for which the partnership bears economic risk of loss with respect to each partnership activity) is allocated to partners as a deductible distributive share. Since a nonrecourse liability means that the partnership bears no economic risk of loss, there is no at-risk loss in the transaction.

Answer (A) is incorrect. A partner is at risk for the money and adjusted basis of property contributed to the activity because there is a risk of economic loss if the activity is unprofitable. Answer (B) is incorrect. The retention of net income by the partnership exposes the partner to the possibility of economic loss. Answer (D) is incorrect. Personal liability for a loan is considered an at-risk activity because the loan must be repaid.

13. Partner C invested $30,000 cash for a 60% interest in ABC Partnership. C materially participates in the partnership's business, and the partnership agreement states he is liable for all of the partnership's debts. The only partnership debt at the year end was a $15,000 loan from Book Bank. Partner C and the other general partner had a separate agreement that C's liability would not exceed $10,000. The partnership reported a $70,000 ordinary loss for the year. What is the amount of C's deductible loss?

A. $40,000

B. $42,000

C. $45,000

D. $70,000

Answer (A) is correct.

REQUIRED: The partner's deductible loss when (s)he signs an agreement that states his or her liability will not exceed a certain amount.

DISCUSSION: A general partner's basis in his or her partnership interest is increased by his or her share of the partnership's recourse liabilities for which (s)he is ultimately liable [Code Sec. 752(a)]. Partner C's ultimate share of the bank debt ($10,000 per the separate agreement) plus his original basis of $30,000 gives him an adjusted basis of $40,000. Although Partner C's share of the partnership loss is 60% of $70,000, or $42,000, his deductible loss is limited to his adjusted basis of $40,000 [Code Sec. 704(d)].

Answer (B) is incorrect. Partner C's total share of the loss is $42,000, not all of which is deductible. Answer (C) is incorrect. The amount of $45,000 includes the total liability of $15,000 and exceeds C's share of the loss. Answer (D) is incorrect. The total partnership loss is not attributable to Partner C.

9.2 Distribution of Partnership Assets

14. The adjusted basis of Stan's partnership interest is $15,000. He receives a distribution of cash of $6,000 and property with an adjusted basis to the partnership of $11,000. (This was not a distribution in liquidation.) What is the basis of the distributed property in Stan's hands?

A. $9,000

B. $11,000

C. $5,000

D. $17,000

Answer (A) is correct.

REQUIRED: The basis of distributive property in the partnership.

DISCUSSION: Sec. 732(a) provides that the basis of property distributed to a partner is the property's adjusted basis to the partnership immediately before such distribution. This basis, however, cannot exceed the adjusted basis of the partner's interest in the partnership minus any money received in the same distribution [Sec. 732(a)(2)]. Stan's basis in the property distributed is

Basis of partnership interest	$15,000
Less: Cash received	(6,000)
Basis in distributed property	$ 9,000

Answer (B) is incorrect. The basis of the distributed property cannot exceed the adjusted basis of the partner's interest in the partnership. Answer (C) is incorrect. The basis of the distributed property will not be equal to the difference between the amount of cash received and the partnership's basis in the property. Answer (D) is incorrect. The basis of the distributed property cannot exceed the adjusted basis of the partner's interest in the partnership.

15. At a time when Nedra's basis in her partnership interest was $5,000, she received a current distribution of $6,000 cash and land with an adjusted basis of $2,000 and a fair market value of $3,000. The partnership had no unrealized receivables or substantially appreciated inventory. What is the result of this distribution to Nedra?

A. $0 gain or loss, $0 basis in land, $(1,000) basis in partnership interest.

B. $3,000 capital gain, $2,000 basis in land, $0 basis in partnership interest.

C. $1,000 ordinary income, $2,000 basis in land, $0 basis in partnership interest.

D. $1,000 capital gain, $0 basis in land, $0 basis in partnership interest.

Answer (D) is correct.

REQUIRED: The tax result of a current distribution to a partner.

DISCUSSION: Gain is not recognized to a partner on a distribution except to the extent that money distributed exceeds the partner's adjusted basis in the partnership interest. Since Nedra received $6,000 when she had a $5,000 basis in the partnership interest, she will recognize a $1,000 gain, which is a capital gain under Sec. 741. The basis in the land is zero under Sec. 732(a)(2) since the basis of property received in a distribution may not exceed the partner's basis in the partnership interest minus any money received in the distribution. Nedra's basis in the partnership interest after the distribution is zero because her basis was reduced by the money distributed to her (Sec. 733).

16. In Year 1, Bob contributed investment land with basis of $14,000 and FMV of $20,000 in exchange for a 20% capital and profits interest in the ABC Partnership. Bob recognized no gain on the contribution. In Year 3, when Bob had a basis in his partnership interest of $35,000, he received a current distribution of machinery with a basis of $34,000 and fair market value of $37,000. Bob has not recognized any of his precontribution gain prior to the distribution. On the distribution, Bob must recognize

A. No gain or loss.

B. $1,000 capital gain.

C. $2,000 capital gain.

D. $6,000 capital gain.

Answer (C) is correct.

REQUIRED: The partner's recognized gain if a current distribution is made when precontribution gain has not previously been recognized.

DISCUSSION: Property distributions made to a partner may cause a partner to recognize any remaining precontribution gain if the FMV of the distributed property exceeds the partner's basis in his or her partnership interest prior to the distribution. The gain recognized under Sec. 737 is the lesser of (1) the remaining precontribution gain or (2) the excess of the FMV of the distributed property over the adjusted basis of the partnership interest immediately before the property distribution (but after any reduction for any money distributed at the same time). The Sec. 737 gain is in addition to any gain otherwise recognized under Sec. 731.

The partnership distribution rules would require Bob to recognize no gain since the adjusted basis of the distributed property ($34,000) is less than Bob's basis in his partnership interest ($35,000). However, under Sec. 737, Bob recognizes a $2,000 capital gain, the lesser of the $6,000 remaining precontribution gain, or the excess of the property's $37,000 fair market value over Bob's $35,000 basis in the partnership interest.

Answer (A) is incorrect. A gain is recognized on the distribution. Answer (B) is incorrect. The gain is not calculated as the basis in the partnership interest minus the basis of the machinery received. Answer (D) is incorrect. Under Sec. 737, Bob should recognize the lesser of the remaining precontribution gain or the excess of the property's fair market value over the basis in the partnership interest.

17. Joan's adjusted basis in the So-Lo Partnership is $15,000. She received a non-liquidating cash distribution of $2,500 and a piece of land with an adjusted basis of $7,500 and a fair market value of $5,000. What is the gain or loss to be recognized at the time of the distribution?

A. $5,000 loss.

B. $2,500 loss.

C. $0

D. $5,000 gain.

Answer (C) is correct.

REQUIRED: The gain or loss to be recognized at the time of the distribution.

DISCUSSION: Gain is not recognized to a partner on a distribution except to the extent that money distributed exceeds the partner's adjusted basis in the partnership interest. Since the $2,500 cash distribution is less than the $15,000 basis, no gain or loss is reported. The basis is reduced by the $2,500 cash distribution and the $7,500 basis in the land.

Answer (A) is incorrect. A loss is not recognized on a distribution to a partner. Answer (B) is incorrect. A loss is not recognized on a distribution to a partner. Answer (D) is incorrect. No gain is reported when the cash distribution is less than the partner's basis.

9.3 Partners Dealing with Their Own Partnership

18. A partnership in which Jane is 50% owner had a profit of $80,000. The partnership agreement provides for a 50-50 sharing of income. Capital is a material income producing factor. During the year, Jane performed services worth $20,000. What is the total income Jane should report from the partnership?

A. $20,000

B. $40,000

C. $50,000

D. $80,000

Answer (C) is correct.

REQUIRED: The total partnership income to be reported by a 50% partner.

DISCUSSION: The partnership agreement is disregarded to the extent a partner receives less than reasonable compensation for services. The $20,000 must be subtracted from the profit of the partnership. Therefore, she receives $20,000 for services performed and $30,000 of partnership income [($80,000 – $20,000) × 50%].

Answer (A) is incorrect. Jane also receives a proportionate share of the profits in addition to the money received for services. Answer (B) is incorrect. Jane does not receive a 50% share of the $80,000 profit. The $80,000 must be reduced by the amount Jane received for services, or $20,000. Answer (D) is incorrect. Jane does not receive the entire profit amount of $80,000. It must be reduced by $20,000 and then divided among the partners.

19. Under a partnership agreement, June is to receive 40% of the partnership income but not less than $12,000 a year. The partnership has <u>net income of $20,000</u>. What is the guaranteed payment that the partnership can deduct in figuring its ordinary income on Page 1 of Form 1065?

A. $0

B. $3,200

C. $4,000

D. $8,000

Answer (C) is correct.

REQUIRED: The amount of the guaranteed payment deducted on Page 1 of Form 1065.

DISCUSSION: Publication 541 states, "Guaranteed payments are those made by a partnership to a partner that are determined without regard to the partnership's income. A partnership treats guaranteed payments . . . as if they were made to a person who is not a partner. This treatment is for purposes of determining gross income and deductible business expenses only. . . If a partner is to receive a minimum payment from the partnership, the guaranteed payment is the amount by which the minimum payment is more than the partner's distributive share of the partnership income before taking into account the guaranteed payment." This is the amount that can be deducted in figuring its ordinary income on Page 1 of Form 1065.

Answer (A) is incorrect. The guaranteed payment is the amount by which the minimum payment is more than the partner's distributive share of partnership income before taking into account the guaranteed payment. Answer (B) is incorrect. The guaranteed payment is not equal to 40% of the difference between partnership income and $12,000. Answer (D) is incorrect. The guaranteed payment is not equal to the difference between partnership income and $12,000.

20. Jasmine, a calendar-year taxpayer, is a partner in Jasmine and Prince Partnership that has a fiscal year ending March 31. Starting April 1, 2013, Jasmine receives a fixed monthly guaranteed payment of $1,000 a month without regard to the income of the partnership. How much of the guaranteed payments will Jasmine report on her 2013 tax return?

A. $0

B. $8,000

C. $9,000

D. $12,000

Answer (A) is correct.

REQUIRED: The amount of guaranteed payment included on tax return.

DISCUSSION: For purposes of determining the partner's gross income, the guaranteed payment is treated as if made to a nonpartner. The partner separately states the guaranteed payment from any distributive share. The payment is ordinary income to the partner. Guaranteed payments are included as income in the recipient's tax year, which includes the end of the partnership tax year in which they were deducted. Thus, the guaranteed payments will not be reported in income until 2014.

Answer (B) is incorrect. Jasmine received 9 months of payments, not 8. Answer (C) is incorrect. The guaranteed payment is reported in 2014. Answer (D) is incorrect. Jasmine only received payments for 9 months of her tax year.

21. Joy and Roger are partners in JR and Associates. Under the terms of the partnership agreement, Joy is to receive 25% of all partnership income or loss plus a guaranteed payment of $60,000 per year. In the current year, the partnership had <u>$50,000 of ordinary income</u> before any deduction for Joy's guaranteed payment. What is the amount of income or loss Joy would report on her current tax return, assuming she materially participates in partnership activities?

A. $15,000 guaranteed payment, $2,500 loss.

B. $57,500 guaranteed payment.

C. $60,000 guaranteed payment.

D. $60,000 guaranteed payment, $2,500 loss.

Answer (D) is correct.

REQUIRED: The amount of income or loss a partner who materially participates in partnership activities would report.

DISCUSSION: Even though a partnership incurs a loss for a tax year, an active partner who receives a guaranteed payment must nevertheless take into account the full amount of such payment [Sec. 707(c)]. This inclusion is required even when the partnership loss is caused by that guaranteed payment to the partner. Furthermore, the partner must also take into account his or her distributive share of the partnership loss. Accordingly, Joy must include her $60,000 guaranteed payment and 25% of the $10,000 loss ($50,000 – $60,000) on her individual return.

Answer (A) is incorrect. The entire guaranteed payment to Joy is included. Answer (B) is incorrect. The $60,000 guaranteed payment is completely recognized, and the partner's share of the loss is also recognized. Answer (C) is incorrect. The partner's share of the loss must be recognized.

22. Under a partnership agreement, Gil is to receive 40% of the partnership income, but not less than $20,000. The partnership has <u>net income of $100,000</u> for Year 1 without regard to the minimum guaranteed and before any allocation. What is the amount and character of the income Gil is to receive for Year 1?

A. $40,000 distributive share.

B. $20,000 guaranteed payment; $32,000 distributive share.

C. $20,000 guaranteed payment; $20,000 distributive share.

D. $20,000 guaranteed payment; $40,000 distributive share.

Answer (A) is correct.
REQUIRED: The amount and character of income the partner is to receive for Year 1.
DISCUSSION: Since the partnership's net income is $100,000, Gil's portion of the net income is $40,000. The $40,000 is greater than the minimum guaranteed. The $40,000 will be received in its entirety regardless of the minimum guaranteed. Therefore, all of the $40,000 is considered distributive share.
    Answer (B) is incorrect. The guaranteed payment is not subtracted from net income before the distributive share is calculated. Answer (C) is incorrect. No portion of the $40,000 from net income is considered guaranteed payment. Answer (D) is incorrect. Gil is not guaranteed $20,000 in addition to his share of the partnership's net income.

23. Jim is a retired partner of HIJ Company, a personal service partnership that has no capital assets. Jim has not rendered any services to HIJ since his retirement in 2005. Under the provisions of Jim's retirement agreement, HIJ is obligated to pay him 10% of the partnership's net income each year. In compliance with this agreement, HIJ paid Jim $20,000 in 2013. The partnership earned only ordinary income during 2013. For tax purposes, how should Jim treat the $20,000 he received?

A. Long-term capital gain.

B. Short-term capital gain.

C. Ordinary income.

D. Not taxable.

Answer (C) is correct.
REQUIRED: The treatment of payments received under a partnership retirement agreement.
DISCUSSION: Payments to a retired partner that are determined by partnership income are distributive shares of partnership income regardless of the period over which they are paid [Sec. 736(a)(1)]. Thus, these payments are taxable to Jim as ordinary income since the partnership income was all ordinary income.

24. Under a partnership agreement, Gary is to receive 25% of the partnership income, but not less than $12,000. At the end of Year 1, the partnership had net income of $30,000. What is the amount the partnership can deduct as a guaranteed payment in Year 1?

A. $3,000

B. $4,500

C. $7,500

D. $12,000

Answer (B) is correct.
REQUIRED: The amount a partnership may deduct as a guaranteed payment.
DISCUSSION: Most guaranteed payments are in the form of a specific amount (e.g., a stated salary amount). Some guaranteed payments are in the form of a guaranteed minimum; that is, the partner is guaranteed a minimum amount from the partnership each year. In such a situation, the guaranteed payment is the excess of the partner's guaranteed minimum over the partner's distributive share. Gary's guaranteed payment is $4,500 [$12,000 guaranteed minimum − ($30,000 × 25%)] and is deductible by the partnership. Gary's 25% distributive share of partnership income before the guaranteed payment ($30,000) is $7,500. He reports it on his individual tax return [Sec. 702(a)]. The guaranteed payment of $4,500 is also reported as ordinary income on his individual tax return.
    Answer (A) is incorrect. Twenty-five percent of the minimum payment is $3,000. Answer (C) is incorrect. Twenty-five percent of net income is $7,500, which is Gary's distributive share of partnership income. Answer (D) is incorrect. Gary's minimum guaranteed amount from the partnership each year is $12,000.

25. Jason owns a 55% capital interest in ABC Partnership. His brother owns 60% interest in XYZ Partnership. ABC sold a piece of property with an adjusted basis of $50,000 and a fair market value of $55,000 to XYZ for $45,000. What is ABC's recognized loss?

   A. $0

   B. $5,000

   C. $5,500

   D. $10,000

Answer (A) is correct.
  REQUIRED: The recognized loss on sale of property between related persons.
  DISCUSSION: Publication 544 states, "A loss on the sale or exchange of property between related persons is not deductible . . . Losses on transactions between members of the same controlled group . . . are deferred rather than denied."

26. Wolf owns a 55% interest in Red Partnership and a 75% interest in Hood Partnership. In February 2012, Red sold land to Hood for $70,000. The land had a basis to Red of $85,000. In July 2013, Hood sold the land to Ride, an unrelated individual, for $76,000. How much gain or (loss) must Hood Partnership recognize in 2013?

   A. $0

   B. $6,000

   C. $(9,000)

   D. $(15,000)

Answer (A) is correct.
  REQUIRED: The amount of gain (loss) recognized on a sale to an unrelated party subsequent to the sale to a related party.
  DISCUSSION: If a taxpayer purchases property from a related party who sustained a loss on the transaction but was not allowed a deduction for the loss due to the related party rules, any gain realized by the taxpayer on a subsequent sale of the property is recognized only to the extent that the gain exceeds the amount of the previously disallowed loss [Sec. 267(d)]. In this question, the $15,000 loss in the sale of the property is disallowed since the two partnerships involved are related parties. Hood Partnership recognizes no loss when it sells the property for $6,000 more than it paid for the property, and it does not recognize a gain since that $6,000 is less than the $15,000 previously disallowed loss. Therefore, the recognized gain is $0.
  Answer (B) is incorrect. No portion of the gain is recognized. Answer (C) is incorrect. The gain on the sale to Ride does not reduce the loss to Red, and Hood does not recognize either. Answer (D) is incorrect. The amount that Red lost when it sold the property to Hood is $15,000.

27. Ted owns a 60% interest in Alpha Partnership and a 55% interest in Beta Partnership. In August 2013, Alpha sold land to Beta for $85,000. The land had a basis to Alpha of $100,000. In September 2013, Beta sold the land to an unrelated individual for $125,000. How much gain or loss must Beta recognize for 2013?

   A. $15,000 loss.

   B. $0

   C. $25,000 gain.

   D. $40,000 gain.

Answer (C) is correct.
  REQUIRED: The gain (loss) a partnership recognizes on a related-party transaction.
  DISCUSSION: If a taxpayer purchases property from a related party who sustained a loss on the transaction but was not allowed a deduction for the loss due to the related party rules, any gain realized by the taxpayer on a subsequent sale of the property is recognized only to the extent that the gain exceeds the amount of the previously disallowed loss [Sec. 267(d)]. In this question, the $15,000 loss in the sale of the property is disallowed since the two partnerships involved are related parties. Beta Partnership recognizes no loss when it sells the property for $40,000 more than it paid for the property, but it does recognize a gain since that $40,000 is greater than the previously disallowed loss of $15,000. Therefore, the recognized gain is $25,000.
  Answer (A) is incorrect. The amount that Alpha lost when it sold the property to Beta is $15,000. Answer (B) is incorrect. A portion of the gain is recognized. Answer (D) is incorrect. The $40,000 gain on the sale by Beta is recognized only to the extent it exceeds the previously disallowed loss.

28. The adjusted basis of Dan's interest in D & P Enterprise at the end of 2013, after allocation of his share of partnership income, was $35,000. This included his $19,000 share of partnership liabilities. The partnership had no unrealized receivables or substantially appreciated inventory items. On December 31, 2013, Dan sold his interest in D & P Enterprise to Joanne for $16,000. It was agreed that she would assume Dan's share of partnership liabilities. What is the amount of Dan's capital gain or (loss)?

A. $1,000

B. $16,000

C. $0

D. $(19,000)

Answer (C) is correct.

REQUIRED: The amount of capital gain (loss) recognized when the amount realized equals the adjusted basis.

DISCUSSION: Because there were no unrealized receivables or inventory, the sale of the interest in the partnership results in capital gain or loss (Sec. 741). The relief from partnership liabilities is treated as an amount realized on the sale [Sec. 752(d)]. Because Dan's amount realized equals his adjusted basis, he will not recognize a gain or loss.

Proceeds ($16,000 cash + $19,000 liabilities assumed by purchaser)	$35,000
Less: Adjusted basis	(35,000)
Capital gain	$ 0

Answer (A) is incorrect. No gain or loss is recognized when the amount realized equals the adjusted basis. Answer (B) is incorrect. A gain is calculated as amount realized minus adjusted basis. Answer (D) is incorrect. The relief from liabilities is treated as an amount realized.

29. Howard has a 60% interest in the profits and losses of Deck Partnership. He also owns a 65% interest in the profits and losses of Card Partnership. On February 5, 2013, Deck sold land to Card for $35,000. At the time of the sale, the land had an adjusted basis to Deck of $40,000 and a fair market value of $45,000. What is the amount of loss that Deck can recognize in 2013?

A. $0

B. $3,250

C. $5,000

D. $6,500

Answer (A) is correct.

REQUIRED: The amount of loss a partnership can recognize on the sale of property to a related partnership.

DISCUSSION: Deck realized a $5,000 loss on the sale. However, Sec. 707(b)(1) provides that losses from sales or exchanges of property between two partnerships in which the same person or persons own more than 50% of the capital or profit interest are not deductible. When the property is subsequently sold, any realized gain is recognized only to the extent that it exceeds the unrecognized loss.

30. In 2013, Barb and Bet Partnership sold land having a $45,000 basis to the PTA Partnership for $35,000. Pat has a 55% capital and profits interest in PTA, and his sister owns 60% of Barb and Bet. In 2014, PTA sells the land to an unrelated individual for $47,000. How much gain or loss should Barb and Bet recognize on the subsequent sale of the land?

A. 2013: $0   2014: $2,000 gain

B. 2013: $10,000 loss   2014: $0

C. 2013: $0   2014: $12,000 gain

D. 2013: $0   2014: $0

Answer (D) is correct.

REQUIRED: The gain or loss a partnership recognizes on a subsequent sale of land.

DISCUSSION: In 2013, Barb and Bet Partnership sold the land to PTA Partnership for a loss of $10,000 ($35,000 sales price – $45,000 basis). However, Barb and Bet will not recognize any of the loss because the sale is to a related party. In addition, Barb and Bet will not recognize any gain or loss on the sale of the land by PTA to the unrelated party. Note that the gain on the sale that must be recognized by PTA will be recognized only to the extent that it exceeds the previously disallowed loss.

Use the additional questions in Gleim **EA Test Prep** to create Practice Exams that emulate Prometric!

STUDY UNIT TEN
DISPOSITION OF A PARTNER'S INTEREST

(5 pages of outline)

The disposition of a partner's interest in a partnership may be accomplished by either a sale or a liquidation. Because the tax consequences differ between the two methods, it is important to understand the differences between them.

10.1 SALE OF A PARTNERSHIP INTEREST

The sale of a partnership interest generally results in a capital gain or loss. The gain or loss is the difference between the amount realized and the adjusted basis of the partnership interest.

1. The amount realized includes the relief of any liabilities that have been assumed by the buyer.

EXAMPLE

Tami sold her share of a partnership for $29,000. Her basis in the partnership is $24,000, including $10,000 of liabilities. The selling price is considered to be $39,000 ($29,000 cash received plus the $10,000 relief of liabilities). Thus, her gain on the sale of the partnership interest is $15,000 ($39,000 – $24,000).

2. The installment method may be used to report a gain from the sale of qualifying partnership interests.

3. The basis of the partnership interest must be adjusted for the current year's distributive share and other allocations.

4. The partnership may make an election for an optional adjustment to the basis of partnership assets in the year the interest is transferred.

    a. The adjustment is the difference between the transferee partner's basis for the partnership interest and the proportionate share of the basis of all partnership property.

5. Any amount of the gain attributable to unrealized receivables or inventory must be reclassified as ordinary income under Sec. 751. This overrides Sec. 741, which normally classifies the gain as capital. Thus, unrealized receivables and inventory are considered Sec. 751 assets.

6. The sale may be made to an outside party or another partner. A sale to the partnership is treated as a liquidating distribution.

7. A portion of the capital gain may be subject to the 25% capital gains rate if there is unrecaptured Sec. 1250 gain within the partnership.

8. Note that a sale of a partnership interest relates to a partner's outside, or adjusted, basis. Inside basis relates to the basis the partnership has in its assets and can be affected by some elections by either the partner or partnership.

Unrealized Receivables

9. If a partner receives money or property in exchange for any part of a partnership interest, the amount due to his or her share of the partnership's unrealized receivables or inventory items results in ordinary income or loss.

    a. Unrealized receivables are defined to include, among other things,

        1) Mining property for which exploration expenses were deducted
        2) Stock in a Domestic International Sales Corporation (DISC)
        3) Certain farmland for which expenses for soil and water conservation or land clearing were deducted
        4) Franchises, trademarks, or trade names
        5) Oil, gas, or geothermal property for which intangible drilling and development costs were deducted
        6) Stock of certain controlled foreign corporations
        7) Market discount bonds and short-term obligations
        8) Property subject to recapture of depreciation under Sections 1245 and 1250

            a) This recapture has a zero basis.

EXAMPLE

T sells a 25% interest (AB = $100,000) in Partnership to B for $200,000. Partnership's assets are cash ($80,000), land (FMV = $300,000, AB = $160,000), and inventory (FMV = $400,000, AB = $280,000). Of T's realized gain of $100,000, at least $30,000 is ordinary income [($400,000 − $280,000) × 25%].

Termination of Partnership

10. A partnership terminates for federal tax purposes only when operations of the partnership cease or when 50% or more of the total partnership interests are sold or exchanged within any 12-month period.

    a. Sale or exchange termination is treated as a distribution of assets immediately followed by the contribution of those assets to a new partnership.

    b. The tax year of a partnership closes with respect to a partner whose entire interest in the partnership terminates by death, liquidation, or other means.

        1) Thus, a deceased partner's allocable share of partnership items up to the date of death will be taxed to the decedent on his final return.
        2) Any items allocated after the date of death will be the responsibility of the successor in interest.

    c. If a former partner is insolvent and cannot pay any of the partnership's debts, the solvent partners may have to pay more than their share of the partnership's debts.

        1) Any partner who pays any part of the insolvent partner's share of the debts can take a bad debt deduction for the amount (s)he pays.

Merger

    d. The merging partnership's tax year is used if the partners of the merged firms own more than 50% of the resulting partnership. Otherwise, a new tax year is started.

Split

    e. The old partnership's tax year continues; however, if partners owned less than 50% of the original partnership, a new tax year should be started.

EXAMPLE 1

On January 7 of the current year, the partners' interests in the capital, profits, and losses of Ripple Partnership were

	Percent of Capital, Profits, and Losses
Pebble	20%
Rock	35%
Stone	45%

On February 8 of the current year, Rock sold his entire interest to an unrelated party. Pebble sold his 20% interest in Ripple to a different unrelated party on December 24. Assuming no other transactions took place in the current year, Ripple Partnership terminated for tax purposes as of December 24 because 50% or more of the total partnership interest in capital and profits had been sold within a 12-month period.

EXAMPLE 2

Tin-Pan-Alley-Cat Partnership is in the manufacturing and wholesaling business. Tin owns a 40% interest in the capital and profits of the partnership, while each of the other partners owns a 20% interest. All of the partners are calendar-year taxpayers. On November 3 of the current year, a decision is made to separate the manufacturing business from the wholesaling business, and two new partnerships are formed. Tin-Pan Partnership takes over the manufacturing business, and Alley-Cat Partnership takes over the wholesaling business. For tax purposes, Tin-Pan is considered to be a continuation of the Tin-Pan-Alley-Cat Partnership because Tin-Pan owned more than 50% (and Alley-Cat owned less than 50%) of the original partnership. Therefore, Alley-Cat Partnership will start a new tax year.

---

11. The conversion from a partnership to an LLC (limited liability company) is not considered a sale, exchange, or liquidation of any partnership interest.

    a. The partnership's tax year does not close, and the LLC can continue to use the partnership's taxpayer identification number.

12. In the abandonment or worthlessness of a partnership interest, an ordinary loss occurs if both of the following tests are met:

    a. The transaction is not a sale or exchange.
    b. The partner has not received an actual or deemed distribution from the partnership.

Stop and review! You have completed the outline for this subunit. Study questions 1 through 19 beginning on page 205.

10.2 LIQUIDATING DISTRIBUTIONS

Distributions liquidating the entire interest of a partner may be due to partnership termination and/or the retirement or death of the partner. Also, sale to the partnership of a partner's entire interest is treated as a liquidating distribution.

1. Payments to a retired partner that are determined by partnership income are treated as a distributive share of partnership income, regardless of the period over which they are paid. The income is characterized at the partnership level.

    a. Payments to a retiring partner in liquidation of an interest that are treated as distributive shares of partnership income or as guaranteed payments are subject to self-employment tax.

2. Amounts received from the partnership in liquidation of a partnership interest are generally treated the same as other (nonliquidating) distributions.

    a. Gain is recognized to the extent money distributed exceeds the liquidating partner's AB in the partnership interest immediately before the distribution.

        1) Decrease of the partner's share of partnership liabilities is treated as a distribution of money.

        2) The gain is capital gain. However, precontribution gain or disproportionate distribution of substantially appreciated inventory (SAI) or unrealized receivables (URs) could result in ordinary income.

b.   The liquidating partner is treated as a partner for tax purposes until all payments in complete liquidation have been made.

3.   Distributions of inventory made in exchange for all or part of a partner's interest in other partnership property are governed by the "substantially appreciated" rule.

a.   Thus, gain from such distributions are taxed as ordinary income if the fair market value exceeds 120% of the partnership's adjusted basis of inventory.

1)   The 120% test applies to the total of all partnership inventory items, not to specific items or group items.

2)   Gains from such distributions are taxed as ordinary income if the fair market value exceeds

a)   120% of the partnership's adjusted basis in the inventory and
b)   10% of the face value of all partnership property other than money.

3)   On the sale of a partnership interest, any increase in value of inventory is considered substantially appreciated.

Loss

4.   A loss is realized when money and the FMV of property distributed are less than the AB of the partnership interest.

a.   No loss is recognized if any property other than money, unrealized receivables, and inventory is distributed in liquidation of the interest.

b.   Loss recognized is limited to any excess of the AB in the partnership interest over the sum of money and the AB in the URs and inventory.

c.   Loss recognized is characterized as if from sale of a capital asset.

EXAMPLE

Amber has a basis in a partnership of $17,000. In complete liquidation of her interest, she received $11,000 in cash and receivables with a basis of $0. Amber will report a capital loss of $6,000 ($17,000 – $11,000 – $0) from the liquidation. The basis of the receivables will be $0 to her. If she had received a capital asset instead of the receivables, she would not qualify to take a loss, and the capital asset would have a basis to her of $6,000 ($17,000 – $11,000).

---

5.   The distributee's basis in (noncash) property received in a distribution in liquidation is any excess of his or her AB in the partnership interest immediately before distribution over any amount of money received.

a.   If the total partnership basis of assets distributed exceeds the partner's basis in the partnership interest, allocate the decrease in the same manner as for current distributions (as described in item 1.d. in Study Unit 9, Subunit 2).

b.   For liquidating distributions only, if the basis in the partnership interest exceeds the total partnership basis of distributed assets, allocate the increase by the following steps:

1)   Determine the amount of basis to be allocated.

        Beginning basis
– Money received
– <u>Unrealized receivables and inventory</u>
        Basis to allocate

2)   Allocate any appreciation to each asset.

3)   Allocate any remaining basis (basis to allocate – appreciation of distributed assets) to the assets based on FMV prior to the distribution.

EXAMPLE

Immediately before receiving the following distribution in the complete liquidation of Scotch Associates, the adjusted basis of Hop's partnership interest in Scotch was $180,000.

	Fair Market Value	Basis Scotch
Cash	$100,000	$100,000
Real estate	96,000	70,000

Hop's basis in the real estate is $80,000 because, in the liquidating distribution, Hop's basis in his partnership interest must be reduced by the amount of money received. The remaining basis is then allocated to other property received, in this case, the real estate.

---

6. The distributee's holding period in the distributed property includes that of the partnership.

Disposition of Distributed Assets

7. Gain on the sale of URs distributed by the partnership is OI.

    a. Gain or loss realized on inventory distributed depends on the nature of the property in the distributee's hands.

        1) If the distributee sells or exchanges the inventory 5 years or more after distribution, capital gain treatment may be available.

Stop and review! You have completed the outline for this subunit. Study questions 20 through 30 beginning on page 212.

QUESTIONS

10.1 Sale of a Partnership Interest

1. Which of the following statements about the sale or exchange of a partner's interest in a partnership is true?

A. Gain or loss is the difference between the amount realized and the adjusted basis of the partner's interest in the partnership.

B. The amount realized by the selling partner does not include any partnership liabilities of which the selling partner is relieved.

C. Any amount realized due to inventory items held by the partnership results in capital gain or loss.

D. The exchange of a limited partnership interest for a limited interest in another partnership is a nontaxable exchange of like-kind property.

Answer (A) is correct.
    REQUIRED: The true statement regarding the sale or exchange of a partnership interest.
    DISCUSSION: The sale or exchange of an interest in a going partnership is similar to the sale of stock in a corporation. The gain or loss on the sale of the partnership interest is a capital gain or loss, subject to long- or short-term treatment depending upon the length of time the selling partner owned the interest in the partnership. The rule also applies to the sale of a partial interest in a partnership. An exception to this rule applies when the partnership owns unrealized receivables or inventory. In this case, the selling partner must allocate a portion of the sales proceeds to the unrealized receivables and to the inventory and, to that extent, will realize ordinary income.
    Answer (B) is incorrect. The amount realized includes any liabilities of which the partner is relieved. Answer (C) is incorrect. Any amount realized due to inventory items is ordinary income. Answer (D) is incorrect. The exchange of limited partnership interests is not a like-kind exchange.

2. The adjusted basis of Rebecca's partnership interest is $17,500. She received a distribution of $9,000 cash and a piece of land with an adjusted basis of $2,500 and a fair market value of $4,000. What is the gain to be recognized at the time of these distributions?

A. $1,500

B. $0

C. $4,500

D. $6,000

Answer (B) is correct.
    REQUIRED: The gain to be recognized at the time of partnership distributions.
    DISCUSSION: A partner generally recognizes gain on a partnership distribution only to the extent any money included in the distribution exceeds the adjusted basis of the partner's interest in the partnership (Publication 541). Since Rebecca's distribution did not exceed her partnership interest, she doesn't recognize any gain. A partnership generally does not recognize any gain or loss because of distributions it makes to partners (Publication 541). Therefore, the partnership does not recognize any gain.

3. Scott became a limited partner in the S&N Partnership with a $10,000 contribution on the formation of the partnership. The adjusted basis of his partnership interest at the end of the current year is $20,000, which includes his $15,000 share of partnership liabilities. He had been paid his share of the partnership income for the year. There are no unrealized receivables or inventory items. Scott sells his interest in the partnership for $10,000. What is the amount and character of Scott's gain (loss) when selling his partnership interest?

A. $5,000 ordinary income.

B. $5,000 capital gain.

C. $10,000 ordinary loss.

D. $25,000 capital gain.

Answer (B) is correct.
REQUIRED: The amount and character of a partner's gain (loss) when selling his or her partnership interest.
DISCUSSION: Sec. 741 provides the general rule that capital gain or loss is recognized on the sale of a partnership interest. A selling partner's relief of liabilities is included in the amount realized [Sec. 752(d)]. Gain or loss recognized by the selling partner is the difference between the amount realized and the adjusted basis of the partner's interest in the partnership [Reg. Sec. 1.741-1(a)]. Therefore, Scott's capital gain is $5,000 ($25,000 amount realized – $20,000 adjusted basis).

4. Which of the following statements with respect to a partner's sale or exchange of a partnership interest is false?

A. The sale or exchange of a partner's interest in a partnership usually results in a capital gain or loss.

B. Gain or loss recognized by the selling partner is the difference between the amount realized and the adjusted basis of the partner's interest in the partnership.

C. The selling partner must include, as part of the amount realized, any partnership liability of which (s)he is relieved.

D. The installment method of reporting cannot be used by the partner who sells a partnership interest at a gain.

Answer (D) is correct.
REQUIRED: The false statement with respect to a partner's sale or exchange of a partnership interest.
DISCUSSION: Sec. 741 provides the general rule that capital gain or loss is recognized on the sale of a partnership interest. A selling partner's relief of liabilities is included in the amount realized [Sec. 752(d)]. Gain or loss recognized by the selling partner is the difference between the amount realized and the adjusted basis of the partner's interest in the partnership [Reg. Sec. 1.741-1(a)]. The installment method is available when at least one payment is received after the tax year in which the sale occurs [Sec. 453(a)]. No exception is provided that prevents the use of the installment method for the sale of a partnership interest.
Answer (A) is incorrect. Generally, capital gain or loss is recognized on the sale of a partnership interest. Answer (B) is incorrect. Gain or loss recognized is computed under Sec. 1001 as the difference between the amount realized and the selling partner's adjusted basis. Answer (C) is incorrect. Relief from liabilities is included in the amount realized [Sec. 752(d)].

5. On December 31 of the current year, Rita's adjusted basis in Diamond Partnership was $40,000, which included her $30,000 share of partnership liabilities. The partnership had no unrealized receivables or inventory. Rita sold her interest for $20,000 cash and was relieved of any partnership liabilities. What is the amount and character of Rita's gain or loss?

A. $0

B. $10,000 ordinary income.

C. $10,000 capital gain.

D. $(20,000) capital loss.

Answer (C) is correct.
REQUIRED: The amount of gain or loss on the sale of a partnership interest.
DISCUSSION: Because there were no unrealized receivables or inventory, the sale of the interest in the partnership results in capital gain or loss (Sec. 741). The relief from partnership liabilities is treated as an amount realized on the sale [Sec. 752(d)]. Rita's gain is

Proceeds ($20,000 cash + $30,000 liabilities assumed by purchaser)	$50,000
Less: Adjusted basis	(40,000)
Capital gain	$10,000

Answer (A) is incorrect. A capital gain or loss is generally recognized on the sale of a partnership interest. Answer (B) is incorrect. The gain on the sale of a partnership interest is a capital gain unless the gain is attributable to inventory or unrealized receivables. Answer (D) is incorrect. The assumption of liabilities by the buyer is included in the amount realized.

6. Abby sells her 50% interest in the ABC partnership to Marty for $1,000 cash. Her outside basis at that time is $775. The partnership has inventory and a capital asset with respective bases of $1,200 and $300 and respective fair market values of $1,500 and $450. Abby should properly recognize

- A. Ordinary income of $300 and a capital loss of $75.
- B. Capital gain of $225 on the sale of her partnership interest.
- C. An ordinary gain of $225, since she received cash of at least that amount.
- D. Ordinary income of $150 and a capital gain of $75.

Answer (D) is correct.
   REQUIRED: The amount and character of the gain (loss).
   DISCUSSION: The total gain Abby realizes is the amount received ($1,000) minus her outside basis ($775). This equals $225. Under Sec. 751, however, a partner is to recognize ordinary income on the sale or exchange of a partnership interest to the extent the consideration received is attributable to unrealized receivables and/or inventory items. The inventory increased in value by $300, and Abby's share of this is $150. Thus, $150 is ordinary income, and the remaining gain $75 ($225 – $150) is treated as a capital gain.
   Answer (A) is incorrect. Ordinary income is recognized only to Abby's share of the unrealized inventory increase, not the whole increase. Abby's share is 50% of the $300 increase in inventory. Answer (B) is incorrect. Ordinary income must be recognized when there is unrealized receivables or inventory items. Answer (C) is incorrect. The sale of a partnership interest results in a capital gain or loss to the extent it is over the ordinary income that is recognized from unrealized receivables or inventory.

7. In a sale or exchange of a partner's interest in a partnership, which of the following partnership assets is (are) treated as unrealized receivables?

- A. Franchises.
- B. Trademarks.
- C. Mining property for which exploration expenses were deducted.
- D. All of the answers are correct.

Answer (D) is correct.
   REQUIRED: The assets treated as unrealized receivables in the sale of partnership assets.
   DISCUSSION: Under Sec. 751(c), unrealized receivables are defined to include, among other things,

- Mining property for which exploration expenses were deducted
- Stock in a Domestic International Sales Corporation (DISC)
- Certain farmland for which expenses for soil and water conservation or land clearing were deducted
- Franchises, trademarks, or trade names
- Oil, gas, or geothermal property for which intangible drilling and development costs were deducted
- Stock of certain controlled foreign corporations
- Market discount bonds and short-term obligations

8. Joseph is a partner in JKL Partnership. The adjusted basis of his partnership interest is $38,000, which includes his $30,000 share of partnership liabilities. The partnership has no unrealized receivables or inventory items. Joseph sells his interest in the partnership for $15,000 in cash. He had been paid his share of the partnership income for the tax year. What is Joseph's gain or loss on the sale?

- A. $7,000
- B. $15,000
- C. $(15,000)
- D. $(23,000)

Answer (A) is correct.
   REQUIRED: The gain or loss on sale of interest in partnership subject to liabilities.
   DISCUSSION: Because there were no unrealized receivables or inventory, the sale of the interest in the partnership results in capital gain or loss (Sec. 741). The relief from partnership liabilities is treated as an amount realized on the sale [Sec. 752(d)]. Because Joseph's amount realized exceeds his adjusted basis, he will recognize a gain of $7,000.
   Answer (B) is incorrect. The gain is not the entire cash received. Answer (C) is incorrect. The cash received does not reduce his liabilities of the partnership. Answer (D) is incorrect. The cash received is not balanced against his basis without the liabilities assumed.

9. Archie sells his 50% interest in XYZ Partnership to Hal for $5,000 cash. His outside basis in the partnership is $3,500. The partnership has inventory and a capital asset with respect to basis of $6,000 and $2,000, respectively. The respective fair market values of the inventory and capital asset are $8,000 and $1,000. Archie should properly recognize

A. Ordinary income of $2,000 and a capital loss of $500.

B. Capital gain of $1,500 on the sale of his partnership interest.

C. Ordinary income of $1,500, the amount of cash he received.

D. None of the answers are correct.

Answer (D) is correct.

REQUIRED: Gain and ordinary income reported from sale of partnership interest.

DISCUSSION: The sale of a partnership interest generally results in a capital gain or loss. The gain or loss is the difference between the amount realized and the adjusted basis of the partnership interest. The total gain would equal $1,500. Only $1,000 of the gain would be classified as ordinary income ($2,000 appreciation of inventory × 50% ownership percentage). Thus, none of the other answers are correct.

Answer (A) is incorrect. The entire amount of inventory appreciation need not be reported by one partner. Answer (B) is incorrect. Only $1,000 of the gain is ordinary income. Answer (C) is incorrect. Not all of the gain is ordinary income.

10. Michael has a partnership interest with a zero basis. The partnership has inventory valued at $250,000. Michael's share of the ordinary income to be received from the sale of the inventory would be $10,000. Michael sells his partnership interest for $30,000. Michael will report the following gain:

A. $30,000 capital gain.

B. $20,000 ordinary gain and $10,000 capital gain.

C. $10,000 ordinary gain and $20,000 capital gain.

D. No gain or loss.

Answer (C) is correct.

REQUIRED: Gain reported from sale of interest in a partnership.

DISCUSSION: The sale of a partnership interest generally results in a capital gain or loss. The gain or loss is the difference between the amount realized and the adjusted basis of the partnership interest. Any amount of gain attributable to unrealized receivables or inventory must be reclassified as ordinary income. Michael's total gain would equal $30,000. Of this gain, $10,000 would be classified as ordinary income. The remaining $20,000 would receive capital gain treatment.

Answer (A) is incorrect. Only $10,000 of the gain would be classified as ordinary income. Answer (B) is incorrect. Only $10,000 of the gain is ordinary income. Answer (D) is incorrect. Michael's basis is $30,000 less than the selling price.

11. Linda sold her partnership interest for $25,000. Her adjusted basis at the time of the sale is $22,500, which includes her $12,500 share of partnership liabilities. When she initially invested in the partnership, she contributed $10,000 worth of equipment. There was no profit or loss at the partnership level at the time she sold her interest. What is the amount and nature of her gain or loss from the sale of her partnership interest?

A. $7,500 ordinary loss.

B. $10,000 capital gain.

C. $12,500 ordinary gain.

D. $15,000 capital gain.

Answer (D) is correct.

REQUIRED: Gain reported from sale of partnership interest.

DISCUSSION: The sale of a partnership interest generally results in a capital gain or loss. The gain or loss is the difference between the amount realized and the adjusted basis of the partnership interest. Her gain would be increased by the amount of liabilities in the partnership. Thus, she would report a capital gain of $15,000 ($25,000 selling price − $22,500 basis + $12,500).

12. Which of the following statements about the liquidation of a partner's interest is false?

A. A retiring partner is treated as a partner until his or her interest in the partnership has been completely liquidated.

B. The retiring partner will recognize a gain on a liquidating distribution to the extent that any money distributed is more than the partner's adjusted basis in the partnership.

C. Payments in liquidation of a partnership interest that are not made in exchange for the interest in partnership property are reported as capital gain by the recipient.

D. Former partners who continue to make guaranteed periodic payments to satisfy the partnership's liability to a retired partner after the partnership is terminated can deduct the payments as business expense in the year paid.

Answer (C) is correct.
REQUIRED: The false statement regarding liquidation of a partner's interest.
DISCUSSION: Amounts received from the partnership in liquidation of a partnership interest are generally treated as distributive shares of partnership income or guaranteed payments.

13. Candy is a partner in LX Partnership. The adjusted basis of her partnership interest is $24,000, of which $19,000 represents her share of the partnership liabilities for which neither Candy, the other partners, nor the partnership has assumed personal liability. Candy's share of unrealized receivables in the partnership is $10,000. Candy sold her partnership interest for $28,000. What is the amount and character of Candy's gain?

A. $10,000 ordinary gain; $13,000 capital gain.

B. $13,000 ordinary gain; $10,000 capital gain.

C. $4,000 ordinary income.

D. $23,000 capital gain.

Answer (A) is correct.
REQUIRED: The amount and character of a gain when a partnership interest is sold.
DISCUSSION: The gain or loss on the sale of the partnership interest is a capital gain or loss, subject to long- or short-term treatment depending upon the length of time the selling partner owned the interest in the partnership. An exception to this rule applies when the partnership owns unrealized receivables or inventory. In this case, the selling partner must allocate a portion of the sale proceeds to the unrealized receivables and to the inventory and, to that extent, will realize ordinary income. Therefore, she must allocate $10,000 of her realized gain of $23,000 ($47,000 amount realized – $24,000 adjusted basis) to ordinary income. This leaves a capital gain of $13,000 ($23,000 – $10,000).
Answer (B) is incorrect. The portion of the gain attributable to unrealized receivables is ordinary income. Answer (C) is incorrect. The liabilities assumed by the buyer are included in the amount realized. Answer (D) is incorrect. The portion of the gain attributable to unrealized receivables is ordinary income.

14. All of the following are considered in determining the basis of a partner's interest in a partnership for purposes of computing gain or loss on the sale or liquidation of that interest except the

A. Partner's distributive share of capital losses.

B. Partnership book value of the partner's interest.

C. Partner's distributive share of nontaxable partnership income.

D. Adjusted basis of property distributed to the partner by the partnership.

Answer (B) is correct.
REQUIRED: The item not used in determining the basis of a partner's interest in a partnership.
DISCUSSION: Once an interest in a partnership is acquired, the partner's basis is adjusted to reflect various partnership activities. Basis is increased by any additional contributions, any increased share of partnership liabilities, and the distributive share of both taxable and nontaxable income. Basis is decreased by any distribution to the partner, any decrease in liabilities, and the distributive share of partnership losses. The partnership book value of a partner's interest (capital account) has no effect on basis.
Answer (A) is incorrect. Basis is reduced by the partner's distributive share of capital losses. Answer (C) is incorrect. Basis is increased by the partner's distributive share of nontaxable partnership income. Answer (D) is incorrect. Basis is decreased by any distribution to the partner.

15. Tracy has a one-fourth interest ih the TANY Partnership. The adjusted basis of his interest at the end of the current year is $30,000. He sells his interest in the TANY Partnership to Roy for $50,000 cash. There was no agreement between Tracy and Roy for any allocation of the sales price. The basis and fair market value of the partnership's assets (there are no liabilities) are as follows:

Assets	Basis	Fair Market Value
Cash	$ 40,000	$ 40,000
Unrealized Receivables	0	36,000
Inventory	40,000	92,000
Land	40,000	32,000
Total	$120,000	$200,000

What is the amount and character of Tracy's gain or loss?

A. $0 ordinary income; $0 capital gain.

B. $20,000 ordinary income; $0 capital gain.

C. $10,000 ordinary income; $10,000 capital gain.

D. $22,000 ordinary income; $2,000 capital loss.

Answer (D) is correct.
REQUIRED: The amount and character of a partner's gain (loss) when selling his or her partnership interest.
DISCUSSION: The gain or loss on the sale of the partnership interest is a capital gain or loss, subject to long- or short-term treatment depending upon the length of time the selling partner owned the interest in the partnership. An exception to this rule applies when the partnership owns unrealized receivables or inventory. In this case, the selling partner must allocate a portion of the sale proceeds to the unrealized receivables and to the inventory and, to that extent, will realize ordinary income. The unrealized receivables and the inventory are Section 751 assets, meaning $22,000 [($52,000 gain from inventory + $36,000 gain from unrealized receivables)(1/4)] is ordinary income. But the gain is only $20,000; thus, there is a $2,000 capital loss.

16. Lloyd is a partner in LG Partnership. The adjusted basis of his partnership interest is $38,000, of which $30,000 represents his share of the partnership liabilities for which neither Lloyd, the other partners, nor the partnership has assumed personal liability. Lloyd's share of unrealized receivables in the partnership is $12,000. Lloyd sold his partnership interest for $45,000 cash. What is the amount and character of Lloyd's gain?

A. $12,000 ordinary gain; $25,000 capital gain.

B. $25,000 ordinary gain; $12,000 capital gain.

C. $7,000 capital gain.

D. $37,000 capital gain.

Answer (A) is correct.
REQUIRED: The amount and character of gain on the sale of a partnership interest including Sec. 751 items.
DISCUSSION: Sec. 741 provides the general rule that capital gain or loss is recognized on the sale or exchange of a partnership interest. A selling partner's relief of liabilities is included in the amount realized [Sec. 752(d)]. However, under Sec. 751(a), gain attributable to unrealized receivables or inventory is ordinary income. The answer assumes that the basis in unrealized receivables is zero.

Total gain ($75,000 amount realized – $38,000 basis)	$37,000
Sec. 751 gain (ordinary) on receivables	(12,000)
Capital gain	$25,000

Answer (B) is incorrect. The portion of gain attributable to unrealized receivables is ordinary income. Answer (C) is incorrect. The liabilities assumed by the buyer are included in the amount realized. Answer (D) is incorrect. The portion of gain attributable to unrealized receivables is ordinary income.

17. You are a partner in ABC Partnership. The adjusted basis of your partnership interest at the end of the current year is zero. Your share of potential ordinary income from partnership depreciable property is $5,000. The partnership has no other unrealized receivables or appreciated inventory items. You sell your interest in the partnership for $11,000 in cash. Which of the following statements is true?

1. You report the entire amount as a gain since your adjusted basis in the partnership is zero.

2. You report $5,000 as ordinary income from the sale of the partnership's depreciable property.

3. You report the remaining $6,000 gain as capital gain.

    A. 2 and 3 are true, but 1 is false.

    B. All of the statements are false.

    C. All of the statements are true.

    D. 1 is true, but 2 and 3 are false.

Answer (C) is correct.
REQUIRED: The true statement(s) regarding the sale of a partnership interest.
DISCUSSION: The sale or exchange of an interest in a going partnership is similar to the sale of stock in a corporation. The gain or loss on the sale of the partnership interest is a capital gain or loss, subject to long- or short-term treatment depending upon the length of time the selling partner owned the interest in the partnership. An exception to this rule applies when the partnership owns unrealized receivables or inventory. In this case, the selling partner must allocate a portion of the sales proceeds to the unrealized receivables and to the inventory and, to that extent, will realize ordinary income.
Answer (A) is incorrect. The entire amount is reported as a gain, although not in the same classification. Answer (B) is incorrect. The gain on the sale of a partnership interest is a capital gain, reduced by the amount attributable to the unrealized depreciable property that is classified as ordinary income. Answer (D) is incorrect. The gain on the sale of a partnership interest is a capital gain, reduced by the amount attributable to the unrealized depreciable property that is classified as ordinary income.

18. A partnership terminates when

1. All of its operations are discontinued and no part of any business, financial operations, or venture is continued by any of its partners in a partnership or a limited liability company classified as a partnership.

2. At least 50% of the total interest in partnership capital and profits is sold or exchanged within a 12-month period, including a sale or exchange to another partner.

    A. 1 and 2 are true in their entirety.

    B. 1 and 2 are false in their entirety.

    C. Only 1 is true.

    D. Only 2 is true.

Answer (A) is correct.
REQUIRED: The condition that terminates a partnership that is not an electing large partnership for tax purposes.
DISCUSSION: Under Sec. 708(b)(1), a partnership terminates for tax purposes only if (1) no part of any business, financial operation, or venture of the partnership continues to be carried on by its partners in a partnership or (2) within a 12-month period there is a sale or exchange of 50% or more of the total interest in partnership capital and profits.
Answer (B) is incorrect. Under Sec. 708(b)(1), a partnership is terminated when either no part of any business, financial operation, or venture of the partnership continues to be carried on by its partners in a partnership or there is a sale or exchange of 50% or more of the total interest in partnership capital and profits within a 12-month period. Answer (C) is incorrect. Under Sec. 708(b)(1), a partnership also terminates if, within a 12-month period, there is a sale or exchange of 50% or more of the total interest in partnership capital and profits. Answer (D) is incorrect. Under Sec. 708(b)(1), a partnership also terminates if no part of any business, financial operation, or venture of the partnership continues to be carried on by its partners in a partnership.

19. Cobb, Danver, and Evans each owned a one-third interest in the capital and profits of their calendar-year partnership. On September 18, Year 1, Cobb and Danver sold their partnership interests to Frank and immediately withdrew from all participation in the partnership. On March 15, Year 2, Cobb and Danver received full payment from Frank for the sale of their partnership interests. For tax purposes, the partnership

    A. Terminated on September 18, Year 1.

    B. Terminated on December 31, Year 1.

    C. Terminated on March 15, Year 2.

    D. Did not terminate.

Answer (A) is correct.
REQUIRED: The date a partnership terminated for tax purposes.
DISCUSSION: Under Sec. 708, a partnership terminates if more than a 50% capital or profits interest is sold or exchanged within a 12-month period. The termination occurs on the date Cobb and Danver sell 66.66% of the partnership to Frank.

10.2 Liquidating Distributions

20. Which of the following statements about the liquidation of a partner's interest is false?

A. A retiring partner is treated as a partner until his or her interest in the partnership has been completely liquidated.

B. The remaining partners' distributive shares of partnership income are reduced by payments in exchange for a retiring partner's interest in partnership property.

C. The retiring partner will recognize a gain on a liquidating distribution to the extent that any money distributed is more than the partner's adjusted basis in the partnership.

D. Payments in liquidation of an interest that are not made in exchange for the interest in partnership property are reported as ordinary income by the recipient.

Answer (B) is correct.
    REQUIRED: The false statement regarding the liquidation of a partner's interest.
    DISCUSSION: Payments made in liquidation of a partner's interest are considered a distribution under Sec. 736(b) to the extent the payments are made in exchange for the interest of the partner in the partnership property. The partnership is not allowed a deduction, and therefore the remaining partners' distributive shares are not affected.
    Answer (A) is incorrect. The liquidating partner is treated as a partner for tax purposes until all payments in complete liquidation have been made. Answer (C) is incorrect. Gain is recognized to the extent money distributed exceeds the liquidating partner's adjusted basis in the partnership interest immediately before the distribution. Answer (D) is incorrect. Payments not made in exchange for the interest in partnership property are reported as ordinary income by the recipient.

21. When payments are made to a retiring partner or successor in interest of a deceased partner for an interest in the partnership property, which of the following is true?

A. Payments that are based on partnership income are not taxable as a distributive share of partnership income but for the interest in the partnership.

B. A retiring partner is treated as a partner until his or her interest in the partnership has been completely liquidated.

C. Payments made for a retiring partner's share of the partnership's unrealized receivables are treated as made in exchange for partnership property if capital is not a material income producing factor and the retiring partner was a general partner.

D. If the amount of the payment is based on partnership income, the payment is treated as a guaranteed payment.

Answer (B) is correct.
    REQUIRED: The true statement about payments made to a retiring partner.
    DISCUSSION: For income tax purposes, a retiring partner or successor in interest of a deceased partner is treated as a partner until his or her interest in the partnership has been completely liquidated (Publication 541).

22. DUG Partnership operates a business. Its tax year ends on December 31. A partner dies on August 20 of the current year. The deceased partner's (and his or her estate's) distributive share of partnership income for the year of death is $18,000. The partner's share of self-employment income from the partnership is

A. $18,000

B. $11,500

C. $12,000

D. $9,000

Answer (C) is correct.
    REQUIRED: The partner's share of self-employment income from a partnership.
    DISCUSSION: The partner's self-employment income includes the partner's distributive share of income earned by the partnership through the end of the month in which the partner's death occurs [IRC Sec. 1402(f)]. Since the partner dies in the eighth month, $12,000 ($18,000 × 8/12) of the distribution is considered self-employment income.

23. Partner A received inventory items with a basis of $20,000 in complete dissolution of a partnership. Within 5 years, Partner A sells the entire inventory for $30,000. What amount and type of gain should Partner A report?

    A. $0

    B. $10,000 short-term capital gain.

    C. $10,000 long-term capital gain.

    D. $10,000 ordinary gain.

Answer (D) is correct.
    REQUIRED: The type of gain reported on partnership assets received in complete liquidation that are later sold.
    DISCUSSION: In order for the gain realized to be capital in nature, the item must have been held for more than 5 years and have been a capital asset in the hands of the distributee partner. The "substantially appreciated" rule applies because the total fair market value ($30,000) is more than 120% of the partnership's adjusted basis for the property ($20,000). When this rule applies, the gain is taxed as ordinary income. Therefore, the $10,000 gain is ordinary.
    Answer (A) is incorrect. An ordinary gain must be recognized. Answer (B) is incorrect. The gain is ordinary, not capital, in nature. Answer (C) is incorrect. The gain is ordinary, not capital, in nature.

24. David Beck and Walter Crocker were equal partners in the calendar-year partnership of Beck & Crocker. On July 1, Year 1, Beck died. Beck's estate became the successor in interest and continued to share in Beck & Crocker's profits until Beck's entire partnership interest was liquidated on April 30, Year 2. At what date was the partnership considered terminated for tax purposes?

    A. April 30, Year 2.

    B. December 31, Year 1.

    C. July 31, Year 1.

    D. July 1, Year 1.

Answer (A) is correct.
    REQUIRED: The date the partnership is considered terminated for tax purposes following a partner's death.
    DISCUSSION: A partnership generally does not terminate for tax purposes on the death of a partner since the deceased partner's estate or successor in interest continues to share in partnership profits and losses (Sec. 708). A partnership terminates when 50% or more of the partnership is sold or exchanged. The Beck & Crocker partnership terminated on April 30, Year 2, because, when Beck's entire partnership interest was liquidated, the business ceased to be operated as a partnership.

25. John's basis in his partnership interest on October 15 of the current year was $30,000. In a distribution in liquidation of his entire interest, he received properties C and D from the partnership on that date, neither of which were inventory or unrealized receivables. On October 15 of the current year, property C had an adjusted basis of $20,000 and a fair market value of $5,000, and property D had an adjusted basis of $30,000 and a fair market value of $20,000. Based on this information, what is John's basis in property C immediately after the distribution?

    A. $5,000

    B. $8,000

    C. $12,000

    D. $20,000

Answer (B) is correct.
    REQUIRED: The basis in property received in liquidation of the partnership interest.
    DISCUSSION: Sec. 732(b) provides that the basis of property distributed by a partnership in a liquidating distribution to a partner is the adjusted basis of the partner's interest in the partnership minus any money received in the same distribution. The basis of distributed property is allocated first to inventory items and unrealized receivables up to the amount of the partnership's adjusted basis in these items, then to other property to the extent of each distributed property's adjusted basis to the partnership. The remaining basis increase or decrease is allocated depending on whether the adjusted basis of the distributed properties exceed the partner's remaining basis in the partnership interest or not. Since the partnership's basis in the distributed properties exceed the partner's remaining basis in the partnership ($50,000 basis in properties and $30,000 basis in partnership), a decrease must be allocated among the properties in proportion to the respective amounts of unrealized depreciation inherent in each property (but only to the extent of any unrealized depreciation). John's basis in property C will be $8,000. The $20,000 basis of property C is reduced by the decline in FMV of property C ($15,000) divided by the decline in FMV of both properties ($15,000 + $10,000) times the $20,000 ($50,000 – $30,000) required reduction in basis for a reduction of $12,000 for property C. The old $20,000 basis – the $12,000 reduction = the new $8,000 basis.
    Answer (A) is incorrect. The adjusted basis of the property is not its fair market value. Answer (C) is incorrect. The basis of the partnership is not allocated to property C based on the basis of the two properties, which is the former rule. Answer (D) is incorrect. The combined basis of the properties received cannot exceed the basis of the partnership interest.

26. On January 1 of the current year, Ruth had a basis in her partnership interest of $55,000. Thereafter, in liquidation of her entire interest, she received an apartment house and an office building. The apartment house has an adjusted basis to the partnership of $5,000 and a fair market value of $40,000. The office building has an adjusted basis to the partnership of $10,000 and a fair market value of $10,000. What is Ruth's basis in each property after the distribution?

A. Apartment house, $40,000; office building, $15,000.

B. Apartment house, $44,000; office building, $11,000.

C. Apartment house, $25,000; office building, $30,000.

D. Apartment house, $45,000; office building, $10,000.

Answer (B) is correct.

REQUIRED: The partner's basis in property after a distribution in liquidation.

DISCUSSION: If a partner's interest is liquidated solely through a distribution of partnership property other than money, no gain is recognized. If the partnership distributes property other than money, the partner's basis in the partnership must be transferred to the distributed assets. When a liquidation occurs and the partner's basis in the partnership exceeds the partnership's basis in the distributed assets, the excess of the partner's basis in the partnership must also be allocated among the distributed assets. Any basis increase required is allocated first to properties with unrealized appreciation in proportion to the respective amounts of unrealized appreciation inherent in each property (but only to the extent of each property's unrealized appreciation). Any remaining increase is then allocated in proportion to the properties' fair market values. The apartment house is first assigned its basis of $5,000, and the office building is assigned $10,000. Another $40,000 ($55,000 partnership basis – $15,000 assigned to properties) must be allocated to the two properties. The apartment house is allocated $35,000 [($35,000 increase in FMV ÷ $35,000 total increase in FMV) × $35,000]. Accordingly, $5,000 still remains to be allocated. It is allocated based on the FMVs of the properties. The apartment house will be allocated $4,000 [$40,000 FMV ÷ ($40,000 FMV of the apartment + $10,000 FMV of the building) × $5,000 remaining increase], and the building will be allocated the remaining $1,000. Thus, the basis in the apartment house will be $44,000 ($5,000 + $35,000 + $4,000), and the basis in the office building will be $11,000 ($10,000 + $1,000).

Answer (A) is incorrect. The bases in the properties will not be based solely on the FMV of the apartment house. Answer (C) is incorrect. The excess of the FMV over the adjusted bases of the properties is not divided equally among the assets. Answer (D) is incorrect. After the initial appreciation, any remaining increase is then allocated in proportion to the properties' fair market values.

27. On September 30, Year 1, Robert retired from his partnership. At that time, his adjusted basis was $40,000, which included his $15,000 share of the partnership's liabilities. In liquidation of Robert's interest in partnership property, he was relieved of his share of the partnership liabilities and received cash retirement payments of $2,500 per month for 15 months, beginning October 1, Year 1. Both Robert and the partnership use a calendar tax year. How much must Robert report as capital gain in Year 1 and Year 2?

	Year 1	Year 2
A.	$18,750	$18,750
B.	$6,250	$6,250
C.	$12,500	$0
D.	$0	$12,500

Answer (D) is correct.

REQUIRED: The amounts of income to be reported for retirement payments received.

DISCUSSION: A retiring partner who receives payments from the partnership is considered to be a partner until the last payment is received [Sec. 706(c)(2)(A)]. Payments made in complete liquidation of a partnership interest are considered distributions by the partnership to the extent they are made in exchange for the interest of the partner in partnership property [Sec. 736(b)(1)]. Gain on a distribution is recognized only to the extent that money distributed exceeds the partner's basis in the interest [Sec. 731(a)]. Thus, gain is recognized after basis is used up, that is, on the payments Robert receives last. AB excluding liabilities is $25,000 ($40,000 – $15,000). Total payments equal $37,500 [($2,500 × 3 months in Year 1) + ($2,500 × 12 months in Year 2)]. The first 10 months of payments go against basis ($2,500 × 10 = $25,000), all of the three payments in Year 1, and seven payments in Year 2. The remaining five payments in Year 2 are capital gains.

Answer (A) is incorrect. A gain is recognized only to the extent that the payments exceed basis. Answer (B) is incorrect. A gain is not recognized until the year basis is used up. Answer (C) is incorrect. A gain is not recognized until the year basis is used up.

28. Jayne's basis in her partnership interest is $55,000. During the current year, in a distribution in liquidation of her entire interest, she receives a rental house and vacant lot, neither of which is inventory or unrealized receivables. The rental house has an adjusted basis to the partnership of $5,000 and a fair market value of $40,000. The vacant lot has an adjusted basis to the partnership of $10,000 and a fair market value of $10,000. What is Jayne's basis in each property after the distribution?

A. Rental house, $40,000; vacant lot, $15,000.

B. Rental house, $44,000; vacant lot, $11,000.

C. Rental house, $25,000; vacant lot, $30,000.

D. Rental house, $45,000; vacant lot, $10,000.

Answer (B) is correct.

REQUIRED: The basis of property distributed to a partner in liquidation of a partner's interest.

DISCUSSION: If a partner's interest is liquidated solely through a distribution of partnership property other than money, no gain is recognized. If the partnership distributes property other than money, the partner's basis in the partnership must be transferred to the distributed assets. When a liquidation occurs and the partner's basis in the partnership exceeds the partnership's basis in the distributed assets, the excess of the partner's basis in the partnership must also be allocated among the distributed assets. Any basis increase required is allocated first to properties with unrealized appreciation in proportion to the respective amounts of unrealized appreciation inherent in each property (but only to the extent of each property's unrealized appreciation). Any remaining increase is then allocated in proportion to the properties' fair market values. The rental house is first assigned its basis of $5,000, and the vacant lot is assigned $10,000. Another $40,000 ($55,000 partnership basis – $15,000 assigned to properties) must be allocated to the two properties. The rental house is allocated $35,000 [($35,000 increase in FMV ÷ $35,000 total increase in FMV) × $35,000]. Accordingly, $5,000 still remains to be allocated. It is allocated based on the FMVs of the properties. The rental house will be allocated $4,000 [$40,000 FMV ÷ ($40,000 FMV of the rental house + $10,000 FMV of the vacant lot) × $5,000 remaining increase], and the lot will be allocated the remaining $1,000. Thus, the basis in the rental house will be $44,000 ($5,000 + $35,000 + $4,000), and the basis in the vacant lot will be $11,000 ($10,000 + $1,000).

Answer (A) is incorrect. The bases in the properties will not be based solely on the FMV of the rental house. Answer (C) is incorrect. The excess of the FMV over the adjusted bases of the properties is not divided equally among the assets. Answer (D) is incorrect. After the initial appreciation, any remaining increase is then allocated in proportion to the properties' fair market values.

29. Mr. K owned a 50% interest in K&L Partnership. It reports income on the accrual basis. On April 1 of the current year, the partnership was dissolved, and it distributed to K one-half of all partnership assets. The partnership had no liabilities. The following assets were distributed to K:

	Basis	Fair Market Value
Cash	$ 5,000	$ 5,000
Accounts receivable	10,000	10,000
Inventory	8,000	10,000
Land	20,000	50,000

K's basis in the partnership interest was $43,000. As of December 31 of the current year, K had sold the inventory for $10,000 and collected all accounts receivable. What gain will K report in the year?

A. $2,000 capital gain.

B. $2,000 ordinary income.

C. $32,000 capital gain.

D. $32,000 ordinary income.

Answer (B) is correct.

REQUIRED: The gain recognized by a partner from partnership assets distributed in liquidation and later sold.

DISCUSSION: Under Sec. 731(a), a partner recognizes no gain when property is distributed by the partnership except to the extent that money distributed exceeds the partner's adjusted basis in the partnership. Since the cash received ($5,000) did not exceed K's basis in the partnership ($43,000), K recognizes no gain under Sec. 731(a).

Under Sec. 732, the basis of property distributed is the partner's adjusted basis in the partnership interest minus any money distributed ($43,000 – $5,000 = $38,000). This basis is first allocated to unrealized receivables and inventory items in an amount not to exceed the adjusted basis of such property to the partnership. K's basis in the inventory is $8,000, and he has a $2,000 gain when it is sold. This gain is ordinary under Sec. 735(a)(2) since the inventory was sold within 5 years of the distribution. K recognizes no gain on collection of $10,000 in accounts receivable since his basis in them is also $10,000. K still holds land with a basis of $20,000 at year end.

Answer (A) is incorrect. A partner does not recognize a gain on the distribution of property unless money received exceeds the adjusted basis in the partnership interest. Answer (C) is incorrect. A partner does not recognize a gain on the distribution of property unless money received exceeds the adjusted basis in the partnership interest. Answer (D) is incorrect. Ordinary income is realized only on the sale of inventory.

30. The adjusted basis of Dave's partnership interest in CDS Partnership is $60,000. In a complete liquidation of his interest, Dave received the following:

	Basis to CDS	Fair Market Value
Cash	$20,000	$20,000
Inventory items	15,000	20,000
Land	24,000	40,000
Building	8,000	10,000

What is Dave's basis in the land and in the building?

	Land	Building
A.	$18,750	$6,250
B.	$24,000	$8,000
C.	$40,000	$10,000
D.	$56,000	$14,000

Answer (A) is correct.

REQUIRED: The bases in properties received in liquidation of the partnership interest.

DISCUSSION: Sec. 732(b) provides that the basis of property distributed by a partnership in a liquidating distribution to a partner is the adjusted basis of the partner's interest in the partnership minus any money received in the same distribution. The basis of distributed property is allocated first to inventory items and unrealized receivables up to the amount of the partnership's adjusted basis in these items, then to other property to the extent of each distributed property's adjusted basis to the partnership. The remaining basis increase or decrease is allocated depending on whether the adjusted bases of the distributed properties exceed the partner's remaining basis in the partnership interest or not. Since the partnership's bases in the distributed properties exceed the partner's remaining basis in the partnership, a decrease must be allocated among the properties with unrealized depreciation in proportion to their respective amounts of unrealized depreciation (to the extent of cash property's depreciation) and then in proportion to the properties' respective adjusted bases (considering the adjustments already made). In this case, a $7,000 decrease is allocated based on the properties' respective adjusted bases as follows:

	Building	Land
Carryover basis	$8,000	$24,000
Allocate decrease (8/32 to building and 24/32 to land)	(1,750)	(5,250)
Basis	$6,250	$18,750

Answer (B) is incorrect. The bases must be reduced by the allocation of the remaining basis in the partnership interest. Answer (C) is incorrect. The FMV of the property does not determine the basis. Answer (D) is incorrect. Basis is first allocated to cash and inventory.

Use the additional questions in Gleim **EA Test Prep** to create Practice Exams that emulate Prometric!

STUDY UNIT ELEVEN
CORPORATIONS

(12 pages of outline)

For tax purposes, the predominant forms of business organizations are C corporations, S corporations, partnerships, and sole proprietorships. A business must choose among the kinds of business organizations based on a number of different factors, including an organization's tax treatment. C corporations are subject to the most rigid tax rules of all the kinds of business organizations, as their earnings are taxed twice. First, the earnings are subject to a corporate tax, and then the profits are taxed at the individual level when they are distributed to shareholders as dividends. A corporation is a business formed by associates to conduct a business venture and divide profits among investors. A corporation files a charter, prepares bylaws, is overseen by a board of directors, and issues stock.

11.1 BUSINESSES TAXED AS CORPORATIONS

Businesses Formed before 1997

1. The following businesses formed before 1997 are taxed as corporations:

    a. A business that is legally chartered as a corporation

    b. A joint-stock company

    c. An insurance company

    d. Any other business formed before 1997 that has more than two of the following characteristics:

        1) Centralization of management
        2) Continuity of life
        3) Free transferability of interests
        4) Limited liability

Businesses Formed after 1996

2. Under a "check-the-box" system, certain business entities are automatically treated as corporations for federal tax purposes, while others may elect to be treated as corporations for federal tax purposes.

    a. If an entity has one owner and is not automatically considered a corporation, it may nevertheless elect to be treated as a corporation or, by default, it will be treated as a sole proprietorship.

    b. Similarly, if an entity has two or more owners and is not automatically considered a corporation, it can elect to be taxed as a corporation for federal tax purposes; otherwise, it will be taxed as a partnership.

    c.   An eligible entity may elect its classification on Form 8832 (*Entity Classification Election*).

        1)   Each member of the entity, or any member of the entity authorized to make the election, must sign the election.

        2)   The taxpayers must indicate the date the election will become effective.

        3)   This effective date cannot be more than 75 days before or 12 months after the date the election was filed.

        4)   If an eligible entity makes an election to change its classification, the corporation cannot change its classification by election again during the 60 months succeeding the effective date of the election.

            a)   EXCEPTION: The IRS may allow a corporation to change its classification prior to the 60 months if more than 50% of the ownership interests are owned by persons other than those who made the prior election.

    d.   The following businesses formed after 1996 are automatically taxed as corporations:

        1)   A business formed under a federal or state law that refers to the business as a corporation, body corporate, or body politic

        2)   A business formed under a state law that refers to the business as a joint-stock company or joint-stock association

        3)   An insurance company

        4)   Certain banks

        5)   A business wholly owned by a state or local government

        6)   A business specifically required to be taxed as a corporation by the Internal Revenue Code, e.g., certain publicly traded partnerships

        7)   Certain foreign businesses

3.   In general, any business formed before 1997 and taxed as a corporation under the old rules will continue to be taxed as a corporation.

4.   A single-member limited liability company (LLC) may elect to be taxed as a corporation.

    a.   If LLCs do not make this election, they are considered disregarded entities, and income is reported as part of the tax return of the owner.

Stop and review! You have completed the outline for this subunit. Study questions 1 and 2 on page 228.

11.2 CONTROLLED GROUPS

A controlled group of corporations includes corporations with a specified degree of relationship by stock ownership.

Parent-Subsidiary

1.   A parent-subsidiary type of controlled group consists of a. and b. presented below:

    a.   Two corporations if one of the corporations owns stock that represents

        1)   80% or more of total voting power **or**

        2)   80% or more of total value outstanding of the stock of the other

    NOTE: Distinguish the controlled group 80% test from that of affiliated groups in which both the 80% voting and 80% value tests must be met.

    b.   Any other corporation that meets the requirements above (if the two corporations discussed there and others in the group own stock in it)

EXAMPLE

Each corporation has a single class of stock. P owns 80% of S stock. P and S own 40% each of O stock. P, S, and O own 30% each of T stock. As shown in the diagram below, per the 80% test, P, S, O, and T are a controlled group.

Diagram

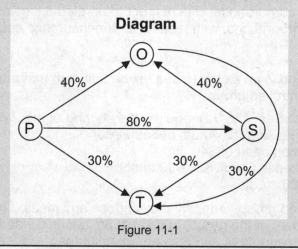

Figure 11-1

Brother-Sister

2. Any two or more corporations are considered a brother-sister controlled group if the stock of each owned by the same five or fewer persons (only individuals, trusts, or estates)

   a. Represents either

      1) 80% or more of voting power of all classes or
      2) 80% or more of value of all classes and

   b. Represents either (counting for each person only the smallest amount owned by that person in any of the corporations)

      1) More than 50% of voting power of all classes or
      2) More than 50% of value of all classes.

EXAMPLE

Alpha, Bravo, and Charley Corporations, each with one class of stock, have the following ownership:

| | 80% Test | | | |
Shareholders	Alpha	Bravo	Charley	50% Test
Mike	45%	5%	30%	5%
Sierra	30%	65%	10%	10%
Oscar	25%	30%	60%	25%
	100%	100%	100%	40%

Alpha, Bravo, and Charley passed the 80% test but not the 50% test. Therefore, they are not a controlled brother-sister group.

3. Rights to acquire stock are treated as the stock would be.

4. Stock both actually and constructively owned is counted. Generally, a person constructively owns stock owned by a

   a. Family member [spouse (not legally separated), child, grandchild, parent, or grandparent] and

   b. Corporation, partnership, estate, or trust

      1) In which (s)he has a 5% or more interest
      2) In proportion to that interest

Excluded Corporations

5.   Without regard to stock ownership, certain types of corporations are excluded from a controlled group, e.g.,

    a.   Tax-exempt corporations, with respect to unrelated income

    b.   Insurance corporations, with respect to non-insurance corporations

Limit on Tax Benefits

6.   Each of the following is an example of a tax benefit item that must be shared by the members of a controlled group:

    a.   Tax brackets. Sec. 1561(a) requires the sharing of the lower tax brackets.

    b.   Sec. 179 expensing maximum of $500,000.

    c.   AMT exemption base of $40,000.

    d.   General Business Credit $25,000 offset.

    e.   AET $250,000 credit.

    NOTE: A controlled group generally may choose any method to allocate the amounts among the members of the group. In default, an item is divided equally among members. If a controlled group adopts or changes an apportionment plan, each member must attach a copy of this consent to his or her tax return.

EXAMPLE

Alpha, Bravo, Charley, and Delta corporations are a controlled group. Each corporation purchased and placed in service $400,000 of qualified Sec. 179 equipment for a total of $1.6 million in qualified equipment for the group. Barring selection of any other allocation, each corporation's Sec. 179 deduction for the year is limited to only $125,000 ($500,000 ÷ 4).

Stop and review! You have completed the outline for this subunit. Study questions 3 through 6 beginning on page 229.

11.3 PERSONAL SERVICE CORPORATION (PSC)

The corporate rates do not apply to PSCs. These corporations are taxed at a flat rate of 35%.

1.   A personal service corporation has two main characteristics:

    a.   Substantially all of its activities must involve the performance of services in the fields of health, law, engineering, architecture, accounting, actuarial science, performing arts, or consulting.

    b.   At least 95% of its stock must be owned by employees who perform the services.

2.   A professional service organization must be both organized and operated as a corporation to be classified as one.

3.   Passive activity limitation rules. If a PSC does not meet material participation requirements, its net passive losses and credits must be carried over to a year in which it has passive income.

Stop and review! You have completed the outline for this subunit. Study questions 7 through 9 beginning on page 230.

11.4 U.S. SOURCE INCOME

Income received by a foreign corporation is considered U.S. source income if the income is effectively connected with the conduct of a trade or business within the United States.

1.   Income is considered "effectively connected" if it satisfies one of the following tests:

    a.   The income was derived from assets used in, or held for use in, the conduct of a U.S. business (the "asset use" test).

    b.   The U.S. trade or business was a material factor in the production of income.

2. An annual withholding tax return (Form 1042) for U.S. source income paid to foreign persons must be filed whether or not any income tax was withheld (Publication 515).

Stop and review! You have completed the outline for this subunit. Study question 10 on page 231.

11.5 TAX RETURN FILING

As a general rule, a corporation's tax return is due by the 15th day of the 3rd month after the end of the corporation's tax year. Every corporation subject to taxation must file a federal income tax return.

1. The corporate tax return is filed on Form 1120.

2. A short-period return must be filed by a new corporation or a dissolved corporation by the 15th day of the 3rd month after a short period ends.

    a. If the 15th falls on a Saturday, Sunday, or holiday, the tax return is due the next succeeding day that is not a Saturday, Sunday, or legal holiday.

3. An extension may be filed by submitting Form 7004 to extend the due date for an additional 6 months.

    a. However, an extension of time to file the return does not extend the time for paying the tax due on the return.

4. If a corporation makes an overpayment of estimated income taxes, it may file an application after the close of the tax year and before the 15th day of the 3rd month after year end for an adjustment.

    a. The adjustment will be allowed only if it is

        1) At least 10% of the amount that the corporation estimates as its income tax liability for the taxable year and

        2) At least $500.

5. The penalty for late filing is 5% of the tax due for each month or part of a month the return is late, but it does not exceed 25%.

    a. However, the minimum penalty for filing a return more than 60 days late is the smaller of the tax due or $135.

6. Corporations having gross receipts for the tax year of less than $250,000 and total assets at the end of the year of less than $250,000 are not required to file a balance sheet per books (Form 1120, Sch. L), a reconciliation of income per books with income per return (Sch. M-1), or an analysis of unappropriated retained earnings per book (Sch. M-2). These forms show the difference between book and tax income.

7. A corporation may make a request for prompt assessment after dissolving.

    a. The period within which the IRS may assess a tax liability is shortened to 18 months from the date the request is filed.

    b. The request does not extend the time within which an assessment may be made, or a proceeding begun, beyond 3 years from the date the return was filed.

        1) EXAMPLE: A request made 20 months after the date the return is filed will **not** extend the limit to 3 years and 2 months (i.e., 20 months + 18 months).

    c. The effect of a request for prompt assessment is to limit the time in which an assessment may be made or a proceeding in court without assessment may be begun.

8. Corporations do not use the address of the registered agent for the state in which the corporation is incorporated. Corporations use the address of the corporations' principal office.

Where to File Your Taxes (for Form 1120)

If the corporation's principal business, office, or agency is located in	And the total assets at the end of the tax year are	Use the following address:
Connecticut, Delaware, District of Columbia, Florida, Georgia, Illinois, Indiana, Kentucky, Maine, Maryland, Massachusetts, Michigan, New Hampshire, New Jersey, New York, North Carolina, Ohio, Pennsylvania, Rhode Island, South Carolina, Tennessee, Vermont, Virginia, West Virginia, Wisconsin	Less than $10 million and Schedule M-3 is not filed	Department of the Treasury Internal Revenue Service Ogden, Utah 84201-0012
	$10 million or more or Schedule M-3 is filed	Department of the Treasury Internal Revenue Service Ogden, UT 84201-0012
Alabama, Alaska, Arizona, Arkansas, California, Colorado, Hawaii, Idaho, Iowa, Kansas, Louisiana, Minnesota, Mississippi, Missouri, Montana, Nebraska, Nevada, New Mexico, North Dakota, Oklahoma, Oregon, South Dakota, Texas, Utah, Washington, Wyoming	Any amount	Department of the Treasury Internal Revenue Service Ogden, UT 84201-0012
A foreign country or U.S. possession (or the corporation is claiming the possessions corporation tax credit under sections 30A and 9936)	Any amount	Internal Revenue Service PO Box 409101 Ogden, UT 84409

This chart does not need to be memorized for the exam.

Stop and review! You have completed the outline for this subunit. Study questions 11 through 19 beginning on page 231.

11.6 ALTERNATIVE MINIMUM TAX (AMT)

The alternative minimum tax is an income tax in addition to the regular income tax.

1. **Formula**

	Taxable income or loss before NOL deduction
+	Tax preference items
+/–	Adjustments to taxable income other than the ACE adjustment and the alternative tax NOL deduction
=	**Pre-adjustment AMTI**
+/–	75% of the difference between pre-adjustment AMTI and adjusted current earnings (ACE)
–	Alternative tax NOL deduction
=	**Alternative minimum taxable income (AMTI)**
–	Statutory exemption
=	**AMTI base**
×	0.20 tax rate
=	**Tentative minimum tax before credits**
–	AMT Foreign Tax Credit (AMT FTC)
=	**Tentative minimum tax (TMT)**
–	Regular (income) tax
=	**Alternative minimum tax (AMT)**

    a.   AMT income (AMTI) is based on taxable income (TI).

        1)   Pre-adjustment AMTI is TI after amounts are added or subtracted for tax preferences, adjustments (other than the ACE adjustment and the alternative tax NOL deduction), and loss limitations.

        2)   AMTI is pre-adjustment AMTI plus or minus 75% of the difference between pre-adjustment AMTI and adjusted current earnings (ACE), minus any alternative tax NOL deduction, and minus any applicable statutory exemption.

    b.   Tentative minimum tax (TMT) is determined by multiplying the 20% corporate rate by AMTI after a reduction for the AMT Foreign Tax Credit (AMT FTC).

    c.   AMT is the excess TMT over regular income tax.

    d.   AMT must be reported and paid at the same time as regular tax liability.

    e.   Estimated payments of AMT are required.

    f.   Corporations having an average of $5 million or less in annual gross receipts for the previous 3-year period are exempt from the AMT.

        1)   Once a corporation is recognized as a small corporation, it will continue to be exempt from the AMT for as long as its average gross receipts for the prior 3-year period do not exceed $7.5 million.

        2)   Corporations not in existence for the entire 3-year period will apply the $5 million test for the period during which they are in existence.

Tax Preference Items

2.   These items generate income tax savings by reducing the taxpayer's taxable income. Therefore, they must be added back to taxable income when computing AMTI.

Small Business Stock

    a.   When computing taxable income, noncorporate taxpayers may exclude up to 50% of gain realized on the sale or exchange of qualified small business stock held more than 5 years. Of the excluded gain, 7% is added as an AMT tax preference item. However, gains from sales made between September 27, 2010, and January 1, 2014, are excluded from tax preferences.

Private Activity Bonds

    b.   Add any tax-exempt interest minus expenses (including interest) attributable to earning it. This does not apply to bonds **issued** in 2009 and 2010.

Percentage Depletion

    c.   Add any excess of deduction claimed over adjusted basis.

Intangible Drilling Costs (IDC)

    d.   Add any excess of IDC amortized over 10 years over 65% of net income from oil, gas, and geothermal properties.

Adjustments

3.   Usually, adjustments eliminate "time value" tax savings from accelerated deductions or deferral of income.

    a.   An adjustment is an increase or a decrease to TI in computing AMTI.

4.   Following are the adjustments affecting corporate taxpayers:

Depreciation

a.   For property placed into service after 1986, taxpayers who, in calculating regular tax liability, depreciate real property under MACRS must use the alternative depreciation system in calculating AMTI.

1)   The difference (+ or −) between the MACRS deduction and the alternative depreciation deduction is treated as a tax preference adjustment.

a)   A positive or negative net adjustment may result.

b)   Real property. The AMT allowable amount is computed using a straight-line method, a 40-year recovery period, and the mid-month convention.

c)   Personal property. Generally, the AMT allowable amount is computed using the 150%-declining-balance method and changing to the straight-line method when it yields a larger amount.

d)   Note that Sec. 1250 property placed in service after December 31, 1998, will **not** require an adjustment.

Installment Sales

b.   The installment method is not allowed for a disposition of stock in trade in the ordinary course of business (e.g., inventory). Add any balance (+ or −) of current-year gain recognized disregarding the installment method, minus gain recognized under the installment method.

Long-Term Contracts

c.   The percentage-of-completion method must be used to determine AMTI. Add any balance (+ or −) if the completed-contract or cash-basis method is normally used.

1)   The same percentage of completion must be used for AMT and regular tax.

2)   Small construction contracts require a simplified method of allocating costs in applying the percentage-of-completion method.

a)   The contract's estimated duration must be less than 2 years.

3)   No AMT adjustment is made for home construction contracts.

Pollution Control Facilities (Certified)

d.   For property placed in service after 1986, the 5-year amortization method for depreciation must be replaced by the alternate depreciation system [Sec. 168(g)]. Add any (+ or −) balance.

Mining Exploration and Development

e.   If these expenditures were expensed for regular tax purposes, the expenditures must be capitalized and amortized over a 10-year period for AMT. Add any balance (+ or −) for the difference.

1)   Tax loss. If a worthless mine is abandoned, expenditures capitalized but unamortized can be deducted from AMTI.

NOL Deduction

f.   Tax preference items are not included for the calculation of AMTI, thereby reducing any NOL from regular taxation.

Adjusted Current Earnings (ACE) Adjustment

5.   A corporation must make an additional adjustment (upward or downward) to TI, called the adjusted current earnings (ACE) adjustment, in computing AMTI.

a.   When computing ACE for AMTI, the AMTI amount is gross of the ACE adjustment and the alternative tax NOL deduction.

    b.   ACE is not the same as earnings and profits, but it is based on undistributed corporate earnings.

    c.   Adjustments to AMTI to compute ACE include the following:

        1)   Organizational expenditures amortized and deducted (Sec. 248) are added.

        2)   Dividends-received deductions attributable to < 20%-owned corporations (70%) are added.

        3)   Life insurance proceeds on a corporate officer are added.

        4)   Installment method on nondealer sales is disregarded unless interest is paid.

        5)   LIFO recapture must be recorded for the excess of FIFO inventory valuation over LIFO inventory valuation.

        6)   Depreciation is computed using the alternative depreciation system method.

           a)   AMT basis is used.

           b)   For corporations, this adjustment is not required for property placed in service after 1993.

    d.   Not requiring adjustment for ACE are the following:

        1)   L-T capital gains

        2)   DRD of 80% or 100% of dividends received

        3)   Discharge of debt income excluded by Sec. 108 (state and local bonds)

    e.   *Amount of ACE adjustment = 75% × (ACE – AMTI)*

        1)   AMTI is gross of the ACE adjustment and NOL deduction.

        2)   Add the ACE adjustment amount if ACE > AMTI.

        3)   Subtract the ACE adjustment amount if ACE < AMTI.

           a)   Limit negative ACE adjustments to prior years'

              i)   Aggregate positive ACE adjustments minus

              ii)   Aggregate negative ACE adjustments.

AMT NOL

6.   The alternative minimum tax net operating loss (AMT NOL) is technically an adjustment to taxable income (TI). After tax preferences have been computed and added to TI and after all other adjustments have been computed and made, one of the two AMT NOL adjustment steps is performed.

    a.   NOL year. Compute the AMT NOL. It is carried back or forward to another tax year.

        1)   The AMT NOL is modified for each of the tax preferences and other adjustments for the current tax year.

    b.   Profit year. An AMT NOL is a final adjustment to TI in computing AMTI in a tax year in which (before reduction by part or all of unused AMT NOLs) there is AMTI.

        1)   Limit: 90% of AMTI. AMT NOL may not offset more than 90% of AMTI (computed without the AMT NOL deduction).

AMT Exemption

7.   An exemption is allowed that reduces gross AMTI to produce AMTI. The basic exemption of $40,000 is phased out at $.25 for each dollar of gross AMTI above $150,000.

AMT Credits

8.   One credit is allowed in computing AMT: the AMT Foreign Tax Credit (FTC). The AMT FTC is the lower of the FTC or 90% of the TMT computed before any alternative tax NOL deduction and the FTC.

Minimum Tax Credit

9. Corporations are allowed a credit for the full amount of AMT paid in a tax year against regular tax liability in 1 or more subsequent tax years to the extent that the regular tax exceeds the TMT for that year. Any Minimum Tax Credit amount is carried forward indefinitely.

10. If a corporation is treated as a small business corporation, it is exempt from AMT for its first taxable year regardless of its gross receipts.

Stop and review! You have completed the outline for this subunit. Study questions 20 through 23 beginning on page 233.

11.7 ACCUMULATED EARNINGS TAX

1. A corporation may be subject to accumulated earnings tax if it does not distribute enough profits beyond what is needed for the conduct of its business.

2. **Formula**

    Taxable Income

    +   Positive Adjustments

        1. Dividends-received deduction claimed
        2. NOL deduction claimed
        3. Excess charitable contributions carried over from a preceding tax year and deducted in determining taxable income
        4. Capital loss carryover deduction

    −   Negative Adjustments

        1. Accrued U.S. and foreign income taxes
        2. Charitable contributions made in excess of the 10% corporate limitation
        3. Net capital losses (if capital losses for the year exceed capital gains)
        4. Net capital gain minus the amount of any income taxes attributed to it

    −   Dividends-paid deduction claimed
    −   Accumulated Earnings Credit
    ─────────────────────────────
    =   Accumulated taxable income
    ×   20%
    ─────────────────────────────
    =   Accumulated earnings tax

3. The Accumulated Earnings Credit reduces accumulated taxable income. It also allows corporations to accumulate E&P up to $250,000 ($150,000 for personal service corporations) or up to the level of its earnings accumulated for the reasonable needs of the business

    a. Reasonable needs of a business include the following:

        1) Specific, definite, and feasible plans for use of the earnings accumulation and
        2) The amount necessary to redeem a corporation's stock included in a deceased shareholder's gross estate. The proceeds are limited to the sum of estate, inheritance, legacy, or succession taxes imposed and the funeral and administrative expenses.

Stop and review! You have completed the outline for this subunit. Study question 24 on page 235.

[Handwritten at top: Estimate Adjustments avg — Average ahead you're last payment — Behind — Immediate catchup]

11.8 ESTIMATED TAX PAYMENTS

A corporation is required to make estimated tax payments unless its estimated tax liability is less than $500. The payments are required on the 15th day of the 4th, 6th, 9th, and 12th months of the tax year. For a calendar-year taxpayer, required quarterly installments are due April 15, June 15, September 15, and December 15.

1. Tax includes the regular income tax and the AMT, net of credits and payments.

2. Each quarterly estimated tax payment required is 25% of the lesser of

    a. 100% of the prior year's tax (provided a tax liability existed and the preceding tax year was 12 months) or *[handwritten: unless PY = 0]*

    b. 100% of the current year's tax.

3. A corporation has the option of annualizing income and paying its estimated taxes accordingly.

    a. Any shortfall is made up in later quarters so that 100% of the tax due is paid on the last installment date (December 15 for calendar-year taxpayers).

4. A corporation with uneven income flows can make its estimated tax payments by annualizing its income.

    a. Corporations are required to use general annualization rules or elect to use one of two sets of optional annualization rules.

5. Paying 100% of the prior year's tax is not an option for a large corporation, i.e., one with taxable income above $1 million during any of the 3 preceding years.

    a. A large corporation must pay 100% of the current year's tax.

    b. However, a large corporation may make its first-quarter estimated tax payment based on the preceding year's tax liability and make up any difference in its second-quarter payment.

6. A corporation must deposit estimated tax payments with a Federal Reserve bank or with an authorized financial institution.

7. A penalty is imposed in the amount by which any required installment exceeds estimated tax paid, multiplied by the federal short-term rate plus 5% (3% for individuals).

    a. The penalty accrues from the installment due date until the underpayment is paid or, if earlier, the due date for filing the tax return.

    b. The penalty is not allowed as an interest deduction.

    c. If any underpayment of estimated tax is indicated by the tax return, Form 2220 should be submitted with the return.

8. No estimated tax penalty is imposed if

    a. Tax liability shown on the return for the tax year is less than $500.

    b. The IRS waives all or part of the penalty for good cause.

    c. An erroneous IRS notice to a large corporation is withdrawn by the IRS.

9. A corporation may obtain a quick refund of estimated tax paid, but adjustment is allowed only if the overpayment is both ≥ $500 and ≥ 10% of the corporation's estimate of its tax liability.

    a. Application is filed (Form 4466) after the close of the tax year but before the return due date (without extensions).

[Handwritten at bottom: Statute of limitations — Generally 3 years from the later of — Due Date of Return — Date Return actually filed — Prompt assessment request — 18 months from date of request]

10. Beginning in 2011, FTD coupons can no longer be used for submitting depository taxes. FTDs must be made electronically unless the payment does not exceed $2,500. It is recommended that Electronic Federal Tax Payment System (EFTPS) be used for making FTD payment.

   a.   If the deposit does not exceed $2,500, payment may be submitted with the quarterly return.

   b.   If the employer does not want to use EFTPS, arrangements may be made for the deposits to be made by the employer's tax professional, financial institution, payroll service, or other trusted third party.

   c.   The mandatory electronic deposit requirement in years prior to 2011 was only for employers with more than $200,000 of total deposits 2 years prior or for employers who were required to deposit electronically the prior year.

   d.   The employer should keep for his or her records a cleared check, bank receipt, or money order as his or her receipt for the deposit.

Stop and review! You have completed the outline for this subunit. Study questions 25 through 30 beginning on page 235.

QUESTIONS

11.1 Businesses Taxed as Corporations

1. Most unincorporated businesses formed after 1996 can choose whether to be taxed as a partnership or a corporation. The new regulations provide for a default rule if no election is made. If an election is not made and the default rules apply, which of the following is true?

A.   Any new domestic eligible entity having at least two or more members is classified as a partnership.

B.   Any new domestic eligible entity with a single member is disregarded as an entity separate from its owner.

C.   If all members of a new foreign entity have limited liability, the entity is classified as an association.

D.   All of the answers are correct.

Answer (D) is correct.
   REQUIRED: The true statement regarding the default rules for the taxation of business if no election is made.
   DISCUSSION: Under a "check-the-box" system, certain business entities are automatically treated as corporations for federal tax purposes, while others may elect to be treated as corporations for federal tax purposes. If an entity has one owner and is not automatically considered a corporation, it may nevertheless elect to be treated as a corporation or, by default, will be treated as a sole proprietorship. Similarly, if an entity has two or more owners and is not automatically considered a corporation, it can elect to be taxed as a corporation for federal tax purposes; otherwise, it will be taxed as a partnership. Further, if all members of a new foreign entity have limited liability, the entity is classified as a corporation. One type of a corporation as defined in the Internal Revenue Code is an association.

2. John and Jim each own 50% of J&J Partnership, which was founded 15 years ago. J&J is a calendar-year taxpayer. On March 20, Year 1, it elected to be treated as a corporation for federal tax purposes by filing a Form 8832. What is the earliest date that J&J can be treated as a corporation?

A.   January 1, Year 1.

B.   March 20, Year 1.

C.   January 4, Year 1.

D.   January 1, Year 2.

Answer (C) is correct.
   REQUIRED: The earliest date a business entity can be treated as a corporation after filing Form 8832.
   DISCUSSION: Instructions for Form 8832 state that, ". . . an election specifying an entity's classification for federal tax purposes can take effect no more than 75 days prior to the date the election is filed . . ."
   Answer (A) is incorrect. January 1, Year 1, is 78 days prior to the date the election was filed. Answer (B) is incorrect. March 20, Year 1, is the date the election was filed, and J&J can be treated as a corporation up to 75 days prior to March 20, Year 1. Answer (D) is incorrect. January 1, Year 2, is 287 days after the date the election was filed.

11.2 Controlled Groups

3. Which of the following statements about a controlled group of corporations is false?

A. John Corporation owns 80% of the voting power and value of James Corporation stock. John Corporation and James Corporation are members of a controlled group.

B. Allen Corporation owns 80% of the voting power and value of Brown Corporation stock. Brown Corporation owns 80% of the voting power and value of Cole Corporation. Allen Corporation, Brown Corporation, and Cole Corporation are members of a controlled group.

C. Members of a controlled group are entitled to one $50,000, one $25,000, and two $9,925,000 taxable income bracket amounts.

D. Members of a controlled group may be either members of an affiliated group, or parent-subsidiary corporations, or brother-sister corporations.

Answer (C) is correct.

REQUIRED: The false statement regarding a controlled group.

DISCUSSION: Sec. 1561(a) entitles a controlled group to one $50,000, one $25,000, and one $9,925,000 taxable income bracket amounts.

4. The Dana Corporation has two subsidiary corporations. In order to determine that the subsidiary corporations are in a controlled corporate group, which of the following must be true?

A. Ten or fewer persons (individuals, estates, or trusts) own at least 80% of the voting stock or value of shares of each of two or more corporations.

B. Ten or fewer persons own more than 50% of the voting power or value of shares of each corporation, considering a particular person's stock only to the extent that it is owned identically with regard to each corporation.

C. A persons' stock ownership is not taken into account for purposes of the 80% requirement unless that shareholder owns stock in all of the corporations considered to be in the group.

D. The subsidiaries must be located in the same state.

Answer (C) is correct.

REQUIRED: Ownership requirements of a controlled corporate group.

DISCUSSION: Stock, both actually and constructively owned, is counted. A person's stock ownership is not taken into account for purposes of the 80% requirement unless that shareholder owns stock in all of the corporations considered to be in the group.

Answer (A) is incorrect. The number of persons considered in the ownership of a controlled group is 5, not 10, and they must own over 50%, not 80%. Answer (B) is incorrect. The number of persons considered in the ownership of a controlled group is 5, not 10. Answer (D) is incorrect. The location of the subsidiaries in the same state does not determine whether the subsidiaries are part of a controlled corporate group.

5. Which of the following statements is false?

A. A controlled group of corporations must file a consolidated return.

B. In addition to regular income tax, a corporation may be liable for accumulated earnings tax if it accumulates profits instead of distributing them to shareholders.

C. In addition to regular income tax, a corporation may be liable for personal holding company tax if a significant portion of its income is dividends, interest, rents, and royalties.

D. Generally, a personal service corporation is one that furnishes personal services performed by employee-owners.

Answer (A) is correct.

REQUIRED: The false statement regarding a controlled group of corporations.

DISCUSSION: Under Sec. 1563(a), a controlled group of corporations may be a parent-subsidiary controlled group, a brother-sister controlled group, or a combined group. Either a parent-subsidiary controlled group or the parent-subsidiary portion of a combined group may file a consolidated tax return because there is a common parent corporation and the includible corporations are all 80%-owned. However, a brother-sister controlled group exists when two or more corporations are owned by five or fewer persons who own at least 80% of the voting stock or 80% of the value of the outstanding stock. There is no common parent corporation, so a consolidated tax return could not be filed. The affiliated group definition requires ownership of 80% of the voting stock and 80% of the value of the controlled corporation. The controlled group definition is an "or" test, and some controlled groups may meet one but not both of the tests and will not be able to file a consolidated return.

6. Which of the following requirements does not have to be met for a group of corporations to be considered a brother-sister controlled group?

A. Five or fewer persons (individuals, estates, or trusts) own at least 80% of the total combined voting power of all classes of voting stock, or at least 80% of the total value of all classes of stock, of each corporation in a group of two or more corporations. A person's stock ownership is considered only if that person owns stock in each of these corporations.

B. Five or fewer persons (individuals, estates, or trusts) own more than 50% of the total combined voting power of all classes of voting stock, or more than 50% of the total value of all classes of stock, of each corporation in a group of two or more corporations. A person's stock ownership is considered only to the extent it is identical with respect to each of these corporations.

C. Five or fewer persons (individuals, estates, or trusts) own 90% or more of the total voting power of all classes of stock, or more than 90% of the total value of all classes of stock.

D. None of the answers are correct.

Answer (C) is correct.
REQUIRED: The requirements that must be met for a group to be considered a brother-sister controlled group.
DISCUSSION: Under Sec. 1563(a), a brother-sister controlled group means two or more corporations of which five or fewer persons who are individuals, estates, or trusts own (1) at least 80% of the voting power or value of each corporation and (2) more than 50% of the voting power or value of the stock of each corporation counting only identical ownership interests (i.e., the smallest amount owned by each person in any of the corporations is all that is counted in the other corporations for the 50% test).

11.3 Personal Service Corporation (PSC)

7. Richard Crepe, M.D., owns 100% of the outstanding stock of Crepe Corporation. All of Crepe Corporation's income and expenditures are derived from the medical services provided by Dr. Crepe. At the end of 2013, Crepe Corporation had $10,000 in reportable taxable income. How much federal income tax was Crepe Corporation required to pay for the 2013 year?

A. $1,500

B. $2,500

C. $3,400

D. $3,500

Answer (D) is correct.
REQUIRED: Taxable liability of a personal service corporation (PSC).
DISCUSSION: The corporate rates do not apply to PSCs. PSCs are taxed at a flat rate of 35%. Crepe Corporation is required to pay $3,500 (35% of $10,000).
Answer (A) is incorrect. The standard corporate tax rates do not apply to personal service corporations. Answer (B) is incorrect. The correct tax rate is 35%, not 25%. Answer (C) is incorrect. The correct tax rate is 35%, not 34%.

8. In 2013, Panda Corp. has passive losses of $250,000 from a rental activity. Its active business income is $150,000 and its portfolio income is $50,000. What is Panda Corp.'s 2013 taxable income if (a) Panda is a closely held corporation, and (b) Panda is a personal service corporation?

A. (a) $50,000   (b) $200,000

B. (a) $50,000 loss   (b) $200,000

C. (a) $50,000   (b) $50,000

D. (a) $200,000   (b) $50,000

Answer (A) is correct.
REQUIRED: The taxable income of a closely held corporation and a personal service corporation.
DISCUSSION: A closely held corporation can offset net active income with its passive activity loss. However, it cannot offset its portfolio income with its passive activity loss. The closely held corporation has $50,000 of portfolio income left. The personal service corporation receives no benefit for its passive loss and has $200,000 taxable income ($150,000 active + $50,000 portfolio income).
Answer (B) is incorrect. A closely held corporation can offset net active income with its passive activity loss but cannot offset its portfolio income with its passive activity loss. Answer (C) is incorrect. The personal service corporation receives no benefit for its passive loss. Answer (D) is incorrect. A closely held corporation can offset net active income with its passive activity loss but cannot offset its portfolio income with its passive activity loss, and the personal service corporation receives no benefit for its passive loss.

9. In 2013, CPAs, Inc., a corporation owned entirely by its employees, all of whom are certified public accountants performing only services in the accounting profession, had taxable income of $110,000. The corporation has never exceeded $5 million in gross receipts. Following is an excerpt from the 2013 corporation income tax rates schedule:

Income at Least	But Not Over	Pay +	% on Excess	Of Amount Over
0	50,000	0	15%	0
50,000	75,000	7,500	25%	50,000
75,000	100,000	13,750	34%	75,000
100,000	335,000	22,250	39%	100,000

What is the tax liability of CPAs, Inc., for 2013?

A. $26,150

B. $17,150

C. Alternative minimum tax preference and adjustment information required.

D. $38,500

Answer (D) is correct.
REQUIRED: The tax liability of a personal service corporation.
DISCUSSION: Under Sec. 448(d)(2), a personal service corporation has two main characteristics: (1) Substantially all of its activities must involve the performance of services in the fields of health, law, engineering, architecture, accounting, actuarial science, performing arts, or consulting, and (2) substantially all of its stock must be owned by employees who perform the services. Section 11(b)(2) provides that the taxable income of a personal service corporation is taxed at a flat rate of 35%. Therefore, CPAs, Inc., will have a $38,500 ($110,000 × 35%) tax liability.

11.4 U.S. Source Income

10. Which of the following statements is false with respect to withholding on nonresident aliens and foreign corporations?

A. Generally, fixed or determinable annual or periodic income from within the United States is subject to withholding unless specifically exempted under the Internal Revenue Code or a tax treaty.

B. Generally, income is from United States sources if it is paid by any domestic or foreign businesses located in the United States.

C. Income effectively connected with the conduct of a trade or business in the United States is usually not subject to withholding if certain conditions are met.

D. Winnings from wagers on blackjack, baccarat, craps, roulette, or big-6 wheel are not subject to income tax withholding or 30% withholding tax.

Answer (B) is correct.
REQUIRED: The false statement with respect to withholding on nonresident aliens and foreign corporations.
DISCUSSION: Under Reg. 1.1441-4(a), no withholding is required for income received by a foreign corporation if the income is effectively connected with the conduct of a trade or business within the U.S. Income is considered effectively connected with the conduct of a trade or business within the U.S. only if the income items satisfy an "asset use" test or if the trade or business activities were a material factor in the production of the income.

11.5 Tax Return Filing

11. ABC Corporation is dissolved on July 9, Year 1. What is the due date, without extensions, for the filing of the final corporate income tax return?

A. March 15, Year 2.

B. December 31, Year 1.

C. October 15, Year 1.

D. October 9, Year 1.

Answer (C) is correct.
REQUIRED: Filing deadline for a dissolved corporation.
DISCUSSION: As a general rule, a corporation's tax return is due by the 15th day of the 3rd month after the end of the corporation's tax year. However, a short-period return must be filed by a new corporation or a dissolved corporation by the 15th day of the 3rd month after a short period ends. The 3rd month following July is October. Thus, the return is due on October 15, Year 1.
Answer (A) is incorrect. The general rule does not apply. The short-period rule must be used in this case. Answer (B) is incorrect. The short-period return must be filed on the 15th day of the 3rd month following the dissolution. Answer (D) is incorrect. The corporation has until the 15th day of the 3rd month. The short-period return is not due exactly 3 months following the dissolution.

12. Generally, a short-period income tax return of a new corporation must be filed by the 15th day of the

A. Fourth month after the short period ends.

B. Third month after the short period ends.

C. Fourth month after the end of its first full tax year.

D. Third month after the end of its first full tax year.

Answer (B) is correct.
REQUIRED: The due date for a short-period income tax return.
DISCUSSION: Section 6072(b) provides that a corporation must file its return on or before the 15th day of the 3rd month following the close of the tax year. A return may cover less than a year if a corporation was formed during the year.

13. Jonas Corporation forgot to request an extension and filed its Form 1120 late for calendar year 2013. It paid the $100 balance due when it filed the return on June 22, 2014. The delinquency penalty will be

A. $20

B. $15

C. $5

D. $100

Answer (D) is correct.
REQUIRED: The delinquency penalty on a return filed late.
DISCUSSION: The penalty for late filing is 5% for each month or part of a month. The penalty would be $100 times 5% times 4 months. However, the minimum penalty for filing a return more than 60 days late is the smaller of the tax due or $135. Therefore, the penalty would be $100.
Answer (A) is incorrect. The return is more than 60 days late, so the penalty is not calculated related to the percentage penalty. Answer (B) is incorrect. The penalty is calculated as the smaller of the tax due or $135, not in reference to the 5% times number of months' penalty. Answer (C) is incorrect. The penalty is calculated as the smaller of the tax due or $135, not in reference to the 5% times number of months' penalty.

14. Generally, if a corporation has dissolved, its final income tax return must be filed by the 15th day of the

A. Third month after the end of the calendar year.

B. Fourth month after the end of its established tax year.

C. Third month after the date it dissolved.

D. Fourth month after the date it dissolved.

Answer (C) is correct.
REQUIRED: The due date for the tax return of a dissolved corporation.
DISCUSSION: A corporation must file a Form 1120 on or before the 15th day of the 3rd month that follows the close of its tax year. In the case of a dissolved corporation, the tax year ends on the date of the dissolution, even if the corporation dissolved on a date other than the last day of the month.
Answer (A) is incorrect. The return due date is established using the dissolution date. Answer (B) is incorrect. The return due date is established using the dissolution date. Answer (D) is incorrect. The return is due 3 months after the dissolution date.

15. Martin Corporation's bookkeeper told the owner that she could not have all the tax information ready for the accountant immediately after the tax year end of June 30. She was having surgery and asked if the tax return could be postponed. The accountant's answer should be

A. No, the return must be filed by September 15.

B. Yes, we can request an extension until October 15.

C. Yes, we can request an extension until the following March 15.

D. No, the return must be filed by October 15.

Answer (C) is correct.
REQUIRED: The allowable extension for a corporation to file its income tax return.
DISCUSSION: Reg. 1.6081-3(a) allows a corporation an automatic extension of 6 months for filing its income tax return if the corporation files the appropriate form (7004) and pays its estimated unpaid tax liability on or before the due date of the return. The IRS may revoke the extension at any time. Martin's tax return is normally due by September 15 but will be due March 15 after the extension.

16. ABC Corporation's tax year ends on October 31, Year 1. When is ABC Corporation's income tax return required to be filed?

A. January 31, Year 2.

B. January 15, Year 2.

C. February 15, Year 2.

D. February 28, Year 2.

Answer (B) is correct.
REQUIRED: A corporation's tax return due date.
DISCUSSION: Publication 542 requires, as a general rule, that a corporation's tax return is due by the 15th day of the 3rd month after the end of the corporation's tax year.
Answer (A) is incorrect. January 31, Year 2, is 3 months after the end of the corporation's tax year. Answer (C) is incorrect. February 15, Year 2, is the 15th day of the 4th month after the end of the corporation's tax year. Answer (D) is incorrect. February 28, Year 2, is 4 months after the end of the corporation's tax year.

17. Which of the following statements concerning the extension of time to file a corporate tax return is false?

A. A corporation will receive an automatic 6-month extension of time for filing by submitting Form 7004.

B. The Internal Revenue Service can terminate the extension to file at any time by mailing a notice of termination to the corporation.

C. Form 7004 must be filed by the due date of the corporation's income tax return.

D. An automatic extension of time for filing a corporate income tax return also extends the time for paying the tax due on the return.

Answer (D) is correct.
REQUIRED: The false statement regarding an extension of time for a corporate tax return.
DISCUSSION: A corporation's entire tax liability is due on the same date as the return. Under Sec. 6072(b), a calendar-year corporation must file its income tax return on or before the 15th day of March following the close of the calendar year. Fiscal-year corporate taxpayers must file by the 15th day of the 3rd month following the close of the fiscal year. Under Sec. 6081(a), in a timely filing of Form 7004, the corporation will receive an automatic 6-month extension for filing the tax return. An extension of time to file the tax return does not provide an extension of time to pay the tax liability without incurring interest and/or penalty.
Answer (A) is incorrect. An extension may be filed to extend the due date for an additional 6 months. Answer (B) is incorrect. The IRS is able to terminate extensions. Answer (C) is incorrect. Form 7004 must be filed by the regular due date of the corporation's income tax return.

18. Abbot Corporation's tax year ends on June 30, Year 1. If Abbot Corporation (a domestic corporation) timely files a Form 7004 for an extension of time to file, what is the extended due date of Abbot Corporation's income tax return for tax year ended June 30, Year 1?

A. March 15, Year 2.

B. March 30, Year 2.

C. April 15, Year 2.

D. May 15, Year 2.

Answer (A) is correct.
REQUIRED: A corporation's extension period.
DISCUSSION: Publication 542 states that an extension may be filed by submitting Form 7004 to extend the due date for an additional 6 months. However, an extension of time to file the return does not extend the time for paying the tax due on the return. The original due date is September 15, Year 1. The extension moves it to 6 months later.
Answer (B) is incorrect. March 30, Year 2, is 6 1/2 months after the required filing deadline. Answer (C) is incorrect. April 15, Year 2, is 7 months after the required filing deadline. Answer (D) is incorrect. May 15, Year 2, is 8 months after the required filing deadline.

19. Bailey Corporation dissolved on December 31, Year 1, and disposed of all its assets by that date. After filing Bailey's final return on March 15, Year 2, the trustee in liquidation filed a written request for a prompt assessment on April 15, Year 2. What is the last day on which the assessment can be made (disregarding Saturdays, Sundays, and holidays)?

A. September 15, Year 3.

B. October 15, Year 3.

C. March 15, Year 5.

D. April 15, Year 5.

Answer (B) is correct.
REQUIRED: The last day an assessment may be made when a request for a prompt assessment is filed.
DISCUSSION: A request for prompt assessment acts to limit the time in which an assessment of tax may be begun to a period of 18 months from the date the request is filed with the proper district director. However, the request does not extend the time within which an assessment may be made, or within which a proceeding in court without assessment may be started, beyond 3 years from the date the return was filed. It is important to note that the 18-month period of limitations does not apply to any return filed after the request was filed. Therefore, the assessment must be made by 10/15/Yr 3.
Answer (A) is incorrect. The assessment is due 18 months after the request for prompt assessment is filed. Answer (C) is incorrect. Prompt assessment limits the time period to 18 months from the time the written assessment is filed. Answer (D) is incorrect. Prompt assessment limits the time period to 18 months from the time the written assessment is filed.

11.6 Alternative Minimum Tax (AMT)

20. Barrett Corporation's 2013 alternative minimum taxable income was $200,000. The exempt portion of Barrett's 2013 alternative minimum taxable income was

A. $0

B. $12,500

C. $27,500

D. $40,000

Answer (C) is correct.
REQUIRED: The corporation's exemption amount for the alternative minimum tax.
DISCUSSION: Under Sec. 55(d), the basic exemption amount for corporations is $40,000. However, this is reduced by 25% of the excess of alternative minimum taxable income over $150,000. Therefore, Barrett's exemption amount is $27,500 [$40,000 – 25% × ($200,000 – $150,000)].
Answer (A) is incorrect. The exemption is not completely phased out until the alternative minimum taxable income reaches $310,000. Answer (B) is incorrect. The amount by which the exemption is reduced is $12,500. Answer (D) is incorrect. The $40,000 exemption must be phased out.

21. In figuring the federal income tax of a corporation, which of the following items is not included in adjustments and preferences for the alternative minimum tax?

A. Installment sales.

B. Long-term contracts.

C. Depreciation of post-1986 property.

D. Amortization of organizational expenses.

Answer (D) is correct.
   REQUIRED: The item not subject to special alternative minimum tax rules.
   DISCUSSION: In determining the alternative minimum tax, taxable income is adjusted for certain items that receive preferential tax treatment. These items are called preferences and adjustments. Any deduction for the amortization of organizational expenses is included in the Adjusted Current Earnings (ACE) adjustment.

22. What is the amount of Anderson, Inc.'s alternative minimum tax based on the following facts?

Taxable income before net operating loss deductions	$85,000
Total adjustments to taxable income	(2,000)
Total tax preference items	45,000
Regular income tax	17,150

A. $0

B. $450

C. $850

D. $1,250

Answer (B) is correct.
   REQUIRED: The calculation of the alternative minimum tax for corporations.
   DISCUSSION: The alternative minimum tax is imposed by Sec. 55 on both individuals and corporations. The term "alternative" is a misnomer because the tax as defined by Sec. 55 is imposed only to the extent that it exceeds the regular tax. It is really an add-on tax. The tax is (1) a tentative tax of 20% of the excess of alternative minimum taxable income over an exemption amount, (2) reduced by the regular tax. Under Sec. 55(d), the basic exemption amount for corporations is $40,000. The alternative minimum tax is computed as follows:

Taxable income	$ 85,000
Plus: preference items	45,000
Less: adjustments	(2,000)
Alternative minimum taxable income	128,000
Less: exemption amount	(40,000)
Net AMTI	88,000
Multiplied by 20% tentative tax	17,600
Less: regular income tax	(17,150)
Alternative minimum tax	$ 450

   Answer (A) is incorrect. The tentative alternative taxable income exceeds the regular income tax. Answer (C) is incorrect. Alternative minimum taxable income is reduced by adjustments to taxable income. Answer (D) is incorrect. Alternative minimum taxable income is reduced by adjustments to taxable income.

23. What would be the alternative minimum tax for a corporation whose tax return reflects the following?

Alternative minimum taxable income	$107,500
Foreign Tax Credit	1,375
Regular tax	6,890

A. $5,235

B. $6,610

C. $12,125

D. $13,500

Answer (A) is correct.
   REQUIRED: The corporation's alternative minimum tax.
   DISCUSSION: Sec. 55 imposes a minimum tax on corporations. First, a tentative tax of 20% is computed on the excess of the alternative minimum taxable income over an exemption amount. The exemption amount is $40,000 provided the alternative minimum taxable income does not exceed $150,000. The minimum tax is the excess of this tentative minimum tax over the regular tax. The corporation's alternative minimum taxable income of $107,500 is reduced by the exemption amount of $40,000. The tentative minimum tax before Foreign Tax Credits is $13,500 ($67,500 × 20%). The minimum tax is $5,235.

Tentative minimum tax	$13,500
Less: Foreign Tax Credit	(1,375)
Tentative minimum tax	$12,125
Less: regular tax	(6,890)
Alternative minimum tax	$ 5,235

   The alternative minimum tax can be reduced by a Foreign Tax Credit, which is limited to 90% of the tentative minimum tax. This limit does not restrict the ability to claim the Foreign Tax Credit here.
   Answer (B) is incorrect. The Foreign Tax Credit reduces the tentative minimum tax. Answer (C) is incorrect. The tentative minimum tax is reduced by the regular tax. Answer (D) is incorrect. The tentative minimum tax is reduced by the Foreign Tax Credit and regular tax.

11.7 Accumulated Earnings Tax

24. Westover Health Services, Inc., a personal service corporation, has two shareholders. Westover was incorporated 17 years ago and has made irregular and infrequent distributions to its shareholders. The balance sheet of Westover Health Services, Inc., reflects unappropriated retained earnings in the amount of $800,000 and no marketable securities. Westover has no specific, definite, and feasible plans for use of the earnings accumulation in its business. It has been determined that the amount needed to redeem a deceased shareholder's stock is $500,000 for estate taxes and administrative expenses. What is the amount of Accumulated Earnings Tax that Westover Health Services, Inc., could be subject to for tax year ended December 31, 2013?

- A. $60,000
- B. $30,000
- C. $130,000
- D. $0

Answer (A) is correct.
REQUIRED: The Accumulated Earnings Tax associated with a redemption.
DISCUSSION: The corporation is allowed an Accumulated Earnings Credit for the greater of $150,000 or the reasonable needs (if there is a definite plan for its use) of the business but not both. The $500,000 qualifies as reasonable needs. The accumulated earnings tax is $60,000 [($800,000 − $500,000) × 20%].
Answer (B) is incorrect. The corporation is allowed an Accumulated Earnings Credit for the greater of $150,000 or the reasonable needs of the business but not both. Answer (C) is incorrect. The corporation is allowed an Accumulated Earnings Credit for the greater of $150,000 or the reasonable needs of the business but not both. The reasonable need is greater. Answer (D) is incorrect. The corporation has an accumulated earnings tax.

11.8 Estimated Tax Payments

25. Corporations generally must make estimated tax payments if they expect their estimated tax (income tax less credits) to be equal to or more than

- A. $1
- B. $500
- C. $600
- D. $1,000

Answer (B) is correct.
REQUIRED: Minimum corporate income that requires estimated tax payments.
DISCUSSION: A corporation is required to make estimated tax payments unless its estimated tax liability is less than $500. The payments are required on the 15th day of the 4th, 6th, 9th, and 12th months of the tax year.

26. If a corporation is required to make estimated tax payments because it expects its tax to be $500 or more for the year, the first installment payment of estimated tax is due by the 15th day of the

- A. Third month of the corporation's tax year.
- B. Fourth month of the corporation's tax year.
- C. Fifth month of the corporation's tax year.
- D. Sixth month of the corporation's tax year.

Answer (B) is correct.
REQUIRED: The due date of the first installment of estimated taxes.
DISCUSSION: A corporation that anticipates a tax bill of $500 or more must estimate its income tax liability for the current tax year and pay four quarterly estimated tax installments. Installments of fiscal-year corporations are due on the 15th day of the 4th, 6th, 9th, and 12th months of the year.

27. The amount required to be paid in estimated tax installments by a corporation is the lesser of 100% of the tax shown on its return for the preceding 12-month tax year (if some tax was reflected), or what percentage of the tax shown on its return for the current year (determined on the basis of actual income or annualized income)?

- A. 100%
- B. 97%
- C. 95%
- D. 90%

Answer (A) is correct.
REQUIRED: The percentage of tax shown on the current-year return that must be paid in estimated tax installments.
DISCUSSION: At least 100% of a calendar-year corporation's final tax must be paid in installments on a quarterly basis. If this 100% requirement is not met, the corporation will be subject to a penalty on the amount by which the installment payments are less than 100% of the tax due. The penalty will not apply if a corporation (other than a large corporation) timely pays an installment based on either 100% of its tax liability for the prior year or 100% of the tax that would be due on its income computed on an annualized or seasonal basis.

28. For Year 2, Corporation N, a calendar-year taxpayer, had a tax liability of $100,000, consisting of $45,000 in regular taxes and $55,000 in alternative minimum taxes. N's Year 1 tax liability was $200,000. What is the amount N must have paid for each quarter for Year 2 to avoid any penalty or interest for underpayment of estimated tax?

A. $11,250

B. $22,250

C. $25,000

D. $50,000

Answer (C) is correct.
   REQUIRED: The corporation's estimated tax payments given a liability for both the regular tax and the alternative minimum tax.
   DISCUSSION: Sec. 6655(d) provides that a corporation will not be considered to have underpaid its income tax if it pays the lesser of (1) 100% of the tax shown on the return for the tax year or (2) 100% of the tax shown on the return for the preceding year. The definition of tax for this purpose is found in Sec. 6655(g). This definition includes the alternative minimum tax. Corporation N has a total tax liability of $100,000 for Year 2. It must pay 100% of this amount in estimated taxes in order to avoid any penalties or interest. The quarterly payment is $25,000 ($100,000 ÷ 4).
   Answer (A) is incorrect. Corporation N must have paid four equal installments of both regular tax and alternative minimum tax. Answer (B) is incorrect. Corporation N must have paid four equal installments of both regular tax and alternative minimum tax. Answer (D) is incorrect. Corporation N must have only paid amounts equal to 100% of the current-year income.

29. Sincere, Inc., a C corporation, overestimated how successful it would be in the Year 1 tax year. Final calculations show it will have a NOL for Year 1 and owe no taxes. It had overpaid its estimated taxes for the year by $700. Sincere, Inc., wants its tax refund as soon as possible. What should it do?

A. File Form 1120, *U.S. Corporation Income Tax Return*, as quickly as possible before the 15th day of the 3rd month after its year ended and wait for the money.

B. File Form 7004, *Application for Automatic Extension of Time to File Certain Business Income Tax, Information, and Other Returns*, as quickly as possible and state on the form that it had overestimated its tax and wishes a quick refund as quickly as possible.

C. File Form 4466, *Corporation Application for a Quick Refund of Overpayment of Estimated Tax*, before the 16th day of the 3rd month after its year end, and use it as a worksheet to show that it had overpaid its estimates by $700.

D. Write a letter to the appropriate IRS Service Center and ask for a quick refund of overpaid corporate tax estimates.

Answer (C) is correct.
   REQUIRED: The proper method to obtain a quick refund of estimated tax paid.
   DISCUSSION: A corporation may obtain a quick refund of estimated tax paid, but adjustment is allowed only if the overpayment is both $500 and 10% of the corporation's estimate of its tax liability. Application is filed (Form 4466) after the close of the tax year but before the return due date (without extensions).
   Answer (A) is incorrect. Form 1120 is filed for corporate income taxes, not estimated taxes. Answer (B) is incorrect. Form 7004 is filed by a corporation to receive an automatic 6-month extension to file their corporate tax return. Answer (D) is incorrect. To obtain a quick refund of estimated tax, the corporation must file a Form 4466.

30. If otherwise qualified, a "large corporation" (defined as a corporation with at least $1 million of modified taxable income in any of the last 3 years) may use all of the following methods to figure all four required installments of estimated tax except

A. The 25% of the corporation's income tax for the current year method.

B. The 25% of the corporation's income tax for the preceding year method.

C. The annualized income installment method.

D. The adjusted seasonal installment method.

Answer (B) is correct.
   REQUIRED: The estimated tax payment method not allowable for a large corporation.
   DISCUSSION: Sec. 6655(d)(2) provides that a large corporation will not be considered to have underpaid its income tax if it pays 100% of the tax shown on the return for the tax year. A large corporation is defined by Sec. 6655(g)(2) as a corporation having $1 million or more taxable income during any of its 3 preceding tax years. Large corporations may not use the option of paying 100% of the tax shown on the return for the preceding year.

STUDY UNIT TWELVE
CORPORATE FORMATION

(4 pages of outline)

Once a decision has been reached to use the corporate form, the investors generally must transfer money, property, or services to the corporation in exchange for a debt or equity interest in the corporation. These transfers may have tax consequences to both the transferor and the corporation. Sec. 351 was enacted to allow taxpayers to incorporate without incurring adverse tax consequences and to prevent taxpayers from recognizing losses while maintaining ownership of the loss assets indirectly through stock ownership.

Realized vs Recognized

12.1 RECOGNIZED GAIN OR LOSS

Sec. 351 requires that no gain or loss be recognized if property is transferred to a corporation by one or more persons solely in exchange for stock (including treasury stock) in the corporation and, immediately after the exchange, such person(s) control the corporation. This nonrecognition treatment is mandatory, not elective.

Control

1. Control is ownership of 80% or more of the voting power of stock and 80% or more of the shares of each class of nonvoting stock of the corporation.

    a. Stock exchanged for services is not counted toward the 80%-ownership test, unless property is also transferred by the service provider.

       1) The FMV of the stock is gross income to the shareholder.

    b. Nonqualified preferred stock is treated as boot received and is not counted as stock toward the 80%-ownership test. Generally, nonqualified preferred stock has any of the following characteristics:

       1) The holder has the right to require the issuer or a related person to redeem or buy the stock.

       2) The issuer or a related person is required to redeem or buy the stock.

       3) The issuer or a related person has the right to redeem the stock and, on the issue date, it is more likely than not that the right will be exercised.

       4) The dividend rate on the stock varies with reference to interest rates, commodity prices, or similar indices.

Solely for Stock

2. To the extent the shareholder receives the corporation's stock in exchange for property, nonrecognition is required.

    a. Inequality of FMV of the stock and property exchanged (i.e., **disparate value**) is not relevant in itself.

       1) The shareholder may have gross income if the disparity represents an (unstated) additional transaction, e.g., payment of compensation, a constructive dividend.

    b. Sec. 351 may apply to an exchange after formation.

    c. Sec. 351 can apply to contributions of property even if the corporation issues no stock in the exchange, e.g., a capital contribution by a sole shareholder who receives no stock in exchange for the contribution.

Losses not recognized

GAIN

Gain

d. Sec. 351 may apply when the corporation exchanges treasury stock as well as newly issued stock.
e. Whenever a shareholder (or group of shareholders) makes a Sec. 351 property exchange for stock in a corporation, a statement of all facts relevant to the exchange must be attached to the individual tax returns, as well as to the corporate return, in the year of the exchange.

Boot

Gain

3. The shareholder recognizes gain realized to the extent of money and the FMV of other property (except the stock of the corporation) received in the exchange.

a. FMV of property given up is used if FMV of property received cannot be ascertained.
b. Character of the gain depends on the property contributed.
c. No loss is recognized on the receipt of boot.

Gain

Liabilities

4. Sec. 351 applies even if the corporation assumes the shareholder's liability or takes property subject to a liability in the exchange.

a. The amount of the liabilities is treated as recognized gain from the sale or exchange of an asset only to the extent it exceeds the adjusted basis (AB) of all property contributed by the shareholder.

1) This rule differs from like-kind exchanges, in which liabilities are considered boot.

b. If tax avoidance was a purpose or if no business purpose was present for the assumption or transfer, a gain may be recognized to the extent of the liability (the full amount) plus the FMV of any property received (not including stock).

5. The corporation recognizes no gain on exchange of its stock for property (including money). No gain or loss is recognized on treasury stock.

a. The corporation recognizes gain on exchanging other property (neither money nor its stock), even when the exchange is with a shareholder, unless an exception applies.

6. Stock is not considered issued in exchange for property if it is issued for services or unsecured debts of transferee or for the interest accrued to the transferor on debts owed by the transferee.

EXAMPLE

John and Mary form a corporation. John transfers a building worth $90,000 to the corporation for stock. Mary receives 10% of the stock in the corporation for services she provided in organizing and setting up the corporation. Mary must recognize $10,000 as ordinary income when she receives the stock.

---

7. Even though a transaction may not qualify as a tax-free transfer under Sec. 351, shareholders may not be able to deduct a loss if they exchange property with an adjusted basis that is higher than the FMV of the property they received.

a. If the shareholder owns more than 50% of the corporation's stock, directly or indirectly, (s)he cannot recognize any losses on an exchange of the property for the corporation's stock or other property.

8. When a transaction does not qualify as a tax-free transfer under Sec. 351, the corporation's initial basis in the property is the FMV of the stock at the time of the exchange.

a. If the FMV of the stock at the time of the exchange cannot be determined, the basis is the FMV of the property received.

Stop and review! You have completed the outline for this subunit. Study questions 1 through 17 beginning on page 241.

12.2 BASIS OF ASSETS TRANSFERRED IN AN EXCHANGE

In a tax-free transaction under Sec. 351, the bases of assets transferred equal the bases of the assets in the hands of the prior owner, with certain adjustments.

Basis of Shareholder in Stock

1. Basis of a controlled group shareholder in the stock of the corporation is an exchanged basis, adjusted.

   — Boot & Liability   *+ Gain*

   ```
   Adjusted basis in contributed property
   –   Boot received
       Money
       Liability (corporation assumes or takes subject to)
       FMV of property received (other than above and the corporation's stock)
   +   Any amount treated as a dividend
   +   Gain recognized (by shareholder)
   =   Basis in stock of issuing corporation
   ```

   a. All liabilities assumed by the corporation are treated as boot when computing stock basis.

   b. Holding period is generally tacked; i.e., the holding period of the property exchanged for stock is added to the holding period of the stock.

   c. If capital assets and other assets (e.g., Sec. 1231 property) are contributed by a **sole proprietor** when incorporating a business, each share received in the exchange has a split holding period.

Basis of Shareholder in Boot

2. Boot generally has a basis equal to fair market value.

Basis of Shareholder in Stock Received for Services *Ordinary Income*

3. The shareholder's basis in the stock exchanged for services is its fair market value.

Basis of Corporation in Property

4. The corporation's initial carryover basis in property exchanged by a control group shareholder for its stock is an adjusted carryover basis.

   ```
       AB in property to shareholder
   +   Gain recognized by shareholder
   =   Basis in property to corporation
   ```

   a. This basis also applies when the shareholder receives nothing in return.

   b. This basis is also the corporation's initial depreciable basis in the property.

      1) Allowable depreciation is apportioned based on the number of months the corporation owned the asset.

   c. Holding period is tacked.

Stop and review! You have completed the outline for this subunit. Study questions 18 through 24 beginning on page 246.

12.3 CORPORATE ORGANIZATION AND START-UP EXPENSES

1. For start-up or organizational expenses incurred, taxpayers are allowed to deduct up to $5,000 of start-up and $5,000 of organizational expenditures in the taxable year in which the business begins.

    a. However, if the cumulative cost of the organizational expenditures exceeds $50,000, the $5,000 amount is reduced (but not below zero).

    b. The same rule applies to start-up expenditures.

    c. After incurring $55,000 of start-up or organizational expenses, no costs are deductible in the year in which the trade or business begins.

    d. Start-up and organizational expenses that are not deducted must be capitalized and amortized over a period of no less than 180 months on a straight-line basis.

Organizational Expenditures

2. Organizational expenditures include those that are incidental to the creation of a corporation, chargeable to a capital account, and amortizable over a limited life if they are expended incident to the creation of a corporation with such a life.

    a. Examples of organizational expenditures include expenses to obtain the corporate charter, fees paid to the state for incorporation, and expenses of temporary directors.

    b. Expenses relating to issuing the corporation's stock are not amortizable expenses. These include commissions for the sale of stock, related professional fees, printing costs for the stock, and costs for listing the stock on an exchange.

    c. If a corporation wants to amortize organizational expenses, it must choose to do so when it files its first return. Otherwise, the expenses are deductible only in the year the corporation liquidates.

        1) In the past, the election to deduct an amortized portion of organizational expenditures was made in a statement attached to the taxpayer's return for the taxable year in which it began business. The return and statement had to be filed no later than the date prescribed by law for filing the return (including any extensions of time) for the taxable year in which the taxpayer began business.

        2) A taxpayer is deemed to have made the election; therefore, a taxpayer is no longer required to attach a separate statement to the return.

Start-Up Expenses

3. Start-up expenses include amounts paid or incurred to create an active trade or business, to investigate the creation or acquisition of a trade or business, and to engage in any activity for profit or for the production of income.

    a. Only expenses that would be deductible if paid or incurred in an existing trade or business may be amortized.

    b. Examples of start-up expenses include surveys of potential markets, grand opening advertisements, training costs, and travel expenses for lining up suppliers, distributors, or customers.

    c. If the taxpayer is not already in the business, the expenses must be capitalized and amortized if the business is entered into.

        1) No deduction is allowed if the taxpayer does not enter into the business.

    d. If the taxpayer is already in the business, a deduction is allowed for the start-up expenses whether or not the business is entered into.

        1) For example, a restaurant chain incurs qualified expenses to open a new location. These expenses may be deducted or amortized regardless of the new location opening.

Stop and review! You have completed the outline for this subunit. Study questions 25 through 30 beginning on page 248.

QUESTIONS

12.1 Recognized Gain or Loss

1. Bob and Charles, as a group, transfer a building with a basis of $100,000 to the ABC Corporation in exchange for 66.67% of each class of stock with a fair market value of $300,000. The other 33.33% of the stock was already issued to Alice. What is the gain, if any, that Bob, Charles, or the ABC Corporation must recognize?

A. Bob and Charles, $0; ABC Corporation, $0.

B. Bob and Charles, $0; ABC Corporation, $300,000.

C. Bob and Charles, $200,000; ABC Corporation, $0.

D. Bob and Charles, $0; ABC Corporation, $200,000.

Answer (C) is correct.
REQUIRED: The gain recognized by the shareholders and corporation upon contribution of property.
DISCUSSION: Bob and Charles combined do not have control over ABC Corporation; therefore, Sec. 351 treatment does not apply. Bob and Charles must recognize a gain of $200,000 ($300,000 FMV – $100,000 adjusted basis), and ABC does not recognize any gain.
Answer (A) is incorrect. Bob and Charles must recognize a gain because, combined, they do not have control of the corporation. Answer (B) is incorrect. Bob and Charles must recognize a gain, and ABC does not recognize a gain. Answer (D) is incorrect. Bob and Charles must recognize a gain, and ABC does not recognize a gain.

2. Theodore has formed the Salsa Corporation in March with only one class of voting stock, and all stock has voting rights. In order to apply Internal Revenue Code Section 351 treatment of nonrecognition of any gain, Theodore has to have what percentage of control of ownership of Salsa Corporation immediately after he transfers his assets to the corporation for stock?

A. At least 75% of the total voting stock.

B. At least 50% of the total voting stock.

C. At least 80% of the total voting stock.

D. At least 20% of the total voting stock.

Answer (C) is correct.
REQUIRED: The percentage of ownership required for nonrecognition under Sec. 351.
DISCUSSION: Sec. 351 requires that no gain or loss be recognized if property is transferred to a corporation by one or more persons solely in exchange for stock in the corporation and immediately after the exchange such person(s) control the corporation. Control is ownership of 80% or more of the voting power of stock and 80% or more of the shares of each class of nonvoting stock of the corporation.
Answer (A) is incorrect. Theodore needs at least 80% of the total voting stock for Sec. 351 treatment. Answer (B) is incorrect. Theodore needs at least 80% of the total voting stock for Sec. 351 treatment. Answer (D) is incorrect. Theodore needs at least 80% of the total voting stock for Sec. 351 treatment.

3. Fran transfers real property and a mortgage to a corporation in exchange for stock. Fran is in control of the corporation immediately after the transfer. The real property has a fair market value of $500,000, and the mortgage transferred to the corporation is $350,000. Fran has an adjusted basis in the real property of $300,000. What is the amount of income required to be recognized by Fran, if any?

A. $350,000

B. $550,000

C. $50,000

D. $0

Answer (C) is correct.
REQUIRED: The amount of recognized gain on the exchange of property for stock in a corporation.
DISCUSSION: Sec. 351 applies even if the corporation assumes the shareholder's liability or takes property subject to a liability in the exchange. However, the amount of the liabilities is treated as a recognized gain from the sale or exchange of an asset only to the extent it exceeds the adjusted basis of all property contributed by the shareholder. Since Fran transferred property with an adjusted basis of $300,000 and a mortgage of $350,000, Fran is required to recognize a $50,000 gain.
Answer (A) is incorrect. Fran is not required to report the entire mortgage as a gain. Answer (B) is incorrect. Fran is not required to report the FMV of the property and the $50,000 as a recognized gain from the exchange. Answer (D) is incorrect. Fran is required to report a gain for the amount the liability exceeds the adjusted basis of the property transferred.

4. Jenny transferred a factory building with an adjusted basis of $70,000 and a fair market value of $110,000 to the Crystal Corporation in exchange for 100% of Crystal Corporation stock and $20,000 cash. The building was subject to a mortgage of $25,000, which Crystal Corporation assumed. The fair market value of the stock was $75,000. What is the amount of Jenny's realized gain and recognized gain?

	Realized	Recognized
A.	$25,000	$25,000
B.	$50,000	$40,000
C.	$50,000	$20,000
D.	$35,000	$20,000

Answer (C) is correct.

REQUIRED: The amount of realized and recognized gain in transfer of property to a corporation.

DISCUSSION: Jenny realized a gain of $50,000 on the transfer of property to the controlled corporation ($75,000 stock + $25,000 mortgage assumed + $20,000 cash – $70,000 basis in building). Because money is received in addition to the stock, any gain realized by the shareholder is recognized up to the amount received. Also, Sec. 351(c) provides that, if the liabilities transferred or assumed do not exceed the basis of all the property transferred, then the liabilities are not recognized as a gain. Thus, Jenny's recognized gain is $20,000, the money received from the corporation.

Answer (A) is incorrect. The amount of $25,000 is the value of the mortgage assumed. Answer (B) is incorrect. The amount of $40,000 is the difference between the adjusted basis of the building and the fair market value of the building. Answer (D) is incorrect. The amount of $35,000 is the difference between the fair market value of the building and the fair market value of the stock.

5. Bob and Sam transfer a building with a basis of $100,000 to the Redwood Corporation in exchange for 75% of each class of stock with a fair market value of $300,000. The other 25% of the stock was already issued to Betty. What is the gain, if any, that Bob, Sam, or the Redwood Corporation must recognize?

A. Bob and Sam, none; Redwood Corporation, none.

B. Bob and Sam, none; Redwood Corporation, $300,000.

C. Bob and Sam, $200,000; Redwood Corporation, none.

D. Bob and Sam, none; Redwood Corporation, $200,000.

Answer (C) is correct.

REQUIRED: The amount of recognized gain, if any, on the transfer of property to a controlled corporation.

DISCUSSION: Publication 542 states, "If you transfer property (or money and property) to a corporation solely in exchange for stock in that corporation, and immediately thereafter you are in control of the corporation, the exchange is usually not taxable." Furthermore, "To be in control of a corporation, you or your group of transferors must own, immediately after the exchange, at least 80% of the total combined voting power of all classes of stock entitled to vote and at least 80% of the outstanding shares of each class of nonvoting stock of the corporation." Thus, Bob and Sam are not in control of the corporation and this transaction does not qualify for Sec. 351 treatment. Bob and Sam must recognize the entire $200,000 realized gain ($300,000 stock received – $100,000 basis of the building). The corporation recognizes no gain on exchange of its stock for property (including money).

Answer (A) is incorrect. The transaction does not qualify for Sec. 351 treatment; thus, a gain must be recognized. Answer (B) is incorrect. Bob and Sam must recognize a gain from the transaction, and the corporation does not recognize any gains on the exchange of its stock for property. Answer (D) is incorrect. Bob and Sam must recognize a gain from the transaction, and the corporation does not recognize any gains on the exchange of its stock for property.

6. Mr. Smith and Mr. Jones each transfer property with a basis of $10,000 to a corporation in exchange for stock with a fair market value of $30,000. The total stock received by them represents 75% of each class of stock of the corporation. The other 25% of each class of stock was issued earlier to Mr. Brown, an unrelated person. The taxable consequences are

A. None because it is transfer of property for stock.

B. Mr. Smith and Mr. Jones each recognize a gain of $20,000.

C. Mr. Smith and Mr. Jones each recognize a gain of $30,000.

D. 80% of the transaction is recognized as a taxable gain.

Answer (B) is correct.

REQUIRED: The tax consequences reported on the transfer of property to a corporation.

DISCUSSION: Sec. 351 requires that no gain or loss be recognized if property is transferred to a corporation by one or more persons solely in exchange for stock in the corporation and, immediately after the exchange, such person(s) control the corporation. Mr. Smith and Mr. Jones combined do not have control over the corporation; therefore, Sec. 351 treatment does not apply. Mr. Smith and Mr. Jones must recognize a gain of $20,000.

Answer (A) is incorrect. Mr. Smith and Mr. Jones must recognize a gain of $20,000. Answer (C) is incorrect. The amount of $30,000 represents the fair market value of the stock. Answer (D) is incorrect. The full $20,000 gain must be recognized.

7. John was one of five incorporators of Builders, Inc. Each received stock valued at $100,000. The other four shareholders each contributed $100,000 for their stock. John contributed $50,000 and his services to build the corporate headquarters. He valued his services at $50,000. How much income must John recognize on this transaction?

A. $100,000 of ordinary income.

B. $50,000 of ordinary income and $50,000 of capital gain income.

C. No income recognition.

D. $50,000 of ordinary income.

Answer (D) is correct.
REQUIRED: The amount and character of income recognized from the transfer of cash and services to a corporation.
DISCUSSION: Sec. 351 requires that no gain or loss be recognized if property is transferred to a corporation by one or more persons solely in exchange for stock in the corporation and, immediately after the exchange, such person(s) control the corporation. Stock is not considered issued in exchange for property if it is issued for services or unsecured debts of transferee. The services John contributed to the corporation do not qualify for the Sec. 351 treatment; therefore, $50,000 must be recognized as ordinary income.
Answer (A) is incorrect. John can exclude the $50,000 contributed to the corporation under Sec. 351. Answer (B) is incorrect. John only recognizes the amount of the services contributed to the corporation as ordinary income. Answer (C) is incorrect. John must include the $50,000 of services contributed as ordinary income.

8. Joseph Jackson had previously incorporated his sole proprietorship by transferring property to his newly formed corporation in exchange for 100% of the stock. These assets, if sold, would produce a gain of $100,000. A week after incorporation, Joseph sells other assets for cash to the corporation that produce a loss of $20,000. Joseph is attempting to avoid Sec. 351 on the transfer of the loss assets in order to recognize the loss for tax purposes. Which statement best explains the tax consequences to him?

A. Joseph has a recognized loss of $20,000 to report.

B. Joseph has a recognized gain of $100,000 and a recognized loss of $20,000 to report.

C. Joseph has neither a recognized gain nor recognized loss to report.

D. Joseph has only a recognized gain of $100,000 to report.

Answer (C) is correct.
REQUIRED: The tax consequences of transferring property to a corporation.
DISCUSSION: Sec. 351(a) provides that no gain or loss is recognized if one or more persons transfer property to a corporation solely in exchange for stock in such corporation and if, immediately after the exchange, such person(s) is (are) in control of the corporation. Control is defined in Sec. 368(c) as the ownership of stock possessing at least 80% of the total combined voting power of all classes of voting stock and at least 80% of the total number of shares of all other classes of stock. Since Joseph transferred property to the corporation in exchange for a total of 100% of the stock, the initial transaction qualifies for tax-free treatment. Under Sec. 267(a)(1), losses are not allowed on sales or exchanges of property between related parties. Related parties include an individual and a corporation in which the individual owns more than 50% of the outstanding stock. Therefore, Joseph and his corporation are treated as related parties and no loss is allowed.
Answer (A) is incorrect. Losses are not allowed on sales or exchanges of property between related parties. Answer (B) is incorrect. Immediately after the initial exchange of property, Joseph had 100% control of the corporation. Therefore, under Sec. 351(a), the $100,000 gain is not recognized. Also, losses are not allowed on sales or exchanges of property between related parties. Answer (D) is incorrect. Under Sec. 351(a), Joseph does not have a recognized gain to report.

9. Ferdinand and Isabella transferred money and a business sailing ship for stock in Columbus Corporation. Immediately after the exchange, Ferdinand owned 30% of the voting power and 49% of the total shares of each of the other classes of stock; Isabella owned 55% of the voting power and 36% of the total shares of each of the other classes of stock. Ferdinand and Isabella are not otherwise related. Assuming Ferdinand and Isabella each realized gains on the transaction, which of the following statements would apply?

A. Only Ferdinand will recognize gain on the exchange.

B. Only Isabella will recognize gain on the exchange.

C. Both Ferdinand and Isabella will recognize gains on the exchange.

D. Neither Ferdinand nor Isabella will recognize gain on the exchange.

Answer (D) is correct.
REQUIRED: The true statement regarding the realized gain of shareholders on a transfer of property to the controlled corporation in exchange for stock.
DISCUSSION: Sec. 351 states that no gain or loss is recognized on the transfer of property by one or more persons solely in exchange for stock if, after the exchange, such person(s) control at least 80% of the voting power and 80% of the nonvoting shares. There is no requirement that the contributions be related. Because Ferdinand and Isabella hold a combined controlling amount in Columbus, each will defer the gain from the transfer.

10. Marlene, Nancy, and Olive formed a new corporation. Solely in exchange for stock, Marlene and Nancy contributed appreciated property, while Olive contributed services. The exchanges of Marlene and Nancy will be nontaxable if

A. Olive receives 30% of the stock.

B. Olive receives 80% of the stock.

C. Olive receives 10% of the stock.

D. Marlene and Nancy receive 50% of the stock.

Answer (C) is correct.
REQUIRED: The true statement regarding the transfer of property and services to a corporation in exchange for stock.
DISCUSSION: Sec. 351 states that no gain or loss is recognized when property is transferred to a corporation in exchange for the corporation's stock if the person(s) transferring the property is (are) in control of the corporation immediately after the transfer. "Control" is defined by the Code as at least 80% ownership of the corporation's voting and nonvoting stock. If Olive receives 10% of the stock, then Marlene and Nancy together will receive the remaining 90%. Thus, 90% ownership interest qualifies Marlene and Nancy for tax-free treatment. Olive is not able to receive the tax-free treatment because she gave services and not property. The FMV of the stock Olive receives will be included in her gross income.
Answer (A) is incorrect. If Olive receives 30% of the stock, then Marlene and Nancy together will receive only 70%. Answer (B) is incorrect. If Olive receives 80% of the stock, then Marlene and Nancy together will receive only 20%. Answer (D) is incorrect. Fifty percent does not satisfy the requirements for tax-free treatment.

11. Bob transfers property worth $50,000 to the Acme Corporation and provides personal services worth $5,000 in exchange for stock valued at $55,000. Immediately after the exchange Bob owns 90% of Acme's outstanding stock. What is Bob's gain if any?

A. No capital gain, no ordinary income.

B. No capital gain, $5,000 ordinary income.

C. No capital gain, $50,000 ordinary income.

D. $5,000 capital gain, no ordinary income.

Answer (B) is correct.
REQUIRED: The amount of income and gain recognized on the exchange of property and services for stock in a corporation.
DISCUSSION: Sec. 351 provides that no gain or loss is recognized if one or more persons transfer property to a corporation solely for stock and, immediately after the exchange, the person(s) is (are) in control of the corporation (i.e., own at least 80% of the stock). However, Sec. 351(d) states that stock issued for services is not issued in return for property. Income must be recognized on such a transfer. The fair market value of stock received for services ($5,000) must be included in Bob's ordinary income. All other stock received was in exchange for property, and no gain or loss is recognized.
Answer (A) is incorrect. The fair market value of stock received for services must be included in income. Answer (C) is incorrect. The fair market value of stock received for services must be included in income. Answer (D) is incorrect. No capital gain is recognized since the transactions fall under Sec. 351, and ordinary income must be recognized to the extent that stock was received for services.

12. Pietro transfers property worth $50,000 to Vino, Inc., and also provides personal services worth $5,000 in exchange for stock valued at $55,000. Immediately after the exchange, Pietro owns 90% of Vino's outstanding stock. What is Pietro's income recognition, if any?

A. $55,000 capital gain, $0 ordinary income.

B. $0 capital gain, $5,000 ordinary income.

C. $0 capital gain, $50,000 ordinary income.

D. $5,000 capital gain, $0 ordinary income.

Answer (B) is correct.
REQUIRED: The amount and character of income recognized on the transfer of cash and services to a corporation.
DISCUSSION: Sec. 351 requires that no gain or loss be recognized if property is transferred to a corporation by one or more persons solely in exchange for stock in the corporation and, immediately after the exchange, such person(s) control the corporation. Stock is not considered issued in exchange for property if it is issued for services or unsecured debts of transferee. The services Pietro contributed to the corporation does not qualify for the Sec. 351 election; therefore, $5,000 must be recognized as ordinary income.
Answer (A) is incorrect. Only the value of the services contributed must be included as ordinary income. Answer (C) is incorrect. Pietro only includes the amount of the services contributed to the corporation. Answer (D) is incorrect. The $5,000 should be classified as ordinary income.

13. Ms. D transferred property having an adjusted basis to her of $20,000 and a fair market value of $27,000 to Corporation F. In exchange for the property, she received $6,000 cash and 100% of Corporation F's only class of stock. If the stock received by Ms. D had a fair market value of $21,000 at the time of the transfer, what is the amount of her recognized gain?

A. $0

B. $6,000

C. $7,000

D. $21,000

Answer (B) is correct.

REQUIRED: The shareholder's recognized gain on the transfer of property to a controlled corporation in return for stock and money.

DISCUSSION: Sec. 351(a) provides for nonrecognition of gain or loss if a person transfers property to a corporation solely in exchange for stock in the corporation and if immediately after the exchange such person is in control (owns at least 80% of the stock). Since money is received in addition to the stock, any gain realized by the recipient is recognized but not in excess of the sum of the money received ($6,000).

Answer (A) is incorrect. A gain is recognized on the transfer. Answer (C) is incorrect. The realized gain is not recognized in excess of the sum of the money received. Answer (D) is incorrect. The gain does not equal the fair market value of the stock received.

14. Frank, an attorney, performed legal services valued at $2,000 for Joey Corporation, a newly formed corporation, in exchange for 1% of the issued and outstanding stock. The fair market value of the shares received was $2,000. Frank would recognize

A. A short-term capital gain of $2,000.

B. Compensation of $2,000.

C. No income until the stock is sold.

D. $2,000 as ordinary income ratably over 60 months.

Answer (B) is correct.

REQUIRED: The treatment of services performed for a corporation in exchange for stock.

DISCUSSION: Frank must recognize the services performed as income, even though he was paid in stock from the corporation. The income is recognized at $2,000, and this amount becomes Frank's tax cost basis in the stock.

Answer (A) is incorrect. The transfer does not involve a capital asset. Answer (C) is incorrect. Income must be recognized when received. Answer (D) is incorrect. The income is not recognized ratably over 60 months.

15. Andrew transferred an office building that had an adjusted basis of $180,000 and a fair market value of $350,000 to Barry Corporation in exchange for 80% of Barry's only class of stock. The building was subject to a mortgage of $200,000, which Barry assumed for valid business reasons. The fair market value of the stock on the date of the transfer was $150,000. What is the amount of Andrew's recognized gain?

A. $0

B. $20,000

C. $170,000

D. $350,000

Answer (B) is correct.

REQUIRED: The shareholder's recognized gain on a transfer of property to a controlled corporation.

DISCUSSION: Sec. 351(a) provides for nonrecognition of gain or loss if a person transfers property to a corporation solely in exchange for stock in the corporation and if, immediately after the exchange, such person is in control (owns at least 80% of the stock). However, Sec. 357(c) provides that, if the liabilities transferred or assumed ($200,000) are greater than the basis of all the property transferred ($180,000), the excess is treated as a gain from the sale or exchange of property. Thus, Andrew's recognized gain is $20,000.

Answer (A) is incorrect. A gain on the transfer is recognized. Answer (C) is incorrect. The amount of $170,000 is the difference between the fair market value of the stock received plus the mortgage assumed and the adjusted basis of the property transferred. Answer (D) is incorrect. The amount of $350,000 is the fair market value of the property transferred.

16. Mr. Carroll transferred the title of a condo he owned in Mexico to his 100%-owned accounting corporation in exchange for stock worth $5,000. Carroll used the condo for personal purposes, and he had no bona fide business reason for the transfer. At the time of the transfer, the condo had a fair market value of $170,000, an adjusted basis of $160,000, and a mortgage of $165,000 (which was assumed by the corporation). What is the amount of Mr. Carroll's recognized gain?

A. $165,000

B. $10,000

C. $5,000

D. $0

Answer (B) is correct.

REQUIRED: The shareholder's recognized gain when (s)he transfers property to a controlled corporation for personal purposes and receives stock in return.

DISCUSSION: If there is no bona fide business purpose in making a transfer, the excess liability rule cannot be used to determine the taxable gain. Instead, the gain is taxable to the extent of all liabilities assumed by the corporation plus the FMV of any property received (other than stock). Mr. Carroll must recognize any gain to the extent of $165,000. Therefore, Mr. Carroll's recognized gain is $10,000 ($170,000 amount realized – $160,000 basis).

Answer (A) is incorrect. The amount of $165,000 equals the liabilities assumed by the transferee corporation. Answer (C) is incorrect. Both the gain on the liabilities assumed and the stock treated as a dividend must be recognized. Answer (D) is incorrect. A gain is recognized on the transfer.

17. Robert transferred an office building that has an adjusted basis of $60,000 and a fair market value of $105,000 to the Wargo Corporation in exchange for 100% of Wargo Corporation stock and $10,000 cash. The building was subject to a mortgage of $25,000, which Wargo Corporation assumed. The fair market value of the stock was $75,000. Which of the following are the amounts of Robert's realized gain and recognized gain?

	Realized	Recognized
A.	$55,000	$30,000
B.	$50,000	$30,000
C.	$50,000	$10,000
D.	$35,000	$10,000

Answer (C) is correct.
    REQUIRED: The amounts of a shareholder's realized and recognized gain on the transfer of property to a controlled corporation.
    DISCUSSION: Robert realized a gain of $50,000 on the transfer of the property to the controlled corporation ($75,000 stock + $25,000 mortgage assumed + $10,000 cash – $60,000 basis in the building). Because money is received in addition to the stock, any gain realized by the shareholder is recognized up to the amount of money received. Also, Sec. 357(c) provides that, if the liabilities transferred or assumed do not exceed the basis of all the property transferred, then the liabilities are not recognized as a gain. Thus, Robert's recognized gain is $10,000, the money received from the corporation.
    Answer (A) is incorrect. The $55,000 realized gain is the difference between the fair market value of the office building and its adjusted basis plus the money received. The $30,000 recognized gain is the difference between the fair market value of the office building and the stock received. Answer (B) is incorrect. The $30,000 recognized gain is the difference between the fair market value of the office building and the stock received. Answer (D) is incorrect. The $35,000 realized gain is the mortgage assumed plus the money received.

12.2 Basis of Assets Transferred in an Exchange

18. The basis of stock received in exchange for property transferred to a controlled corporation is the same as the basis of the property transferred with certain adjustments. All of the following would decrease the basis of the stock except

A. The fair market value of other property received.

B. Any amount treated as a dividend.

C. Any money received.

D. Any loss recognized on the exchange.

Answer (B) is correct.
    REQUIRED: The item that does not decrease the basis of the stock received in a tax-free transfer to a controlled corporation.
    DISCUSSION: Sec. 358(a)(1) provides that, in a Sec. 351 exchange, the basis of the stock received by the transferors (shareholders) is the basis of the property transferred decreased by the fair market value of other property received, the amount of any money received, and the amount of loss that was recognized by the taxpayer. The basis is increased by the amount of gain recognized by the taxpayer. Any amount treated as a dividend increases the basis.

19. Mr. Kahr transferred property with an adjusted basis of $17,500 and a fair market value of $21,500 to Corporation G. In exchange, Mr. Kahr received $2,000 cash and 85% of Corporation G's only class of stock. The stock received by Kahr had a fair market value of $19,500. What is Corporation G's basis in the property received in this exchange?

A. $0

B. $17,500

C. $19,500

D. $21,500

Answer (C) is correct.
    REQUIRED: The corporation's basis in property contributed by a shareholder.
    DISCUSSION: Sec. 362(a) provides that the basis to a corporation of property acquired in a Sec. 351 transaction is the same as the basis in the hands of the transferor, increased by the gain recognized by the transferor. Here, the transfer qualifies as a Sec. 351 transaction since greater than 80% of all stock was held by the shareholder after the exchange.
    Mr. Kahr received $2,000 cash in addition to the stock. He recognizes a gain on the $2,000 received. Thus, Corporation G's basis in the property is $19,500 ($17,500 Mr. Kahr's adjusted basis + $2,000 gain recognized by Mr. Kahr).
    Answer (A) is incorrect. The corporation has a basis in the property. Answer (B) is incorrect. The basis is increased by the amount of gain recognized by the transferor. Answer (D) is incorrect. The basis does not equal the fair market value of the property.

20. Ms. White transferred property having an adjusted basis of $145,000 and a fair market value of $160,000 to Corporation T in exchange for 100% of T's only class of stock and $20,000 cash. At the time of the transfer, the stock had a fair market value of $115,000. What is the basis of the stock Ms. White received in this transaction?

A. $160,000

B. $145,000

C. $125,000

D. $115,000

Answer (C) is correct.

REQUIRED: The basis of stock received in a tax-free transfer to a controlled corporation.

DISCUSSION: Sec. 358(a)(1) provides that, in a Sec. 351 exchange, the basis of the stock received by the transferors (shareholders) is the basis of the property transferred decreased by the fair market value of other property received, the amount of any money received, and the amount of loss that was recognized by the taxpayer. The basis is increased by the amount of gain recognized by the taxpayer. When boot (the cash) is received, gain must be recognized to the extent of the lesser of the transferor's realized gain or the fair market value of boot property received. Ms. White has a realized loss of $10,000 ($115,000 stock received + $20,000 cash – $145,000 basis). A loss is never recognized in an exchange qualifying under Sec. 351, whether boot is received or not. Therefore, the basis equals the adjusted basis of the property transferred ($145,000) less the boot property received ($20,000 cash), or $125,000.

Authors' Note: When the fair market value received ($115,000) is different from fair market value of property given up ($160,000), use FMV received as the selling price.

Answer (A) is incorrect. The basis does not equal the fair market value of the property transferred. Answer (B) is incorrect. The basis must be reduced by the amount of cash received. Answer (D) is incorrect. The basis does not equal the fair market value of the stock received.

21. Mr. Garza transferred property with an adjusted basis of $37,000 and a fair market value of $50,000 to Corporation K. In exchange, Mr. Garza received $6,000 cash and 90% of Corporation K's only class of stock. The stock received by Garza had a fair market value of $40,000. What is Corporation K's basis in the property received in this exchange?

A. $50,000

B. $43,000

C. $40,000

D. $37,000

Answer (B) is correct.

REQUIRED: The corporation's basis in property contributed by a shareholder.

DISCUSSION: Sec. 362(a) provides that the basis to a corporation of property acquired in a Sec. 351 transaction is the same as the basis in the hands of the transferor, increased by the gain recognized by the transferor. Here, the transfer qualifies as a Sec. 351 transaction since greater than 80% of all stock was held by the shareholder after the exchange. Mr. Garza received $6,000 cash in addition to the stock. Mr. Garza recognizes a gain on the $6,000 received. Thus, Corporation K's basis in the property is $43,000 ($37,000 Mr. Garza's adjusted basis + $6,000 gain recognized by Mr. Garza).

Answer (A) is incorrect. The basis does not equal the fair market value of the transferred property. Answer (C) is incorrect. The basis does not equal the fair market value for the stock received. Answer (D) is incorrect. The basis must be increased by the gain recognized by the shareholder.

22. For bona fide business purposes, Mr. D transferred the following property to Corporation X. X assumed the $50,000 mortgage.

	Asset Basis	Mortgage	Fair Market Value
Building and land	$120,000	$50,000	$160,000
Various equipment	60,000	0	40,000

In the exchange, Mr. D received 100% of X's only class of stock. What is Corporation X's basis in the property received in the exchange?

A. $130,000

B. $150,000

C. $180,000

D. $200,000

Answer (C) is correct.

REQUIRED: The basis of assets transferred to a corporation subject to a mortgage.

DISCUSSION: Sec. 362(a) provides that the basis to a corporation of property acquired in a Sec. 351 transaction is the same as the basis in the hands of the transferor, increased by the gain recognized by the transferor. Here, the transfer qualifies as a Sec. 351 transaction since greater than 80% of all stock was held by the shareholder after the exchange. Sec. 357(c) would not cause any recognition of gain on the contribution of the mortgage since the liability did not exceed the adjusted basis of all property transferred. The basis of the property received by Corporation X is therefore the adjusted basis of the property in the hands of the shareholder, which was $180,000 ($120,000 + $60,000).

23. During the year, Yasmine transferred land with an adjusted basis of $40,000 and a fair market value of $95,000 to Nadir Corporation in exchange for 100% of Nadir Corporation's only class of stock. The land was subject to a liability of $45,000, which Nadir Corporation assumed. The fair market value of Nadir Corporation's stock at the time of the transfer was $50,000. What amount of gain must Yasmine recognize and what is her basis in the Nadir Corporation stock?

A. $0 recognized gain, $40,000 basis.

B. $55,000 recognized gain, $95,000 basis.

C. $5,000 recognized gain, $0 basis.

D. $5,000 recognized gain, $45,000 basis.

Answer (C) is correct.
REQUIRED: The gain recognized on the exchange and basis in stock received.
DISCUSSION: Liabilities transferred to a corporation in a Sec. 351 transaction are not boot. However, if the liabilities exceed the basis of the assets, boot is received for the excess liabilities. Gain is recognized for the excess of liabilities over basis so that there is not a negative basis in the stock. The stock basis is zero. The basis of the asset to the corporation is $45,000.
Answer (A) is incorrect. A gain must be recognized to the extent of excess of the liabilities over the basis of the assets. Answer (B) is incorrect. The gain is simply the excess of the liabilities over the basis and the basis is zero. Answer (D) is incorrect. The basis is zero because the discharge of indebtedness by the corporation is part of her amount realized, not her basis in the stock.

24. On August 15 of last year, the ABC Partnership purchased telephone equipment for $10,000. The equipment is 5-year property under the MACRS rules. Depreciation in the amount of $2,000 was claimed by ABC on the equipment last year. On April 1 of the current year, ABC Partnership was incorporated with its assets being exchanged for King Corporation stock and notes. Gain of $1,000 was recognized on the transfer of the equipment that was purchased last year. What amount of depreciation is claimed by ABC and King on the equipment in the current year?

	ABC	King
A.	$800	$2,400
B.	$800	$2,600
C.	$1,600	$1,600
D.	$888	$2,640

Answer (B) is correct.
REQUIRED: The amount of depreciation claimed by the transferor of property and the recipient of the property.
DISCUSSION: Under Sec. 1012, the basis of property is generally the cost of the property. ABC's basis in the telephone equipment is therefore initially $10,000. Sec. 362 provides that, when property is transferred to a corporation in a transaction to which Sec. 351 applies, the corporation's basis in the property is the same as the transferor's basis, increased in the amount of any gain recognized by the transferor on the transfer. Therefore, King's basis in the property is $8,200 [$7,200 ($10,000 – $2,000 – $800) transferor's adjusted basis + $1,000 gain recognized by ABC on the transfer].
Because the property was transferred during the second year of its life, the depreciation must be apportioned between ABC and King. The depreciation is apportioned based on the number of complete months the property was owned. The step-up in basis of $1,000 is treated as a second property whose depreciation commences on April 1 of the current year. Under IRS depreciation tables, depreciation rates of 20% and 32% are applied to 5-year property in its first and second years, respectively. ABC's depreciation deduction is $800 ($10,000 basis × 32% × 3/12). King's depreciation deduction is $2,600 [($10,000 basis × 32% × 9/12) + ($1,000 basis × 20%)].
Answer (A) is incorrect. The recognized gain that increases basis must also be depreciated by King. Answer (C) is incorrect. The depreciation is apportioned based on the number of months the property was held and the recognized gain that increases basis must also be depreciated by King. Answer (D) is incorrect. The recognized gain that increases basis is only depreciated by King.

12.3 Corporate Organization and Start-Up Expenses

25. The Lucky Corporation has just been formed. It has organizational costs that the corporation wishes to amortize. Which of the following tests must the Lucky Corporation meet before it can amortize the organizational costs?

A. The costs are for the creation of the corporation.

B. The costs are chargeable to a capital account.

C. The costs could be amortized over the life of the corporation if the corporation had a fixed life.

D. All of the answers are correct.

Answer (D) is correct.
REQUIRED: The required tests that must be met before an organization can amortize its organizational costs.
DISCUSSION: Organizational expenditures include those that are incidental to the creation of a corporation, chargeable to a capital account, and expenditures that could be amortized over the limited life of a corporation if the corporation had a fixed life. In order for an organizational cost to be eligible for amortization, it must be: (1) incurred for the creation of the corporation, (2) chargeable to a capital account, and (3) amortizable over a limited life.

26. In November of 2013, Pine Corporation opened for business and has elected to amortize its start-up expenses. What is the minimum number of months over which the start-up costs can be amortized?

A. 180
B. 80
C. 60
D. 36

Answer (A) is correct.
REQUIRED: The minimum period over which a corporation may amortize its start-up costs.
DISCUSSION: Businesses can choose to amortize start-up costs for setting up your business over a period of 180 months. The minimum amortization period is 180 months.
Answer (B) is incorrect. The minimum number of months over which the start-up costs can be amortized is 180 months. Answer (C) is incorrect. Start-up costs must be amortized over 180 months. Sixty months is for expenses incurred prior to October 23, 2004. Answer (D) is incorrect. Start-up costs must be amortized over 180 months.

27. Holover Corporation started business on July 1 of last year and has elected to amortize its organizational expenses of $60,000. The maximum deduction that can be claimed for organizational expense on Holover's current-year federal income tax return is

A. $0
B. $2,000
C. $4,000
D. $60,000

Answer (C) is correct.
REQUIRED: The maximum deduction for organizational expense on a corporation's second income tax return.
DISCUSSION: Sec. 248 allows a corporation to elect to amortize its organizational expenditures over at least 180 months, beginning with the month in which the corporation starts business. A taxpayer is deemed to have made the election. Therefore, Holover Corporation may deduct $4,000 ($60,000 × 12/180 months) of organizational expense in its second year.
Answer (A) is incorrect. The organization may amortize organizational expenses over at least 180 months. Answer (B) is incorrect. This is the amount of organizational expenses amortized in the first year. Answer (D) is incorrect. The entire $60,000 is not deductible in the second year.

28. During November and December of 2012, Doyle, Inc., incurred $60,000 in potential market feasibility costs, $72,000 in legal fees for setting up the corporation, $21,000 in advertising costs for the opening of the business, and $18,000 for the purchase of equipment. Doyle began business operations on January 1, 2013. If Doyle chooses to amortize its organizational and start-up expenses over the minimum 180-month period, how much can Doyle deduct as an amortization expense in 2013?

A. $4,800
B. $5,400
C. $10,200
D. $11,400

Answer (C) is correct.
REQUIRED: The amount of expenses amortized over 180-month period for organizational and start-up expenditures incurred.
DISCUSSION: Any start-up or organizational expenses incurred may be capitalized and amortized over a period of no less than 180 months that begins with the month in which the corporation begins business. Organizational expenditures include those that are incidental to the creation of a corporation, chargeable to capital account, and amortizable over a limited life if they are expended incident to the creation of a corporation with such a life. Start-up expenses include amounts paid or incurred to create an active trade or business, to investigate the creation or acquisition of a trade or business, and to engage in any activity for profit or for the production of income. The $5,000 first year deduction for both types of cost expenses is nullified by the dollar-for-dollar reduction of cost or expense over $50,000.
Doyle incurred $72,000 of organizational expenditures and $81,000 ($60,000 + $21,000) of start-up expenditures. The amortization of the organizational expenditures would equal $4,800 [($72,000 ÷ 180) × 12] and the amortization of the start-up expenditures would equal $5,400 {[($21,000 + $60,000) ÷ 180] × 12}. Thus, the total amount of amortization expense would equal $10,200 ($4,800 + $5,400).
Answer (A) is incorrect. In addition to the amortized expenses for organizational costs, Doyle may also deduct $5,400 {[($21,000 + $60,000) ÷ 180] × 12} of start-up expenditures. Answer (B) is incorrect. In addition to the amortized expenses for start-up expenditures, Doyle may also deduct $4,800 [($72,000 ÷ 180) × 12] of organizational expenditures. Answer (D) is incorrect. The $18,000 purchase of equipment is not an organizational nor start-up expense.

29. Which of the following costs qualify as business "start-up costs"?

A. Deductible interest.

B. State and local taxes.

C. A survey of potential markets.

D. Research and experimental costs.

Answer (C) is correct.
REQUIRED: The item qualifying as a start-up expense.
DISCUSSION: Start-up expenses include amounts paid or incurred to create an active trade or business, to investigate the creation or acquisition of a trade or business, and to engage in any activity for profit or for the production of income. Examples of start-up expenses include surveys of potential markets, grand opening advertisements, training costs, and travel expenses for lining up suppliers, distributors, or customers (Publication 542).

30. The Lux Corporation incurred $10,000 in start-up costs when it opened for business in 2013. What is the minimum amortization period over which these expenses can be recovered?

A. 12 months.

B. 36 months.

C. 60 months.

D. 180 months.

Answer (D) is correct.
REQUIRED: The correct amortization period for start-up expenses incurred in 2013.
DISCUSSION: For start-up expenses incurred, taxpayers are allowed to deduct up to $5,000 of start-up and $5,000 of organizational expenditures in the taxable year in which the business begins. Start-up and organization expenses that are not deducted must be capitalized and amortized over 180 months on a straight-line basis. Thus, the minimum amortization period is 180 months.
Answer (A) is incorrect. The amortization period is 180 months. Answer (B) is incorrect. The amortization period is 180 months. Answer (C) is incorrect. The amortization period was 60 months for organizational and start-up expenses incurred on or before October 22, 2004.

Use the additional questions in Gleim **EA Test Prep** to create Practice Exams that emulate Prometric!

STUDY UNIT THIRTEEN
CORPORATE INCOME AND LOSSES

(4 pages of outline)

Although many of the Code's provisions apply to all forms of business organizations, some areas of the law are specially tailored for each type. Corporations have many special rules, including a different tax schedule, restrictions on losses, and rules for related party transactions. This study unit examines some of the unique corporate tax laws.

13.1 INCOME TAX LIABILITY

1. Corporations are subject to the following tax rates on their taxable income:

If taxable income is:			
Over	But not over	Tax is	Of the amt. over
$ 0	$ 50,000	15%	$ 0
50,000	75,000	$ 7,500 + 25%	50,000
75,000	100,000	13,750 + 34%	75,000
100,000	335,000	22,250 + 39%	100,000
335,000	10,000,000	113,900 + 34%	335,000
10,000,000	15,000,000	3,400,000 + 35%	10,000,000
15,000,000	18,333,333	5,150,000 + 38%	15,000,000
18,333,333	—	6,416,667 + 35%	18,333,333

2. Unlike the capital gains of individuals, capital gains of corporations are taxed at the same rates as ordinary income.

3. Two of the rate brackets include surtaxes.

   a. A surtax of 5% is charged on taxable income (TI) between $100,000 and $335,000, which eliminates the tax savings on the first $100,000 of taxable income.

   b. A 3% surtax is charged on TI between $15,000,000 and $18,333,333, which recaptures the tax savings from $335,000 to $10,000,000.

4. If the corporation has less than $250,000 of assets and less than $250,000 of gross receipts, it is not required to include a balance sheet (Schedule L), a reconciliation of income per book with income per return (Schedule M-1), and an analysis of unappropriated retained earnings per book (Schedule M-2).

Stop and review! You have completed the outline for this subunit. Study questions 1 and 2 beginning on page 254.

13.2 INCOME FROM BONDS AND DEBT OBLIGATIONS

1. **Bonds issued at a premium.** For bonds issued at a premium, income is recognized to the extent of the amortized bond premium. The premium is amortized over the life of the bond.

2. **Discharge of indebtedness.** A gain is recognized on the discharge of indebtedness.

    a. If a corporation transfers stock to its creditors to pay off the debt, it will recognize income to the extent that the amount or adjusted issue price of the debt satisfied exceeds the value of the distributed stock. Exclusion from income for discharge of indebtedness is allowed when bankrupt or insolvent.

Stop and review! You have completed the outline for this subunit. Study questions 3 through 5 on page 255.

13.3 NET OPERATING LOSS (NOL)

An NOL is any excess of deductions over gross income.

Modified Deductions

1. Modified deductions for some items are used in computing an NOL.

    a. An NOL carried over from other tax years is not allowed in computing a current NOL.

    b. A dividends-received deduction (DRD) may produce or increase an NOL.

        1) A corporation is entitled to disregard the limitations on a DRD when calculating an NOL (limitations are covered in Study Unit 14, Subunit 1). The DRD would increase the NOL.

    c. Charitable contributions are not allowed in computing a current NOL.

Applying NOLs as a Deduction

2. Generally, a corporation's NOL is carried back 2 years and forward 20 years.

    a. For 2008 or 2009, taxpayers may elect to extend the carryback period to 3, 4, or 5 years.

    b. A corporation may elect to forgo carryback and elect to only carry the NOL forward.

        1) Election is for a particular year's NOL and is irrevocable once made.

    c. The NOL must be applied to the earliest tax year to which it can be carried and used to the fullest extent possible in that year.

    d. The NOL reduces taxable income (TI) but only up to zero for that year.

    e. TI for the carryover year is adjusted TI.

    f. Federally declared disasters creating NOLs may be carried back 5 years.

    g. A charitable contribution allowable in a carryback year remains deductible because the charitable contribution 10%-of-TI limit is applied before an NOL carryback.

    h. Applying an NOL as a deduction in a subsequent tax year and computing excess NOL carryover from the subsequent year are complex when the charitable contribution 10%-of-TI limit applies.

Carryback Procedure

3. Carryback of an NOL results in overpayment in a prior tax year.

    a. Claiming a refund requires filing an amended return (Form 1120X), which must be filed during the statute of limitations period.

        1) Once the election is made for any taxable year, it becomes irrevocable for that taxable year.

      b.   Quick refund. Application for quick refund of tax as a result of an NOL carryback is permitted (Form 1139).

          1)   The application window is the date the loss-year return is due until 12 months from the close of the tax year.

Stop and review! You have completed the outline for this subunit. Study questions 6 through 15 beginning on page 256.

13.4 CAPITAL LOSSES

Net capital gains (NCGs) constitute gross income.

1.   Net capital gains (net LTCG – net STCL) are currently taxed as ordinary income.

    a.   The 35% alternative tax on NCGs does not apply at current rates.

    b.   Net STCGs (STCGs – STCLs) are treated as ordinary income (OI) unless offset by LTCLs.

2.   A corporation's capital losses are deductible only to the extent of capital gains, whether they are short- or long-term.

    a.   A net capital loss (NCL) is not deductible against OI.

        1)   It cannot produce or increase an NOL.
        2)   NCL = CLs (ST & LT) – CG (ST & LT).

    b.   When figuring a current-year net capital loss, capital losses carried from other years are not included.

3.   A corporation's NCL for a particular tax year may be carried back to each of the 3 preceding tax years and forward to the 5 succeeding tax years.

    a.   The corporation may not elect to forgo the carryback.

    b.   The NCL must be used to the extent possible in the earliest applicable tax year.

    c.   The oldest unused NCL is applied first.

4.   The NCL is treated as an STCL in a carryover tax year. It offsets only a net capital gain before the carryover, but it may not produce or increase an NOL.

5.   A corporation may not carry a capital loss from, or to, a year during which it is an S corporation.

Stop and review! You have completed the outline for this subunit. Study questions 16 through 24 beginning on page 259.

13.5 RELATED PARTY TRANSACTIONS

These rules limit tax avoidance between related parties.

1.   If gain is recognized on the transfer of an asset and the recipient can depreciate the asset, gain is ordinary income.

2.   Loss realized on sale or exchange of property to a related person is not deductible. The transferee takes a cost basis. Holding periods are not added.

    a.   Gain realized on a subsequent sale to an unrelated party is recognized only to the extent it exceeds the previously disallowed loss.

        1)   Loss realized on a subsequent sale to a third party is recognized, but the previously disallowed loss is not added to it.

3. For purposes of these provisions, related parties generally include

    a. An individual's brothers and sisters (whether by whole or half blood), spouse, ancestors, and lineal descendants

    b. An individual and a corporation that the individual **controls** (directly or indirectly owns more than 50% in value of the outstanding stock)

    c. Two corporations that are members of the same **controlled group** (a chain of corporations connected through stock ownership with a common parent when at least 50% of the total combined voting power, or value, of all classes of stock is owned by one corporation)

    d. A partnership and a corporation **owned by the same person** (ownership of more than 50% of value of corporate stock and more than 50% of capital interest in the partnership)

    e. An S corporation and a C corporation if owned by the same person

    f. A personal service corporation and any employee-owner

4. Generally, a corporation cannot do the following:

    a. Deduct losses on the sale or exchange of properties between itself and related parties

    b. Deduct certain unpaid business expenses and interest on transactions with related parties

    c. Treat an exchange of property between related taxpayers as a like-kind exchange if, within 2 years of the exchange, either party sells the property

Stop and review! You have completed the outline for this subunit. Study questions 25 through 30 beginning on page 262.

QUESTIONS

13.1 Income Tax Liability

1. HY-Text, Inc., a calendar-year cash-basis corporation, had the following transactions during the year:

Net income per books (after tax estimates)	$100,000
Federal income tax paid	22,250
Excess of capital losses over capital gains	5,000
Interest from municipal bonds	11,000
Expenses related to municipal bond interest	500

What is HY-Text's taxable income?

A. $116,750

B. $139,000

C. $127,750

D. $77,750

Answer (A) is correct.

REQUIRED: The true taxable income for a cash-method corporation.

DISCUSSION: The federal income taxes paid, excess capital losses, and expenses related to the municipal bond interest must be added back because they are not deductible for purposes of federal income tax. Additionally, the municipal bond interest is subtracted because it is tax-exempt income. Therefore,

Net income per books	$100,000
Add back:	
Federal income taxes	22,250
Excess of capital losses over capital gains	5,000
Expenses related to municipal interest	500
	$127,750
Subtract:	
Interest from municipal bonds	(11,000)
	$116,750

Answer (B) is incorrect. The federal income taxes paid are added back to arrive at taxable income. Answer (C) is incorrect. The municipal bond interest is tax-exempt income and is subtracted. Answer (D) is incorrect. The federal income taxes paid are added back to net income before books along with the excess capital losses and the expenses related to the municipal bond interest.

2. For the calendar year, Cincy Corporation had operating income of $80,000, exclusive of the following capital gains and losses:

Long-term capital gain	$14,000
Short-term capital gain	6,000
Long-term capital loss	(2,000)
Short-term capital loss	(8,000)

What is Cincy's income tax liability for the year?

- A. $22,250
- B. $18,850
- C. $18,250
- D. $15,450

Answer (B) is correct.
    REQUIRED: The current-year income tax liability of a calendar-year corporation.
    DISCUSSION: Sec. 11 imposes a tax on the taxable income of every corporation. Cincy Corporation's taxable income includes $80,000 of operating income and a net long-term capital gain of $10,000 [($14,000 − $2,000) + ($6,000 − $8,000)], or $90,000. The current-year tax liability of Cincy Corporation is

$50,000 × 15%	$ 7,500
$25,000 × 25%	6,250
$15,000 × 34%	5,100
Total	$18,850

13.2 Income from Bonds and Debt Obligations

3. Sierra Corporation issued $40,000, 5-year bonds for $43,000 on March 1 of the current year. How much of the bond premium must Sierra report on its current-year income tax return?

- A. $3,000
- B. $600
- C. $500
- D. $0

Answer (C) is correct.
    REQUIRED: The income reported from the issuance.
    DISCUSSION: Under Reg. 1.61-12(c)(2), in the case of a bond, the amount of amortizable bond premium for the taxable year is included in income. The amount is amortized over the life of the bond. Thus, Sierra must report $600 each year [($43,000 − $40,000) ÷ 5]. In the current year, Sierra has to recognize only $500 because the bonds were issued for only 10 months [$600 × (10 months ÷ 12 months)].
    Answer (A) is incorrect. The premium is amortized over the life of the bond. Answer (B) is incorrect. The bond was issued for only 10 months. Answer (D) is incorrect. The amortizable value of the premium is included in income.

4. Sanders Corporation issued a $10,000, 10-year debenture for $12,000 on January 1, 2009. In 2013, how much income must Sanders report on its income tax return from issuance of this bond?

- A. $2,400
- B. $2,000
- C. $200
- D. $0

Answer (C) is correct.
    REQUIRED: The amortizing bond premium.
    DISCUSSION: Under Reg. 1.61-12(c)(2), in the case of a bond, the amount of amortizable bond premium for the taxable year is included in income. The amount is amortized over the life of the bond. Thus, Sanders must report $200 [($12,000 − $10,000) ÷ 10].
    Answer (A) is incorrect. The amount of $2,400 incorrectly amortizes the issue price over 5 years. Answer (B) is incorrect. The amount of $2,000 is the total premium. Answer (D) is incorrect. The premium may be amortized over the life of the bond.

5. Scott Corporation transferred stock with a fair market value of $20,000 to its creditor in satisfaction of indebtedness of $30,000. The stock's book value was $15,000. How much ordinary income from this transaction should Scott include in its income tax return?

- A. $0
- B. $5,000
- C. $10,000
- D. $15,000

Answer (C) is correct.
    REQUIRED: The amount of income included from the transfer of stock used to satisfy a debt.
    DISCUSSION: Under Sec. 61(a)(12), taxpayers, including corporations, must recognize gain from the discharge of indebtedness. If a corporation transfers stock to its creditors in satisfaction of indebtedness, it will have income from the discharge of the indebtedness to the extent that the amount or adjusted issue price of the debt satisfied exceeds the value of the distributed stock. The exception that existed under Sec. 108(a), whereby a corporation would not have income from the discharge of indebtedness if it is insolvent or is involved in bankruptcy, does not apply because Scott Corporation is neither insolvent nor involved in bankruptcy. Therefore, the amount of ordinary income included on Scott's return is $10,000.
    Answer (A) is incorrect. A gain is recognized as the difference between the value of the debt satisfied and the value of the stock that is given to the creditor. Answer (B) is incorrect. The gain recognized is not the difference between the fair market value and the book value of the stock. Answer (D) is incorrect. The fair market value, not book value, is used to determine the gain to be included on the income tax return.

13.3 Net Operating Loss (NOL)

6. The Workit Corporation has a loss for the year 2013. In computing the net operating loss, which of the following statements is true regarding either limiting or allowing deductions?

A. The corporation can deduct any NOL carryovers from 2012.

B. A corporation can take the deduction for dividends received, without regard to the limits based on taxable income that normally apply.

C. A corporation cannot figure the deduction for dividends paid on certain preferred stock of public utilities without limits to its taxable income for the year.

D. The corporation can deduct any NOL carryovers from prior years, subject to possible special limitations.

Answer (B) is correct.
REQUIRED: The true statement regarding net operating losses.
DISCUSSION: An NOL is any excess of deductions over gross income. A dividends-received deduction may produce or increase an NOL. A corporation is entitled to disregard the limitations on a dividends received deduction when calculating an NOL.
Answer (A) is incorrect. An NOL from other tax years is not allowed in computing a current NOL. Answer (C) is incorrect. A corporation can figure the deduction for dividends paid on certain preferred stock of public utilities without regard to the limits based on taxable income for the year. Answer (D) is incorrect. An NOL from other tax years is not allowed in computing a current NOL.

7. Ace Corporation had $700,000 of gross income from business operations and $725,000 of allowable business expenses. It also received $50,000 in dividends from a domestic corporation for which it can take an 80% deduction, ordinarily limited to 80% of its taxable income before the dividends received deduction. What is Ace's net operating loss (NOL)?

A. $15,000

B. $0

C. $40,000

D. $65,000

Answer (A) is correct.
REQUIRED: The net operating loss for Ace Corporation.
DISCUSSION: Ace Corporation's NOL is computed as follows:

Gross Income	$750,000
Less: Expenses	(725,000)
Net Income before DRD	25,000
Less: DRD	(40,000)
NOL	$ 15,000

Ordinarily, a DRD is limited to 80% of taxable income unless the DRD creates an NOL. If an NOL is created, then this limit does not apply.
Answer (B) is incorrect. The dividends-received deduction was not taken. Answer (C) is incorrect. This is the amount of the DRD. Answer (D) is incorrect. The dividends-received deduction was not included when computing the NOL.

8. Sea Corporation reported gross income from operations of $100,000 and operating expenses of $150,000. Sea also received dividend income of $90,000 from a domestic corporation in which Sea is a 20% shareholder. What is the amount of Sea Corporation's net operating loss?

A. $0

B. $23,000

C. $32,000

D. $40,000

Answer (C) is correct.
REQUIRED: The net operating loss when there is dividend income.
DISCUSSION: Sec. 172(c) defines a net operating loss as the excess of deductions over gross income, with certain modifications. One modification is that the dividends-received deduction is computed without regard to the 80% of taxable income limitation in Sec. 246(b). Thus, Sea's NOL is $32,000 as computed below.

Gross income from operations	$100,000
Dividend income	90,000
Less: Operating expenses	(150,000)
Net income before DRD	$ 40,000
Less: Dividends-received deduction ($90,000 × 80%)	(72,000)
Net operating loss	$(32,000)

Answer (A) is incorrect. Sea's deductions exceed gross income. Answer (B) is incorrect. The amount of $23,000 incorrectly deducts only 70% of the dividends received. Answer (D) is incorrect. The amount of $40,000 is Sea's gross income.

9. Page Corporation reported gross income from operations of $200,000 and operating expenses of $300,000. Page also received dividend income of $180,000 from Taylor, Inc., a domestic corporation, of which Page is a 10% shareholder. What is the amount of Page Corporation's net operating loss?

A. $0

B. $46,000

C. $64,000

D. $100,000

Answer (B) is correct.

REQUIRED: The net operating loss when there is dividend income.

DISCUSSION: Sec. 172(c) defines a net operating loss as the excess of deductions over gross income, with certain modifications. One modification is that the dividends-received deduction is computed without regard to the 70% of taxable income limitation in Sec. 246(b). Thus, Page's NOL is $46,000 as computed below.

Gross income from operations	$200,000
Dividend income	180,000
Less: Operating expenses	(300,000)
Gross income	$ 80,000
Less: Dividends-received deduction	
($180,000 × 70%)	(126,000)
Net operating loss	$ (46,000)

Answer (A) is incorrect. Page's deductions exceed gross income. Answer (C) is incorrect. The amount of $64,000 incorrectly deducts 80% of the dividends received. Answer (D) is incorrect. Dividends received and the dividends-received deduction are included in the calculation.

10. Word Corporation reported gross income from operations of $450,000 and operating expenses of $480,000. Word Corporation also received dividend income of $100,000 from Knit, Inc., a domestic corporation, of which Word is a 10% shareholder. What is the amount of Word Corporation's net operating loss?

A. $0

B. $10,000

C. $30,000

D. $70,000

Answer (A) is correct.

REQUIRED: The net operating loss when there is dividend income.

DISCUSSION: Sec. 172(c) defines a net operating loss as the excess of deductions over gross income, with certain modifications. One modification is that the dividends-received deduction is limited to 70% of taxable income before the dividends-received deduction unless the full deduction creates or increases an NOL. Since an NOL is not created, the dividends-received deduction is limited to $49,000. Thus, Word has net income rather than an NOL.

Gross income from operations	$450,000
Dividend income	100,000
Less: Operating expenses	(480,000)
Net income before dividends-received deduction	$ 70,000
Less: Dividends-received deduction	
($70,000 × 70%)	(49,000)
Net income	$ 21,000

Answer (B) is incorrect. The amount of $10,000 incorrectly deducts 80% of the dividends received. Answer (C) is incorrect. Dividends received and the dividends-received deduction are included in the calculation. Answer (D) is incorrect. Dividends received must be included in gross income.

11. How much of Corporation A's Year 2 net operating loss of $100,000 may be deducted in Year 1 based on the following information pertaining to A's Year 1 return?

Taxable income before the net operating loss deduction	$81,000
Charitable contribution deduction	9,000
Total charitable contributions for Year 1	12,000

A. $69,000

B. $81,000

C. $90,000

D. $93,000

Answer (B) is correct.

REQUIRED: The corporation's use of a prior year's net operating loss.

DISCUSSION: The amount of Year 2 NOL carryback that may be deducted on the Year 1 return is the Year 1 taxable income. A charitable contribution allowable in a carryback year remains deductible because the charitable contribution 10%-of-TI limit is applied before an NOL carryback. Thus, Corporation A's NOL carryback deduction is limited to its Year 1 taxable income of $81,000.

12. Tilden, Inc., had gross income from business operations of $500,000 and allowable business expenses of $625,000. Tilden also received $150,000 in dividends from Jefferson Corporation. Tilden owns 23% of the voting power and value of Jefferson. What is the amount of Tilden's net operating loss for the year?

A. $125,000

B. $80,000

C. $95,000

D. $0

Answer (C) is correct.

REQUIRED: The net operating loss when there is dividend income.

DISCUSSION: Sec. 172(c) defines a net operating loss as the excess of deductions over gross income, with certain modifications. One modification is that the dividends-received deduction is computed without regard to the 80% of taxable income limitation in Sec. 246(b). Thus, Tilden's NOL is $95,000 as computed below.

Gross income from operations	$500,000
Dividend income	150,000
Less: Operating expenses	(625,000)
Net income before dividends-received deduction	$ 25,000
Less: Dividends-received deduction ($150,000 × 80%)	(120,000)
Net operating loss	$ (95,000)

Answer (A) is incorrect. Dividends received and the dividends-received deduction must be included in the calculation. Answer (B) is incorrect. This amount incorrectly deducts only 70% of the dividends received. Answer (D) is incorrect. Tilden's deductions exceed gross income.

13. Corporation R incurred a net operating loss of $96,000 in 2013 and carried it back to 2011. In 2011, Corporation R had gross income of $470,000 and business expenses of $390,000, including charitable contributions of $1,000. A net operating loss of $70,000 from 2012 had also been carried back to 2011. How much of Corporation R's 2013 net operating loss can be deducted against 2011 income?

A. $0

B. $10,000

C. $11,000

D. $80,000

Answer (B) is correct.

REQUIRED: The amount of the 2013 NOL that may be carried back to 2011.

DISCUSSION: Under Sec. 172(b)(1), a net operating loss may be carried back to each of the 2 preceding taxable years and forward to the 20 succeeding taxable years. Unless an election to forgo the carryback is made, the loss must be carried back to the earliest possible year. The charitable contribution is still deductible in 2011 because the limitation is on taxable income before a net operating loss carryback [Sec. 170(b)(2)(C)]. For 2011, Corporation R had gross income of $470,000 and business expenses of $390,000, producing taxable income of $80,000. Since a $70,000 NOL from 2012 was carried back to 2011, $10,000 of income remains for that year to which the 2013 NOL may be applied.

Answer (A) is incorrect. An NOL may be carried back 2 years and used to offset income. Answer (C) is incorrect. The charitable contribution is deductible because the limitation applies only to taxable income before an NOL carryback. Answer (D) is incorrect. The 2012 NOL carryback must be offset first.

14. Spring Corporation's income from business in the year 2013 is $500,000, and it has business expenses of $750,000. Spring also received dividends from Acme Corporation of $100,000. Spring owns 25% of Acme. What is Spring Corporation's net operating loss for the year 2013?

A. $(150,000)

B. $0

C. $(220,000)

D. $(230,000)

Answer (D) is correct.

REQUIRED: The net operating loss for Spring Corporation for the year 2013.

DISCUSSION: If a corporation has a 20% or greater interest in a corporation, it normally can deduct 80% of the dividends received but cannot if it exceeds 80% of the taxable income. The 80% of taxable income cap is disregarded if the corporation is determining an NOL for the year. Therefore, Spring's NOL for the year is calculated as follows:

Income from business	$ 500,000
Dividends	100,000
Gross income	$ 600,000
Deductions (expenses)	(750,000)
Taxable income (loss before special deductions)	$(150,000)
Minus deduction for dividends received (80% of $100,000)	(80,000)
Net operating loss	$(230,000)

Answer (A) is incorrect. The full $80,000 DRD is permitted in calculating the NOL. Answer (B) is incorrect. Spring is allowed to take a deduction for the expenses and the dividends received. Answer (C) is incorrect. The DRD permitted is 80%, not 70%.

15. For tax year 2013, Myer Corporation had taxable income of $60,000 before using any of the $30,000 net operating loss from 2012. Myer has never elected to forgo the carryback of its losses since incorporation in 2008. Myer's books and records reflect the following income (loss) since its incorporation:

2008	$10,000
2009	(35,000)
2010	20,000
2011	25,000

What amount of taxable income (loss) should Myer report on its 2013 tax return?

A. $30,000

B. $40,000

C. $50,000

D. $60,000

Answer (C) is correct.

REQUIRED: The taxable income (loss) and the net operating loss deduction for 2013 when losses are carried back to previous years.

DISCUSSION: Under Sec. 172, a net operating loss may be carried back 2 years and forward 20 years. Unless an election is made under Sec. 172(b)(3)(c) to forgo the carryback, the loss must be carried to the earliest possible taxable year. The amount of loss that may be carried to any tax year is equal to the taxable income after any earlier net operating losses. Myer's 2013 net operating loss deduction is

(1) 2009 net operating loss	$35,000
Carried back to 2008	(10,000)
Carried forward to 2010	(20,000)
Carried forward to 2011	(5,000)
Remaining net operating loss	$ 0

(2) 2012 net operating loss	$30,000
Carried back to 2011 ($25,000 – $5,000 2009 net operating loss used)	(20,000)
Carryover to 2013	$10,000

Therefore, Myer will report $50,000 income on its 2013 tax return ($60,000 taxable income – $10,000 NOL carryover).

Answer (A) is incorrect. The 2012 NOL must be carried back before it is carried forward. Answer (B) is incorrect. Only $10,000 of the 2012 NOL is carried over. Answer (D) is incorrect. Only $10,000 of the 2012 NOL is carried over.

13.4 Capital Losses

16. Which of the following statements concerning capital losses by corporations other than S corporations is true?

A. Assuming no capital gains to offset the corporation's capital losses, the maximum deduction is $3,000.

B. A capital loss may never be carried forward.

C. A net capital loss may be carried back 3 years and carried forward for up to 15 years.

D. Capital losses can be deducted only up to the amount of the capital gains.

Answer (D) is correct.

REQUIRED: The true statement regarding capital losses by corporations.

DISCUSSION: Sec. 1211 provides that a corporation may deduct capital losses only to the extent of capital gains (without regard to whether they are short- or long-term). The remaining capital losses will be carried back 3 years or carried over to the next year.

Answer (A) is incorrect. Capital losses may be deducted only to the extent of capital gains. Answer (B) is incorrect. A capital loss may be carried forward for up to 5 years. Answer (C) is incorrect. A net capital loss may be carried back 3 years and carried forward for up to 5 years.

17. Iron Corporation incurred net short-term capital gains of $40,000 and net long-term capital losses of $90,000 during 2013. Taxable income from other sources was $500,000. How are the capital gains and losses treated on the 2013 tax return, Form 1120?

A. $3,000 of the excess net long-term capital losses are deducted currently, and the $47,000 remainder is carried forward indefinitely.

B. None of the excess net long-term capital losses are currently deductible but may be carried back to the 3 preceding years and then forward 5 years as short-term capital losses.

C. Excess net long-term capital losses are fully deductible in 2013.

D. Excess net long-term capital losses of $50,000 are carried back 2 years and then carried forward 20 years as short-term capital losses.

Answer (B) is correct.

REQUIRED: The corporation's tax treatment of capital gains and losses.

DISCUSSION: Under Sec. 1211, a corporation's capital losses are deductible only to the extent of capital gains, whether they are short- or long-term. A net capital loss is not deductible against ordinary income in the tax year incurred. It cannot increase an NOL. A corporation's NCL for a particular tax year may be carried back to each of the 3 preceding tax years and forward to the 5 succeeding tax years. No election to forgo the carryback is provided. The NCL must be used to the extent possible in the earliest applicable tax year. The oldest unused NCL is applied first.

Answer (A) is incorrect. Individuals, not corporations, are allowed to deduct $3,000 of the excess NCL and allowed to carry over the remaining NCL indefinitely. Answer (C) is incorrect. Corporations may only deduct capital losses to the extent of capital gains. Answer (D) is incorrect. Corporations may only deduct capital losses to the extent of capital gains. Any remaining NCL may be carried back to each of the 3 preceding tax years and forward to the 5 succeeding tax years.

18. Which of the following statements is false regarding corporate capital losses?

A. Excess net capital losses may not be deducted in the current year.

B. Capital losses may only offset capital gains.

C. Net capital losses may be carried back to the 3 preceding tax years.

D. Net capital loss carryovers may be carried forward to 7 succeeding tax years from the year of the loss.

Answer (D) is correct.
   REQUIRED: The false statement regarding corporate capital losses.
   DISCUSSION: When applying the carryback, carryforward rules for corporate capital losses, the losses may be carried forward for 5 years, not 7 years.

19. With regard to the treatment of capital losses by a corporation other than an S corporation, which of the following statements is false?

A. If a corporation has a net capital loss, it cannot deduct the loss in the current year.

B. When a corporation carries a long-term net capital loss to another year, it is treated as a short-term loss.

C. A corporation may not carry a capital loss from, or to, a year during which it is an S corporation.

D. When figuring a current-year net capital loss, you must include any capital loss carried from another year.

Answer (D) is correct.
   REQUIRED: The false statement regarding the treatment of capital losses by a corporation other than an S corporation.
   DISCUSSION: A corporation's capital losses are deductible only to the extent of capital gains, whether they are short- or long-term. A net capital loss is not deductible against OI in the tax year incurred. It cannot produce or increase an NOL. Net capital loss (NCL) = CLs (ST + LT) – CG (ST + LT). When figuring a current-year net capital loss, capital losses carried from other years are not included.
   Answer (A) is incorrect. Capital losses can be used only to offset capital gains (Sec. 1211). Answer (B) is incorrect. A capital loss carried to another year is treated as a short-term loss. Answer (C) is incorrect. A capital loss cannot be carried from, or to, any year during which the corporation was classified as an S corporation.

20. With regard to carrybacks and carryforwards of a corporation's capital losses, which of the following statements is false?

A. When figuring the current year's net capital loss, you cannot use any capital loss carried from another year.

B. If you carry capital losses from 2 or more years to the same year, you should deduct the loss from the latest year first.

C. You cannot use a capital loss carried from another year to produce or increase a net operating loss in the year to which you carry it.

D. There is no offset against ordinary income for a corporation.

Answer (B) is correct.
   REQUIRED: The false statement regarding carrybacks and carryforwards of corporation's capital losses.
   DISCUSSION: If capital losses are carried from 2 or more years to the same year, the loss should be deducted from the earliest year first. When that loss is fully deducted, the loss from the next earliest year should be deducted.
   Answer (A) is incorrect. Capital losses from another year cannot be used to create a capital loss in the current year. Answer (C) is incorrect. Capital losses from another year cannot be used to create an NOL. Answer (D) is incorrect. Capital losses can offset only capital gains for a corporation. There is no offset against ordinary income.

21. Taxpayer, Inc., a C corporation, had the following transactions during 2013:

Long-term gain from sale of land $10,000
Short-term gain from sale of stock   20,000
Long-term losses from sale of securities   (40,000)

What is the amount of long-term capital loss that may be taken as a deduction by Taxpayer in 2013?

A. $0

B. $10,000

C. $30,000

D. $40,000

Answer (C) is correct.
   REQUIRED: The amount of capital losses allowed as a deduction.
   DISCUSSION: Sec. 1211 provides that a corporation may deduct capital losses only to the extent of capital gains (without regard to whether they are short- or long-term). Therefore, Taxpayer can deduct only $30,000 of its net long-term capital loss in 2013. The remaining $10,000 long-term capital loss will be carried back 3 years or carried forward to the 5 succeeding tax years.
   Answer (A) is incorrect. Capital losses are deductible when there are capital gains in the same year. Answer (B) is incorrect. Capital losses may be deducted up to the extent of capital gains, regardless if they are short- or long-term. Answer (D) is incorrect. Capital losses may be deducted only to the extent of capital gains.

22. In tax year 2013, Sun Corporation had a $10,000 long-term capital loss and a $5,000 short-term capital gain. In tax year 2009, Sun reported $1,000 in long-term capital gains and $4,000 in short-term capital gains. Sun Corporation reported no other capital gains or losses in any other tax year. How much net capital loss will be available for Sun to carry into tax year 2014?

A. $0

B. $1,000

C. $4,000

D. $5,000

Answer (D) is correct.
  REQUIRED: The amount of available carryforward of capital losses.
  DISCUSSION: A corporation's capital losses are deductible only to the extent of capital gains, whether they are short- or long-term. A net capital loss is not deductible against OI in the tax year incurred. It cannot produce or increase an NOL. A corporation's NCL for a particular tax year may be carried back to each of the 3 preceding tax years and forward to the 5 succeeding tax years. The last time capital gains and losses were reported was 2009, which is beyond the 3-year carryback period. Sun Corporation may offset $5,000 of the gain in 2013 against the loss in 2013. The remaining $5,000 loss will carry forward for the 5 succeeding tax years.
  Answer (A) is incorrect. The IRC allows a corporation to carry forward capital losses. Answer (B) is incorrect. The carryforward amount is $5,000 ($10,000 – $5,000). Answer (C) is incorrect. The carryforward amount is $5,000 ($10,000 – $5,000).

23. Waco, Inc., reported net capital gains as follows:

Tax year 2009 at $6,000
Tax year 2011 at $8,000
Tax year 2012 at $1,000

In tax year 2013, Waco had $40,000 in long-term capital losses and $25,000 in short-term capital gains. How much net capital loss will be available for Waco to carry into tax year 2014?

A. $0

B. $6,000

C. $14,000

D. $15,000

Answer (B) is correct.
  REQUIRED: The capital loss carryover of a corporation.
  DISCUSSION: The net capital loss for the corporation may be carried back 3 years and forward 5 years. The current year's net capital loss will be carried back first to 2011, where it will offset $8,000 of net capital gains, then to 2012, where it will offset $1,000 of net capital gains. The remaining net capital loss of $6,000 will be carried over to 2014.
  Answer (A) is incorrect. The net capital loss from 2009 cannot be used. The corporation may only carry back 2 years since the third year did not have a gain to offset. Answer (C) is incorrect. A capital loss amount of $8,000 in 2011 may be used to offset the capital gain in the current year. Answer (D) is incorrect. The capital loss may only be taken back to the 2 preceding tax years since the third year did not have a gain to offset.

24. With regard to the treatment of capital losses by corporations other than S corporations, which of the following statements is true?

A. When a corporation carries a long-term net loss to another tax year, the character is automatically changed to a short-term loss.

B. Assuming no capital gains to offset the corporation's capital losses, the maximum deduction is $3,000.

C. A net capital loss may be carried back 3 years and carried forward for up to 15 years.

D. None of the answers are correct.

Answer (A) is correct.
  REQUIRED: The true statement regarding the treatment of capital losses by corporations.
  DISCUSSION: A capital loss that cannot be offset in the current year may be carried back 3 years and carried forward for up to 5 years. When a capital loss is carried to another tax year, it is treated as a short-term loss regardless of its original characterization.
  Answer (B) is incorrect. A corporation may deduct capital losses only to the extent of capital gains. Answer (C) is incorrect. A net capital loss may be carried forward for up to 5 years. Answer (D) is incorrect. One of the statements is correct.

13.5 Related Party Transactions

25. Sandra sold her Lavender Corporation stock to her mother, Beth, for $8,000. Sandra's cost basis in the stock was $15,000. Beth later sold this stock to Harry, an unrelated party, for $20,000. What is Sandra's recognized gain or loss?

A. $2,000

B. $7,000

C. $7,500

D. $0

Answer (D) is correct.

REQUIRED: The gain or loss recognized on a sale to a related party.

DISCUSSION: Sandra does not recognize any gain or loss on the transaction because it is a related party transaction. However, Beth may recognize the $7,000 loss to offset her gain on the sale to the unrelated party.

26. Chandler Corporation has 500 shares of common stock outstanding. Scott owns 150 shares; Scott's mother, Mabel, owns 50 shares; his brother, Ted, owns 40 shares; and Scott's son, Fred, owns 60 shares. Borus Corporation owns 50 shares of Chandler, and Scott owns 70% of the stock in Borus. How many shares does Scott own in Chandler, applying the rules of ownership attribution, for purposes of determining whether a loss on the sale or trade of property between related parties is deductible?

A. 335 shares.

B. 295 shares.

C. 350 shares.

D. None of the answers are correct.

Answer (A) is correct.

REQUIRED: The proper application of attribution of ownership rules in determining related parties.

DISCUSSION: Sec. 267 contains the constructive ownership rules of ownership of stock with respect to losses on the sale or trade of property between related taxpayers. An individual is considered to own stock owned by his or her brothers and sisters (whether by whole or half blood), spouse, ancestors, and lineal descendants [Sec. 267(c)(4)]. If a shareholder owns 50% or more in value of the stock of a corporation, (s)he is considered to own the stock the corporation owns in proportion to the value of the stock that (s)he owns in the corporation. Therefore, Scott constructively owns 35 shares (50 shares × 70%) of the stock Borus owns in Chandler. Also, Scott constructively owns the shares his relatives (Mabel, Ted, and Fred) own in Chandler. As a result, Scott constructively owns 335 shares (150 + 50 + 40 + 60 + 35) in Chandler.

Answer (B) is incorrect. Under Sec. 267, an individual is considered to own stock owned by his or her brothers and sisters. Answer (C) is incorrect. Since Scott owns more than 50% of Borus, he is considered to own the stock the corporation owns in proportion to the value of the stock that he owns in the corporation, not all 50 shares. Answer (D) is incorrect. Scott constructively owns 335 shares of Chandler.

27. The Cole Corporation distributes $75,000 in cash along with land having a $50,000 adjusted basis and a $60,000 FMV to its shareholder. What gain, if any, must Cole recognize?

A. $10,000

B. $75,000

C. $25,000

D. $0

Answer (A) is correct.

REQUIRED: The amount of gain Cole Corporation should recognize.

DISCUSSION: A corporation recognizes gain realized on the distribution of appreciated property on the amount the fair market value of the property exceeds the adjusted basis. Gain is not recognized on the distribution of cash; therefore, Cole must recognize a gain of $10,000 ($60,000 FMV – $50,000 adjusted basis).

Answer (B) is incorrect. Only gain on the distribution of the appreciated property is recognized. Answer (C) is incorrect. The amount of $25,000 is the difference between the amount of the cash and the adjusted basis of the land. Answer (D) is incorrect. Cole must recognize a gain on the distribution of the appreciated property.

28. Which of the following related parties can recognize a loss on the sale or exchange of an asset between themselves for tax purposes?

A. Corporation and sole shareholder.

B. Grandfather and granddaughter.

C. Brother and sister.

D. Daughter-in-law and mother-in-law.

Answer (D) is correct.

REQUIRED: The related parties that can recognize a loss on the sale or exchange of an asset between themselves.

DISCUSSION: The loss on the sale or exchange of property is not deductible if the transaction occurs between related parties. Sec. 267 lists related parties for purposes of sale and exchange transactions. In-laws are not considered related parties because, for purposes of this rule, members of a family include brothers, sisters, half-brothers, half-sisters, spouses, ancestors, and lineal descendants.

29. Which of the following are not related persons for purposes of disallowing an accrual deduction for interest payable to a cash-basis person until payment of the interest is made?

   A. Two corporations that are members of the same controlled group.

   B. The grantor and fiduciary, and the fiduciary and beneficiary of any trust.

   C. A personal service corporation and any employee-owner, regardless of the amount of stock owned by the employee-owner.

   D. Any two S corporations if the same person owns 25% in value of the outstanding stock of each corporation.

Answer (D) is correct.

   REQUIRED: The situation that does not describe related taxpayers.

   DISCUSSION: A related person relationship exists if the same person owns more than 50% in value of the outstanding stock of each S corporation.

30. When Jill formed a corporation during the year, she transferred property with a basis of $100,000 to the corporation in exchange for 75% of the stock. The fair market value of the stock she received was $50,000. How should Jill report this transaction on her tax return?

   A. No reporting required because the exchange is non-taxable.

   B. Report a $50,000 capital loss.

   C. Report a non-deductible $50,000 loss.

   D. Report a $50,000 ordinary loss.

Answer (C) is correct.

   REQUIRED: The treatment of property transferred for stock.

   DISCUSSION: If an individual transfers property to a corporation upon its formation and owns, directly or through attribution, more than 50% of its stock, any loss generated is not deductible. Therefore, the $50,000 loss would not be permitted as a deduction.

   Answer (A) is incorrect. Reporting is required even though the loss is disallowed. Answer (B) is incorrect. A loss is not allowed because the sale or exchange occurs between related parties. Answer (D) is incorrect. A loss is not allowed because the sale or exchange occurs between related parties.

Use the additional questions in Gleim **EA Test Prep** to create Practice Exams that emulate Prometric!

STUDY UNIT FOURTEEN
CORPORATE DEDUCTIONS

(8 pages of outline)

In computing the taxable income of a corporation, ordinary and necessary expenses of carrying on its trade or business are generally allowed as deductions. In addition, a corporation is entitled to special deductions, including charitable contributions, dividends-received deductions, etc. This study unit also discusses the reconciliation of book income to taxable income on Schedule M-1.

14.1 DIVIDENDS-RECEIVED DEDUCTION

A special corporate deduction for dividends received (DRD) from domestic taxable corporations is allowed. However, all dividends constitute gross income.

1.   Amounts deductible vary with the percentage of the stock of the distributing corporation (by voting and value) owned by the recipient.

% Ownership	% of Dividends Deductible	Limit: % of TI of Recipient
< 20%	70%	70%
≥ 20%, < 80%	80%	80%
≥ 80% & affiliated	100%	100%

   a.   A small business investment company operating under the Small Business Investment Act of 1958 may deduct 100% of dividends received.

   b.   Members of an affiliated group of corporations may deduct 100% of the dividends received from a member of the same affiliated group.

2.   To be eligible for the DRD, a corporation must hold the stock at least 46 days during the 90-day period that begins 45 days before the dividends are paid (i.e., the ex-dividend date).

3.   A corporation cannot take a DRD if it holds a short position in substantially similar or related property.

4.   Regulated investment company dividends can qualify for the DRD.

   a.   However, capital gain dividends do not qualify for the deduction.

   b.   The DRD may be reduced when the investment company receives substantial amounts of income from sources other than dividends from domestic corporations eligible for the DRD.

Limit

5.   The DRD is limited by the recipient corporation's adjusted taxable income. The TI limit amount varies with the recipient's stock ownership of the corporation.

   a.   To compute the limit, use TI before any of the following:

      1)   Dividends-received deduction
      2)   Domestic production activities deduction
      3)   NOL deduction
      4)   Capital loss carryback
      5)   Certain extraordinary dividend adjustments

b.   If dividends are received from both 20%-owned and non-20%-owned corporations, the limit is first computed with respect to 20%-and-more-owned corporate dividends.

c.   The TI limit does not apply if a current NOL exists or an NOL results from the DRD.

EXAMPLE

A corporation has taxable income of $1,000, including $10,000 in dividends received from a less-than-20%-owned domestic taxable corporation, before the DRD. The DRD before applying the TI limit is $7,000 ($10,000 × 70%). Because the DRD produces an NOL, it is not limited to 70% of taxable income before the deduction ($700). The corporation may deduct the entire $7,000, which results in a $6,000 NOL.

---

6.   The DRD on debt-financed portfolio stock is restricted. Debt-financed portfolio stock is stock purchased with a loan. In this case, the DRD is limited to the greater of

a.   The DRD minus the interest deduction on the portfolio debt or

b.   The dividend times 70% (80% for a 20%-owned corporation) of 100% minus average indebtedness percentage.

$$Dividend \times 70\% \ (or \ 80\%) \times (100\% - Average\ indebtedness\ \%)$$

$$Average\ indebtedness\ \% = \frac{Average\ amt.\ of\ portfolio\ indebtedness\ during\ period}{Average\ amt.\ of\ AB\ in\ the\ stock\ during\ period}$$

Foreign Corporations

7.   The DRD is allowable for dividends received from foreign corporations if the distribution corporation

a.   Is at least 10%-owned by the recipient domestic corporation,
b.   Is subject to U.S. federal income tax,
c.   Has income effectively connected with a trade or business in the U.S., and
d.   Is not a foreign personal holding company.

8.   An S corporation may not claim the DRD.

Disqualified Dividends

9.   A deduction is not allowed, or it is further restricted, for dividends received from the following:

a.   Mutual savings banks (they are like interest)
b.   Real estate investment trusts
c.   Domestic international sales corporations (generally)
d.   Public utilities on preferred stock
e.   A corporation exempt from tax during the distribution year

Stop and review! You have completed the outline for this subunit. Study questions 1 through 11 beginning on page 273.

14.2 CHARITABLE CONTRIBUTIONS   1st Deduction

A corporation's charitable contribution is deductible only if it is made to a qualified organization (Publications 542 and 526).

1.   Deductible amounts must be paid during the tax year.

a.   An accrual-method corporation may elect to deduct amounts paid no later than 2 1/2 months after the close of the tax year.   March 15

Ordinary Income Property

2. A corporation may deduct the adjusted basis (AB) of inventory and other ordinary income property contributed.

    a. Half of the FMV-AB difference (i.e., appreciation/would-be gain) is also deductible when inventory (e.g., food) is donated solely for the care of infants, the ill, or the needy.

    $$Deduction = AB + \frac{1}{2} \times (FMV - AB)$$

    1) The deduction may not exceed two times the equipment's basis.

Capital Gain Property

3. In general, the deduction for the contribution of long-term capital gain property is the property's FMV.

    a. The deduction is FMV minus the amount of ordinary income if the asset had been sold.

4. To qualify for a FMV deduction, the tangible personal property must be used in a manner related to the organization's exempt purpose.

    a. It must not be disposed of for value.

    b. The deducting corporation must receive a statement indicating that the property use will comply with these conditions.

Limit

5. Deductions are limited to 10% of taxable income. Allowable is 10% of TI before any

    a. Charitable contribution deduction
    b. Dividends-received deduction
    c. Domestic production activities deduction
    d. Net operating loss (NOL) carryback
    e. Capital loss carryback

    Include
    Not carry forward

6. Excess over the TI limit may be carried over and is deductible during the succeeding 5 tax years.

    a. No carryback is allowed.

    b. Current-year contributions are deducted first.

    c. FIFO treatment applies to carryforwards.

    d. The charitable contribution carryover cannot be deducted to the extent it increases an NOL carryover to a succeeding tax year.

7. Charitable contributions of tangible personal property are not treated as tax preference items for AMT purposes.

Stop and review! You have completed the outline for this subunit. Study questions 12 through 18 beginning on page 276.

14.3 OTHER CORPORATE DEDUCTIONS

<u>Gifts</u>

1.   Distinguish gifts from charitable contributions, which are made to qualified organizations. A deduction for business gifts is allowable only to the extent of $25 per donee per year. The following are not treated as gifts:

   a.   Promotional materials, such as signs and display racks used on the recipient's business premises

   b.   One of a number of identical items costing less than $4 and having a permanent imprint of the donor's name

<u>Compensation</u>

2.   Compensation, e.g., salary, wages, or bonuses, is a deductible business expense unless the services are capital in nature.

   a.   Unreasonable compensation to a shareholder is generally treated as a dividend to the extent of earnings and profits (discussed in Study Unit 15).

   b.   Accrued compensation is not deductible unless paid within 2 1/2 months after year end.

      1)   If paid after 2 1/2 months, it is deferred compensation and deductible when paid.

   c.   A publicly held corporation may not deduct compensation in excess of $1 million paid in any tax year to a covered employee.

      1)   The term "covered employee" is determined by reference to SEC rules and includes the chief operating officer and any individual who is among the four highest-compensated officers.

         a)   No amount of a "parachute payment" made to an officer, shareholder, or highly compensated person is deductible.

      2)   The following forms of remuneration are not included in computing the $1 million limit:

         a)   Income from pension plans, annuity plans, and specified employer trusts

         b)   Benefits that are tax-free under the Code

         c)   Commissions based on income generated by the individual performance of the employee

         d)   Compensation based on performance goals

         e)   Income payable under a pre-February 17, 1993, contract

      3)   The disallowance of the deduction for the compensation payment does not change the employee's reporting of the compensation for income tax purposes.

         a)   The $1 million and any excess is generally compensation gross income.

         b)   The salary, bonus, or other payment is not required to be treated as a dividend.

         c)   However, dividend reporting for part of the compensation may be required if part or all of the compensation is not reasonable in amount.

<u>Stock</u>

   d.   FMV of property received for services is gross income to the corporate employee when it is not subject to a substantial risk of forfeiture and its value can be ascertained with reasonable certainty.

      1)   Deduction of the compensation by the corporation is allowed when the amount is included as gross income, but only if federal income tax on the compensation is withheld.

         a)   The amount of the deduction is the FMV of the stock on the date of transfer.

       b)   If the stock has appreciated, the corporation must also recognize a gain on the deemed sale.

EXAMPLE

Employee purchases stock (FMV = $1,000) in 2011 for $500. In 2013, when its FMV is $2,000, Employee's rights in it are no longer subject to a substantial risk of forfeiture. Employee includes $1,500 in gross income in 2013. Employer may deduct $1,500 in 2013.

---

    2)   Sale prior to vesting in a non-arm's-length transaction results in gross income computed from the current FMV of the property. Further, gross income is includible upon a subsequent arm's-length sale.

EXAMPLE

Employee, from the above example, sold the stock to Spouse in 2012 for $750 when its FMV was $1,500. Spouse sold the stock for $2,000 in 2013. Employee includes and Employer deducts $1,000 in 2012 and $500 in 2013.

---

    3)   The amount of the deduction is FMV of the stock on the date of transfer.

       a)   The employee's basis is also the FMV of the stock received.

       b)   If an employee is paid in cash and stock, the cash is deducted from the stock FMV and the difference is the employee's basis in the stock.

       c)   If the stock splits, the split shares are allocated basis.

Education

    e.   An employer's expenditures for employee education are deductible as a business expense.

       1)   The corporate employer is not required to document incidental travel costs related to education as travel and entertainment expenses.

       2)   An individual, in contrast, may deduct only educational expenses required to maintain or improve skills in a present position.

Travel and Meals

  3.   Travel and meals are deductible business expenses.

    a.   Fifty percent of the cost of meals bought while traveling or served on the business premises are deductible.

    b.   However, meals bought and served on the business premises are 100% deductible if considered de minimis (i.e., little value) and provided to more than half of the employees.

    c.   Fifty percent of expenses for entertainment that are ordinary and necessary to the business are deductible.

Insuring an Employee

  4.   Reasonable amounts of expenditures to promote employee health, goodwill, and welfare are deductible. This includes employee life insurance.

    a.   Premiums for life insurance covering an officer or employee are not deductible if the corporation is a direct or indirect beneficiary.

       1)   The excess of the insurance proceeds minus the premiums and other amounts paid for the policy is included in income.

    b.   A deduction is denied for interest expense incurred with respect to corporate-owned life insurance policies or to endowment or annuity contracts.

       1)   An exception is provided for debt on contracts involving key employees.

R&E Expenditures

5.   Qualified research and experimental expenditures may be capitalized, amortized, or currently deducted.

   a.   Generally, costs incidental to development of a model, process, or similar property are included.

   b.   Not included are costs of market research, sociological research, or development of art.

Fines

6.   Fines and penalties paid to a governmental entity are not deductible.

Bad Debts

7.   The reserve method is not allowed. A corporation must use the direct charge-off method or the nonaccrual-experience method.

Worthless Securities

8.   Loss incurred when a security becomes worthless is generally treated as a capital loss subject to the capital loss limitations.

   a.   Loss incurred when a security of an affiliated corporation becomes worthless may be treated as an ordinary loss.

Stock Redemptions

9.   Deduction of amounts paid or incurred with respect to a stock redemption or to the redemption of the stock of any related person is not allowed.

   a.   Deductions for interest paid or accrued within the tax year on indebtedness are allowed.

Original Issue Discount

10.   OID is treated as deductible interest expense.

   a.   Pre-1982 issue bonds. OID is deductible ratably over the term (in months) of the bond.

   b.   Effective yield method. For bonds issued after July 1, 1982, OID is deductible as interest using the yield method to amortize the discount.

   1)   Effective yield to maturity is computed and applied to adjusted issue price (AIP) to compute deductible interest.

   2)   The OID portion does not include cash interest payments made to the holder during the period.

   3)   AIP is the original issue price adjusted for OID previously taken into account.

   4)   Yield to maturity is determined on the basis of compounding at the end of each accrual period (typically 6 months).

   5)   Daily portions of OID must be computed. It is the ratable daily portion of the excess of AIP multiplied by yield to maturity over cash interest payable for the bond year.

EXAMPLE

Consider a 5-year 10% bond issued on June 30, Year 1, with a $10,000 face value, a $9,250 original issue price, and 12% yield.

Year 1 Amortization

$$\$9,250 \ \times \ 12\% \ \times \ \frac{6 \text{ months}}{12 \text{ months}} \ = \ \$555 - \$500 \left(\$10,000 \ \times \ 10\% \ \times \ \frac{6 \text{ months}}{12 \text{ months}} \right) \text{cash paid} \ = \ \$55$$

Year 2 Amortization

$$(\$9,250 \ + \ 55) \ \times \ 12\% \ = \ \$1,116.60 - \$1,000 \ (\$10,000 \ \times \ 10\%) \text{ cash paid} \ = \ \$116.60$$

      c.   The original issue discount rules do not apply to U.S. savings bonds.

      d.   An original issue discount can be treated as zero if it is less than one-fourth of 1% of the stated redemption price at maturity multiplied by the number of years from the date of issue to maturity.

(.25%) × Stated redemption price at maturity × No. of years from the date of issue to maturity

Repurchase at Premium

11.   A corporation that repurchases its bonds may deduct as interest expense the excess of the repurchase price over the issue price. Issue price is adjusted for OID deducted.

      a.   No more than the normal call premium on nonconvertible debt is allowable unless the corporation can show that the excess is not attributable to a conversion feature.

           1)   A call premium not exceeding 1 year's interest at the rate stated in the bond is considered normal.

Interest Expense

12.   Interest expense incurred on borrowings used to repurchase stock is deductible in the period in which it is paid or incurred.

      a.   However, other expenses related to a stock purchase on reorganization are generally not deductible.

Casualty Losses

13.   Casualty losses are deductible by a corporation.

      a.   When business property is partially destroyed, the deductible amount is the lesser of the decline in FMV or the property's adjusted basis (prior to the loss).

      b.   When business property is completely destroyed, the deductible amount is the property's adjusted basis (prior to the loss).

      c.   There is no $100-per-loss or 10%-of-AGI floor for corporations.

Expenses between Related Taxpayers

14.   A deduction for accrued expenses or interest owed by a corporation to a controlling shareholder or by a controlling shareholder to a corporation cannot be taken when

      a.   The two parties use different accounting methods and

      b.   The payee will include the accrued expense in gross income at a date later than when the expense is taken by the payor.

EXAMPLE

John, a cash-basis taxpayer, owns 100% of Gatlin, Inc., an accrual-basis taxpayer. Throughout 2012, John leased a building to Gatlin but received no cash payments until July 2013, when Gatlin made a payment for the entire lease. Gatlin properly accrued the expense associated with the building lease. Gatlin is not permitted to take a deduction for the accrued expense until the payment is made to John because they use different accounting methods, and the payee (John) will not include the income until 2013. Thus, Gatlin will be allowed to deduct the expense in 2013, and John will include the lease income in his personal income in 2013.

---

           1)   For purposes of determining control, this includes both direct and indirect interests.

Stop and review! You have completed the outline for this subunit. Study questions 19 through 25 beginning on page 278.

14.4 CORPORATE TAX RETURN SCHEDULES

Corporations file federal returns using Form 1120.

Reconciliation

1. Reconciliation of income per books (book income) with income per tax (tax income) is reported on Schedule M-1.

    a. For corporate tax groups with more than $10 million of assets at year end, reconciliation of book income with tax income is reported on Schedule M-3.

    b. Corporate tax groups with year-end assets of less than $10 million may file the Schedule M-3 in lieu of the Schedule M-1.

    c. These schedules reconcile differences, both permanent and temporary, for financial reporting and tax accounting.

2. To reconcile income per books with income per tax, the following adjustments are made to net income (loss) per books (similar to Schedule M-1):

    Net income (loss) per books
    +   Federal income tax
    +   Excess of capital losses over capital gains
    +   Income subject to tax not recorded on books
    +   Expenses recorded on books not deducted on the tax return [including contributions in excess of 10% taxable income limitation, book depreciation expense in excess of allowable tax depreciation, disallowed travel and entertainment costs (50% of meals and entertainment expenses are nondeductible), life insurance premiums on key personnel when the corporation is the beneficiary, tax-exempt interest expense, and political contributions]
    –   Income recorded on books not subject to tax (including prepaid rent or interest previously received and recorded for tax purposes but not earned until the current year, and tax-exempt interest)
    –   Deductions on this return not charged against book income (e.g., depreciation)
    =   Taxable income

3. Changes in the unappropriated retained earnings account from the beginning of the year to the end are reported on Schedule M-2.

    a. This schedule gives the IRS information regarding dividends paid during the year and any special transactions that caused a change in retained earnings for the year.

4. Changes in the unappropriated retained earnings account for the year are calculated as follows (similar to Schedule M-2):

    Beginning balance in unappropriated retained earnings account
    +   Net income per books
    +   Other increases (including a refund of federal income taxes paid in a prior year that is taken directly to the retained earnings account instead of used to reduce federal income tax expenses)
    –   Dividends paid (cash or property)
    –   Other decreases (including appropriation of retained earnings made during the tax year)
    =   Ending balance in unappropriated retained earnings account

Stop and review! You have completed the outline for this subunit. Study questions 26 through 30 beginning on page 281.

QUESTIONS

14.1 Dividends-Received Deduction

1. Which of the following statements regarding the corporate dividends-received deduction is false?

A. Generally, a corporation can deduct 70% of the dividends received from a corporation of which it owns less than 20%.

B. Generally, a corporation can deduct 80% of the dividends received from a corporation of which it owns 20% or more.

C. The dividends-received deduction is unlimited.

D. No deduction is allowed for dividends from tax-exempt corporations.

Answer (C) is correct.
REQUIRED: The false statement regarding the corporate dividends-received deduction.
DISCUSSION: The dividends-received deduction is limited by, among other things, the recipient corporation's adjusted taxable income unless an NOL results from the DRD.

2. Copper Corporation had the following income and expenses during its calendar year:

Income from operations	$250,000
Expenses from operations	175,000
Qualifying dividends from domestic corporations (10% ownership)	15,000

What is Copper Corporation's dividends-received deduction for the year?

A. $15,000

B. $10,500

C. $12,000

D. None of the answers are correct.

Answer (B) is correct.
REQUIRED: The proper computation of the dividends-received deduction.
DISCUSSION: Sec. 243 permits a corporation to deduct 70% of dividends received from a domestic taxable corporation of which it owns less than 20% of the stock, 80% of dividends received if the stock is 20% or more (but less than 80%) owned, and 100% of dividends received if the stock is 80% or more owned. In the case of dividends received from a less-than-20%-owned corporation, the dividends-received deduction is limited to the lesser of 70% of dividends received or 70% of taxable income computed without regard to any NOL deduction, any capital loss carryback, or the dividends-received deduction itself. Thus, Copper's dividends-received deduction equals $10,500 ($15,000 dividends received × 70%) because the dividend payment is less than taxable income.
Answer (A) is incorrect. A 100% deduction is not applicable. Answer (C) is incorrect. The deduction does not equal 80% of the dividends received. Answer (D) is incorrect. Sec. 243 permits a corporation to deduct 70% of dividends received from a domestic taxable corporation of which it owns less than 20% of the stock.

3. In Year 1, Green, Inc., had gross receipts from sales of $500,000, dividends of $100,000 from a domestic corporation in which Green owned 50% of the stock, and operating expenses of $800,000. What is the Year 1 net operating loss for Green?

A. $200,000

B. $280,000

C. $300,000

D. $330,000

Answer (B) is correct.
REQUIRED: The dividends-received deduction when increasing an NOL.
DISCUSSION: If a corporation has a 20% or greater interest in a corporation, it normally can deduct 80% of taxable income. The 80% of taxable income cap is disregarded if the corporation is determining an NOL for the year. Therefore, Green's NOL for the year is calculated as follows:

Income from business	$ 500,000
Dividends	100,000
Gross income	$ 600,000
Deductions (expenses)	(800,000)
Taxable income (loss) before special deductions	$(200,000)
Minus: Deduction for dividends received (80% of $100,000)	(80,000)
Net operating loss	$(280,000)

Answer (A) is incorrect. The DRD is computed without regard to the NOL. Answer (C) is incorrect. A DRD for 100% of the dividends received only applies to corporate ownership levels of greater than or equal to 80%. Answer (D) is incorrect. The dividends-received deduction is $80,000. The NOL should equal $280,000 ($200,000 + $80,000).

4. Croaker, Inc., is a taxable domestic corporation. Dana Corporation, a large manufacturing corporation, owns 15% of Croaker's outstanding stock. In Year 1, Dana received $100,000 in dividends from Croaker. Dana received no other dividends in Year 1. Dana may deduct, within certain limits, what percentage of the dividends received?

A. 15%

B. 70%

C. 80%

D. 100%

Answer (B) is correct.

REQUIRED: The dividends-received deduction percentage given the ownership percentage.

DISCUSSION: A special corporate deduction for dividends received (DRD) from domestic taxable corporations is allowed. However, all dividends constitute gross income. For ownership percentages of less than 20%, a corporation may deduct 70% of the dividends. Thus, Dana may deduct 70% of the dividends it receives from Croaker.

Answer (A) is incorrect. The dividends-received deduction does not necessarily equal the ownership percentage. The dividends-received deduction equals either 70%, 80%, or 100%. Answer (C) is incorrect. The 80% of dividends deductible is for ownership percentages from 20% to less than 80%. Answer (D) is incorrect. The 100% dividends-received deduction is for affiliated corporations (ownership of 80% or more).

5. During the current year, Zack Corporation experienced a $15,000 loss from operations. It received $100,000 in dividends from a domestic corporation of which Zack owns 15% of total stock outstanding. Zack's taxable income before the dividends-received deduction was $85,000. What is the amount of Zack's dividends-received deduction?

A. $59,500

B. $70,000

C. $80,000

D. $100,000

Answer (A) is correct.

REQUIRED: The corporate shareholder's amount of dividends-received deduction.

DISCUSSION: The dividends-received deduction for dividends received from a 15%-owned corporation cannot exceed 70% of taxable income for the year. Zack's taxable income is $85,000 ($100,000 dividends – $15,000 loss). The tentative dividends-received deduction of $70,000 would not cause an NOL; therefore, the dividends-received deduction is limited to 70% of taxable income, or $59,500 ($85,000 × 70%).

Answer (B) is incorrect. The taxable income limitation applies. Answer (C) is incorrect. An 80% dividends-received deduction cannot apply. Answer (D) is incorrect. The deduction is limited to 70% of taxable income.

6. In the current year, Pine Corporation had losses of $20,000 from operations. It received $180,000 in dividends from a 25%-owned domestic corporation. Pine's taxable income is $160,000 before the dividends-received deduction. What is the amount of Pine's dividend-received deduction?

A. $0

B. $144,000

C. $128,000

D. $180,000

Answer (C) is correct.

REQUIRED: The dividends-received deduction of a corporation.

DISCUSSION: A corporate deduction for dividends received from domestic taxable corporations is allowed. Pine Corporation may deduct 80% of dividends received from a domestic corporation in which Pine owned between 20% and 80% of the stock. The dividends-received deduction is limited to 80% of taxable income if the tentative dividends-received deduction does not cause an NOL. Without regard to the limitation, Pine could deduct $144,000 ($180,000 × 80%). Pine, however, is limited to a $128,000 deduction ($160,000 taxable income × 80%) because the tentative deduction does not cause an NOL. Thus, Pine's dividends-received deduction is $128,000.

Answer (A) is incorrect. Pine is entitled to a dividends-received deduction. Answer (B) is incorrect. Pine's dividends-received deduction is limited to 80% of taxable income. Answer (D) is incorrect. Pine may not deduct all of the dividends received.

7. During Year 1, the initial year of operations, Robert wholly owned a limited liability company (LLC) that manufactured air compressors that were sold to retail outlets within the United States. At the end of Year 1, the LLC had net income from the manufacturing activity of $100,000, interest income of $5,000, and dividend income of $10,000. If Robert had no other items of income or loss in Year 1, he should compute his tax liability on which amount?

A. $75,000

B. $85,000

C. $100,000

D. $115,000

Answer (D) is correct.

REQUIRED: The computation of tax when LLC has operations that are incidental to main business.

DISCUSSION: The LLC should compute its tax liability based on the income generated from the manufacturing activity, interest income, and dividend income. The tax liability should be computed from $115,000 of taxable income ($100,000 manufacturing operations + $5,000 interest income + $10,000 dividend income).

8. Marisa Corporation purchased 20% of Mantle Corporation's common stock in August of the current year and paid for the purchase with $100,000 cash and $100,000 borrowed from its bank. During the current year, Marisa received $30,000 in dividends from Mantle and paid $10,000 in interest expense on the bank loan. Marisa did not make any principal payments on the loan during the year. If Marisa had taxable income of $50,000 before special deductions, what is its dividends-received deduction for the year?

A. $0

B. $12,000

C. $14,000

D. $24,000

Answer (C) is correct.

REQUIRED: The corporate dividends-received deduction when stock is debt financed.

DISCUSSION: Sec. 246A restricts the dividends-received deduction when portfolio stock is debt financed. Debt-financed portfolio stock is any stock of a corporation if the taxpayer does not own at least 50% of the stock of such corporation and if, at some time during the base period, portfolio indebtedness exists with respect to the stock. The dividends-received deduction (when the recipient owns 20% or more of the payor corporation) is limited to a percentage equal to 80% times 100% minus the average indebtedness percentage. This percentage is the average amount of portfolio indebtedness divided by the average amount of adjusted basis of the stock during the period. However, the reduction in the dividends-received deduction cannot be more than the interest deducted for the portfolio indebtedness.

Marisa's average indebtedness percentage is 50% ($100,000 ÷ $200,000), so the allowable deduction is 40% [80% × (100% – 50%)], giving a dividends-received deduction of $12,000 ($30,000 × 40%). The full deduction would have been $24,000 ($30,000 × 80%). The total reduction in the dividends-received deduction ($24,000 – $12,000 = $12,000) is greater than the interest-expense deduction for the period ($10,000), so the reduction is limited by Sec. 246A(e) to the $10,000 of interest expense. Marisa's dividends-received deduction is thus $14,000 [($30,000 × 80%) – $10,000].

Answer (A) is incorrect. A deduction is allowable for debt-financed stock. Answer (B) is incorrect. The reduction is limited to the $10,000 interest expense. Answer (D) is incorrect. The deduction is limited for debt-financed stock.

9. For a domestic corporation to deduct a percentage of the dividends it receives from a foreign corporation, certain tests must be met. Which of the following conditions need not be present?

A. The domestic corporation owns at least 10% of the foreign corporation.

B. The foreign corporation has income effectively connected with a trade or business in the U.S.

C. The corporation is not a foreign personal holding company.

D. The foreign corporation has derived income effectively connected with its U.S. business amounting to at least 50% of its gross income from all sources for a 36-month period.

Answer (D) is correct.

REQUIRED: The condition that need not be met for a domestic corporation to deduct a percentage of dividends received from a foreign corporation.

DISCUSSION: Sec. 245 lists requirements that must be met for the dividends of a foreign corporation to qualify for the dividends-received deduction. These requirements include that the foreign corporation (1) not be a foreign personal holding company, (2) be subject to U.S. federal income taxation, (3) be 10% or more owned by the domestic corporation, and (4) have income from effectively connected business sources within the United States. For dividends received before 1987, prior law required the foreign corporation to have derived 50% or more of its gross income from effectively connected business sources within the U.S.

10. Corporations can take a deduction for dividends received from which of the following?

A. A real estate investment trust.

B. A corporation exempt from tax for the tax year of the distribution.

C. A corporation whose stock has been held for 90 days.

D. None of the answers are correct.

Answer (C) is correct.

REQUIRED: The true statement regarding the dividends-received deduction.

DISCUSSION: A dividends-received deduction is disallowed for dividends received on any share of stock that the corporate shareholder has held for 45 days or less. The holding-period rule prevents a corporation from claiming a dividends-received deduction if it purchases stock immediately before the ex-dividend date and sells the stock immediately thereafter.

Answer (A) is incorrect. Sec. 243(d) provides that amounts received from real estate investment trusts are not eligible for a deduction. Answer (B) is incorrect. Sec. 246(a) disallows a deduction if the corporation is exempt from tax during the distribution year. Answer (D) is incorrect. Corporations can take a deduction for dividends received from a corporation whose stock has been held for 90 days.

11. Corporations cannot take a deduction for dividends received from any of the following entities except

    A. A regulated investment company.

    B. A real estate investment trust.

    C. A corporation whose stock has been held less than 46 days during the 90-day period beginning 45 days before the stock becomes ex-dividend with respect to the dividend.

    D. Any corporation under an obligation (pursuant to a short sale or otherwise) to make related payments for positions in substantially similar or related property.

Answer (A) is correct.
    REQUIRED: The entity from which a corporation can take a dividends-received deduction.
    DISCUSSION: A corporation may take a deduction for dividends received from a regulated investment company. However, in determining the deduction, dividends received from a regulated investment company shall be subject to the regulations provided in Sec. 854.
    Answer (B) is incorrect. A corporation cannot take a deduction for dividends received from a real estate investment trust. Answer (C) is incorrect. A corporation cannot take a deduction for dividends received from a corporation whose stock has been held less than 46 days during the 90-day period beginning 45 days before the stock becomes ex-dividend with respect to the dividend. Answer (D) is incorrect. A corporation cannot take a deduction if it holds a short position in substantially similar or related property.

14.2 Charitable Contributions

12. Norwood Corporation is an accrual-basis taxpayer. For the year ended December 31, Year 1, it had book income before tax of $450,000 after deducting a charitable contribution of $50,000. The contribution was authorized by the board of directors in December, Year 1, but was not actually paid until March 1, Year 2. How should Norwood treat this charitable contribution for tax purposes to minimize its Year 1 taxable income?

    A. It cannot claim a deduction in Year 1 but must apply the payment against Year 2 income.

    B. Make an election claiming a deduction for Year 1 of $50,000 with no carryover.

    C. Make an election claiming a deduction for Year 1 of $45,000 with no carryover.

    D. Make an election carrying the deduction back 3 years.

Answer (B) is correct.
    REQUIRED: The corporation's maximum charitable contribution deduction.
    DISCUSSION: Sec. 170(a)(2) allows an accrual-basis corporation to deduct a charitable contribution if authorized during the taxable year and paid within 2 1/2 months after year end. Since the contribution was paid by March 15, Year 2, it is deductible in Year 1. Sec. 170(b)(2) provides that the charitable contribution deduction may not exceed 10% of a corporation's taxable income computed before certain special deductions and the charitable contribution deduction. Norwood's maximum Year 1 deduction is $50,000, which is within the limit as shown below.

Taxable income after contribution	$450,000
Add: Charitable contributions made	50,000
Taxable income before contribution	$500,000
Times: Limit percentage	× 10%
Year 1 contribution deduction limit	$ 50,000

    Answer (A) is incorrect. A deduction may be claimed in Year 1. Answer (C) is incorrect. The deduction is limited to 10% of taxable income before deducting the charitable contribution. Answer (D) is incorrect. Carrying the deduction back would not minimize Year 1 taxable income.

13. Grey Corporation made cash contributions totaling $20,000 to qualified charitable organizations. Grey received $30,000 in dividends from a domestic corporation in which it holds 24% stock ownership. Grey was able to deduct 80% of the dividends received from the domestic corporation. Grey's taxable income for the year was $150,000 after the dividends-received deduction but before the deduction for charitable contributions. What is Grey's charitable contribution deduction for the year?

    A. $12,600

    B. $15,000

    C. $17,400

    D. $20,000

Answer (C) is correct.
    REQUIRED: The corporation's charitable contribution deduction.
    DISCUSSION: Under Sec. 170, charitable contributions made to qualified organizations and paid within the taxable year may be deducted from taxable income. A corporation's charitable deduction is limited to 10% of taxable income computed before the charitable contribution deduction, net operating loss carryback, capital loss carryback, and the dividends-received deduction. The dividends-received deduction of $24,000 ($30,000 × 80%) must be added back to the taxable income of $150,000. Grey's charitable contribution deduction is $17,400 ($174,000 × 10%).
    Answer (A) is incorrect. The dividends-received deduction is not deducted twice from income before the 10% limit is applied. Answer (B) is incorrect. The dividends-received deduction is not deducted from income before the 10% limit is applied. Answer (D) is incorrect. The total cash contributions are limited to 10% of income before the charitable contributions deduction, net operating loss carryback, capital loss carryback, and the dividends-received deduction.

14. During the year, HOOS Corporation had the following income and expenses:

Gross receipts	$700,000
Salaries	300,000
Contributions to qualified charitable organizations	60,000
Capital gains	7,000
Depreciation expense	28,000
Dividend income	60,000
Dividends-received deduction	42,000

What is the amount of HOOS Corporation's charitable contribution deduction for the year?

A. $33,700

B. $39,700

C. $43,900

D. $60,000

Answer (C) is correct.

REQUIRED: The corporation's charitable contribution deduction.

DISCUSSION: Under Sec. 170, charitable contributions made to qualified organizations and paid within the taxable year may be deducted from taxable income. A corporation's charitable deduction is limited to 10% of taxable income computed before the charitable contribution deduction, net operating loss carryback, capital loss carryback, and the dividends-received deduction. HOOS's charitable contribution deduction for the year is $43,900, as computed below.

Gross receipts	$700,000
Capital gains	7,000
Dividend income	60,000
Less: Salaries	(300,000)
Less: Depreciation expense	(28,000)
Taxable income before special deductions	$439,000
Times: Limit percentage	× 10%
Charitable contribution deduction	$ 43,900

Answer (A) is incorrect. The charitable contributions and dividends-received deduction were incorrectly deducted before the 10% limit was applied. Answer (B) is incorrect. The dividends-received deduction was incorrectly deducted before the 10% limit was applied. Answer (D) is incorrect. The charitable contribution deduction is limited to 10% of taxable income before special deductions.

15. Which of the following statements concerning the charitable contribution deduction by a corporation is true?

A. A corporation cannot deduct contributions in the current year that exceed 10% of its taxable income.

B. A corporation can deduct contributions to charitable organizations only if they are made in cash.

C. A corporation using the accrual basis of accounting must have made the charitable donation by the close of its tax year.

D. A corporation is not permitted to carry over any charitable contributions that were not deducted in the current year.

Answer (A) is correct.

REQUIRED: The true statement concerning the charitable contribution deduction by a corporation.

DISCUSSION: A corporation's allowable charitable contribution deduction for a given tax year cannot exceed 10% of the corporation's taxable income for the year. Any excess amount can be carried forward to the following tax year.

Answer (B) is incorrect. Noncash contributions are also deductible. Answer (C) is incorrect. An accrual-method corporation may elect to deduct an amount authorized by the board during the current tax year and paid no later than 2 1/2 months after the close of the tax year. Answer (D) is incorrect. Excess charitable contributions over the taxable income limit may be carried over and are deductible during the succeeding 5 tax years.

16. Corporation D donated meat products inventory with a cost of $8,500 and a fair market value of $10,000 to a public charity. The conditions regarding the special rule on appreciation have been met (e.g., the charity used the inventory for the care of the needy). Corporation D's taxable income before the contribution deduction is $95,000. What is Corporation D's allowable contribution deduction?

A. $750

B. $8,500

C. $9,250

D. $9,500

Answer (C) is correct.

REQUIRED: The corporation's allowable deduction for charitable contributions of inventory.

DISCUSSION: Normally, the deduction for a contribution of inventory is limited to its basis by Sec. 170(e)(1). However, Sec. 170(e)(3) provides that, when a corporation contributes inventory to be used by the donee for the care of the needy, the qualified contribution is the FMV reduced by only one-half the amount of potential ordinary income if the property had instead been sold at its fair market value. Corporation D's allowable contribution deduction is $9,250 and is not limited since it does not exceed $9,500 ($95,000 adjusted taxable income × 10%).

Contributions	$10,000
Less: Potential ordinary income if sold [($10,000 FMV − $8,500 basis) × 50%]	(750)
Contribution deduction	$ 9,250

Answer (A) is incorrect. A deduction is allowed for the FMV minus one-half of ordinary income potential. Answer (B) is incorrect. One-half of ordinary income potential may also be deducted. Answer (D) is incorrect. The deduction is limited to one-half of potential income plus basis.

17. In Year 2, Green Corporation had a net operating loss and has a net operating loss carryback of $4,400 available to Year 1. Green had the following income and expenses for Year 1 when it was originally reported:

Gross profit	$205,000
Other deductions (including $1,700 of charitable contributions)	194,200

What is Green Corporation's deduction for contributions when the Year 1 taxable income is recomputed?

A. $640

B. $810

C. $1,080

D. $1,250

Answer (D) is correct.

REQUIRED: The corporation's contribution deduction when there are NOL carrybacks.

DISCUSSION: Sec. 170(b)(2) limits a corporation's charitable deduction to 10% of the corporation's taxable income computed before the charitable contribution deduction, net operating loss carryback, capital loss carryback, and dividends-received deduction. Green's contribution deduction is $1,250 because the 10% limit is less than actual contributions. This limitation does not change because of Year 2's NOL that is carried back.

Gross profit	$ 205,000
Less: Deductions	(194,200)
Add: Charitable contributions made	1,700
Taxable income before special deductions	$ 12,500
Times: Limitation percentage	× 10%
Contribution deduction limitation	$ 1,250

Answer (A) is incorrect. An NOL deduction is not calculated into the limitation amount. Answer (B) is incorrect. An NOL deduction is not calculated into the limitation amount. Answer (C) is incorrect. The deduction is limited to income before the charitable contribution deduction.

18. Kelli Corporation had the following income and expense items during the current year:

Dividends received (10% owned)	$ 10,000
Revenue from operating activities	130,000
Expenses from operating activities	100,000
Charitable contributions paid	5,000

In addition to the above items, Kelli had a $1,000 unused charitable contribution from 4 years ago. The proper treatment of Kelli Corporation's charitable contributions when calculating its current-year tax liability is to

A. First apply the carryover from 4 years ago and then use the current contributions.

B. First use the current contributions and then apply the carryover from 4 years ago.

C. Lump both amounts together and treat the total as contributions made in the current year.

D. Use only the current contributions since unused charitable contributions can be carried forward for only 3 succeeding tax years.

Answer (B) is correct.

REQUIRED: The proper treatment of charitable contribution carryovers.

DISCUSSION: Sec. 170(d)(2) requires that the current contributions be used first and then requires that carryovers be applied in a first-in, first-out (FIFO) manner. Excess contributions may be carried forward for 5 years.

Answer (A) is incorrect. Current contributions should be deducted first. Answer (C) is incorrect. Carryover contributions are applied on a FIFO basis. Answer (D) is incorrect. Excess contributions may be carried forward up to 5 years.

14.3 Other Corporate Deductions

19. On December 31, Year 1, PSC Corporation, a personal service corporation, accrued a $25,000 bonus to Mrs. Adams, an employee-owner. She owns 3% of the outstanding stock of the corporation. Mrs. Adams is a cash-basis taxpayer and received the bonus on April 15, Year 2. PSC Corp., a calendar-year taxpayer, may take a deduction on its Year 1 return of which of the following amounts?

A. $25,000

B. $21,250

C. $3,750

D. $0

Answer (D) is correct.

REQUIRED: The deduction for a PSC when the bonus is distributed the following year to a cash-basis taxpayer.

DISCUSSION: Under Sec. 162(a), a reasonable allowance for salaries or other compensation for personal services actually rendered is deductible by the corporation if paid or incurred during the tax year. PSC Corporation is denied the deduction for the accrual in Year 2 since compensation paid to employees must not only meet the economic performance requirement but must also be paid within 2 1/2 months after the end of the employer's tax year in which the services are rendered. Payments made after the end of the 2 1/2-month period are presumed to be deferred compensation, and the deduction is deferred until the year in which payment occurs [Temp. Reg. 1.404(b)-1T(A-2)(b)(1)].

Answer (A) is incorrect. The bonus is not deductible until Year 2. Answer (B) is incorrect. The 3% ownership is irrelevant. Answer (C) is incorrect. The 3% ownership is irrelevant.

20. The Charlie Corporation, a calendar-year, accrual-basis taxpayer, distributed shares of the David Corporation stock to Charlie's employees in lieu of salaries. The salary expense would have been deductible as compensation if paid in cash. On the date of the payment, Charlie's adjusted basis in David's stock was $20,000, and the stock's fair market value was $100,000. What is the tax effect to Charlie Corporation?

A. $100,000 deduction.

B. $20,000 deduction.

C. $20,000 deduction and $80,000 recognized gain.

D. $100,000 deduction and $80,000 recognized gain.

Answer (D) is correct.

REQUIRED: The tax effect of a distribution of stock held by a corporation to its employees.

DISCUSSION: Publication 535 states, "If you transfer property (including your company's stock) to an employee as payment for services, you can generally deduct it as wages. The amount you can deduct is its fair market value on the date of the transfer minus any amount the employee paid for the property. . . . You treat the deductible amount as received in exchange for the property, and you must recognize any gain or loss realized on the transfer. Your gain or loss is the difference between the fair market value of the property and its adjusted basis on the date of transfer."

Answer (A) is incorrect. The corporation must recognize the $80,000 gain. Answer (B) is incorrect. The deduction is equal to the FMV of the property distributed, and the corporation must recognize the $80,000 gain. Answer (C) is incorrect. The deduction is equal to the FMV of the property distributed.

21. Carol provides services in Year 1 to Bragg Corporation. Her service contract with Bragg listed her fee at $50,000 receivable in cash and/or stock. At the time her fee was due, Bragg stock was trading for $1,000 per share. Carol elected to receive $30,000 in cash and 20 shares of Bragg stock. In Year 4, the Bragg stock split, increasing the number of Carol's shares to 40. In Year 6, Carol sells 20 shares of her Bragg stock for $1,500 per share. What is Carol's basis in the Bragg Corporation shares she still owns?

A. $10,000

B. $20,000

C. $30,000

D. $40,000

Answer (A) is correct.

REQUIRED: The adjusted basis of a shareholder's remaining shares.

DISCUSSION: The adjusted basis of stock is usually its cost. However, since Carol rendered services for $50,000 (of which $30,000 was paid in cash), Carol's basis in her original 20 shares equals $20,000, the fair market value of the stock. The stock split reduces her basis per share to $500. Since she sold 20 shares with a $500 per share basis, her remaining 20 shares have a $500 per share basis, for a total basis of $10,000.

22. On May 15, Corporation A issued callable 20-year convertible bonds at a face value of $200,000 bearing interest at 5% per year. Under the terms of the bonds, the call price before May 15 of next year is $210,000. On July 1 of the current year, Corporation A calls the bonds for $210,000. What amount of the premium can Corporation A deduct on its current-year income tax return?

A. $0

B. $5,000

C. $10,000

D. $150,000

Answer (C) is correct.

REQUIRED: The amount of premium a corporation may deduct as a result of calling its convertible bonds.

DISCUSSION: Reg. 1.163-4(c) provides that, if bonds are issued and subsequently repurchased by the corporation at a price greater than the issue price, the excess of the purchase price over the issue price is deductible as interest expense for the taxable year. Corporation A can deduct $10,000 (redemption price of $210,000 minus issue price of $200,000) in the current year.

Sec. 249 limits the deduction to the amount of the normal call premium on convertible debt. Excess amounts can be deducted only if the taxpayer can show that the excess is not attributable to the conversion feature. Reg. 1.249-1(d)(1) holds that a normal call premium on a convertible obligation is an amount equal to the normal call premium (in dollars) on a nonconvertible obligation that is comparable to the convertible obligation. Since the call premium does not exceed 1 year's interest, it is considered under the safe harbor rule of Reg. 1.249-1(d)(2) to be a normal call premium and can be deducted in full.

Answer (A) is incorrect. A premium may be deducted when a convertible bond is called. Answer (B) is incorrect. A corporation can deduct the difference between the redemption price and the issue price. Answer (D) is incorrect. A corporation can deduct the difference between the redemption price and the issue price.

23. All of the following are true except

    A. An original issue discount must be included in income as it accrues over the term of the debt instrument, whether or not any payments are received from the issuer.

    B. The original issue discount rules do not apply to U.S. savings bonds.

    C. The amount of original issue discount is the difference between the stated redemption price at maturity and the par value.

    D. An original issue discount can be treated as zero if it is less than one-fourth of 1% (.0025) of the stated redemption price at maturity multiplied by the number of years from the date of issue to maturity.

Answer (C) is correct.

    REQUIRED: The false statement regarding original issue discount (OID).

    DISCUSSION: An original issue discount (OID) is equal to the difference between the issue price and the stated redemption price at maturity. OID exists only if the discount exceeds 1/4 of 1% of the stated redemption price times the number of years to maturity [Sec. 1273(a)(3)].

24. Mr. Doering owns 2% of the outstanding stock of Dowd Corporation and 80% of Turner Partnership, which owns 90% of the outstanding stock of Dowd Corporation. Mr. Doering is a cash-basis taxpayer, and Dowd is an accrual-basis taxpayer. Both use the calendar tax year. During Year 1, Doering performed legitimate business services for Dowd. His wages were accrued and paid as follows:

- Accrued $6,000 June 10, Year 1; paid September 3, Year 1
- Accrued $2,000 August 6, Year 1; paid October 1, Year 1
- Accrued $3,500 October 15, Year 1; paid January 28, Year 2

What amount can Dowd Corporation deduct as wages to Mr. Doering on its income tax return for Year 1?

    A. $0

    B. $3,500

    C. $8,000

    D. $11,500

Answer (C) is correct.

    REQUIRED: The deduction for expenses occurring between related taxpayers.

    DISCUSSION: A controlling shareholder is defined as one who owns more than 50% (in value) of the corporation's stock. In determining whether a shareholder owns more than 50% of a corporation's stock, a shareholder is considered to own not only his or her own stock but also stock owned by entities in which the shareholder has an ownership or beneficial interest. Mr. Doering is a controlling shareholder because he constructively owns over 50% of Dowd Corporation. Sec. 267(a)(2) defers a deduction for accrued expenses or interest owed by a corporation to a controlling shareholder or by a controlling shareholder to a corporation when the two parties use different accounting methods and the payee will include the accrued expense as part of gross income at a date that is later than when it is accrued by the payer. Accrued expenses of the corporation may not be deducted until the day the controlling shareholder includes the payment in gross income. Thus, the $3,500 payment accrued on October 15, Year 1, will not be deductible until Year 2, when the controlling shareholder is paid.

    Answer (A) is incorrect. The corporation can deduct a portion of the expenses. Answer (B) is incorrect. The $3,500 is not deductible until Year 2, but $8,000 of the accrued expenses is deductible. Answer (D) is incorrect. All of the accrued expenses are not deductible in Year 1.

25. If a corporation transfers its stock to an employee as payment for services, the amount the corporation can deduct would be

    A. The corporation's basis in the stock transferred.

    B. The fair market value of the stock on the date of the transfer.

    C. The fair market value of the stock when the corporation issues the W-2.

    D. None of the answers are correct.

Answer (B) is correct.

    REQUIRED: The corporation's deduction amount related to its stock.

    DISCUSSION: Under Sec. 83(a), the employee includes in income the fair value of property received for services. Under Sec. 83(h), the employer is allowed a deduction for the amount the employee must include in income when the employee includes it in income. However, when property other than cash is distributed in exchange for services, the employer must recognize a gain on the deemed sale. The fair market value of property is gross income to the employee when no longer subject to a substantial risk of forfeiture.

    Answer (A) is incorrect. The employee must include in his or her gross income the FMV of any stock received, and the corporation can deduct the FMV of the stock. The corporation is also required to recognize a gain if the stock has appreciated. Answer (C) is incorrect. The amount the corporation can deduct is the FMV on the date of transfer. Answer (D) is incorrect. A correct answer is given.

14.4 Corporate Tax Return Schedules

26. For the tax year, Sting Corporation had net income per books of $65,000, tax-exempt interest of $1,500, excess contributions of $3,000, excess tax depreciation over book depreciation of $4,500, premiums paid on term life insurance on corporate officers of $10,000 (Sting is the beneficiary), and accrued federal income tax of $9,700. Based on this information, what is Sting Corporation's taxable income as it would be shown on Schedule M-1 of its corporate tax return?

A. $59,000

B. $68,700

C. $81,700

D. $87,700

Answer (C) is correct.
   REQUIRED: The taxable income for Sting Corporation.
   DISCUSSION: Schedule M-1 reconciles income or loss per books with income or loss per tax return.

Net income per books	$65,000
Add back:	
Federal income taxes	9,700
Excess contributions	3,000
Life insurance premiums	10,000
	$87,700
Subtract:	
Tax-exempt interest	(1,500)
Excess depreciation	(4,500)
Taxable income	$81,700

   Answer (A) is incorrect. The tax liability, excess contributions, and life insurance premiums must be added. Answer (B) is incorrect. The excess contributions and the life insurance premiums must be added. Answer (D) is incorrect. The tax-exempt interest and the excess depreciation must be subtracted.

27. Everyday Corporation realized net book income in the amount of $300,000 for tax year ended December 31, Year 1. Included in the net book income are the following:

Federal income taxes	$ 4,000
Excess capital losses over capital gains	10,000
Tax exempt interest income	5,000

What is Everyday Corporation's taxable income?

A. $290,000

B. $304,000

C. $280,000

D. $309,000

Answer (D) is correct.
   REQUIRED: The taxable income for Everyday Corporation.
   DISCUSSION: To reconcile income per books with income per tax, the following adjustments are made to net income (loss) per books: net income (loss) per books plus federal income tax, excess of capital loss over capital gains, income subject to tax not recorded on books, and expenses recorded on books not deducted on tax return; minus income recorded on books not subject to tax and deductions on this return not charged against book income. Everyday Corporation's taxable income is computed as follows:

Net book income		$300,000
Add:	Excess capital losses over capital gains	10,000
	Federal income taxes	4,000
Less:	Tax exempt interest income	(5,000)
Taxable income		$309,000

   Answer (A) is incorrect. Only the excess capital losses over capital gains was deducted from net book income. Answer (B) is incorrect. Only the federal income taxes was added to net book income. Answer (C) is incorrect. The federal income taxes, the excess capital losses or capital gains, and the tax exempt interest income were added to net book income.

28. Net income per books of Pat Jordan's psychology clinic was $140,825 for the year ended September 30, Year 1. Select from the following account information those items that would be necessary to reconcile book income to the income to be reported on the return, and compute taxable income per return.

Capital gains	$ 3,600
Capital losses	8,200
Entertainment expenses (before limitation)	10,850
Federal income tax expense	62,225
Tax-exempt interest income	5,000
Net income	140,825
Cash distribution to shareholders	20,000

A. $203,050

B. $208,075

C. $202,225

D. $207,650

Answer (B) is correct.
   REQUIRED: The taxable income per return computed from the items necessary to reconcile book income to the income to be reported.
   DISCUSSION: Schedule M-1 reconciles income or loss per books with income or loss per tax return.

Net income per books	$140,825
Add back:	
Federal income taxes	62,225
Excess net capital losses	4,600
Excess entertainment	5,425
	$213,075
Subtract:	
Tax-exempt interest	(5,000)
Taxable income	$208,075

29. Agress Corporation, a calendar-year taxpayer reporting on the accrual basis, showed the following balances on its books for the year:

Sales	$130,000
Cost of sales	70,000
Operating expenses	40,000
Contributions	2,500
Net life insurance premiums on officer with Agress as the beneficiary	4,000
Accrued federal income tax	3,230
Book income	$ 10,270

What is the amount of Agress Corporation's taxable income as it would be shown on Schedule M-1 of its corporate income tax return?

A. $13,500

B. $14,270

C. $18,000

D. $20,000

Answer (C) is correct.
REQUIRED: The taxable income for Agress Corporation.
DISCUSSION: Schedule M-1 reconciles income or loss per books with income or loss per tax return. Taxable income before the charitable contribution is $20,000 ($130,000 – $70,000 – $40,000). The charitable contribution is limited to $2,000 ($20,000 × 10%).

Net income per books	$10,270
Add back:	
Federal income taxes	3,230
Excess contributions	500
Life insurance premiums	4,000
Taxable income	$18,000

Answer (A) is incorrect. Excess contributions and life insurance premiums must be added back to book income. Answer (B) is incorrect. Taxes and excess contributions must be added back to book income. Answer (D) is incorrect. Excess contributions must be added back to book income, not the entire contribution.

30. For the current tax year, Task Corporation had an unappropriated retained earnings beginning balance of $115,000 and net income per books of $155,000. During the current year, Task had a loss on a sale of securities of $10,700, paid cash dividends of $85,000, and received a refund of last year's income taxes of $24,000. What is Task Corporation's unappropriated retained earnings ending balance for the current year?

A. $185,000

B. $209,000

C. $219,700

D. $270,000

Answer (B) is correct.
REQUIRED: The corporation's unappropriated retained earnings balance.
DISCUSSION: A corporation's unappropriated retained earnings balance is computed on Schedule M-2 of Form 1120. The balance at the end of the year is the beginning balance; plus net income per books; minus distributions of cash, property, or stock. Other adjustments may be made as necessary. Task's unappropriated retained earnings balance is as follows:

Beginning balance	$115,000
Add:	
Net income per books	155,000
Income tax refund	24,000
Less:	
Cash dividends paid	(85,000)
Unappropriated retained earnings	$209,000

The loss on the sale of securities is already included in the net income per books amount. Thus, no further adjustment is needed.
Answer (A) is incorrect. The income tax refund must be added. Answer (C) is incorrect. The loss on the sale of securities is already included in the net income per books. Answer (D) is incorrect. The income tax refund must be added, and the dividends paid must be subtracted.

Use the additional questions in Gleim **EA Test Prep** to create Practice Exams that emulate Prometric!

STUDY UNIT FIFTEEN
CORPORATE DISTRIBUTIONS

(8 pages of outline)

A **distribution** is any transfer of property by a corporation to any of its shareholders with respect to the shareholder's shares in the corporation. Property is defined as money; bonds or other obligations (also of the distributing corporation); stock in other corporations (not issued by the distributor); and other property, including receivables.

The amount of a distribution is calculated as follows:

> Money
> + Obligations (FMV), e.g., a bond
> + Property (FMV), other
> − Related liabilities, recourse or not
> = Amount of distribution

15.1 EARNINGS AND PROFITS

Significance

1. The amount of a distribution is treated as a dividend to the extent of the corporation's earnings and profits (E&P).

   a. Distributions are presumed to come from the corporation's E&P, unless there are no E&P.

   b. An E&P account provides an approximate measure of a corporation's ability to pay a dividend (in the generic sense) to its shareholders.

   c. A corporate shareholder may prefer dividend treatment for a distribution it receives because of the availability of a dividends-received deduction.

      1) Between 70% and 100% of the dividend amount may represent a current deduction.

   d. An individual shareholder may benefit from nondividend treatment for a portion of a distribution (Form 5452).

      1) Portions treated as recovery of capital are not subject to federal income taxes.

      2) Portions treated as LTCG can offset capital losses and may be taxed at a lower maximum rate of 0%, 15%, or 20%, depending on the taxpayer's total taxable income.

Computing E&P: The Formula

2. The IRC does not provide a mechanical definition of E&P. Sec. 312 and regulations provide rules that indicate how certain transactions or events are reported.

   a. Taxable income (TI). TI is the starting point for computing E&P.

b. Adjustments. TI is adjusted up and down to compute the approximate dividend-paying ability of the corporation. Adjustment items may be categorized as follows:

Adjustment Category	Adjustment Needed to Compute E&P
1) Income excluded from TI	• Add to TI
2) Expenses and losses that are nondeductible for TI	• Subtract from TI
3) Deferred income recognition items	• Add to or subtract from TI
4) Accelerated deduction items	• Add to or subtract from TI
5) Deductions not allowed for E&P	• Add to TI

Income Excluded From TI

3. TI is adjusted upward for (most) items of economic income not included as gross income when computing TI.

a. Add economic income that is

1) Not a contribution to capital but
2) Increases dividend-paying capacity.

b. Add the following:

1) Refunds of prior years' federal income tax
2) Recoveries of deduction items that produced no tax benefit, e.g.,

a) Bad debts
b) Casualty losses

3) Tax-exempt interest income
4) The excludable portion of life insurance proceeds paid to the corporation

Nondeductible Expenses and Losses

4. TI is adjusted downward for expenditures and losses to the extent they are not allowed as a deduction from GI in computing TI.

a. Subtract the following from TI:

1) Charitable contributions (excess over 10% of TI)
2) Capital losses (current year's carried over)
3) Disallowed losses (e.g., sale to related party)
4) Federal income taxes
5) Penalties and fines
6) Political contributions
7) Tax-exempt-income-related expenses
8) The excludable portion of life insurance premiums (with the corporation as the beneficiary)

b. Timing. The adjustment for corporations using the cash method of accounting is made when the item is paid.

1) A corporation using the accrual method of accounting generally reports the adjustment when it is accrued.

c. Capacity. Each corporate item, including those previously listed, must be considered for its effect on dividend-paying capacity and on TI.

1) For example, life insurance premiums on policies in which the corporation is the beneficiary are subtracted net of the cash surrender value increase.

Deferred Recognition Items

5. Most income for which an exception defers recognition when determining TI is not included in E&P until recognized.

    a. Exceptions

        1) Add to TI any unrecognized realized income/gain on an installment sale.

EXAMPLE

Delaware Corp. engages in an installment sale of land that it has held as a potential plant site. Delaware is to receive 60% of the sales proceeds in the following tax year. Delaware's realized gain on the sale is $1 million. Taxable income does not include realized gain not recognized, or $600,000 ($1,000,000 × 0.60). E&P include the gain that is currently recognized as well as the $600,000 deferred gain.

---

        2) Recalculate income reported on a long-term contract reported using the completed-contract method as if the percentage-of-completion method were used.

Accelerated Deduction Items

6. TI is adjusted to the extent deductions reduce TI in excess of economic costs due to premature recognition of anticipated economic decline.

    a. Adjust TI upward or downward for the difference between

        1) Sec. 179 expense deducted and the amount deducted as if the cost is expensed ratably over 5 years
        2) Realty depreciation deducted using the MACRS rules and depreciation computed over 40 years
        3) ACRS deductions and straight-line ACRS deductions with extended recovery periods
        4) MACRS deductions and the alternative depreciation system (ADS) deductions

            a) ADS applies straight-line depreciation over the property's class life using a half-year convention.

        5) Percentage depletion deductions claimed and cost depletion amounts
        6) Intangible drilling costs (IDC) deducted and the IDC amounts amortized over 60 months

Deductions Not Allowed for E&P

7. TI is adjusted upward for items that are currently deductible from gross income (GI) in computing TI but do not currently reduce capacity to pay dividends. These items may have already reduced E&P in a prior tax year or may never reduce E&P.

    a. Add to TI any amounts deducted for

        1) Charitable contribution carryovers
        2) NOL carryovers
        3) Capital loss carryovers
        4) Dividends-received deductions

Distributions

8. A distribution by the corporation to one or more shareholders may trigger both upward and then downward adjustments to E&P (which may affect tax treatment of distributions to the distributee and other shareholders).

    a. Although distributions can occur at any time during the tax year, current E&P are determined at the end of the tax year.

        1) Once current E&P are determined, the tax consequences of each distribution can be determined.

b. When a corporation distributes property that has appreciated in value, the corporation must recognize a gain as if the corporation had sold its property for its FMV.

1) However, a corporation does not recognize any loss when it makes a distribution of property even if the sale would have resulted in a loss.

2) Gain recognized by the corporation on the distribution of appreciated property is included in TI.

3) Before distributions of appreciated property (other than the corporation's obligations), earnings and profits must be increased by the excess of the FMV over the adjusted basis of the appreciated property.

4) If a liability attached to a distributed asset exceeds the FMV of the asset, the selling price is equal to the amount of the liability.

5) When noncash property is distributed, the gain included in TI may be different from the gain that is reported for E&P purposes.

6) When depreciable property is distributed, the gain reported for TI purposes is calculated using the property's AB after reduction for MACRS depreciation.

a) The AB used when calculating the E&P gain is reduced for the slower ADS depreciation.

b) This difference reduces the gain (increases the loss) reported for E&P purposes.

c) If liabilities exceed basis, FMV is treated as not less than the liabilities assumed by the shareholder.

c. E&P are reduced by the property's basis in the case of distributed property that is not appreciated property.

d. Only after determining shareholder tax treatment for the tax year, reduce current E&P by the amounts constituting distributions from the corporation during the year, but not below zero. The amount of the E&P reduction is

1) Amount of money

2) Principal amounts of the corporation's own obligations

a) When a bond is issued with OID, use the issue price.

3) FMV of appreciated property

a) Less any liability assumed or acquired by the shareholder

4) AB of other property

a) Less any liability assumed or acquired by the shareholder

e. A distribution cannot produce a deficit in (i.e., reduce below zero) current E&P.

f. For corporate distributions from E&P, there are four scenarios:

1) When both current and accumulated E&P are positive, the corporation is required to allocate the current portion of E&P to all of the distributions and then apply accumulated E&P in chronological order.

2) If both are negative E&P, all distributions (to the extent of basis) are a return of basis. Any distributions in excess of basis are treated as capital gains on the stock to the investor.

3) If current E&P are positive and accumulated E&P are negative, the corporation does not net the two. Instead, all distributions to the extent of the current E&P are dividends, and the remainder are returns of basis.

4) If current E&P are negative and accumulated E&P are positive, the corporation prorates negative E&P up to the point of each distribution, nets it with accumulated E&P, and all distributions to the extent of the positive E&P netted amount are considered dividends, with the remainder being returns of basis.

> 5) For all of the above, once E&P are exhausted, the remainder of distributions are returns of basis to the extent of shareholder basis. Once shareholder basis is exhausted, the remainder of distributions are treated as if the underlying stock had been sold, and capital gain treatment is applied.

9. When a corporation has a loss in the current year, the loss is prorated over the year to determine the accumulated E&P at the time of a distribution.

EXAMPLE

A corporation has accumulated E&P of $100,000 at the beginning of the year and a loss for the current year of $80,000. The corporation makes a distribution of $90,000 on April 1. Only $80,000 is considered a dividend since there are only $80,000 of accumulated E&P at the time of the distribution [$100,000 − ($80,000 × 1/4)]. The $80,000 loss is prorated over the year.

Stop and review! You have completed the outline for this subunit. Study questions 1 through 11 beginning on page 291.

15.2 SHAREHOLDER TREATMENT OF DISTRIBUTIONS

A distribution to a shareholder is equal to the FMV of the property distributed. This amount must be decreased by any liabilities that are assumed by the shareholder or to which the property is subject.

Dividend

1. The amount of a distribution is first a dividend to the extent of any current E&P and then to the extent of any accumulated E&P.

   a. When distributions during the year exceed current E&P, pro rata portions of each distribution are deemed to be from current E&P.

   b. Treatment of a distribution is determined by reference to accumulated E&P (acc. E&P) only after any current E&P have been accounted for.

      1) Acc. E&P constitute the remaining balance of E&P from prior tax years.

      2) A deficit in acc. E&P never results from a distribution. It results from any aggregate excess of current E&P deficits over unused positive acc. E&P.

         a) A deficit in acc. E&P does not offset current E&P.

      3) Current E&P are added to acc. E&P after determining treatment of distributions.

   c. When distributions exceed both current E&P and acc. E&P, allocate acc. E&P to distributions in their chronological order.

Constructive Dividend

   d. Constructive dividends are tangible benefits to shareholders other than declared dividends and are included as income to the shareholder.

      1) The corporate deduction taken for such expenses should be reversed, thereby increasing corporate E&P.

      2) The following are examples:

         a) Excessively high salaries
         b) Forgiveness of shareholder debt
         c) Personal use of corporate equipment
         d) Excessive lease or purchase payment to shareholder
         e) Transfer of property to shareholder for less than FMV

   e. A constructive distribution will be treated as a dividend for tax purposes if sufficient E&P are available.

   f. If the corporation makes any payment that may be a dividend but is unable to confirm whether such payment is a dividend by the time the Form 1099-DIV must be filed, the entire amount of the payment must be reported as a dividend or as an amount paid with respect to a dividend.

Capital Recovery

2.   A shareholder treats the amount of a distribution in excess of dividends as tax-exempt return of capital to the extent of his or her basis in the stock.

    a.   Basis in the stock is reduced (but not below zero).

    b.   Apportion the distribution among the shares if they have different bases.

EXAMPLE

Corporation distributes $90,000 when E&P are $60,000. Shareholder N receives $30,000 of the distribution, of which $20,000 is a dividend (2/3).

	# of Shares	Basis	Dividend	Capital Recovery	Gain
Block 1	1,000	$ 3,000	$10,000	$3,000	$2,000
Block 2	1,000	$15,000	$10,000	$5,000	0

Gain on Sale

3.   Any excess of the amount of a distribution over E&P and basis is treated as gain on the sale of the stock (e.g., the $2,000 above).

    a.   Character depends on the nature of the stock in the hands of the shareholder as a capital asset or dealer property.

    b.   Loss may be recognized only if the stock becomes worthless or is redeemed.

Basis in Distributed Property

4.   The shareholder's basis in property received in a nonliquidating distribution is generally its FMV at the time of the distribution.

    a.   Obligations of the distributing corporations have a basis equal to their FMV.

    b.   If liabilities assumed or liabilities of property taken are

        1)   Less than FMV, then basis in the property is its FMV.

        2)   Greater than FMV, then the basis should equal the liability if the distributee shareholder assumes personal liability.

Stop and review! You have completed the outline for this subunit. Study questions 12 through 20 beginning on page 294.

15.3 STOCK DISTRIBUTIONS

A corporation recognizes no gain or loss on distribution of its own stock.

1.   A proportionate distribution of stock issued by the corporation to the shareholders is generally not gross income to the shareholders.

    a.   Generally, a shareholder does not include a distribution of stock or rights to acquire stock in gross income unless it is a

        1)   Distribution in lieu of money;

        2)   Disproportionate distribution;

        3)   Distribution on preferred stock;

        4)   Distribution of convertible preferred stock; or

        5)   Distribution of common and preferred stock, resulting in receipt of preferred stock by some shareholders and common stock by other shareholders.

    b.   A shareholder allocates the aggregate adjusted basis (AB) in the old stock to the old and new stock in proportion to the FMV of the old and new stock.

        1)   Basis is apportioned by relative FMV to different classes of stock if applicable.

    c.   The holding period of the distributed stock includes that of the old stock.

    d.   E&P are not altered for a tax-free stock dividend.

Stock Rights

2. Treat a distribution of stock rights as a distribution of the stock.

   a. Basis is allocated based on the FMV of the rights.

      1) Basis in the stock rights is zero if their aggregate FMV is less than 15% of the FMV of the stock on which they were distributed, unless the shareholder elects to allocate.

   b. Basis in the stock, if the right is exercised, is any basis allocated to the right, plus the exercise price.

   c. The holding period of the stock begins on the exercise date.

   d. No deduction is allowed for basis allocated to stock rights that lapse.

      1) Basis otherwise allocated remains in the underlying stock.

3. **Taxable Stock Distribution**

   a. The amount of a distribution subject to tax is the FMV of distributed stock or stock rights. Distributions of stock are subject to tax when

      1) Any shareholder has an option to choose between a distribution of stock or a distribution of other property.

         a) The amount of the distribution is the greater of

            i) The FMV of stock or
            ii) The cash and FMV of other property.

      2) Some shareholders receive property, and other shareholders receive an increase in their proportionate interests.

         a) Such a distribution of stock is treated as if it were a distribution of property.

      3) Some common shareholders receive common stock, but others receive preferred.

      4) Distribution is on preferred stock.

         a) Limited change in conversion ratios, by itself, does not trigger taxability.

      5) Convertible preferred stock is distributed, and the effect is to change the shareholder's proportionate stock ownership.

      6) Constructive stock distributions change proportionate interests resulting from a transaction, such as a change in conversion ratio or redemption price.

   b. E&P are reduced by the FMV of stock and stock rights distributed.

   c. Basis in the underlying stock does not change. Basis in the new stock or stock rights is their FMV.

   d. The holding period for the new stock begins on the day after the distribution date.

   e. If a distribution of a stock dividend or stock right is taxable when received, the basis is the fair market value on the date of acquisition.

      1) When the dividend is taxable, there is no tacking of the holding period for the underlying stock.

         a) The holding period begins the day following the acquisition date.

Stock Split

4. A stock split is not a distribution.

   a. Basis in the old stock is also "split" and allocated to the new stock.
   b. The holding period of the new stock includes that of the old stock.

Stop and review! You have completed the outline for this subunit. Study questions 21 through 26 beginning on page 297.

15.4 BACKUP WITHHOLDING

1. Although investment income is generally not subject to regular withholding, it may be subject to backup withholding to ensure that income tax is collected.

    a. A corporation may be required to withhold tax equal to 28% of the dividends paid to certain shareholders (e.g., a shareholder who does not furnish a taxpayer identification number).

2. Backup withholding may be required on certain types of payments.

    a. Interest payments
    b. Dividends
    c. Patronage dividends, but only if at least half the payment is in money

Form 1099-DIV

3. A corporation is required to file Form 1099-DIV with the IRS no later than February 28 of the following year.

    a. Form 1099-DIV must be mailed to the shareholders no later than January 31 of the following year.

    b. Form 1099-DIV is required for each shareholder

        1) To whom it paid gross dividends of $10 or more during the calendar year,
        2) To whom it paid a liquidating distribution of $600 or more, or
        3) From whose dividend income it withheld taxes.

Form 1042

4. A corporation is generally required to withhold tax on dividends to any nonresident alien, foreign corporation, or foreign partnership (see Publication 515).

    a. Form 1042 is used for withholding from a nonresident alien, foreign partnership, or foreign corporation. Form 1042-S gives the names and addresses of the payee and withholding agent.

        1) Both forms are due March 15.

    b. If the shareholder changes his or her address from a place outside the United States to a place within the United States, the tax shall be withheld on dividends unless proof is furnished showing that an individual is a citizen or resident of the United States or, in the case of a partnership or corporation, it is a domestic partnership or corporation.

Stop and review! You have completed the outline for this subunit. Study questions 27 through 30 beginning on page 299.

QUESTIONS

15.1 Earnings and Profits

1. Foghorn Corporation, an accrual-method taxpayer, had accumulated earnings and profits of $75,000 as of December 31, Year 1. For the Year 2 tax year, Foghorn's books and records reflect the following:

Taxable income per return	$175,000
Tax-exempt interest received	2,000
Federal income taxes	60,000
Business meals in excess of 50% limitation	4,000
Contributions in excess of limitation	1,000

Based on the above, what is the amount of Foghorn Corporation's accumulated earnings and profits as of December 31, Year 2?

A. $112,000

B. $187,000

C. $250,000

D. $313,000

Answer (B) is correct.

REQUIRED: The earnings and profits (E&P) balance as of December 31, Year 2.

DISCUSSION: Calculation of E&P begins with taxable income according to the tax return. Tax-exempt income is added to the taxable income, and nondeductible expenditures are subtracted, e.g., federal income taxes, charitable contributions in excess of the 10% limitation, and excess business meals.

Acc. E&P at December 31, Year 1	$ 75,000
Taxable income for Year 2	175,000
Add: Tax-exempt interest	2,000
Deduct: Excess contributions	(1,000)
Excess business meals	(4,000)
Federal income taxes	(60,000)
Acc. E&P at December 31, Year 2	$187,000

Answer (A) is incorrect. The previous accumulated E&P are added to current-year E&P. Answer (C) is incorrect. E&P are adjusted by tax-exempt income and nondeductible expenditures. Answer (D) is incorrect. E&P are reduced by nondeductible expenses and increased by tax-exempt interest.

2. The following information is available from the record of Emute, Inc. Compute current-year earnings and profits.

Taxable income, Form 1120	$50,000
Federal income taxes paid	7,500
Nondeductible portion of travel and entertainment	500
Excess of capital losses over capital gains	1,000

A. $41,500

B. $48,500

C. $41,000

D. $42,000

Answer (C) is correct.

REQUIRED: The computation of the current year's E&P.

DISCUSSION: Earnings and profits (E&P) are designed to measure a corporation's true ability to pay a dividend to its shareholders. In computing E&P, certain adjustments are made to taxable income (TI). One such adjustment is subtracting from TI expenses and losses that are nondeductible. Accordingly, current E&P are calculated as follows:

Taxable income	$50,000
Less:	
Federal income taxes paid	(7,500)
Nondeductible travel and entertainment expense	(500)
Excess capital losses	(1,000)
Current E&P	$41,000

Answer (A) is incorrect. The nondeductible portion of travel and entertainment expense is subtracted to arrive at E&P. Answer (B) is incorrect. The federal income taxes paid are subtracted from taxable income. Answer (D) is incorrect. The excess capital losses are subtracted from taxable income to arrive at current E&P.

3. Hampshire, Inc., a calendar-year taxpayer, had an accumulated earnings and profits balance at the beginning of Year 1 of $20,000. During Year 1, Hampshire distributed $30,000 to its sole individual shareholder. On December 31, Year 1, Hampshire reported taxable income of $50,000, reported federal income taxes of $7,500, and had tax-exempt interest on municipal bonds of $2,500. What is Hampshire, Inc.'s accumulated earnings and profits balance at the beginning of Year 2?

A. $15,000

B. $25,000

C. $30,000

D. $35,000

Answer (D) is correct.

REQUIRED: E&P after adjustments.

DISCUSSION: Taxable income is the starting point for computing E&P. Appropriate adjustments are made for E&P for items that are not used to compute taxable income.

Beginning E&P	$ 20,000
Distribution to shareholder	(30,000)
Taxable income	50,000
Federal income taxes	(7,500)
Tax exempt interest	2,500
Ending E&P	$ 35,000

Answer (A) is incorrect. The amount of $15,000 does not include the beginning E&P balance of $20,000. Answer (B) is incorrect. Beginning E&P is added, not subtracted, and the distribution to the shareholder is subtracted, not added. Answer (C) is incorrect. The ending E&P calculation is not merely the taxable income less the distribution to the shareholder.

4. Buffalo, Inc., owned and displayed a collection of watercolors in its main office. When the 75% owner retired, he was presented with his choice from the collection. He selected a painting with a fair market value of $250,000. Buffalo's basis in the painting was $150,000. How should the distribution be reported on the return of Buffalo?

A. No reporting required.

B. $150,000 distribution reduces assets on the balance sheet but no effect on tax.

C. $100,000 taxable gain.

D. $250,000 taxable gain.

Answer (C) is correct.

REQUIRED: The treatment of distribution of property subject to appreciation.

DISCUSSION: If a corporation distributes property other than its own obligations to a shareholder and the property's FMV exceeds the corporation's adjusted basis, the property is treated as sold at the time of distribution. The corporation recognizes gain on the excess of the FMV over the adjusted basis of the property.

FMV of property distributed	$250,000
Less adjusted basis	150,000
Gain recognized under Sec. 311(b)	$100,000

Answer (A) is incorrect. A gain is recognized on the distribution of appreciated property. Answer (B) is incorrect. The corporation recognizes a taxable gain on the excess of the FMV over the adjusted basis of the property. Answer (D) is incorrect. The gain is limited to the FMV of the property less its adjusted basis.

5. Heritage Corporation distributed an antique automobile to Rene, its sole shareholder. On the date of distribution, the automobile had a fair market value of $30,000 and an adjusted basis to Heritage of $22,000. What is the amount of Heritage Corporation's recognized gain on the distribution?

A. $30,000

B. $12,000

C. $8,000

D. $0

Answer (C) is correct.

REQUIRED: The corporation's recognized gain on the distribution of property.

DISCUSSION: If a corporation distributes property other than its own obligations to a shareholder and the property's FMV exceeds the corporation's adjusted basis, the property is treated as sold at the time of distribution. The corporation recognizes gain on the excess of the FMV over the adjusted basis of the property.

FMV of property distributed	$30,000
Less adjusted basis	22,000
Gain recognized under Sec. 311(b)	$ 8,000

Answer (A) is incorrect. The gain is limited to the FMV of the property less its adjusted basis. Answer (B) is incorrect. The gain is limited to the FMV of the property less its adjusted basis. Answer (D) is incorrect. A gain is recognized on the distribution of appreciated property.

6. Which of the following statements regarding corporate distributions is false?

A. Under no circumstances may a distribution, whether in cash or property, generate a deficit in E&P.

B. Under no circumstances may a distribution, whether in cash or property, add to a deficit in E&P.

C. In a corporate distribution, the E&P account is reduced by the amount of money distributed.

D. In a corporate distribution, the E&P account is reduced by the lesser of the FMV or the adjusted basis of the property distributed.

Answer (D) is correct.

REQUIRED: The false statement regarding distributions.

DISCUSSION: If a corporation distributes property other than its own obligations to a shareholder and the property's FMV exceeds the corporation's adjusted basis, the property is treated as sold at the time of distribution. The corporation recognizes gain on the excess of the FMV over the adjusted basis of the property. A distribution cannot produce a deficit in (i.e., reduce below zero) E&P. If current E&P are exhausted, the balance reduces prior-year E&P. The reductions do not produce or increase a deficit accumulated E&P. Any distributions in excess of E&P reduce paid-in capital.

Answer (A) is incorrect. If current E&P are exhausted, the balance reduces prior-year E&P. Any distributions in excess of accumulated E&P reduce paid-in capital. Answer (B) is incorrect. If current E&P are exhausted, the balance reduces prior-year E&P. Any distributions in excess of accumulated E&P reduce paid-in capital. Answer (C) is incorrect. E&P may also be reduced by the following distributions: principal amounts of the corporation's own obligations, FMV of appreciated property (less any liability assumed by the shareholder), or the adjusted basis of other property (less any liability assumed by the shareholder).

7. The Smart Corporation distributes an office building to Collin, a shareholder of the corporation. The fair market value of the building exceeds its basis to the corporation. Which of the following statements is true with regard to this transaction?

    A. Smart realizes but does not recognize gain on this distribution.

    B. Smart elects not to report the gain on this distribution.

    C. Smart must recognize gain on this distribution.

    D. Collin must recognize the losses on this distribution on his return as a shareholder.

Answer (C) is correct.
    REQUIRED: The treatment of an office building distributed to a shareholder.
    DISCUSSION: If a corporation distributes property other than its own obligations to a shareholder and the property's fair market value exceeds corporation's adjusted basis, the property is treated as sold at the time of distribution. The corporation recognizes gain on the excess of the FMV over the adjusted basis of the property.
    Answer (A) is incorrect. The corporation recognizes gain on the excess of the FMV over the adjusted basis of the property. Answer (B) is incorrect. There is no election enabling a corporation not to report the gain on the distribution. Answer (D) is incorrect. There are no losses for Collin to recognize.

8. Yappa Corporation distributed depreciable personal property having a fair market value of $9,500 to its shareholders. The property had an adjusted basis of $2,000 to the corporation. Yappa had correctly deducted $7,000 in depreciation on the property. What is the amount of Yappa's ordinary income due to this distribution?

    A. $9,500

    B. $7,500

    C. $7,000

    D. $0

Answer (C) is correct.
    REQUIRED: The corporation's ordinary income upon the distribution of depreciable property.
    DISCUSSION: Sec. 311(b) requires that gain on the distribution of appreciated property be recognized as if the property had been sold. Therefore, Yappa will recognize $7,500 ($9,500 fair market value – $2,000 basis) of total gain. $7,000 of this gain will be ordinary income as a result of Sec. 1245 depreciation recapture.
    Answer (A) is incorrect. Ordinary income is limited to the depreciation actually taken. Answer (B) is incorrect. Ordinary income is limited to the depreciation actually taken. Answer (D) is incorrect. Sec. 1245 recaptures depreciation taken as ordinary income.

9. On July 1, Year 1, VAL, a calendar-year C corporation, distributed an auto used 100% in its business to its sole shareholder. At the time of the distribution, the auto, which originally cost $18,000, had an adjusted basis of $6,000 and a fair market value of $5,000. No liabilities were attached to the auto. No other distributions were made during Year 1. As of January 1, Year 1, VAL's accumulated earnings and profits were $(5,000). For Year 1, VAL's earnings and profits were $8,000. By what amount will VAL reduce its earnings and profits as a result of the distribution of the auto?

    A. $3,000

    B. $4,000

    C. $5,000

    D. $6,000

Answer (D) is correct.
    REQUIRED: The reduction of E&P resulting from a distribution of unappreciated property.
    DISCUSSION: In the case of distributed property that is not appreciated property, E&P are reduced by the property's basis. However, the distribution cannot create negative E&P. In determining whether negative E&P are created, first look to current year's E&P. Since the distributed property's basis ($6,000) is less than current year's E&P ($8,000), no deficit in E&P is created. Thus, E&P are reduced by the full $6,000.

10. In figuring the amount of a distribution by a corporation to its shareholders, the term "property" includes all of the following except

    A. Money.

    B. Securities.

    C. Indebtedness of the distributing corporation.

    D. Stock of the distributing corporation.

Answer (D) is correct.
    REQUIRED: The item not considered property for distribution purposes.
    DISCUSSION: Under Sec. 317(a), "property" is defined as money, securities, and any other property except stock or stock rights of the distributing corporation.
    Answer (A) is incorrect. Money of the distributing corporation is specifically defined as property under Sec. 317(a). Answer (B) is incorrect. Securities of the distributing corporation are specifically defined as property under Sec. 317(a). Answer (C) is incorrect. Indebtedness of the distributing corporation is specifically defined as property under Sec. 317(a).

11. Ball, a calendar-year C corporation, had accumulated earnings and profits of $50,000 as of January 1, Year 1. Ball had a deficit in earnings and profits for Year 1 of $65,000. Ball distributed $25,000 to its shareholders on July 1, Year 1. What is the amount of Ball Corporation's accumulated earnings and profits as of December 31, Year 1?

A. $0

B. $(15,000)

C. $(32,500)

D. $(40,000)

Answer (C) is correct.

REQUIRED: The accumulated E&P after a distribution is made when a current accumulated E&P deficit exists.

DISCUSSION: When a distribution is made during the course of the year, the E&P must be prorated for the year to reflect the accumulated E&P balance on the date of the distribution. Because the distribution occurred on July 1, the accumulated E&P were $17,500 [$50,000 – (6 months ÷ 12 months × $65,000)]. The $25,000 distribution reduces the E&P balance to zero. The accumulated E&P balance as of December 31, Year 1, is a $32,500 deficit, or the remainder of the current E&P deficit.

Answer (A) is incorrect. An accumulated E&P deficit may exist when the current-year deficit is larger than the previous balance. Answer (B) is incorrect. The distribution decreases the accumulated E&P when a positive balance exists. Answer (D) is incorrect. The distribution cannot reduce the E&P balance below zero.

15.2 Shareholder Treatment of Distributions

12. For 10 years, Ben has owned all 100 outstanding shares of N and M Corporation's stock. Ben's basis for the stock is $50,000. In the current year, N and M have earnings and profits of $100,000. The corporation redeemed 25 shares of Ben's stock for $75,000 in the current year. How will Ben report this?

A. $75,000 gain.

B. $75,000 dividend.

C. $50,000 gain.

D. None of the answers are correct.

Answer (B) is correct.

REQUIRED: The treatment of a distribution to a shareholder owning 100% of the corporation when the distribution is less than E&P.

DISCUSSION: Because Ben owns 100% of the stock before and after the redemption, the transaction is a dividend to the extent that N and M Corporation has earnings and profits. Because the distribution ($75,000) is less than earnings and profits ($100,000), the entire amount is taxable as a dividend.

Answer (A) is incorrect. Ben owns 100% of the stock before and after the redemption, and the transaction is a dividend to the extent that N and M has earnings and profits. Answer (C) is incorrect. The distribution is less than earnings and profits; the entire amount is taxable as a dividend. Answer (D) is incorrect. Ben owns 100% of the stock before and after the redemption, and the transaction is a dividend to the extent that N and M has earnings and profits.

13. Heron, Inc., made a distribution of real estate with a FMV of $100,000 to its only shareholder, Jennifer, on December 31, Year 1. Heron's basis in the property was $60,000. Current year earnings and profits of Heron (before the distribution) is $10,000, and it has accumulated $20,000 earnings and profits from prior years. Jennifer's basis in her Heron stock is $5,000. What will be the tax effect to Jennifer?

A. $30,000 dividend and $25,000 capital gain.

B. $30,000 dividend and $65,000 capital gain.

C. $100,000 dividend.

D. $70,000 dividend and $25,000 capital gain.

Answer (D) is correct.

REQUIRED: The tax effect of a property distribution.

DISCUSSION: The $100,000 distribution of an asset with a $60,000 basis will create a $40,000 gain. The $40,000 gain will be added to current earnings and profits. Thus, dividend income would be $70,000 because of the earnings and profits ($10,000 + $40,000 + $20,000). A corporate distribution is a dividend that must be included in the recipient's gross income under Sec. 301(c)(1) to the extent it comes from current or accumulated E&P of a corporation. To the extent the distribution exceeds current and accumulated E&P, it is treated as a return of capital to the shareholder. Once the basis of the stock has been reduced to zero, any distributions received are treated as a gain from the sale of the stock. Therefore, Jennifer will treat $5,000 of the $30,000 excess ($100,000 property distribution – $70,000 current and accumulated E&P) as return of capital and $25,000 of the excess as a capital gain.

Answer (A) is incorrect. The $40,000 gain will increase current earnings and profits. Answer (B) is incorrect. The $40,000 gain will increase current earnings and profits. Answer (C) is incorrect. Dividend income is limited to earnings and profits.

14. Adam Corporation is a calendar-year C corporation that had accumulated earnings and profits of $30,000 as of January 1, Year 1. On April 1, Year 1, Adam distributed $55,000 in cash to its sole shareholder. For Year 1, Adam had earnings and profits of $20,000. The shareholder's adjusted basis in the stock of Adam was $12,000 before the distribution. What are the shareholder's ordinary dividend income and the return of capital due to this distribution?

	Dividend Income	Return of Capital
A.	$55,000	$0
B.	$50,000	$5,000
C.	$30,000	$25,000
D.	$50,000	$12,000

15. Corporation A, a calendar-year C corporation that began conducting business 18 years ago, had accumulated earnings and profits of $26,000 as of January 1 of the current year. On April 1, A distributed $40,000 in cash to Ms. X, Corporation A's sole shareholder. Corporation A had earnings and profits of $4,000 for the current year. Ms. X had an adjusted basis of $18,000 in her stock before the distribution. What are Ms. X's ordinary dividend income and the return of capital due to this distribution?

	Dividend Income	Return of Capital
A.	$40,000	$0
B.	$22,000	$18,000
C.	$30,000	$10,000
D.	$10,000	$30,000

16. James Corporation made various payments and transfers to and for its shareholders, Rob and Jim, during the year. Which of the following is not a reportable distribution? (Assume sufficient earnings and profits.)

A. Monthly cash payments of $500 to Rob.

B. Transfer of stocks held for investment to both Rob and Jim.

C. Use of a company vehicle by Jim's daughter at college.

D. Reasonable salary to both Rob and Jim.

Answer (B) is correct.
REQUIRED: The amount considered taxable dividend income and the amount considered return of capital.
DISCUSSION: A corporate distribution is a dividend that must be included in the recipient's gross income under Sec. 301(c)(1) to the extent it comes from accumulated or current E&P of a corporation. To the extent the distribution exceeds current and accumulated E&P, it is treated as a return of capital to the shareholder to the extent of the shareholder's basis in the stock. The distribution of $55,000 cash exceeds the corporation's total E&P of $50,000 ($30,000 accumulated + $20,000 current). Therefore, $50,000 of the distribution is dividend income, and the remaining $5,000 is a return of capital.
Answer (A) is incorrect. The distribution exceeds the E&P. Answer (C) is incorrect. The distribution is treated as coming from both accumulated and current E&P. Answer (D) is incorrect. The distribution is a return of capital only to the extent that it exceeds E&P.

Answer (C) is correct.
REQUIRED: The dividend income and return of capital resulting from a distribution.
DISCUSSION: A corporate distribution is a dividend that must be included in the recipient's gross income under Sec. 301(c)(1) to the extent it comes from accumulated or current E&P of a corporation. To the extent the distribution exceeds current and accumulated E&P, it is treated as a return of capital to the shareholder. Once the basis of the stock has been reduced to zero, any distributions received are treated as a gain from the sale of the stock. The distribution of $40,000 exceeds the corporation's total E&P balance of $30,000 ($26,000 accumulated + $4,000 current). Therefore, $30,000 of the distribution will be dividend income, and the remaining $10,000 will be a return of capital and will reduce the shareholder's basis.
Answer (A) is incorrect. The distribution exceeds E&P. Answer (B) is incorrect. A distribution depletes E&P before it is considered a return of capital. Answer (D) is incorrect. The distribution is dividend income to the extent that an E&P balance exists.

Answer (D) is correct.
REQUIRED: The item that is not a reportable distribution.
DISCUSSION: Reasonable salaries are not distributions. However, if a portion of the salary is deemed to be excessive and therefore unreasonable, the excess would be a distribution. The salaries are an expense of the corporation.
Answer (A) is incorrect. Cash payments to Rob are distributions. Answer (B) is incorrect. The transfer of stock is deemed to be a distribution. Answer (C) is incorrect. Use of the vehicle is considered a distribution.

17. Olympic Corporation distributed real estate with a FMV of $500,000 to its sole shareholder, Joshua. Olympic's basis in the real estate is $400,000. What is the tax effect of the distribution to Olympic and what is Joshua's basis in the real estate?

A. $0 gain/loss to Olympic; $400,000 basis to Joshua.

B. $100,000 gain to Olympic; $400,000 basis to Joshua.

C. $0 gain/loss to Olympic; $500,000 basis to Joshua.

D. $100,000 gain to Olympic; $500,000 basis to Joshua.

Answer (D) is correct.
REQUIRED: The tax effect of a distribution of appreciated property of a corporation to its sole shareholder.
DISCUSSION: Sec. 301(b) provides that the amount distributed to a shareholder (corporate or noncorporate) is equal to the amount of money received, plus the fair market value of other property received. Additionally, Sec. 311(b) provides if a corporation distributes property to a shareholder and the FMV is greater than the adjusted basis, the gain shall be recognized by the distributee corporation.
Answer (A) is incorrect. The corporation must recognize the gain on the appreciation and the basis to the shareholder is the property's FMV. Answer (B) is incorrect. The basis to Joshua is the FMV, not the corporation's basis. Answer (C) is incorrect. The $100,000 gain must be recognized on the appreciated property to the corporation.

18. Walnut, Inc., is a C corporation that was started 10 years ago. At the beginning of the current year, Walnut has accumulated earnings and profits of $100,000. During the current year, Walnut makes a $5,000 distribution to its 100% shareholder in the first month of each quarter. At the end of the current year, Walnut had $150,000 in gross income and $140,000 in allowable expenses from ordinary business operations. Walnut also received $5,000 in fully tax-exempt interest from state bonds. What part of the second quarter distribution is treated as a distribution of accumulated earnings and profits?

A. $1,250

B. $2,500

C. $3,750

D. $5,000

Answer (A) is correct.
REQUIRED: The amount of the distribution from accumulated earnings and profits.
DISCUSSION: Distributions are deemed to come from current E&P and then from accumulated E&P if the current E&P is insufficient. The amount of the distribution from accumulated earnings and profits is calculated as follows:

Gross income	$150,000
Add: Tax-exempt income	5,000
Total income	$155,000
Less: Annual expenses	140,000
Total annual current E&P	$ 15,000

Current earnings and profits ÷ 4 quarters = $3,750 current E&P/quarter	
Amount of distributions per quarter	$ 5,000
Less: Amount of distribution from current E&P	3,750
Amount of distribution from accumulated E&P	$ 1,250

Answer (B) is incorrect. The amount of $2,500 does not include the tax-exempt interest in current E&P. Answer (C) is incorrect. The amount deemed from current E&P is $3,750. Answer (D) is incorrect. The total distribution for the quarter is $5,000. Only the excess distribution over current E&P is from accumulated E&P.

19. Rose Corporation, a calendar-year corporation, had accumulated earnings and profits of $40,000 as of January 1, Year 1. However, for the first 6 months of Year 1, Rose had an operating loss of $36,000 and finished the year with a total net operating loss for Year 1 tax year of $55,000. Rose distributed $15,000 to its shareholders on July 1, Year 1. Which of the following is true?

A. The entire distribution of $15,000 is taxable.

B. The entire distribution is not taxable.

C. The part of the distribution that is taxable is $12,500.

D. The part of the distribution that is taxable is $14,000.

Answer (C) is correct.
REQUIRED: The amount of a distribution taxable when it exceeds current and accumulated E&P.
DISCUSSION: When a distribution is made during the course of the year, the E&P must be prorated to reflect the accumulated E&P balance on the date of the distribution. Because the distribution occurred on July 1, the accumulated E&P were $12,500 {$40,000 − [$55,000 × (6 months ÷ 12 months)]}. A corporate distribution is a dividend that must be included in the recipient's gross income under Sec. 301(c)(1) to the extent it comes from current or accumulated E&P of a corporation. To the extent the distribution exceeds current and accumulated E&P, it is treated as a return of capital to the shareholder. Once the basis of the stock has been reduced to zero, any distributions received are treated as a gain from the sale of the stock. Therefore, each shareholder will recognize $12,500 of ordinary income.

20. Which of the following statements regarding distributions of stock is not true?

A. Distributions of stock and stock rights are never treated as property.

B. Stock rights are distributions by a corporation of rights to acquire its stock.

C. Distributions of stock dividends and stock rights are generally tax free to shareholders.

D. Expenses of issuing a stock dividend are not deductible but must be capitalized.

Answer (A) is correct.
REQUIRED: The false statement regarding distributions of stock.
DISCUSSION: Distributions of stock and stock rights are generally not treated as property.
Answer (B) is incorrect. Stock rights are distributions by a corporation of rights to acquire its stock. Answer (C) is incorrect. Distributions of stock dividends and stock rights are generally tax free to shareholders. Answer (D) is incorrect. Expenses of issuing a stock dividend are not deductible but must be capitalized.

15.3 Stock Distributions

21. A distribution of stock or stock rights is generally considered a dividend unless it is which of the following?

A. Distribution of convertible preferred stock.

B. Distribution in lieu of money.

C. Distribution with respect to preferred stock.

D. Proportionate distribution.

Answer (D) is correct.
REQUIRED: The distribution of stock or stock rights that would not be considered a dividend.
DISCUSSION: A proportionate distribution of stock or stock rights would not be considered a dividend under Sec. 305(a) and would not be included in the gross income of the distributee.
Answer (A) is incorrect. A distribution of convertible preferred stock is an exception under Sec. 305(b) to the general rule, and such a distribution would receive dividend treatment. Answer (B) is incorrect. A distribution in lieu of money is an exception under Sec. 305(b) to the general rule, and such a distribution would receive dividend treatment. Answer (C) is incorrect. A distribution with respect to preferred stock is an exception under Sec. 305(b) to the general rule, and such a distribution would receive dividend treatment.

22. A distribution of taxable stock rights or dividends generally is treated the same as

A. Any other property distribution, and the holding period begins on the day after the distribution date.

B. The distribution of an obligation of the distributing corporation.

C. A cash distribution.

D. Any other property distribution, but the holding period begins on the day of the issue of the underlying stock.

Answer (A) is correct.
REQUIRED: The proper treatment of a distribution of taxable stock rights or dividends.
DISCUSSION: If a distribution of a stock dividend or stock right is taxable when received, the basis is the fair market value on the date of distribution. When the dividend is taxable, there is no tacking of the holding period for the underlying stock. The holding period begins the day following the acquisition date.
Answer (B) is incorrect. A distribution of taxable stock rights or dividends is not treated the same as the distribution of an obligation of the distributing corporation. Answer (C) is incorrect. A distribution of taxable rights or dividends is not treated the same as a cash distribution. Answer (D) is incorrect. The holding period of the stock begins on the day following the acquisition date.

23. Corporation H, a calendar-year, accrual-basis taxpayer, distributed shares of Corporation B stock to H's employees in lieu of salaries. The salary expense would have been deductible as compensation if paid in cash. On the date of the payment, H's adjusted basis in Corporation B stock was $15,000 and the stock's fair market value was $85,000. What is the tax effect to Corporation H?

A. $85,000 deduction.

B. $15,000 deduction.

C. $85,000 deduction and $70,000 recognized gain.

D. $15,000 deduction and $70,000 recognized gain.

Answer (C) is correct.
REQUIRED: The tax effect to Corporation H of satisfying a salary liability with appreciated property.
DISCUSSION: Under Sec. 83(a), the employee includes in income the fair value of property received for services. Under Sec. 83(h), the employer is allowed a deduction for the amount the employee must include in income when the employee includes it in income. However, when property other than cash is distributed in exchange for services, the employer must recognize a gain on the deemed sale. Since the employees will include the $85,000 FMV of shares in income, Corporation H may deduct the $85,000. However, H must also recognize a $70,000 gain ($85,000 FMV – $15,000 adjusted basis) on the deemed sale.
Answer (A) is incorrect. A $70,000 gain is recognized as if the shares were sold to a third party. Answer (B) is incorrect. The employer may deduct the FMV of property relinquished and must recognize a gain. Answer (D) is incorrect. H's adjusted basis in the stock is $15,000, not the FMV of the property given up.

24. Which one of the following statements is false with regard to property distributions?

A. All stock distributions are treated as property distributions.

B. Property distributions to shareholders are measured by their FMV on the distribution date adjusted for liabilities.

C. The distributing corporation treats the property distributed as though sold to the shareholder at FMV or the amount of liabilities the shareholder assumes, whichever is greater.

D. The shareholder's basis in the property distributed is usually the FMV on the date of distribution.

Answer (A) is correct.

REQUIRED: The false statement with regard to property distributions.

DISCUSSION: According to Publication 542, in order for a stock distribution to be treated as a property distribution, one of the following five conditions must be met:

1. The shareholder has a choice to receive cash or other property instead;

2. The distribution gives cash or other property to some and an increase in percentage interests to others;

3. The distribution is comprised of convertible preferred stock and results like 2. above;

4. Some common shareholders get preferred stock, while others get common shares; or

5. The distribution is preferred stock.

Answer (B) is incorrect. The property distributions are measured by their FMV on the distribution date adjusted for liabilities. Answer (C) is incorrect. The distributed property is treated as though it was sold to the shareholder at its FMV or the amount of liabilities assumed, whichever greater, by the distributing corporation. Answer (D) is incorrect. The basis to the shareholder normally is the FMV on the date of the distribution.

25. A distribution of stock or rights to acquire stock in the distributing corporation is not included in the recipient's gross income unless

A. It is a disproportionate distribution.

B. It is a distribution instead of money or other property.

C. The distribution of stock or rights is greater than 15% of the value of the stock or rights with respect to which the rights were distributed.

D. It is either a disproportionate distribution, or a distribution instead of money or other property.

Answer (D) is correct.

REQUIRED: The situation in which a distribution of stock, or rights to acquire stock in the distributing corporation, is included in the recipient's gross income.

DISCUSSION: Usually, a shareholder does not include a distribution of stock or rights to acquire stock in gross income unless it is (1) a distribution in lieu of money, (2) a disproportionate distribution, (3) a distribution on preferred stock, (4) a distribution of convertible preferred stock, or (5) a distribution of common and preferred stock, resulting in receipt of preferred stock by some shareholders and common stock by other shareholders.

Answer (A) is incorrect. A distribution of stock or rights to acquire stock in the distributing corporation is included in the recipient's income if it is a distribution instead of money or other property. Answer (B) is incorrect. A distribution of stock or rights to acquire stock in the distributing corporation is included in the recipient's income if it is a disproportionate distribution. Answer (C) is incorrect. It is not a requirement for inclusion in the recipient's gross income.

26. Which of the following statements is false with regard to stock dividends and stock rights?

A. If stock dividends are not taxable, there is no reduction in the corporation's E&P account.

B. If stock dividends are taxable, the distribution is treated by the distributing corporation in the same manner as any other taxable property dividend.

C. A disproportionate distribution of stock rights is not includible in gross income.

D. If stock rights are taxable; basis to the shareholder-distributee is the FMV of the rights.

Answer (C) is correct.

REQUIRED: The false statement regarding stock dividends and stock rights.

DISCUSSION: Generally, a shareholder does not include a distribution of stock or rights to acquire stock in gross income unless it is (1) a distribution in lieu of money, (2) a disproportionate distribution, (3) a distribution on preferred stock, (4) a distribution of convertible preferred stock, or (5) a distribution of common and preferred stock, resulting in receipt of preferred stock by some shareholders and common stock by other shareholders.

15.4 Backup Withholding

27. When is a corporation required to file a Form 1099-DIV for a liquidating distribution?

    A. Never, liquidating distributions do not require a Form 1099-DIV.

    B. When the liquidating distribution equals or exceeds $10 in a calendar year.

    C. When the liquidating distribution equals or exceeds $600 in a calendar year.

    D. Always, liquidating distributions in any amount require the filing of a Form 1099-DIV.

Answer (C) is correct.
    REQUIRED: The situation in which a Form 1099-DIV must be filed for a liquidating distribution.
    DISCUSSION: When a corporation makes distributions to a shareholder, in partial or complete liquidation, that exceed $600 in any one calendar year, the corporation must furnish the shareholder with Form 1099-DIV.
    Answer (A) is incorrect. Liquidating distributions that exceed $600 require the filing of Form 1099-DIV. Answer (B) is incorrect. Liquidating distributions that exceed $600 require the filing of Form 1099-DIV. Answer (D) is incorrect. Only liquidating distributions that exceed $600 require the filing of Form 1099-DIV.

28. A corporation is not required to file Form 1099-DIV under which of the following circumstances?

    A. The corporation made a payment to an individual of $10 or more in distributions (such as dividends, capital gains, or nontaxable distributions) that were made on stock.

    B. The corporation sold stock held for investment purposes through a short sale.

    C. The corporation withheld federal income tax under the backup withholding rules.

    D. The corporation made payments of $600 or more as part of a liquidation.

Answer (B) is correct.
    REQUIRED: The circumstance under which a corporation is not required to file Form 1099-DIV.
    DISCUSSION: Although investment income is generally not subject to regular withholding, it may be subject to backup withholding to ensure income tax is collected. Most corporations use Form 1099-DIV to show the amounts distributed to shareholders. A corporation is required to file a 1099-DIV if (1) distributions in excess of $10 were made as dividends, capital gains, or nontaxable distributions; (2) tax was withheld under the backup withholding rules; or (3) a liquidating payment of exactly $600 was distributed. The corporation's sale of stock is not a distribution.

29. With regard to the filing of Form 1099-DIV, all of the following are true except

    A. Corporate payers file this form to report dividends and other distributions of stock of $10 or more.

    B. Corporate payers file this form for every person for whom any federal income taxes were withheld under the backup withholding rules.

    C. Corporate payers file this form for each person to whom payments of $600 or more were made as a part of a liquidation.

    D. This form is filed by payers for royalties paid to authors.

Answer (D) is correct.
    REQUIRED: The false statement regarding the filing of Form 1099-DIV.
    DISCUSSION: A corporation is required to file a 1099-DIV if (1) distributions of $10 or more were made as dividends, capital gains, or nontaxable distributions; (2) tax was withheld under the backup withholding rules; or (3) a liquidating payment of $600 was distributed.
    Answer (A) is incorrect. A corporation is required to file Form 1099-DIV if distributions of $10 or more were made as dividends, capital gains, or nontaxable distributions. Answer (B) is incorrect. A corporation is required to file Form 1099-DIV if tax was withheld under the backup withholding rules. Answer (C) is incorrect. A corporation is required to file Form 1099-DIV if a liquidating payment of $600 was distributed.

30. Corporation X, a U.S. corporation, paid a dividend to Corporation U, a foreign corporation. What form or forms must Corporation X or its designated agent use to report the dividends and income tax withheld?

    A. Forms 1096 and 1099-DIV.

    B. Form 1040NR.

    C. Forms 1042 and 1042-S.

    D. Forms 8804, 8805, and 8813.

Answer (C) is correct.
    REQUIRED: The forms used to report backup withholding for dividends paid to a foreign corporation.
    DISCUSSION: An annual return is required to be filed on Form 1042 for withholdings from a nonresident alien, foreign partnership, or foreign corporation. The form must be filed, regardless of whether any tax is withheld, by March 15 of the year following the end of the calendar year. Form 1042-S, which gives the names and addresses of the payee and withholding agent, must also be filed by March 15.

Use the additional questions in Gleim **EA Test Prep** to create Practice Exams that emulate Prometric!

STUDY UNIT SIXTEEN
CORPORATE LIQUIDATIONS AND REDEMPTIONS

(5 pages of outline)

A stock redemption occurs when a corporation acquires its stock from its shareholders in return for cash or property. Whether the redemption is treated as a sale or an exchange or a dividend depends on numerous factors. For instance, if the distribution is considered a partial liquidation under Sec. 302, noncorporate shareholders will receive sale or exchange treatment. In contrast, at some point in the life of a corporation, it may be determined that the corporation should be liquidated. If so, the corporation's shareholders will surrender all of their stock in the corporation and receive their pro rata shares of any remaining assets after all creditors are paid.

16.1 REDEMPTIONS

Stock is redeemed when a corporation acquires its own stock from a shareholder in exchange for property. The stock may be canceled, retired, or held as treasury stock. A shareholder is required to treat the amount realized on redemption (not in liquidation) as either a distribution (a corporate dividend) or a sale of the stock redeemed.

1. Redemptions of stock by a corporation are treated as <u>dividends</u> unless certain conditions are met. If any of the following <u>conditions are met</u>, the exchange is treated as a sale, and the gains or losses are <u>capital gains and losses.</u>

    a. The redemption is not essentially equivalent to a dividend.
    b. The redemption is substantially disproportionate.
    c. The distribution is in complete redemption of all of a shareholder's stock in the corporation.
    d. The distribution is to a noncorporate shareholder in partial liquidation.
    e. The distribution is received by an estate.

Corporation

2. A corporation recognizes gain realized on a distribution

    a. As if the property distributed were sold at FMV to the distributee immediately prior to the distribution
    b. Even if stock is redeemed by the distribution

3. A corporation recognizes ordinary income on the distribution of depreciated property to the extent of depreciation or amount realized, whichever is less.

4. No recognition of loss realized is allowed the corporation, unless the redemption is

    a. In complete liquidation of the corporation or
    b. Of stock held by an estate (to pay death taxes).

Shareholder

5. A shareholder treats a nonqualifying redemption in the same manner as a regular distribution (not in redemption). The amount is a dividend to the extent of E&P.

    a. Any unrecovered basis in the redeemed stock is added to the shareholder's basis in stock retained.
    b. A distribution that redeems all of a shareholder's shares is treated as a sale irrespective of earnings and profits.

6.   The expenses incurred in connection with any reacquisition by a corporation of its own stock or the stock of a related person (50% relationship test) are not deductible.

    a.   Such transactions may include stock sales, tax-free reorganizations, and dividends.

    b.   An exception exists for any cost allocable to an indebtedness and amortized over the life of the indebtedness (e.g., financial advisory costs).

Sale Treatment

7.   The shareholder treats qualifying redemptions as if the shares redeemed were sold to a third party.

    a.   Gain or loss is any difference between the adjusted basis (AB) of the shares and the fair market value (FMV) of property received.

    b.   Character of gain or loss depends on the nature of the stock in the shareholder's hands.

    c.   Basis in distributed property is its FMV.

    d.   Holding period for the property starts the day after the redemption exchange.

    e.   Treatment of a redemption as a sale is determined separately for each shareholder.

Not Essentially Equivalent

8.   Not essentially equivalent to a dividend means that there is a meaningful reduction in the shareholder's proportionate interest in the corporation.

    a.   Reduction in voting power is generally required.

        1)   Majority control (over 50%) reduction to deadlock (50%) has been determined sufficient.

        2)   Minimal reduction by a minority shareholder may be meaningful.

    b.   Attribution can be used to determine essential equivalence.

Substantially Disproportionate

9.   Substantially disproportionate means that the amount received by shareholders is not in the same proportion as their stock holdings.

    a.   It is tested by determining the shareholders' applicable ownership percentages (including constructive ownerships) both before and after the redemption.

    b.   A redemption is substantially disproportionate with respect to a shareholder if, immediately after the redemption, (s)he owns

        1)   Less than 50% of the voting power of outstanding voting stock and

        2)   Less than 80% each of interest in

            a)   The voting stock (s)he owned before the redemption and

            b)   The common stock (s)he owned before the redemption.

Termination

10.   Termination of a shareholder's interest must be complete to qualify.

    a.   All the stock owned by the shareholder in the corporation, actually and through family attribution, must be redeemed in the exchange for the property.

    b.   The family attribution rules may be waived if the following three requirements are met:

        1)   The shareholder may not retain any interest, except as a creditor, in the corporation.

        2)   The shareholder may not acquire an interest, except by bequest or inheritance, for 10 years.

        3)   A written agreement must be filed with the IRS stating that the IRS will be notified if a prohibited interest is acquired.

Partial Liquidation

11. Partial liquidations are one kind of redemption.

Estate

12. An estate may treat a qualifying redemption (to pay death taxes) as a sale.

    a. The stock included in the estate must be valued at more than 35% of the gross estate net of deductions allowed.

        1) Deductions allowed are administration expenses, funeral expenses, claims against the estate (including death taxes), and unpaid mortgages.

Constructive Ownership

13. The (redeemed) shareholder is treated as owning shares owned by certain related parties. The following ownership is considered to be constructively owned by the shareholder through related parties:

    a. Stock owned directly or indirectly by or for the shareholder's spouse, children, grandchildren, or parents

---

EXAMPLE

A corporation has 100 shares outstanding. A husband, wife, child, and grandchild (the child's child) each own 25 shares. The husband, wife, and child are each considered as owning 100 shares. The grandchild is considered as owning only 50 shares (25 shares of the grandchild + 25 shares of the child).

---

    b. Stock owned directly or indirectly by or for a partnership (or S corporation) in which the shareholder is a partner

        1) The reverse also applies (i.e., partnership owns stock owned by a partner).

    c. Stock owned directly or indirectly by an estate or trust in which the shareholder is treated as a beneficiary or an owner

    d. Stock owned directly or indirectly by or for a corporation (other than an S corporation) in which the shareholder owns directly or indirectly at least 50% of the value of the stock

    e. Stock on which the shareholder holds an option to buy

Stop and review! You have completed the outline for this subunit. Study questions 1 through 12 beginning on page 306.

16.2 COMPLETE LIQUIDATION

Under a plan of complete liquidation, a corporation redeems all of its stock in a series of distributions.

Corporate Gains

1. A corporation recognizes any gain or loss realized on distributions in complete liquidation as if the property were sold at its FMV to the shareholder immediately before its distribution.

    a. Gain or loss is computed on an asset-by-asset basis.

    b. FMV of distributed property is treated as not less than related liabilities that the shareholder assumes or to which the property is subject.

    c. Character of amounts recognized depends on the nature of the asset in the hands of the distributing corporation, e.g., Secs. 1245 and 1250.

Corporate Losses

2. A corporation generally recognizes any losses realized on liquidating distributions.

   a. Certain realized losses are not recognized when the shareholder and corporation are related.

      1) A more-than-50% shareholder, actually or constructively, is a typical related distributee.

      2) Applicable distributions are of assets non-pro rata or acquired within 5 years by a contribution to capital or a Sec. 351 exchange.

      3) Permanent disallowance results, even if postcontribution.

   b. Precontribution loss. The amount of a loss inherent on a contribution reduces loss recognized on distribution.

      1) In other words, no loss on assets originally contributed at a loss (either as a capital contribution or by a Sec. 351 exchange) can be recognized on the distribution.

         a) *Loss allowable = Loss on liquidation – Loss on contributed property*

   c. Carryovers. Unused, unexpired NOLs; capital losses; and charitable contribution carryover amounts are lost.

Shareholder Treatment

3. A shareholder treats amounts distributed in complete liquidation as realized in exchange for stock.

   a. Capital recovery to the extent of basis is permitted before recognizing gain or loss.
   b. Holding period will not include that of the liquidated corporation.
   c. Amounts realized include money and the FMV of other distributed property received.

      1) Liabilities assumed or to which property is subject reduce the amount realized.
      2) Allocation of amounts realized to each block of stock is required.

EXAMPLE

Consider a single liquidating distribution to Shareholder R on February 1, 2013, of $70 cash and a car (FMV = $25) subject to a liability of $15. R's amount realized is $80 [$70 + ($25 – $15)].

Block	Shares	Acquired	Basis	Amount Realized	Gain (Loss) Realized
A	1	5/04	$10	$20	$10
B	3	10/10	$90	$60	$(30)

---

   d. When a series of liquidating distributions is made, the shareholder must use the cost recovery method for recognition of gain or loss.

      1) Each payment received is first applied against the basis of the stock.
      2) When basis is exceeded, a gain must be recognized.
   e. Character of recognized gain or loss depends on the nature of each block of the stock in the hands of the shareholder.

EXAMPLE

If R, in the previous example, held the stock for investment, R would recognize LTCG on Block A and STCL on Block B.

---

   f. Basis in distributed property is its FMV but only after gain or loss on its receipt has been recognized.

Reporting

4. A corporation must file an information return (Form 966, *Corporate Dissolution or Liquidation*) reporting adoption of a plan or resolution for its dissolution, or partial or complete liquidation, within 30 days of adoption.

    a. The IRS requires a corporation to file Forms 1099-DIV for each calendar year it makes partial distribution(s) of $600 or more under a plan of complete liquidation.

    b. Expenses incurred in connection with the liquidation are deductible by the dissolved corporation.

    c. A corporation may file Form 4810 with the IRS requesting a prompt assessment of tax liability. If granted, this request limits the time for assessment to 18 months from the date the request was filed.

        1) The period for assessing the tax will not be shortened if the taxpayer

            a) Filed a false return,

            b) Willfully attempted to evade tax,

            c) Did not file a return, or

            d) Omitted from gross income greater than 25% of the amount of gross income stated in the return.

Stop and review! You have completed the outline for this subunit. Study questions 13 through 24 beginning on page 310.

16.3 PARTIAL LIQUIDATION

A noncorporate shareholder treats a distribution as a sale to the extent it is (in redemption) in partial liquidation of the corporation.

1. The corporation making the distribution recognizes gain but not loss.

2. A corporation receiving a distribution that partially liquidates another corporation treats the distribution as a dividend to the extent of E&P of the distributing corporation.

    a. The distributee corporation is eligible for the dividends-received deduction.

3. Partial liquidation refers to contraction of the corporation's business. Focus is not on the shareholders but on genuine reduction in size of the corporation's business.

    a. Partial liquidation must be pursuant to a plan, and the distribution must not be essentially equivalent to a dividend. The partial liquidation must be complete within either

        1) The tax year of plan adoption or
        2) The succeeding tax year.

    b. Pro rata distributions do not preclude partial liquidation sale treatment. Furthermore, shareholders are not required to surrender stock to the corporation.

    c. Safe harbor. Noncorporate shareholders apply partial liquidation sale treatment to distributions received if the following conditions are satisfied:

        1) The corporation ceases conduct of a trade or business that it actively conducted for at least 5 years ending with the date of the distribution.

            a) The distribution must be attributable to the discontinued operations.

        2) Immediately after the distribution, the corporation continues to conduct at least one active trade or business it has conducted for 5 years.

Stop and review! You have completed the outline for this subunit. Study questions 25 through 30 beginning on page 313.

QUESTIONS

16.1 Redemptions

1. Two unrelated individuals, Ward and June, own all the stock of Wally Corporation, which has earnings and profits of $300,000. Because of his inactivity in the business for the last several years, Ward has decided to retire from the business completely and move to Oregon. Accordingly, Wally will redeem all the stock owned by Ward and, in return, Ward will receive a distribution of $450,000. Ward's adjusted basis in the stock is $250,000. What will be the tax effect to Ward?

A. $150,000 capital gain.

B. $300,000 dividend.

C. $400,000 dividend.

D. $200,000 capital gain.

Answer (D) is correct.
    REQUIRED: The tax effect of a redemption to a shareholder.
    DISCUSSION: Under Sec. 302(b)(3), if a corporation redeems all of its stock owned by a shareholder, the redemption is treated as a distribution in partial payment or full payment in exchange for the stock. Since Wally Corporation redeemed all of Ward's stock, the $450,000 distribution is treated as payment for the stock, and any gain is treated as capital gain. The amount of the gain is computed under Sec. 1001 and is the amount by which the distribution exceeds the shareholder's basis in the stock. In this case, the gain is $200,000 ($450,000 distribution – $250,000 basis). Because the stock is a capital asset, the recognized gain is a capital gain. Because the distribution is treated as an exchange for the stock and not as a dividend, the amount of the corporation's earnings and profits is irrelevant. Earnings and profits affect distributions only when those distributions have the character of dividends.
    Answer (A) is incorrect. The gain is reduced by the shareholder's basis in the stock. Answer (B) is incorrect. The gain is reduced by the shareholder's basis in the stock, and the distribution is in redemption of a shareholder's entire interest. Answer (C) is incorrect. The gain is reduced by the shareholder's basis in the stock, and the distribution is in redemption of a shareholder's entire interest.

2. With respect to the redemption of stock, which of the following tests does not establish that the redemption can be treated as an exchange of stock rather than as a dividend?

A. The redemption is substantially disproportionate with respect to the shareholder.

B. The redemption is not substantially equivalent to a dividend.

C. The redemption terminates the shareholder's entire interest in the corporation.

D. The redemption is of stock held by a corporate shareholder and is made in partial liquidation of the redeeming corporation.

Answer (D) is correct.
    REQUIRED: The test that does not establish that the redemption can be treated as an exchange of stock rather than a dividend.
    DISCUSSION: A redemption qualifies for sale or exchange treatment if the redemption is (1) substantially disproportionate, (2) a complete termination of the shareholder's interest, (3) not essentially equivalent to a dividend, (4) a partial liquidation of the distributing corporation in redemption of part or all of a noncorporate shareholder's stock, or (5) made in order to pay death taxes. A redemption of stock held by a noncorporate shareholder in a partial liquidation will receive sale or exchange treatment but not a redemption of stock held by a corporate shareholder.

3. Belle Corporation owns as an investment 10% of the stock of Gaston Corporation, with an adjusted basis of $4,000 and a fair market value of $44,000. Belle uses the Gaston stock to redeem approximately 1%, or $10,000 par value, of its own outstanding stock from unrelated, noncorporate shareholders. As a result of this transaction, Belle must report a gain of

A. $0

B. $2,000

C. $40,000

D. $44,000

Answer (C) is correct.
    REQUIRED: The gain a corporation must report on the redemption of stock with property.
    DISCUSSION: A corporation that distributes property in redemption of its stock generally recognizes gain, but not loss, if it pays all or part of the redemption price by transferring property whose fair market value exceeds its basis to the corporation. Thus, Belle Corporation must recognize the $40,000 gain inherent in the difference between the value of the Gaston stock ($44,000) and its basis ($4,000).
    Answer (A) is incorrect. The corporation must recognize a gain. Answer (B) is incorrect. The corporation's gain does not equal $2,000. Answer (D) is incorrect. The corporation's gain does not equal the fair market value of the property.

4. Gus Corporation, a C corporation, is owned equally by Al, Bill, and Charlie. Their stock basis on December 31 is as follows: Al $20,000, Bill $40,000, and Charlie $40,000. Gus Corporation has earnings and profits of $90,000 at the end of the calendar year and will continue as a viable entity. Al wants to exit the corporation and pursue other interests. He surrenders all his shares and receives $15,000. What are the tax consequences to Al of this complete redemption?

A. $5,000 capital loss.

B. $5,000 capital gain.

C. $15,000 ordinary dividend.

D. None of the answers are correct.

Answer (A) is correct.

REQUIRED: The tax consequences of a complete redemption of shareholder's stock.

DISCUSSION: Under Sec. 302(b)(3), if a corporation redeems all of its stock owned by a shareholder, the redemption is treated as a distribution in part or full payment in exchange for the stock. Since Gus Corporation redeemed all of Al's stock, the $15,000 distribution is treated as payment for the stock, and any loss is treated as capital loss. The amount of the loss is computed under Sec. 1001 and is the amount by which the distribution is less than the shareholder's basis in the stock. Because the distribution is treated as an exchange for the stock and not as a dividend, the amount of the corporation's earnings and profits is irrelevant. Earnings and profits affect distributions only when those distributions have the character of dividends. In this case, the loss is $5,000 ($15,000 distribution – $20,000 basis). Additionally, since the stock is a capital asset, the recognized loss is a capital loss.

Answer (B) is incorrect. The redemption generates a $5,000 loss, not gain. Answer (C) is incorrect. The complete redemption is treated as a payment for the stock, not a dividend. Answer (D) is incorrect. Al will experience a $5,000 capital loss because of his complete redemption.

5. Turbo Corporation distributed land to shareholder Lea in partial liquidation of her interest. At the time of the distribution, the land had an adjusted basis of $80,000 and a fair market value of $125,000. Lea exchanged 90 of 100 shares of Turbo stock for the land. At the time of the partial liquidation, Lea's adjusted basis in the 90 shares was $60,000. Other unrelated shareholders of Turbo own a combined 150 shares outstanding. Just prior to the distribution, Turbo had earnings and profits of $150,000. What are the amounts and the character of income that Turbo Corporation and Lea must recognize on the partial liquidation?

	Turbo	Lea
A.	$0	$65,000 capital gain
B.	$0	$65,000 dividend
C.	$45,000 capital gain	$65,000 capital gain
D.	$45,000 capital gain	$125,000 dividend

Answer (C) is correct.

REQUIRED: The amount and the character of income that a shareholder and a corporation recognize on a partial liquidation.

DISCUSSION: A redemption distribution is substantially disproportionate with respect to a shareholder (and qualifies for capital gains treatment) if, after the redemption, (s)he owns less than 50% of the total combined voting power of all classes of voting stock and his or her percentage of voting stock and ownership percentage of common stock after the redemption are less than 80% of each such stock owned immediately before the redemption. Lea meets these criteria and has $65,000 of capital gain ($125,000 land value – $60,000 stock basis). Turbo has capital gain of $45,000 because a corporation that makes an in-kind distribution of property that has a fair market value ($125,000) that exceeds its basis ($80,000) recognizes gain as if it had sold the property to the shareholder at its fair market value.

Answer (A) is incorrect. The corporation must recognize a gain on the partial liquidation. Answer (B) is incorrect. The redemption is substantially disproportionate with respect to the shareholder. Answer (D) is incorrect. The redemption is substantially disproportionate with respect to the shareholder and is reduced by basis in the stock.

6. Danny owns 35% of Batch Corporation's only class of stock outstanding. His daughter Ann and son-in-law Tony each own 20%. Ann is legally separated from Tony. Danny's father owns 25% of Batch's outstanding stock. What is Ann's percentage of stock ownership under the attribution rules for stock redemption?

A. 55%

B. 75%

C. 80%

D. 100%

Answer (A) is correct.

REQUIRED: The shareholder's percentage of stock ownership under the attribution rules for stock redemption.

DISCUSSION: A shareholder is treated as owning shares owned by certain related parties. Stock owned directly or indirectly by or for a spouse, child, grandchild, or parent is considered to be constructively owned. However, a spouse who is legally separated is not considered a related party. Danny's father constructively owns Ann's shares, but Ann does not constructively own Danny's father's shares. Therefore, Ann is considered to own 55% of Batch's stock (20% personally owned + 35% of father's stock).

Answer (B) is incorrect. A spouse that is legally separated is not a related party for calculating a grandchild's ownership. This is not the same as a grandchild being related for calculating the grandparent's ownership. Answer (C) is incorrect. A grandfather is not a related party. Answer (D) is incorrect. A legally separated spouse and a grandfather are not related parties.

7. Larry, Jane, Robert, and Mary each own 250 shares of XYZ, Inc., for which they paid $100 each. They started XYZ, Inc., this year. Current earnings and profits are $40,000. Which of the following is most true?

A. If XYZ cancels (redeems) 25 shares of each shareholder's stock, the $2,500 paid to each owner will be taxable as a dividend.

B. If Robert redeems all of his stock (and Larry, Jane, and Mary redeem none), the $25,000 Robert receives will not be taxed as a dividend.

C. If XYZ cancels (redeems) 25 shares of each shareholder's stock, the $2,500 paid to each owner will be taxable as a dividend, or if Robert redeems all of his stock (and Larry, Jane, and Mary redeem none), the $25,000 Robert receives will not be taxed as a dividend.

D. None of the answers are correct.

Answer (C) is correct.
REQUIRED: The true statement regarding the effects of liquidation or redemption.
DISCUSSION: The redemption of 25 shares each does not result in a substantially disproportionate redemption. The $2,500 will be a dividend. In addition, Robert's total redemption is treated as an exchange for stock and not as a dividend.
Answer (A) is incorrect. In addition to it being a true statement, under Sec. 302(b)(3), if a corporation redeems all of its stock owned by a shareholder, the redemption is treated as a distribution in part or full payment in exchange for the stock. Since XYZ, Inc., redeemed all of Robert's stock, the $25,000 distribution is treated as payment for the stock, and any gain is treated as capital gain. The amount of the gain is computed under Sec. 1001 and is the amount by which the distribution exceeds the shareholder's basis in the stock.
Because the distribution is treated as being in exchange for the stock and not as a dividend, the amount of the corporation's earnings and profits is irrelevant. Earnings and profits affect distributions only when those distributions have the character of dividends.
Answer (B) is incorrect. In addition to it being a true statement, Sec. 302 determines whether a redemption is considered a distribution equivalent to a dividend or payment for the stock eligible for capital gain or loss treatment. Under Sec. 302(b)(2), a substantially disproportionate redemption qualifies for capital gain or loss treatment. For a redemption to be substantially disproportionate, the shareholder must own less than 50% of all outstanding voting stock immediately after the redemption, and his or her total percentage of ownership must be less than 80% of his or her ownership percentage immediately before the redemption.
Each of the three shareholders owns less than 50% of all outstanding voting stock immediately after the redemption, so the first test is met. However, the percentage of stock owned by each shareholder has not changed as a result of the redemption. Therefore, the second test is not met, and the redemption is not substantially disproportionate. The redemption is considered to be equivalent to a dividend since a meaningful reduction in the shareholders' ownership interests did not occur [Sec. 302(b)(1)].
Answer (D) is incorrect. One of the answers is true.

8. Arnold acquired 10 shares of Klesco, Inc., stock in Year 1 for $50 per share. Klesco, Inc., decided in Year 5 to reacquire all of its outstanding stock, which it did for $200 per share. What amount of capital gain in Year 5 must Arnold report on the redemption of his Klesco, Inc., stock?

A. $0

B. $500

C. $1,500

D. $2,000

Answer (C) is correct.
REQUIRED: The capital gain a shareholder must report from a stock redemption.
DISCUSSION: Under Sec. 302(b)(3), if a corporation redeems all of its stock owned by a shareholder, the redemption is treated as a distribution in part or full payment in exchange for the stock. Since Klesco, Inc., decided to redeem all of Arnold's stock, the $2,000 distribution is treated as a capital gain. The amount of the gain is computed under Sec. 1001 and is the amount by which the distribution exceeds the shareholder's basis in the stock. In this case, the gain is $1,500 ($2,000 distribution – $500 basis). Because the distribution is treated as being in exchange for the stock and not as a dividend, the amount of the corporation's earnings and profits is irrelevant. Earnings and profits affect distributions only when those distributions have the character of dividends.
Answer (A) is incorrect. Arnold realized a gain of $1,500 ($2,000 distribution – $500 basis). If a corporation redeems all of its stock owned by a shareholder, the redemption is treated as a distribution in payment in exchange for the stock (not a dividend). Answer (B) is incorrect. Arnold's basis in the stock is $500. His gain is $1,500 ($2,000 distribution – $500 basis). Answer (D) is incorrect. The $2,000 distribution is reduced by Arnold's basis of $500 for a gain of only $1,500.

9. Wargo Corporation has two equal shareholders, Karen and Bob. Each shareholder owns 10 shares of Wargo stock and has owned the stock for several years. Each share has a $100 basis and a $150 FMV. Wargo, which has sufficient E&P, redeems five shares from each shareholder at the $150 FMV. What income, if any, do Karen and Bob each recognize as a result of the redemption of Wargo Corporation stock?

A. $750 dividend income.

B. $1,500 capital gain.

C. $0

D. $1,500 dividend income.

Answer (A) is correct.

REQUIRED: The treatment of a distribution in redemption of stock.

DISCUSSION: Since the distribution is proportionate among the shareholders, it is not a redemption of stock and is treated as a dividend. Each shareholder would report $750 as dividend income (5 shares × $150 per share).

Answer (B) is incorrect. The distribution is a dividend. Answer (C) is incorrect. There is a dividend income. Answer (D) is incorrect. The combined dividend income is $1,500.

10. Art, Betty, and Cora are equal partners in ABC Partnership. ABC Partnership and Betty are the only two shareholders in Angel, Inc., with direct ownership of 60% and 40%, respectively. Based upon the constructive-ownership rules for stock redemptions, what are ABC's and Betty's percentages of constructive ownership of Angel?

	ABC	Betty
A.	60%	60%
B.	100%	40%
C.	100%	60%
D.	100%	100%

Answer (C) s correct.

REQUIRED: The percentage of stock a taxpayer is considered to own under the constructive-ownership rules.

DISCUSSION: Stock owned by a partnership is considered to be owned proportionately by the partners. Accordingly, Art, Betty, and Cora each own 33.33% of the ABC partnership. ABC owns 60% of the stock of Angel, Inc.; therefore, all of the partners of ABC Partnership constructively own 20% (60% × 33%) of Angel. Betty directly owns 40% of the stock of Angel and constructively owns 20%. All together Betty owns 60% (20% + 40%). Stock owned, directly or indirectly, by a partner shall be considered as owned by the partnership. Therefore, we must consider all of the stock that Betty owns in Angel as being owned by the partnership, resulting in the partnership owning 100% of Angel's stock.

11. Ranger Corporation's only class of stock is owned as follows:

Matthew	40%
Darlene, Matthew's sister	25%
Matthew and Darlene's father	25%
Matthew and Darlene's grandfather	10%

What is Matthew's percentage of stock ownership under the attribution rules for stock redemption?

A. 65%

B. 75%

C. 90%

D. 100%

Answer (A) is correct.

REQUIRED: The shareholder's percentage of stock ownership under the attribution rules for stock redemption.

DISCUSSION: An individual is treated as constructively owning stock owned directly or indirectly by his or her spouse, children, grandchildren, and parents. Thus, Matthew is treated as owning his shares (40%) and his father's shares (25%).

Answer (B) is incorrect. Matthew is not treated as owning the grandfather's stock. Answer (C) is incorrect. Matthew is not treated as owning the sister's stock. Answer (D) is incorrect. Matthew is not treated as owning the sister's and grandfather's stock.

12. A stock redemption is the acquisition by a corporation of its stock from a shareholder. A shareholder who owns all of the stock of a corporation sells back one half of his stock for cash. Assume that the current E&P is greater than the redemption amount. Which of the following statements is true with regard to this stock redemption?

A. This sale back to the corporation of one half will cause no percentage change in the shareholder's ownership.

B. After the redemption the shareholder will own all of the stock in the corporation.

C. The stock redemption resembles a dividend distribution and will be taxed accordingly.

D. All of the answers are correct.

Answer (D) is correct.

REQUIRED: The true statement regarding stock redemptions.

DISCUSSION: Stock is redeemed when a corporation acquires its own stock from a shareholder in exchange for property. The redemption occurs whether or not the stock is canceled, retired, or held as treasury stock. A shareholder is required to treat amounts realized on a redemption (not in liquidation) either as a distribution (a corporate dividend) or as a sale of the stock redeemed. Because the shareholder owns 100% of the stock before and after the redemption, the transaction is a dividend to the extent that the corporation has earnings and profits.

16.2 Complete Liquidation

13. A fiduciary representing a dissolving corporation may request a prompt assessment of tax under Internal Revenue Code section 6501(d). This will limit the time the Internal Revenue Service has to assess additional tax or to begin court action to collect the tax from the date the fiduciary files the request to

A. 6 months.

B. 12 months.

C. 18 months.

D. 24 months.

Answer (C) is correct.
REQUIRED: The time limit for a prompt assessment of tax for a dissolving corporation.
DISCUSSION: Sec. 6501(d) allows a corporation to file Form 4810 with the IRS requesting a prompt assessment of tax liability. If granted, this request limits the time for assessment to 18 months from the date the request was filed.

14. Annual statement Form 1099-DIV must be furnished to recipients of which of the following?

A. Liquidating distributions of $600 or more.

B. Patronage dividends.

C. Both liquidating distributions of $600 or more and patronage dividends.

D. None of the answers are correct.

Answer (A) is correct.
REQUIRED: The situation when a Form 1099-DIV must be provided.
DISCUSSION: A Form 1099-DIV must be provided to recipients who have received dividends (including capital gains dividends) and other distributions on stock of $10 or more, recipients for whom the payer has withheld and paid any foreign tax on dividends and other distributions on stock, recipients for whom the payer has withheld any federal income tax under the backup withholding rules, and recipients for whom the payer has paid $600 or more as part of a liquidation. Patronage dividends are reported on 1099-PATR. Note, the original EA exam did not include "of $600 or more" in the answer choice of liquidating distributions.

15. Which of the following will not shorten the period for assessing the tax when a fiduciary representing a dissolving corporation requests a prompt assessment of tax under Internal Revenue Code section 6501(d) by filing a Form 4810?

A. Where the taxpayer did not report substantial amounts of gross income.

B. Where the taxpayer was filing a final return.

C. Where the taxpayer filed a false return.

D. Both where the taxpayer did not report substantial amounts of gross income and where the taxpayer filed a false return.

Answer (D) is correct.
REQUIRED: The event(s) that will not shorten the period for assessing tax for a dissolving corporation.
DISCUSSION: Under Sec. 6501, the period for assessing the tax will not be shortened if the taxpayer filed a false return, willfully attempted to evade tax, did not file a return, or omitted from gross income greater than 25% of the amount of gross income stated in the return.
Answer (A) is incorrect. A case where the taxpayer did not report substantial amounts of gross income is one of two exceptions to prompt assessment under Sec. 6501. Answer (B) is incorrect. A case where the taxpayer was filing a final return is not an exception under Sec. 6501. Answer (C) is incorrect. A case where the taxpayer filed a false return is one of two exceptions to prompt assessment under Sec. 6501.

16. In Year 1, pursuant to a complete liquidation, Richards Corporation distributes the following to a shareholder: inventory, basis $10,000, FMV $20,000; and land held as an investment, basis $5,000, FMV $40,000. The land is subject to a $30,000 liability. What are the amounts and character of income to be recognized by Richards Corporation?

A. $10,000 ordinary income; $35,000 capital gain.

B. $10,000 ordinary income; $65,000 capital gain.

C. $0 ordinary income; $0 capital gain.

D. $10,000 ordinary income; $5,000 capital gain.

Answer (A) is correct.
REQUIRED: The amounts and character of income to be recognized by Richards Corporation.
DISCUSSION: Sec. 311(b) requires that gain on the distribution of appreciated property be recognized as if the property had been sold. Therefore, Richards Corporation recognizes $10,000 as ordinary income ($20,000 FMV – $10,000 basis) and $35,000 as capital gain ($40,000 FMV – $5,000 basis). The $30,000 liability is irrelevant when considering the corporate gain. If the liability exceeds the FMV of the property, however, the liability amount would be considered the new "selling price" and shareholder basis in the property.
Answer (B) is incorrect. The amount of $65,000 includes the $30,000 liability. Answer (C) is incorrect. Richards Corporation must recognize a gain on appreciated property. Answer (D) is incorrect. The amount of $35,000 must be reported as a capital gain.

17. Lantern Corporation is in the process of dissolving and has filed a request with the IRS for a prompt assessment. Assuming all other requirements are met, if the request is granted, the period within which the IRS may assess a tax liability is shortened to how many months?

A. 24
B. 18
C. 36
D. 12

18. Individual Y owns 55% of Beta Corporation. Five years ago, Y contributed property with an adjusted basis of $20,000 and a fair market value of $8,000 to Beta in a transaction qualifying under Sec. 351. In the current year, Beta adopted a plan of complete liquidation and distributed this same property to Y. At this time, the property had an adjusted basis of $18,000 and a fair market value of $5,000. How much loss will Beta recognize on the distribution?

A. $0
B. $1,000
C. $12,000
D. $13,000

19. Six years ago, Adam purchased 100 shares of Call Corporation stock for $50 per share. During the current year, Call completely liquidated. After paying its liabilities, Call distributed to its shareholders $10,000 in cash and appreciated property sold for $90,000. Adam's portion received a liquidating distribution from Call of $10,000. Adam must report what amount of capital gains income from this distribution?

A. $4,500
B. $5,000
C. $22,500
D. $25,000

20. Vernon receives a truck from Berry Trucking Company as a distribution in complete liquidation. Vernon's basis in the stock of Berry Trucking Company is $2,000. The fair market value of the truck on the date of the distribution is $30,000. There is a $15,000 loan on the truck, which Vernon assumed. What is the basis of the truck to Vernon?

A. $28,000
B. $13,000
C. $15,000
D. $30,000

Answer (B) is correct.
REQUIRED: The amount of time for a prompt assessment of tax by the IRS for a dissolving corporation.
DISCUSSION: Form 4810 states, "The fiduciary representing a dissolving corporation or a decedent's estate may request a prompt assessment of tax under the Internal Revenue Code (IRC) Sec. 6501(d). This will limit the time to 18 months from the date the fiduciary files the request."

Answer (A) is correct.
REQUIRED: The loss recognized in a liquidation on the distribution of recently contributed property to a related shareholder.
DISCUSSION: Normally gain or loss is recognized on a liquidating distribution of assets [Sec. 336(a)]. However, under Sec. 336(d)(1), a loss is not recognized in a liquidation on the distribution of property to a related person (which includes a greater-than-50% shareholder) unless the property is distributed to all shareholders on a pro rata basis and the property was not acquired in a Sec. 351 transaction or contribution to capital during the 5 preceding years (also known as disqualified property). Since the distribution was of property acquired in a Sec. 351 transaction within the 5 preceding years, no loss is recognized on the distribution of the disqualified property to the related person. The fact that the distribution was not pro rata does not affect the ability to recognize the loss.

Answer (B) is correct.
REQUIRED: The shareholder treatment of proceeds received from a complete liquidation.
DISCUSSION: A shareholder treats amounts distributed in complete liquidation as realized in exchange for stock. Capital recovery to the extent of basis is permitted before recognizing gain or loss. Amounts realized include money and the FMV of other distributed property received. Adam should recognize $5,000 of gain ($10,000 value of distribution received – $5,000 basis in stock).
Answer (A) is incorrect. A gain of $5,000 is reported. The value of the distribution received less the basis in the stock is the amount of gain reported. Answer (C) is incorrect. A gain of $5,000 is reported. The value of the distribution received less the basis in the stock is the formula used to calculate the gain income from the distribution. Answer (D) is incorrect. A gain of $5,000 is reported. The value of the distribution received less the basis in the stock is the formula used to calculate the gain income from the distribution.

Answer (D) is correct.
REQUIRED: The basis of property subject to a liability received by a shareholder in a complete liquidation of a corporation.
DISCUSSION: If a shareholder assumes a liability of the liquidating corporation, or receives property that is subject to a liability, then the liability reduces the amount realized by the shareholder, thus reducing the shareholder's gain or increasing the shareholder's loss. Nevertheless, the shareholder's basis for the property is the property's fair market value, in this case $30,000.
Answer (A) is incorrect. The basis does not equal the fair market value less basis of stock. Answer (B) is incorrect. The basis does not equal the fair market value less the loan and the basis of the stock. Answer (C) is incorrect. The basis does not equal the fair market value less the loan.

21. In Year 1, Daniel inherited 100% of Candy Corporation's outstanding stock from his mother. The stock had a fair market value of $250,000 at the date of death and was reflected on Candy's balance sheet as follows:

Cash	$250,000
Capital stock	150,000
Accumulated earnings & profits	100,000

Daniel immediately withdrew $50,000 out of Candy Corporation as a dividend distribution. Later in Year 1, pursuant to a plan of liquidation, Daniel withdrew the remaining $200,000 out of Candy. For Year 1, how much will Daniel be required to report as ordinary dividend income and capital gain or loss?

	Ordinary Dividend	Capital Gain or Loss
A.	$0	$0
B.	$50,000	$(50,000)
C.	$100,000	$(100,000)
D.	$50,000	$(250,000)

Answer (B) is correct.
REQUIRED: The reporting of a complete liquidation.
DISCUSSION: Because Daniel received the stock through inheritance, he takes a stepped-up basis of $250,000 (fair market value at the date of the transferor's death). The $50,000 dividend is ordinary dividend income and does not affect Daniel's basis. Thus, when he liquidated the corporation and received the remaining $200,000, he had a capital loss of $50,000 ($200,000 distribution minus $250,000 basis).
Answer (A) is incorrect. Daniel must report the distributions made by the corporation. Answer (C) is incorrect. The stock basis is stepped up because Daniel received the stock through inheritance. Answer (D) is incorrect. The loss does not equal the basis in the stock.

22. Ann owned two blocks of Lou Corporation stock, which had the following characteristics:

Block	Shares	Acquired	Basis
1	200	6/01/Yr 1	$20,000
2	50	7/01/Yr 2	12,500

Ann's two blocks of stock combined represented 10% of Lou Corporation's outstanding stock. Pursuant to Lou's complete liquidation, Ann received a $50,000 cash distribution on December 1, Year 2, in exchange for her 250 shares. Lou's earnings and profits balance immediately before any liquidating distributions was $50,000. What are the amount and the character of Ann's gain or loss?

A. $50,000 dividend income.

B. $17,500 long-term capital gain.

C. $20,000 long-term capital gain and $2,500 short-term capital loss.

D. No gain or loss.

Answer (C) is correct.
REQUIRED: The amount and the character of gain or loss to be reported as a result of a complete liquidation.
DISCUSSION: Sec. 331 provides capital gain or loss treatment for distributions received by a shareholder in complete liquidation of a corporation. The gain or loss will be long-term or short-term, depending on the length of time the stock has been held (Sec. 1222).
The shareholder's gain or loss is the difference between the amount realized and the basis in the stock. The amount realized by Ann is $200 per share ($50,000 distribution ÷ 250 shares owned). The sale of Block 1 produces a gain of $20,000 [200 shares × ($200 selling price – $100 per share basis)]. The gain is long-term because the stock was held for more than 1 year. The sale of Block 2 produces a loss of $2,500 [50 shares × ($250 per share basis – $200 per share selling price)]. The loss is short-term because the stock was held less than 1 year.
Answer (A) is incorrect. The figure of $50,000 is the amount of the distribution, not the amount of the gain (loss). Answer (B) is incorrect. The gain and loss should be allocated to the different blocks of stock. The amounts should not be aggregated ($50,000 distribution – $32,500 total basis). Answer (D) is incorrect. A gain and a loss are recognized because the transaction is treated as a sale.

23. When Paul formed his corporation 5 years ago, he invested $5,000 in corporate stock. In the current year, when his basis in the stock was $10,000, he liquidated his corporation receiving $15,000 cash. How should Paul report this disposal on his return?

A. No reporting required for liquidating distributions.

B. Report $10,000 long-term capital gain.

C. Report $5,000 long-term capital gain.

D. Report $5,000 ordinary income.

Answer (C) is correct.
REQUIRED: The correct reporting of a complete liquidation to its sold shareholder.
DISCUSSION: Sec. 331 provides capital gain or loss treatment for distributions received by a shareholder in complete liquidation of a corporation. The gain or loss will be long-term or short-term depending on the length of time the stock has been held (Sec. 1222). The shareholder's gain or loss is the difference between the amount realized and the basis in the stock. Therefore, Paul will realize a long-term capital gain of $5,000 ($15,000 – $10,000) because the stock was held for 5 years.
Answer (A) is incorrect. Reporting is required for the liquidation. Answer (B) is incorrect. The long-term capital gain is the difference between the amount realized and the basis at liquidation, not creation. Answer (D) is incorrect. The gain is characterized as a capital gain, not ordinary income.

24. In Year 1, Mark purchased 100 shares of Roman, Inc., for $10 per share. In Year 5, Roman completely liquidated and distributed $8,000 to Mark. Mark must report income from this distribution as

A. Ordinary other income.

B. Dividends.

C. Capital gains.

D. Return of capital.

Answer (C) is correct.

REQUIRED: The proper shareholder treatment of gains realized from liquidation of a corporation.

DISCUSSION: A shareholder treats amounts distributed in complete liquidation as realized in exchange for stock. Capital recovery to the extent of basis is permitted before recognizing gain or loss. Holding period will not include that of the liquidated corporation. Capital gains treatment is afforded a complete liquidation. The character of the recognized gain or loss depends on the nature of each block of the stock in the hands of the shareholder.

Answer (A) is incorrect. The liquidation gain is a capital gain, not ordinary income. Answer (B) is incorrect. The liquidation gain is a capital gain, not dividends. Answer (D) is incorrect. The liquidation gain is a capital gain.

16.3 Partial Liquidation

25. Oak Corporation had earnings and profits of $500,000 before distributions. Due to economic conditions, Oak, in partial liquidation, distributed land having an adjusted basis to Oak of $135,000 and a fair market value of $150,000 to Mr. Brown for 95% of his interest in Oak Corporation. Mr. Brown's adjusted basis in the stock at the time of the distribution was $180,000. What is the amount of Oak Corporation's recognized gain or loss?

A. $(45,000)

B. $(30,000)

C. $0

D. $15,000

Answer (D) is correct.

REQUIRED: The amount of gain or loss recognized by the corporation when it distributes property in a partial liquidation.

DISCUSSION: If a corporation makes a distribution of property to a noncorporate shareholder in partial liquidation, the distribution is treated as being in exchange for stock. Since the corporation makes a distribution of property whose fair market value ($150,000) exceeds its basis ($135,000), the corporation will recognize a gain of $15,000 as if it had sold the property to the shareholder at its fair market value.

26. Rachel purchased 100 shares of Comet Corporation stock for $500 in Year 1. In Year 4, Rachel received $5,000 in a distribution from the partial liquidation of Comet Corporation. On her personal Year 4 income tax return, Rachel must report income from this transaction as

A. Dividends.

B. Capital gains.

C. Other.

D. None of the answers are correct.

Answer (B) is correct.

REQUIRED: The character of distribution from a partial liquidation.

DISCUSSION: Sec. 302(b)(4) allows noncorporate shareholders who receive redemptions in partial liquidation to treat the distribution as payment for their stock. Any gain on the redemption is eligible for capital gain treatment.

Answer (A) is incorrect. A corporation, not a noncorporate shareholder, that receives a distribution in redemption in partial liquidation of another corporation treats the distribution as a dividend to the extent of E&P of the distributing corporation. Answer (C) is incorrect. A noncorporate shareholder must report the income as capital gains. Answer (D) is incorrect. Rachel must report income from this transaction as capital gains.

27. Ivana Dolla received property with a fair market value of $60,000 and an adjusted basis of $33,000 from Candid Corporation in partial liquidation. Candid's earnings and profits for the year prior to the distribution were $250,000. Ms. Dolla's basis in the stock she exchanged was $44,000. What is the amount of Ms. Dolla's recognized gain?

A. $11,000

B. $16,000

C. $27,000

D. $60,000

Answer (B) is correct.

REQUIRED: The amount of gain recognized by a noncorporate shareholder in a partial liquidation.

DISCUSSION: Under Sec. 302(b)(4), a redemption of an interest held by a noncorporate shareholder made in partial liquidation of the corporation is treated as a distribution in exchange for the stock. The shareholder will treat any gain on the redemption as a capital gain. The amount of the gain is computed under Sec. 1001. Under Sec. 301(b)(1), the amount of the distribution is the fair market value of the property. Ms. Dolla will recognize a gain of $16,000 on the distribution ($60,000 fair market value of the distributed property – $44,000 basis in the stock).

Answer (A) is incorrect. The gain is not the difference between the adjusted basis of the stock and the adjusted basis of the property. Answer (C) is incorrect. The gain is not the difference between the fair market value of the property and the adjusted basis of the property. Answer (D) is incorrect. The gain does not equal the fair market value of the property.

28. Which of the following statements is true in order for a distribution of corporate assets to be treated as being in exchange for stock in a partial liquidation of a corporation?

A. A distribution must be essentially equivalent to a dividend.

B. A distribution must occur in the taxable year the plan is adopted.

C. A distribution of corporate assets to a corporate shareholder is treated as being in exchange for stock.

D. A distribution of corporate assets is treated as an exchange for stock in a partial liquidation of a corporation, whether or not the stock is actually surrendered.

Answer (D) is correct.
   REQUIRED: The true statement regarding an exchange for stock in a partial liquidation of a corporation.
   DISCUSSION: A distribution of corporate assets is treated as an exchange for stock in a partial liquidation of a corporation, regardless of whether the stock is actually surrendered.
   Answer (A) is incorrect. A distribution must not be essentially equivalent to a dividend. Answer (B) is incorrect. The distribution can occur in a year after the plan is adopted. Answer (C) is incorrect. The partial liquidation treatment applies only to noncorporate shareholders.

29. Which of the following is not a requirement for a distribution to be treated as a partial liquidation of a corporation?

A. The distribution is not essentially equivalent to a dividend, which is determined at the shareholder level rather than at the corporate level.

B. The distribution is attributable to the distributing corporation's ceasing to conduct a qualifying trade or business that was actively conducted throughout the 5-year period ending on the date of the redemption.

C. The distribution is pursuant to a plan and occurs within the taxable year in which the plan is adopted or within the succeeding taxable year.

D. All of the answers would be treated as a distribution in partial liquidation of a corporation.

Answer (A) is correct.
   REQUIRED: The statement that is not a requirement for a distribution to be treated as a partial liquidation of a corporation.
   DISCUSSION: The determination of whether a distribution is not essentially equivalent to a dividend is made at the corporate level. The distribution must be the result of a bona fide contraction of the corporation's business. A distribution satisfies the "not essentially equivalent to a dividend" standard if it meets the safe harbor rule under Sec. 302(e)(2).
   Answer (B) is incorrect. A distribution must be attributable to the distributing corporation's ceasing to conduct a qualifying trade or business that was actively conducted throughout the 5-year period ending on the date of the redemption for it to be treated as a partial liquidation of a corporation. Answer (C) is incorrect. A distribution must be pursuant to a plan and occur within the taxable year in which the plan is adopted or within the succeeding taxable year for it to be treated as a partial liquidation of a corporation. Answer (D) is incorrect. One of the statements is not a requirement for a distribution to be treated as a partial liquidation of a corporation.

30. With respect to a partial liquidation under Sec. 302(b)(4), which of the following statements are false?

1. The redemption must be part of a plan.

2. The shareholder may be a corporation.

3. The redemption may be pro rata.

4. The distribution may not be made in the year after the plan was adopted.

A. 1 and 2.

B. 1 and 3.

C. 2 and 4.

D. 3 and 4.

Answer (C) is correct.
   REQUIRED: The false statements regarding the partial liquidation of a corporation.
   DISCUSSION: The redemption must be part of a plan, and the redemption may be pro rata. However, a shareholder that is a corporation does not qualify for partial liquidation treatment. Furthermore, a distribution may be made in the year the plan is adopted or in the succeeding tax year.
   Answer (A) is incorrect. The redemption must be part of a plan. Also, the distribution can be made in the year after the plan was adopted. Answer (B) is incorrect. The distribution can be made in the year after the plan was adopted and that the shareholder may be a corporation. It is true that the redemption must be part of a plan and that the redemption may be pro rata. Answer (D) is incorrect. It is not true that the shareholder may be a corporation, but it is true that the redemption may be pro rata.

Use the additional questions in Gleim **EA Test Prep** to create Practice Exams that emulate Prometric!

STUDY UNIT SEVENTEEN
S CORPORATIONS

(13 pages of outline)

An S corporation is generally not subject to a federal tax on its income. The corporation's items of income, loss, deduction, and credit are passed through to its shareholders on a per-day and per-share basis. Each shareholder is taxed on his or her share of the S corporation's income as it is earned. Distributions of cash or property generally are not income to its shareholders.

17.1 ELIGIBILITY AND ELECTION

A corporation is treated as an S corporation only for those days for which each specific eligibility requirement is met and the required election is effective.

Eligibility

1. Eligibility depends on the nature of the corporation, its shareholders, and its stock.

   a. An S corporation must have only one class of stock.

      1) One class of stock means that the outstanding shares of the corporation must be identical as to the rights of the holders in the profits and in the assets of the corporation.

         a) Variation in voting rights of that one class of stock is permitted.

      2) Rights to profits and assets on liquidation must be identical.

      3) Debt may be treated as a disqualifying second class of stock.

   b. The number of shareholders may not exceed 100. Related taxpayers and their estates are considered a single shareholder for this purpose.

      1) A husband and wife are considered a single shareholder for this purpose.

      2) Family members in a six-generation range are also considered one shareholder.

      3) A nonresident alien (NRA) may not own any shares.

      4) Each shareholder must be an individual, an estate (including estates of individuals in bankruptcy), or a qualified trust.

         a) Certain small business trusts and tax-exempt organizations can be shareholders.

         b) Partnerships, corporations, and nonresident aliens may not be shareholders.

         NOTE: Single-member LLCs are not partnerships or corporations. However, they may elect corporation status.

         c) Charitable Remainder Unitrusts and Charitable Remainder Annuity Trusts are not eligible to be shareholders.

        5)   The following is a list of qualified trusts that are allowed as shareholders of an S corporation:

             a)   A trust, all of which is treated as owned by an individual who is a citizen or resident of the United States.

             b)   A trust that was described in a) immediately before the death of the deemed owner and that continues in existence after such death.

                  i)   This provision applies for only a 2-year period beginning on the day of the deemed owner's death.

             c)   A trust with respect to stock transferred to it pursuant to the terms of a will.

                  i)   The 2-year period begins on the day the stock was transferred.

             d)   A trust created primarily to exercise the voting power of stock transferred to it. This shall not apply to any foreign trust.

             e)   An electing small business trust.

    c.   The corporation must be domestic and eligible.

        1)   Ineligible corporations include insurance companies and financial institutions, such as banks that use the reserve method of bad debts.

    d.   S corporations can own C corporations or Qualified Subchapter S Subsidiaries (QSSS).

        1)   A QSSS is an electing domestic corporation and is 100% owned by an S corporation parent.

             a)   The IRS now refers to a QSSS as a QSub.

        2)   A C corporation cannot own shares in an S corporation.

Election

2.   An eligible corporation must make the election for S corporation status.

    a.   All shareholders at the time the election is made must file a consent.

        1)   A shareholder's consent is binding and may not be withdrawn after a valid election is made by the corporation unless the shareholders vote to terminate the election.

        2)   Each person who is a shareholder at the time of the election must consent by signing Form 2553, *Election by a Small Business Corporation*.

        3)   In addition, each person who was a shareholder at any time during the part of the tax year before the election is made must also consent.

        4)   If any former shareholders do not consent, the election is considered made for the following year.

    b.   Election made within the first 2 months and 15 days of the beginning of the corporation's tax year is effective from the first day of that tax year.

    c.   Election made after the first 2 months and 15 days of the corporation's tax year will become effective on the first day of the following tax year.

    d.   The IRS can treat a late-filed election as having been timely filed if a determination is made that reasonable cause existed for a corporation's failure to file the election in a timely manner.

    e.   The IRS can waive the effect of an invalid election resulting from a corporation's failing to qualify as an S corporation and/or failing to obtain the necessary shareholder consents.

    f.   To make the election, the corporation must file Form 2553.

Late S Corporation Elections

3. Rev. Proc. 2007-62 provides a simplified method to request relief for late S corporation elections.

   a. The new method streamlines the process and allows submission of Form 2553, along with the business Form 1120S for its first year.

   b. An entity may request relief if it satisfies several requirements:

      1) It failed to qualify as an S corporation solely because it failed to timely file a Form 2553, *Election by a Small Business Corporation*, with the correct IRS campus;

      2) It has reasonable cause for failing to timely file;

      3) It has not filed a tax return for the first year for which the election is intended;

      4) The application for relief is filed no later than 6 months after the due date of the tax return (excluding extensions) for the first year of the election; and

      5) No taxpayer (including the S corporation shareholders) has reported inconsistently with the S corporation status on any affected return.

Termination

4. Upon the occurrence of a terminating event, an S corporation becomes a C corporation.

   a. The IRS may waive termination.

      1) The terminating event must be inadvertent and corrected within a reasonable time.

   b. An S corporation election is terminated by any of the following:

      1) An effective revocation. Shareholders collectively holding more than 50% of the outstanding shares of stock on the day of the revocation (voting and nonvoting) must consent.

         a) In order for the revocation to be effective as of the first day of the current tax year, the election must be made within the first 2 months and 15 days unless a prospective date is selected.

      2) Any eligibility requirement not being satisfied on any day.

      3) Passive investment income (PII) termination.

   c. The termination is effective as of the date the disqualifying event, other than a PII termination, occurs.

   d. PII termination occurs when, for 3 consecutive tax years, the corporation has both Subchapter C E&P on the last day and PII that is greater than 25% of gross receipts.

      1) An S corporation does not have E&P unless it was formerly a C corporation or acquired E&P in a tax-free reorganization, e.g., a merger.

      2) Gross receipts are gross receipts of the S corporation for the tax year reduced by capital losses (other than on stock and securities) to the extent of capital gains.

      3) PII is generally the total amount received or accrued from investments, as opposed to operations, with some adjustments.

         a) PII consists of gross receipts from dividends, interest, royalties, rents, and sales and exchanges of stock and securities, reduced by

            i) Losses on sales or exchanges of stock and securities to the extent of gains thereon

               - For tax years beginning after May 25, 2007, receipts from sales and exchanges of stock and securities will not be considered PII.

        ii)   Interest on accounts receivable (notes) for inventory sold in the ordinary course of trade or business

        iii)   Rents from a lease under which significant services are rendered to the lessee (those not customarily rendered)

      b)   Interest includes tax-exempt interest

    4)   Termination is effective at the end of the tax year.

  e.   After revocation or termination of an election, a new election cannot be effectively made for 5 years without the consent of the IRS.

Accounting Method

5.   An S corporation is not required to use the accrual method.

  a.   Accounting method election is generally made by the S corporation.

  b.   Shareholders, however, personally elect

    1)   Credit or a deduction for foreign income taxes

    2)   Percentage or cost depletion for oil and gas properties

    3)   Treatment of mining exploration expenditures

Tax Year

6.   An S corporation generally must adopt a calendar tax year.

  a.   With IRS consent, it may adopt a fiscal year (if it establishes a valid business purpose for doing so) that

    1)   Does not result in deferral of income to shareholders but

    2)   Coincides with a natural business year.

      a)   A natural business year may end with or after the end of the peak period of a cyclical business.

  b.   An S corporation that deposits the equivalent amount of the deferred tax may elect a fiscal year under Sec. 444.

    1)   A new S corporation is limited to no more than 3 months' deferral of income to its shareholders.

    2)   An existing S corporation may continue to use the fiscal year previously adopted.

  c.   To change its tax year, other than by a Sec. 444 election, an S corporation should file Form 1128 by the 15th day of the 2nd month of the new tax year.

  d.   A Sec. 444 election may be made on Form 2553 when the corporation elects S corporation status or, if subsequent to the election, by filing Form 8716.

  e.   A Sec. 444 election may be terminated by filing a short-year return and writing "Sec. 444 election terminated" across the top.

  f.   When S status is terminated and creates a short year, nonseparately computed income is allocated on a pro rata basis unless certain exceptions apply or an election is made.

Administration

7.   The tax treatment of S corporation items of income, loss, deduction, and credit is determined at the corporate level.

  a.   The S corporation files a tax return (Form 1120S).

  b.   Each shareholder must report his or her pro rata share of items on his or her personal tax return, similar to a partnership, consistent with the corporate return, unless (s)he notifies the IRS of the inconsistency.

  c.   Administrative and judicial proceedings to determine proper treatment of items are unified at the level of the S corporation.

    1)   Shareholders are notified and given the opportunity to participate.

EXAMPLE

Compliance Corporation is a calendar-year S corporation. Compliance has two shareholders: Shelly, with a year end of June 30 of the current year, and Julie, with a year end of December 31 of the current year. Because Julie is a calendar-year taxpayer, she will report any current-year income from Compliance on her current-year return. Shelly, on the other hand, will report any current-year income from Compliance on her return for the following year.

Stop and review! You have completed the outline for this subunit. Study questions 1 through 8 beginning on page 328.

17.2 OPERATIONS

Governance and Exempt Taxes

Provisions that govern taxation of C corporations also govern taxation of S corporations, unless a specific exception applies. S corporations are expressly exempt from the following taxes:

- Corporate income tax
- Alternative minimum tax (AMT)
- Accumulated earnings tax (AET)
- Personal holding company (PHC) tax

Pro Rata Share and Separately Stated Items

1. The items of income, deduction (including losses), and credit of an S corporation are reported by the corporation.

   a. A shareholder is required to take the pro rata share of items passed through into account in computing the shareholder's personal taxable income for his or her tax year within which the tax year of the S corporation (in which the S corporation accounted for and reported the items) ended.

EXAMPLE

Super, Inc., an S corporation, properly reported non-separately stated net income from operations of $100,000 for its tax year ending November 30, 2013. Steve, a calendar-year taxpayer who owns 5% of the shares of Super, Inc., must include $5,000 of ordinary income in his tax return for 2013, which is due on or before April 15, 2014.

---

2. S corporation items of income, deduction, and credit, which could alter the tax liability of shareholders if taken into account by them on their personal returns, are required to be stated (and are passed through) separately. Separately stated items include

   a. Sec. 1231 gains and losses
   b. Net short-term capital gains and losses
   c. Net long-term capital gains and losses
   d. Dividends
   e. Charitable contributions
   f. Taxes paid to a foreign country or to a U.S. possession
   g. Tax-exempt interest and related expense
   h. Investment income and related expense
   i. Amounts previously deducted (e.g., bad debts)
   j. Real estate activities
   k. Sec. 179 deduction (immediate expensing of new business equipment)
   l. Credits
   m. Deductions disallowed in computing S corporation income

3. Items not required to be separately stated (e.g., organizational costs) are combined at the corporate level, and a net amount of ordinary income or loss is passed through to shareholders.

4.   A shareholder's Sec. 179 deduction is subject to limits. For 2013, the maximum Sec. 179 deduction is $500,000.

a.   If the cost of Sec. 179 property placed in service during the year exceeds $2 million, the maximum deduction limit must be reduced by the amount of cost that exceeds $2 million.

b.   The maximum deduction limit is applied to each taxpayer, not each separate business.

5.   If an S corporation makes a contribution of property to a charity, each shareholder reduces his or her basis in the stock of the S corporation by his or her pro rata share of the AB of the contributed property.

EXAMPLE

The S corporation contributed a capital asset held long term to a charity. The basis of the asset was $12,000, and the fair market value was $20,000. The sole shareholder has a $20,000 charitable contribution and reduces basis in the stock by $12,000.

6.   Shareholders (who are individuals) may elect to ratably deduct the expenses incurred during the tax year for

a.   Research and experimentation costs (over a 10-year period)

b.   Mining exploration and development costs (over a 10-year period)

c.   Increasing the circulation of a newspaper, magazine, or periodical (over a 3-year period)

d.   Intangible drilling costs (over a 5-year period)

7.   The amount of each item that each shareholder takes into account is computed on a per-day and then a per-share basis.

a.   A shareholder's holding period does not include the date of acquisition and does include the date of disposition.

1)   All allocations are made on a per-share, per-day basis.

EXAMPLE

Axel transfers 100 shares of GNR Corp., an S corporation, to fellow shareholder Duff on March 14, Year 1. Therefore, Axel is allotted 73 days of ownership (January 1 – March 14) amounting to 20% (73 days/365 days) of net income from the 100 shares. Duff will receive the other 80% (292 days/365 days) of net income from the 100 shares.

b.   Upon a termination of a shareholder's interest during the tax year, an election is available to allocate items according to the books and records of the corporation (its accounting methods) instead of by daily proration.

8.   Pro rata shares of S corporation items passed through may be reallocated by the IRS among shareholders who are members of the same family.

a.   Distributive shares must reflect reasonable compensation for services or capital furnished to the corporation by family members.

b.   The IRS may disregard a stock transfer (by gift or sale) motivated primarily by tax avoidance, e.g., as evidenced by retention of control over the stock.

9.   The shareholder characterizes each item (e.g., long-term capital gain) as the corporation would.

10. A person who directly or by attribution owns more than 2% of the stock of an S corporation (voting power or amount) on any day during its tax year is treated as not being an employee entitled to employee benefits (i.e., they are partners, not employees).

a.   The S corporation must treat an amount paid for fringe benefits as deductible compensation, and the shareholder must include the amount in gross income.

b.   This rule does not apply to pension and profit-sharing plans.

Debt Discharge

11. Ordinarily, a taxpayer realizes income when indebtedness is forgiven or otherwise canceled. However, if the discharge of debt occurs in a bankruptcy case, when the taxpayer is insolvent, or when the discharge of indebtedness is with respect to qualified real property business indebtedness, the income realized upon the discharge is excluded from income, and the amount excluded is applied to reduce the tax attributes of the taxpayer, including any net operating loss (NOL) of the taxpayer.

    a. Income from the discharge of indebtedness of an S corporation that is excluded from the S corporation's income is not taken into account as an item of income by any shareholder. As a result, it does not increase the basis of any shareholder's stock in the corporation.

Carryovers

12. Carryovers (e.g., NOL) between S and C corporations are not permitted. This rule applies to corporations that change their status from C to S or from S to C.

    NOTE: Do not confuse this rule with the carryover rules for built-in gains tax explained in Subunit 17.4.

Stock Basis

13. Generally, if a shareholder purchases stock, the shareholder's original basis in the stock is its cost.

    a. If a shareholder receives stock in exchange for property, the basis is the same as the property's basis.

    b. If a shareholder lends money to the S corporation, the basis is usually the amount of the loan.

    c. If a shareholder guarantees a third-party loan to an S corporation, the loan does not increase the shareholder's basis.

        1) If, however, the shareholder makes payments on the loan, the payments increase the shareholder's basis.

        2) The shareholder receives basis if the shareholder is the primary signer on the note and the S corporation is the guarantor.

14. Almost every transaction of an S corporation affects shareholder basis. The adjusted basis of the shareholder's stock is calculated at year end with increases for the shareholder's pro rata share of the following:

    a. All income items of the S corporation, including tax-exempt income, that are separately stated

    b. Any non-separately stated income of the S corporation

    c. The amount of the deduction for depletion (other than oil and gas) that is more than the basis of the property being depleted

---

EXAMPLE

The taxpayer's basis in the S corporation is $12,000 at the beginning of the year. The corporation has ordinary income of $6,000, tax-exempt interest of $2,000, and a long-term capital gain of $1,500. The taxpayer's basis will be increased by $9,500 ($6,000 + $2,000 + $1,500) to $21,500 at the end of the year.

---

15. An exception to the rules concerning increases to shareholder pro rata share is discharged debt that is excluded from the S corporation's income. The income does not flow through to any shareholder or increase any shareholder's basis in the S corporation.

16. The adjusted basis of the shareholder's stock must also be decreased by the shareholder's pro rata share of the following:

    a. Distributions by the S corporation that were not included in income (this is done before determining the allowable loss deduction)

    b. All separately stated loss and deduction items

    c. Any non-separately stated loss of the S corporation

    d. Any expenses of the S corporation that are not deductible in figuring its taxable income or are not properly capitalized

    e. The shareholder's deduction for depletion of oil and gas property held by the S corporation to the extent it is not more than the shareholder's share of the adjusted basis of the property

---

EXAMPLE

The taxpayer's basis at the beginning of the year is $22,000. The taxpayer withdraws $16,000 during the year, and the corporation has an ordinary loss of $9,000. Basis in the corporation is first reduced by the $16,000 distribution to $6,000. Only $6,000 of the loss is deductible by the shareholder, limited to basis.

---

17. The basis is not reduced below zero. After basis in the shareholder's S corporation stock has been reduced to zero, the shareholder's basis in debt of the S corporation to that shareholder is reduced (but not below zero) by his or her share of items of loss and deduction.

    a. In a subsequent tax year, items passed through must restore the basis in the debt before basis in the stock.

    b. Limit. A shareholder's share of loss and deduction items in excess of basis in the debt is not deductible.

        1) The excess is suspended and carried over indefinitely. It may be deducted in a subsequent tax year in which basis is restored to debt or to stock.

EXAMPLE

If the taxpayer's basis in the corporation is made up of $19,500 stock basis and $2,500 debt basis, the stock basis is reduced to $3,500 by the distribution and then to zero by the loss pass-through. Next, the loan basis is reduced to zero by the loss pass-through, with $3,000 of loss carried forward ($9,000 – $3,500 – $2,500).

At-Risk Rules

18. At-risk rules are applied at the shareholder level.

    a. Any excess of each shareholder's pro rata share of passed-through losses for the tax year over his or her amount at risk at the close of his or her tax year is not deductible in the current tax year.

        1) It is suspended and carried forward indefinitely until the shareholder's amount at risk with regard to the particular activity has increased.

    b. Each shareholder's at-risk amount equals, basically, the sum of the following:

        1) Money and the adjusted basis of property contributed to the corporation (to the extent unencumbered)

        2) Amounts borrowed and lent to the corporation to the extent the shareholder has personal liability for repayment or (s)he has pledged as security for repayment property not used in the activity (of the corporation)

            a) However, it does not include other debts of the corporation to third parties, even if the repayment is guaranteed by the shareholder.

            b) The shareholder's amount at risk is increased or decreased by the shareholder's pro rata share of passed-through income and deduction (tax-exempt related also) and by distributions to the shareholder.

    c.   The shareholder's basis in his or her stock and debt of the corporation is reduced (subject to prior application of the basis loss limitation) even if current deductibility of the loss is prohibited by the at-risk rules.

Passive Activity Loss Rules

19. If the S corporation engages in rental activity or if a shareholder does not materially participate (even if the S corporation materially participates) in the trade or business conducted by the corporation, current deductibility of any losses passed through is limited at the shareholder level to passive activity income.

    a.   A shareholder's amount at risk must be reduced by the full amount allowable as a current deduction after application of the at-risk rules, even if part of it must be suspended (i.e., disallowed as a current deduction) by the passive loss rules.

20. If the S corporation's total receipts and its total assets at the end of the year are less than $250,000, the corporation is not required to complete the balance sheet and the reconciliation of income per book with income per return.

21. An S corporation's tax return is due by the 15th day of the 3rd month after the end of the corporation's tax year. An application for an extension of an S corporation tax return is filed on Form 7004. The extension is for 6 months after the original due of the return.

Failure to File Penalty

22. The penalty is imposed in the amount of the number of persons who were shareholders during any part of the year, multiplied by $195 for each of up to 12 months (including a portion of one) that the return was late or incomplete.

Stop and review! You have completed the outline for this subunit. Study questions 9 through 20 beginning on page 330.

17.3 DISTRIBUTIONS

These include nonliquidating and liquidating distributions of money or other property but not of the S corporation's own stock or obligations. The amount of a particular distribution is the sum of any money plus the FMV of property distributed.

AAA, OAA, PTI

1. S corporations maintain records for each shareholder referred to as accumulated adjustments account (AAA), other adjustments account (OAA), and previously taxed income accounts (PTI accounts).

    a.   These records, together with a shareholder's basis in his or her stock and any Subchapter C earnings and profits (E&P) in the corporation, are used to determine the manner in which shareholders must treat distributions of property from the S corporation for tax purposes.

    b.   Note that AAA, OAA, and PTI records and information are needed by S corporations only for purposes of helping shareholders determine taxability of distributions when the S corporation has E&P.

    c.   The AAA represents the current cumulative balance of all the separately stated items and non-separately stated items (ordinary) of the S corporation.

        1) AAA adjustments parallel those made to basis for separately and non-separately stated items.

            a) It is calculated without regard to any net negative adjustments (excess of losses and deductions over income and gains).

            b) AAA is not affected by any transactions related to when it was a C corporation (i.e., federal income tax).

        2)   Expenditures that are not deductible by the S corporation decrease basis in stock and the AAA.

             a)   Charitable contributions pass through to the shareholder and reduce stock basis. For 2013, the reduction of basis is equal to AB of contributed property rather than FMV.

        3)   Adjustment is not made to the AAA for tax-exempt income (which increases basis) or nondeductible expenses related thereto (which reduce basis).

             a)   These adjustments are made to OAA.

        4)   The AAA balance can be reduced below zero. (Basis may not.)

    d.   The OAA represents a cumulative balance of tax-exempt interest earned and life insurance proceeds, reduced by expenses incurred in earning it.

    e.   The PTI account represents a balance of undistributed net income on which the shareholders were already taxed prior to 1983.

    f.   Subchapter C E&P. An S corporation does not have E&P unless it was formerly a C corporation or acquired E&P in a tax-free reorganization, e.g., a merger.

        1)   Subchapter C E&P are not adjusted for any S corporation items of income (or loss, deduction, or credit) passed through to shareholders.

2.   **Distributions of Property**

    a.   An S corporation recognizes gain realized on the distribution of appreciated property (FMV > basis).

        1)   The amount and character of the gain and its treatment are determined as if the distributed property were sold to the shareholder at its FMV.

             a)   Ordinary income results if the property is depreciable in the hands of a more-than-50% shareholder.

        2)   The gain is passed through pro rata to each shareholder, and the shareholder's basis in his or her stock and the AAA is increased by his or her shares as if the S corporation had sold the property.

             a)   The distributee shareholder must determine the proper treatment of the distribution.

EXAMPLE

The S corporation sells an investment asset with a basis of $15,000 for $23,000. The corporation reports an $8,000 gain, which flows through to the shareholders.

---

    b.   When loss property (basis > FMV) is distributed, no loss may be recognized by the S corporation.

        1)   No loss is passed through to the shareholders.

             a)   Each shareholder must reduce the basis in his or her stock in the S corporation and take a FMV basis in the property distributed.

             b)   The distributee shareholder must determine the proper treatment of the distribution.

        2)   Sale to a non-related party instead of distribution results in pass-through of loss.

EXAMPLE

The S corporation has a capital asset with a basis of $7,000 and a FMV of $5,000, which it distributes to the sole shareholder. The corporation has a nondeductible loss of $2,000. The shareholder reduces basis by $7,000 and has a $5,000 basis in the asset. If the corporation sold the asset and distributed the proceeds, the shareholder would have a $2,000 deductible loss.

---

c. An S corporation is not required to recognize gain on the liquidating distributions of certain installment obligations.

1) The shareholder treats each payment as a passed-through item from the S corporation.

Shareholder Treatment

3. Shareholder treatment of distributions from the S corporation is determined at the end of the S corporation's tax year. The AAA, OAA, basis in shareholders' stock, and basis in corporate-shareholder debt must be adjusted for the S corporation's items of income, deduction, etc., for the entire tax year before determining the proper treatment by the shareholders for the distributions.

a. S corporations with no E&P. Shareholder treatment of distributions is straightforward when the S corporation has no Subchapter C E&P.

1) That portion of distributions that does not exceed the basis in the shareholder's stock in the S corporation is treated as tax-free return of capital.

2) Excess over basis is treated as gain on sale of the stock.

a) The character depends on the nature of the stock in the hands of the shareholder and his or her holding period.

b. If there are Subchapter C E&P, the distribution is first treated as return of capital (tax-free) to the extent of the shareholder's AAA balance and then to PTI (up to any basis in the shareholder's stock).

1) Excess distribution beyond AAA and PTI is dividend income to the extent of Subchapter C E&P in the corporation.

2) Excess distribution beyond Subchapter C E&P is return of capital to the extent of OAA.

3) Excess distribution beyond OAA is return of capital to the extent of any remaining basis in the stock.

4) Any excess distribution over remaining basis distributed is treated as gain from the sale of the stock.

S Corporation without C Corporation E&P

Shareholder Distribution	Tax Result
To extent of basis in stock	Not subject to tax; reduces basis in stock
In excess of basis of stock	Taxed as capital gain

S Corporation with C Corporation E&P

Shareholder Distribution	Tax Result
To extent of AAA	Not subject to tax; reduces AAA and basis in stock
To extent of PTI	Already taxed previously; reduces basis in stock
To extent of C corporation E&P	Taxed as a dividend; does not reduce basis in stock
To extent of OAA	Not subject to tax; reduces basis in stock
To extent of basis in stock	Not subject to tax; reduces basis in stock
In excess of basis	Taxed as capital gain

NOTE: In the above determination of shareholder treatment of distributions, any amount to be treated as tax-free return of capital reduces the shareholder's basis in his or her stock.

EXAMPLE

A single-owner S corporation has AAA of $12,000, PTI of $4,000, and E&P of $8,000. The shareholder's basis is $25,000. The first $12,000 of any distribution reduces AAA and shareholder basis by $12,000 and is nontaxable. The next $4,000 of distributions reduces PTI and shareholder basis by $4,000 and is nontaxable. The next $8,000 of distributions is classified as dividend income and reduces E&P. The next $9,000 of distributions is a tax-free reduction of basis ($25,000 − $12,000 − $4,000). Any distributions above $33,000 will be taxed as capital gain income.

    c.   An election may be made to treat distributions as coming first from Subchapter C E&P.

         1)   This results in ordinary dividend income to the distributee shareholder to the extent of the E&P.

             a)   Any excess distribution is treated as a return of capital or gain on the sale of stock.

    d.   Cash distributions within a relatively short transition period subsequent to termination of an S-election are treated as return of capital to the extent of the AAA.

         1)   Basis in shareholder stock is reduced.

    e.   Form 1099-DIV is used to report any distribution that is in excess of the accumulated adjustments account and that is treated as a dividend to the extent of accumulated earnings and profits.

Stop and review! You have completed the outline for this subunit. Study questions 21 through 27 beginning on page 334.

17.4 SPECIAL TAXES

Although S corporations are not generally subject to income tax, the following four special taxes are imposed on S corporations that either were formerly C corporations or acquired E&P in a tax-free reorganization.

Passive Investment Income (PII) Tax

    1.   An S corporation with Subchapter C E&P at the close of its tax year and more PII than 25% of its gross receipts is subject to tax of 35% of excess net passive income.

    a.   Gross receipts are gross receipts of the S corporation for the tax year reduced by capital losses to the extent of capital gains.

         1)   PII is generally the total amount received or accrued from investments, as opposed to operations, with some adjustments.

             a)   PII does not include capital gain from stock or securities.

    b.   Net passive income (NPI) is PII reduced by expenses directly attributable to its production.

EXAMPLE

Slash Enterprises is a manufacturer of doodads, and its gross receipts for the current year were $2,000,000. Slash had no capital losses during the year. Also, Slash receives a substantial amount of income from passive investments. For the current year, its passive investment income was $700,000, and its net passive income was $600,000. To determine the excess NPI, one must first subtract 25% of the gross receipts for the year from the PII for the current year. This is equal to $200,000 [$700,000 − ($2,000,000 × .25)]. The excess PII is then divided by the PII for the current year and multiplied times the NPI for the current year. This results in excess NPI of $171,429 [$600,000 × ($200,000 ÷ $700,000)].

$$\text{NPI for the year} \times \frac{\text{Excess of PII over 25\% of the gross receipts for the year}}{\text{PII for the year}} = \text{Excess NPI}$$

    c.   PII tax liability is allocated to the PII items and reduces the amount of the item passed through to shareholders.

    d.   S corporations are required to make estimated payments of PII tax.

Built-In Gains (BIG) Tax

2. An S corporation that, upon conversion from C to S status after 1986, had net appreciation inherent in its assets is subject to tax of 35% on net gain recognized (up to the amount of built-in gain on conversion) during the recognition period.

    a. The recognition period normally is the 10-year period beginning on the date the S election became effective.

        1) For 2009 and 2010, the 10-year period is reduced to a 7-year period.

            a) If 2008 was the seventh year of S election, then the recognition period has ended for sales in 2009.

            b) If 2009 is the seventh year, then the recognition period has ended for sales in 2010.

        2) For 2011 through 2013, the 7-year period is further reduced to a 5-year period.

            a) If 2010 is the fifth year, then the recognition period has ended for sales in 2011.

            b) If 2011 is the fifth year, then the recognition period has ended for sales in 2012.

    b. The tax liability is passed through, as a loss, pro rata to its shareholders.

        1) It reduces basis in each shareholder's stock and any AAA balance.
        2) Subchapter C E&P are not reduced by BIG tax liability.

    c. If the S corporation is also liable for the tax on excess net passive income, it should figure that tax before it figures its capital gains tax. Then it should reduce its capital gains, to the extent that they are subject to the tax on excess net passive income, and calculate its taxable income.

    d. S corporations are required to make estimated payments of BIG tax.

    e. Any net operating or capital loss carryover arising in a tax year in which the S corporation was a C corporation can offset the built-in gain for the tax year.

LIFO Recapture

3. Any excess of the FIFO inventory value over LIFO inventory value at the close of the last tax year of C corporation status (before the S corporation election becomes effective) is gross income to a corporation that used the LIFO method to inventory goods.

    a. Basis of the inventory is increased by the amount on which the recapture tax is imposed.

    b. The income is spread over 4 years, the last C corporation year and the first 3 years of the S corporation.

EXAMPLE

Mile, Inc., switched from a C corporation to an S Corporation at the beginning of the current year. Mile used the LIFO inventory valuation method during its existence as a C corporation. Mile's inventory for the previous year was $2,750,000 and, if Mile used the FIFO method, would be valued at $3,000,000. Therefore, for the previous year tax return, Mile must include an additional $250,000 of gross income due to the LIFO recapture, and the tax associated with this additional gross income will be paid over four equal annual installments beginning with the previous year.

General Business Credit Recapture

4. An S corporation remains liable for any recapture attributable to credits during C corporation tax years.

Stop and review! You have completed the outline for this subunit. Study questions 28 through 30 on page 336.

QUESTIONS

17.1 Eligibility and Election

1. Which of the following characteristics can disqualify a corporation from S corporation status?

A. Corporation Z has as one of its shareholders a trust that is treated as entirely owned by an individual who is a U.S. citizen.

B. Corporation M has 101 shareholders, including a husband and wife.

C. Corporation B has voting and nonvoting stock.

D. Corporation T has as its shareholders an individual, an estate, and a partnership.

Answer (D) is correct.

REQUIRED: The action that will prevent a current-year S corporation election.

DISCUSSION: An S corporation may not have more than 100 shareholders; shareholders who are not individuals, estates, or certain kinds of trusts and exempt organizations; a nonresident alien as a shareholder; or more than one class of stock [Sec. 1361(b)]. Having a partnership as a shareholder will prevent a corporation from making an S corporation election.

Answer (A) is incorrect. These characteristics will not disqualify a corporation from S corporation status. Answer (B) is incorrect. Related taxpayers are considered one taxpayer for purposes of qualifying under the 100 shareholder limit. Answer (C) is incorrect. These characteristics will not disqualify a corporation from S corporation status.

2. All of the following events will cause the termination of an S corporation's S election except

A. Transaction that results in over 100 shareholders.

B. Donation of stock to a tax-exempt organization under 501(c)(4).

C. Sale of stock to a resident alien.

D. Failing the passive income test for 3 consecutive years.

Answer (C) is correct.

REQUIRED: The event that will not cause the termination of an S corporation's S election.

DISCUSSION: Upon the occurrence of a terminating event, an S corporation becomes a C corporation. The IRS may waive termination that is a result of the corporation's ceasing to be a small business corporation or failing the passive income test for 3 consecutive years when it has Subchapter C earnings and profits (E&P) if the terminating event is found to be inadvertent and is corrected within a reasonable time after it is discovered. An S corporation election is terminated by any of the following: (1) an effective revocation, which requires the consent of a majority of the shareholders (voting and nonvoting); (2) any eligibility requirement not being satisfied on any day; or (3) passive investment income (PII) termination. One eligibility requirement is that shareholders be individuals who are citizens or resident aliens of the United States. Therefore, sale of stock to a resident alien does not terminate the election.

Answer (A) is incorrect. An S corporation cannot have over 100 shareholders. Answer (B) is incorrect. Only charitable organizations under Sec. 501(c)(3), not civic leagues under Sec. 501(c)(4), are eligible shareholders. Answer (D) is incorrect. The election is terminated if the corporation has passive investment income exceeding 25% of its gross receipts for 3 consecutive years.

3. Nevertoolate Corporation was established on January 1, Year 1. One hundred percent of the shareholders elected to adopt S status for the company and properly completed IRS Form 2553. However, the company's tax accountant did not file the form. On July 1, Year 1, the new accountant discovered the filing omission. Select the best available remedy for the corporation to elect S status from the following:

A. File the Form 2553, as originally prepared, on or before the end of the first tax year of the corporation.

B. Prepare a new Form 2553 and adopt a "short year" period for S status.

C. File the original Form 2553, on or before the due date of the initial return "pursuant to Rev-Ruling 2007-62" and show cause as to why the election is being filed late.

D. The company may file the prepared Form 2553, however, consent for S status will not be effective earlier than January 1, Year 2.

Answer (C) is correct.

REQUIRED: The process to remedy a late filing of Form 2553.

DISCUSSION: All shareholders, at the time of the election, must file a consent by signing Form 2553. Elections made after the first 2 months and 15 days of the corporation's tax year will become effective on the first day of the following tax year. The IRS can treat a late-filed election as having been timely filed if a determination is made that reasonable cause existed for a corporation's failure to file the election in a timely manner.

Answer (A) is incorrect. Form 2553 will not be valid for the Year 1 tax year if it is filed at year end. Answer (B) is incorrect. The original Form 2553 should be filed and a "short year" should not be adopted. Answer (D) is incorrect. The IRS can treat late-filed elections as having been timely filed if there was a reasonable cause for the corporation's failure to file the election in a timely manner.

4. Which of the following is not eligible to be a shareholder of an S corporation?

A. A domestic partnership.

B. Individuals who are not nonresident aliens.

C. Estates.

D. Exempt organizations described in Sec. 401(a) or 501(c)(3).

Answer (A) is correct.

REQUIRED: The participants that are not eligible in an S corporation.

DISCUSSION: The number of shareholders may not exceed 100. A husband and wife, and their estates, are considered a single shareholder for this purpose. A nonresident alien (NRA) may not own any shares. Each shareholder must be either an individual, an estate (including estates of individuals in bankruptcy), or a qualified trust. Certain small business trusts and tax-exempt organizations can be shareholders. Partnerships, corporations, and nonresident aliens may not be shareholders. Additionally, Charitable Remainder Unitrusts and Charitable Remainder Annuity Trusts are not eligible to be shareholders.

Answer (B) is incorrect. These individuals are eligible to qualify as a shareholder of an S corporation. Answer (C) is incorrect. Estates are eligible to qualify as a shareholder of an S corporation. Answer (D) is incorrect. Exempt organizations described in Sec. 401(a) or 501(c)(3) are eligible to qualify as a shareholder of an S corporation.

5. Bob and Dianne are merchants. They decided to combine their businesses and start a mail-order business. They also decided that the corporate structure would be in their best interest. On January 1, Year 1, they formed the B & D Corporation, but they did not file Form 2553 when they formed the corporation. Bob and Dianne filed an 1120S return at the end of the Year 1 calendar tax year, and reported their respective shares of earnings on their individual tax returns. All of the following statements are true except

A. Bob and Dianne have until March 15, Year 2, to make a valid election for Year 1.

B. Bob and Dianne were not permitted to file an 1120S return because they did not make a valid election for Year 1.

C. Bob and Dianne should have filed Form 1120, *U.S. Corporation Income Tax Return*, and should not report earnings and losses on their individual tax returns.

D. Both Bob and Dianne are required to consent to the election.

Answer (A) is correct.

REQUIRED: The false statement about S corporation election.

DISCUSSION: The election to be taxed under Subchapter S is made on Form 2553 (election by small business corporation to tax corporate income directly to shareholders). This form may be filed during the previous tax year or within 2 months and 15 days of the beginning of the current tax year to qualify for S corporation status for the current tax year [Sec. 1362(b)]. In the case of a calendar-year corporation, this would mean filing before March 15 of the current year. Under Sec. 1362(b)(5), the IRS may treat a late-filed election as timely filed if reasonable cause existed (for tax years beginning after 12/31/82). Each person who is a shareholder at the time of election must consent by signing Form 2553. In addition, each person who was a shareholder at any time during the part of the tax year before the election is made must also consent. If any former shareholders do not consent, the election is considered made for the following year. Accordingly, a valid S election has not been made by Bob and Dianne for Year 1.

Answer (B) is incorrect. A valid election made through Form 2553 must be completed before an 1120S return can be filed. Answer (C) is incorrect. A valid election must be made before an 1120S return can be filed. Thus, Bob and Dianne should have filed Form 1120. Answer (D) is incorrect. Each person who is a shareholder at the time of election must consent by signing Form 2553. In addition, each person who was a shareholder at any time during the part of the tax year before the election is made must also consent. If any former shareholders do not consent, the election is considered made for the following year.

6. Which of the following statements regarding the termination of an S corporation election is true?

A. The election may be revoked with the consent of shareholders who, at the time the revocation is made, hold more than 50% of the number of issued and outstanding shares.

B. The election may be revoked by the board of directors of the corporation only if they are not shareholders.

C. The election terminates automatically if the corporation derives more than 25% of its gross receipts from passive investment income during the year.

D. The election may be revoked by the Internal Revenue Service if there is a history of 10 years of operating losses.

Answer (A) is correct.

REQUIRED: The true statement regarding the termination of an S corporation election.

DISCUSSION: Upon the occurrence of a terminating event, an S corporation becomes a C corporation. An S corporation election is terminated if shareholders collectively holding more than 50% of the outstanding shares of stock on the day of the revocation (voting and nonvoting) consent, any eligibility requirement not being satisfied on any day, and/or a passive income investment income (PII) termination.

Answer (B) is incorrect. Shareholders holding more than 50% of both the voting and nonvoting shares of the corporation may consent to the termination in an effective revocation. The board of directors may not terminate the election. Answer (C) is incorrect. The passive investment income (PII) termination occurs when, for 3 consecutive tax years, the corporation has both Subchapter C E&P on the last day and PII that is greater than 25% of gross receipts. Answer (D) is incorrect. No such rule exists. The IRS will not terminate an S corporation election if the corporation has 10 years of operating losses.

7. Mary and Paul are plumbers. They went into business together and decided that the corporation structure would be in their best interest. On January 1, Year 1, they formed the M & P Corp. They did not file a Form 2553. Mary and Paul filed an 1120S return at the end of the year and paid self-employment tax on their respective shares of the income. All of the following statements are true except

- A. They are not permitted to file an 1120S return because they have not made a valid election.
- B. The income distributed by a corporation is not subject to self-employment tax.
- C. Mary and Paul have until March 15, Year 2, to make a valid election for Year 1.
- D. Both Mary and Paul must sign Form 2553 to make a valid election.

Answer (C) is correct.
REQUIRED: The false statement regarding the business structure.
DISCUSSION: The election to be taxed under Subchapter S is made on Form 2553 (election by small business corporation to tax corporate income directly to shareholders). This form may be filed during the previous tax year or within 2 months and 15 days of the beginning of the current tax year to qualify for S corporation status for the current tax year [Sec. 1362(b)]. In the case of a calendar-year corporation, this would mean filing before March 15 of the current year. Under Sec. 1362(b)(5), the IRS may treat a late-filed election as timely filed if reasonable cause existed (for tax years beginning after 12/31/82). Each person who is a shareholder at the time of election must consent by signing Form 2553. In addition, each person who was a shareholder at any time during the part of the tax year before the election is made must also consent. If any former shareholders do not consent, the election is considered made for the following year. Accordingly, a valid S election has not been made by Mary and Paul for Year 1.
Answer (A) is incorrect. A valid election made through Form 2553 must be completed before an 1120S return can be filed. Answer (B) is incorrect. S corporation distributions are not considered self-employment income (Rev. Rul. 59-221). Answer (D) is incorrect. Each person who is a shareholder at the time of election must consent by signing Form 2553. In addition, each person who was a shareholder at any time during the part of the tax year before the election is made must also consent. If any former shareholders do not consent, the election is considered made for the following year.

8. All of the following events would cause an S corporation to cease qualifying as an S corporation except

- A. Having more than 100 shareholders.
- B. The transfer of its stock to a corporation.
- C. The transfer of its stock to a resident alien.
- D. The election is revoked with the consent of shareholders who, at the time the revocation is made, had 55% of the stock.

Answer (C) is correct.
REQUIRED: The event that would not cause an S corporation disqualification.
DISCUSSION: A resident alien is an individual who qualifies to be a shareholder of an S corporation. Therefore, the transfer of stock to a resident alien does not disqualify a corporation from S corporation status.

17.2 Operations

9. Foster's RV Sales, Inc., is an S corporation with the following activity during 2013:

Gross sales of RV's and campers	$500,000
Operating expenses	300,000
Interest income	1,000
Charitable contributions	3,000
Sec. 179 expense	10,000

How much ordinary income from trade or business activities will be reported on Schedule K, *Shareholder's Pro Rata Items*?

- A. $188,000
- B. $190,000
- C. $198,000
- D. $200,000

Answer (D) is correct.
REQUIRED: The income reported on Schedule K for an S corporation.
DISCUSSION: Items of income, gain, expense, loss, and credit must be separately stated if those items are specially treated for tax purposes at the shareholder level. These items include interest income, charitable contributions, and the Sec. 179 expense. Therefore, Foster will report $200,000 ($500,000 – $300,000) as ordinary income on Schedule K.
Answer (A) is incorrect. Interest income, charitable contributions, and Sec. 179 expense are separately stated items. Answer (B) is incorrect. The Sec. 179 expense is not included. Answer (C) is incorrect. The interest income and charitable contributions are not included.

10. Which of the following are considered separately stated items for Form 1120S shareholders?

A. Charitable contributions.

B. Low-income housing credit.

C. Sec. 179 expense deduction.

D. All of the answers are correct.

Answer (D) is correct.
REQUIRED: The items considered separately stated items for Form 1120S.
DISCUSSION: An S corporation passes a pro rata share of its total income (loss) through to the individual shareholders except for items that require separate treatment by the shareholder. Charitable contributions made by the corporation, Sec. 179 deduction, and low-income housing credit are all items that must be separately stated.

11. What is the total amount of separately stated income items of a calendar-year S corporation operating on an accrual basis with the following information:

Net income of rental real estate activities	$300,000
Interest income	25,000
Royalty income	10,000
Sec. 1231 gain (from equipment sale)	20,000
Gross receipts	700,000

A. $355,000

B. $1,055,000

C. $300,000

D. $720,000

Answer (A) is correct.
REQUIRED: The separately stated income items for an S corporation.
DISCUSSION: Items of income, gain, expense, loss, and credit must be separately stated if those items are specially treated for tax purposes at the shareholder level. These items include interest income, rental income, royalty income, and net long-term capital gains.
Answer (B) is incorrect. Gross receipts are not separately stated. Answer (C) is incorrect. The royalty income, interest income, and capital gain are also included. Answer (D) is incorrect. Gross receipts are not separately stated. Also, royalty income, interest income, and real estate income are included.

12. What is the non-separately stated income amount of a calendar-year S corporation operating on an accrual basis with the following items?

Gross receipts	$300,000
Interest income	25,000
Royalty income	10,000
Salary paid to shareholder	20,000

A. $300,000

B. $55,000

C. $320,000

D. $280,000

Answer (D) is correct.
REQUIRED: The non-separately stated income amount for an S corporation.
DISCUSSION: Items of income, gain, expense, loss, and credit must be separately stated if those items are specially treated for tax purposes at the shareholder level. These items include interest income and royalty income.
Answer (A) is incorrect. Compensation paid to a shareholder is not separately stated. Answer (B) is incorrect. Interest income and royalty income are not included, but gross receipts are included. Also, the salary paid to the shareholder is an expense. Answer (C) is incorrect. The salary paid to the shareholder is not income; it is an expense.

13. On December 31 of last year, Mr. Hyde purchased 50% of Z Corporation's only class of outstanding stock for $150,000. Z is an electing S corporation. On November 30 of the current year, he purchased the other 50% of Z's stock for $150,000. For the current year, Z incurred an ordinary loss of $237,250. How much of the loss can Mr. Hyde deduct on his personal income tax return for the year?

A. $237,250

B. $217,750

C. $128,700

D. $118,625

Answer (C) is correct.
REQUIRED: The ordinary loss allocable to a shareholder of an S corporation who bought his or her stock during the year.
DISCUSSION: An S corporation shareholder includes his/her pro rata share of loss from the S corporation [Sec. 1366(a)]. Sec. 1377(a) defines pro rata share as the taxpayer's share of loss determined on a per-day and then a per-share basis.
The loss for the whole year was $237,250, which is $650 per day ($237,250 ÷ 365 days). Therefore, Hyde's share is $128,700 [($650 × 50% × 365 days) + ($650 × 50% × 31 days)] because Hyde owned 50% of the stock for the full year and the other 50% for 31 days.
Answer (A) is incorrect. The entire ordinary loss may not be deducted. Answer (B) is incorrect. The amount of $217,750 is 100% ownership for 335 days. Answer (D) is incorrect. The amount of $118,625 does not include the 50% the shareholder held for 31 days.

14. Ben and Jerry were the only shareholders of Water Ice, Inc., an S corporation. On January 1, Year 1, Ben owned 40 shares, and Jerry owned 60 shares. Ben sold his shares to Joe for $10,000 on March 31, Year 1. The corporation reported a $50,000 loss at the end of Year 1. How much of the loss is allocated to Joe?

A. $20,000

B. $15,068

C. $12,500

D. $10,000

Answer (B) is correct.
REQUIRED: The loss allocated to an S corporation shareholder owning 40% of the company.
DISCUSSION: An S corporation shareholder includes his or her pro rata share of loss from the S corporation [Sec. 1366(a)]. Sec. 1377(a) defines pro rata share as the taxpayer's share of loss determined on a per-day and then a per-share basis. Since Joe bought Ben's shares on March 31, Year 1, his per-day basis is 275. The loss must be allocated based on the number of days Joe was a shareholder. Therefore, the loss allocated to Joe is $15,068 ($50,000 × 40% × 275 ÷ 365).
Answer (A) is incorrect. The allocation also is done by the amount of time held for the year. Answer (C) is incorrect. The amount of the loss must be allocated as determined by the taxpayer's pro rata share [Sec. 1377(a)]. Answer (D) is incorrect. The amount of the loss must be allocated as determined by the taxpayer's pro rata share [Sec. 1377(a)].

15. Which of the following would not increase the basis of a shareholder's stock in an S corporation?

A. All separately stated income items of the S corporation, including tax-exempt income.

B. Any non-separately stated income of the S corporation.

C. Capital gains tax paid by the shareholder.

D. The amount of deductions for depletion that is more than the basis of the property being depleted.

Answer (C) is correct.
REQUIRED: The item that would not increase the basis of a shareholder's stock in an S corporation.
DISCUSSION: If the shareholder paid capital gains in disposing of the stock, this tax does not increase the basis of the shareholder's remaining stock.

16. Magnolia Corporation, a calendar-year S corporation, was formed on January 1, Year 1. Kathy owns 25% of Magnolia's outstanding stock, which she purchased for $20,000. In Year 1, Kathy guaranteed a corporate loan for $40,000. In Year 2, Kathy made payments on the loan totaling $10,000. Magnolia had losses of $90,000 and $60,000 in Year 1 and Year 2, respectively. What is the amount of the unallowed loss that Kathy can carry over to Year 3?

A. $0

B. $7,500

C. $10,000

D. $17,500

Answer (B) is correct.
REQUIRED: The amount of loss deductible by an S corporation shareholder carried over to future years.
DISCUSSION: A shareholder of an S corporation may include a pro rata share of loss in income, limited to the shareholder's basis in the stock. Generally, the shareholder's original basis is its cost. If a shareholder guarantees a loan to an S corporation, the loan does not increase the shareholder's basis. If, however, the shareholder makes payments on the loan, the payments increase the shareholder's basis. Kathy's basis in the stock was $20,000, the cost. Kathy may deduct only $20,000 of her $22,500 loss in Year 1 ($90,000 × 25%). After deducting the loss, her basis is $0. In Year 2, Kathy makes loan payments of $10,000. This makes her basis $10,000 for Year 1. Kathy may deduct the remaining loss of $2,500 from Year 1 in Year 2 ($22,500 – $20,000). Therefore, Kathy may deduct up to only $7,500 ($10,000 – $2,500) of her $15,000 loss from Year 2 ($60,000 × 25%). She may, however, carry the remaining $7,500 loss over to Year 3.
Answer (A) is incorrect. The loss deduction is limited to the basis in the stock. Answer (C) is incorrect. The loss deduction is limited to the basis in the stock. Answer (D) is incorrect. The payment of an S corporation's loan obligations increases basis.

17. On January 1, Year 1, Mr. Karl purchased 50% of Olive, Inc., an S corporation, for $75,000. At the end of Year 1, Olive, Inc., incurred an ordinary loss of $160,000. How much of the loss can Mr. Karl deduct on his personal income tax return for Year 1?

A. $160,000

B. $80,000

C. $75,000

D. $37,500

Answer (C) is correct.
REQUIRED: The amount of loss a shareholder can deduct on his or her personal income tax return.
DISCUSSION: The amount of losses and deductions an S corporation shareholder can claim is limited to the adjusted basis of the shareholder's stock. Thus, for Year 1, Karl can deduct only $75,000 of the $80,000 loss allocated to him.
Answer (A) is incorrect. The shareholder may not deduct the entire ordinary loss. Answer (B) is incorrect. The loss may not reduce Mr. Karl's basis below zero. Answer (D) is incorrect. Half of the shareholder's basis is not the limit on deductibility.

18. John is the sole shareholder of Maple Corporation, a qualified S corporation. At January 1, Year 1, John has a basis in Maple Corporation of $2,000. The corporation's Year 1 tax return shows the following:

Ordinary income	$10,000
Interest income	$1,000
Nondeductible expenses	$2,000
Real estate rental loss	$5,000
Section 179 deduction	$1,500
Distributions to John	$3,000

What is John's basis in Maple Corporation at the end of Year 1?

A. $0

B. $3,500

C. $4,500

D. $1,500

Answer (D) is correct.
  REQUIRED: The resulting shareholder's basis in an S corporation.
  DISCUSSION: The shareholder of an S corporation's stock must increase his or her basis for all items of income to the S corporation that are both separately and nonseparately stated. The basis in John's stock would equal the following:

Beginning basis	$ 2,000
Ordinary income	10,000
Interest income	1,000
Nondeductible expenses	(2,000)
Real estate rental loss	(5,000)
Sec. 179 deduction	(1,500)
Distributions to John	(3,000)
Ending basis	$ 1,500

19. Rap, Inc., was organized in January 2013 and immediately made an S election. Rap's stock is entirely owned by Howard, who contributed $40,000 to start the business. Rap reported the following results for the 2013 year:

Ordinary income	$36,000
Short-term capital loss	4,000
Charitable contributions	1,000
Tax-exempt income	1,000
Sec. 179 deduction	10,000

On April 12, 2013, Howard received a $30,000 cash distribution from the corporation. What is the adjusted basis of his stock on January 1, 2014?

A. $41,000

B. $32,000

C. $31,000

D. $10,000

Answer (B) is correct.
  REQUIRED: The basis of an S corporation shareholder's stock after a distribution.
  DISCUSSION: The adjusted basis of the shareholder's stock is figured at year end with increases for the shareholder's pro rata share of all income items, including tax-exempt income, that are separately stated and any nonseparately stated income. Also, all separately and nonseparately stated losses and deduction items decrease the basis of the shareholder's stock on a pro rata basis. Howard's stock basis on January 1, 2014, is $32,000.

Original basis	$40,000
Ordinary income	36,000
Tax-exempt income	1,000
Short-term capital loss	(4,000)
Charitable contributions	(1,000)
Sec. 179 deduction	(10,000)
Cash distribution	(30,000)
Adjusted basis	$32,000

  Answer (A) is incorrect. The Sec. 179 deduction and charitable contributions reduce the basis. Answer (C) is incorrect. The charitable contributions reduce the basis. Answer (D) is incorrect. Other factors besides the cash distribution are considered.

20. Which of the following would not reduce a shareholder's basis in S corporation stock?

A. A shareholder's pro-rata share of an expense not deductible in computing the corporation's taxable income and not chargeable to the capital account.

B. A shareholder's share of all loss and deduction items of the S corporation that are separately stated and passed through to the shareholder.

C. A shareholder's pro-rata share of any non-separately stated loss of the S corporation.

D. The excess of the corporation's deductions for depletion over the basis of the property subject to depletion.

Answer (D) is correct.
  REQUIRED: The item that would not reduce a shareholder's basis in an S corporation's stock.
  DISCUSSION: Per Sec. 1367(a)(2)(E), the shareholder's basis in S corporation stock is reduced by the amount of the shareholder's deduction for depletion only to the extent it is not in excess of the shareholder's proportionate share of the adjusted basis of the property. Allocations of income increase a shareholder's basis, not decrease basis.
  Answer (A) is incorrect. The pro rata share of a nondeductible expense and one not changeable to a capital account would reduce the basis. Answer (B) is incorrect. The separately stated items of loss and deduction do decrease the basis. Answer (C) is incorrect. The pro rata share of non-separately stated losses reduces the shareholder's basis in the stock.

17.3 Distributions

21. If an S corporation, which has accumulated earnings and profits (AE&P), is allowed to treat shareholder distributions as being made from the AE&P account, how will those distributions be taxed, if at all?

    A. They will be taxed as dividend income.

    B. They will be taxed as ordinary earned income.

    C. They will be taxed as capital gain income.

    D. They will not be taxed, as it would be deemed a return of shareholder capital.

Answer (A) is correct.
    REQUIRED: The tax treatment of AE&P distributions.
    DISCUSSION: Any part of a distribution from either current or accumulated earnings and profits is reported to the shareholder as dividend income.

22. Jenny Corporation (an S corporation) is owned entirely by Craig. At the beginning of Year 1, Craig's adjusted basis in his Jenny Corporation stock was $20,000. Jenny reported ordinary income of $5,000 and a capital loss of $10,000. Craig received a cash distribution of $35,000 in November Year 1. What is Craig's gain from the distribution?

    A. $0

    B. $10,000

    C. $20,000

    D. $35,000

Answer (B) is correct.
    REQUIRED: The sole shareholder's gain from the distribution of an S corporation.
    DISCUSSION: The basis is increased by the ordinary income to $25,000. The $35,000 distribution is taken next, and there is a $10,000 gain since it exceeds the basis. The capital loss is nondeductible because there is no basis, and it is carried over.
    Answer (A) is incorrect. If the distribution is greater than the basis, the excess is taxable as a sale or an exchange of property (a taxable capital gain). Answer (C) is incorrect. The distribution is taken before the deduction for the capital loss. Answer (D) is incorrect. Only the difference between the distribution and the basis, not the entire distribution, is taxable.

23. Twister, an S corporation, has no earnings and profits. In Year 1, Twister distributed property with a fair market value of $65,000 and an adjusted basis of $52,000 to Carlos, its sole shareholder. After recognizing his share of any corporate gain or loss, his adjusted basis in Twister's stock at year end was $50,000. How should the distribution be handled by Carlos?

    A. $50,000 as return of capital and $15,000 as nontaxable distributions.

    B. $50,000 as return of capital and $15,000 as taxable capital gain.

    C. $50,000 as return of capital and $2,000 as taxable capital gain.

    D. $50,000 as nontaxable distributions.

Answer (B) is correct.
    REQUIRED: The treatment of an S corporation distribution when the S corporation has no accumulated earnings and profits (E&P).
    DISCUSSION: If the S corporation has no accumulated E&P, any distribution a shareholder receives is a return of capital to the extent of the shareholder's basis. Any excess will be a gain from the sale of property. Therefore, Carlos will treat the distribution as a $50,000 return of capital and the remaining $15,000 as a taxable capital gain.
    Answer (A) is incorrect. The remaining $15,000 is treated as a taxable capital gain. Answer (C) is incorrect. If property other than cash is distributed, the amount of the distribution is the FMV of the property. Answer (D) is incorrect. The distribution is nontaxable only to the extent of the shareholder's basis.

24. Thunder, an S corporation, has no earnings and profits (E&P). Thunder distributed $100,000 to Ben, its only shareholder. His adjusted basis in Thunder's stock is $40,000. The amount that exceeds his adjusted basis in the stock is treated as

    A. Previously taxed income.

    B. A nontaxable distribution.

    C. A taxable dividend.

    D. A taxable capital gain.

Answer (D) is correct.
    REQUIRED: The treatment of a distribution to a shareholder that exceeds the shareholder's adjusted basis.
    DISCUSSION: S corporation distributions to a shareholder are generally a nontaxable return of the shareholder's basis if the S corporation does not have any accumulated E&P. However, if the distributions are more than the shareholder's basis, the excess is taxable as a sale or an exchange of property (a taxable capital gain).
    Answer (A) is incorrect. The amount does not constitute previously taxed income. Answer (B) is incorrect. The amount exceeds the shareholder's adjusted basis. Answer (C) is incorrect. The corporation had no accumulated E&P.

25. Quantum Leap, an S corporation, has $10,000 in accumulated earnings and profits. In Year 1, Quantum Leap distributed property with a fair market value of $75,000 and an adjusted basis of $62,000 to Edward, its sole shareholder. After recognizing his share of any corporate gain or loss, his adjusted basis in Quantum Leap's stock at the end of the year was $60,000. How should Edward handle the distribution?

A. $60,000 as return of capital and $15,000 is nontaxable distributions.

B. $10,000 as ordinary income, $60,000 as return of capital, and $5,000 as taxable capital gain.

C. $60,000 as return of capital and $2,000 as taxable capital gain.

D. $70,000 is a nontaxable distribution.

Answer (B) is correct.
REQUIRED: The character of a distribution to an S corporation shareholder.
DISCUSSION: The problem does not give the amount of the accumulated adjustment account (AAA), which is distributed first as a tax-free return of basis. However, the amount of AAA cannot exceed $60,000 since the basis of the stock is $60,000. Therefore, the accumulated earnings and profits would be fully distributed as ordinary income of $10,000. Next, the remaining basis ($60,000 minus the AAA balance) is distributed tax-free. The remaining $5,000 is a taxable capital gain ($75,000 distribution minus the $60,000 basis in the stock and the $10,000 dividend).
Answer (A) is incorrect. The $15,000 is taxable. Answer (C) is incorrect. The shareholder treats the distribution as a dividend only up to the accumulated E&P amount. The shareholder also treats the remaining distribution as a return of capital up to the amount of basis. Any amount left over is treated as a taxable capital gain. Answer (D) is incorrect. The shareholder treats the distribution as a dividend only up to the accumulated E&P amount. The shareholder also treats the remaining distribution as a return of capital up to the amount of basis. Any amount left over is treated as a taxable capital gain.

26. At the end of 2005, Green, Inc., was a C corporation with $50,000 in earnings and profits. Green elected to be treated as an S corporation beginning with the 2006 year. At the end of 2013, Green has a balance of $10,000 in its other adjustments account, a balance of $20,000 in its accumulated adjustment account, and a balance of $50,000 in earnings and profits. Green made cash distributions of $25,000 to each of its 50% shareholders. Green makes no elections relating to the source of distributions. What is the remaining Green, Inc., earnings and profits balance after the shareholder distributions?

A. $50,000

B. $40,000

C. $30,000

D. $20,000

Answer (D) is correct.
REQUIRED: The effect on earnings and profits after a distribution.
DISCUSSION: The accumulated adjustments account represents the cumulative income and loss recognized for S corporations after 1982. Regulation Sec. 1.1368-2 provides that distributions from an S corporation reduce stock basis to the extent the AAA is positive and sufficient basis exists in the stock. The distribution is tax-free to the extent of AAA. If the distribution exceeds the AAA, then the additional distribution is taxable and is treated as coming from accumulated E&P. Since Green, Inc., had $20,000 in its accumulated adjustment account and $50,000 in its earnings and profits, the first $20,000 is treated as coming from the AAA. The remaining $30,000 distribution is subtracted from E&P. The remaining balance in E&P is $20,000 ($50,000 E&P – $30,000 distribution).
Answer (A) is incorrect. E&P was reduced by $30,000. Answer (B) is incorrect. Distributions cannot be treated as coming from the other adjustments account (OAA). Answer (C) is incorrect. Distributions cannot come from the OAA.

27. If an S corporation has no accumulated earnings and profits from prior operations as a C corporation, any amount distributed to a shareholder

A. Must be returned to the S corporation.

B. Increases the shareholder's basis in the stock.

C. Decreases the shareholder's basis in the stock.

D. Has no effect on the shareholder's basis in the stock.

Answer (C) is correct.
REQUIRED: The distribution treatment of an S corporation, previously a C corporation, when no accumulated earnings and profits exist.
DISCUSSION: Sec. 1368(d) provides that if there are no accumulated earnings and profits, the S corporation treats distributions as a reduction in the shareholder's basis and therefore a nontaxable return of capital. If the entire basis is exhausted, any additional distribution is treated as a gain on the sale or exchange of property [Reg. 1.1368–1(c)].
Answer (A) is incorrect. The distribution does not have to be returned to the corporation. Answer (B) is incorrect. It decreases, not increases, the shareholder's basis. Answer (D) is incorrect. There is an effect on the basis: a decrease.

17.4 Special Taxes

28. An S corporation will be subject to excess net passive income tax

    A. Even if it has always been an S corporation.

    B. If it has passive investment income for the year that is at least 20% of gross receipts.

    C. Even if it has always been an S corporation and it has passive investment income for the year that is at least 20% of gross receipts.

    D. None of the answers are correct.

Answer (D) is correct.
    REQUIRED: The S corporation's requirements to be subject to excess net passive income tax.
    DISCUSSION: Sec. 1375 provides that an S corporation with Subchapter C E&P at the close of its tax year and more PII than 25% of its gross receipts is subject to tax of 35% of excess net passive income.
    Answer (A) is incorrect. The S corporation must have accumulated earnings and profits and an S corporation that has never been a C corporation cannot have accumulated earnings and profits. Answer (B) is incorrect. The S corporation must have passive investment income for the year that is at least 25% of gross receipts. Answer (C) is incorrect. It is not a requirement for an S corporation to be subject to excess net passive income tax, and the S corporation must have passive investment income for the year that is at least 25% of gross receipts.

29. With regard to built-in gains, which of the following statements is false?

    A. Any net operating or capital loss carryover arising in a tax year in which the S corporation was a C corporation can offset the built-in gain for the tax year.

    B. Gasoline tax credits may be used to offset the tax on built-in gains.

    C. Built-in gains are used to compute the tax on excess net passive income.

    D. The tax on built-in gains is effective for tax years beginning after 1986 but only for corporations that have made S corporation elections after 1986.

Answer (C) is correct.
    REQUIRED: The false statement concerning the built-in gains tax applicable to certain S corporations.
    DISCUSSION: An S corporation that had net appreciation inherent in its assets, upon conversion from C to S status after 1986, is subject to tax of 35% on net gain recognized (up to the amount of built-in gain on conversion) during the recognition period. The built-in gains, however, are not used to compute the tax on excess net passive income.

30. We Converted, Inc., elected S corporation status in Year 2, after 10 years as a C corporation. At the date of conversion, the company had a $50,000 net operating loss (NOL) carryover, which it incurred in Year 1, and a $25,000 capital loss carryover. In Year 5, the company sold a vacant piece of property it owned for 11 years. The sales price of the property was $100,000 and an original cost of $25,000. Given the circumstances as stated above, which of the following statements is true?

    A. No amount of gain is taxable to the S corporation, because the total of the NOL and capital loss carryover ($75,000) can be used to offset the capital gain on the sale of the property.

    B. Only $50,000 of the $75,000 capital gain is subject to S corporation tax.

    C. $75,000 of the capital gain is taxable, since the S corporation cannot succeed to the beneficial tax attributes of a former C corporation.

    D. No amount of gain is taxable to the S corporation because all income items are separately stated to the shareholders.

Answer (A) is correct.
    REQUIRED: The effects of a net operating loss carryforward.
    DISCUSSION: No amount of the gain is taxable because the total NOL can be used to offset the capital gain on the sale of the property. The S corporation is still able to receive the beneficial tax attributes of the former C corporation. This is a Built-In Gains (BIG) tax issue. Even though the built-in gain (FMV at date of conversion – cost) is not given, it would not be greater than the gain at the date of sale ($75,000).
    Answer (B) is incorrect. The S corporation is allowed to use the full $75,000 NOL to offset the capital gain. Answer (C) is incorrect. The S corporation can use the tax attributes of the former C corporation. Answer (D) is incorrect. The gain is taxable but is offset against the $75,000 NOL.

Use the additional questions in Gleim **EA Test Prep** to create Practice Exams that emulate Prometric!

STUDY UNIT EIGHTEEN
DECEDENT, ESTATE, AND TRUST
INCOME TAX RETURNS

(9 pages of outline)

This study unit addresses different kinds of income taxes. Estates and trusts (also called fiduciaries) are legal entities defined by the assets they hold. These assets produce income. The entities are subject to tax on that income. This is referred to as fiduciary income taxation. The formula for computing this fiduciary tax is the individual income tax formula, modified for the distribution deduction and other special rules. Furthermore, the beneficiaries of these fiduciary entities, rather than the fiduciary, are personally subject to income tax on certain fiduciary income.

18.1 DECEDENT'S FINAL INCOME TAX RETURN

The final individual income tax return is due at the same time the decedent's return would have been due had death not occurred.

Inclusions in Income

1. The decedent's income includible on the final return is generally determined as if the person were still alive except that the taxable period ends on the date of death.

   a. Cash-method taxpayers include only the income that was actually received or constructively received before the date of death, that is, income that was made available for use by the decedent without restriction.

   b. Accrual-method taxpayers include any amounts earned and accrued before death.

   c. Partnership income. The death of a partner does not generally close the partnership's tax year.

      1) For partnership tax years ending on or before a partner's death, the distributive share should be included on the final return.

      2) For partnership tax years ending after the date of death, the partner's distributive share before death is included on the final tax return.

      3) These rules apply for cash- and accrual-method taxpayers in all situations except for self-employment tax purposes.

   d. The person who is required to file the final income tax return of the decedent can elect to include all interest earned on bonds transferred as a result of death if the cash-method decedent had chosen not to report the interest each year.

2. **Deductions and Credits**

   a. A personal exemption may be taken unless the decedent was another person's dependent.

   b. A full standard deduction may be taken unless deductions are itemized.

    c.   If deductions are itemized, medical expenses paid before death by the decedent are deductible.

        1)   This includes amounts paid for the decedent, the decedent's spouse, and the decedent's dependents.

        2)   If medical expenses are paid out of the estate during the 1-year period beginning with the day after death, an election may be made to also deduct them on the return for the year incurred.

        3)   Any medical expenses claimed on the decedent's final income tax return may not be claimed on the estate tax return.

    d.   A decedent's deduction for NOLs from business must be taken on the final return or carried back to prior years.

        1)   Any deduction for capital losses must be taken on the final return.

            a)   The capital loss deduction is limited to $3,000 in any year.

        2)   There are no carryforwards of unused losses and deductions, and the limitations on losses and deductions still apply in this situation.

    e.   Any credits, taxes, and payments that the decedent would have applied had (s)he not died during the year are applied in full in the final return.

Self-Employment Tax

    3.   Self-employment income for a decedent includes income actually or constructively received or accrued, depending on the decedent's accounting method.

        a.   For self-employment tax purposes only, the decedent's self-employment income includes the decedent's distributive share of a partnership's income or loss through the end of the month in which death occurred.

    4.   The return should only be signed by the personal representative and/or an individual who prepares the return for pay.

        a.   If an individual prepares the return free of charge, (s)he should not sign the return.

Stop and review! You have completed the outline for this subunit. Study questions 1 through 3 beginning on page 345.

18.2 INCOME IN RESPECT OF A DECEDENT (IRD)

    IRD is all amounts to which a decedent was entitled as gross income but that were not includible in computing taxable income on the final return. The person had a right to receive it prior to death, e.g., salary was earned or sale contract was entered into.

    1.   Not includible on the final income tax return of a cash-method (CM) taxpayer are amounts not received. Not includible on the final income tax return of an accrual-method (AM) taxpayer are amounts not properly accrued. Examples follow:

Not IRD	IRD
Salary earned and accrued by AM taxpayer	**Salary** earned prior to, but not received before, death of a CM taxpayer
Collection of A/R by AM taxpayer	**Collection** after death of A/R of CM taxpayer
Gain on sale of property received before death	**Gain** on sale of property by CM taxpayer not received before death
Rent received before death	**Rent** accrued but not received before death by CM taxpayer
Interest on installment debt accrued after death by AM taxpayer	**Interest** on installment debt accrued before death by CM taxpayer
Installment contract income recognized before death	**Installment** income recognized after death on contract entered into before death

2. IRD is reported by the person receiving the income when it is received.

    a. The cash method applies to income once designated IRD.
    b. IRD received by a trust or estate is fiduciary income.

3. A right to receive IRD has a transferred basis. The basis is not stepped-up to FMV on the date of death, as is generally the case for property acquired from a decedent. For 2010, the estate has a choice of electing an estate tax with stepped-up basis or no estate tax with modified carryover basis.

EXAMPLE

Mrs. Hart had earned 2 weeks' salary of $2,000 that had not been paid when she died. As a cash-method taxpayer, her basis in the right to receive the $2,000 was $0. When her estate received the income, it had $2,000 of ordinary income because its basis in the right to receive it was also $0. Note that the $2,000 is not reported on Mrs. Hart's final return.

---

4. IRD has the same character it would have had in the hands of the decedent.

5. IRD is taxable as income to the recipient and is includible in the gross estate. Double tax is mitigated by deductions.

    a. Deductions in respect of a decedent.

        1) Expenses accrued before death, but not deductible on the final return because the decedent used the cash method, are deductible when paid if otherwise deductible.

            a) They are deductible on a fiduciary income tax return.
            b) They are also deductible on the estate tax return.

    b. Deduction for estate tax. Estate taxes attributable to IRD included in the gross estate are deductible on the fiduciary income tax return.

        1) Administrative expenses and debts of a decedent are deductible on the estate tax return (Form 706). Some of them may also be deductible on the estate's income tax return (Form 1041).

            a) Double deductions are disallowed.
            b) The right to deduct the expenses on Form 706 must be waived in order to claim them on Form 1041.

        2) Deduction (on Form 1041) is allowed for any excess of the federal estate tax over the amount of the federal estate tax if the IRD had been excluded from the gross estate.

Stop and review! You have completed the outline for this subunit. Study questions 4 and 5 beginning on page 346.

18.3 INCOME TAXATION OF ESTATES AND TRUSTS

Tax is imposed on taxable income of a trust or estate at the following rates for 2013:

Fiduciary Taxable Income Brackets	Applicable Rate
$ 0 – $2,450	15%
> 2,450 – 5,700	25% (+ $367.50)
> 5,700 – 8,750	28% (+ $1,180.00)
> 8,750 – 11,950	33% (+ $2,034.00)
> 11,950	39.6% (+ $3,090.00)

Fundamentals

1.   Following are some basic definitions and a discussion of filing requirements:

   a.   A simple trust is formed under an instrument having the following characteristics:

      1)   Requires current distribution of all its income
      2)   Requires no distribution of the res (i.e., principal)
      3)   Provides for no charitable contributions by the trust

   b.   A complex trust is any trust other than a simple trust.

      1)   A complex trust can accumulate income, provide for charitable contributions, and distribute amounts other than income.

   c.   A grantor trust is any trust to the extent the grantor is the effective beneficiary. Income attributable to the portion of a trust principal owned by the grantor is taxed to the grantor. The trust is disregarded.

      1)   A trust is considered a grantor trust when the grantor retains a greater than 5% reversionary interest.

      2)   Under Sec. 677(a), a grantor is treated as the owner of a trust, the income of which may be distributed or accumulated for the grantor's spouse (without the approval or consent of an adverse party).

      3)   The grantor is also taxed on income from a trust in which the income may be applied for the benefit of the grantor [Sec. 677(a)].

         a)   Use of income for the support of a dependent is considered the application of income for the benefit of the grantor.

         b)   Under Sec. 677(b), however, the income of a trust that may be applied for the support of a dependent is not taxable to the grantor if it is not actually used.

      4)   The grantor or other owners with substantial interests have not given up complete dominion and control over the trust property. The trust is not considered a separate legal entity for tax purposes.

      5)   Grantor trusts are not subject to the Net Investment Income Tax (NIIT).

   d.   The rules for classifying trusts are applied on a year-to-year basis.

   e.   An estate with gross income greater than or equal to $600 is required to file a tax return. A trust is required to file a return if it has either any taxable income or more than $600 of gross income.

      1)   The trustee, executor, or administrator must file the return no later than the 15th day of the 4th month after the close of the entity's tax year.

      2)   Form 1041, *U.S. Income Tax Return for Estates and Trusts*, must be used.

      3)   If a domestic estate has a beneficiary who is a nonresident alien, the representative must file a return regardless of income.

      4)   Estate gross income includes the gain from the sale of property (not gross proceeds).

2.   An estate may adopt any tax year ending within 12 months after death.

   a.   A trust must adopt a calendar tax year.

   b.   Tax-exempt and wholly charitable trusts may qualify to use a fiscal tax year.

   c.   A beneficiary includes his or her share of trust income in his or her return for his or her tax year in which the trust's tax year ends.

      1)   When distributions are made is irrelevant.

3.   Any permissible accounting method may be adopted.

4.   The alternative minimum tax applies to trusts and estates. It is determined in the same manner as for individuals.

Principal vs. Income

5. Tax is imposed on taxable income (TI) of trusts and estates, not on items treated as fiduciary principal.

   a. State law defines what is principal and what is income of a trust or estate for federal income tax purposes.

      1) Many states have adopted the Revised Uniform Principal and Income Act, some with modifications.

         a) The act and state laws provide that the trust instrument controls designations of fiduciary principal and interest components.

         b) They also provide default designations.

   b. Generally, principal is property held to eventually be delivered to the remainderman.

      1) Income is return on or for use of the principal. It is held for or distributed to the income beneficiary.

         a) Principal is also referred to as the corpus or res.

      2) Change in form of principal is not taxable income.

Allocation of Fiduciary Receipts and Disbursements	
Principal	**Income**
Receipts	
Consideration for property, e.g., gain on sale	Business income
	Insurance proceeds for lost profits
Replacement property	Interest
Nontaxable stock dividends	Rents
Stock splits	Dividends (taxable)
Stock rights	Extraordinary dividends
Liquidating dividends	Taxable stock dividends
Royalties (27 1/2%)	Royalties (72 1/2%)
Disbursements	
Principal payments on debt	Business (ord. & nec.) expenses, e.g., interest expense
Capital expenditures	Production of income expenses,
Major repairs	e.g., maintenance or repair,
Modifications	insurance, rent collection fee
Fiduciary fees	Tax on fiduciary income
Tax on principal items, e.g., capital gains	Depreciation

Income Tax Formula

6. TI of a trust or an estate is computed similarly to that of an individual.

   a. Gross income is computed as for individuals.

      1) It includes dividends, interest, rents, royalties, gain from the sale of property, and income from business, partnerships, trusts, and other sources.

   b. Life insurance proceeds are generally includible in the value of the gross estate but are not considered income of the estate.

   c. Income in respect of a decedent is also taxed as income if it is received by the estate.

   d. Capital gains are taxed to the estate; then the gain must be added to the principal of the estate.

   e. Losses from a passive activity owned by the estate or trust cannot be used to offset portfolio (interest, dividends, royalties, annuities, etc.) income of the estate or trust in determining taxable income.

f. AGI does apply to fiduciaries for purposes of computing deduction limits.

  1) The standard deduction is not allowed.

g. Deductions. They generally follow those allowable to an individual. Trustee, or administrator, fees and tax return preparation fees are deductible in full.

  1) Administration expenses are deductible in full if not deducted on the estate tax return. The amount of trustee fees deductible is not limited to the excess over 2% of AGI.

  2) Depreciation. In default of a trust instrument designation, the act charges depreciation to income.

    a) Absent provisions in the estate instrument apportioning the deduction, the allowable amount must be allocated between the estate and each beneficiary in proportion to the amount of fiduciary income taxable to each party.

    b) Trusts. The trust may deduct depreciation only to the extent a reserve is required or permitted under the trust instrument or local law, and income is set aside for the reserve and actually remains in the trust.

      i) Any part of the deduction in excess of the trust income set aside for the reserve is then allocated between the parties according to the trust instrument.

      ii) If the instrument is silent, allocation of the excess between the trust and each beneficiary is in proportion to the amount of fiduciary income taxable to each.

  3) Fiduciary NOLs are computed without regard to charitable contributions or distribution deductions. Carryover by the fiduciary is permitted.

    a) Pass-through for deduction on personal returns of beneficiaries is allowed only in the year the trust or estate terminates.

    b) Pass-through NOLs and capital loss carryovers are used to calculate the beneficiary's AGI and taxable income.

    c) Estates can claim a deduction for an NOL. The NOL is calculated in the same manner as an individual taxpayer's deduction, except that an estate cannot deduct any distributions to beneficiaries or charitable contributions in arriving at the NOL or NOL carryover.

    d) An unused NOL in the final year of the estate may carryover to the beneficiaries succeeding to the property of the estate.

  4) A fiduciary may deduct a capital loss to the extent of capital gains plus $3,000. Carryover is permitted.

  5) Miscellaneous itemized deductions are subject to the 2%-of-AGI floor.

  6) Charitable contributions are deductible only if the governing instrument (e.g., trust) authorizes them. Deduction is not subject to limits based on AGI.

  7) Expenses attributable to tax-exempt income are not deductible.

  8) Personal exemption. A deduction is allowable but not for the year the trust or estate terminates. The amount is $600 for an estate, $300 for a simple trust, and $100 for a complex trust.

h. Credits. Gross regular tax of a fiduciary is offset by most of the same credits available to individuals.

  1) Certain "personal" credits are unavailable.

    a) A fiduciary, for example, has no dependents.

Distribution Deduction

7. The deduction for distributions allocates taxable income of a trust or estate (gross of distributions) between the fiduciary and its beneficiaries.

    a. Simple trust. The deduction is the lesser of the amount of the distributions (required) minus net tax-exempt income or distributable net income minus tax-exempt interest (DNI – tax-exempt interest).

        1) Generally, DNI is current net accounting income of the fiduciary reduced by any amounts allocated to principal.

    b. Estates and complex trusts. The deduction is the lesser of DNI (minus tax-exempt interest) or distributions.

        1) The amount distributed is the lesser of the FMV of the property or the basis of the property in the hands of the beneficiary.

        2) The trustee(s) of a complex trust may elect to treat distributions made during the first 65 days of the (trust's) tax year as if they were made on the last day of the preceding tax year.

        3) Specific bequests distributed or credited to a beneficiary in no more than three installments are not included as amounts distributed.

        4) The fiduciary recognizes no gain on distribution of property unless an estate executor so elects.

        5) A fiduciary's basis in distributed property is transferred, along with adjustments for any gain recognized, to the beneficiary. Every $1 of value distributed is treated as if (first) from any current DNI.

            a) The instrument might allocate the $1 to current income, accumulated income, or principal.

            b) Principal (after DNI) is distributed tax-free.

Distributable Net Income (DNI)

8. Distributable net income (DNI) is the maximum deductible at the fiduciary level for distributions and the maximum taxable at the beneficiary level. It is taxable income of the fiduciary (trust or estate), adjusted by the following items:

	TI of fiduciary (before the distribution deduction)
+	Personal exemption deduction ($600 estate, $300 simple trust, $100 complex trust)
+	Tax-exempt interest minus any related expenses
+	Capital losses allocated to principal
–	Capital gains allocated to principal
–	Taxable stock dividends allocated to principal
–	Extraordinary dividends allocated to principal
=	DNI

    a. Expenses directly related are allocated first (e.g., interest expense allocated to taxable and exempt interest income). The remaining balance is used to allocate indirect expenses to all income.

    b. No adjustment to fiduciary TI is made for the following:

        1) Dividends, other than as previously noted.
        2) NOL deductions
        3) Depreciation, if a reserve is established and all income is not distributable
        4) Certain expenditures charged to principal, such as trustee fees

            a) They reduce income taxable to the beneficiary.

9.   **Beneficiary's Taxable Income**

Simple Trust

    a.   A beneficiary of a simple trust is taxed on the lower of the two amounts listed below.

        1)   Trust income required to be distributed (even if not distributed)
        2)   The beneficiary's proportionate share of the trust's DNI

Estates and Complex Trusts

    b.   A beneficiary of a complex trust is taxed on amounts of fiduciary income required to be distributed plus additional amounts distributed to the beneficiary.

        1)   The taxable amount is limited to the beneficiary's share of DNI.

Character

    c.   The character of the income in the hands of the beneficiary is the same as in the hands of the trust or estate.

EXAMPLE

A simple trust distributes all its $10,000 income to its sole beneficiary. Its DNI is also $10,000. Included in the trust income was $1,000 of tax-exempt income. The beneficiary treats $1,000 of the income from the trust as tax-exempt interest and excludes it from his or her personal gross income.

Schedule K-1

    d.   Schedule K-1 (Form 1041) is used to report the beneficiary's share of income, deductions, and credits from a trust or an estate. The income is reported on the beneficiary's tax return for the year in which the trust or estate year ends.

10.   Trusts and estates are required to remit payments of estimated tax. The required amount and due dates of installments are determined in the same manner as for individuals.

    a.   An estate is not required to pay estimated tax for its first 2 tax years.

    b.   A trustee may elect to treat any portion of an estimated tax payment by the estate as made by the beneficiary.

        1)   The amount would also be treated as paid or credited to the beneficiary on the last day of the tax year.

    c.   An estate of a domestic decedent or a domestic trust that had no tax liability for the full 12-month preceding tax year is not required to make estimated tax payments in the current year.

11.   Most estate and trust income tax returns are due on April 15. An extension of up to 5 months may be granted.

Net Investment Income Tax (NIIT)

12.   The NIIT affects income tax returns of estates and trusts with their first tax year beginning on or after January 1, 2013. Estates and trusts will be subject to the NIIT, at a rate of 3.8%, if they have undistributed net investment income and also have adjusted gross income over the dollar amount at which the highest tax bracket for an estate or trust begins ($11,950 for 2013). Net investment income includes interest, dividends, capital gains, rental and royalty income, and nonqualified annuities.

Stop and review! You have completed the outline for this subunit. Study questions 6 through 29 beginning on page 347.

18.4 FRAUDULENT TRUSTS

1. All trusts must comply with the tax laws as set forth by the Congress in the Internal Revenue Code, Sections 641-683.

   a. Trusts established to hide the true ownership of assets and income or to disguise the substance of financial transactions are considered fraudulent trusts.

   b. Abusive techniques used to reduce income taxes include

      1) Depreciating personal assets (such as a home);
      2) Deducting personal expenses;
      3) Splitting income over multiple entities, often filed in multiple locations;
      4) Underreporting income;
      5) Avoiding filing returns;
      6) Wiring income overseas and failing to report it; and
      7) Attempting to protect transactions through bank secrecy laws in tax haven countries.

   c. Violations of the Internal Revenue Code may result in civil penalties and/or criminal prosecution.

      1) Civil sanctions can include a fraud penalty up to 75% of the underpayment of tax attributable to the fraud in addition to the taxes owed.
      2) Criminal convictions may result in fines up to $250,000 and/or up to 5 years in prison for each offense.

Stop and review! You have completed the outline for this subunit. Study question 30 on page 354.

QUESTIONS

18.1 Decedent's Final Income Tax Return

1. Alice, a cash-basis taxpayer, died August 31 of the current year. During the current year, the following amounts were paid to her estate:

- $1,000 dividend from the ABC Corp., which was declared on August 25 and received in the mail on September 2.
- $5,000 distributive share of XYZ Partnership income received on October 3 of the current year. This distribution was for the partnership's tax year ended September 30 of the current year.

What income must be included on Alice's final individual income tax return for the dividend and partnership payments?

A. The $1,000 dividend and a pro rata portion of the $5,000 partnership income.

B. The $1,000 dividend but no portion of the partnership income.

C. A pro rata portion of the partnership income but not the $1,000 dividend.

D. No income from either payment.

Answer (C) is correct.
REQUIRED: The amount of income included on the final income tax return.
DISCUSSION: If the decedent accounted for income under the cash method, only the items actually or constructively received before the date of death are included on the final return. Constructive receipt would have occurred if the income had become available for use by the decedent without restriction. Because the dividends were not available for use before the date of death, they were not constructively received. For a partnership whose tax year ends after the partner's date of death, the decedent's distributive share of income is income in respect of the decedent and will be reported on the final tax return to the extent of the pro rata portion prior to death.
Answer (A) is incorrect. The dividend income is not included in income. Answer (B) is incorrect. The dividend is not included in income and a pro rata portion of the $5,000 is included in income. Answer (D) is incorrect. A portion of the partnership income should be included.

2. Mr. Benson, a cash-method, calendar-year taxpayer, leased his farm for pasture land each August for 1 year at $2,000 per year, payable when the lease was signed. He died on June 30 of the current year. Your review of his records, as a personal representative, reflected that, as of the date of his death, he had received interest of $8,000. You also found a dividend check in the amount of $650, which was undeposited and had been received on June 15 of the current year. What is the amount of income to be included on Mr. Benson's final income tax return?

A. $8,000

B. $8,650

C. $10,000

D. $10,650

Answer (B) is correct.
REQUIRED: The amount of income included on the final income tax return.
DISCUSSION: If the decedent accounted for income under the cash method, only the items actually or constructively received before the date of death are included on the final return. Constructive receipt occurred if the income became available for use by the decedent without restriction. The interest received ($8,000) and the dividends constructively received ($650) are included in income. The rent is not included because it was not constructively received.
Answer (A) is incorrect. The dividend check was available for use by the decedent. Answer (C) is incorrect. The rent was not constructively received, but the dividend check was because it was available for use by the decedent. Answer (D) is incorrect. The rent was not constructively received.

3. John, a self-employed carpenter, died on January 8 of the current year. Which of the following, if allowable, could be deducted on John's final Form 1040?

A. Unused net operating loss carryover from last year.

B. The full amount of his personal exemption (without proration).

C. Medical expenses paid by the estate within 1 year of death.

D. All of the answers are correct.

Answer (D) is correct.
REQUIRED: The allowable deductions on a decedent's final return.
DISCUSSION: For a decedent's final return, a personal exemption may be taken unless the decedent was another person's dependent. If medical expenses are paid out of the estate during the 1-year period beginning with the day after death, an election may be made to also deduct them on the final return. A deduction for NOLs must be taken on the final return or carried back to prior periods.

18.2 Income in Respect of a Decedent (IRD)

4. Which one of the following statements concerning the consequences of income being classified as "income in respect of a decedent" is true?

A. It receives no step-up in basis upon the decedent's death.

B. It is all treated as ordinary income to recipient.

C. It is all taxable to the decedent's estate.

D. It must be included in the decedent's final return.

Answer (A) is correct.
REQUIRED: The true statement of the consequences of income in respect of a decedent.
DISCUSSION: Sec. 1014(a) provides that the basis of property acquired from a decedent is generally the fair market value of the property on the date of the decedent's death. Sec. 1014(c) provides that property that constitutes a right to receive income in respect of a decedent does not receive a step-up in basis. Therefore, it has a carryover basis.
Answer (B) is incorrect. Income in respect of a decedent is treated as having the same character it would have had in the hands of the decedent [Sec. 691(a)(3)]. Answer (C) is incorrect. Income in respect of a decedent is included when received (as if on a cash basis) by the person who receives it [Sec. 691(a)(1)]. Answer (D) is incorrect. Income in respect of a decedent is income that is earned by the taxpayer but not received prior to his or her death nor accrued prior to his or her death if on the accrual method, so it is not included in the decedent's final return.

5. Fred, a calendar-year, cash-basis taxpayer who died in June of the current year, was entitled to receive a $10,000 accounting fee that had not been collected before the date of death. The executor of Fred's estate collected the full $10,000 in July of the current year. This $10,000 should appear in

A. Only the decedent's final individual income tax return.

B. Only the estate's fiduciary income tax return.

C. Only the decedent's estate tax return.

D. Both the fiduciary income tax return and the estate tax return.

Answer (D) is correct.

REQUIRED: The true treatment of income earned before death but not received until after death.

DISCUSSION: Income that a decedent had a right to receive prior to death but which was not includible on his or her final income tax return is income in respect of a decedent. The $10,000 is properly includible in the estate's (fiduciary) income tax return because Fred was a cash-basis taxpayer and would not properly include income not yet received at the time of death in his final return. Since the money was owed to Fred (he has a right to receive it), it is an asset of the estate and must be included on the estate tax return also.

Answer (A) is incorrect. Fred was a cash-basis taxpayer and would not properly include income not received at the time of death. Answer (B) is incorrect. The $10,000 is an asset of the estate and must also be included on the estate tax return. Answer (C) is incorrect. The $10,000 is income to the estate and must also be included on its income tax return.

18.3 Income Taxation of Estates and Trusts

6. Which of the following statements is true regarding estate income tax returns filed on Form 1041?

A. Form 1041 has its own tax rate schedule.

B. Estates are never liable for the alternative minimum tax.

C. All estates are subject to the same estimated tax rules that apply to Form 1040.

D. None of the answers are correct.

Answer (A) is correct.

REQUIRED: The true statement regarding estate income tax returns filed on Form 1041.

DISCUSSION: Form 1041 is subject to a tax rate schedule that reaches the 39.6% tax bracket in 2013 for taxable incomes exceeding $11,950.

Answer (B) is incorrect. Estates may be subject to the alternative minimum tax. Answer (C) is incorrect. Estates may be subject to estimated payments after 2 years. Answer (D) is incorrect. One of the answers is correct.

7. Which of the following statements is not true regarding the income taxation of trusts?

A. A trust (except for a grantor-type trust) is a separate legal entity for federal tax purposes.

B. A trust may be created only during the life of the grantor.

C. A trust figures its gross income in much the same manner as an individual.

D. A trust is allowed an income distribution deduction for distributions to beneficiaries.

Answer (B) is correct.

REQUIRED: The income taxation requirements of trusts.

DISCUSSION: A trust is created when a grantor conveys title to property to a trustee. A trust may be created before or after the death of a grantor. A trust created by the terms of a will is called a testamentary trust. A testamentary trust does not come into existence until the estate's personal representative completes the administration of the estate or transfers assets to the trust prior to the close of the estate. An *inter vivos* trust is created while the grantor is still alive.

8. As a general rule, a trust may qualify as a simple trust if

A. The trust instrument requires that all income must be distributed currently.

B. The trust does not distribute amounts allocated to the corpus of the trust.

C. The trust has no provisions for charitable contributions.

D. All of the answers are correct.

Answer (D) is correct.

REQUIRED: The criteria to qualify as a simple trust.

DISCUSSION: A simple trust is formed under an instrument having the following characteristics:

1) Requires current distribution of all its income
2) Requires no distribution of the rest (i.e., principal)
3) Provides for no charitable contributions by the trust

Thus, all of the answers are correct.

Answer (A) is incorrect. A trust that does not distribute amounts allocated to the corpus of the trust and one that has no provisions for charitable contributions also qualify as simple trusts. Answer (B) is incorrect. A trust that requires all income be distributed currently and one that has no provisions for charitable contributions also qualify as simple trusts. Answer (C) is incorrect. A trust that requires all income be distributed currently and one that does not distribute amounts allocated to the corpus of the trust also qualify as simple trusts.

9. Which of the following statements regarding the various types of trusts is not true?

A. A trust may qualify as a simple trust if all income must be distributed currently.

B. A trust may qualify as a simple trust if the trust does not distribute amounts allocated to the corpus of the trust.

C. A grantor trust is a separate taxable entity in which the grantor has not relinquished complete dominion and control over the trust.

D. A complex trust is any trust that does not qualify as a simple or grantor trust.

Answer (C) is correct.
  REQUIRED: The false statement regarding the various types of trusts.
  DISCUSSION: A grantor-type trust is a legal trust under applicable state law that is not recognized as a separate taxable entity for income tax purposes because the grantor or other substantial owners have not relinquished complete dominion and control over the trust.

10. With respect to simple trusts, all of the following statements are true except

A. The trust instrument requires that all the income must be distributed currently.

B. The trust instrument provides that amounts set aside for charitable purposes are deductible only to the trust.

C. The trust does not distribute amounts allocable to the corpus of the trust.

D. The exemption amount for a simple trust is $300.

Answer (B) is correct.
  REQUIRED: The false statement with respect to simple trusts.
  DISCUSSION: A simple trust is formed under an instrument that (1) requires current distribution of all its income, (2) requires no distribution of the res (i.e., principal), and (3) provides for no charitable contributions by the trust.
  Answer (A) is incorrect. A simple trust is formed under an instrument requiring current distribution of all its income. Answer (C) is incorrect. The distributable net income of the trust does not include amounts allocable to principal (corpus). Answer (D) is incorrect. A deduction for a personal exemption of $300 is allowable for a simple trust.

11. Christopher wants to create a revocable grantor trust that will own all of his stocks and rental properties. Which statement regarding income of the trust is true?

A. Christopher will be taxed only income that is distributed to him.

B. Christopher will be taxed on all income of the trust, regardless of distributions.

C. State law will determine how much of the trust income is taxable to Christopher.

D. If the rental income is passive, it will not be taxable to him.

Answer (B) is correct.
  REQUIRED: The true statement regarding grantor trusts.
  DISCUSSION: In general, a grantor trust is ignored for tax purposes, and all of the income, deductions, etc., are treated as belonging directly to the grantor. This also applies to any portion of a trust that is treated as a grantor trust.
  Answer (A) is incorrect. Christopher will be taxed on the income earned by the trust whether distributed to him or not. Answer (C) is incorrect. Federal law states that all income earned by the trust, whether distributed to him or not, is taxable the year earned. State law defines the criteria to be classified as a grantor trust. Answer (D) is incorrect. The passive rental income may be taxed to Christopher.

12. The Large Trust is a simple trust. Bert Little is the sole beneficiary of the trust. Capital gains are allocable to corpus. Based on the following information, what is the trust's distribution deduction?

Interest	$1,700
Dividends	300
Capital gains	2,000
Fiduciary fee	1,000

A. $1,000

B. $1,500

C. $2,000

D. $3,000

Answer (A) is correct.
  REQUIRED: The distribution deduction for the trust.
  DISCUSSION: Since capital gains are allocated to corpus, distributable net income is $1,000 ($1,700 + $300 – $1,000).
  Answer (B) is incorrect. The fiduciary fee is not allocated to the capital gains. Answer (C) is incorrect. The full fiduciary fee is deductible. Answer (D) is incorrect. The capital gains are allocated to corpus.

13. James Smith, a cash-basis taxpayer, received $35,000 in wages before his death on July 7 of the current year. In addition, his stock portfolio paid $12,000 in dividends, $11,500 of which was paid to him before his death. By what date is Form 1041 required to be filed?

    A. Form 1041 is not required to be filed.

    B. Nine months after date of death.

    C. By the 15th day of the 4th month after the end of the tax year selected by the estate's personal representative.

    D. By the 15th day of the 3rd month after the end of the tax year selected by the estate.

Answer (A) is correct.
    REQUIRED: The due date for Form 1041.
    DISCUSSION: Under Sec. 6012(a)(3), every estate that has gross income of $600 or more must file an income tax return. Under Reg. 1.6012-3, the return to be filed by a fiduciary for an estate or a trust is Form 1041. Sec. 6072 requires the return to be filed on or before the 15th day of the 4th month after the end of the tax year. Because Mr. Smith's income after death is less than $600, the estate does not have to file a return.

14. Rudy, a cash-basis taxpayer, received $50,000 in wages before his death. In addition, his stock portfolio paid $4,000 in dividends, $2,500 of which was paid to him before his death. By what date is Form 1041, *U.S. Income Tax Return for Estates and Trusts*, required to be filed?

    A. Form 1041 is not required to be filed.

    B. Nine months after death.

    C. By the 15th day of the 4th month after the end of the tax year selected by the estate's personal representative.

    D. By the 15th day of the 3rd month after the end of the tax year selected by the estate.

Answer (C) is correct.
    REQUIRED: The due date for Form 1041.
    DISCUSSION: Under Sec. 6012(a)(3), every estate that has gross income of $600 or more must file an income tax return. Under Reg. 1.6012-3, the return to be filed by a fiduciary for an estate or a trust is Form 1041. Sec. 6072 requires the return to be filed on or before the 15th day of the 4th month after the end of the tax year.
    Answer (A) is incorrect. The taxpayer's estate has gross income in excess of $600. Answer (B) is incorrect. Form 1041 is not the estate tax return. Answer (D) is incorrect. Form 1041 must be filed by the 15th day of the 4th month.

15. Which of the following receipts should be allocated exclusively to income by a trustee?

    A. A stock dividend.

    B. A very large year-end cash dividend.

    C. A stock split.

    D. A liquidating dividend whether in complete or partial liquidation.

Answer (B) is correct.
    REQUIRED: The receipts that should be allocated exclusively to income.
    DISCUSSION: Cash dividends are exclusively allocable to income. Cash dividends are not a change in the form of the principal; rather, they represent earnings from the principal (corpus). For simple trusts (i.e., trusts that must distribute all of their income currently), extraordinary dividends (whether paid in cash or property) or taxable stock dividends can be excluded from income if they are not distributed or credited to a beneficiary because the fiduciary in good faith determines that the governing instrument and local law allocate such amounts to corpus [Sec. 643(a)(4)].
    Answer (A) is incorrect. Stock dividends are allocated exclusively to principal. Answer (C) is incorrect. Stock splits are allocated exclusively to principal. Answer (D) is incorrect. Liquidating dividends are allocated exclusively to principal.

16. After Mary's death on August 1 of the current year, her estate received the following:

- $50,000 life insurance proceeds
- $1,000 interest income from a certificate of deposit that matured on August 5 of the current year
- $2,000 annual royalty on a patent

What amount of taxable income must be reported on the current-year *U.S. Income Tax Return for Estates and Trusts* (Form 1041)?

    A. $53,000

    B. $52,400

    C. $3,000

    D. $2,400

Answer (D) is correct.
    REQUIRED: The amount of taxable income that must be reported on Form 1041.
    DISCUSSION: An estate's gross income includes accrual and receipt of all income items for the year, including, among others, interest and royalties. The estate is also permitted a $600 exemption deduction. The life insurance proceeds are exempt from inclusion.
    Answer (A) is incorrect. The life insurance proceeds are not included in income, and the estate is allowed an exemption. Answer (B) is incorrect. The insurance proceeds are excluded. Answer (C) is incorrect. The estate is permitted an exemption.

17. Which of the following statements is false?

    A. The beneficiary of an estate or trust may be taxed on money required to be distributed whether actually distributed or not.

    B. Money distributed to a beneficiary from an estate is taxed twice—on the estate return and on the beneficiary's return.

    C. Tax-exempt interest distributed to a beneficiary is not taxable to the beneficiary.

    D. Losses of estates and trusts are generally not deductible by the beneficiaries.

Answer (B) is correct.
    REQUIRED: The false statement concerning taxes on estates.
    DISCUSSION: Money distributed to a beneficiary from an estate is not taxed twice. DNI is allocated to either the estate or beneficiary and is only taxed to whichever of the two it is allocated.
    Answer (A) is incorrect. According to Sec. 662, the beneficiary may be taxed on money required to be distributed, whether actually distributed or not. Answer (C) is incorrect. The character of income in the hands of the beneficiary is the same as in the hands of the trust or estate. Answer (D) is incorrect. This is generally a true statement. However, an estate's unused net operating loss carryover or capital loss carryover existing upon termination of the estate can be used by a beneficiary succeeding to property of the estate. A beneficiary entitled to an unused loss carryover or an excess deduction is the beneficiary who, upon the estate's termination, bears the burden of any loss for which a carryover is allowed or of any deductions more than gross income.

18. Ms. Brown died on June 30 last year. During the current year, her estate received the following:

Interest income	$2,500
Dividend income	5,000
Long-term capital gain	2,500

Pursuant to her will, 50% of all income was to be distributed to a specific qualifying charitable organization. The executor complied with the provision in a timely manner. Assuming all income was accumulated, what is the estate's taxable income for the current year?

    A. $10,000

    B. $2,500

    C. $5,000

    D. $4,400

Answer (D) is correct.
    REQUIRED: The taxable income of an estate.
    DISCUSSION: The total income of the estate is $10,000. A deduction for the charitable contribution reduces the income to $5,000. A $600 exemption deduction is then permitted, making the taxable income $4,400.
    Answer (A) is incorrect. A deduction for the charitable contribution and an exemption deduction is permitted. Answer (B) is incorrect. The long-term capital gain and interest income are includible. Answer (C) is incorrect. An exemption deduction of $600 is permitted.

19. Given the following information, compute the distribution deduction for a simple trust:

Interest income	$80,000
Dividend income	30,000
Tax-exempt interest	20,000
Capital gains	25,000
Expenses attributable to all interest income	5,000
Trustee's commissions allocable to all income including capital gains	15,000

- A. $125,000
- B. $110,000
- C. $95,400
- D. $85,500

Answer (C) is correct.
REQUIRED: The distribution deduction for a simple trust.
DISCUSSION: The expenses and commissions must be allocated to the various forms of income. The $5,000 expense for interest is attributed $4,000 to taxable interest and $1,000 to tax-exempt interest. This reduces taxable interest to $76,000 and tax-exempt interest to $19,000. The trustee commission is allocated to income of $150,000 ($76,000 taxable interest + $19,000 tax-exempt interest + $30,000 dividend income + $25,000 capital gains). The commission allocated to taxable interest is $7,600 [($76,000 ÷ $150,000) × $15,000], making taxable interest $68,400. The commission allocated to dividends is $3,000 [($30,000 ÷ $150,000) × $15,000], making taxable dividends $27,000.
Tax-exempt interest and capital gains are not included in the distribution deduction. Therefore, the distribution deduction for this simple trust equals $95,400 ($68,400 taxable interest + $27,000 taxable dividends).
Answer (A) is incorrect. The commissions and expenses must be allocated to the various forms of income and will reduce the distribution. Answer (B) is incorrect. Tax-exempt interest and capital gains are not included, and the expenses must be allocated to the various forms of income. Answer (D) is incorrect. All of the expenses and commissions reduce the deduction.

20. Trust B has distributable net income of $60,000, which includes $5,000 of tax-exempt income. The trustee distributed $75,000 to the trust's sole beneficiary. What amount will be shown as the distribution deduction on the trust's Form 1041?

- A. $55,000
- B. $60,000
- C. $70,000
- D. $75,000

Answer (A) is correct.
REQUIRED: The distribution deduction for a trust.
DISCUSSION: The distribution deduction for a trust is equal to the lesser of distributable net income (DNI) of the trust reduced by any tax-exempt income or the distributed amount reduced by any tax-exempt income. The DNI is less than the distribution. The $60,000 of DNI for Trust B is reduced by the $5,000 of tax-exempt income for a total of $55,000. This amount is then shown as the distribution deduction on the trust's Form 1041.
Answer (B) is incorrect. The DNI is reduced by the $5,000 of tax-exempt income. Answer (C) is incorrect. The DNI is reduced by the $5,000 of tax-exempt income, not the actual amount distributed. Answer (D) is incorrect. The actual amount distributed is not used on the Form 1041.

21. If you are the beneficiary of an estate that must distribute all its income currently (and none is tax-exempt), you must report your share of

- A. The distributable net income plus all other amounts actually paid to you.
- B. The distributable net income that you have actually received.
- C. The distributable net income whether or not you have actually received it.
- D. None of the answers are correct.

Answer (C) is correct.
REQUIRED: The amount of income to be reported by a beneficiary of an estate.
DISCUSSION: Under Sec. 662, a beneficiary of an estate (or complex trust) must include in gross income the amounts required to be distributed currently and any additional amounts actually distributed, but both amounts are limited to distributable net income (DNI). Therefore, if all income is taxable and required to be distributed currently, the beneficiary must include all DNI in income even if not actually received.
Answer (A) is incorrect. DNI is the limit on a beneficiary's taxable income from an estate (or complex trust). Answer (B) is incorrect. DNI is included when required to be distributed even if not actually received. Answer (D) is incorrect. DNI must be included in income when required to be distributed even if it is not actually received.

22. Under the terms of the will of Rick Waters, $6,000 a year is to be paid to his widow and $3,000 a year to his daughter out of the estate's income during the period of administration. There are no charitable contributions. For the year, the estate's distributable net income is only $6,000. How much must the widow and the daughter include in their gross incomes?

	Widow	Daughter
A.	$6,000	$3,000
B.	$4,000	$2,000
C.	$3,000	$3,000
D.	$2,000	$1,000

Answer (B) is correct.
REQUIRED: The amount each beneficiary should include in gross income from an estate.
DISCUSSION: Under Sec. 662, a beneficiary of an estate includes in gross income the amount distributed from an estate, limited to the distributable net income (DNI) of the estate. If the amount distributed exceeds DNI, each beneficiary includes a proportionate amount of the DNI based on the total amount distributed to all beneficiaries [Sec. 662(a)(1)]. The widow received 2/3 of total distributions to beneficiaries, so she will include $4,000 in her gross income ($6,000 DNI × 2/3). The daughter includes the other 1/3 of the $6,000 of DNI.
Answer (A) is incorrect. The income recognized is limited to the DNI. Answer (C) is incorrect. The income recognized is the proportionate amount based on the total amount distributed to all beneficiaries. Answer (D) is incorrect. The income recognized is the proportionate amount based on the total amount distributed to all beneficiaries.

23. Mrs. A died on June 30 of the current year. According to the terms of her will, $20,000 was paid to each of her three children prior to the end of the year. Additionally, the estate was to pay from earnings $20,000 to each child in the current year. In the current year, the estate had net earnings of $30,000. Assuming no charitable contributions were made, how much income will each child report?

A. $30,000 ordinary income.

B. $40,000 ordinary income.

C. $10,000 ordinary income.

D. $0

Answer (C) is correct.
REQUIRED: The amount each beneficiary should include in gross income from an estate.
DISCUSSION: Under Sec. 662, beneficiaries of an estate (and a complex trust) are required to include in gross income the amounts of fiduciary income that are required to be distributed and all other amounts that are distributed, limited to DNI. The amounts included in the beneficiaries' gross income retain the same character as in the hands of the estate or trust and are treated as consisting of the same proportion of each classified item entering into the computation of DNI. Since DNI is $30,000, each of the three children must include $10,000 in gross income.
Answer (A) is incorrect. DNI is distributed among the three children when calculating the amount of income to include. Answer (B) is incorrect. The amount includible in income is limited to the estate's DNI. Inheritances specified in the will are not included. Answer (D) is incorrect. DNI is $30,000 and must be distributed among three children.

24. With regard to a trust, which of the following statements is false?

A. A trust is a separate taxable entity.

B. The income allocated to a beneficiary retains the same character in his or her hands as it had in the hands of the trust.

C. If income is required to be distributed currently or is properly distributed to a beneficiary, the trust is regarded as a conduit with respect to that income.

D. Generally, the trust is taxed on the income currently distributed and on the portion it has accumulated.

Answer (D) is correct.
REQUIRED: The false statement regarding trusts.
DISCUSSION: A trust is allowed a distribution deduction for amounts required to be distributed currently and any other amounts properly paid, credited, or required to be distributed.

25. The trustee of a simple trust has prepared Form 1041 for the tax year ending December 31 of the current year. After determining the proportionate share of distributable net income for each beneficiary, the trustee must provide the beneficiary a copy of which federal form for inclusion on the beneficiary's Form 1040 for the current year?

A. Form 1099-MISC.

B. Schedule K-1 (Form 1041).

C. Form 1099-T.

D. No form, since a simple trust does not distribute income.

Answer (B) is correct.

REQUIRED: The federal form that the trustee must provide a copy of to the beneficiary.

DISCUSSION: Schedule K-1 (Form 1041) is used to report the beneficiary's share of income, deductions, and credits from a trust or an estate.

Answer (A) is incorrect. The trustee does not need to provide the beneficiary a copy of Form 1099-MISC after determining the proportional share of distributable net income. Answer (C) is incorrect. The trustee does not need to provide the beneficiary a copy of Form 1099-T after determining the proportional share of distributable net income. Answer (D) is incorrect. A simple trust does distribute income.

26. In which circumstance must an estate of a decedent make estimated tax payments?

A. An estate is never required to make estimated tax payments.

B. The estate has a first tax year that covers 12 months.

C. The estate has income in excess of $400.

D. The estate has a tax year ending 2 or more years after the date of the decedent's death.

Answer (D) is correct.

REQUIRED: The true statement concerning estimated tax payments for an estate.

DISCUSSION: Sec. 6654(l) requires an estate to make estimated payments of income tax in all tax years except during its first 2 taxable years of existence. No estimated payments are required during its first 2 taxable years.

Answer (A) is incorrect. Estates are required to make payments of estimated tax after the first 2 years of existence. Answer (B) is incorrect. Estimated tax payments are required only after the estate's first 2 years of existence without regard to the length of the first tax year. Answer (C) is incorrect. An estate need not make estimated tax payments for its first 2 years of existence without regard to the amount of its gross income.

27. On December 15, Year 1, Kyle received a $10,000 distribution from his father's estate. On March 30, Year 2, Kyle was issued Schedule K-1 for the estate's first fiscal year (February 1, Year 1, through January 31, Year 2). The Schedule K-1 from the estate showed taxable interest income of $200 and had no other entries. Based on the information above, which of the following statements are true?

A. Kyle must report income of $10,000 on his Year 2 return.

B. Kyle must report $200 interest income on his Year 2 return.

C. Kyle may claim a deduction on Schedule A for a pro rata share of the estate tax that was paid by the estate.

D. Kyle must report $200 interest income on his Year 2 return and he may also claim a deduction on Schedule A for a pro rata share of the estate tax that was paid by the estate.

Answer (B) is correct.

REQUIRED: The true statement concerning the amount of estate income to be reported on the beneficiary's return.

DISCUSSION: Publication 559 states, "income in respect of a decedent is . . . taxed when received by the recipient (estate or beneficiary). However, an income tax deduction is allowed to the recipient for the estate tax paid on the income." The information in the question does not indicate whether there was any IRD. From the information, it must be assumed that the $10,000 was a nontaxable distribution of estate assets. It also should be assumed that the $200 represented income earned by the estate that flowed through to Kyle and was not IRD. Thus, Kyle would report only the $200 as income.

Answer (A) is incorrect. The $10,000 distribution was a nontaxable distribution of estate assets. Answer (C) is incorrect. No estate tax would have been paid since there was no income in respect of a decedent. Therefore, no deduction may be claimed. Answer (D) is incorrect. No estate tax would have been paid since there was no income in respect of a decedent. Therefore, no deduction may be claimed.

28. Stan is the personal representative of his brother, Bruce, who died June 30, 2013. Stan has obtained an identification number for Bruce's estate and has notified the IRS on Form 56 that he has been appointed executor. He has filed his brother's final return for 2013 and has the following information regarding Bruce's remaining estate. What will be the taxable income of the estate?

Unpaid salary not received by Bruce before he died	$ 6,000
Dividend check on XYZ stock received August 15, 2013	600
Form 1099 interest earned on savings after death	2,000
Sales price of coin collection sold to unrelated person	10,000
Value of the coins at the date of death	9,000
Attorney's fees for administration of the estate	1,000

    A. $8,600

    B. $17,600

    C. $8,000

    D. None of the answers are correct.

Answer (C) is correct.

    REQUIRED: The taxable income of the estate.

    DISCUSSION: Administration expenses (and debts of a decedent) are deductible on the estate tax return under Sec. 2053, and some may also qualify as deductions for income tax purposes on the estate's income tax return. Sec. 642(g), however, disallows a double deduction and requires a waiver of the right to deduct them on Form 706 in order to claim them on Form 1041. Therefore, the attorney's fees for administration of the estate can be deducted on the estate return since it is not stated that a waiver was filed. The income earned by the decedent but taxable to the estate is calculated as follows:

Unpaid salary	$ 6,000
Gain on sale of coins	1,000
Dividend income	600
Interest income	2,000
Less: Administrative expense	(1,000)
Exemption deduction	(600)
Estate's taxable income	$ 8,000

    Answer (A) is incorrect. An exemption deduction of $600 is allowed for estates. Answer (B) is incorrect. The sales price of the coins must be reduced by their basis and an exemption deduction of $600 is allowed. Answer (D) is incorrect. The taxable income of the estate is $8,000.

29. Trust A is a simple trust with two equal beneficiaries, Jim and Randy. In 2013, the trust had $30,000 of distributable net income, all from taxable interest. During the year, the trust distributed $5,000 to Jim and $10,000 to Randy. Based on this information, the trustee should issue K-1s as follows:

    A. Jim $5,000; Randy $10,000.

    B. Jim $15,000; Randy $15,000.

    C. Jim $10,000; Randy $20,000.

    D. Jim $30,000; Randy $30,000.

Answer (B) is correct.

    REQUIRED: The amount of DNI to include on Schedule K-1.

    DISCUSSION: Beneficiaries of a simple trust are taxed on the distributable net income (DNI) of the trust, whether the income is distributed or not. Even though Jim and Randy only received $5,000 and $10,000, respectively, they are taxed on the full $30,000 of trust income. Since they are equal beneficiaries, they each have $15,000 of taxable income.

    Answer (A) is incorrect. Jim and Randy are taxed on the full amount of DNI from the trust, not just the amount distributed. Answer (C) is incorrect. Jim and Randy are equal beneficiaries and therefore share the $30,000 of DNI equally. Answer (D) is incorrect. Jim and Randy are only responsible for their share of DNI.

18.4 Fraudulent Trusts

30. Which of the following is not an abusive technique used to reduce income taxes?

    A. Depreciation of personal assets.

    B. Reporting income wired overseas.

    C. Deduction of personal expenses.

    D. Splitting income over multiple entities.

Answer (B) is correct.

    REQUIRED: The transaction that is not considered abusive.

    DISCUSSION: Some abusive techniques used to reduce income tax include:

1. Depreciation of personal assets (such as a home)

2. Deduction of personal expenses

3. Splitting income over multiple entities, often filed in multiple locations

4. Underreporting income

5. Avoiding filing returns

6. Wiring income overseas and failing to report it

7. Attempting to protect transactions through bank secrecy laws in tax haven countries

Use the additional questions in Gleim **EA Test Prep** to create Practice Exams that emulate Prometric!

STUDY UNIT NINETEEN
RETIREMENT PLANS FOR SMALL BUSINESSES

(11 pages of outline)

This study unit discusses retirement plans that the owner of a small business, including a self-employed person, can set up and maintain for employees. The IRS tests three types of plans: simplified employee pension (SEP) plans, SIMPLE plans, and Keogh plans. A SEP is a simple plan that allows contributions to retirement plans without involvement with the more complex Keogh plan. However, some advantages available to Keogh plans, such as special tax treatment that may apply to Keogh plan lump-sum distributions, do not apply to SEP.

19.1 SIMPLIFIED EMPLOYEE PENSION (SEP)

1. A simplified employee pension (SEP) is a written agreement (a plan) that allows an employer to make contributions toward his or her retirement (if a self-employed individual) and his or her employees' retirement without becoming involved in more complex retirement plans.

   a. Under a SEP, IRAs are set up for, at a minimum, each qualifying employee and/or self-employed individual.

      1) The employer must make contributions to the SEP plan by the due date of the employer's return, including extensions.

         a) Contributions are reported on Form 5498.

Self-Employed Individual

2. A self-employed individual is an employee for SEP purposes. (S)he is also the employer.

   a. Even if the self-employed individual is the only qualifying employee, (s)he can have a SEP-IRA.

   b. A qualified employer plan set up by a self-employed person is sometimes called a Keogh plan.

Qualifying Employee

3. A qualifying employee is one who meets all of the following conditions:

   a. (S)he is at least 21 years old.

   b. (S)he has worked for the employer during at least 3 of the 5 years immediately preceding the tax year.

   c. (S)he has received from the employer at least $550 in compensation during the tax year.

Excludable Employees

4. The following groups of employees can be excluded from coverage under a SEP:

   a. Employees who are covered by a union agreement and whose retirement benefits were bargained for in good faith by their union and their employer

   b. Nonresident alien employees who have no U.S.-source earned income from their employer

5.   A SEP does not require contributions every year, but it must not discriminate in favor of highly compensated employees.

Highly Compensated Employee

a.   A highly compensated employee is any employee who meets either of the following two conditions:

1)   The employee owns (or owned last year) more than 5% of

a)   The capital or profits interest in the employer,
b)   The outstanding stock, or
c)   The total voting power of all stock of the employer corporation.

2)   The employee's compensation from the employer for the preceding year (i.e., 2012) was more than $115,000, and (if the employer elects to apply this clause for last year) the employee was in the top 20% when ranked on the basis of last year's compensation.

6.   **Contributions**

a.   An employer is permitted to contribute (and deduct) each year to each participating employee's SEP up to the lesser of

1)   25% of the employee's compensation (limited to $255,000 of compensation) or
2) $51,000.

b.   A 10% excise tax is generally imposed on the employer on contributions in excess of the deductible amount under Sec. 4972(a).

7.   Special rules apply for self-employed individuals who contribute to their own SEPs.

a.   Compensation for the self-employed is equal to net earnings from self-employment.

1)   For SEP purposes, the individual's net earnings must take into account the deduction for contributions to a SEP.

a)   Because the deduction amount and net earnings are dependent on each other, the following worksheets must be used.

b)   The maximum rate becomes 20% after the computation.

2)   First, a new rate must be determined to take into account the contribution deduction.

Self-Employed Person's Rate Worksheet	
(1) Plan contribution rate as a decimal (for example, 10 1/2% would be 0.105)	_____
(2) Rate in line 1 plus one (for example, 0.105 plus one would be 1.105)	_____
(3) Self-employed rate as a decimal (divide line 1 by line 2)	_____

3) Then the maximum deduction may be computed.

Self-Employed Person's Deduction Worksheet	
Step 1: Enter the rate from the "Self-Employed Person's Rate Worksheet."	_____
Step 2: Enter net earnings from self-employment.	$_____
Step 3: Enter the deduction for self-employment tax.	$_____
Step 4: Subtract Step 3 from Step 2 and enter the result.	$_____
Step 5: Multiply Step 4 by Step 1 and enter the result.	$_____
Step 6: Multiply $255,000 by the plan contribution rate. Enter the result but not more than $51,000.	$_____
Step 7: Enter the smaller of Step 5 or Step 6. This is the **maximum deductible contribution**.	$_____

8. Income passed through to shareholders of S corporations is not considered to be earnings from self-employment.

9. Unlike contributions to IRAs, contributions to SEP-IRAs are excluded from an employee's income rather than deducted from it. Any excess employer contributions must be included in income without any offsetting deduction.

10. An employee's deduction for contributions to a qualified plan, including a SEP, is generally allowed for the tax year in which contributions are paid.

    a. Contributions paid on or before the due date of returns, including extensions, for a particular tax year are deemed paid on the last day of that tax year.

Credits

11. When an employer starts up a SEP, SIMPLE, or qualified retirement plan, the firm may be eligible for a credit, which is equal to 50% of all ordinary and necessary costs of starting up the plan (maximum $500) for the first 3 years of the plan.

    a. Eligible small businesses are those that have fewer than 100 employees who receive at least $5,000 in compensation from the employer in the year preceding the start-up of the retirement plan.

Stop and review! You have completed the outline for this subunit. Study questions 1 through 8 beginning on page 366.

19.2 SAVINGS INCENTIVE MATCH PLANS FOR EMPLOYEES (SIMPLE)

1. Employers with 100 or fewer employees who received at least $5,000 in compensation from the employer in the preceding year are eligible.

EXAMPLE

A corporation has 70 eligible employees, and its subsidiary has 50 eligible employees. The corporation is not eligible for a SIMPLE plan.

---

2. Employers cannot maintain another qualified plan.

3. The plan allows employees to make elective contributions of up to $12,000 for 2013 ($14,500 if 50 or older) and requires employers to make matching contributions.

4.   A SIMPLE plan is not subject to nondiscrimination rules or other complex requirements applicable to qualified plans.

   a.   An employer can choose to cover all employees without restriction, or (s)he can limit the employees covered to those who received at least $5,000 in compensation during any 2 preceding years and who are reasonably expected to receive at least $5,000 in the current year.

5.   SIMPLE plans may be structured as an IRA or as a 401(k) qualified cash or deferred compensation.

6.   Contributions to a SIMPLE IRA account are limited to employee elective contributions and require employer matching contributions or nonelective contributions.

7.   There are two formulas for employer matching:

Matching

   a.   Matching contribution formula

   1)   Employers are generally required to match employee contributions on a dollar-for-dollar basis up to 3% of an employee's compensation for the year.

   2)   However, an employer also may elect to match contributions for all eligible employees for a given year at a rate not less than 1% of each employee's compensation upon notification to the employees.

   3)   The lower percentage cannot drop below 3% of employee compensation in more than 2 years in a 5-year period ending with that year.

Alternative

   b.   Alternative formula

   1)   An employer may elect to make a nonelective contribution of 2% of compensation for each eligible employee who has earned at least $5,000 in compensation from the employer during the year.

   a)   Only the first $255,000 of compensation is considered [Sec. 401(a)(17)].

8.   The employees vest immediately in employer SIMPLE contribution.

9.   Self-employed individuals may participate in a SIMPLE plan.

10.   An employer may establish a SIMPLE plan even if none of its employees wish to participate.

Employer Contributions

11.   Employer contributions are expressed as a percentage of compensation, not as a flat dollar amount.

   a.   Employers must continue to make contributions even in lean years of at least 1% of employee compensation.

   b.   Employers must contribute an employee's elective deferral to the employee's SIMPLE account no later than 30 days after the last day of the month for which the contributions are made.

   c.   An employer must make matching contributions by the due date of the tax return, including extensions.

Deduction

12. Employers may deduct contributions for the year in which they are made.

    a. Matching contributions are deductible for the year only if made by the due date of the tax return, including extensions.

13. Distributions from a SIMPLE IRA plan are generally taxed like distributions from an IRA.

    a. Distributions can be rolled over tax-free from one SIMPLE account to another SIMPLE account.
    b. Distributions can be rolled over tax-free to an IRA after 2 years.
    c. Distributions can be rolled over to a qualified plan after 2 years.

Penalties

14. Withdrawals

    a. Withdrawals before age 59 1/2 are subject to the 10% tax.
    b. Withdrawals within the first 2 years are subject to a 25% penalty.
    c. Distributions from a SIMPLE account are includible in a participant's income when withdrawn.

15. An employee's elective contributions will be treated as wages for purposes of employment tax.

    a. The employer's matching or nonelective contributions are not wages.

Stop and review! You have completed the outline for this subunit. Study questions 9 through 13 beginning on page 369.

19.3 KEOGH PLANS

1. A qualified employer plan set up by a self-employed person is sometimes called a Keogh or HR10 plan.

    a. Only a sole proprietor or a partnership may set up a Keogh plan.
    b. Qualified plans must be set by year end.

2. For Keogh plan purposes, a self-employed person is both an employer and an employee.

3. To set up a Keogh plan, an employer must either

    a. Adopt an IRS-approved prototype or master plan offered by a sponsoring organization or

    b. Prepare and adopt a written plan that satisfies the qualification requirements of the Internal Revenue Code.

Minimum Participation Requirements

4. An employee must be allowed to participate in the plan if (s)he

    a. Has reached age 21 and
    b. Has at least 1 year of service (2 years if the plan provides that, after not more than 2 years of service, the employee has a nonforfeitable right to all of his or her accrued benefits).

        1) The employee must complete at least 1,000 hours of service within the 1 year of service.

5. A plan cannot exclude an employee because (s)he has reached a specified age.

6. **Two Basic Kinds of Keogh Plans**

Defined Contribution Plan

a. A defined contribution plan provides an individual account for each participant in the plan. It provides benefits to a participant largely based on the amount contributed to that participant's account. Benefits are also affected by any income, expenses, gains and losses, and any forfeitures of other accounts that may be allocated to an account. There are two types of defined contribution plans:

1) Profit-sharing plan. A profit-sharing plan is a plan for sharing employer profits with the firm's employees.

   a) An employer does not have to make contributions out of net profits to have a profit-sharing plan.

2) Money purchase pension plan. Contributions to a money purchase pension plan are fixed and are not based on the employer's profits.

   a) This applies even if the compensation of a self-employed individual as a participant is based on earned income derived from business profits.

Defined Benefit Plan

b. A defined benefit plan is any plan that is not a defined contribution plan. Contributions to a defined benefit plan are based on a computation of the contributions needed to fulfill the requirements established by an employer.

Contributions

7. Generally, contributions made to a Keogh plan, including those made for a self-employed individual's own benefit, are deductible and subject to limits.

a. Self-employed individuals may make contributions on their own behalf only if they have net earnings from self-employment.

1) For Keogh plan purposes, common-law employees are not self-employed with respect to income from their work, even if that income is self-employment income for Social Security tax purposes.

   a) A common-law employee is a person who performs services for an employer who has the right to control and direct both the results of the work and the way it is done.

      i) For example, common-law employees who are ministers, full-time insurance salespeople, or U.S. citizens employed in the U.S. by foreign governments may not establish Keogh plans.

      ii) A common-law employee can be self-employed as well.

b. Limits

1) Defined contribution plan. A defined contribution plan's annual contributions and other additions (excluding earnings) to the account of a participant cannot exceed the lesser of

   a) 100% of the employee's compensation or
   b) $51,000.

2) Defined benefit plan. For 2013, the annual benefit for a participant under a defined benefit plan cannot be more than the lesser of

   a) 100% of the participant's average compensation for his or her highest 3 consecutive calendar years or

   b) $205,000.

   NOTE: Compensation is the pay a participant receives from an employer for personal services for a year. It includes wages and salaries, fees, commissions, tips, fringe benefits, and bonuses. It does not include reimbursement or other expense allowances.

Employer Deduction

8. The deduction is limited based on the type of plan.

   a. Profit-sharing plan. The deduction for contributions to a profit-sharing plan cannot be more than 25% of the compensation from the business paid to all common-law employees participating in the plan.

   b. Money purchase pension plan. The deduction for contributions to a money purchase pension plan is generally limited to 25% of the compensation paid to participating common-law employees.

   c. Defined benefit plan. Because the deduction for contributions to a defined benefit plan is based on actuarial assumptions, an actuary must compute the deduction.

   d. If an employer contributes more than can be deducted in the current year, the excess may be carried over and deducted in later years, in addition to contributions for those years.

9. **Elective Deferrals [401(k) Plans]**

   a. A Keogh plan can include a cash or deferred arrangement under which eligible employees can elect to have part of their before-tax pay contributed to the plan rather than receive the pay in cash.

      1) This contribution, called an elective deferral, remains tax-free until it is distributed.

   b. An employer may, under a qualified 401(k) plan, also make contributions (other than matching contributions) for participating employees without giving them a choice to take cash instead.

   c. For 2013, the basic limit on elective deferrals is $17,500 ($23,000 if 50 or older).

   d. If an excess deferral exists and is not withdrawn by April 15 of the following year, the amount will be included in income and not included in cost basis when determining a future gain.

      1) If it is withdrawn by April 15, it will be included in gross income but no penalty will apply.

10. **Rollovers**

    a. The recipient of an eligible rollover distribution from a Keogh plan can defer the tax on it by rolling it over into an IRA or another eligible retirement plan.

    b. Rollovers may be subject to withholding tax. If a recipient receives an eligible rollover distribution that is expected to total more than $200, the payor must withhold 20% of each distribution for federal income tax.

       1) Tax will not be withheld if the taxpayer has the plan administrator pay the eligible rollover distribution directly to another qualified plan or an IRA in a direct rollover.

    c. An eligible rollover distribution is any distribution that is not

       1) A required distribution

       2) An annual (or more frequent) distribution under a long-term (10 years or more) annuity contract or as part of a similar long-term series of substantially equal periodic distributions

       3) The portion of a distribution that represents the return of an employee's nondeductible contributions to the plan

       4) A distribution, such as a return of excess contributions or deferrals under a 401(k) plan

11. **Tax on Premature Distributions**

    a.   If a distribution is made to an employee under the plan before (s)he reaches age 59 1/2, the employee may have to pay a 10% additional tax on the premature distribution. This tax applies to the amount received that the employee must include in income.

Exceptions

    b.   The 10% tax will not apply if distributions before age 59 1/2

        1)   Are made to a beneficiary (or to the estate of the employee) on or after the death of the employee

        2)   Result from the employee having a qualifying disability

        3)   Are part of a series of substantially equal periodic payments beginning after separation from service and made at least annually for the life or life expectancy of the employee or the joint lives or life expectancies of the employee and his or her designated beneficiary

        4)   Are made to an employee after (s)he separated from service if the separation occurred during or after the calendar year in which the employee reached age 55

        5)   Are made to an employee for medical care up to the amount allowable as a medical expense deduction (determined without regard to whether the employee itemizes deductions)

        6)   Are timely made to reduce excess contributions or excess deferrals under a 401(k) plan

        7)   Are made to an alternate payee under a Qualified Domestic Relations Order (QDRO)

        8)   Are timely made to reduce excess employee or matching employer contributions (excess aggregate contributions)

        9)   Are timely made to reduce excess elective deferrals

        10)   Are made because of an IRS levy on the plan

        11)   Are made as a qualified reservist distribution

        12)   Are made as a permissible withdrawal from an eligible automatic contribution arrangement (EACA)

12. **Prohibited Transactions**

    a.   Certain transactions between a plan and a disqualified person are prohibited and are subject to a 15% excise tax on the amount involved.

        1)   If the transaction is not corrected within the taxable period, an **additional** tax of 100% of the amount involved is imposed.

            a)   Both taxes are payable by any disqualified person who participated in the transaction.

    b.   Prohibited transactions generally include

        1)   A transfer of plan income or assets to, or use of them by or for the benefit of, a disqualified person

        2)   Dealing with plan income or assets by a fiduciary in his or her own interest

        3)   The receiving of consideration by a fiduciary for his or her own account from a party that is dealing with the plan in a transaction that involves plan income or assets

        4)   Any of the following acts between the plan and a disqualified person:

            a)   Selling, exchanging, or leasing property

            b)   Lending money or extending credit

            c)   Furnishing goods, services, or facilities

Disqualified Persons

    c.   The following are disqualified persons:

        1) An employer of any participants in the plan

        2) A 10% (or more) partner in a partnership having the plan

        3) A fiduciary of the plan

        4) A highly compensated employee (earning 10% or more of the employer's yearly wages)

        5) An employee organization, any of whose members are covered by the plan

        6) A person providing services to the plan

        7) A related party to a disqualified person

Exemption

    d.   Prohibited transactions do not take place if a disqualified person receives benefits to which (s)he is entitled as a plan participant and beneficiary. However, the same terms apply as for other qualified persons.

EXAMPLE

The owner of a business with an established plan must meet the age requirement of 59 1/2 before receiving a distribution.

Keogh Plan Qualification Rules

13. To qualify for the tax benefits available to qualified plans, a Keogh plan must meet certain requirements of the tax law:

    a.   Plan assets must not be diverted.

    b.   Minimum coverage requirements must be met. To be a qualified plan, a defined benefit plan must benefit at least the lesser of

        1) 50 employees or

        2) The greater of

            a) 40% of all employees or

            b) 2 employees.

        NOTE: If there is only one employee, the plan must benefit that employee.

    c.   Contributions must not discriminate in favor of highly compensated employees.

    d.   Contribution and benefit limits must not be exceeded.

    e.   Minimum vesting standards must be met. A benefit becomes vested when it becomes nonforfeitable.

    f.   Benefit payments must begin when required, except in the case of early retirement payments.

    g.   Benefits must not be assigned or alienated.

    h.   Benefits must not be reduced for Social Security increases.

    i.   Elective deferrals must be limited.

14. If an employer contributes to a defined contribution retirement plan (a plan under which an individual account is set up for each participant), annual additions to an account are limited to the lesser of

    a.   100% of the participant's compensation or

    b. $51,000.

        1) For purposes of these limits, contributions to more than one such plan must be added.

        2) Since a SEP is considered a defined contribution plan for purposes of these limits, employer contributions to a SEP must be added to other contributions to defined contribution plans.

15. In order to be eligible to file Form 5500-EZ, the plan must meet the following criteria:

a. Be a one-participant plan;

1) A one-participant plan is one in which the coverage is for the owner or owner and spouse of a business, regardless of incorporated or not or if coverage is given to one or more partners or partners and spouses in a business partnership.

b. Meet the minimum coverage required by Sec. 410(b) without being combined with any other plan; and

c. Provide benefits only for the individual, the individual and a spouse, or one or more partners and their respective spouses.

Stop and review! You have completed the outline for this subunit. Study questions 14 through 28 beginning on page 370.

19.4 RETIREMENT DISTRIBUTIONS AND LOANS

1. **Distributions from Qualified Plans**

Lump-Sum Distributions

a. Annuity distributions are taxed using the Sec. 72 exclusion ratio.

1) Joint and survivorship annuity stops being paid when both spouses are deceased.

2) Single life annuity stops being paid when the employee dies.

3) A nonannuity distribution made on or after an annuity starting date is generally included in full in gross income.

Early Distribution

b. Early distributions received by a participant before attaining age 59 1/2 are subject to a 10% (25% for a SIMPLE plan during the first 2 years) penalty tax in addition to the regular income tax. The following exceptions apply:

1) Post employee death
2) On account of disability
3) Substantially equal periodic payments
4) Separation from service after 55 (not applicable to IRA)
5) Dividends on employer securities
6) Levy
7) Medical expenses (without regard to employee itemizing deductions)
8) Alternate payees
9) Additional exceptions for IRAs
10) Medical insurance premiums
11) Education expenses
12) First-time homebuyer expenses
13) U.S. military reservists called to active duty

2. **Excess Accumulations and Required Minimum Distributions**

a. Failure to meet the required minimum distributions can result in a 50% penalty.

b. The RMD amount for a year is generally equal to the participant's accrued benefit or account balance as of the end of the prior year, divided by the appropriate distribution period.

1) Before-death distributions
2) After-death distributions

a) Death before RMDs begin
b) Death on or after RMDs begin

c. Required beginning dates

1) Generally, the required beginning date is April 1 of the calendar year following the later of the employee attaining age 70 1/2 or retiring.

2) For a traditional IRA, the required beginning date is April 1 of the calendar year following the employee attaining age 70 1/2.

3) The required distribution date each year following the initial beginning date is December 31.

EXAMPLE

Lurlene is an unmarried participant in a qualified defined contribution plan. Her account balances for 5 years are as follows:

Date	Account Balance
December 31, Year 1	$275,000
December 31, Year 2	$295,000
December 31, Year 3	$320,000
December 31, Year 4	$350,000
December 31, Year 5	$340,000

Lurlene retired January 1, Year 1, and reached age 70 on May 1, Year 2. The initial RMD is based on the year in which she reached 70 1/2 (Year 2), since it is later than her retirement date. The deadlines and amounts associated with the first four RMDs are shown below:

	Distribution			Calculation	
No.	RMD Date	Relevant Balance Date (Dec. 31)	Relevant Age (Dec. 31)	Balance ÷ Life Expectancy	RMD Amount
1st	April 1, Yr 3	Year 1	Yr 2: 70	$275,000 ÷ 27.4	$10,037
2nd	Dec 31, Yr 3	Year 2	Yr 3: 71	[$295,000 − $10,037] ÷ 26.5	$10,753
3rd	Dec 31, Yr 4	Year 3	Yr 4: 72	$320,000 ÷ 25.6	$12,500
4th	Dec 31, Yr 5	Year 4	Yr 5: 73	$350,000 ÷ 24.7	$14,170

---

3. **Borrowing from the Plan**

a. The terms of a qualified plan may permit the plan to lend money to participants without adverse income or excise tax results, if certain requirements are met.

b. Code Sec. 72(p) basically treats loans as distributions.

1) A loan will not be treated as a distribution to the extent loans to the employee do not exceed the lesser of

a) $50,000 or

b) The greater of one-half of the present value of the employee's vested accrued benefit under such plans or $10,000.

2) The $50,000 maximum sum is reduced by the participant's highest outstanding balance during the preceding 12-month period.

c. Plan loans generally have to be repaid within 5 years, unless the funds are to acquire a principal residence for the participant.

d. Plan loans must be amortized in level payments, made not less frequently than quarterly over the term of the loan.

e. A pledge of the participant's interest under the plan or an agreement to pledge such interest as security for a loan by a third party, as well as a direct or indirect loan from the plan itself, is treated as a loan.

Stop and review! You have completed the outline for this subunit. Study questions 29 and 30 on page 375.

QUESTIONS

19.1 Simplified Employee Pension (SEP)

1. Joaquin is a small business owner who maintains a SEP for his employees:

- Jan, a 42-year-old part-timer who has worked for Joaquin in this business since 2003. She works 15 hours per week. She earned $13,600 in 2013.
- Malik, a 72-year-old seasonal worker who works from September through December. He has worked for Joaquin in this business since 2005 and earned $6,100 in 2013.
- Monica is 21 years old and works 10 hours per week all year. She has worked for Joaquin since June 2011 and earned $4,900 in 2013.

Joaquin's business had net taxable income in 2012 of $62,300. All employees and Joaquin are U.S. citizens, and none of them are union members. Which of the individuals listed below can be excluded from coverage under the SEP in 2013?

A. Jan.

B. Malik.

C. Monica.

D. Joaquin.

Answer (C) is correct.
    REQUIRED: The excludable individual from coverage under the SEP.
    DISCUSSION: In order for an employee to be eligible for coverage under a SEP, the employee must be 21 years old, have worked for the employer in at least 3 of the last 5 years, and have earned at least $550 in compensation. Therefore, Monica is excludable because she has not been working for Joaquin for the necessary time.

2. Which of the following is required for an individual to qualify for a simplified employee pension (SEP)?

A. The individual must not be covered by another retirement plan.

B. Self-employment net loss is subtracted from any salaries and wages when figuring total compensation.

C. The individual must not be age 70 1/2 by the end of the tax year.

D. None of the answers are correct.

Answer (D) is correct.
    REQUIRED: The requirement for an individual to qualify for a self-employed retirement plan.
    DISCUSSION: A self-employed individual is an employee for SEP purposes. (S)he is also the employer. Even if the self-employed individual is the only qualifying employee, (s)he can have a SEP-IRA. A qualifying employee is one who meets all of the following conditions: (1) (S)he is at least 21 years old, (2) (s)he has worked for the employer during at least 3 of the 5 years immediately preceding the tax year, and (3) (s)he has received from the employer at least $550 in compensation in the tax year.
    Answer (A) is incorrect. This is not a requirement to qualify for a SEP. Answer (B) is incorrect. This is not a requirement to qualify for a SEP. Answer (C) is incorrect. There is no age limitation.

3. Mike is self-employed. He is a calendar-year taxpayer. If he wants to set up a SEP plan for his business for the year 2013, he must do so by (including extensions)

A. December 31, 2013.

B. January 31, 2014.

C. April 15, 2014.

D. October 15, 2014.

Answer (D) is correct.
    REQUIRED: The latest date that a SEP plan can be set up for a given year.
    DISCUSSION: A deduction for contributions to a qualified plan, including a SEP, is generally allowed for the tax year in which contributions are paid. Contributions paid on or before the due date of returns, including extensions, for a particular tax year are deemed paid on the last day of that tax year. Therefore, Mike would be allowed until October 15, 2014 (April 15, 2014, the normal due date plus a 6-month extension).
    Answer (A) is incorrect. Mike is allowed beyond the 2013 tax year. He is entitled to the normal due date plus an extension. Answer (B) is incorrect. January 31, 2014, is before the normal due date of April 15, 2014. Answer (C) is incorrect. April 15, 2014, does not include the 6-month extension allowed by the IRS to set up a SEP.

4. Antonio is an ordained minister. As a minister, Antonio is a common-law employee of the church where he works, but his earnings and parsonage allowance are treated as self-employment income on which he pays self-employment tax. If the church had no retirement plan under which Antonio was covered, which of the following would Antonio be permitted to establish for himself?

    A. Traditional IRA.

    B. Savings Incentive Match Plan for Employees (SIMPLE) IRA.

    C. Simplified employee pension (SEP).

    D. Both a traditional IRA and a Savings Incentive Match Plan for Employees (SIMPLE) IRA.

Answer (A) is correct.

REQUIRED: The retirement plan that may be used by a self-employed individual.

DISCUSSION: Since SEP and SIMPLE plans are plans that are established by the employer, Antonio may not participate in these plans. Although his income is considered self-employment income for tax considerations, he is still an employee of the church. The only reason that he is required to pay self-employment tax on his income is because the church is a tax-exempt organization. So, unless the church has established a retirement plan, Antonio can only establish a traditional IRA, because it does not require the participation of an employer.

Answer (B) is incorrect. A SIMPLE plan requires the participation of the employer and, although he must pay self-employment tax on his income, the church is considered his employer and is not participating in his retirement plan. Answer (C) is incorrect. A SEP requires the participation of the employer and, although he must pay self-employment tax on his income, the church is considered his employer and is not participating in his retirement plan. Answer (D) is incorrect. A SIMPLE plan requires the participation of the employer and, although he must pay self-employment tax on his income, the church is considered his employer and is not participating in his retirement plan.

5. John, a self-employed taxpayer, has a SEP plan for his business. He has three eligible employees, Sara (age 35), Joseph (age 37), and Jean (age 45), who have worked for him for the past 10 years. For the year 2013, Sara earned $15,000, Joseph earned $25,000, and Jean earned $30,000. John wants to elect the 25% contribution rate so he can put as much as possible in for himself. If he elects 25%, how much must he contribute to the plan for his employees?

    A. $0

    B. $2,100

    C. $17,500

    D. $51,000

Answer (C) is correct.

REQUIRED: The amount of money that must be contributed to a SEP plan.

DISCUSSION: A SEP does not require contributions every year, but it must not discriminate in favor of highly compensated employees. If John wants to contribute 25% to his own SEP, he must also contribute the lesser of 25% of the participating employee's compensation (limited to $255,000 of compensation) or $51,000. Therefore, 25% of $70,000 ($15,000 + $25,000 + $30,000) is $17,500.

Answer (A) is incorrect. John is required to contribute to the plan if he elects the 25% contribution rate. Answer (B) is incorrect. John must contribute 25% of the total of his three employees' salaries. Answer (D) is incorrect. The amount of $51,000 is the upper limit of how much John would be able to contribute if his employees were eligible.

6. Crispian is employed by Pied Piper, Inc. Pied Piper, Inc., has a simplified employee pension (SEP) plan for its employees in which Crispian participates. Crispian's compensation for 2013, before Pied Piper's contribution to his SEP-IRA, was $270,000. What is the maximum contribution that Pied Piper can contribute to Crispian's SEP-IRA?

    A. $65,000

    B. $51,000

    C. $30,000

    D. $20,000

Answer (B) is correct.

REQUIRED: The maximum deductible contribution that can be made to a SEP.

DISCUSSION: Under Sec. 404(h), the amount of deductible contributions for a simplified employee pension shall not exceed 25% of the employee's compensation (limited to $255,000) during the taxable year. Pied Piper's maximum deductible contribution is $51,000 (limited to the lesser of $255,000 × 25%, or $51,000).

7. Amy, a self-employed consultant, contributes more to her profit-sharing plan than she can deduct for the year. Amy can carry over and deduct the excess in later years combined with her normal contributions. Her contribution in later years is limited to which of the following?

A. 15% of the participating employee compensation.

B. 10% of the participating employee compensation.

C. 25% of the participating employee compensation.

D. None of the answers are correct.

Answer (D) is correct.
REQUIRED: The self-employed taxpayer's deduction limitation for contributions to a profit-sharing plan.
DISCUSSION: Publication 560 states, "Your deduction for contributions to a profit-sharing plan cannot be more than 15% (25% for year beginning after December 31, 2001) of the compensation paid (or accrued) during the year to your eligible employees participating in the plan. You must reduce this limit in figuring the deduction for contributions you make for your own account." For years after 2001, the plan contribution rate is 25%. Special rules apply for self-employed individuals who contribute to their own SEPs, since their compensation is the net earnings from self-employment. A special rate is used for self-employed individuals, which takes into account the allowable deductions to arrive at net earnings. The rate is determined by taking the plan contribution rate and dividing it by the rate plus one. Thus, if the plan contribution rate is 25%, a self-employed taxpayer's maximum contribution would be 20% [.25 ÷ (1 + .25)].

8. When Bob is figuring the deduction for contributions made to his own SEP-IRA, compensation is his net earnings from self-employment, which takes the following into account:

A. A reduction for all of Bob's self-employment tax.

B. A reduction for the maximum allowable contribution to Bob's own SEP-IRA.

C. The deduction for one-half of Bob's self-employment tax and the deduction for contributions to his own SEP-IRA.

D. A reduction for all of Bob's self-employment tax and a reduction for the maximum allowable contribution to Bob's own SEP-IRA.

Answer (C) is correct.
REQUIRED: The item that is taken into account when figuring net earnings from self-employment.
DISCUSSION: Special rules apply for self-employed individuals who contribute to their own SEPs. Compensation for the self-employed is equal to net earnings from self-employment. For SEP purposes, the individual's net earnings must take into account the deduction for contributions to a SEP. Because the deduction amount and net earnings are dependent on each other, the following worksheets must be used:

1. First, a new rate must be determined to take into account the contribution deduction.

Self-Employed Person's Rate Worksheet

(1) Plan contribution rate as a decimal (for example, 10 1/2% would be 0.105) _____

(2) Rate in line 1 plus one (for example, 0.105 plus one would be 1.105) _____

(3) Self-employed rate as a decimal (divide line 1 by line 2) _____

2. Then the maximum deduction may be computed.

Self-Employed Person's Deduction Worksheet

Step 1: Enter the rate from the "Self-Employed Person's Rate Worksheet." _____

Step 2: Enter net earnings from self-employment. $ _____

Step 3: Enter the deduction for self-employment tax. $ _____

Step 4: Subtract Step 3 from Step 2 and enter the result. $ _____

Step 5: Multiply Step 4 by Step 1 and enter the result. $ _____

Step 6: Multiply $255,000 by the plan contribution rate. Enter the result but not more than $51,000. $ _____

Step 7: Enter the smaller of Step 5 or Step 6. This is the maximum deductible contribution. $ _____

Answer (A) is incorrect. A reduction of only 50% of the self-employment tax should be taken into account. Answer (B) is incorrect. Bob is also allowed a reduction of 50% of the self-employment tax. Answer (D) is incorrect. A reduction of only 50% of the self-employment tax should be taken into account.

19.2 Savings Incentive Match Plans for Employees (SIMPLE)

9. The SIMPLE plan must be available to every employee who

A. Received at least $5,000 in compensation from the employer during any 2 preceding years and is reasonably expected to receive at least $5,000 in compensation during the current year.

B. Received at least $5,000 in compensation from the employer during the 2 preceding years and is reasonably expected to receive at least $5,000 in compensation during the current year.

C. Received at least $5,000 in compensation from the employer during any 2 preceding years.

D. Is reasonably expected to receive at least $5,000 in compensation during the current year.

Answer (A) is correct.

REQUIRED: The employee who is eligible to participate in a SIMPLE plan.

DISCUSSION: The SIMPLE plan must be available to every employee who (1) received at least $5,000 in compensation from the employer during any 2 preceding years and (2) is reasonably expected to receive at least $5,000 in compensation during the current year. Individuals who are self-employed may also participate in a SIMPLE plan. However, certain nonresident aliens and employees who are covered by a collective bargaining agreement may be unable to participate (Publication 4334).

Answer (B) is incorrect. The employee is required to have received at least $5,000 in compensation during any 2 preceding years, not just in the last 2 years. Answer (C) is incorrect. The employee is also required to reasonably expect to receive at least $5,000 in compensation during the current year. Answer (D) is incorrect. The employee is also required to have received at least $5,000 in compensation during any 2 preceding years.

10. Participants of SIMPLE plans who take early withdrawals are generally subject to

A. A 10% withdrawal penalty.

B. A 25% withdrawal penalty.

C. A 25% withdrawal penalty on the first $10,000 and a 10% withdrawal penalty on the remainder.

D. A 25% withdrawal penalty on withdrawals made during the 2-year period beginning on the date the participant began participating in the plan and a 10% withdrawal penalty on all other early distributions.

Answer (D) is correct.

REQUIRED: The applicable early withdrawal penalty for SIMPLE plans.

DISCUSSION: Participants are considered to have taken early withdrawals if the distributions are made before age 59 1/2. These distributions are generally subject to a 10% early withdrawal penalty. However, employees who withdraw contributions during the 2-year period beginning on the date the participant began participating in the SIMPLE plan will be assessed a 25% early withdrawal penalty tax.

11. The SIMPLE 401(k) plan is a qualified retirement plan. It is not subject to nondiscrimination and top-heavy rules if it meets all of the following conditions except

A. Under the plan, the employee may choose salary reduction contributions to a trust up to $12,000 for 2013.

B. Participants age 50 and over can make a catch-up contribution up to $2,500.

C. Employers must make matching contributions of 3% of compensation for the year or nonelective contributions of 2% of compensation on behalf of each eligible employee who has at least $5,000 of compensation from his employer for the year.

D. The employee's rights to any contributions are forfeitable.

Answer (D) is correct.

REQUIRED: The condition not required to exclude the SIMPLE 401(k) plan from nondiscrimination and top-heavy rules.

DISCUSSION: The SIMPLE 401(k) plan is available to employers with 100 or fewer employees who received at least $5,000 in compensation from the employer in the preceding year. Employers are not permitted to maintain another qualified plan. Employers are generally required to match employee contributions on a dollar-for-dollar basis up to 3% of an employee's compensation for the year. An employer may elect to make a nonelective contribution of 2% of compensation for each eligible employee who has earned at least $5,000 in compensation from the employer during the year. The employees vest immediately in employer SIMPLE contributions; therefore, the funds are not forfeitable.

Answer (A) is incorrect. An employee is permitted to make salary reduction contributions to a trust up to $12,000 for 2013. Answer (B) is incorrect. Participants age 50 and up are allowed to make a catch-up contribution of $2,500 a year. Answer (C) is incorrect. The contribution percentages are properly stated.

12. All of the following are true statements about contributions to SIMPLE IRA plans except

    A. Employer contributions have to be expressed as a percentage of the employee's compensation and cannot exceed $12,000 in 2013 for employees under age 50.

    B. Unless an election is made otherwise, the employer must match the elective contribution of an employee in an amount not exceeding 3% of the employee's compensation.

    C. An employee's SIMPLE IRA contribution cannot exceed 3% of the employee's compensation.

    D. An employer may elect to limit its matching contribution for all eligible employees to a smaller percentage of compensation, but not less than 1%.

Answer (C) is correct.
    REQUIRED: The contribution requirements to a SIMPLE IRA plan.
    DISCUSSION: A SIMPLE IRA must allow each eligible employee to elect to have the employer make payments either directly to the employee in cash or as a contribution, expressed as a percentage of compensation, to the SIMPLE account. Elective contributions are limited to $12,000 for employees under age 50 for 2013, but there is no limit based on a percentage of compensation. The employer must match the elective contribution of an employee in an amount not exceeding 3% of the employee's compensation. However, an employer may elect to limit its match to a smaller percentage of compensation not to fall below 1%.
    Answer (A) is incorrect. Employer contributions must be expressed as a percentage of compensation and cannot exceed $12,000 if the employee is under age 50. Answer (B) is incorrect. The employer must match the employee's elective contribution that does not exceed 3% of compensation unless an election is made otherwise. Answer (D) is incorrect. An employer may elect to match a smaller elective contribution, but not less than 1% of compensation.

13. Lenore, who is 43 years old, opened a SIMPLE IRA on January 19, 2012. On September 22, 2013, she withdrew the entire $10,000 value of the account. The distribution does not meet any early withdrawal exceptions to the additional tax on early distributions. How much additional tax (penalty) is the distribution subject to?

    A. $600

    B. $1,000

    C. $1,500

    D. $2,500

Answer (D) is correct.
    REQUIRED: The additional tax (penalty) assessed on early distributions from a SIMPLE IRA.
    DISCUSSION: If an early distribution occurs from a SIMPLE IRA within 2 years of commencing to participate in the program, the penalty assessed increases from 10% to 25%. Therefore, Lenore would be penalized $2,500 ($10,000 × .25). (See Publication 560.)
    Answer (A) is incorrect. The penalty is 25%, not 6%. Answer (B) is incorrect. The penalty assessed is 25%, not 10%. Answer (C) is incorrect. The penalty is 25%, not 15%.

19.3 Keogh Plans

14. Your qualified 401(k) plan can include what type of contribution arrangement?

    A. Cash.

    B. Elective deferral.

    C. Both cash and elective deferral arrangements.

    D. None of the answers are correct.

Answer (C) is correct.
    REQUIRED: The permissible qualified 401(k) contribution arrangements.
    DISCUSSION: Qualified 401(k) plans can include contribution arrangements that are either cash or elective deferral arrangements. (See Publication 560.)

15. Which of the following correctly states the maximum allowable catch-up contribution for a participant age 50 or over for the year 2013?

    A. $5,500 for a 401(k) plan.

    B. $1,500 for a SIMPLE plan.

    C. $1,500 for a traditional IRA.

    D. $6,000 for a Roth IRA.

Answer (A) is correct.
    REQUIRED: The maximum catch-up contribution for a participant age 50 and older on a qualified retirement plan.
    DISCUSSION: For 2013, the catch-up contribution is $5,500 for qualified 401(k) plans (Publication 571). However, the catch-up contribution is only $2,500 for a SIMPLE plan and $1,000 for traditional and Roth IRAs.
    Answer (B) is incorrect. The catch-up contribution for a SIMPLE plan is $2,500 for 2013. Answer (C) is incorrect. The catch-up contribution for a traditional IRA is $1,000 for 2013. Answer (D) is incorrect. The amount of $6,000 includes the $1,000 catch-up contribution and the maximum ordinary contribution.

16. Which of the following statements is false with respect to Keogh plans?

A. If a plan is a defined benefit plan subject to the minimum funding requirements, the employer must make quarterly installment payments of the required contributions.

B. If a defined contribution plan is a profit-sharing plan, the employer can make contributions for common-law employees out of net profits only.

C. An employer can have more than one Keogh plan.

D. A separate account is set up for each participant under a defined contribution plan.

Answer (B) is correct.

REQUIRED: The false statement regarding Keogh plans.

DISCUSSION: A profit-sharing plan is a plan for sharing employer profits with the firm's employees. However, an employer does not have to make contributions out of net profits to have a profit-sharing plan.

Answer (A) is incorrect. The employer must make quarterly installment payments of required contributions if the plan is defined benefit subject to minimum funding requirements. Answer (C) is incorrect. Employers can have multiple Keogh plans. Answer (D) is incorrect. Separate accounts are set up for each participant of a defined contribution plan.

17. If persons in the following positions are treated as having earnings from self-employment, the only ones who can establish Keogh plans with regard to those earnings are

A. Ministers.

B. Full-time insurance salespeople.

C. Accountants.

D. U.S. citizens employed in the United States by foreign governments.

Answer (C) is correct.

REQUIRED: The person who may establish a Keogh plan.

DISCUSSION: For Keogh plan purposes, common-law employees are not self-employed with respect to income from their work, even if that income is self-employment income for Social Security tax purposes. A common-law employee is a person who performs services for an employer who has the right to control and direct both the results of the work and the way it is done. For example, common-law employees who are ministers, full-time insurance salespeople, or U.S. citizens employed in the U.S. by foreign governments may not establish Keogh plans. However, a common-law employee can be self-employed as well. For example, an accountant can be an employee during regular working hours and also practice in the evening as a self-employed person.

Answer (A) is incorrect. Ministers are common-law employees and therefore are not eligible to establish a Keogh plan. Answer (B) is incorrect. Full-time insurance salespeople are common-law employees and therefore are not eligible to establish a Keogh plan. Answer (D) is incorrect. U.S. citizens employed in the United States by foreign governments are common-law employees and therefore are not eligible to establish a Keogh plan.

18. Max, a fiduciary, pledged his client's traditional IRA of $300,000 as security for a loan. If Max is found liable for engaging in a prohibited transaction, what is the minimum penalty he is most likely to pay if the transaction is not corrected?

A. $45,000

B. $30,000

C. $300,000

D. $345,000

Answer (D) is correct.

REQUIRED: The minimum penalty for engaging in a prohibited transaction.

DISCUSSION: Certain transactions between a plan and a disqualified person are prohibited and are subject to a 15% excise tax on the amount involved. If the transaction is not corrected within the taxable period, an additional tax of 100% of the amount involved is imposed. Both taxes are payable by any disqualified person who participated in the transaction. The receiving of consideration by a fiduciary for his or her own account from a party that is dealing with the plan in a transaction that involves plan income or assets is prohibited. As an extra note, the IRS accepted both $45,000 and $300,000 as correct answers in this question because the question stated that the transaction was not corrected, but it did not give a time frame. The IRS failed to combine the penalties for a total of $345,000.

Answer (A) is incorrect. Max must also pay an additional 100% penalty for failure to correct the transaction. Answer (B) is incorrect. The amount of $30,000 is only a 10% excise tax, and the correct excise tax is 15% plus an additional penalty for failure to correct the violation. Answer (C) is incorrect. The amount of $300,000 only includes the 100% additional penalty.

19. With regard to a Keogh plan, which of the following statements is true?

A. Only a sole proprietor or a partner can establish a Keogh plan.

B. An employee must be allowed to participate in the plan if the employee is at least age 21, but not over age 59 1/2, and has at least 1 year of service (2 years if the plan provides that, after not more than 2 years of service, the employee has a nonforfeitable right to all of his or her accrued benefits).

C. For Keogh plan purposes, a self-employed individual is both an employer and an employee. As an employer, the individual can usually deduct, subject to limits, contributions made to a Keogh plan, excluding those made for his or her own retirement.

D. You can choose not to have tax withheld on long-term periodic distributions and required distributions.

Answer (D) is correct.
REQUIRED: The true statement regarding Keogh plans.
DISCUSSION: If a participant receives a distribution that is not eligible for rollover treatment, such as a long-term periodic distribution or a required distribution, the 20% withholding requirement does not apply. Although other withholding rules may apply, a taxpayer may still choose not to have tax withheld from these distributions.
Answer (A) is incorrect. A partnership, not a partner, can establish a Keogh plan. Answer (B) is incorrect. A plan cannot exclude an employee because (s)he has reached a certain age. Answer (C) is incorrect. A self-employed individual may deduct contributions to his or her own account.

20. Which of the following retirement plans does not have a salary reduction (elective deferral) component to it?

A. Simplified employee pension plan.

B. SIMPLE IRA plan.

C. SIMPLE 401(k) plan.

D. Qualified 401(k) plan.

Answer (A) is correct.
REQUIRED: The retirement option that does not have a salary reduction (elective deferral) component.
DISCUSSION: Many retirement options offer an elective deferral component. The simplified employee pension plan does not offer a salary reduction, however.

21. Which of the following statements with respect to a Sec. 401(k) plan is false?

A. Any Keogh plan can include a 401(k) plan.

B. Eligible employees can elect to have their employer contribute part of their before-tax pay to the 401(k) plan rather than receive the pay in cash.

C. The amount contributed to a 401(k) plan within applicable limits, and any earnings on it, remain tax-free until it is distributed by the plan.

D. A 401(k) plan may not require, as a condition of participation, that an employee complete a period of service beyond the later of age 21 or the completion of 1 year of service.

Answer (A) is correct.
REQUIRED: The false statement regarding a Sec. 401(k) plan.
DISCUSSION: A Keogh plan can include a cash or deferred arrangement [401(k) plan] under which eligible employees can elect to have an employer contribute part of their before-tax pay to the plan rather than receive the pay in cash. However, a Keogh plan can include a 401(k) plan only if the Keogh is

1) A profit-sharing plan or
2) A money purchase pension plan in existence on June 27, 1974.

Answer (B) is incorrect. Eligible employees can elect to have their employer contribute part of their before-tax pay to the 401(k) plan rather than receive the pay in cash. Answer (C) is incorrect. The amount contributed to a 401(k) plan within applicable limits, and any earnings on it, remains tax-free until it is distributed by the plan. Answer (D) is incorrect. A 401(k) plan may not require, as a condition of participation, that an employee complete a period of service beyond the later of age 21 or the completion of 1 year of service.

22. Which of the following distributions would be subject to the 10% additional tax that is imposed upon premature distributions from a Keogh plan prior to an employee reaching age 59 1/2?

A. A distribution made to an employee after separation from service, if the separation occurred during or after the calendar year in which the employee reached age 55.

B. A distribution made to an employee for medical care to the extent that the distribution does not exceed the amount allowable as a medical expense deduction (determined without regard to whether the employee itemizes deductions).

C. A timely made distribution to reduce excess employee or matching employer contributions (excess aggregate contributions).

D. A distribution made to permit the employee to purchase a vacation home.

Answer (D) is correct.
   REQUIRED: The situation subject to the 10% additional tax.
   DISCUSSION: Section 72(t)(2) lists many exceptions to the 10% tax on early distributions from qualified retirement plans. One of these exceptions is an early distribution qualified first-time home buyer distribution. A qualified first-time home buyer distribution is a payment received to the extent the payment is used before the close of the 120th day after the day on which the distribution is received to pay qualified acquisition costs with respect to a principal residence of a first-time home buyer. However, the purchase of a second personal residence does not meet the exception from the additional tax.

23. The 2013 basic limit on elective deferrals in 401(k) plans (excluding SIMPLE plans) for participants under age 50 is

A. $12,000

B. $14,500

C. $17,500

D. $23,000

Answer (C) is correct.
   REQUIRED: The 2013 basic limit on elective deferrals in 401(k) plans for participants under age 50.
   DISCUSSION: A 401(k) plan can include a cash or deferred arrangement under which eligible employees can elect to have part of their before-tax pay contributed to the plan rather than receive the pay in cash. This contribution, called an elective deferral, remains tax-free until it is distributed. For 2013, the basic limit on elective deferrals is $17,500 ($23,000 if 50 or older).

24. Which of the following statements with respect to self-employed retirement plan prohibited transactions is false?

A. The tax on a prohibited transaction is 15% of the amount involved.

B. Disqualified persons include a fiduciary of the plan.

C. Exchanging property between a disqualified person and a plan is a prohibited transaction.

D. If the prohibited transaction is not corrected within the taxable period, an additional tax of 80% of the amount involved is imposed.

Answer (D) is correct.
   REQUIRED: The false statement regarding prohibited transactions.
   DISCUSSION: The tax on a prohibited transaction is 15% of the amount involved for each year in the taxable period. If the transaction is not corrected within the taxable period, an additional tax of 100% of the amount involved is imposed. Both taxes are payable by any disqualified person who participated in the transaction.
   Answer (A) is incorrect. The tax on prohibited transactions is 15% of the amount involved. Answer (B) is incorrect. A fiduciary of the plan is a disqualified person. Answer (C) is incorrect. Exchanging property between a disqualified person and a plan is a prohibited transaction.

25. Benjamin, a sole proprietor, has a retirement plan for himself and all eligible employees. For 2013, Benjamin paid salaries of $75,000 on which contributions to the plan were based. With regard to the tax on prohibited transactions, all of the following are considered disqualified persons with respect to the retirement plan except

- A. Benjamin.
- B. Benjamin's employee and plan participant, Marcie, who received wages of $7,000.
- C. Benjamin's grandson, Bryan.
- D. Tate, who provides services to the retirement plan.

Answer (B) is correct.

REQUIRED: The individual who is not a disqualified person regarding prohibited transactions.

DISCUSSION: Any prohibited transaction between a plan and a disqualified person is subject to an excise tax of 15% on the amount involved. An individual is a disqualified person if (s)he is

1) An employer of any participants in the plan
2) A 10% or more partner in a partnership having the plan
3) A fiduciary of the plan
4) A highly compensated employee (10% or more of the employer's yearly wages)
5) An employee organization
6) A person providing services to the plan
7) A related party to a disqualified person

Marcie is not a disqualified person because she made less than $7,500 (10% of $75,000).

Answer (A) is incorrect. Benjamin is the employer. Answer (C) is incorrect. Bryan is a related party to a disqualified person. Answer (D) is incorrect. Tate provides services to the plan.

26. To qualify for the tax benefits available to qualified plans, a Keogh plan must meet certain requirements of the tax law. In this regard, which of the following statements is true?

- A. Under the plan, contributions or benefits to be provided may discriminate in favor of highly compensated employees.
- B. The plan must satisfy certain requirements regarding when benefits vest. A benefit is vested when it becomes forfeitable.
- C. The plan must make it impossible for its assets to be used for or diverted to purposes other than for the benefit of employees and their beneficiaries.
- D. The plan cannot provide for payment of retirement benefits before the normal retirement age.

Answer (C) is correct.

REQUIRED: The statement that is a requirement for a qualified Keogh plan.

DISCUSSION: In order for a Keogh plan to qualify for the tax benefits, the benefits must not be assigned or alienated.

Answer (A) is incorrect. Contributions and benefits may not discriminate. Answer (B) is incorrect. A benefit is vested when it becomes nonforfeitable. Answer (D) is incorrect. A plan can provide for early retirement distributions.

27. Which of the following plan provisions or benefits will preclude a Keogh plan from qualifying for the tax benefits available to qualified plans?

- A. The plan benefits at least the fewer of 50 employees or 40% of all employees.
- B. The defined benefit plan provides for automatic survivor benefits in the form of a qualified preretirement survivor annuity for a vested participant who dies before the annuity starting date and who has a surviving spouse.
- C. The plan permits a benefit reduction for a post-separation increase in the Social Security benefit level or wage base for any participant receiving benefits under the plan.
- D. The plan permits loans to a participant or beneficiary if the loan is secured by the participant's accrued nonforfeitable benefit and is exempt from the tax on prohibited transactions.

Answer (C) is correct.

REQUIRED: The provision that disqualifies a plan from the tax benefits available to qualified plans.

DISCUSSION: To qualify for the tax benefits available to qualified plans, a Keogh plan must meet certain requirements of the tax law. In order to qualify as a Keogh plan, the plan must not reduce benefits because of Social Security increases. A plan must not permit a benefit reduction for a post-separation increase in the Social Security benefit level or wage base for any participant or beneficiary who is receiving benefits under the plan or is separated from service and has nonforfeitable rights to benefits.

Answer (A) is incorrect. A Keogh plan must benefit the fewer of 50 employees or 40% of all employees. Answer (B) is incorrect. Automatic survivor benefits must be provided for in the Keogh plan. Answer (D) is incorrect. Loans to a participant or beneficiary are allowed in a Keogh plan if the loan is secured by the participant's accrued nonforfeitable benefit and is exempt from the tax on prohibited transactions.

28. A Keogh plan must meet certain requirements. Which of the following is not a requirement of a Keogh plan?

A. The plan must make it impossible for its assets to be used for or diverted to purposes other than for the benefit of employees and their beneficiaries.

B. Contributions or benefits must not discriminate in favor of highly compensated employees.

C. Minimum coverage requirements must be met.

D. The plan cannot provide for payment of retirement benefits before the normal retirement age.

Answer (D) is correct.
   REQUIRED: The item that is not a requirement of a Keogh plan.
   DISCUSSION: To qualify for the tax benefits available to qualified plans, a Keogh plan must meet certain requirements of the tax law.

● Plan assets must not be diverted.
● Minimum coverage requirements must be met.
● To be a qualified plan, a defined benefit plan must benefit at least the lesser of 50 employees or the greater of 40% of all employees or two employees.
● If there is only one employee, the plan must benefit that employee.
● Contributions must not discriminate in favor of highly compensated employees.
● Contribution and benefit limits must not be exceeded.
● Minimum vesting standards must be met.
● A benefit becomes vested when it becomes nonforfeitable.
● Benefit payments must begin when required, except in the case of early retirement payments.
● Benefits must not be assigned or alienated.
● Benefits must not be reduced for Social Security increases.
● Elective deferrals must be limited.

   Answer (A) is incorrect. Prohibited transactions generally include a transfer of plan income or assets to, or use of them by or for the benefit of, a disqualified person. Answer (B) is incorrect. It is a requirement that contributions must not discriminate in favor of highly compensated employees. Answer (C) is incorrect. The minimum coverage requirements of a Keogh plan must be met.

19.4 Retirement Distributions and Loans

29. Rick reached age 70 1/2 on July 24, 2012. Rick must receive the required minimum distribution from his IRA for 2012 and 2013 by

A. April 1, 2013, and December 31, 2013.

B. December 31, 2012, and December 31, 2013.

C. April 15, 2013, and December 31, 2013.

D. April 15, 2013, and April 15, 2014.

Answer (A) is correct.
   REQUIRED: The due date of a required minimum distribution from an IRA after obtaining age 70 1/2.
   DISCUSSION: Owners of a traditional IRA must start receiving the required minimum distribution (required beginning date) from an IRA by April 1 of the year following the year in which they reach age 70 1/2. The required minimum distribution for any year after the year the owner turns 70 1/2 must be made by December 31 of that year.

30. Charles retired 3 years ago at age 72 from working at his family's laminating business. His required minimum distribution for 2013 is $2,000. Charles elects to only withdraw $1,500 from his IRA account. How much excise tax may Charles have to pay for that year?

A. $50

B. $100

C. $200

D. $250

Answer (D) is correct.
   REQUIRED: The amount of excise tax Charles may have to pay for excess accumulation.
   DISCUSSION: Failure to meet the required minimum distributions can result in a 50% penalty (excise tax) for the year on the amount not distributed as required.

Use the additional questions in Gleim **EA Test Prep** to create Practice Exams that emulate Prometric!

STUDY UNIT TWENTY
EXEMPT ORGANIZATIONS

(4 pages of outline)

Certain organizations may qualify for exemption from federal income tax under Sec. 501(a). They are referred to as nonprofit organizations. Most organizations seeking recognition of exemption from federal income tax must use application forms specifically prescribed by the IRS.

20.1 EXEMPT ORGANIZATIONS

Exempt Status

1. Exempt status generally depends on the nature and purpose of an organization.

   a. An organization is tax-exempt only if specifically designated exempt by the IRC.

   b. It may be organized as a corporation, trust, foundation, fund, society, etc.

      1) An organization operated for the primary purpose of carrying on a trade or business for profit is generally not tax-exempt.

   c. Examples of organization types that may be exempt are

      1) Religious or apostolic organizations

         a) The Salvation Army is an example of a religious organization.

      2) Political organizations
      3) Chambers of commerce
      4) Real estate boards
      5) Labor organizations
      6) American Red Cross
      7) State-chartered credit unions
      8) Civic welfare organizations

         a) Organizations that combat community deterioration and juvenile delinquency, such as a Boys & Girls Club, qualify.

      9) Certain domestic and foreign corporations
      10) Child and animal protection organizations
      11) Public safety testing organizations
      12) Athletic clubs

         a) Organizations that foster national or international amateur sports competition provided they do not provide athletic facilities or equipment

      13) Fraternal beneficiary associations

         a) Associations that operate under a lodge system and provide payment of life, sick, accident, or other benefits to members and their dependents

      14) Social organizations

         a) No part of net earnings may benefit a private shareholder.
         b) Exempt status is lost if 35% or more of its receipts are from sources other than membership fees, dues, and assessments.

      15) Schools

Prohibited Transactions

d. Certain employee trusts lose exempt status if they engage in prohibited transactions.

1) Examples include lending without adequate security or reasonable interest or paying unreasonable compensation for personal services.

Religious, Charitable, Scientific, Educational, Literary

e. Organizations formed and operated exclusively for religious, charitable, scientific, educational, literary, or similar purposes are a broad class of exempt organizations.

1) No part of net earnings may inure to the benefit of any private shareholder or individual.

2) No substantial part of its activities may be attempts to influence legislation or a political candidacy (e.g., political action committees).

a) In general, if a substantial part of the activities of an organization consists of attempting to influence legislation, the organization will lose its exempt status.

i) However, most organizations can elect to replace the substantial part of activities test with a lobbying expenditure limit.

b) If an election for a tax year is in effect for an organization and that organization exceeds the lobbying expenditure limits, an excise tax of 25% will be imposed on the excess amount.

c) Exempt status will be lost if the organization directly participates in a political campaign.

Private Foundations

f. Each domestic or foreign exempt organization is a private foundation unless, generally, it receives more than a third of its support (annually) from its members and the general public. In this case, the private foundation status terminates, and the organization becomes a public charity.

1) Exempt status of a private foundation is subject to statutory restrictions, notification requirements, and excise taxes.

2) A charitable, religious, or scientific organization is presumed to be a private foundation unless it either

a) Is a church or has annual gross receipts under $5,000 or

b) Notifies the IRS that it is not a private foundation (on Form 1023) within 15 months from the end of the month in which it was organized.

Feeder Organization

g. An organization must independently qualify for exempt status. It is not enough that all of its profits are paid to exempt organizations.

Homeowners' Association

h. It is treated as a tax-exempt organization.

1) A homeowners' association is one organized for acquisition, construction, management, maintenance, etc., of residential real estate or condominiums. A cooperative housing corporation is excluded.

2) A condominium management association, to be treated as a tax-exempt housing association, must file a separate election for each tax year by the return due date of the applicable year.

Requirements for Exemption

2.   An organization other than an employee's qualified pension or profit-sharing trust must apply in writing to its IRS district director for a ruling or a determination that it is tax-exempt.

   a.   To establish its exemption, an organization must file a **written application** with the key director for the district in which the principal place of business or principal office of the organization is located.

      1)   Religious, charitable, scientific, educational, etc., organizations (public charities) use Form 1023. Form 1024 is used by most others.

      2)   If filed within the 15-month period, retroactive treatment is available.

Annual Information Return

   b.   Exempt organizations are generally required to file annual information returns on or before the 15th day of the 5th month following the close of the taxable year.

      1)   Exempt status may be denied or revoked for failure to file.

      2)   The organization reports all gross income, receipts, and disbursements.

         a)   The amount of contributions received is reported.
         b)   All substantial contributions are identified.

      3)   Those exempted from the requirement include

         a)   A church or church-affiliated organization;

         b)   An exclusively religious activity or any religious order;

         c)   An organization (other than a private foundation) having annual gross receipts that are not more than $50,000; and

         d)   A stock bonus, pension, or profit-sharing trust that qualified under Sec. 401.

      4)   Private foundations are required to file annual information returns on Form 990 or Form 990-PF regardless of the amounts of their gross receipts.

      5)   Organizations with under $50,000 in gross receipts that do not have to file an annual notice will be required to file a Form 990-N, *Electronic Notice (e-Postcard) for Tax-Exempt Organizations Not Required to File Form 990 or 990-EZ*.

         a)   The form is due by the 15th day of the 5th month following the close of the tax year and can be filed electronically and free of charge.

         b)   Form 990-N requires the organization to provide the name and mailing address of the organization, any other names used, a web address (if one exists), the name and address of the principal officer, and a statement confirming the organization's annual gross receipts are $50,000 or less.

         c)   Failure to file the annual report for 3 years in a row will subject the organization to loss of its exempt status, requiring the organization to reapply for recognition.

      6)   A central or parent organization may file Form 990, *Return of Organization Exempt from Income Tax*, for two or more local organizations that are not private foundations. However, this return is in addition to the central or parent organization's separate annual return if it must file one.

         a)   Form 990-EZ is a shortened version of Form 990. It is designed for use by small exempt organizations and nonexempt charitable trusts. An organization may file Form 990-EZ instead of Form 990 if it meets both of the following requirements:

            i)   Its gross receipts during the year were less than $200,000.
            ii)   Its total assets at the end of the year were less than $500,000.

Unrelated Business Taxable Income Tax

3.   Tax-exempt organizations are generally subject to tax on income from unrelated business taxable income (UBTI).

    a.   An unrelated business is a trade or business activity regularly carried on for the production of income (even if a loss results) that is not substantially related to performance of the exempt purpose or function, i.e., that does not contribute more than insubstantial benefits to the exempt purposes.

        1)   Certain qualified sponsorship payments received by an exempt organization are not subject to UBTI tax.

            a)   A qualified sponsorship payment is one from which the payor does not expect any substantial return or benefit, other than the use or acknowledgment of the payor's name or logo.

                i)   The payor may not receive a substantial return.

        2)   Bingo games that are not an activity ordinarily carried out on a commercial basis or do not violate state or local law are not considered an unrelated trade or business.

        3)   Exempt organizations subject to tax on UBTI are required to comply with the Code provisions regarding installment payments of estimated income tax by corporations.

        4)   A UBTI tax return (Form 990-T) is required of an exempt organization with at least $1,000 of gross income used in computing the UBTI tax for the tax year.

Charitable Deduction

4.   Solicitations for contributions or other payments by tax-exempt organizations must include a statement if payments to that organization are not deductible as charitable contributions for federal income tax purposes. Donations to the following organizations are tax deductible:

    a.   Corporations organized under an Act of Congress
    b.   501(c)(3) organizations except those testing for public safety
    c.   Cemetery companies
    d.   Cooperative hospital service organizations
    e.   Cooperative service organizations of operating educational organizations
    f.   Childcare organizations

Stop and review! You have completed the outline for this subunit. Study questions 1 through 15 beginning on page 380.

QUESTIONS

20.1 Exempt Organizations

1. Which of the following is not an exempt organization?

A.   American Society for the Prevention of Cruelty to Animals.

B.   Red Cross.

C.   State-chartered credit unions.

D.   Privately owned nursing home.

Answer (D) is correct.

    REQUIRED: The organization that does not qualify as exempt.

    DISCUSSION: Exempt status generally depends on the nature and purpose of an organization. Among the types of organizations that may qualify as exempt are corporations, trusts, foundations, funds, community funds, etc. A more complete list can be found in Sec. 501(c) along with the permitted stated purposes and requirements.

    Answer (A) is incorrect. The American Society for the Prevention of Cruelty to Animals is an exempt organization according to Sec. 501(c). Answer (B) is incorrect. The Red Cross is an exempt organization according to Sec. 501(c). Answer (C) is incorrect. State-chartered credit unions are exempt organizations [Sec. 501(c)(14)(A)].

2. Which of the following organizations may request exempt status under the Internal Revenue Code as exempt organizations?

A. Religious organization.

B. School.

C. Animal welfare organization.

D. All of the answers are correct.

Answer (D) is correct.

REQUIRED: The organization that could request tax-exempt status under Sec. 501(c)(3) as a charitable organization.

DISCUSSION: Exempt status generally depends on the nature and purpose of an organization. An organization is tax-exempt only if it is a class specifically described by the IRC as one on which exemption is conferred. An organization operated for the primary purpose of carrying on a trade or business for profit is generally not tax-exempt. Religious organizations, schools, and animal welfare organizations are all considered exempt because their activities do not involve making a profit.

3. Of the organizations listed below, which organization could not receive approval for tax-exempt status under Internal Revenue Code Sec. 501(c)(3)?

A. A local chapter of the Salvation Army.

B. A partnership for scientific research.

C. A college alumni association.

D. A local boys club.

Answer (B) is correct.

REQUIRED: The organization that qualifies as a tax-exempt organization.

DISCUSSION: Organizations formed and operated exclusively for religious, charitable, scientific, educational, literary, or similar purposes are a broad class of exempt organizations. No part of the net earnings may accrue to the benefit of any private shareholder or individual.

Answer (A) is incorrect. The Salvation Army operates exclusively for charitable purposes, with no part of net earnings accrued for the benefit of a private shareholder or individual. Answer (C) is incorrect. A college alumni association does not accrue any part of its net earnings for the benefit of an individual. Answer (D) is incorrect. A boys club operates exclusively for charitable purposes, with no part of net earnings accrued for the benefit of a private shareholder or individual.

4. Which of the following is not an organization exempt from federal income taxes under Subchapter F of the Internal Revenue Code (Sec. 501 et seq.)?

A. Civic leagues or organizations operated exclusively for the promotion of social welfare.

B. Fraternal benefit societies.

C. Labor, agricultural, or horticultural organizations.

D. Blue Cross and Blue Shield organizations.

Answer (D) is correct.

REQUIRED: The organization that is not tax-exempt.

DISCUSSION: Tax-exempt status is available to various classes of nonprofit organizations under Sec. 501(a). Sec. 501(c)(2) through (25) lists several organizations that may qualify for tax-exempt status, including civic leagues; fraternal benefit societies; and labor, agricultural, or horticultural organizations. Blue Cross and Blue Shield organizations are not qualifying organizations.

5. Which of the following organizations, exempt from federal income tax under Sec. 501(a), must file an annual information return on Form 990 or Form 990-PF?

A. An organization, other than a private foundation, having gross receipts in each year that normally are not more than $50,000.

B. A school below college level, affiliated with a church or operated by a religious order, that is not an integrated auxiliary of a church.

C. A private foundation exempt under Sec. 501(c)(3) of the Internal Revenue Code.

D. A stock bonus, pension, or profit-sharing trust that qualifies under Sec. 401 of the Internal Revenue Code.

Answer (C) is correct.

REQUIRED: The organization that is required to file an annual information return.

DISCUSSION: Most exempt organizations are required to file various returns and reports at some time during or following the close of their accounting periods. Private foundations are required to file annual information returns on Form 990 or Form 990-PF regardless of the amounts of their gross receipts.

6. Which of the following statements is true with respect to tax-exempt organizations?

A. A foundation may qualify for exemption from federal income tax if it is organized for the prevention of cruelty to animals.

B. A partnership may qualify as an organization exempt from federal income tax if it is organized and operated exclusively for one or more of the purposes found in Sec. 501(c)(3).

C. An individual can qualify as an organization exempt from federal income tax.

D. In order to qualify as an exempt organization, the organization must be a corporation.

Answer (A) is correct.
   REQUIRED: The true statement with respect to tax-exempt organizations.
   DISCUSSION: Exempt status generally depends on the nature and purpose of an organization. Among the types of organizations that may qualify as exempt are corporations, trusts, foundations, funds, community funds, etc. A more complete list can be found in Sec. 501(c) along with the permitted stated purposes and requirements.
   Answer (B) is incorrect. A partnership is, by definition, a for-profit association. Also, a partnership is not listed as a type of organization that may qualify for exempt status in Sec. 501(c) or (d). Answer (C) is incorrect. An individual is not an organization described in Sec. 501(c) or (d) that may qualify for exempt status. Answer (D) is incorrect. Other types of organizations listed in Sec. 501(c) or (d) may also qualify.

7. With respect to tax-exempt organizations, which of the following statements is false?

A. A foundation may qualify for exemption from federal income tax if it is organized for the prevention of cruelty to children.

B. An individual may qualify as an organization exempt from federal income tax.

C. A corporation organized for the prevention of cruelty to animals may qualify for exemption from federal income tax.

D. A trust organized and operated for the purpose of testing for public safety may qualify for exemption from federal income tax.

Answer (B) is correct.
   REQUIRED: The false statement regarding tax-exempt organizations.
   DISCUSSION: To qualify for tax-exempt status, an organization must be a corporation, community chest fund, or foundation. An individual or a partnership cannot qualify.

8. Which return might a tax-exempt organization be required to file?

A. Employment tax returns.

B. Annual information return, Form 990.

C. Report of cash received.

D. All of the answers are correct.

Answer (D) is correct.
   REQUIRED: The return that a tax-exempt organization might be required to file.
   DISCUSSION: Publication 557 states that annual information returns, employment tax returns, and a report of cash received are all returns that might be required of a tax-exempt organization.

9. With respect to the filing requirements of an exempt organization (including private foundations), which of the following statements is true?

A. A central or parent organization may file Form 990, *Return of Organization Exempt from Income Tax*, for two or more local organizations that are not private foundations. However, this return is in addition to the central or parent organization's separate annual return if it must file one.

B. Every organization exempt from income tax must file an annual information return.

C. Forms 990, 990-EZ, and 990-PF are required to be filed by the 15th day of the third month after the end of the organization's accounting period.

D. An exempt organization must have at least $5,000 gross income from an unrelated business before it is required to file Form 990-T, *Exempt Organization Business Income Tax Return*.

Answer (A) is correct.
   REQUIRED: The true statement regarding the filing requirements of an exempt organization.
   DISCUSSION: A parent or central exempt organization files a separate return for itself. If it chooses, the organization may also file a group information return for two or more local organizations as long as none of the local organizations are private foundations.
   Answer (B) is incorrect. Several organizations are exempt from filing an annual information return. Answer (C) is incorrect. The return is required to be filed by the 15th day of the 5th month after the end of the organization's accounting period. Answer (D) is incorrect. Some organizations, including private foundations, must file a return regardless of the amount of gross income.

10. A tax-exempt organization with a calendar tax year was required to file Form 990, *Return of Organization Exempt from Income Tax*, for Year 1. Disregarding any extensions, when is the return due (do not consider Saturdays, Sundays, or holidays)?

A. March 15, Year 2.

B. April 15, Year 2.

C. May 15, Year 2.

D. June 15, Year 2.

Answer (C) is correct.
REQUIRED: The date the tax-exempt organization's tax return is due.
DISCUSSION: Under Sec. 6072(e), the income tax return of an organization exempt from tax under Sec. 501(a) must be filed on or before the 15th day of the 5th month following the close of the taxable year.

11. Which of the following organizations, which are exempt from federal income tax, must generally file an annual information report?

A. An organization, other than a private foundation, with annual gross receipts that normally are not more than $50,000.

B. A private foundation.

C. A church.

D. A religious order.

Answer (B) is correct.
REQUIRED: The organization that must file an annual information return.
DISCUSSION: Most organizations exempt from tax under Sec. 501(a) must file annual information returns on Form 990, *Return of Organization Exempt from Income Tax*. Those excepted from the requirement are

1. A church or church-affiliated organization

2. An exclusively religious activity or religious order

3. An organization (other than a private foundation) having annual gross receipts that are not more than $50,000

4. A stock bonus, pension, or profit-sharing trust that qualified under Sec. 401

5. A Keogh plan whose total assets are less than $100,000

Answer (A) is incorrect. Such an organization is specifically exempt from filing annual information returns. Answer (C) is incorrect. A church is specifically exempt from filing annual information returns. Answer (D) is incorrect. A religious order is specifically exempt from filing annual information returns.

12. Individuals may claim a charitable deduction for a contribution to which of the following?

A. Civic leagues or organizations operated exclusively for the promotion of social welfare.

B. Organizations operated exclusively for scientific or educational purposes.

C. Cemetery companies operated exclusively for the benefit of their members.

D. Civic leagues or organizations operated exclusively for the promotion of social welfare and organizations operated exclusively for scientific or educational purposes.

Answer (D) is correct.
REQUIRED: The organization(s) to which individuals may make a deductible charitable contribution.
DISCUSSION: Solicitations for contributions or other payments by tax-exempt organizations must include a statement if payments to that organization are not deductible as charitable contributions for federal income tax purposes. Donations to the following organizations are tax deductible:

1. Corporations organized under an Act of Congress

2. All 501(c)(3) organizations except those testing for public safety

3. Cemetery companies

4. Cooperative hospital service organizations

5. Cooperative service organizations of operating educational organizations

6. Childcare organizations

Although contributions to cemetery companies are generally tax deductible, a cemetery company that operates exclusively for the benefit of its members is not a tax-exempt organization.
Answer (A) is incorrect. Organizations operated for scientific or educational purposes also qualify for deductible contributions. Answer (B) is incorrect. Civic leagues operated for the promotion of social welfare also qualify for deductible contributions. Answer (C) is incorrect. If it operates exclusively for the benefit of its members, a cemetery company is not a tax-exempt organization.

13. Which of the following organizations is not required to file an annual information return, such as Form 990, *Return of Organization Exempt from Income Tax*?

    A. All are required to file with no exceptions.

    B. Any exempt organization with annual gross receipts exceeding $50,000.

    C. A convention or an association of churches with annual gross receipts exceeding $50,000.

    D. Any chamber of commerce with annual gross receipts exceeding $50,000.

Answer (C) is correct.
    REQUIRED: The organization that is not required to file an annual information return.
    DISCUSSION: Most organizations exempt from tax under Sec. 501(a) must file annual information returns on Form 990, *Return of Organization Exempt from Income Tax*. Those exempt from the requirement are

1. A church or church-affiliated organization

2. An exclusively religious activity or religious order

3. An organization (other than a private foundation) having annual gross receipts that are not more than $50,000

4. A stock bonus, pension, or profit-sharing trust that qualified under Sec. 401

    Answer (A) is incorrect. Most organizations exempt from tax under Sec. 501(a) must file annual information returns on Form 990, *Return of Organization Exempt from Income Tax*. Answer (B) is incorrect. An organization having annual gross receipts of not more than $50,000 is not required to file Form 990. Answer (D) is incorrect. An organization having annual gross receipts of not more than $50,000 is not required to file Form 990.

14. An incorporated exempt organization subject to tax on its current-year unrelated business taxable income (UBTI)

    A. Must make estimated tax payments if its tax can reasonably be expected to be $100 or more.

    B. Must comply with the Code provisions regarding installment payments of estimated income tax by corporations.

    C. Must pay at least 70% of the tax due as shown on the return when filed, with the balance of tax payable in the following quarter.

    D. May defer payment of tax for up to 9 months following the due date of the return.

Answer (B) is correct.
    REQUIRED: The timing of payment obligations with respect to UBTI tax.
    DISCUSSION: Exempt organizations subject to tax on UBTI are required to comply with the Code provisions regarding installment payments of estimated income tax by corporations [Sec. 6655(g)(3)].
    Answer (A) is incorrect. Like a corporation, quarterly payments of estimated tax are required of an exempt organization that expects estimated tax on UBTI to equal or exceed $500 for the tax year. Answer (C) is incorrect. Tax on UBTI is due in full when the UBTI return and annual information return are due. Answer (D) is incorrect. Tax on UBTI is due in full when the UBTI return and annual information return are due.

15. Which of the following forms is intended for an exempt organization with gross receipts of $100,000 and total assets of $400,000 on December 31, 2013?

    A. Form 990.

    B. Form 990 Schedule M.

    C. Form 990-EZ.

    D. Form 990 Schedule O.

Answer (C) is correct.
    REQUIRED: The form designed for use by small exempt organizations.
    DISCUSSION: Form 990-EZ is a shortened version of Form 990. It is designed for use by small exempt organizations and nonexempt charitable trusts. An organization may file Form 990-EZ instead of Form 990 if it meets both of the following requirements:

1. Its gross receipts during the year were less than $200,000.

2. Its total assets at the end of the year were less than $500,000.

The amounts in this question pass both of these tests.
    Answer (A) is incorrect. Form 990 is designed for use by all (large or small) exempt organizations. Answer (B) is incorrect. Schedule M is for noncash contributions. Answer (D) is incorrect. Schedule O is for supplemental information to Form 990.

Use the additional questions in Gleim **EA Test Prep** to create Practice Exams that emulate Prometric!

INDEX